THE ROUGH

Holland

There are more than one hundred and fifty Rough Guide titles
covering destinations from Amsterdam to Zimbabwe

Forthcoming titles include
Alaska • Copenhagen • Ibiza & Formentera • Iceland

Rough Guide Reference Series
Classical Music • Country Music • Drum 'n' Bass • English Football
European Football • House • The Internet • Jazz • Music USA • Opera
Reggae • Rock Music • Techno • Unexplained Phenomena • World Music

Rough Guide Phrasebooks
Czech • Dutch • Egyptian Arabic • European Languages • French • German
Greek • Hindi & Urdu • Hungarian • Indonesian • Italian • Japanese
Mandarin Chinese • Mexican Spanish • Polish • Portuguese • Russian
Spanish • Swahili • Thai • Turkish • Vietnamese

Rough Guides on the Internet
www.roughguides.com

ROUGH GUIDE CREDITS

Text editors: Andrew Tomičić and Cameron Wilson
Series editor: Mark Ellingham
Editorial: Martin Dunford, Jonathan Buckley, Jo Mead, Kate Berens, Amanda Tomlin, Ann-Marie Shaw, Paul Gray, Helena Smith, Judith Bamber, Orla Duane, Olivia Eccleshall, Ruth Blackmore, Geoff Howard, Claire Saunders, Gavin Thomas, Alexander Mark Rogers, Polly Thomas, Joe Staines, Lisa Nellis, Richard Lim, Duncan Clark, Peter Buckley, Sam Thorne (UK); Andrew Rosenberg, Mary Beth Maioli, Don Bapst, Stephen Timblin (US)
Production: Susanne Hillen, Andy Hilliard, Link Hall, Helen Ostick, Julia Bovis, Michelle Draycott, Katie

Pringle, Robert Evers, Niamh Hatton, Mike Hancock, Robert McKinlay
Cartography: Melissa Baker, Maxine Repath, Nichola Goodliffe, Ed Wright
Picture research: Louise Boulton, Sharon Martins
Online editor: Kelly Cross, Anja Mutic-Blessing (US)
Finance: John Fisher, Gary Singh, Edward Downey, Mark Hall, Tim Bill
Marketing & Publicity: Richard Trillo, Niki Smith, David Wearn, Jemima Broadbridge (UK); Jean-Marie Kelly, Myra Campolo, Simon Carloss (US)
Administration: Tania Hummel, Demelza Dallow

ACKNOWLEDGEMENTS

Thanks on this edition due to Ruth Rigby for her assistance with Basics; Tricia Allan for her help with South Holland; Marlien Meijer at the Netherlands Board of Tourism in London; and Els Wamsteeker of the Amsterdam Tourist Board. Thanks also to Matthew Teller for proofreading; and at Rough Guides Mike Hancock for typesetting and Ed Wright for cartography.

We'd like to thank all those readers who wrote in with comments and updates to the previous edition: Helen Akitt, Tessa Baars, Marilyn Barton, B.

Bedwell, Tricia Brady, Jared Butcher, Philip Chklar, G. Curran, Claudia Dimmer, John Fanning, Jackie Follos, H. Gill, Patrick Goldsmith, JoAnn Hadden, Dustin Haferbecker, Arthur Hampton, B. van Hoecke, Simon Huggins, Annie Katata, Veronica Keycke, Lori Lang, Ian Leatt, Chris Melia, Mark Oliver, Kim Pogorelsky, J. Reynolds, Graeme Ritchie, David Ryan, Kate Sanders, Mvrna Savers, Toby Screech, Craig Smith, Dave Stern, Andrew Sykes, J. Turner, Jenni Wagstaff, David Walker and Antony Young.

PUBLISHING INFORMATION

This second edition published July 2000 by Rough Guides Ltd, 62–70 Shorts Gardens, London, WC2H 9AB.
Distributed by the Penguin Group:
Penguin Books Ltd, 27 Wrights Lane, London W8 5TZ
Penguin Putnam, Inc. 375 Hudson Street, NY 10014, USA
Penguin Books Australia Ltd, 487 Maroondah Highway, PO Box 257, Ringwood, Victoria 3134, Australia
Penguin Books Canada Ltd, 10 Alcorn Avenue, Toronto, Ontario, Canada M4V 1E4
Penguin Books (NZ) Ltd, 182–190 Wairau Road, Auckland 10, New Zealand
Typeset in Linotron Univers and Century Old Style to an original design by Andrew Oliver.
Printed in England by Clays Ltd, St Ives PLC
Illustrations in Part One and Part Three by Edward Briant.

Illustrations on p.1 & p.339 by Henry Iles
© Martin Dunford, Jack Holland and Phil Lee 2000
No part of this book may be reproduced in any form without permission from the publisher except for the quotation of brief passages in reviews.
416pp – Includes index
A catalogue record for this book is available from the British Library
ISBN 1-85828-541-0

The publishers and authors have done their best to ensure the accuracy and currency of all the information in *The Rough Guide to Holland*, however, they can accept no responsibility for any loss, injury, or inconvenience sustained by any traveller as a result of information or advice contained in the guide.

THE ROUGH GUIDE TO

Holland

written and researched by

Martin Dunford, Jack Holland and Phil Lee

with additional contributions by

Sharon Harris

ROUGH GUIDES

We set out to do something different when the first Rough Guide was published in 1982. Mark Ellingham, just out of university, was travelling in Greece. He brought along the popular guides of the day, but found they were all lacking in some way. They were either strong on ruins and museums but went on for pages without mentioning a beach or taverna. Or they were so conscious of the need to save money that they lost sight of Greece's cultural and historical significance. Also, none of the books told him anything about Greece's contemporary life – its politics, its culture, its people, and how they lived.

So with no job in prospect, Mark decided to write his own guidebook, one which aimed to provide practical information that was second to none, detailing the best beaches and the hottest clubs and restaurants, while also giving hard-hitting accounts of every sight, both famous and obscure, and providing up-to-the-minute information on contemporary culture. It was a guide that encouraged independent travellers to find the best of Greece, and was a great success, getting shortlisted for the Thomas Cook travel guide award, and encouraging Mark, along with three friends, to expand the series.

The Rough Guide list grew rapidly and the letters flooded in, indicating a much broader readership than had been anticipated, but one which uniformly appreciated the Rough Guide mix of practical detail and humour, irreverence and enthusiasm. Things haven't changed. The same four friends who began the series are still the caretakers of the Rough Guide mission today: to provide the most reliable, up-to-date and entertaining information to independent-minded travellers of all ages, on all budgets.

We now publish more than 150 titles and have offices in London and New York. The travel guides are written and researched by a dedicated team of more than 100 authors, based in Britain, Europe, the USA and Australia. We have also created a unique series of phrasebooks to accompany the travel series, along with an acclaimed series of music guides, and a best-selling pocket guide to the Internet and World Wide Web. We also publish comprehensive travel information on our Web site:

www.roughguides.com

HELP US UPDATE

We've gone to a lot of effort to ensure that the second edition of The Rough Guide to Holland is accurate and up-to-date. However, things change – places get "discovered", opening hours are notoriously fickle, restaurants and rooms raise prices or lower standards. If you feel we've got it wrong or left something out, we'd like to know, and if you can remember the address, the price, the time, the phone number, so much the better.

We'll credit all contributions, and send a copy of the next edition (or any other Rough Guide if you prefer) for the best letters. Please mark letters: "Rough Guide Holland Update" and send to:

Rough Guides, 62–70 Shorts Gardens, London WC2H 9AB, or Rough Guides, 4th Floor, 345 Hudson St, New York, NY 10014.

Or send email to: mail@roughguides.co.uk
Online updates about this book can be found on Rough Guides' Web site at www.roughguides.com

Martin Dunford and **Jack Holland** first met at the University of Kent at Canterbury. Following jobs as diverse as insurance collection, beer-barrel rolling and EFL teaching in Greece they co-founded the Rough Guides in the mid-1980s. After co-authoring several other titles, Martin is now editorial director of Rough Guides and Jack lives in the Cotswolds.

Phil Lee has worked as a freelance author with the Rough Guides for the last thirteen years – his other titles include Norway; Toronto; and Mallorca and Menorca. Phil lives in Nottingham, where he was born and raised.

CONTENTS

Introduction ix

LIST OF MAPS

MAP SYMBOLS

– – –	Chapter division boundary	⚊	Campsite
▬▪▬▪▬	International boundary	△	Youth hostel
▬▬ ▪ ▪	Provincial boundary	◉	Hotel
═══	Road	✈	Airport
▬▬	Railway	⚲	Museum
- - - - -	Footpath	▇	Building
▒▒▒	River/canal	⊞	Church
— —	Ferry route	✡	Synagogue
▓	Urban area	⊠	Post office
▒	Park	*i*	Tourist information (VVV)
♦	Point of interest	Ⓗ	Hospital

INTRODUCTION

Holland, or, to give the country its proper name, The Netherlands, is a country reclaimed in part from the waters of the North Sea, an artificially created land, around half of which lies at or below sea level. Land reclamation has been the dominant motif of its history, the result a country of resonant and unique images: flat, fertile landscapes punctuated by windmills and church spires; ornately gabled terraces flanking peaceful canals; huge, open skies; and mile upon mile of grassy dune, backing onto wide stretches of pristine, sandy beach.

A major colonial power, its mercantile fleets once challenged the best in the world for supremacy, and its standard of living (for the majority at least) was second to none. Today, Holland is one of the most developed countries in the world, small and urban, with the highest population density in Europe, its fifteen million or so inhabitants concentrated into an area about the size of the US state of Maine. It's an international, well-integrated place too: many people speak English, at least in the heavily populated west of the country; communications and infrastructure are efficient; and its companies – Philips and Shell for instance – are at the forefront of the new, free-trading Europe. On the political scene, successive Dutch governments have steered towards consensus and, despite something of a conservative backlash in recent years, the country is one of Europe's most liberal, with relaxed laws regarding soft drugs and prostitution underpinned by forward-thinking attitudes on social issues.

Where to go

If you say you're going to Holland, everyone will immediately assume you're going to **Amsterdam**. Indeed for such a small and accessible country, Holland is, apart from Amsterdam, relatively unknown territory. Some people may confess to a brief visit to Rotterdam or The Hague, but for most visitors Amsterdam *is* Holland, the assumption being that there's nothing remotely worth seeing elsewhere – a prejudice shared, incidentally, by many Amsterdammers. It is certainly true that Amsterdam has more cosmopolitan dash than any other Dutch city, but to write off the rest of the country would be to miss much, especially considering the modest size of the place and the efficiency of its transport system, which makes everywhere easily accessible.

Although throughout the Guide we have used the name Holland to mean the whole country, technically the term refers to just two of The Netherlands' twelve provinces – **North** and **South Holland**, in the west of the country. For the most part, this is unrelentingly flat territory, much of it reclaimed land that has become home to a grouping of towns known collectively as the **Randstad** (literally "rim town"), an urban sprawl which holds all the country's largest cities and the majority of its population. Travelling in this part of the country is easy, with trains and buses cheap and efficient and no language barrier for the English-speaking visitor. Amsterdam is rightly the main focus: no other city has its vitality and flair, or, indeed, its features of interest, particularly its lattice of handsome canal houses and trio of first-rate art museums. But the other Randstad towns are worth a visit,

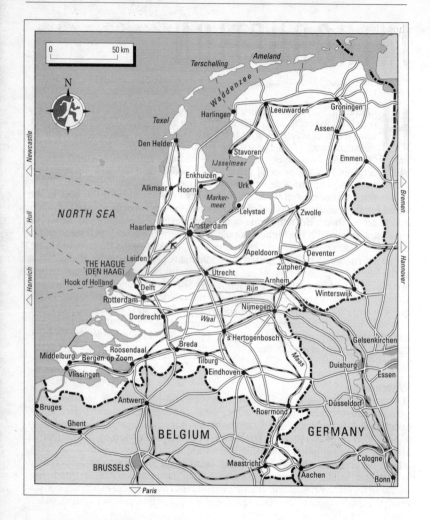

too: **Haarlem**, **Leiden** and **Delft** with their old canal-girded centres; the gritty port city of **Rotterdam**; the dignified architecture and stately air of **The Hague**, home of the government and the Dutch royal family; not to mention the **bulb-fields** which spread all around – in spring, justifiably, the one thing that never fails to draw tourists out of Amsterdam.

Beyond the Randstad is a quieter, more rural Holland, especially in the far north where a chain of low-lying **islands** marks the northern boundary of the Waddenzee. Prime resort territory, the islands possess a blustery, bucolic charm all of their own and thousands of Dutch families come here every summer for their holidays. Most of the islands lie offshore from the coast of the province of **Friesland**, named after the Germanic Frisians who first settled the region and whose language – Frysk – is still spoken by some of the locals. Friesland's capital, **Leeuwarden**, is a likeable, eminently visitable city, and neighbouring **Groningen** is one of the country's busiest cultural centres, given verve by its large resident student population. To the south, the provinces of **Overijssel** and **Gelderland** are dotted with charming old towns, most notably **Deventer** and **Zutphen**, whilst their eastern portions herald Holland's first few geophysical bumps as the landscape rolls up towards the German frontier. Here also are two lively and diverting towns, **Arnhem**, a hop and a skip from the open heaths of the **Nationaal Park de Hoge Veluwe**, and the lively college town of **Nijmegen**. Further south still lie the predominantly Catholic provinces of **Limburg**, **North Brabant** and **Zeeland**. The last of these is well named – literally "Sealand", made up of a series of low-lying islands connected by road and protected from the encroaching waters of the North Sea by one of Holland's most ambitious projects, the Delta Plan. Heading east from here, you reach **North Brabant**, gently rolling scrub and farmland which centres on the historic cities of **Breda** and **'s Hertogenbosch**, and, not least, the modern manufacturing hub of **Eindhoven**, home to the electronics giant Philips. Lastly, **Limburg** occupies the slim scythe of land that reaches down between the Belgian and German borders, its landscape, in the south at least, truly hilly, and with a charming cosmopolitan capital in **Maastricht**.

Climate

Holland enjoys a **temperate climate**, with fairly mild summers and cold winters. Generally speaking, temperatures rise the further south you go, with the south of the country perhaps a couple of degrees warmer than the north and east for much of the year. This is offset by the prevailing westerlies that sweep in from the North Sea, making the coastal provinces both warmer in winter and colder in summer than the eastern provinces, where the more severe climate of continental Europe begins to assert itself. As far as showers go, be prepared for them at any time – rain is a strong possibility all year round.

AVERAGE DAILY TEMPERATURES (°C)											
Jan	Feb	March	April	May	June	July	Aug	Sept	Oct	Nov	Dec
2	2	5	8	12	15	17	17	15	11	6	3

PART ONE

THE

BASICS

GETTING THERE FROM BRITAIN

There are many ways to reach Holland, but basically it comes down to deciding between a low-cost but time-consuming journey by bus, or ferry and train, and a swift but slightly more expensive flight. However, travelling by train through the Channel Tunnel is an attractive alternative, little cheaper than a flight, but with the advantage of taking you direct from London to the heart of Amsterdam, Rotterdam or Maastricht. Whichever method you opt for, you'll find a variety of competitive fares.

BY AIR

Flying to any of the **major airports** in Holland – Amsterdam Schiphol (*skip-oll*), Rotterdam, Eindhoven or Maastricht – saves a lot of time over the ferry or train connections: Schiphol, for example, is just an hour's flying time from London. What's more, there are plenty of direct flights from the UK, both from London and a range of regional airports – Schiphol is the easiest Dutch airport to get to (a ninety-minute journey from Scotland and the north of England).

For **Amsterdam** both British Airways and KLM run a large number of daily **scheduled flights** to Schiphol from London, while regional airports are well served by KLMuk and British Midland, who fly at least twice a day from those airports detailed in the box overleaf. Of the **smaller operators**, EasyJet's budget, ticketless service operates three or four flights daily from Luton, plus two or three from Liverpool; ScotAirways has

two or three daily flights on weekdays from Cambridge and Southampton, with a reduced service at the weekend; and Transavia flies from Gatwick at least twice a day. You may also find **long-haul** airlines offering reasonable prices on the London–Amsterdam route, as they stop off on their way to more distant destinations: Air Kenya, Cathay Pacific and Qantas are three such operators.

For other Dutch cities there's a choice of airlines flying to **Rotterdam**, with around four daily flights from London City, London Heathrow, London Gatwick and Manchester, and two flights a day from Birmingham; most of these are provided by British Airways franchise holders – CityFlyer and BAse Airlines, or KLMuk franchise holders, VLM. There are also daily flights to **Eindhoven** from London Heathrow and Gatwick, Birmingham and Manchester and flights most days to **Maastricht** from London Stansted with KLM Exel.

The amazing number of flights to Amsterdam Schiphol has led to a price war between the airlines. As a result it's reasonably easy to find **return fares** from London for £70 to £120, with Apex fares (which usually have to be booked fourteen days in advance and require you to spend a Saturday abroad) between £150 and £210. Flights from regional airports are likely to be around twice the price, with the exception of those operated by EasyJet, which start at around £60 return, plus airport tax. Return flights to other Dutch cities range from £130 to £300, depending on where you're flying from and your destination city: flying to Rotterdam from London City with VLM, for example, costs £180 return. To help you find the best bargains, all major airlines have **Web sites** providing the latest information about timetables and fares, and, increasingly, an online booking service. There are also a growing number of flight agents' Web sites offering instant access to the best deals; while we've listed some of these below, others can be found through the online service Cheapflights, at *www.cheapflights.co.uk*, which will signpost you to the booking agent or airline offering the lowest prices.

Alternative sources of **discounted tickets** include Ceefax, which hosts a large number of travel agents touting last-minute deals, the weekend travel sections of the quality newspapers, or, if you live in London, the back pages of the listings magazine *Time Out* or the *Evening Standard*. Alternatively, contact a discount flight agent such as STA Travel, Trailfinders or UsitCAMPUS, who specialize in youth flights and, if you're under 26 (or a student under 32), can offer substantial savings; they also sell ordinary discounted tickets to non-students.

BY TRAIN

The simplicity of the Eurostar passenger service is likely to make it the first, although not usually the cheapest, choice for anyone travelling by **train** to Holland. The alternatives all involve using the ferries, and are consequently more time-consuming; the fastest of them is the competitively priced Stena Line ferry route.

ROUTES

Eurostar's rapid passenger service from London through the Channel Tunnel can cut the journey time to Holland to a manageable six hours, with a change at Brussels Midi station for the last leg of the journey; the London–Brussels leg takes a little less than three hours. The Eurostar service from **London Waterloo** to **Brussels** runs roughly ten times a day from Monday to Saturday, and eight times on Sunday, usually stopping at Ashford in Kent and always at Lille, France (if you need a

visa to visit France, you'll have to get one in order to use the Eurostar). Travel is simple: you're required to check in twenty minutes before departure and passports are checked on arrival in Brussels, which can mean a delay, but rarely of more than half an hour. From Brussels there are onward **connections** direct to Rotterdam (hourly; 2hr) and Amsterdam Centraal Station (hourly; 3hr). Another connecting service runs to Maastricht via Liège-Guillemins in just under 2 hours via either Dordrecht or Roosendaal and Breda.

There is a wide range of **fares** on Eurostar, which start at around £70 return if you're under 26 (no single fare), but can cost up to £250 for a **standard return** (£125 one-way), which offers you travel between Monday and Friday with flexible return dates and ticket exchanges or refunds for up to two months after departure. One way of reducing the cost is to take advantage of deals such as the "**Excursion**" and "**Leisure Return**" tickets; at around half the price of the standard return (£100 for an Excursion and £130 for a Leisure return ticket) you can travel any day, are required to stay a minimum of one Saturday night before returning (or alternatively three nights, for the Leisure Return) and you cannot exchange or refund your return ticket after departure. If you're planning to take a **bicycle**, Eurostar will charge £20 per journey to carry it as "registered

DISCOUNT FLIGHT AGENTS

North South Travel, Moulsham Mill Centre, Parkway, Chelmsford, Essex CM2 7PX ☎01245/608291. Friendly, competitive travel agency, offering discounted fares worldwide – profits are used to support projects in the developing world, especially the promotion of sustainable tourism.

STA Travel, 86 Old Brompton Rd, London SW7 3LQ; 117 Euston Rd, London NW1 2SX; 38 Store St, London WC1 (all: ☎020/7361 6161); 38 North St, Brighton ☎01273/728 282; 25 Queens Rd, Bristol BS8 1QE ☎0117/929 4399; 38 Sidney St, Cambridge CB2 3HX ☎01223/366966; 75 Deansgate, Manchester M3 2BW ☎0161/834 0668; 78 Bold Street, Liverpool L1 4HR ☎0151/707 1123; 88 Vicar Lane, Leeds LS1 7JH ☎0113/244 9212; 9 St Mary's Place, Newcastle-upon-Tyne NE1 7PG ☎0191/233 2111; 36 George St, Oxford OX1 2OJ ☎01865/792800; 27 Forrest Rd, Edinburgh ☎0131/226 7747; 184 Byres Rd, Glasgow G1 1JH ☎0141/338 6000; 30 Upper Kirkgate, Aberdeen ☎01224/658222; and branches on university campuses in London, Birmingham, Bristol, Canterbury, Cardiff, Coventry, Durham, Glasgow, Leeds, Loughborough, Nottingham, Sheffield and Warwick; *www.statravel.co.uk* Worldwide specialists in low-cost flights and tours for students and under-26s, though other customers are also welcome.

Travel CUTS, 295a Regent St, London W1R 7YA ☎020/7255 1944; 33 Prince's Square, London W2 4NG ☎020/7792 3770; *www.travelcuts.co.uk* British branch of Canada's main youth and student travel specialist.

Trailfinders, 1 Threadneedle Street, London EC2R 8JX (all destinations ☎020/7628 7628); 42–50 Earls Court Rd, London W8 6FT (☎020/7938 3366); 194 Kensington High St, London W8 7RG (☎020/7938 3939); 215 Kensington High St, London W8 6BD (☎020/7937 5400); 58 Deansgate, Manchester M3 2FF ☎0161/839 6969; 254–284 Sauchiehall St, Glasgow G2 3EH ☎0141/353 2224; 22–24 The Priory Queensway, Birmingham B4 6BS ☎0121/236 1234; 48 Corn St, Bristol BS1 1HQ ☎0117/929 9000; 7–9 Ridley Place, Newcastle NE1 8 JQ ☎0191/261 2345; *www.trailfinder.com* One of the best informed and most efficient agents for independent travellers; their Web site offers "best buy" information, provides a brochure ordering service and sells travel insurance.

The Travel Bug, 125 Gloucester Rd, London SW7 4SF ☎020/7835 2000; 597 Cheetham Hill Rd, Manchester M8 5EJ ☎0161/721 4000; *www.travel-bug.co.uk* Large range of discounted tickets; the Web site offers a flight price "wizard" as well as a brochure request service.

UsitCAMPUS, 52 Grosvenor Gardens, London SW1W 0AG ☎020/7730 3402; 541 Bristol Rd, Selly Oak, Birmingham B29 6AU ☎0121/414 1848; 61 Ditchling Rd, Brighton BN1 4SD ☎01273/570226; 39 Queen's Rd, Clifton, Bristol BS8 1QE ☎0117/929 2494; 5 Emmanuel St, Cambridge CB1 1NE ☎01223/324283; 53 Forrest Rd, Edinburgh EH1 2QP ☎0131/668 3308; 105–106 St Aldates, Oxford OX1 1BU ☎01865/484730; *www.usitcampus.co.uk* Student/youth travel specialists, with branches also in YHA shops and on university campuses all over Britain.

TELEPHONE AND ONLINE DISCOUNT AGENTS

Dial-a-Flight ☎0870/333 4488, *www.dialaflight.com* Telephone sales of scheduled flights, with a Web site useful for tracking down bargains.

Expedia UK *expedia.co.uk* Microsoft's venture into the Internet travel market, with a "flight wizard" listing many (but not all) airline options, its own special fares and an online booking service.

Flightline ☎01702/715151, *www.flightline.co.uk* Another telephone-based outfit offering online searches for cheap charter and scheduled flights.

Lastminute.com *www.lastminute.com* Vast Web site selling everything from holidays to mobile phones, but with a particular emphasis on cheap travel.

Busabout, 258 Vauxhall Bridge Rd, London SW1V 1BS ☎020/7950 1661, *www.busabout.com* European coach operator.

Deutsche Bahn UK, 18 Conduit St, London W1R 9TD ☎020/7317 0919, *www.db-ag.de* European rail tickets and passes.

Eurolines, 52 Grosvenor Gardens, London SW1W 0AU ☎0870/580 8080, *www.eurolines.co.uk* European coach operator, offering scheduled coach services to European cities as well as passes for Europe-wide travel.

Eurostar, Eurostar House, Waterloo International Station, London SE1 8SE; 102–104 Victoria St, London SW1E 5JL (both ☎0870/518 6186); ticket purchase also available at Ashford International and principal train stations; *www.eurostar.com* Channel tunnel services to Paris or Brussels via Lille.

Eurotunnel, PO Box 300, Dept 302, Folkestone, Kent CT19 4QD ☎0870/535 3535, *www.eurotunnel.co.uk* Shuttle train via the Channel Tunnel for passengers and their vehicles.

Holland Rail, Chase House, Gilbert St, Ropley, Hants SO24 0BY ☎01962/773646; *www.ukconsultants.com/hollandrail* British agents for tickets on Netherlands Railways.

Nederlandse Spoorwegen *www.ns.nl* Netherlands Railway. This site has a useful online timetable, covering both national and international routes.

Rail Europe, 179 Piccadilly, London W1V BA ☎08705/848848, *www.raileurope.co.uk* European rail tickets and passes.

Wasteels, by platform 2, Victoria Station, London SW1V 1JT ☎020/7834 7066. Youth train and coach ticket specialists.

---

baggage"; you can retrieve it at Brussels, but not at intermediate stations. It's possible to check your bike in up to ten days in advance, to ensure it's waiting for you on arrival; if you check it in on the day of travel Eurostar only guarantees that you will be reunited within 24 hours, which obviously poses problems if you're travelling on to Holland.

A longer and cheaper rail route is available through **Stena Line** in conjunction with several local rail operators – Scotrail, Anglia, First North Western, First Great Western and Virgin – and utilizes the fast **Harwich** to **Hook of Holland** ferry crossing (3hr 40min). The London Liverpool Street to Amsterdam journey takes around eight hours and operates twice daily. Prices from London start at £50 return for a three-day Apex fare, which must be booked at least a week in advance, with the return journey being made within three days. A standard return costs £60 with a young person's railcard, £80 for an adult. Tickets are available from the rail agents listed in the box above or from larger stations.

RAIL PASSES

Though you're hardly likely to buy a **rail pass** (see p.3) simply to get to Holland it's worth knowing that, whilst not entitling UK and Irish nationals to free rail travel within Britain and Ireland, the **InterRail** pass does entitle the holder to dis-counted fares en route to the continent via rail/ferry routes; check for specific details. See p.32 for full details of the available options.

BY BUS

Travelling by long-distance **bus** is generally the cheapest way of reaching Holland from the UK, but it is very time-consuming: the main route, London to Amsterdam, takes ten hours or more. There are three **Eurolines** coaches daily from **London Victoria** Coach Station to Amsterdam's **Amstel** Station, southeast of the city centre, leaving at 8.30am, 8pm and 10.30pm, and crossing the Channel with Eurotunnel. Prices for under-26s and over-60s are a fixed £42 return (£28 one-way); a standard fare is £47 return (£31 one-way).

Alternatively, if you prefer to travel by **ferry** from either Newcastle to IJmuiden or Hull to Rotterdam (see ferries below), you can book and pay for the coach along with your ferry ticket. Coaches meet the ferries and leave from the respective quays to Amsterdam Centraal Station. A return trip from **Newcastle** to **Amsterdam**, via IJmuiden, costs around £70 in low season (£100 in high season) and takes approximately fifteen hours. Travelling from **Hull** to **Amsterdam** via the Rotterdam Europoort takes around the same time, including the hour's coach journey, and costs £86 in low season (£104 in high season).

BY CAR: THE CHANNEL TUNNEL AND FERRIES

If you're looking to travel to Holland by **car**, your options are either to take the train through the Channel tunnel, or to opt for one of the many ferry routes.

Eurotunnel operates the car-carrying rail service which operates between Folkestone and Coquelles, near Calais, through the Channel tunnel. The train journey takes around 35 minutes, and trains run three times an hour during the day and once hourly at night. Tickets can be bought on arrival, but advance booking (by phone or via the Internet) is advised at peak times. The recommended check-in time is 25 minutes before departure, with final boarding fifteen minutes later. **Prices** vary seasonally, but more noticeably depending on the time of day, with the cheapest fares available on journeys made between 10pm and 6am. Prices are charged per vehicle, with no additions for passengers, and one-way fares are charged at half the price of an economy return. Return trips made within five days entitle you to mini-break prices which, for a **car**, range from £140 (£150 in high season) for a night train to £170 (£215 in high season) during the day; for a **motorbike** the corresponding prices are £80 and £125 (£160) respectively. If you wish to stay longer, an economy return (the confusing name for the standard return ticket) by car will cost £220 for overnight travel and £250 (£330) by day; for a motorbike it's £120 and £190 (£250). A trailer or caravan costs more or less the equivalent of another car; bicycles and foot passengers are not carried on Eurotunnel. From Calais, it's around 130 miles (200km) to Rotterdam, over 300 miles (around 500km) to Amsterdam, and, in the east, about 160 miles (260km) to Arnhem.

There are three direct **ferry** crossings into Holland from the UK: the twice daily Stena Line route from **Harwich** to the **Hook of Holland** (3hr 40min), which leaves you with roughly an hour's drive to Amsterdam; the DFDS Seaways route, sailed three times weekly from **Newcastle** to **IJmuiden** (14hr), which is twenty minutes' drive from Amsterdam; and the once daily **Hull** to **Rotterdam** (Europoort) crossing (13hr) with P&O North Sea Ferries. P&O also operate a **Hull** to **Zeebrugge** service (13hr), leaving you with a drive of around two to three hours to Amsterdam, a couple of hours more to the east of the country around Arnhem, more of course to the provinces in the far north. **Prices**, perhaps surprisingly given the differing lengths of the crossings, are broadly similar. The cost of a return for a single person and car taking the Stena Line route from Harwich varies from £160 (low season) to £260 (high season) with additional passengers charged at £11 per person. On the two longer routes, the price of a return crossing for a car and two people in a basic two-berth cabin will work out at between £235 (low season) and £390 (high season) with DFDS Seaways, although there's a discount of up to £30 per passenger for those under 26 or over 60. DFDS also have "all-in-a-car" discounts and special deals on the larger cabins. The P&O North Sea Ferries routes cost around £265 return from October to June and £325 from July to September, with reductions of up to £42 for each person under 26 or over 60; they also have an all-in-one price that includes the cost of the car and

FERRY OPERATORS

DFDS Seaways, Scandinavia House, Parkeston Quay, Harwich, Essex CO12 4QG ☎0870/533 3000; 15 Hanover St, London W1R 9HG ☎020/7409 6060; Tyne Commission Quay, North Shields, NE29 6EA ☎0191/296 0101; *www.dfdsseaways.co.uk* Newcastle to IJmuiden.

Hoverspeed ☎08705/240241, *www.hoverspeed.co.uk* Dover to Oostende and Calais.

P&O North Sea Ferries, King George Dock, Hedon Rd, Kingston-upon-Hull HU9 5QA

☎01482/377177, *www.ponsf.com* Hull to Rotterdam and Zeebrugge.

P&O Stena Line, Channel House, Channel View Rd, Dover CT17 9TJ ☎08706/000611, *www.posl.com* Dover to Calais.

Seafrance, Eastern Docks, Dover, Kent CT16 1JA ☎08705/711711, *www.seafrance.com* Dover to Calais.

Stena Line, Charter House, Park St, Ashford, Kent TN24 8EX ☎0870/570 7070, *www.stenaline.co.uk* Harwich to Hook of Holland.

up to four people. If you're looking for a short break, all three companies offer five-day/night deals that bring down the cost of the crossing yet again.

If you want to spend less time actually at sea, **Hoverspeed** "fly" from **Dover** to **Oostende** in Belgium. Otherwise there are countless Channel crossings to France, but you'll need to consider the additional time and cost involved in making your way north. If you're planning to take your bike, Stena Line charge just £5, while DFDS Seaways and P&O North Sea Ferries make no charge at all. For more on cycles and cycling see p.34.

PACKAGE HOLIDAYS

Don't automatically dismiss the idea of going on a **package holiday**; most consist of no more than travel and accommodation (from two nights to two weeks or more) and can work out an easy way of cutting costs and hassle. For example, short breaks to Amsterdam on Eurostar, giving two nights' accommodation with breakfast in a two-star hotel, start at around £170 per person. The same package with return flights from a London airport works out around the same, with supplements of £10–50 for a flight from a regional airport. Operators can also arrange accommodation plus ferry tickets if you want to design your own self-drive package (both P&O North Sea Ferries and DFDS Seaways – see box on p.7 – offer all-inclusive short breaks). Day-trips to Amsterdam, available through the Amsterdam Travel Service (see box), cost between £120 and £185. The price includes a return flight and the trains between Schiphol and the city centre.

SELECTED TOUR OPERATORS

Amsterdam Travel Service, Bridge House, 55–59 High Rd, Broxbourne, Herts EN10 7DT ☎01992/456056, *www.bridge-travel.co.uk* The largest collection of Amsterdam holidays, and a variety of short breaks, including cycling breaks.

Anglo-Dutch Sports Ltd, 177a High St, Beckenham, Kent BR3 1AH ☎020/8289 2808, *www.anglodutchsports.co.uk* Offering a range of countryside cycling holidays, some incorporating sailing and travel by barge.

Cresta Holidays, Tabley Court, Victoria St, Altrincham, Cheshire WA14 1EZ ☎0161/927 7000. Popular short-break specialists with a broad range of Amsterdam packages.

Euro Villages, Hartford Manor, Greenbank Lane, Northwich, Cheshire CW8 1HW ☎01606/787776, *www.eurovillages.co.uk* The company's six Netherlands holiday villages are mainly water-based activity centres, with cabin-style family accommodation.

Inntravel, Hovingham, York YO62 4JZ ☎01653/628811, *www.inntravel.co.uk* Classy short breaks, by air, rail or car.

Stena Line Holidays, Charter House, Park St, Ashford, Kent TN24 8EX ☎0870/574 7474, *www.stenaline.co.uk* A reasonable selection of Amsterdam package holidays, along with eight other Dutch city destinations.

GETTING THERE FROM IRELAND

Taking into account the time and inconvenience of crossing the UK and then the Channel, travelling by air is by far the simplest way to reach Holland from Ireland. Unless you're on the tightest of budgets, the extra money spent on a flight is well worthwhile.

BY AIR

Aer Lingus flies direct from **Dublin** to **Amsterdam**, with around five flights daily, and connections from Cork, Galway, Kerry, Shannon and Sligo. From **Belfast**, there are no direct flights to Amsterdam, but British Midland operate around three flights daily via London Heathrow, from around £160 plus tax. Other flight options also involve **transfers** in the UK, which almost always mean switching carriers for the second leg of your journey. However flying with Ryanair to London Stansted (which could cost as little as IR£30 each way), then with KLMuk to Amsterdam (from around £80 return), can work out cheaper than a direct Aer Lingus flight. UsitNOW, or any of the discount agents listed in the box below can advise you on the latest and cheapest deals.

TRANSPORT COMPANIES

AIRLINES

Aer Lingus, 40/41 Upper O'Connell St, Dublin 1 ☎01/705 3333; 46/48 Castle St, Belfast BT1 1HB ☎0845/9737747; 2 Academy St, Cork ☎021/327 155; 136 O'Connell St, Limerick ☎061/474 239; *www.aerlingus.ie* Direct flights from Dublin to Amsterdam, codesharing with KLMuk, plus flights via Dublin from Cork, Shannon, Galway, Sligo and Kerry.

British Midland, Nutley, Merrion Rd, Dublin 4 ☎01/283 8833; Suite 2, Fountain Centre, College St, Belfast 1 ☎0870/607 0555; *www.britishmidland.com* Belfast and Dublin to Amsterdam via London Heathrow and East Midlands.

Ryanair, Phoenix House, Conyngham Rd, Dublin ☎01/609 7800, *www.ryanair.ie* From Dublin, Cork, Knock and Kerry to London Stansted.

BUS COMPANY

Bus Éireann, Busáras, Store St, Dublin 1 ☎01/830 2222, *www.buseireann.ie* Irish Eurolines agents.

FERRY COMPANIES

DFDS Seaways, c/o Stena Line, Ferry Terminal, Dún Laoghaire ☎01/204 7777; c/o SeaCat, SeaCat Terminal, Donegal Quay, Belfast BT1 3AL ☎028/9031 4918; *www.dfdsseaways.co.uk* Dún Laoghaire to Holyhead, Rosslare to Fishguard, and Belfast to Stranraer.

Irish Ferries, 2–4 Merrion Row, Dublin 2 ☎01/638 3333 or ☎01/661 0715; St Patrick's Buildings, Cork ☎021/551995; *www.irishferries.ie* Rosslare to Roscoff and Cherbourg, or Dublin to Holyhead.

TRAIN COMPANY

Iarnrod Éireann, Connolly Station, Amiens St, Dublin 1 ☎1-850/366222, *www.irishrail.ie* National rail company.

BY TRAIN

The **train** journey from Dublin to the Netherlands is a real endurance test. There are three daily departures, taking between seventeen and 24 hours. The favoured route is Dublin to Holyhead on the ferry and then a train from Holyhead to London Euston (changing at Crewe or Birmingham). From London Euston, you must make your own way across the city to Waterloo station to catch the **Eurostar** train through to Brussels, with connecting trains direct to Amsterdam and Rotterdam (see p.4 for more on Eurostar). The cost of the ticket is little less than the IR£200 cost of an InterRail pass and is available from Iarnród Éireann (see box p.9).

There's a great variety of **InterRail** passes on offer, but bear in mind that to travel from Ireland you must buy a pass for two zones in order to cover travel across the UK and Holland. For **under-26s** resident in Ireland who buy the pass before they leave, an InterRail giving a month's unlimited travel throughout Zone A (UK) and Zone E (France, Belgium, Luxembourg and the Netherlands) costs around IR£200; this also gives reductions on the ferries. Those **over 26** buy a two-zone InterRail pass for IR£275, but it cannot be used in Belgium or France, which means that the only way of getting there from the UK is by taking a ferry route directly into Holland. For travel around The Netherlands, the **Euro Domino** pass is a better bet (see p.3 for details of the options available); note, too that Euro Domino pass-holders are entitled to fifty-percent reductions on the ferries between Ireland and the UK, and between the UK and the Netherlands, as well as a 25 percent discount on the train journey across the UK to Harwich.

BY BUS

The **bus** journey from Dublin to Holland takes around 25 hours, but it's cheap enough to appeal to those watching every punt. The best way to reach Holland by bus is to use the twice daily **Eurolines** service to Amsterdam. Beginning at the Dublin Busáras, the route takes you across the Irish Sea by ferry to Holyhead, the Eurotunnel via London, Antwerp, Rotterdam and The Hague, before reaching Amsterdam. From Dublin, a standard adult return costs IR£83 (IR£99 high season), with an **under-26** ticket of IR£77 (IR£94); prices from elsewhere in Ireland are fixed at IR£103 (IR£119) for an adult, IR£94 (IR£108) if you're under 26. Alternatively, you could try the Busabout service, which provides a series of bus routes intended to link major European cities – the bus equivalent of the Interrail and Euro Domino passes. Bookings can be made through UsitNOW.

BY FERRY

There are no **ferries** direct from Ireland to either Belgium or Holland – the nearest ferries get is the northwest of France. However, **Irish Ferries** will arrange your travel via the UK. The route is Dublin

---

DISCOUNT TRAVEL AGENTS

Aran Travel, Granary Hall, 58 Dominick St, Galway ☎091/562595, *arantvl@iol.ie* Well-informed and competitive holiday agent, but with flight-only bargains.

Dial-a-Flight Ireland, 11/12 Warrington Place, Dublin 2 ☎01/662 9933. Scheduled flight specialists.

Fahy Travel, 3 Bridge St, Galway ☎091/563055, *fahytrav@iol.ie* Has a good selection of last-minute bargains.

Joe Walsh Ltd, 8–11 Baggot St, Dublin 2 ☎01/676 3053; 117 St Patrick St, Cork ☎021/277 959. Package holiday and flight agent, with occasional discount offers.

Thomas Cook, 11 Donegal Place, Belfast BT1 5AJ ☎028/9024 0833; 118 Grafton St, Dublin ☎01/677 1360; *www.thomascook.com* Package holiday and flight agent, with occasional discount offers.

Twohigs Travel, 8 Burgh Quay, Dublin ☎01/677 2666; 13 Duke St, Dublin ☎01/670 9750. General budget fares agent.

UsitNOW, O'Connell Bridge, 19–21 Aston Quay, Dublin 2 ☎01/602 1600; Fountain Centre, Belfast BT1 6ET ☎028/9032 4073; 66 Oliver Plunkett St, Cork ☎021/270900; 33 Ferryquay St, Derry ☎028/7137 1888; Victoria Place, Eyre Sq, Galway ☎091/565177; Central Buildings, O'Connell St, Limerick ☎061/415064; 36–37 Georges St, Waterford ☎051/872601; *www.usitnow.com* Ireland's main student and youth travel specialists.

to Holyhead by ferry, then overland to Hull to pick up the P&O North Sea Ferries service to Rotterdam or Zeebrugge (see p.7). Either way, this is a long way from being a competitive option.

PACKAGE HOLIDAYS

Package holidays – which can simply mean flights plus accommodation – are a feasible and

sensible method of eliminating snags, and can easily cut costs as well. Both KLMuk and Aer Lingus offer several different "weekend break" packages to suit various budgets and styles; travel agents should have the relevant brochures, or you can call the airlines direct for information. Many travel agents can also give deals on city breaks in Amsterdam (see box overleaf).

GETTING THERE FROM NORTH AMERICA

Amsterdam's Schiphol airport is among the most popular and least expensive gateways to Europe from North America, and getting a convenient and good-value flight is rarely a problem. Virtually every region of the United States and Canada is well served by the major airlines, though only two scheduled carriers offer nonstop flights – KLM/ Northwest Airlines and Delta Air Lines. The rest fly via London and other European centres. Look out, too, for deals offered by the Dutch charter company Martinair, which offers mid-priced seats on nonstop flights from a number of cities in the USA and Canada.

SHOPPING FOR TICKETS

Barring special offers, the cheapest fare is usually an **Apex** ticket, although this will carry certain restrictions: you have to book – and pay – at least fourteen days in advance (more often 21 days),

spend at least seven days abroad (maximum stay three months), and you tend to get penalized if you change your schedule. On transatlantic routes, there are also winter **Super Apex** tickets, sometimes known as "Eurosavers" – slightly cheaper than an ordinary Apex, but limiting your stay to between seven and 21 days. Some airlines also issue **Special Apex** tickets to people younger than 24, often extending the maximum stay to a year. Many airlines offer youth or student fares to **under-25s**; a passport or driver's licence is sufficient proof of age, though these tickets are subject to availability and can have eccentric booking conditions. It's worth remembering that most cheap return fares will only give a percentage refund if you need to cancel or alter your journey, so make sure you check the restrictions carefully before buying.

You can normally cut costs further by going through a **specialist flight agent** – either a **consolidator**, who buys up blocks of tickets from the airlines and sells them at a discount, or a **discount agent**, who wheels and deals in tickets offloaded by the airlines, and often offers special student and youth fares and a range of other travel-related services, such as travel insurance, car rental and tours. Bear in mind, though, that the penalties for changing your plans can be stiff. Remember too that these companies make their money by dealing in bulk, so don't expect them to answer lots of questions. Some agents specialize in **charter flights**, which may be cheaper than any scheduled flight available, but again departure dates are fixed and withdrawal penalties are high (check the refund policy). If you travel a lot, **discount travel clubs** are another option – the annual membership fee may be worth it for benefits such as cut-price air tickets and car rental.

A further possibility is to see if you can arrange a **courier flight**, although the hit-and-miss nature of these makes them most suitable for the single traveller who travels light and has a very flexible schedule. In return for shepherding a package through customs and possibly giving up your baggage allowance, you can expect to get a heavily discounted ticket. See p.14 or, for more options, consult *A Simple Guide to Courier Travel* (Pacific Data Sales Publishing).

Regardless of where you buy your ticket, the fare will depend on the **season**. Fares are highest in December, June, July and August, and fares during these months can cost between $100 and $300 more, depending on the airline. Flying on weekends can add $100 to the cost of a return ticket: prices quoted below assume midweek travel. In addition, any Apex fares quoted entail a maximum stay of thirty days.

FLIGHTS FROM THE USA

KLM and Northwest Airlines, which operate a joint service from the United States and Canada to Amsterdam, offer the widest range of flights, with nonstop or direct services from eleven US cities on KLM and connections from dozens more via Northwest. Their Apex fares are usually identical to those offered by other carriers, so for convenience at least, KLM/Northwest is your best bet. It's also worth looking into deals offered by the Dutch carrier **Martinair**, which flies regularly scheduled nonstop flights from five US cities – though note that three of them are served in summer only.

One-way fares are rarely good value, but if you're set on one, the best source is the seat consolidators that advertise in the back pages of the travel sections of the major Sunday newspapers – or see the box below.

Travelling from the **East Coast**, KLM's nonstop flights out of New York JFK start at around $400 in low season, rising by around $150 in May and peaking at around $780 in July and August. Nonstop fares out of Washington DC, Atlanta, Detroit, Chicago and Minneapolis typically cost $50–100 more; connecting flights from other major cities are usually thrown in for free. Delta has similar fares on its nonstop flights out of New York and Atlanta, as does United from Washington DC, and most carriers match these prices on their flights via London Heathrow. Especially during winter, many airlines have special offers that can reduce fares to well under $500 return, and discount travel agents and consolidators can often find you fares as low as $350 (low season) or $650 (high season). Martinair also offers good deals in the summer out of Newark, with fares as low as $640 at the height of the peak season, and a year-round service from Miami (six days a week) and Orlando (four days per week) with similarly low prices.

As for the **West Coast**, KLM/Northwest Airlines' round-trip Apex fares on nonstop flights out of Los Angeles start at around $570 in low season, rising to $700 in May and $1200 in July and August. Consolidators can probably get you a seat for less than $550 (low season) or $750 (high

---

AIRLINES

British Airways US: ☎1-800/247-9297; Canada: ☎1-800/247-9297; *www.british-airways.com* Daily nonstop flights to London from major US and Canadian cities, with connections to Amsterdam.

Delta Air Lines ☎1-800/241-4141, *www.delta-air.com* Daily nonstop service to Amsterdam from New York and Atlanta.

KLM/Northwest Airlines US: ☎1-800/447-4747; Canada: ☎1-800/361-5073; *www.nwa.com* Daily nonstop or direct services to Amsterdam from major US and Canadian cities.

Martinair US: ☎1-800/627-8462; Canada: ☎416/364-3672; *www.martinairusa.com*

Regularly scheduled nonstop flights to Amsterdam from Miami and Orlando (year-round), and Los Angeles, Newark and Oakland (April–Oct). Charter flights (April–Oct) from Toronto, Vancouver, Calgary and Edmonton.

United Airlines, ☎1-800/241-6522, *www.ual.com* Daily nonstop to Amsterdam from Washington DC.

Virgin Atlantic Airways, ☎1-800/862-8621, *www.virgin-atlantic.com* Daily nonstop flights to London from New York, with connections to Amsterdam.

DISCOUNT FLIGHT AGENTS, TRAVEL CLUBS AND CONSOLIDATORS

Air Brokers International, 323 Geary St, Suite 411, San Francisco, CA 94102 ☎1-800/883-3273, *www.airbrokers.com* Consolidator and specialist in round-the-world tickets.

Air Courier Association, 15000 W. 6th Ave, Suite 203, Golden, CO 80401 ☎1-800/282-1202 or 303/279-3600, *www.aircourier.org* Courier flight broker – $25 membership plus $39 annual fee.

Airhitch, 2641 Broadway, New York, NY 10025 ☎1-800/326-2009 or 212/864-2000, *www.airhitch.org* Standby-seat broker. For a set price, they guarantee to get you on a flight as close to your preferred destination as possible, within a week.

Council Travel, 205 E 42nd St, New York, NY 10017 ☎1-800/226-8624, *www.counciltravel.com* Agent specializing in student/budget fares, with branches in forty US cities.

Encore Short Notice, 4501 Forbes Blvd, Lanham, MD 20706 ☎1-800/444-9800, *www.emitravel.com* East Coast travel club – $69 membership fee.

Flight Center, 3030 S Granville St, Vancouver, BC V6H 3J9 ☎604/739-9539. Discount air fares from Canadian cities.

High Adventure Travel Inc., 442 Post St, Suite 400, San Francisco, CA 94102 ☎1-800/350-0612, *www.airtreks.com* Round-the-world tickets.

Interworld Travel, 3400 Coral Way, Miami, FL 33145 ☎1-800/468-3796 or 305/443-4929, *www.interworld.com* Southeastern US consolidator.

Last-Minute Travel Club, 132 Brookline Ave, Boston, MA 02215 (☎617/267-9800 or 1-800/LAST-MIN). Package tour specialist.

Nouvelles Frontières US: 12 E 33rd St, New York, NY 10016 ☎1-800/366-6387 or 212/779-0600; Canada: 1000 Sherbrook East, Suite 720, Montréal, H2L 1L3 ☎514/871-3060; *www.nouvelles-frontieres.com* Main US and Canadian branches of the French discount travel outfit. Other branches in LA, San Francisco and Québec City.

Now Voyager, 74 Varick St, Suite 307, New York, NY 10013 ☎212/431-1616, *www.nowvoyagertravel.com* Courier flight broker and consolidator.

Overseas Tours, 199 California Drive, suite 188 Millbrae, CA 94030 ☎1-800/323-8777, *www.overseastours.com* Discount agent.

Pan Express Travel, 65 Wellesely St East, Suite 401, Toronto, ON M4Y 1H6 ☎416/964-6888. Discount travel agent.

Rebel Tours, 25050 Avenue Kearny, Suite 215, Valencia, CA 91355 ☎1-800/227-3235 or 661/294-0900, *www.rebeltours.com* Good source of deals with Martinair.

STA Travel, 10 Downing St, New York, NY 10014 ☎1-800/777-0112 or 212/627-3111, *www.sta-travel.com* Worldwide discount firm specializing in student/youth fares, student IDs, travel insurance, car rental, and rail passes. Other branches in the Los Angeles, San Francisco, Minneapolis, Chicago, Philadelphia and Boston areas.

TFI Tours, 34 W 32nd St, 12th Floor, New York, NY 10001 ☎1-800/745-8000 or 212/736-1140. Consolidator with the very best East Coast deals, especially if you only want to fly one-way.

Travac, 989 6th Ave, 16th Floor, New York, NY 10018 ☎1-800/872-8800, fax 1-888/872-8327, *www.thetravelsite.com* Consolidator and charter broker. They will fax current fares from their fax line.

Travel CUTS, 187 College St, Toronto, ON M5T 1P7 ☎416/979-2406, *www.travelcuts.com* Main office of the Canadian student travel organization. Many other offices nationwide.

Travelers Advantage, 3033 S Parker Rd, Suite 1000, Aurora, CO 80014 ☎1-800/548-1116, *www.travelersadvantage.com* Reliable discount travel club; annual membership of $59.95 required.

Travel Avenue, 10 S Riverside Plaza, Suite 1404, Chicago, IL 60606, ☎1-800/333-3335 or 312/876-6866, *www.tipc.com* Discount travel agent.

Travelocity *www.travelocity.com* Online consolidator.

Unitravel, 11737 Administration Dr, Suite 120, St Louis, MO 63146 ☎1-800/325-2222, *www.flightsforless.com* Reliable consolidator.

season). Fares from San Francisco or Seattle usually cost $50–100 more and most international carriers charge similar prices. Special offers sometimes bring the fares down to under $500, though these are usually only available during winter.

Martinair's service from the West Coast is now limited to flights from Los Angeles (three weekly) and Oakland (two weekly), and is only available between April and October, but if you are willing to work within these restrictions, the reward is low fares – with flights from either LA or Oakland to Amsterdam for as little as $538 (April to mid-June). Even their peak fare (mid-June to August) is low at $768.

ROUND-THE-WORLD TICKETS AND COURIER FLIGHTS

If you plan to visit Holland as part of a major world trip, then you might want to think about getting a **round-the-world ticket** that includes the city as one of its stops. A sample route from the West Coast, using a combination of airlines, might be Los Angeles–Hong Kong–Bangkok–Amman–Cairo–Amsterdam–New York–Los Angeles, which costs $1677. A ticket covering the same route from the East Coast (New York) costs $1536. See the box on p.13 for details of agents specializing in round-the-world tickets.

Return **courier flights** to Amsterdam from major US cities are available for around $200–250, with last-minute specials booked within three days of departure going for as little as $100. For more information about courier flights, contact The Air Courier Association or Now Voyager (see box on p.13).

FLIGHTS FROM CANADA

KLM/Northwest Airlines has the best range of routes from Canada, with nonstop flights from all the major airports, and fares approximately the same as those from the USA. Return tickets out of **Toronto** start at around C$708 in the low season, stepping up to C$1000 in May and C$1300 in July and August. Fares from **Vancouver** start at around C$900, climbing to C$1400 and C$1700.

Canadian **charter** operations, such as Air Transat and Fiesta West/Canada 3000 offer some of the best deals on spring through fall travel, with fares as low as C$659 from Toronto and C$819 from Vancouver and Calgary. Neither Air Canada nor Canadian Airlines serves Amsterdam, though Martinair flies nonstop charters out of Toronto, Vancouver, Calgary and Edmonton (April–Oct): low-season fares from Toronto start at C$620, rising to C$820 in high season.

Canadian departures for **round-the-world** tickets can usually be arranged for around C$150 more than the US fare (see above).

TRAVELLING VIA EUROPE

Even though many flights from North America to Holland are routed via London, because of the various special fares it's often cheaper to stay on the plane all the way to Amsterdam. In general you can't stop over and continue on a later flight, as US and Canadian airlines are not allowed to provide services between European cities.

However, if you want to combine a trip with visits to other European cities, **London** makes the best starting point, as onward flights are relatively inexpensive. Besides having the best range of good-value transatlantic flights (New York to London is the busiest and cheapest route), London also has excellent connections on to Amsterdam. **Paris**, too, is becoming a popular gateway to Europe. United and American Airlines, as well as British Airways and the British carrier Virgin Atlantic, all have frequent flights to London from various parts of the US, BA flying from Canada too; Air France, United and American fly daily to Paris. See "Getting There from Britain", p.3, for details on travel from Britain to Amsterdam and other Dutch cities.

RAIL PASSES

If you intend Holland to form just part of your European travels, or envisage using the European rail network extensively, then you should consider investing in a **Eurail train pass**. These are good for unlimited travel within seventeen European countries, including Holland, and they should be purchased before you leave, as they cost ten percent more in Europe: you can get them from most travel agents in the USA and Canada or from Rail Europe (US: ☎1-800/438-7245; Canada ☎1-800/361-7245; *www.raileurope.com*), who can also supply you with up-to-date information and fares). The **standard** Eurail pass is valid for unlimited first-class travel on consecutive days for periods of fifteen days ($554), 21 days ($718), one month ($890), two months ($1260), or three months ($1558). If you're **under 26** the Eurail Youthpass allows second-class rail travel, the prices for which, respectively, are $388, $499, $623, $882 or $1089. There's also the Eurail **Flexipass**, which may be a better buy, as it allows for a certain number of non-consecutive days travel within a two-month period, and also comes in first-class/under-26 versions: ten days costs $654/$458, and fifteen days, $862/$599. Parties of between two and five can save fifteen percent with the Eurail **Saver Flexipass**, allowing for travel within a two-month period on ten days ($556) or fifteen days ($732).

If you intend to move about within the Netherlands only there's also a **Holland Railpass** which might be worth purchasing. It can be bought in 1st/2nd-class forms, with travel on any three days in a month costing $98/$65; and five days $147/$98. The discount offered for

two adults travelling together brings the price for three days, each, down to $73/$49; and five days down to $110/$73 each. The under-26 version of this pass costs $52 for three days and $79 for five days. If you're planning to cross over into Holland's immediate neighbours as well, you might want to consider the **Benelux Tourrail Pass** (for unlimited travel in Belgium, the Netherlands and Luxembourg), which can be purchased in similar variations, with travel on any five days in a month going for $217/$155, the discounted ticket for two adults costing $163/$116.50 and for under-26s $104.

INCLUSIVE TOURS

There are any number of **packages and organized tours** from North America to Amsterdam and elsewhere in Holland. Prices vary, with some

SPECIALIST TOUR OPERATORS

Abercrombie & Kent ☎1-800/323-7308, *www.abercrombiekent.com* Six-night river and canal cruising tours from Amsterdam to Bruges starting at $1100. Airfare extra.

AESU Travel ☎1-800/638-7640, *www.aesu.com* Tours, independent city stays, discounted air fares. 37-day "Grand Europe" tour includes one day in Amsterdam (with biking and a visit to a diamond-cutting factory) and a stop in Brussels; $3300 plus airfare.

Air Transat Holidays ☎604/688-3350. Canadian charter company offering discount fares from major Canadian cities, tours and fly-drive trips. Contact travel agents for brochures.

American Airlines Vacations ☎1-800/321-2121, *www.aavacations.com* Package tours and fly-drive programmes.

British Airways Holidays ☎1-800/359-8722, *www.british-airways.com/vacations* Package tours and fly-drives.

Canada 3000/FiestaWest Discount charter flights, car rental, accommodation and package tours. Book through travel agents or by calling BCAA TeleCentre in Canada: ☎1-800/663-1956.

CBT Bicycle Tours ☎1-800/736-BIKE, *www.biketrip.net* Affordable tours in Holland, Belgium and Luxembourg. Two-week Amsterdam to Brussels trip, with one week in each country, starts at $2395. A one-week tour through

Holland during the tulip season (May) costs $1565. Airfare extra. Available through travel agents.

Contiki Tours ☎1-800/CONTIKI, *www.contiki.com* Budget tours to Europe for those aged 18 to 35, including a large number of multi-country tours with stops in Holland. A twenty-day tour of eleven countries, including two days in Amsterdam, starting in London, costs $1390.

Euro Bike Tours ☎1-800/321-6060, *www.eurobike.com* Upscale cycling tours: fourteen days in Holland, Belgium, Luxembourg and Germany starts at $3095; and eight days in Holland, including Amsterdam, for $1995. Airfare extra.

Europe Through the Back Door ☎425/771-8303, *www.ricksteves.com* Small-group travel off-the-beaten track, with an enthusiastic guide team. 21-day "Best of Europe" Tour, including stops in Amsterdam and Haarlem, costs $2700.

Kemwel's Premier Selections ☎1-800/234-4000, *www.premierselections.com* Rail journeys and barge cruises – also a discount auto rental agency.

KLM/Northwest World Vacations ☎1-800/447-4747, *www.nwa.com* Hotel and sightseeing packages and escorted tours.

United Vacations ☎1-800/538-2929, *www.ual.com* Flight and hotel packages.

operators including the air fare, while others cover just accommodation, sightseeing and activities such as cycling or hiking. In addition, many airlines offer fly-drive deals that include a week's hotel accommodation, but again the prices vary according to season and can even change daily.

You'll find that most European tours include Amsterdam on their itineraries, too. Among the best of the Europe-wide operators are Europe Through the Back Door, a specialist in independent budget travel, with the emphasis on simple accommodation and meeting local people.

GETTING THERE FROM AUSTRALIA AND NEW ZEALAND

There is no shortage of flights to the Netherlands from Australia and New Zealand, though all of them involve at least one stop. When buying a ticket, as well as the price, you might want to take into account the airline's route – whether, for example, you'd rather stop in Moscow or Bali. Some of the airlines allow free stopovers (see the box opposite).

Air fares to Holland vary significantly with the season: **low season** runs from mid-January to the end of February and during October and November; **high season** runs from mid-May to the end of August and December to mid-January; the rest of the year is counted as shoulder season. Tickets purchased direct from the airlines tend to be expensive, with published fares ranging from A$2000/NZ$2500 (low season) to A$2500–3000/NZ$3000–3600 (high season).

Travel agents offer better deals on fares, specifically to Amsterdam, and have the latest information on special deals, such as free

stopovers en route and fly-drive-accommodation packages. Flight Centres and STA generally offer the best discounts, especially for students and those under 26. For a **discounted ticket** from Sydney, Melbourne or Auckland, expect to pay A$1600–2500/NZ$2000–2700. Fares from Perth and Darwin are slightly cheaper via Asia, rather more expensive via Canada and the US, and fares from Christchurch and Wellington are around NZ$150–300 more than those from Auckland.

For flights to **other European cities**, the lowest fares are with Britannia to London, during its limited charter season (Nov–March), when you can expect to pay A$1000–1600/NZ$1200–1900; from London you could pick up a cheap flight to Amsterdam or consider going overland (see "Getting there from Britain", p.3). For a scheduled flight, including any connections, count on paying A$1500–2260/NZ$1900–2800 on Alitalia or KLM; A$1900–2500/NZ$2280–3000 on SAS, Thai Airways or Lufthansa; A$2400–2850/NZ$2700–3400 on British Airways, Qantas, Singapore Airlines, Air New Zealand or Canadian Airways depending on the season. See the box opposite for a full rundown of airlines and routes.

ROUND THE WORLD TICKETS

For extended trips, **round-the-world tickets**, valid for up to a year, can be good value. These are mileage-based tickets used with a combination of airlines – which airlines you use depends to a degree on your route, but also on seat availability. The cheapest tickets usually involve three to four stopovers, with prices rising the further you travel or the more stops you add – you can backtrack as much as you like within the mileage of the ticket. RTW tickets can be booked through any of the partner airlines, or through travel

AIRLINES

Aeroflot, 44 Market St, Sydney ☎02/9262 2233. Four flights a week to Amsterdam from Sydney via Moscow. There is a code-sharing arrangement with Qantas to either Bangkok or Singapore for the first leg.

Air New Zealand Australia: 90 Arthur St, North Sydney ☎13/2476; NZ: Customs/Albert St, Auckland ☎0800/737000; *www.airnz.co.nz* Daily flights to London or Frankfurt via LA, from where you can get a connecting flight.

Alitalia Australia: 118 Albert St, Milsons Point, Sydney ☎1300/653757; NZ: 229 Queen St, Auckland ☎09/379 4457; *www.alitalia.it* Six flights a week from Sydney, with Ansett connections from the other major cities, direct to Amsterdam (code sharing with KLM) or via Milan.

Britannia Airways Australia: c/o UK Flight Shop, 7 Macquarie Place, Sydney ☎02/9247 4833, *www.ukflightshop.com.au*; NZ: c/o World Aviation, Trustbank Building, 229 Queen St, Auckland ☎09/308 3355. Charter flights to London from Sydney and Auckland via Indonesia and Abu Dhabi (both stops for refuelling only).

British Airways Australia: Level 4, 50 Franklin St, Melbourne ☎03/9603 1133; 70 Hunter St, Sydney ☎02/8904 8800; NZ: 154 Queen St, Auckland ☎09/356 8690; *www.british-airways.com* Daily to London from Sydney, Perth or Brisbane with onward connections to Amsterdam.

Cathay Pacific Australia: 8 Spring St, Sydney ☎13/1747; NZ: Floor 11, 205 Queen St, Auckland ☎09/379 0861. Several flights a week from major Australasian cities via Hong Kong. Code-sharing with Qantas for the Australia–Hong Kong leg of the journey.

Garuda Indonesia Australia: 55 Hunter St, Sydney ☎1300/365330; NZ: Westpac Trust Tower, 120 Albert St, Auckland ☎09/366 1862. Three flights a week to Amsterdam from Bali and Jakarta, both of which are connected to major Australian and New Zealand cities by regular flights.

KLM Australia: Nauru House, 80 Collins St, Melbourne ☎03/9654 5222; 5 Elizabeth St, Sydney ☎02/9231 6333; toll-free ☎1800/500747; *www.klm.com.au*; NZ: 369 Queen St, Auckland ☎09/309 1782. Six times a week from Sydney to Amsterdam, with Ansett

connections from other major Australasian cities. There may be some code-sharing with Alitalia.

Lauda Air, Level 7, 84 William St, Melbourne ☎03/9600 4000; Level 11, 143 Macquarie St, Sydney ☎02/9251 6155, toll-free 1800/642438; *www.laudaair.com* Four departures a week from Sydney and three from Melbourne, both via Vienna to Amsterdam.

Lufthansa, Australia: 143 Macquarie St, Sydney ☎1300/655727; NZ: 36 Kitchener St, Auckland ☎0800/945220 (toll-free); *www.lufthansa.com* Daily flights from major cities via Bangkok or Singapore and Frankfurt. Code-sharing with Thai or Singapore Airlines for the first leg.

Malaysia Airlines Australia: 16 Spring St, Sydney ☎13/2627; NZ: 12th Floor, 12–26 Swanson St, Auckland ☎09/373 2741, toll-free 0800/777747. Daily flights to Amsterdam from major Australian cities and five flights a week from Auckland with a transfer or stopover in Kuala Lumpur.

Olympic Airways, 37 Pitt St, Sydney ☎02/9251 2044, toll-free ☎1800/221663. Three flights a week to Amsterdam from Sydney and Melbourne, with a transfer or stopover in Athens.

Qantas Australia: 70 Hunter St, Sydney ☎13/1313, *www.qantas.com.au*; NZ: 154 Queen St, Auckland ☎09/357 8900, toll-free ☎0800/808767.Daily from major cities with code-sharing arrangements via Asian gateway cities, or European cities with connections to Amsterdam.

SAS, Level 15, 31 Market St, Sydney ☎02/9299 9800, *www.flysas.com* No flights from Australia or New Zealand, but can organize connections through other airlines to Amsterdam via Bangkok, Beijing, Singapore or Tokyo and Copenhagen.

Singapore Airlines Australia: 17 Bridge St, Sydney ☎13/1011; NZ: West Plaza Building, Fanshawe/Albert St, Auckland ☎09/303 2129, toll-free 0800/808909; *www.singaporeair.com* Daily flights to Amsterdam via Singapore from most major Australasian cities.

Thai Airways Australia: 75 Pitt St, Sydney ☎1300/651960; NZ: 22 Fanshawe St, Auckland ☎09/377 3886; *www.thaiairways.com* Daily flights to Amsterdam from Sydney and Auckland via Bangkok.

agents, who may have cheaper deals. Those that take in Amsterdam include the "Star Alliance" (Ansett, Air Canada, Air New Zealand, Lufthansa, SAS, Thai and United Airlines) which starts at A$2800/NZ$3350, and the One World Alliance "Global Explorer" (American, British Airways, Canadian, Cathay, Finnair, Iberia and Qantas) which starts at A$2400–2900/NZ$2900–3400.

RAIL PASSES

If you're planning to travel around the Netherlands or the rest of Europe by **train**, then it's best to get hold of a rail pass before you go. **Eurail passes** are available through most travel agents or specialist operators like CIT or Thomas Cook (see box), and there are various kinds.

The **Eurail Youthpass** for under-26s is available in fifteen-day, 21-day, one-month, two-month and three-month versions and varies in price from A$615/NZ$765 for the fifteen-day pass to A$1730/NZ$2135 for the three-month one; if you're **over 26** you have to buy a first-class pass, which has the same options and costs between A$880/NZ$1090 for fifteen days and A$2475/NZ$3055 for three months. A **Eurail Flexipass** is good for a certain number of travel days in a two-month period and also comes in youth/first-class versions: ten days cost A$725/1040 (NZ$900/1285); and fifteen days, A$950/1370 (NZ$1175/1700). A scaled-down version of the Flexipass, the **Europass** allows travel in France, Germany, Italy, Spain and Switzerland for (youth/first-class) A$370/550 (NZ$460/675) for five days in two months, on up to A$815/1155 (NZ$1020/1435) for fifteen days in two months; you also have the option of adding adjacent

DISCOUNT TRAVEL AGENTS

Anywhere Travel, 345 Anzac Parade, Kingsford, Sydney ☎02/9663 0411, *anywhere@ozemail.com.au*

Budget Travel, 16 Fort St, Auckland ☎09/366 0061; other branches around the city ☎0800/808040 (toll-free), *www.budgettravel.co.nz*

CIT, 422 Collins St, Melbourne ☎03/9650 5510; 263 Clarence St, Sydney ☎02/9267 1255; also Brisbane, Adelaide and Perth.

Destinations Unlimited, 3 Milford Rd, Milford, Auckland ☎09/373 4033.

European Travel Office (ETO), 122 Rosslyn St, West Melbourne ☎03/9329 8844; 20th Floor, 133 Castlereagh St, Sydney ☎02/9267 7727.

Flight Centre Australia: branches nationwide; phone ☎13/1600 (24hr) for your nearest office. NZ: National Bank Towers, 205–225 Queen St, Auckland ☎0800/354448, plus branches nationwide; *www.flightcentre.com*

Harvey World Travel, 631 Princes Highway, Kogarah, Sydney ☎02/9567 6099 or 13/2757, plus branches nation wide; *www.harveyworld.com.au*

Northern Gateway, 22 Cavenagh St, Darwin ☎08/8941 1394.

Passport Travel, Suite 11, 401 St Kilda Rd, Melbourne ☎03/9867 3888, toll-free 1800/337031; *www.travelcentre.com.au*

STA Travel Australia: nationwide ☎1300/360960; 256 Flinders St, Melbourne ☎03/9654 7266; 855 George St, Sydney (☎02/9212 1255; toll-free 1800/637444), plus other offices in state capitals and major universities; *www.statravelaus.com.au*; NZ: Travellers' Centre, 10 High St, Auckland ☎09/309 0458; 90 Cashel St, Christchurch ☎03/379 9098; 130 Cuba St, Wellington ☎04/385 0561, plus offices in Dunedin, Palmerston North, Hamilton and major universities; *www.statravel.co.nz*

Thomas Cook Australia: 257 Collins St, Melbourne ☎03/9282 0222 or 13/1771; 175 Pitt St, Sydney ☎02/9231 2877, toll-free 1800/801002; branches in other state capitals. NZ: 159 Queen St, Auckland ☎09/379 3924, toll-free 0800/353535; plus other branches.

Topdeck Travel, 65 Glenfell St, Adelaide ☎08/8232 7222.

Trailfinders, 8 Spring St, Sydney ☎02/9247 7666, *www.trailfinders.com.au*

Travel.com, 80 Clarence St, Sydney ☎02/9290 1500, *www.travel.com.au*

Tymtro Travel, 428 George St, Sydney ☎02/9223 2211.

UTAG Travel, 122 Walker St, North Sydney ☎02/9956 8399 or 13/1398, plus offices nationwide; *www.utag.com.au*

SPECIALIST OPERATORS

All the following can arrange sightseeing tours, car rental and accommodation in Holland, starting from about A$100/NZ$130 twin share.

Adventure World, Australia: 73 Walker St, North Sydney (☎02/9956 7766, toll-free 1800/221931), plus branches in Adelaide, Brisbane, Melbourne and Perth; *www. adventureworld.com.au*. NZ: 101 Gt South Rd, Remuera, Auckland ☎09/524 5118, *www.adventureworld.co.nz* Agents for a vast array of international adventure travel companies.

CIT, 422 Collins St, Melbourne ☎03/9650 5510; 263 Clarence St, Sydney ☎02/9267 1255, plus branches in Brisbane, Adelaide and Perth; *www.cittravel.com.au* City tours and accommodation packages, and also handles Eurail passes.

Eurolynx, 20 Fort St, Auckland ☎09/379 9716.

National World Travel, Level 1, 1 Mclaren St, North Sydney ☎13/1435, *www.natworldtravel.com.au*

Travel Plan, 118 Edinburgh St, Castlecraig, Sydney ☎02/9438 1333, *www.travelplan.com.au*

YHA Travel Centre, 38 Stuart St, Adelaide ☎08/8231 5583; 154 Roma St, Brisbane ☎07/3236 1680; 191 Dryandra St, O'Connor, Canberra ☎02/6248 0177; 69a Mitchell St, Darwin ☎08/8981 2560; 28 Criterion St, Hobart ☎03/6234 9617; 83 Hardware Lane, Melbourne ☎03/9670 9611; 236 William St, Northbridge, Perth ☎08/9227 5122; 422 Kent St, Sydney ☎02/9261 1111; *www.yha.com.au* Budget accommodation throughout Europe for YHA members.

UsitBEYOND (formerly YHA Travel), Shortland St/Jean Batten Place, Auckland ☎09/379 4224, plus offices in Hamilton, Palmerston North, Wellington and Christchurch; *www.usitbeyond.co.nz*

"associate" countries. There are also "**saver**" versions of all three passes, which are first-class passes valid for between two and five people who must be travelling together on all journeys. The cost is slightly less than the full first class passes.

Once you get to the Netherlands, you can also buy a **Euro Domino** pass – see p.3.

RED TAPE AND VISAS

gaining legal resident's status in the Netherlands without pre-arranged work is extremely slim. To work legally, non-EU nationals need a work permit (*werkvergunning*), and these are even harder to get than a residence permit. EU citizens take priority in the job market, the only exceptions being Australians and New Zealanders aged between 18 and 25, who are eligible to apply for year-long Working Holiday visas (which vary slightly between the two countries).

CUSTOMS

Within the EU, **EU nationals** can take goods for personal consumption across international borders without incurring duty, as long as they've paid the local tax imposed at the place of purchase. Thus, for them at least, **tax-free goods** as such no longer exist. Instead, shop owners at Amsterdam Schiphol airport have come up with a discount "See Buy Fly" scheme, in which the businesses pre-pay the duty (the only exceptions being alcohol and cigarettes, for which you pay local prices). Call ☎020/312 7447 or have a look at the airport's Web site, *www.schiphol.nl*, for further details.

For **non-EU nationals**, the following export/import limits apply: 200 cigarettes or 250g tobacco or 50 cigars; 1 litre spirits or 2 litres fortified wine or 2 litres sparkling wine; and 60cl perfume. Non-EU nationals who spend more than *f*300 in one shop in one day, and then export the goods within three months of purchase, can

Citizens of the UK, Ireland, Australia, New Zealand, Canada and the USA need only a valid passport to stay for three months in Holland. On arrival, be sure to have enough money to convince officials you can support yourself. Poorer-looking visitors are often checked out, and if you come from outside the EU and can't flash a credit card, or a few travellers' cheques or notes, you may not be allowed in.

If you want to stay longer than three months, you need a *verblijfsvergunning* or residence permit from the Aliens' Police. Even for EU citizens, however, this is far from easy to obtain (impossible if you can't show means of support), and the bureaucracy involved is byzantine.

Non-EU nationals should always have their documents in order, but even so the chance of

DUTCH EMBASSIES AND CONSULATES

Australia *Embassy*: 120 Empire Circuit, Yarralumla, Canberra ACT 2600 ☎02/6273 3111, *nlgovcan@ozemail.com.au*; *Consulates-General*: 499 St Kilda Rd, Melbourne ☎03/9867 7933; 500 Oxford St, Bondi Junction, Sydney ☎02/9387 6644.

Canada Suite 2020, 350 Albert St, Ottawa, ON K1R 1A4 ☎613/237 5030, *nlgovott@netcom.ca*

Ireland 160 Merrion Rd, Dublin 4 ☎01/269 3444, *nethemb@indigo.ie*

New Zealand *Embassy*: Investment House, Featherston/Ballance St, Wellington ☎04/471

6390, *nlgovwel@compuserve.com*; *Consulates*: 1st Floor, 57 Symonds St, Auckland ☎09/379 5399; 161–163 Kilmore St, Christchurch ☎03/366 9280.

UK 38 Hyde Park Gate, London SW7 5DP ☎020/7590 3200, *london@netherlands-embassy.org.uk*

USA 4200 Linnean Ave NW, Washington DC 20008 ☎202/244 5300, *www.netherlands-embassy.org*

FOREIGN EMBASSIES IN THE NETHERLANDS

Australia Carnegielaan 4, 2517 KH The Hague
☎070/310 8200.
Canada Sophialaan 7, 2514 JP The Hague
☎070/361 1600,
hague@hague01.x400.gc.ca
Ireland Dr Kuyperstraat 9, 2514 BA The Hague
☎070/363 0993,
postbus@irish.embassy.demon.nl
New Zealand Carnegielaan 10, 2517 KH The
Hague ☎070/365 8037.

UK *Embassy.* Lange Voorhout 10, 2514 ED The
Hague ☎070/427 0427;
Consulate-General: Koningslaan 44, 1075 AE
Amsterdam ☎020/676 4343.
USA *Embassy:* Lange Voorhout 102, 2514 EJ The
Hague ☎070/310 9209, *www.usemb.nl*;
Consulate-General: Museumplein 19, 1071 DJ
Amsterdam ☎020/575 5309.

reclaim the VAT (sales tax); shops displaying the "Tax Free for Tourists" logo will help with the formalities, or alternatively check out the Web site *www.globalrefund.com*.

HEALTH AND INSURANCE

As a member of the European Union, Holland has free reciprocal health agreements with other member states. To take advantage of this, UK citizens will need form E111, available over the counter from most post offices, which entitles you to free treatment within the Netherlands' public health care system; other EU nationalities need comparable documentation. Australians are able to receive treatment through a reciprocal arrangement with Medicare (check with your local office

for details). Anyone planning to stay for three months or more is required by Dutch law to have private health insurance.

Taking out your own **private medical insurance** means you will cover the cost of items not within the purview of the EU scheme, such as dental treatment and repatriation on medical grounds. It will usually also cover your baggage and tickets in case of theft, as long as you get a crime report from the local police. **Non-EU residents**, apart from Australians, will need to insure themselves against all eventualities, including medical costs. In the case of major expense the more worthwhile policies promise to sort matters out before you pay rather than after, but if you do have to pay up-front, make sure you get and keep the receipts.

HEALTH

If you should fall ill, minor ailments can be remedied at a **drugstore** (*drogist*). These sell non-prescription drugs as well as toiletries, tampons, condoms and the like. A **pharmacy** or *apotheek* (generally open Mon–Fri 9.30am–6pm; often closed Mon mornings) is where you go to get a prescription filled. There aren't any 24-hour pharmacies, but the local VVV (see p.23), as well as

In medical emergencies, telephone ☎112.

most of the better hotels, will supply addresses of ones that are open late.

In more serious cases, you can get the address of an English-speaking **doctor** from your local pharmacy, tourist office or hotel. There's also a 24-hour medical **helpline**, Centrale Doktorsdienst (☎0900/503 2042), where you can seek general advice about medical symptoms and get the details of duty doctors. If you're entitled to free treatment under EU health agreements, double-check that the doctor is both working within, and regarding you as a patient of, the public health care system; bear in mind though that even within the EU agreement you may still have to pay a significant portion of the prescription charges (senior citizens and children are exempt). Most private health insurance policies don't help cover prescription charges either, and although their "excesses" are usually greater than the cost of the medicines, it's worth keeping receipts just in case.

Minor accidents can be treated at the outpatients department of most hospitals (*ziekenhuis*), but in **emergencies**, telephone ☎112. Again if you're reliant on free treatment within the EU health scheme, try to remember to make this clear to the ambulance staff, and, if you're whisked off to hospital, to the medic you subsequently encounter. If possible, it's a good idea to hand over a photocopy of your E111 on arrival at the hospital to ensure your non-private status is clearly understood. In terms of describing symptoms, you can anticipate that someone will speak English. Without an E111 you won't be turned away from a hospital, but you will have to pay for any treatment you receive and should therefore get an official receipt, a necessary preamble to the long-winded process of trying to get at least some of the money back.

Dental treatment is not within the scope of the EU's health agreement: again, enquire at the local tourist office or your hotel reception for an English-speaking dentist. However, in Amsterdam you can ring the Dentist Administration Bureau on ☎0990/821 2230 (ƒ1 per min) who will find a dentist for you 24 hours a day.

For advice about **AIDS** there's a free national **helpline** (Mon–Fri 2–10pm) on ☎0800/022 2220, and in Amsrerdam there's also an HIV Plus Line (☎020/685 0055; Mon, Wed & Fri 1–4pm, Tues & Thurs 8–10.30pm), which counsels people who are HIV positive.

INSURANCE

A typical **travel insurance policy** usually provides cover for the loss of baggage, tickets and – up to a certain limit – cash or cheques, as well as cancellation or curtailment of your journey. Most of them exclude so-called dangerous sports unless an extra premium is paid: in Holland this can mean windsurfing and sailing. Read the small print and benefits tables of prospective policies carefully; coverage can vary wildly for roughly similar premiums. Many policies can be chopped and changed to exclude coverage you don't need – for example, sickness and accident benefits can often be excluded or included at will. If you do take medical coverage, ascertain whether benefits will be paid as treatment proceeds or only after returning home, and whether there is a 24-hour medical emergency number. When securing baggage cover, make sure that the per-article limit – typi-

---

ROUGH GUIDES TRAVEL INSURANCE

Rough Guides now offer their own **travel insurance**, customized for our readers by a leading UK broker and backed by a Lloyds underwriter. It's available for anyone, of any nationality, travelling anywhere in the world, and we are convinced that this is the best-value scheme you'll find.

There are two main Rough Guide insurance plans: **Essential**, for effective, no-frills cover, starting at £11.75 for 2 weeks; and **Premier** – more expensive but with more generous and extensive benefits. Each offer European or Worldwide cover, and can be supplemented with a "Hazardous Activities Premium" if you plan to indulge in sports considered dangerous, such as skiing, scuba-diving or trekking. Unlike many policies, the Rough Guides schemes are calculated by the day, so if you're travelling for 27 days rather than a month, that's all you pay for. You can alternatively take out annual **multi-trip insurance**, which covers you for all your travel throughout the year (with a maximum of 60 days for any one trip).

For a **policy quote**, call the Rough Guides Insurance Line on UK freefone ☎0800/0150906, or, if you're calling from outside Britain, on ☎+44-1243/621046. Alternatively, get an online quote at *www.roughguides.com/insurance*

cally under £500 equivalent – will cover your most valuable possession. If you need to make a claim, you should keep receipts for medicines and medical treatment, and in the event you have anything stolen, you must obtain an official statement from the police. Bank and credit cards often have certain levels of medical or other insurance included and you may automatically get travel insurance if you use a major credit card to pay for your trip.

It's always advisable to take out an insurance policy before travelling to cover against theft, loss and illness or injury. **UK** and **Ireland** residents are likely to find themselves pressed to take travel insurance by the travel agent or tour operator when booking a package holiday, though according to UK law they can't make you buy their own (other than a £1 premium for "schedule airline failure"). If you have a good all-risks home insurance policy it *may* cover your possessions against loss or theft even when overseas. Many private medical schemes such as BUPA or PPP also offer coverage plans for abroad, including baggage loss, cancellation or curtailment and cash replacement as well as sickness or accident.

Americans and **Canadians** should also check that they're not already covered. Canadian provincial health plans usually provide partial cover for medical mishaps overseas. Holders of official student/teacher/youth cards are entitled to meagre accident coverage and hospital in-patient benefits. Students will often find that their student health coverage extends during the vacations and for one term beyond the date of last enrolment. Homeowners' or renters' insurance often covers theft or loss of documents, money and valuables while overseas, though conditions and maximum amounts vary from company to company.

INFORMATION AND MAPS

Information on the Netherlands is easy to get hold of in advance, either via the Internet or from the Netherlands Board of Tourism.

After arrival, you'll find that just about every town (and even most large villages) has a tourist office. These are known by the acronym "VVV".

INFORMATION

It's not essential, but before you leave for Holland, you might consider contacting the highly efficient **Netherlands Board of Tourism** (see box) as they issue (or sell) a wide range of glossy leaflets. One of their most useful publications is their country-wide Accommodation guide, complete with hotel prices, addresses, phone numbers, email addresses and Web sites, as well as photographs of the hotels and brief (if sometimes rather flattering) descriptions. The NBT also has useful leaflets on the main tourist attractions, annual

NETHERLANDS BOARD OF TOURISM OFFICES

Britain 18 Buckingham Gate, London SW1E 6LB
☎0906/871 7777, *goholland.co.uk*
Canada 25 Adelaide St East, Suite 710, Toronto, ON M5C 1Y2 ☎416/363 1577, fax 363 1470, *goholland.com*

USA 355 Lexington Ave, 21st floor, New York, NY 10017 ☎212/370-7360, *goholland.com*

There are no offices in Australia or New Zealand.

THE NETHERLANDS ON THE NET

Netherlands Board of Tourism
www.goholland.com Well-presented guide to the
country and its various attractions for the tourist,
providing information in a number of languages
including English. Well worth a visit.

NL-menu
www.nl-menu.nl/nlmenu.eng/nlmenu.html
No slick presentation here, but an extremely useful link site. Established in 1992, and designed to
provide an educational resource, it acts as a
signpost to information on a broad range of
topics – art, health, leisure.

Amsterdam *www.amsterdam.nl*
The city's official Web site contains a raft of
information about the operation of local government in the city, but is elegantly presented and
has an extremely useful map facility, which
allows you to pinpoint and print out a map for
any address in the city.

Amsterdam Hotspots
www.amsterdamhotspots.nl A clearly presented
and well informed guide to the city, including
maps, with a particular emphasis on events listings, particularly music and the club scene. The
site is kept bang up-to-date and offers a useful
guide to the gay scene, the city's coffee houses
and the Red Light District as well as the more
standard information. You can add your own
review online and read those of others.

De Museumserver *www.museumserver.nl*
This site is designed as a platform for Dutch
museums represented on the Internet, giving
details of over 250. Although the English text is a

hit-and-miss affair (work is still in progress on
the English version of the site), it's a fascinating
resource.

The Official Ajax site *www.ajax.nl*
As its name suggests, the virtual home of the
world-famous football team, giving you a comprehensive rundown of its history, fixture information and current news. It doesn't however, sell
match tickets, which are only available to Club
Card holders.

Bloemenbureau Holland *www.bbh.nl*
The Flower Council of Holland's Web site, which
provides a useful guide to all flower-related
events in the country, as well as a detailed
account of the how the industry works and its
significance both on a national and international
level.

Van Gogh Museum *www.vangoghmuseum.nl*
A guide to the gallery, which includes a selection
of accessible, expertly written essays on a handful of Van Gogh's major works.

JazzFacts *www.netcetera.nl/jazzfacts*
A site dedicated to the Dutch jazz scene, giving
details of artists, venues, specialist record shops
and events, including the large number of
regional festivals around the country. Also provides links to Dutch bands/musicians' Web
sites.

Clogs *www.woodenshoes.nl*
Probably the only site on the Internet providing a
Clog-o-paedia, a guide to the history and manu-
facture of the familiar Dutch wooden shoe.
Includes an online ordering service, too.

events, campsites and special interest leaflets on
such things as cycling and watersports. They publish a reasonable map of the country too.

Once you're in the Netherlands, almost every
place you visit will have a **VVV**. In towns, the
majority are either in the centre on the Grote
Markt (the main square) or by the train station. In
addition to handing out basic maps (often free)
and English information on the main sights, many
VVVs keep lists of local accommodation options
and, for a small fee, will book rooms for you,
some of which will be lodgings in private houses
(see p.35) accessible only to them. Where this is
the case, we've mentioned it in the Guide. Most
VVV offices also keep information on neighbouring towns, which can be a great help for forward

planning. Hours vary, and are detailed – along
with phone numbers – in the text.

It's also well worth accessing the **Internet** prior
to travelling. The Dutch have a very positive attitude
to the Net and as a result there's a large amount of
information available about the country online.
Most large organizations in the country have well-
established Web sites, usually of a very high quality. All the sites given in the box provide all or most
information in English, unless otherwise stated.

MAPS

A wide range of **road maps** of The Netherlands
is readily available both inside the country and
abroad. The AA/Baedeker *Netherlands*
(1:250,000) is as good as any and comes complete

MAP OUTLETS IN BRITAIN AND IRELAND

Blackwell's Map and Travel Shop, 53 Broad St, Oxford OX1 3BQ ☎01865/792792, *bookshop.blackwell.co.uk*

Daunt Books, 83 Marylebone High St, London W1M 3DE ☎020/7224 2295; 193 Haverstock Hill, London NW3 4QL ☎020/7794 4006.

Easons Bookshop, 40 O'Connell St, Dublin 1 ☎01/873 3811, *www.eason.ie*

Fred Hanna's Bookshop, 27–29 Nassau St, Dublin 2 ☎01/677 1255, *www.hannas.ie*

Heffers Map and Travel, 3rd Floor, in Heffers Stationery Department, 19 Sidney St, Cambridge CB2 3HL ☎01223/568467, *www.heffers.co.uk*.

Hodges Figgis Bookshop, 56–58 Dawson St, Dublin 2 ☎01/677 4754, *www.hodgesfiggis.ie*

James Thin Melven's Bookshop, 29 Union St, Inverness IV1 1QA ☎01463/233500, *www.jthin.co.uk*

National Map Centre, 22–24 Caxton St, London SW1H 0QU ☎020/7222 2466, *www.mapsworld.com*

Newcastle Map Centre, 55 Grey St, Newcastle upon Tyne NE1 6EF ☎0191/261 5622, *nmc@enterprise.net*

John Smith and Sons, 57–61 St Vincent St, Glasgow G2 5TB ☎0141/221 7472, *www.johnsmith.co.uk*

Stanfords, 12–14 Long Acre, London WC2E 9LP ☎020/7836 1321; within Campus Travel at 52 Grosvenor Gardens, London SW1W 0AG ☎020/7730 1314; within the British Airways offices at 156 Regent St, London W1R 5TA ☎020/7434 4744; 29 Corn Street, Bristol BS1 1HT ☎0117/929 9966; *www.stanfords.co.uk*

The Travel Bookshop, 13–15 Blenheim Crescent, London W11 2EE ☎020/7229 5260, *www.thetravelbookshop.co.uk*

Waterstone's, 91 Deansgate, Manchester, M3 2BW ☎0161/837 3000; Queens Bldg, 8 Royal Ave, Belfast BT1 1DA ☎028/9024 7355; 7 Dawson St, Dublin 2 ☎01/679 1415; 69 Patrick St, Cork ☎021/276 522; *www.waterstones.co.uk*

MAP OUTLETS IN THE USA AND CANADA

ADC Map and Travel Center, 1636 1st St, Washington DC 20006 ☎202/628 2608.

The Complete Traveler Bookstore, 199 Madison Ave, New York, NY 10016 ☎212/685-9007; 3207 Fillmore St, San Francisco, CA 94123 ☎415/923-1511; *www.CompleteTraveler.com*

Curious Traveler Travel Bookstore, 101 Yorkville Ave, Toronto, ON M5R 1C1 ☎1-800/268-4395.

Elliott Bay Book Company, 101 S Main St, Seattle, WA 98104 ☎206/624-6600, *www.elliottbaybook.com*

Map Link, 30 S La Petera Lane, Unit #5, Santa Barbara, CA 93117 ☎805/692-6777, *www.maplink.com*

Open Air Books and Maps, 25 Toronto St, Toronto, ON M5R 2C1 ☎416/363-0719.

Phileas Fogg's Books & Maps, #87 Stanford Shopping Center, Palo Alto, CA 94304 ☎1-800/533-FOGG.

Rand McNally, 444 N Michigan Ave, Chicago, IL 60611 ☎312/321-1751; 150 E 52nd St, New York, NY 10022 ☎212/758-7488; 595 Market St, San Francisco, CA 94105 ☎415/777-3131; call ☎1-800/333-0136 (ext 2111) for other locations, or for maps by mail order; *www.randmcnally.com*

Traveler's Choice Bookstore, 22 W 52nd St, New York, NY 10019 ☎212/941-1535.

Ulysses Travel Bookshop, 4176 St-Denis, Montréal ☎514/843-9447, *www.ulysses.ca*

World Wide Books and Maps, 552 Seymour St, Vancouver, BC V6B 3J5 ☎604/687-3320, *www.itmb.com*

MAP OUTLETS IN AUSTRALIA AND NEW ZEALAND

Map Land, 372 Little Bourke St, Melbourne ☎03/9670 4383, *mapland@lexicon.net*

The Map Shop, 16a Peel St, Adelaide ☎08/8231 2033, *www.mapshop.net.au*

Map World, 371 Pitt St, Sydney ☎02/9261 3601.

Mapworld, 173 Gloucester St, Christchurch ☎03/374 5399, *www.mapworld.co.nz*

Perth Map Centre, 884 Hay St, Perth ☎09/9322 5733, *www.perthmap.com.au*

Speciality Maps, 58 Albert St, Auckland ☎09/307 2217.

Travel Bookshop, Shop 3, 175 Liverpool St, Sydney ☎02/9261 8200.

Worldwide Maps and Guides, 187 George St Brisbane ☎07/3221 4330, *www.powerup.com.au/~wwmaps*

with a number of city-centre plans – but not an index. In general terms, note that Holland is a crowded country, so any road map above the 1:250,000 scale is going to be difficult, if not impossible, to use for driving. Inside the country, our maps are adequate for most purposes, but if you need one on a larger scale, or with a street index, there's a bewildering variety, which you'll find in most VVVs and decent bookshops. The best **regional maps** are those produced for the VVV at the 1:37,500 scale, and for **cities** the Cito series (1:5200) and the Falkplan maps, produced at a variety of scales, are especially good. In **Amsterdam**, most good bookshops sell Geocart's clear and easy-to-use *Amsterdam Tourist Special* (1:10,000), whilst the pick of several handily compact, spiral-bound street atlases is produced by Falk. Prices are reasonable, with most city maps costing between ƒ4 and ƒ6, regional maps between ƒ8 and ƒ10.

MONEY, BANKS AND COSTS

Holland is a cash society; as a general rule, people prefer to pay for most things with notes and coins. Indeed, quite a lot of smaller shops and a surprising number of restaurants still refuse all other forms of payment, though most hotels and the larger shops almost invariably take one or other of the major credit cards.

MONEY

Until the fully-fledged introduction of the EU's "euro" (€), the Dutch **currency** remains the guilder, generally indicated by "ƒ" or "fl" (guilders were originally florins); other abbreviations include "Hfl", "Dfl" and, increasingly, "NLG". Each guilder is divided into 100 cents. There are notes of ƒ1000, ƒ250, ƒ100, ƒ50 and ƒ10; coins come as ƒ5 (thick bronze), ƒ2,50, ƒ1, 25c, 10c (all silver) and 5c (thin bronze). As in the rest of Europe, decimal points are indicated by a comma, thousands by a full stop. Thus "ƒ2,50" means two guilders and fifty cents; "ƒ2.500" means two thousand five hundred guilders. Round figures are often indicated with a little dash: "ƒ3,-" means three guilders exactly. Although some prices (mostly in supermarkets) are still marked in individual cents, these are always rounded up or down to the nearest 5c.

Guilders are available in advance from any high street bank: current **exchange rates** are around ƒ3,60 (€1.62) to £1, ƒ2,20 (€1) to US$1, and there are no restrictions on bringing currency into the country.

THE EURO

The Netherlands is one of eleven European Union countries who on January 1, 1999, formed an economic and monetary union (EMU) and started using a single currency, the **euro**. The exchange rate is fixed at one guilder to 0.45 euros. Initially, however, it will only be possible to make paper transactions in the new currency (if you have, for example, a euro bank or credit-card account), and the guilder will remain, in effect, the normal unit of currency in Holland. Euro notes and coins will be issued at the beginning of 2002, and will replace the guilder entirely by July of that year.

TRAVELLERS' CHEQUES, ATMS AND CREDIT CARDS

The safest way to carry your funds is in **travellers' cheques**; the usual fee for their purchase is one percent of face value. Make sure you keep the purchase agreement and a record of cheque serial numbers safe and separate from the cheques themselves. In the event that cheques are lost or stolen, the issuing company will expect you to report the loss immediately; consequently, when you buy your travellers' cheques, ensure you have details of the company's emergency contact numbers or the addresses of their local offices. Most companies claim to replace lost or stolen cheques within 24 hours. American Express cheques are sold through most North American, Australasian and European banks, and they are the most widely accepted cheques in The Netherlands. When you cash your cheques, you'll find that almost all banks make a percentage charge per transaction on top of a basic minimum charge. Note also that there is no charge for American Express cheques cashed at any of their Amsterdam offices.

For a while at least, if you have an ordinary British/EU bank account you can use **Eurocheques** (with the respective guarantee card) in many banks, as well as in most shops and hotels, up to a value of around *f*450. In terms of exchange rates, this works out slightly more expensive than travellers' cheques, but can be more convenient; however the Eurocheque system is only in operation until December 2000, after which you'll need to use other options

Most Eurocheque cards (for the moment), many Visa, Mastercard and British bank/cash cards, as well as cards in the Cirrus or Plus systems, can also be used for withdrawing cash from **ATMs**, often the quickest and easiest way of obtaining money. There are dozens dotted across every

EMERGENCY NUMBERS FOR LOST AND STOLEN CARDS AND CHEQUES

Access/Mastercard/Eurocard
☎030/283 5888

American Express
cards   ☎020/504 8000 before 6pm,
         ☎020/504 8666 after 6pm
travellers' cheques ☎0800/022 0100
Diners Club ☎020/557 3557
Visa ☎020/660 0789

major city and a reasonable number in smaller places too. They usually give instructions in a variety of languages. Check with your bank to find out about reciprocal arrangements.

Credit cards are predictably useful for car rental, cash advances (though these attract a high rate of interest from the date of withdrawal) and hotel bills, and of course shopping. American Express, Visa and Mastercard are all widely accepted.

CHANGING MONEY

If you need to change money, Dutch **banks** usually offer the best deals. Hours are Monday to Friday 9am to 4pm, with a few big-city banks also open Thursday until 9pm or on Saturday morning; all are closed on public holidays (see p.45). Outside these times, changing money is rarely a problem – there's a nationwide network of **GWK exchange offices**, usually at train stations, which are open late every day (sometimes, as in for instance at Amsterdam Centraal Station and Schiphol Airport, even 24 hours). GWK offers competitive rates and charges reasonable commissions, but some other agencies do not, so be cautious. The VVV tourist office also changes money, as do most hotels and campsites and some hostels, but their rates are generally poor.

WIRING MONEY

Having money wired from home is never convenient or cheap, and should only be considered as a last resort. One option is to have your own **bank** send the money through, and for that you need to nominate a receiving bank in The Netherlands – any local branch will do. Naturally, you need to confirm the cooperation of the local bank before you set the wheels in motion back home. The sending bank's fees are geared to the amount being transferred and the urgency of the service you require – the fastest transfers, taking two or three days, start at around £20/$32 for the first £300–400/$450–600.

You can also have money wired via **American Express**, with the funds sent by one office and available for collection at the company's local office within minutes. All transactions are done in US dollars and the service is only open to American Express card holders. Again, charges depend on the amount being sent, but as an example, wiring $400 from Britain to Amsterdam will cost $20, $5000 about $190.

COSTS

In terms of **accommodation**, Holland is, by western European standards at least, moderately expensive, though this is partly offset by low-priced public transport and the availability of inexpensive cafés. Hotel prices in Amsterdam are around thirty percent more than in the rest of the country. More precise costs for places to stay and eat are given in the Guide.

On average, if you're prepared to buy your own picnic lunch, stay in youth hostels, and stick to the less expensive bars and restaurants, you could get by on around £25/US$40 a day. Staying in two-star hotels, regularly eating out in medium-range restaurants and going to bars, you'll get through at least £70/$110 a day, the main variable being the cost of your room – plus the higher prices paid in Amsterdam. On £100/$160 a day and upwards, you'll be limited only by your energy reserves – though if you're planning to stay in a five-star hotel anywhere in the country and have a big night out, this still won't be enough. **Restaurants** don't come cheap, but costs remain manageable if you avoid the extras and concentrate on the main courses, for which around £10/$14 will normally suffice – twice that with a drink, starter and dessert. You can, of course, pay a lot more – a top restaurant can be twice as expensive again, and then some. As always, if you're travelling alone you'll spend much more on accommodation than you would in a group of two or more: most hotels do have single rooms, but they're fixed at about 75 percent of the price of a double.

As for incidental expenses, ƒ2,75 buys a cup of coffee, a small glass of beer or a wedge of apple cake; today's English newspaper costs ƒ7; and developing a roll of film an amazing ƒ40. Museum admission prices hover around the ƒ5–15 mark. Just so you know, hashish and marijuana both come in ƒ10 and ƒ25 bags; the more powerful it is, the less you get.

POST, PHONES AND MEDIA

Holland has an efficient postal system and a first-rate telephone network. Telephone and mail boxes are liberally distributed across every town and village in the country – and charges are reasonable.

POST

Dutch **post offices** are plentiful and mostly open Monday to Friday 8.30am to 5pm, though some big-city branches also open on Saturday from 8.30am to noon. Postal **charges** right now are: ƒ1 for an airmail letter (up to 20g) to anywhere within the EU; ƒ1,60 airmail to the rest of the world (ƒ1,20 by surface mail); postcards to all destinations cost ƒ1. Stamps are sold at a wide range of outlets including many shops and hotels. **Postboxes** are everywhere, but be sure to use the correct slot – labelled *overige* for non-local deliveries. All major post offices offer a **poste restante** service; to collect items, you need your passport.

TELEPHONES

Although there are some coin-operated **public telephones** in Holland, the vast majority only take phone cards and often credit cards too. It is worth bearing in mind however that phone boxes are provided by different companies and their respective phone cards aren't mutually compatible, so when you buy your card check which phones you'll have access to. Phone cards can be bought at many outlets, including post offices, tobacconists and VVV offices, in denominations

INTERNATIONAL DIALLING CODES

Australia	☎00 61	UK	☎00 44
Ireland	☎00 353	USA and Canada	☎00 1
New Zealand	☎00 64		

USEFUL NUMBERS

Operator (domestic and international)
☎0800/0410; free

Domestic directory enquiries
☎0900/8008; 60c per call

International directory enquiries
☎0900/8418; ƒ1,05 per call

Emergencies (Police, Ambulance, Fire Brigade)
☎112

of ƒ10 and ƒ25. Brightly-coloured, public phones are both easy to spot and use: most are multilingual, switching between different languages, including English, when you press the appropriately labelled button. International direct dialling is straightforward – just follow the instructions. The cheap rate period for international calls is between 8pm and 8am during the week and all day at weekends. All the more expensive hotel rooms also have phones, but note that there is nearly always an exorbitant surcharge for their use.

Calling The Netherlands from abroad, dial your international access number, followed by ☎31, then the city/area code (without the initial 0) and the number. ☎0800 numbers are freephone, while Dutch premium lines are usually prefixed by ☎0900; at the start of these premium calls, a pre-recorded message warns you of the tariff applied, but it's usually also in Dutch. The multilingual international operator (see box) is able to place collect calls. Note also that various telephone companies, including British Telecom, issue phone cards to their subscribers for use abroad: you tap in an account and PIN number on any phone (or extension) and the subsequent call is automatically billed to your home telephone number; for further details, ask your phone company.

INTERNET AND EMAIL

Holland, and particularly Amsterdam, is also well geared for **Internet** access. In most large cities you'll find either Internet cafés, which charge around ƒ2 to ƒ2,50 for every twenty minutes spent online. Occasionally, you may also come across *internetzuilen* – "Internet poles" – fixed pillars with a screen and keyboard, which you access by using a card (available from VVVs); the

minimum-value card is ƒ10 and every twenty minutes spent online costs around ƒ5.

MEDIA

There's no difficulty in finding **British newspapers** – they are on sale in every major city on the day of publication for around ƒ7. The newsagent at the train station will almost always have copies if no one else does. Current issues of **UK and US magazines** are widely available too, as is the *International Herald Tribune*.

Of the **Dutch newspapers** *NRC Handelsblad* is a right-of-centre paper that has perhaps the best news coverage and a liberal stance on the arts; *De Volkskrant* is a progressive, leftish daily; the popular right-wing *De Telegraaf* boasts the highest circulation figures in the country and has a well-regarded financial section; *Algemeen Dagblad* is a right-wing broadsheet, while the middle-of-the-road *Het Parool* ("The Password") and the news magazine *Vrij Nederland* ("Free Netherlands") are the successors of underground Resistance newspapers printed during wartime occupation. The Protestant *Trouw* ("Trust"), another former underground paper, is centre-left in orientation with a focus on religion. Bundled in with the weekend *International Herald Tribune* is *The Netherlander*, a small but useful business-oriented review of Dutch affairs in English.

Dutch TV isn't up to much, although the quantity of English-language programmes broadcast is high. If you're staying somewhere with cable TV (which covers almost ninety percent of Dutch households), it's also possible to find many foreign TV channels: Britain's BBC1 and BBC2 are available everywhere, along with TV10 Gold, which shows reruns of old British sitcoms and dramas. There's also a host of German, French, Spanish,

Italian, Turkish and Arabic stations, some of which occasionally show undubbed British and American movies. Most hotels also pick up some European-wide cable and satellite stations, such as Superchannel – an at times dreadfully amateurish mix of videos, soaps, and movies; MTV – 24-hour pop videos; CNN, which gives 24-hour news coverage; or Eurosport – up-to-the-minute footage of contests like the women's world curling championships or European handball league. Other Dutch and Belgian TV channels, cable and non-cable, regularly run English-language movies with Dutch subtitles.

As for **Dutch radio**, Radio Honderd at 98.3FM is a stalwart of the squat movement and has an eclectic programming style – world music and dance rubbing shoulders with hardcore noise and long sessions of beat-free bleeps. Radio London (90.4FM) has no discernible English connection, but does have a play-list covering Latin, reggae and African music. Jazz Radio, at 99.8FM, speaks for itself. The Dutch Classic FM, at 101.2FM, like the British version, has bits of well-known classical music jumbled together, with jazz after 10pm. There's next to no English-language programming, but the BBC World Service broadcasts all day in English on 648kHz (medium wave), with occasional news in German; between 2am and 7am it also occupies 198kHz (long wave).

GETTING AROUND

Getting around is never a problem in The Netherlands: it's a small country, and the longest journey you'll ever make – say from Amsterdam to Maastricht – takes under three hours by train or car. Furthermore, the public transport system is exemplary, a fully integrated network of trains and buses that brings even the smallest of villages within easy reach – and all at very reasonable prices. Train and bus stations are almost always next door to each other and in several of the larger cities there are trams too.

TRAINS

The best way of travelling around The Netherlands is to take the **train**. The system, run by Nederlandse Spoorwegen or NS (Dutch Railways), is one of the best in Europe: trains are fast, modern, frequent and, normally, very punctual; fares are relatively low, and the network of lines comprehensive. **Ordinary fares** are calculated by the kilometre, diminishing proportionately the further you travel. As a rough guide, reckon on spending about ƒ15 to travel 50km or so. Same-day return tickets (*dagretour*) knock about ten percent off the price of one-way tickets for the same journey, but otherwise returns are simply double the price of singles; first-class fares cost about fifty percent on top of the regular fare. With any ticket, you're free to stop off anywhere en route and continue your journey later that day, but you're not allowed to backtrack. For a one-way ticket ask for an *enkele reis*; a return trip is a *retour*.

In addition, NS offers several **discounted day tickets**, including a Day Pass for unlimited travel on any train (first-class ƒ110; second-class ƒ70), and the OV-Day Pass (ƒ120; ƒ80), which includes the country's trams and buses. Otherwise, amongst other options, a **Rail Idee** ticket is a special discounted ticket which combines the price of admission to selected sights (say, the Hoge Veluwe) with the price of a return train journey. There are nearly 200 possible excursions in all – get further information from any major station.

Dutch Railways publishes mounds of **information** on its various services, passes and fares – and some of it is in English. They also run an

information line (☎0900/9292) and an excellent Web site, *www.ns.nl*. Their comprehensive and easy-to-use timetable (*spoorboekje*; ƒ10,50) is available at major stations and in advance from the Netherlands Board of Tourism (see p.23 for addresses).

RAIL PASSES

If you're travelling extensively around Holland by train, you should consider buying a **rail pass** before you go (see the box on p.6 for contact details), of which there are a number of options.

The **Euro Domino** pass (also called the "Freedom" pass) is valid for unlimited travel within a single country, though you can buy several to run concurrently in different countries. There are no residence requirements or age restrictions and they can be remarkably good value. Euro Dominos are valid for between three and eight days' travel within any one month, with three categories of pass – youth (under 26), first- and second-class. **Prices** for a three-day pass in Holland cost £29, £59 and £39, for a five-day pass £49, £99 and £59, and for an-eight day pass, £79, £149 and £99, respectively. An equivalent national discount card, the **Holland Rail Pass**, enables unlimited travel within Holland during either a three- or five-day period in a given month; the cost is the same as for a Euro Domino pass except for additional discounts on the cost of a second pass for two people travelling together, and an extra "senior" category, which enables people aged over 60 to purchase the pass for the same price as the youth option.

If the Netherlands is only part of your travel plans, and you intend to go further afield, there are a number of different passes available. The **InterRail pass**, available to European residents only, provides unlimited rail travel on national rail networks across Europe (though supplements are often payable on high-speed trains). The price of the pass depends on whether you're under or over 26 (the former faring considerably better), as well as the number of zones you wish to travel in. Europe is divided into eight zones, the Netherlands falling into Zone E, along with France, Belgium and Luxembourg, with the neighbouring zones, C and B, comprising Germany, Austria, Denmark and Switzerland, and Norway, Sweden and Finland, respectively. A pass enabling travel within a single zone for a 22-day period costs £159 for under-26s, £229 or more for over-26s; all other passes last a full month, with a two-zone pass costing £209 (£279), a three-zone £229 (£309) and an all-zone pass £259 (£349). If you're over 26, the InterRail 26-Plus pass covers some, but not all, of the countries in the scheme, including the Netherlands, Denmark, Norway, Sweden, Finland, and Germany, but excluding France or Belgium. Passes can be bought from larger train stations, student/youth travel agents, or at a discounted price, online at *www. inter-rail.co.uk*. One of the most popular deals if you're under 26 is to purchase a **BIJ ticket** (International Youth Ticket), which gives around a thirty-percent discount on city-to-city fares, allowing as many stopovers as you like within a two-month period. Tickets are available either direct from the rail operators, or from youth and student travel agents. Alternatively, if you're sixty or over, the Rail Europe Senior Card gives up to thirty percent discounts on any journeys which cross international boundaries (but not on journeys within countries) in most of western Europe. You can get one free if you have a Senior Citizen Rail Card (£18 from any UK train station).

TREINTAXIS

In NS's **treintaxi** scheme, rail passengers can get a taxi to or from most major stations. To get to the station, call the local *treintaxi* number at least half an hour before you want to make your journey; within the city limits, the fare is a flat-rate ƒ9,50. On arrival at the local station, you can either book a *treintaxi* for your destination station when you buy your ticket (ƒ7,50), or wait till you get there and pay the taxi driver the flat-rate ƒ9,50. Most major stations have *treintaxi* buttons at the entrance, which you press to summon a taxi. Again, taxis will take you from the train station to anywhere within the city limits.

BUSES

Supplementing the extensive train network are **buses** – run by local companies but again amazingly efficient, spreading out to span the local surroundings from ranks of bus stops almost always located bang next to the train station. Ticketing is simple, organized on a universal, nationwide system. You need to buy just one kind of ticket wherever you are, a **strippenkaart** – a piece of card made out of strips. The country is divided into zones: the driver will cancel one strip on your *strippenkaart* for your journey plus one for each of the zones you travel through – but note that on city trams and metro systems you cancel it yourself in the franking machines provided. In the larger towns and cities two strips will suffice to take you anywhere in the centre. You can buy 2- or 3-strip *strippenkaarts* from bus drivers, or pick up the better-value 15-strip (ƒ11,75) or 45-strip (ƒ34,50) *strippenkaarts* in advance from train stations, tobacconists and local public transport offices. Some long-distance routes are covered by fast and reliable Interliner coaches (*www.interliner.nl*); these express buses don't accept *strippenkarten* – pay the driver for your journey.

Bear in mind that in more rural areas, some bus services only operate when passengers have made advance bookings. Local timetables indicate where this applies.

DRIVING

Driving around The Netherlands is pretty much what you would expect – painless and quick. The country has a uniformly good and comprehensive road network, most of the major towns are linked by some kind of motorway or dual carriageway, and things only get congested on the outskirts of the major cities. **Rules of the road** are similar to other mainland European countries: you drive on the right; speed limits are 50kph in built-up areas, 80kph outside, 120kph on motorways – though some motorways have a speed limit of 100kph, indicated by small yellow signs on the side of the road. Drivers and front-seat passengers are required by law to wear seatbelts, and penalties for drunken driving are severe. There are no toll roads, and although petrol isn't particularly cheap, at around ƒ2.20 per litre, the short distances mean this isn't much of a factor.

EU **driving licences** are honoured in the Netherlands, but other nationals will need an International Driver's Licence (available at minimal cost from your home motoring organization). Any sort of provisional licence is, however, not acceptable. If you're bringing your own car, you must have vehicle registration papers, adequate insurance, a first-aid kit, a warning triangle and a green card (available from your insurers or motoring organization). Extra insurance coverage for unforeseen legal costs is also well worth having, as is an appropriate **breakdown policy** from a motoring organization back home. In Britain, for example, the RAC and AA charge members and non-members about £95 for one month's Europe-wide breakdown cover, with all the appropriate documentation, including green card, provided.

CAR RENTAL

All the major international **car rental** companies are represented in Holland, and useful addresses are given in the "Listings" section at the end of those parts of the Guide describing the larger cities. To rent a car, you'll have to be 21 or over (and have been driving for at least a year), and you'll need a credit card – though the occasional agency will accept a hefty cash deposit. Rental **charges** are fairly high, beginning around ƒ600 per week for unlimited mileage in the smallest vehicle, but include collision damage waiver and vehicle (but not personal) insurance. To cut costs, watch for special deals offered by the bigger companies. If you go to a smaller, local company (of which there are many), you should proceed with care. In particular, check the policy for the excess applied to claims and ensure that it includes a collision damage waiver (applicable if an accident is your fault) as well as adequate levels of financial cover. Bear in mind, too, that it's almost always

---

CAR RENTAL COMPANIES

IN AUSTRALIA AND NEW ZEALAND

Avis Australia freephone ☎1800/225 533, lowcall ☎13/6333; New Zealand ☎09/526 2847; *www.avis.com*

Budget Australia ☎1300/362 848, *www.budget.com.au*; New Zealand ☎09/375 2222, *www.budget.co.nz*

Hertz Australia freephone ☎1800/550 067, lowcall ☎13/3039; New Zealand ☎09/309 0989, freephone ☎0800/655 955; *www.hertz.com*

IN NORTH AMERICA

Avis ☎1-800/331-1084, *www.avis.com*

Budget ☎1-800/527-0700, *www.budget.com*

Dollar ☎1-800/421-6868, *www.dollar.com*

Hertz US: ☎1-800/654-3131; Canada: ☎1-800/263-0600; *www.hertz.com*

IN THE UK AND IRELAND

Avis UK: ☎0870/590 0500; Ireland: ☎01/605 7555; *www.avis.co.uk*

Budget UK: ☎0800/418 1181; Ireland: ☎01/844 5919; *www.budget.com*

Europcar UK: ☎0345/222 525; Ireland: ☎01/812 0410; *www.europcar.com*

National Car Rental UK: ☎0870/536 5365; Ireland: ☎01/844 4927; *www.nationalcar.com*

Hertz UK: ☎0870/599 6699; Ireland: ☎01/844 5466; *www.hertz.co.uk*

Holiday Autos UK: ☎0870/530 0400; Ireland: ☎01/872 9366; *www.holidayautos.co.uk*

Thrifty UK: ☎0870/516 8238; Ireland: ☎01/679 9420; *www.thrifty.co.uk*

less expensive to rent your car before you leave home and pick it up at the airport on arrival.

If you break down in a rented car, you'll get roadside assistance from the particular repair company the rental firm has contracted. The same principle works with your own vehicle's breakdown policy (see above).

CYCLING

If you've got time to spare, **cycling** is the way to see the country. Holland's largely flat landscape makes travelling by bike an almost effortless pursuit, and the short distances involved make it possible to see most of the country with relative ease using the nationwide system of well-marked cycle paths – which often divert away from the main roads into the countryside. Dutch bookshops heave with cycling books, many of them in English, but the maps and route advice provided by most VVVs are perfectly adequate for all but the longest trips.

Most people, however, either **bring their own** bike or **rent one**. Bikes can be rented from all main train stations for ƒ8 a day or ƒ32 per week

plus a ƒ50 deposit (ƒ200 in larger centres); if you have a valid train ticket, it costs just ƒ6 a day or ƒ24 per week with a *treinfiets* voucher. You'll also need some form of ID. The snag is that cycles must be returned to the station from which they were rented, making onward hops by rented bike impossible. Most bike shops rent bicycles out for around the same amount as train stations, though they may be more flexible on deposits – some accept a passport in lieu of cash; otherwise, again expect to leave ƒ50–200. Wherever you're intending to rent your bike from, in summer it's a good idea to reserve one in advance.

It is possible to take your bike **on trains**, but it isn't encouraged, and a ticket costs ƒ9–25 depending on the day and time of year. Be warned that space is limited and you're not allowed to load your bike on at all during the rush hour – between 6.30am and 9am and 4.30pm and 6pm. Bear in mind that you should never, ever, leave your bike unlocked, even for a few minutes. In the larger cities especially, used bikes are big business, the prey of thieves armed with bolt-cutters. Almost all train stations have somewhere you can store your bike safely for a minimal fee.

ACCOMMODATION

With prices comparable to those of most of western Europe, few would claim that hotel accommodation is much of a bargain in Holland, though a wide network of inexpensive HI youth hostels and generally well-equipped campsites can, if needs must, keep costs down. Wherever you stay, you should book ahead of time during the summer and over holiday periods like Easter when rooms can run short. In Amsterdam,

shortages are commonplace throughout the year, so advance booking is always required, and note also that Amsterdam hotel prices are on average about thirty percent higher than elsewhere.

HOTELS

All **hotels** in The Netherlands are graded on a star system up to five stars. One-star and no-star hotels are rare, and prices for two-star establishments start at around ƒ100 for a double room without private bath or shower; count on paying at least ƒ150 if you want your own facilities. Three-star hotels cost upwards of about ƒ150; for four- and five-star places you'll pay ƒ250-plus, which won't necessarily include breakfast, though it usually does.

During the summer, in all parts of the country but especially in Amsterdam and the major tourist centres, it's a good idea to **reserve** a room in

PRICE CODES

All the **hotels** we have listed in the Guide have been graded according to the following categories. They are above all a guide to price, and give little indication of the facilities you might expect to find. The prices given are for the cheapest double room – without private bath, etc. – during high season. In the case of **hostels** we've given the code if they have double rooms, otherwise we've stated the actual price per dorm bed per night. You will find many bottom-end hotels have a mixture of rooms, some with private facilities, some without; thus you may find that a good standard ③ category hotel has quite a number of ④ rooms as well.

① up to ƒ100/€45	⑤ ƒ250–300/€112.50–135
② ƒ100–150/€45–67.50	⑥ ƒ300–400/€135–180
③ ƒ150–200/€67.50–90	⑦ ƒ400–500/€180–225
④ ƒ200–250/€90–112.50	⑧ ƒ500/€225+

advance. You can do this most easily by calling the hotel direct – we've listed phone numbers throughout the Guide – and English is almost always spoken so there should be no language problem. You can also contact the **Netherlands Reservations Centre** (☎+31-70/419 5500), who coordinate three Web sites where you can view availability and prices and make hotel and apartment bookings online. The three sites are *www.hotelres.nl*, *www.visitamsterdam.nl* and *www.visitholland.com*. You'll find a similar service at *www.hotels-holland.com*. In The Netherlands itself, you can make advance bookings in person through any VVV office for a nominal fee.

PRIVATE ROOMS

One way of cutting costs is, wherever possible, to use **private accommodation** – rooms in private homes that are let out to visitors on a bed and breakfast basis; they're sometimes known as pensions. Prices are usually quoted per person and are normally around ƒ30–35; breakfast is usually included, but if not will cost about ƒ5 on top. You have to go through the VVV to find private rooms: they will either give you a list to follow up independently or will insist they book the accommodation themselves and levy the appropriate (but minimal) booking fee. Bear in mind, also, that not all VVVs are able to offer private accommodation; generally you'll find it only in the larger towns and tourist centres.

HOSTELS AND STUDENT ROOMS

There are just over thirty **official youth hostels** in Holland, all affiliated to Hostelling International (HI) and open to members for between ƒ25 and ƒ40 per person per night, including breakfast, depending on the season and the hostel's facilities. Accommodation is usually in small dormitories, though some hostels have single- and double-bedded rooms. Meals are often available – about ƒ16 for a filling dinner – and in some hostels there are kitchens where you can cook your own food. It is possible for non-members to stay in official hostels, though there's normally a small surcharge (around ƒ5). You should book in advance if possible during the summer, as some places get crammed. For a full list of Dutch hostels, contact the Nederlandse Jeugdherberg Centrale (NJHC), Professor Tulpstraat 2, 1018 HA Amsterdam (☎020/551 3155, fax 639 0199, *www.njhc.org*).

In addition to official hostels, the larger cities – particularly Amsterdam – sometimes have a number of **unofficial hostels** offering dormitory accommodation (and invariably double- and triple-bedded rooms, too) at broadly similar prices, though inevitably standards are frequently not as high or as reliable as the official HI places (and some are extremely poor). We've detailed possibilities in the Guide. In some cities you may also come across something known as a **Sleep-in** – dormitory accommodation established and run by the local council, which is often cheaper than regular hostels and normally only open during the summer. Locations vary from year to year; again, we've tried to give some indication of locations in the Guide, but for the most current information contact the VVV. The same goes for student accommodation, which is sporadically open to travellers during the summer holidays in some university towns. We've detailed definite possibilities in the guide, but the VVV usually has up-to-date information.

CAMPING

Camping is a serious option in The Netherlands: there are plenty of sites, most are very well equipped, and they represent a good saving on other forms of accommodation. Prices vary greatly, mainly depending on the facilities available, but you can generally expect to pay around ƒ5–10 per person, plus another ƒ5–10 for a tent, and another ƒ5–10 or so if you have a car or motorcycle. Everywhere the VVV will have details of the nearest site, and we've mentioned campsites where appropriate throughout the Guide. A list of selected sites is available from the Dutch camping association, Stichting Vrije Recreatie,

Broeksweg 75–77, 4231 VD Meerkerk (☎0183/352 741, fax 351 234). Good Dutch bookshops also carry a variety of publications on the country's campsites.

Some campsites also offer **cabins**, known as *trekkershutten* – frugally furnished wooden affairs that can house a maximum of four people for around ƒ55 a night. The Dutch camping association can provide a list of these and advance booking is advised – either by phoning the site direct or through the Netherlands Reservations Centre (address and phone number on p.35). There's also a modest network of hikers' cabins spread across much of the country. Listings are available from Stichting Trekkershutten Nederland, Ruigeweg 49, 1752 HC Sint Maartensbrug ☎0224/563 318 (fax only).

FOOD AND DRINK

Quite rightly, Holland is not renowned for its cuisine, but although much is unimaginative, it's rarely unpleasant (sometimes delicious) and prices won't generally break the bank. There's a good supply of ethnic restaurants too, especially Indonesian and Chinese, and even Dutch food holds one or two surprises. Drinking is easily affordable – indeed, downing a Dutch beer at one of the country's many good bars is one of the real pleasures of a visit.

FOOD

Dutch food tends to be higher in protein content than variety: steak, chicken and fish, along with filling soups and stews, are staple fare, usually served up in enormous quantities. It can, however, at its best, be excellent, some restaurants offering increasingly adventurous crossovers with French cuisine at good-value prices, especially *eetcafés* and bars.

BREAKFAST

In all but the cheapest of hostels, **breakfast** (*ontbijt*) will be included in the price of the room. Though usually nothing fancy, it's always substantial: rolls, cheese, ham, hard-boiled eggs, jam and honey or peanut butter are the principal ingredients. If you don't have a hotel breakfast, many bars and cafés serve rolls and sandwiches in similar mode.

The **coffee** is normally good and strong, served with a little tub of *koffiemelk* (evaporated milk); ordinary milk is rarely used. If you want coffee with warm milk, ask for a *koffie verkeerd*. **Tea** generally comes with lemon if anything – if you want milk you have to ask for it. **Chocolate** (*chocomel*) is also popular, hot or cold: for a real treat, drink it hot with a layer of fresh whipped cream (*slagroom*) on top. Some coffeeshops also sell aniseed-flavoured warm milk or *anijsmelk*.

SNACKS, CAKES, CHEESES

Beyond breakfast, eating cheaply, particularly on your feet, is no real problem, although those on the tightest of budgets may find themselves dependent on the dubious delights of **Dutch fast food**. This has its own peculiarities. Chips – *frites* or *patat* – are the most common standby (*vlaamse* or "Flemish" *frites* are the best), sprinkled with salt and smothered with huge gobs of mayonnaise (*fritesaus*) or, alternatively, curry, sateh, goulash, or tomato sauce. If you just want salt, ask for "*patat zonder*"; fries with salt and mayonnaise are "*patat met*". Chips are complemented with *krokken* – spiced minced meat (usually either veal or beef), often in hash, covered with breadcrumbs and deep fried – or *fricandel*, a frankfurter-like sausage. All these are available over the counter at evil-smelling fast-food places, or, for a guilder or so, from heated glass compartments on the street.

Tastier, and good both as a snack and a full lunch, are the **fish specialities** sold by street vendors: salted raw herring, smoked eel (*gerookte paling*), mackerel in a roll (*broodje makreel*), mussels, and various kinds of deep-fried fish. Look out, too, for "green" or *maatje* herring, eaten raw with onions in early summer. Tip your head back and dangle the fish into your mouth, Dutch-style.

Another fast snack you'll see everywhere is **shoarma** – kebabs, sold in numerous Middle Eastern restaurants and takeaways. A *shoarma* in pitta will set you back about *f*6 on average. Other, though far less common, street foods include **pancakes** (*pannekoeken*), sweet or spicy, also widely available at sit-down restaurants; **waffles** (*stroopwafels*), doused with syrup; and, in November and December, **oliebollen**, greasy doughnuts sometimes filled with fruit (often apple) or custard (a berliner) and traditionally eaten on New Year's Eve.

Dutch **cakes and cookies** are always good, and filling, best eaten in a *banketbakkerij* with a small serving area; or buy a bag and eat them on the hoof. Apart from the ubiquitous *appelgebak* – wedges of apple and cinnamon tart – things to try include *speculaas*, a crunchy cinnamon cookie with gingerbread texture; *stroopwafels*, butter wafers sandwiched together with runny syrup, and *amandelkoek*, cakes with a crisp cookie outside and melt-in-the-mouth almond paste inside. In Limburg you should also sample *Limburgse Vlaai* – a pie with various fruit fillings.

As for the kind of food you can expect to encounter in bars, there are **sandwiches and rolls** (*boterham* and *broodjes*) – often open, and varying from a slice of tired cheese on old bread to something so embellished it's almost a complete meal – as well as different kinds of more substantial fare. A sandwich made with French bread is known as a *stokbrood*. In the winter, *erwtensoep* (or *snert*) – thick pea soup with smoked sausage, served with a portion of smoked bacon on pumpernickel – is available in many bars, and at about *f*8 a bowl makes a great buy for lunch. Or there's an *uitsmijter* (literally, "bouncer"): one, two, or three fried eggs on buttered bread, topped with a choice of ham, cheese, or roast beef – at about *f*10, another good budget lunch.

Holland's **cheeses** have an unjustified reputation abroad for being bland. This is because the Dutch tend to export the lower quality products and keep the best for themselves. In fact, Dutch cheese can be delicious, although there isn't the variety you get in, say, France or Italy. Most are based on the same soft creamy Goudas, and differences in taste come with the varying stages of maturity – *jong*, *belegen*, or *oud*. *Jong* cheese has a mild flavour, *belegen* is much tastier, while *oud* can be pungent and strong, with a flaky texture not unlike Parmesan. Among the other cheeses you'll find, best known is the round red Edam, made principally for export and not eaten much by the Dutch; Leidse, simply Gouda with cumin seeds; Leerdammer and Maasdammer, strong, creamy, and full of holes; and Dutch-made Emmentals and Gruyères. The best way to eat cheese here is the way the Dutch do it, in thin slices (cut with a cheese slice or *kaasschaaf*) rather than in large hunks.

SIT-DOWN EATING

The majority of **bars** serve food, everything from sandwiches to a full menu, in which case they may be known as an **eetcafé**. This type of place tends to be open all day, serving both lunch and dinner. Full-blown **restaurants**, on the other hand, tend to open in the evening only, usually from around 5.30pm or 6pm until around 11pm. Bear in mind that everywhere, especially in the smaller provincial towns, the Dutch tend to eat early, usually around 7.30pm or 8pm, and that after about 10pm you'll find many restaurant kitchens closed.

If you're on a budget, stick to the **dagschotel** (dish of the day) wherever possible, for which you pay around *f*15–20 for a meat or fish dish, heavily garnished with potatoes and other vegetables and salad; note, though, that it's often only served at lunchtime or between 6pm and 8pm. Otherwise, you can pay up to *f*30 for a meat course in an average restaurant; fish is generally high quality but rarely cheap at *f*25–35. The three-course *tourist menu*, which you'll see displayed at some mainstream restaurants, is – at *f*25 or so – reasonable value, but the food is often dull. Surprisingly enough, train station restaurants are a good standby: every station has one serving full meals, in huge portions, for *f*10–15. Consider also The Netherlands' cheapest option for eating out, the university **mensa restaurants** in larger towns, where – with international student ID – you can get a filling, if not especially exciting, meal for under *f*12.

Eating **vegetarian** isn't a problem in Holland. Many *eetcafés* and restaurants have at least one meat-free menu item, and you'll find a few vegetarian restaurants in most of the larger towns, offering full-course set meals for *f*10–15. Bear in mind that vegetarian restaurants often close early.

Of foreign cuisines, **Italian** food is ubiquitous: pizzas and pasta dishes start at a fairly uniform *f*15 or so in all but the ritziest places. To eat Spanish and Tex-Mex costs a little more. **Surinamese** restaurants are a good bet for eating on a budget: try *roti*, flat pancake-like bread served with a spicy curry, hardboiled egg, and vegetables. **Chinese** and **Indonesian** restaurants, too, are widespread (sometimes they're combined), and are normally well worth checking out. You can eat à la carte – *Nasi Goreng* and *Bami Goreng* (rice or noodles with meat) are good basic dishes, though there are normally more exciting things on the menu, some very spicy and chicken or beef in peanut sauce (*sateh*) is always available. Or try a *rijstaffel*: boiled rice and/or noodles served with a huge number of spicy side dishes and hot *sambal* sauce on the side. Eaten with the spoon in the right hand, fork in the left, and with dry white or rosé wine, or beer, this doesn't come cheap, but it's delicious and is normally more than enough for two; indeed that's the usual way to order it – reckon on paying around f85 for two people.

DRINKING

Most **drinking** is done either in the cosy surroundings of a **brown café** (*bruin kroeg*) – so named because of the colour of the walls, often stained by years of tobacco smoke – or in more modern-looking places, everything from slick **designer bars**, minimally furnished and usually catering for a younger crowd, to homely neighbourhood bars. Most bars stay open until around 1am during the week and 2am at weekends, though some don't bother to open until lunchtime, a few not until around 4pm. There is another drinking establishment that you may come across, though they're no longer all that common – **proeflokaalen** or tasting houses, originally the sampling houses of small distillers, now small, old-fashioned bars that only serve spirits (and maybe a few beers) and sometimes close early around 8pm.

BEER

Other than in tasting houses, the most commonly consumed beverage is **beer**. This is usually served in small measures (just under a British half-pint) – ask for *een pils*. "May I have?" is *mag ik?*, as in "*mag ik een pils?*". The Dutch like their beer with a foaming head. Prices are fairly standard: you don't pay much over the odds for sitting outside or drinking in a swanky bar or club; reckon on paying about f3 a glass pretty much everywhere. Some bars, particularly those popular with the local English community, serve beer in larger measures, similar to the British pint, for which you can expect to pay f6–8. Beer is much cheaper from a supermarket, most brands retailing at a little over f1 for a half-litre bottle (a little less than a pint).

The most common names are Heineken, Amstel, Oranjeboom and Grolsch, all of which you can find more or less nationwide. Expect them to be stronger and more distinctive than the watery approximations brewed under licence outside The Netherlands. In the southern provinces of North Brabant and Limburg you'll also find a number of locally brewed beers – Bavaria from Brabant, De Ridder, Leeuw, Gulpen and Brand (the country's oldest brewer) from Limburg, all of which are worth trying. For something a little less strong, look out for Donkenbier, which is about half the strength of an ordinary pilsener beer.

You will also, of course, see plenty of the better-known **Belgian brands**, like Stella Artois and the darker De Koninck, available on tap, and bottled beers like Duvel, Chimay and various brands of the cherry-flavoured *Kriek*. There are also a number of beers which are seasonally available: *Bokbier* (bock beer) is widespread in autumn; white beers (*witbieren*) like *Hoegaarden*, *Dentergems* and *Raaf* are available in summer, often served with a slice of a lemon – refreshing and potent in equal measure.

WINE AND SPIRITS

Wine is reasonably priced – expect to pay around f8 or so for an average bottle of French white or red, though it will cost you f30 in a restaurant. As for **spirits**, the indigenous drink is **jenever**, or Dutch gin – not unlike British gin, but a bit weaker and oilier, made from molasses and flavoured with juniper berries: it's served in small glasses and is traditionally drunk straight, often knocked back in one gulp with much hearty back-slapping. There are a number of varieties: *Oud* (old) is smooth and mellow, *Jong* (young) packs more of a punch – though neither is extremely alcoholic. *Zeer oude* is very old *jenever*. The older *jenevers* are a little more expensive but are stronger and less oily. In a bar, ask for a *borreltje* (straight jenever) or a *bittertje* (with angostura); if you've a sweet tooth, try a *bessenjenever* – blackcurrant-flavoured gin; for a glass of beer with a jenever chaser, ask for a *kopstoot*. A glass of *jenever* in a bar will cost you around f3; in a supermarket bottles sell for around f15. Imported spirits are considerably more expensive.

Other drinks you'll see include numerous Dutch **liqueurs**, notably *advocaat* or eggnog, the sweet blue *curaçao* and luminous green *pisang ambon*, as well as an assortment of luridly coloured fruit brandies best left for experimentation at the end of an evening. There's also the Dutch-produced **brandy**, *Vieux*, which tastes as if it's made from prunes but is in fact grape-based, and various regional firewaters, such as *elske* from Maastricht – made from the leaves, berries and bark of alder bushes.

DUTCH FOOD AND DRINK TERMS

BASICS

Boter	Butter	*Kaas*	Cheese	*Vis*	Fish
Brood	Bread	*Koud*	Cold	*Vlees*	Meat
Broodje	Sandwich/roll	*Nagerechten*	Desserts	*Voorgerechten*	Appetizers, hors d'oeuvres
Dranken	Drinks	*Peper*	Pepper		
Eieren	Eggs	*Pindakaas*	Peanut butter		
Gerst	Barley	*Sla/salade*	Salad	*Vruchten*	Fruit
Groenten	Vegetables	*Smeerkaas*	Cheese spread	*Warm*	Hot
Honing	Honey	*Stokbrood*	French bread	*Zout*	Salt
Hoofdgerechten	Main courses	*Suiker*	Sugar		

STARTERS AND SNACKS

Erwtensoep/snert	Thick pea soup with bacon or sausage	*Patats/Frites*	Chips/French fries
		Soep	Soup
Huzarensalade	Potato salad with pickles	*Uitsmijter*	Ham or cheese with eggs on bread
Koffietafel	Light meal of cold meats, cheese, bread, and perhaps soup		

MEAT AND POULTRY

Biefstuk (hollandse)	Steak	*Karbonade*	Chop
Biefstuk (duitse)	Hamburger	*Kip*	Chicken
Eend	Duck	*Kroket*	Spiced veal or beef in hash, coated in breadcrumbs
Fricandeau	Roast pork		
Fricandel	A frankfurter-like sausage	*Lamsvlees*	Lamb
Gehakt	Ground meat	*Lever*	Liver
Ham	Ham	*Rookvlees*	Smoked beef
Kalfsvlees	Veal	*Spek*	Bacon
Kalkoen	Turkey	*Worst*	Sausages

FISH

Forel	Trout	*Kabeljauw*	Cod	*Schol*	Flounder
Garnalen	Shrimp	*Makreel*	Mackerel	*Schelvis*	Shellfish
Haring	Herring	*Mosselen*	Mussels	*Tong*	Sole
Haringsalade	Herring salad	*Paling*	Eel	*Zalm*	Salmon

TERMS

Belegd	Filled or topped, as in *belegde broodjes* (small rolls topped with cheese etc)	*Geraspt*	Grated
		Gerookt	Smoked
		Gestoofd	Stewed
Doorbakken	Well done	*Half doorbakken*	Medium
Gebakken	Fried/baked	*Hollandse saus*	Hollandaise (a milk and egg sauce)
Gebraden	Roasted		
Gegrild	Grilled	*Rood*	Rare
Gekookt	Boiled		

VEGETABLES

Aardappelen	Potatoes	*Champignons*	Mushrooms
Bloemkool	Cauliflower	*Erwten*	Peas
Bonen	Beans	*Hutspot*	Mashed potatoes and carrots

Knoflook	Garlic	Stampot Andijvie	Mashed potato and
Komkommer	Cucumber		endive
Prei	Leek	Uien	Onions
Rijst	Rice	Wortelen	Carrots
Stampot Boerenkool	Mashed potato and cabbage	Zuurkool	Sauerkraut

INDONESIAN DISHES AND TERMS

Ajam	Chicken	Nasi Rames	Rijsttafel on a single plate
Bami	Fried noodles with meat/chicken and vegetables	Pedis	Hot and spicy
		Pisang	Banana
Daging	Beef	Rijsttafel	Collection of different spicy dishes served with plain rice
Gado gado	Vegetables in peanut sauce		
Goreng	Fried	Sambal	Hot, chilli-based sauce
Ikan	Fish	Satesaus	Peanut sauce to accompany meat broiled on skewers
Katjang	Peanut		
Kroepoek	Shrimp crackers	Seroendeng	Spicy fried, shredded coconut
Loempia	Egg rolls	Tauge	Beansprouts
Nasi	Rice		
Nasi Goreng	Fried rice with meat/chicken and vegetables		

SWEETS AND DESSERTS

Appelgebak	Apple tart or cake	Oliebollen	Doughnuts
Drop	Dutch liquorice, available in zoet (sweet) or zout (salted) varieties – the latter an acquired taste	Pannekoeken	Pancakes
		Poffertjes	Small pancakes, fritters
		(Slag) room	(Whipped) cream
		Speculaas	Spice- and honey-flavoured biscuit
Gebak	Pastry		
Ijs	Ice cream	Stroopwafels	Waffles
Koekjes	Cookies	Vla	Custard

FRUIT AND NUTS

Aardbei	Strawberry	Druif	Grape	Peer	Pear
Amandel	Almond	Framboos	Raspberry	Perzik	Peach
Appel	Apple	Hazelnoot	Hazelnut	Pinda	Peanut
Appelmoes	Apple purée	Kers	Cherry	Pruim	Plum/prune
Citroen	Lemon	Kokosnoot	Coconut		

DRINKS

Anijsmelk	Aniseed-flavoured warm milk	Melk	Milk
		Met ijs	With ice
Appelsap	Apple juice	Met slagroom	With whipped cream
Bessenjenever	Blackcurrant gin	Pils	Dutch beer
Chocomel	Chocolate milk	Proost!	Cheers!
Citroenjenever	Lemon gin	Sinaasappelsap	Orange juice
Droog	Dry	Thee	Tea
Frisdranken	Sodas	Tomatensap	Tomato juice
Jenever	Dutch gin	Vieux	Dutch brandy
Karnemelk	Buttermilk	Vruchtensap	Fruit juice
Koffie	Coffee	Wijn	Wine
Koffie verkeerd	Coffee with warm milk	(wit/rood/rosé)	(white/red/rosé)
Kopstoot	Beer with a jenever chaser	Zoet	Sweet

MUSEUMS, GALLERIES AND CHURCHES

The Netherlands is strong on museums and galleries. Every town and most of the larger villages have at least one small collection of Dutch art worth investigating and many places heave with general and special-interest museums. Predictably enough, there are literally hundreds of churches too – most of the more interesting are in the major cities.

MUSEUMS AND GALLERIES

There are a number of different kinds of **museum** you'll come across time and again: a *Rijksmuseum* is a state-run museum, housing a national collection on a specific theme; a *Stedelijk* or *Gemeente* museum is run by the local town council and can vary from a small but quality collection of art to dusty arrays of local archeological finds. A *tentoonstelling* is a temporary exhibition, usually of contemporary art. **Hours** are fairly uniform across the country – generally Tuesday to Saturday 10am to 5pm, Sunday 1pm or 2pm to 5pm, though in recent years some of the larger museums in the cities have tended to open on Monday as well; entry prices for the more ordinary collections are usually around ƒ2–5, children

halfprice, but for huge state-run affairs such as Amsterdam's Rijksmuseum you're looking at somewhere between ƒ10 and ƒ15. Most museums offer at least some English information, even if it's just a returnable leaflet.

CHURCHES

Dutch **churches** are normally rather austere – the older ones stripped bare after the Reformation, their spartan, white-painted walls emphasizing the effect of their often soaring Gothic lines. Organs are often the only embellishment, with great, ornate cases that put out a terrific – and awesome – noise, and only in the Catholic south of the country does the occasional church still retain anything of the mystery of pre-Calvinist rituals. **Hours** for visitors vary, though northern churches do usually have set times when visits are possible – assuming, of course, that there's something inside worth seeing. Falling attendances, however, also mean that some churches have been pragmatically turned over to other purposes – exhibition halls, concert halls, even apartments. In the south, unless there's something of special interest, you may find you can only get in during a service.

MUSEUM DISCOUNTS

If you're planning to visit a fair number of museums in Holland, you'd be well advised to buy a **Museumjaarkaart** ("museum year card"), which allows you free or reduced admission to more than 400 museums throughout the country for an entire year. They're sold at VVVs and museums (you'll need a passport photo), and cost ƒ55 (ƒ25 for under-25s and ƒ45 for over-55s) – a bargain, considering you'll fork out a hefty total of ƒ27,50 to get into Amsterdam's Rijksmuseum and Van Gogh museum alone. Bear in mind, though, that some museums *don't* give reductions for museum-card-holders; we've usually indicated this in the Guide. An alternative for those under 26 is the **Cultureel Jongeren Passport** or **CJP**, which for ƒ20 gets you reductions on entry to museums all over the Netherlands, though these can vary wildly and are sometimes not that substantial. CJPs can be bought from the AUB Uitburo in Amsterdam (see p.119). Incidentally, if you're travelling as a family, ask at the larger museums about discounted family tickets.

POLICE, CRIME AND PERSONAL SAFETY

By comparison with other, more troubled parts of Europe, Holland is relatively free of crime, so there's little reason why you should ever come into contact with the Dutch police force. Bar-room brawls are highly unusual, muggings uncommon, and street crime much less conspicuous than in many other countries. Even in Amsterdam and the larger cities you shouldn't have problems, though it's obviously advisable to be on your guard against petty theft: secure your things in a locker when staying in hostel accommodation, and never leave any valuables in a tent or car. That said, if you're on a bike, make sure it is well locked up – bike theft and resale is a major industry here.

PETTY CRIME

Almost all the problems tourists encounter in The Netherlands are to do with **petty crime** – pickpocketing and bag-snatching – rather than more serious physical confrontations, so it's as well to be on your guard and know where your possessions are at all times. Thieves often work in pairs and, although theft is far from rife, you should be aware of certain ploys, such as: the "helpful" person pointing out "birdshit" (actually shaving cream or similar) on your coat, while someone else relieves you of your money; being invited to read a card or paper on the street to distract your attention; someone in a café moving for your drink with one hand while the other is in your bag

as you react; and if you're in a crowd of tourists, watch out for people moving in unusually close.

Sensible **precautions** against petty crime include: carrying bags slung across your neck and not over your shoulder; not carrying anything in pockets that are easy to dip into; having photocopies of your passport, airline ticket and driving licence, and leaving the originals in your hotel; and noting down travellers' cheque and credit card numbers. When you're looking for a hotel room, never leave your bags unattended, and similarly if you have a car, don't leave anything in view when you park: vehicle theft is still fairly uncommon, but luggage and valuables do make a tempting target. Again, if you're using a bicycle, make sure it is well locked up.

If you are robbed, you'll need to go to the police to report it, not least because your insurance company will require a police report; remember to make a note of the report number – or, better still, ask for a copy of the statement itself. Don't expect a great deal of concern if your loss is relatively small – and don't be surprised if the process of completing forms and formalities takes ages.

PERSONAL SAFETY

Although it's generally possible to walk around without fear of **harassment or assault**, certain parts of all the big cities – especially Rotterdam and Amsterdam – are decidedly shady, and wherever you go at night it's always better to err on the side of caution. In particular, Amsterdam's Red Light District has an unpleasant, threatening undertow, with hang-around junkies concentrated on some of the narrow streets, whilst Rotterdam's docklands are similarly edgy. As general **precautions** avoid unlit or empty streets, don't go out brimming with valuables, and try not to appear hopelessly lost – doubly so if you're travelling alone. Using public transport, even late at night, isn't usually a problem, but if in doubt take a taxi.

In the unlikely event that you are **mugged**, or otherwise threatened, never resist, and try to reduce your contact with the robber to a minimum; either just hand over what's wanted, or throw money in one direction and take off in the other. Afterwards go straight to the police, who will be much more sympathetic and helpful on these occasions. Most police officers speak at least some English.

DRUGS

Thousands of visitors come to Holland in general, and Amsterdam in particular, just to get stoned. This is the one Western country where the purchase of **cannabis** is entirely legal, and the influx of people drawn here by this fact creates problems: many Amsterdammers, for instance, get mightily hacked off with "drug tourism".

However, the Dutch government's attitude to **soft drugs** is actually more complex than you would think. The use of cannabis is tolerated but not condoned, with the result being a rather complicated set of **rules and regulations**. Where the local administration permits it, the sale of cannabis is only sanctioned at specified coffeeshops, but these are not allowed to sell alcohol (or hard drugs) or sell drugs to under-18s, and neither are they allowed to advertise. Furthermore, over-the-counter sales of cannabis are limited to 5g (under one-fifth of an ounce) per purchase – sold in ƒ10 and ƒ25 bags (the more powerful it is, the less you get); possession of over 30g (1oz) is illegal. In practice, the 5g and 30g laws are pretty much unenforceable and busts are rare, but note that if the police search you they are technically entitled to confiscate any quantity they find, regardless of whether or not it's less than the legal limit. Outside the coffeeshops, it's acceptable to smoke in some bars, but many are strongly against it so don't make any automatic assumptions – especially outside the cities. If in doubt, ask the barperson. "**Space cakes**" (cakes baked with hashish and sold by the slice), although widely available, count as

hard drugs and are illegal; if you choose to indulge, spend a few days working your way up to them, since the effect can be exceptionally powerful and long-lasting (and you can never be entirely sure what's in them anyway). And a word of warning: since all kinds of cannabis are so widely available in coffeeshops, there's no need to buy any on the street – if you do, you're asking for trouble. Needless to say, the one thing you shouldn't attempt to do is take cannabis out of the country – a surprising number of people think (or claim to think) that if it's bought in Amsterdam it can be taken back home legally; customs officials and drug enforcement officers always ignore this story.

As far as **other drugs** go, the Dutch law surrounding magic mushrooms is that you can legally buy and possess any amount so long as they are fresh, but as soon as you tamper with them in any way (dry or process them, boil or cook them), they become as illegal as crack. Despite the existence of a lively and growing trade in cocaine and heroin, possession of either could mean a stay in one of the Netherlands' lively and growing jails. And ecstasy, acid and speed are as illegal in the Netherlands as they are anywhere else.

BEING ARRESTED

If you're **detained** by the police, you don't automatically have the right to a phone call, although in practice they'll probably phone your consulate for you – not that consular officials have a reputation for excessive helpfulness. If your alleged offence is a minor matter, you can be held for up to six hours without questioning; if it is more serious, you can be detained for up to 24 hours.

OPENING HOURS AND PUBLIC HOLIDAYS

Although there's recently been some movement towards greater flexibility, opening hours for shops, businesses and tourist attractions – including museums – remain a little restrictive. Travel plans can be disrupted on public holidays, when most things close down, apart from restaurants, bars and hotels, and public transport is reduced to a Sunday timetable.

The Dutch weekend fades painlessly into the working week with many smaller **shops** and businesses staying closed on Monday mornings until noon. Normal opening hours are, however, Monday to Friday 8.30/9am to 5.30/6pm and – for shops, not businesses – Saturday 8.30/9am to 4/5pm. That said, shops are allowed to open seven days a week from 9am–10pm and an increasing number are doing so; where this isn't the case, many open late on Thursday or Friday evenings. In the cities, a handful of **night shops** – *avondwinkels* – stay open round the clock. Most towns have a market day, usually midweek (and sometimes Saturday morning), and this is often the liveliest day to be in a town, particularly when the stalls fill the central square, the *markt*.

Museums, especially those that are state-run, tend to follow a pattern: closed on Monday, open Tuesday to Saturday from 10am to 5pm, and from 1 to 5pm on Sunday and public holidays, though things are slowly changing in favour of seven-day opening. Though closed for Christmas and New Year, the state-run museums adopt Sunday hours on the remaining public holidays, when most shops and banks are closed. **Galleries** tend to be open from Tuesday to Sunday noon to 5pm. For precise details of opening hours, see the Guide.

Most **restaurants** are open for dinner from about 5 or 6pm, and though many close as early as 9pm, a few stay open past 11pm. **Bars**, **cafés** and **coffeeshops** are either open all day from around 10am or don't open until about 5pm; both varieties close at 1am during the week and 2am at weekends. **Nightclubs** generally function from 11pm to 4am during the week, staying open until 5am at weekends.

PUBLIC HOLIDAYS (NATIONALE FEESTDAGEN)

Jan 1, New Year's Day	April 30, the Queen's Birthday	Whit Sunday and Monday
Good Friday (many shops open)	May 5, Liberation Day	Dec 25, Christmas Day
Easter Sunday and Monday	Ascension Day	Dec 26

FESTIVALS AND ANNUAL EVENTS

The Netherlands has few national annual events, and aside from the carnivals that are celebrated in the southern part of the country and a sprinkling of religious-oriented celebrations, most annual shindigs are arts- or music-based affairs, confined to a particular town or city. In addition there are also markets and folkloric events; traditionally, locals turned out in peasant costume on market day and in remoter towns and vil-

FESTIVALS DIARY

JANUARY

Mid-Jan Leiden. Jazz Week, featuring mainly Dutch performers; contact the Leiden VVV for details (☎0900/222 2333).

FEBRUARY

Mid- to late Feb Bovenkarspel. Westfriese Flora (West Frisian Flora exhibition; ☎0228/511 644) – the world's largest covered flower show held over ten days.

Late Feb to early March Carnivals at the beginning of Lent in Breda, 's Hertogenbosch, Maastricht and in other southern towns.

MARCH

Sunday closest to March 15 Amsterdam. Stille Ommegang procession through the city streets to the Oude Kerk. Information on ☎023/524 5415.

Late March to late May Keukenhof Gardens, Lisse (☎0252/465 555). World renowned floral displays in the bulbfields and hothouses of this 23-hectare park.

APRIL

April–Sept Alkmaar. "Traditional" Cheese Market on Friday mornings.

Second week Nationaal Museumweekend. Free entrance to all of the country's museums

Third weekend Groningen. Avant-garde jazz festival; contact the Groningen VVV (☎0900/202 3050) for information.

Penultimate weekend North Holland. Flower Parade from Noordwijk to Haarlem.

Last Sunday Rotterdam Marathon.

April 30 All Holland: Koninginnedag (Queen's Birthday), celebrated by street markets and fireworks.

MAY

May 5 Bevrijdingfestival. Outdoor festivals around the country celebrating liberation at the end of World War II.

Early May Amersfoort. Jazz Festival, featuring mainly national talent; information from Amersfoort VVV (☎0900/112 2364).

Mid-May Amsterdam. Drum Rhythm Festival, two-day outdoor rhythm and roots music festival. Details from Amsterdam VVV (☎0900/400 4040).

End May Breda. Traditional Jazz Festival, with open-air concerts and street parades. Information from Breda VVV (☎076/521 8530).

May 30 Scheveningen. Vlaggetjesdag ("Flag Day"). The town's boats are decorated with flags at this gala held to celebrate the commencement of the Dutch herring season. Further details from Scheveningen VVV (☎0900/340 3505).

Mid-May to early June Scheveningen. Sand Sculpture Festival. A serious business this, with hard-working teams descending on the resort from all over Europe to create amazing sand sculptures, which are left for three weeks for visitors to admire. Details on ☎070/324 8487.

JUNE

Throughout June Amsterdam, The Hague and Rotterdam. Holland Festival. A month-long arts festival, covering all aspects of both national and international music, theatre, dance and the contemporary arts Details from Amsterdam VVV (☎0900/400 4040).

June to September Maastricht. European Summer Cultural Programme, with music, theatre, etc. Details from Maastricht VVV (☎043/325 2121).

Early June Landgraaf. Pink Pop festival – a top-notch, three-day, open-air rock festival. Programme details on ☎046/475 2500.

lages this practice still survives, though some are rather bogusly sustained for tourists – the Alkmaar cheese market (see p.161) being a prime example. Most festivals, as you might expect, take place during the summer. Contact the local VVV for up-to-date details – and remember that wherever you might be staying, large swathes of the country are no more than a short train ride away.

Of the country's **annual cultural events**, the **Holland Festival**, held in June in Amsterdam, Rotterdam and The Hague, is probably the most diverse, with most performing arts represented and an increasingly international feel; the Web site *www.hollandfestival.nl* provides programme

Early June Bolsward. Frisian "eleven cities" cycle race, using bicycles instead of the ice skates used in the traditional Elfstedentocht (see overleaf and p.241).

Mid-June Scheveningen. International Kite Festival, with stunt kite tournaments held on the beach. Details from Scheveningen VVV (☎0900/340 3505).

Mid-June Terschelling. Oerol Festival, a ten-day event featuring location theatre and stand-up comedy.

Mid-June to mid-July Middleburg. International Festival of new avant-garde music. Details from Middleburg VVV (☎0118/659 900).

JULY

July–Aug Bloemendaal. "Woodstock" festival held on Bloemendaal beach and featuring live percussion, dance acts and plenty of revelry.

July 1–Sept 30 The Hague. International Rose Exhibition, with participants competing for the prestigious "Golden Rose". Details from The Hague VVV (☎0900/340 3505).

Early July The Hague. North Sea Jazz Festival. Outstanding three-day jazz festival showcasing international names as well as local talent. Thirteen stages and a thousand musicians. Programme details on ☎015/214 8900.

Mid-July Drentse Rijwielvierdaagse. A four-day cycling event, with routes ranging from 30km to 150km, and departure points at Assen, Emmen, Hoogeveen and Meppel.

Late July Nijmegen. Vierdaagse. One of the world's largest walking events, with over 30,000 participants walking between thirty and fifty kilometres per day over four days. Details on ☎070/360 4141.

AUGUST

Early Aug Sneek Week. The Netherlands' international sailing event at Sneek, with around 1000 boats competing in over thirty classes.

First or second weekend. Amsterdam Pride. The city's gay community celebrates, with street parties and performances, as well as a "Canal Pride" flotilla of boats parading along the Prinsengracht.

Mid-Aug Scheveningen. International Firework Festival, with two displays each evening. Further details from Scheveningen VVV (☎0900/340 3505).

Last week Amsterdam. The Grachtenfestival. International musicians perform classical music at twenty historical locations in the city, including the Prinsengracht, one of the world's most prestigious open-air concerts.

SEPTEMBER

Early Sept Aalsmeer. The Bloemencorso, a flower parade to Amsterdam. Route details on ☎0297/325 100.

Mid-Sept Brabantse Fietsdag. For one day 100 cycle routes are laid out in North Brabant, ranging in length from fifteen to fifty kilometres.

OCTOBER

Early/mid-October Amsterdam. City marathon. Further information from Amsterdam VVV (☎0900/400 4040).

NOVEMBER

Mid-Nov Parades throughout the country celebrating the arrival of St Nicholas.

DECEMBER

Dec 5 Pakjesavond. Though it tends to be a private affair, this is the day Dutch kids receive their Christmas presents. If you have Dutch friends, it's worth knowing that it's traditional to give a present together with a rude poem you have written caricaturing the recipient.

details a couple of months in advance. The country's keen interest in **jazz** is reflected in the large number of regional jazz festivals, of which The Hague's North Sea Jazz Festival in July is the most prestigious, attracting all the big names. Check out also the Europe-renowned Pink Pop Festival, held in Landgraaf near Maastricht early the same month, as this three-day event also attracts top-level performers.

Outside summer, **other annual events** include, of course, viewing the **bulbfields** – at their best between March and May (tulips from mid-April to mid-May). There are a number of places you can visit in the bulbfield areas of North and South Holland, notably the dazzling Keukenhof Gardens and – for a taste of the industry in action – the Aalsmeer flower auction.

A good source of information on everything flora-related in Holland is the Bloemenbureau Holland Web site at *www.bbh.nl*, which provides, in English, details of flower auctions and other events during the course of the year. If you're visiting the country in February/March, a number of towns in The Netherlands' southern provinces host **Mardi Gras carnivals**, notably Maastricht (well documented at *www.cybercomm.nl/~karneval*); while an event to look out for also in January (though really any time when the weather is cold enough) is the Elfstedentocht, Friesland's uniquely exciting, and gruelling, canal skating race between the province's eleven towns – though it's only actually been held once in the last twenty years so don't plan your trip around it.

TRAVELLERS WITH DISABILITIES

Despite its general social progressiveness, Holland is far from well equipped to deal with the particular requirements of people with mobility problems. In Amsterdam and most of the other major cities the most obvious difficulty you'll face is in negotiating the cobbled streets and narrow, often broken pavements of the older districts, where the key sights are usually located. Similarly, provision for people with disabilities on the country's urban public transport is only average, although in fairness it is improving – many new buses are, for instance, wheelchair accessible. And yet, while it can be difficult simply to get around, practically all public buildings, including museums, theatres, cinemas, concert halls and hotels, are obliged to provide access, and do. Bear in mind, however, that a lot of the older, narrower hotels are not allowed to install lifts, so check first. The Netherlands Tourist Board produces specific information for disabled tourists, providing access information and local contact numbers.

In terms of travel to the Netherlands, most **airlines** are now reasonably accommodating of wheelchair users and if you're thinking of travelling on **Eurostar**, their Web site, *www.eurostar.com*, is likely to provide much of the information you'll need. If you're planning to use the Dutch train network at all during your stay, it is worth calling the Head Office of **Netherlands Railways** (☎030/235 5555) in Utrecht well beforehand; as well as producing informative leaflets on train travel for people with disabilities, they can provide practical help during your journey.

USEFUL CONTACTS

THE NETHERLANDS

Mobility International Nederland, Heidestein 7, 3971 ND Driebergen ☎0343/521795, *bijning@worldonline.nl* Largest Dutch information and advice service for people with disabilities.

Stadsmobiel, Postbus 2131, 1000 CC Amsterdam ☎ & fax 020/613 4769.Provides an accessible shuttle service from Amsterdam's Schiphol Airport.

Stichting Informatie Gehandicapten (SIG), Zakkedragershof 34–44, Postbus 70, 3500 AB Utrecht ☎030/234 5611.General disability information.

UK AND IRELAND

Holiday Care Service, 2nd floor, Imperial Building, Victoria Rd, Horley, Surrey RH6 9HW ☎01293/774535. *Information on all aspects of travel.*

Irish Wheelchair Association, Blackheath Drive, Clontarf, Dublin 3 ☎01/833 8241. National organization working for people with disabilities; related services for holidaymakers.

RADAR, 12 City Forum, 250 City Rd, London EC1V 8AS (☎020/7250 3222, minicom 4119). An excellent source of advice on holidays and travel abroad.

Tripscope, The Courtyard, Evelyn Rd, London W4 5JL (☎020/8994 9294, minicom ☎0845/758 5641). A national telephone information service offering free transport and travel advice.

US AND CANADA

Directions Unlimited, 720 N Bedford Rd, Bedford Hills, NY 10507 ☎1-800/533 5343. Travel agency specializing in custom tours for people with disabilities.

Jewish Rehabilitation Hospital, 3205 Place Alton Goldbloom, Chomedy Laval, Québec H7V 1RT ☎514/688-9550 (ext. 226). Guidebooks and travel information.

Society for the Advancement of Travel for the Handicapped (SATH), 347 5th Ave, Suite 610, New York, NY 10016 ☎212/447-0027, fax 725-8253, *www.sath.org* Non-profit travel-industry referral service that passes queries on to its members as appropriate; allow plenty of time for a response.

Travel Information Service, Moss Rehabilitation Hospital, 1200 West Tabor Rd, Philadelphia, PA 19141 ☎215/456-9600, *www.mossresourcenet.org/travel.htm* Telephone service, plus an excellent Web site offering information and resources, including travel agents, tourist offices and airline information.

Twin Peaks Press, Box 129, Vancouver, WA 98666-0129 (☎360/694-2462 or 1-800/637-2256). Publisher of the *Directory of Travel Agencies for the Disabled*, listing more than 350 agencies worldwide, and *Travel for the Disabled* which lists many free access guides; plus the *Directory of Accessible Van Rentals* and *Wheelchair Vagabond*, loaded with personal tips.

AUSTRALIA AND NEW ZEALAND

ACROD (Australian Council for Rehabilitation of the Disabled), PO Box 60, Curtin, ACT 2605 ☎06/6282 4333; 24 Cabarita Rd, Cabarita, NSW 2137 ☎02/9743 2699; 55 Charles St, Ryde ☎02/9809 4488; PO Box 8136, Perth Business Centre, Perth, WA 6849 ☎08/9221 9066; *www.acrod.org.au* Provides lists of travel agencies and tour operators for people with disabilities.

Barrier Free Travel, 36 Wheatley St, North Bellingen, NSW 2454 ☎02/6655 1733.

Disability Information & Resource Centre, 195 Gilles St, Adelaide, SA 5000 ☎08/8223 7522, *www.dircsa.org.au* Provides details of organizations offering holiday and travel information.

Disabled Persons Assembly (DPA), Level 4, Wellington Trade Centre, 173–175 Victoria St, Wellington ☎04/801 9100.

Wheelchair Travel, 29 Ranelagh Dr, Mt Eliza VIC 3930 ☎03/9787 8861, toll-free ☎1800/674468, *www.travelability.com*

DIRECTORY

ADDRESSES These are written, for example, as Haarlemmerstraat 15 III, meaning the third-floor (US – fourth-floor) apartment at no. 15 Haarlemmerstraat. The ground floor is indicated by hs (*huis*, "house") after the number; the basement is sous (*sousterrain*). The figures 1e, 2e, 3e and 4e before a street name are an abbreviation for Eerste, Tweede, Derde and Vierde, respectively – first, second, third and fourth streets of the same name. Some sidestreets, rather than have their own name, take the name of the street which they run off, but with the addition of the word *dwars*, meaning crossing, so Palmdwarsstraat is a sidestreet of Palmstraat. T/O (*tegenover*, or "opposite") in an address shows that the address is a boat: hence "Prinsengracht T/O 26" would indicate a boat to be found opposite building no. 26 on Prinsengracht. Dutch post codes – made up of four figures and two letters – can be found in the directory kept at post offices.

CLOGS You'll see these on sale in all the main tourist centres, usually brightly painted and not really designed for wearing. It's estimated that about three million clogs are still made annually in The Netherlands; interestingly, only about half are for the tourist market, the rest being worn mainly by industrial workers as foot protection.

ELECTRIC CURRENT 220v AC – British equipment needs only a plug adaptor; American apparatus requires a transformer and will need new plugs or an adaptor.

EMERGENCIES The Netherlands has one emergency number for the Police, Ambulance and the Fire Brigade – ☎112.

FLOWERS It doesn't take long to notice the Dutch enthusiasm for flowers and plants of all kinds: windows are often festooned with blooms and greenery, and shops and markets sell sprays and bunches for next to nothing. Flowers are grown year-round, though obviously spring is the best time to come if this is your interest, when the bulbfields (and glasshouses) of North and South Holland are dense with colour – tulips, hyacinths, and narcissi are the main blooms. Later in the year there are rhododendrons and, in Friesland and Groningen, fields of yellow rapeseed; in summer roses appear, while the autumn sees late chrysanthemums. For more on Holland's flowers, consult the NBT's Flowers booklet.

GAY AND LESBIAN HOLLAND As you might expect, it's in The Netherlands' cities that gay life is most visible and enjoyable. Amsterdam is probably the best city in Europe in which to be gay – attitudes are tolerant, bars are excellent and plentiful, and support groups and facilities are unequalled. Elsewhere in The Netherlands, while the scene isn't anywhere near as extensive, it's well organized: Rotterdam, The Hague, Nijmegen and Groningen each has an enjoyable nightlife. The native lesbian scene is smaller and more subdued than the gay one. Many politically active lesbians move within tight circles, and it takes time for foreign visitors to find out what's happening. All cities of any size have a branch of COC, the national organization for gay men and women, which can offer help, information and usually a coffee bar. The national HQ is at Rozenstraat 14, Amsterdam (Mon–Fri 9am–5pm; ☎020/626 8300).

ISIC CARDS Student ID is useful for mensas (university canteens), but won't help you gain reduced admission to very much, and certainly not museums or mainstream tourist attractions.

LEFT LUGGAGE At all train stations. Where there is no actual office, there will always be coin-operated lockers.

LONG-STAY For those planning a long-term stay in the Netherlands, a good source of information is a non-profit organization called Access, Societeit de Witte, Plein 24, 2511 CS Den Haag

(☎070/346 2525). They operate a very useful English-language information line on everything from domestic services to legal matters, as well as running courses on various aspects of Dutch administration and culture.

MOSQUITOES These pesky blighters thrive in The Netherlands' watery environment and can be particularly bad at campsites. An antihistamine cream such as Phenergan is the best antidote, although this can be difficult to find in The Netherlands – in which case preventative sticks like Autan or Citronella are the best idea.

TIME One hour ahead of GMT; six hours ahead of Eastern Standard Time; nine hours ahead of Pacific Standard Time.

TIPPING Appreciated (at around 10–15 percent), but not essential since restaurants, hotels, taxis, etc, must include a fifteen percent service charge by law. In public toilets, it's normal to leave about 25c.

TRAVEL AGENTS NBBS is the nationwide student/youth travel organization and the best source of BIJ tickets, discount flights and the like. They have branches in all the main Dutch cities.

WAR CEMETERIES There was fierce fighting in parts of The Netherlands during the last war, notably at Arnhem, where several thousand British and Polish servicemen are remembered at the Oosterbeek cemetery. There are other military cemeteries in the east and south of the country, not least at Margraten, where around eight thousand US soldiers lie buried.

WINDMILLS The best place to see windmills is at Kinderdijk near Dordrecht (see p.212); they're also still very much part of the landscape in the polderlands north of Amsterdam. Some, too, have been moved and reassembled out of harm's way in the open-air museums at Zaanse Schans (see p.160) and the Netherlands Open-Air Museum just outside Arnhem (see p.291).

N

CHAPTER 4
THE NORTH AND
THE FRISIAN ISLANDS

CHAPTER 2
NORTH
HOLLAND

CHAPTER 1
AMSTERDAM

CHAPTER 5
OVERIJSSEL, FLEVOLAND
AND GELDERLAND

CHAPTER 3
SOUTH HOLLAND
AND UTRECHT

CHAPTER 6
ZEELAND, NORTH BRABANT
AND LIMBURG

GERMANY

BELGIUM

CHAPTER ONE

AMSTERDAM

Amsterdam is a compact, instantly likeable city. It's appealing to look at and pleasant to walk around, an intriguing mix of the parochial and the international; it also has a welcoming attitude towards visitors and a uniquely youthful orientation, shaped by the liberal counter-culture of the last three decades. Also engaging are the buzz of open-air summer events and the intimacy of its clubs and bars, not to mention the Dutch facility with languages: just about everyone you meet in Amsterdam will be able to speak near-perfect English, on top of their own native Dutch and often French and German too.

The city's layout is determined by a web of **canals**. The historical centre, which dates from the thirteenth century, is girdled by five concentric canals dug in the seventeenth century as part of a planned expansion to create a uniquely elegant urban environment. It is here that the city's merchant class built their grand mansions, typified by tall, gracefully decorated gables, whose fine proportions are reflected in the still, olive-green waters below. The city council exercised strict control over this expansion – proscribing, for example, the width and length of every building lot – resulting in the homogeneous architecture that survives today. With its antique houses, cobbled streets, humpback bridges and tree-lined canals Amsterdam is – at its best – acutely beautiful.

The conventional sights are for the most part low-key, the most promoted being the **Anne Frank House**. What sways the balance however is Amsterdam's world-class group of museums and galleries. For many, the **Van Gogh Museum** alone is reason enough to visit the city, but add to this the **Rijksmuseum**, with its collections of medieval and seventeenth-century Dutch paintings, and the contemporary and experimental art of the **Stedelijk Museum** and the international quality of the art on display in the city is self-evident.

But it's Amsterdam's **population and politics** that constitute its most enduring characteristics. Notorious during the 1960s and 1970s as the zenith – or nadir – of radical permissiveness, the city mellowed only marginally during the Eighties, and, despite the gentrification of the last ten years or so, retains a uniquely laid-back feel, with much to it that is both innovative and comfortably familiar. Indeed, Amsterdammers make much of their city and its attractions being *gezellig*, a rather over-used Dutch word roughly corresponding to "cosy", "appealingly lived-in" and "warmly convivial" all at the same time. The city's unparalleled selection of *gezellig* drinking-places is a delight, whether you choose to visit a traditional, bare-floored **brown café** or one of the many designer bars and grand cafés. Furthermore, Amsterdam's unique approach to combating hard-drug abuse – embodied in the effective decriminalization of cannabis – has led to a proliferation of **coffeeshops**, which sell coffee only as a sideline to high-quality marijuana and hashish. Entertainment has a similarly innovative edge, exemplified by **multimedia complexes**, whose offerings are at the forefront of contemporary European film, dance, drama and music. There is any amount of affordable live music from all genres – although the Dutch have a particular soft spot for jazz – and Amsterdam has one of the world's leading classical orchestras, with generously subsidized ticket prices. The club scene is by contrast relatively subdued, even modest by the standards of other capital cities, though gay men will find that Amsterdam has Europe's most active and convivial nightlife network, largely justifying its claim to be the "Gay Capital of Europe" (gay women, on the other hand, with far fewer options, may feel the tag to be unwarranted).

Arrival, information and city transport

Schiphol, Amsterdam's international airport, is both a quick and convenient train ride away from Centraal Station, the city's international train station, which is itself a ten-minute metro ride from Amstel Station, the terminus for long-distance and international buses. For information, there are three central tourist offices. Centraal Station is also the hub of an excellent public transport network, whose trams, buses and metro combine to delve into every corner of the city. The system is supplemented by a host of companies offering canal trips and tours.

> The telephone code for Amsterdam is ☎020

Arrival

Amsterdam's **Schiphol airport** is located about 18km southwest of the city centre. The Arrivals hall, arranged around a large plaza, has all the standard facilities, including a VVV tourist office (daily 7am–10pm), two bureaux de change – the GWK (24hr) and ABN/Amro bank – plus left luggage facilities. Most of the major car hire companies are represented – Hertz, Avis, Budget, National and Europcar – and there's an NS railway ticket office. You'll find several credit card operated cash dispensers on the plaza too. From the airport, trains run to Amsterdam's Centraal Station (often abbreviated to C.S.) – a fast service leaving every fifteen minutes during the day, and every hour at night (1–6am); the journey takes between fifteen and twenty minutes and costs just ƒ6,50. The **taxi** fare from Schiphol to the city centre is around ƒ60 to ƒ65.

Centraal Station (C.S.), Amsterdam's **international train station**, has regular connections with key cities in Germany, Belgium and France, as well as all the larger towns and cities of the Netherlands. Its facilities include a GWK bank and bureau de change (24hr), a VVV tourist office on platform 2 (see box on p.57), coin-operated luggage lockers, a staffed left-luggage office (daily 6.30am–11.30pm) and ATMs. If you arrive late at night, it's best to take a taxi to your hotel or hostel – and you should certainly avoid wandering aimlessly around the station: it's not a dangerous place by any means, but there are too many shifty characters to make hanging around advisable. Stationsplein also possesses a second VVV office (see box on p.57) and a GVB public transport office.

Eurolines long-distance **international buses** arrive at **Amstel Station**, about 3.5km to the southeast of Centraal Station. The station concourse has a GWK bank and bureau de change (Mon–Sat 7.30am–9pm, Sun 10am–6pm), as well as a GVB municipal transport office. The metro journey to Centraal Station takes about ten minutes.

By car, coming in on either the A4 (E19) from The Hague or the A2 (E35) from Utrecht, you should experience few traffic problems, and the city centre is clearly signposted as soon as you approach Amsterdam's southern reaches. Both the A4 and the A2 lead to the A10 (E22) ring road; on its west side, leave the A10 at either the Osdorp or Geuzenveld exits for the city centre. However, be warned that driving in central Amsterdam – never mind parking – is extremely difficult; if you are travelling by car the best thing is to use the city's "Park and Ride" scheme.

Information

The Amsterdam Tourist Board runs three **tourist offices** (see box below) in the city centre. These offices, known here as elsewhere in the Netherlands as the **VVV** (pronounced "fay-fay-fay"), offer a wide range of services and issue a comprehensive assortment of literature (though few publications are free) – the bad news is that they are amazingly popular, so come early if you want to beat the queues, especially in the summer. In addition they operate a **money exchange** and an excellent **hotel reservation** service, which costs ƒ6 (plus a refundable deposit which is subtracted from your final hotel bill) and is especially useful in the summer when accommodation gets mighty tight, and sell telephone cards, maps and guidebooks, as well as tickets for public transport and canal cruises.

In terms of the city's cultural **events**, the VVV sells a comprehensive, but bland, monthly listings magazine, *What's On in Amsterdam* (ƒ4), detailing everything from theatre and ballet through to rock concerts. They also operate a premium-rate **information line** on ☎0900/400 4040, and sell **tickets** for concerts, museums and the theatre. Another source of tickets for events is Amsterdam's Uitburo, or AUB, part of the city council, which has a walk-in booking centre tucked away in a corner at Leidseplein 25 (☎621 1211).

You can also buy **tourist passes** at the VVV. The "Amsterdam Pass" (ƒ39,50) contains 31 coupons providing a range of discounts at museums, on boat trips and at several restaurants. Its lead feature is free entry to either the Rijksmuseum or the Van Gogh Museum, but all in all you'll need to be quite diligent to recoup your outlay. Another option is the Museumjaarkaart ("museum year-card"), which gives free entry to most museums in the country for a year; it costs ƒ55 and there are concessionary rates for senior citizens and the under-18s.

City transport

Almost all of Amsterdam's leading attractions are clustered in or near the city centre, within easy walking distance of each other. For longer jaunts, the city has an excellent **public transport system**, the mainstay of which is its trams. It also has a good bus network, which is supplemented by a modest metro and four passenger ferries across the river to the northern suburbs. Centraal Station is the hub

---

VVV OFFICES IN CENTRAL AMSTERDAM

On platform 2, Centraal Station (Mon–Sat 8am–8pm, Sun 9am–5pm).
On Stationsplein, across from the entrance to Centraal Station (daily 9am–5pm).
On Leidsestraat, just off the Leidseplein (daily 9am–5pm, Thurs–Sat till 7pm).

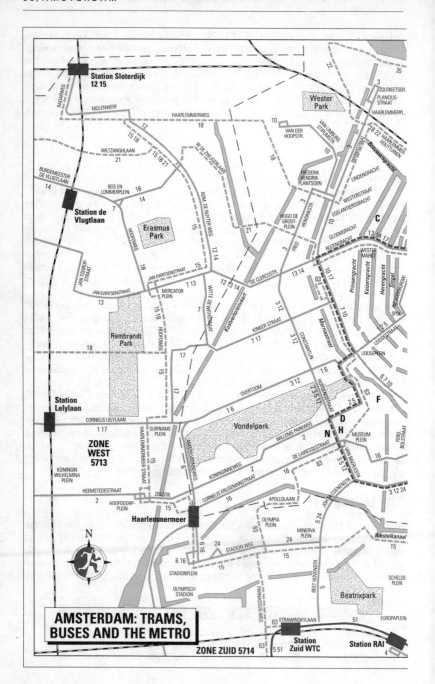

AMSTERDAM: TRAMS, BUSES AND THE METRO

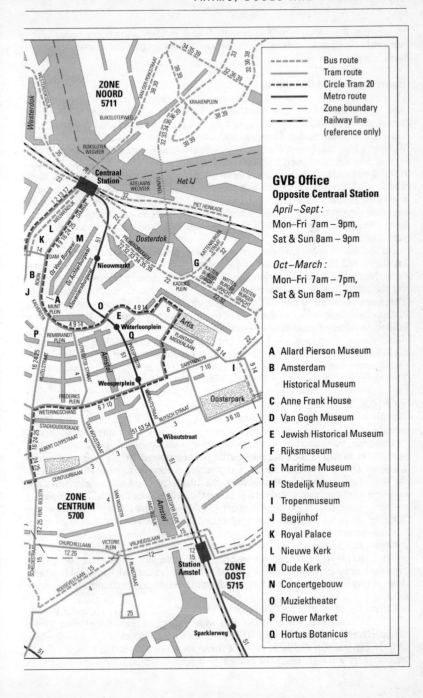

Bus route
Tram route
Circle Tram 20
Metro route
Zone boundary
Railway line (reference only)

GVB Office
Opposite Centraal Station
April–Sept:
Mon–Fri 7am – 9pm,
Sat & Sun 8am – 9pm

Oct–March:
Mon–Fri 7am – 7pm,
Sat & Sun 8am – 7pm

A Allard Pierson Museum
B Amsterdam Historical Museum
C Anne Frank House
D Van Gogh Museum
E Jewish Historical Museum
F Rijksmuseum
G Maritime Museum
H Stedelijk Museum
I Tropenmuseum
J Begijnhof
K Royal Palace
L Nieuwe Kerk
M Oude Kerk
N Concertgebouw
O Muziektheater
P Flower Market
Q Hortus Botanicus

of the transit system, which is operated by a publicly owned company, GVB. Amsterdam's **canals** present yet more possibilities for travelling between attractions by boat.

Trams, buses and the metro

The city centre is crisscrossed by **trams**, which operate on about twenty different routes. For the tourist, the most useful service is **Circle Tram #20** (daily 9am–7pm; every 10min); this links all the main attractions, running south from Centraal Station along Damrak and Rokin before threading east across Waterlooplein, southwest via Museumplein to Leidseplein, and then back to the station. For the most part, trams are entered at the rear doors (push the button). If the doors start to close before you've got on, put your foot on the bottom step, which will keep them open. To signal to the driver that you want to get off, push one of the buttons dotted at regular intervals down the length of the cars. This is especially important out in the suburbs or after dark, when drivers will blithely keep driving until someone tells them to stop. To get on a tram after dark, stick your hand out.

Buses, which are always entered at the front, are mainly useful for going to the outskirts, and the same applies to the **metro**, which has just two downtown stations, Nieuwmarkt and Waterlooplein. The metro is clean, modern and punctual, but the number of dodgy characters on it at night can make it a bit intimidating. The same operating hours (Mon–Fri 6am–midnight, Sat 6.30am–midnight, Sun 7.30am–midnight) apply to the bulk of the transport system, supplemented by a limited number of nightbuses (*nachtbussen*). All tram and bus stops display a detailed map of the network. For further details on all services, head for the main **GVB information office** (April–Sept Mon–Fri 7am–9pm, Sat & Sun 8am–9pm; Oct–March Mon–Fri 7am–7pm, Sat & Sun 8am–7pm) in front of Centraal Station. Their free, English-language *Tourist Guide to Public Transport* is very helpful.

TICKETS

The most common type of ticket, used on all forms of GVB transport, is the **strippenkaart** – a piece of card divided into strips. On the city's trams, unless there's a conductor, you insert your *strippenkaart* into the on-board franking machine: fold it over to expose only the last of the strips required for your journey before doing so. One person making a journey within a zone costs two strips – one for the passenger and one for the journey. On the metro, the franking machines are on the station concourse and on the buses the driver does the job. To complicate matters, Amsterdam's public transport system is divided into eleven **zones**; the "Centre" zone covers the city centre and its immediate surroundings (well beyond Singelgracht), but for longer journeys you'll have to dock your *strippenkaart* one additional strip for each zone you cross (thus a journey across two zones requires three strips, and so on). More than one person can use a *strippenkaart*, as long as the requisite number of strips is stamped; once this has been done, it can be used to transfer between trams, buses and the metro for up to an hour.

Currently, a two-strip *strippenkaart* costs ƒ3, a fifteen-strip ƒ11,75, and a 45-strip ƒ34,50. The last two are available at a wide variety of outlets including tobacconists, the GVB, the VVV, post offices and metro station ticket offices – the two-strip is generally available at most of these locations too, but not always. Most tram drivers will only issue the two-strip *strippenkaart*, and the same applies to bus drivers within the city, though on longer distances (beyond the city limits), you can expect the fifteen-strip to be on sale. To avoid all this stamping, you can instead opt for a *dagkaart* or "day ticket", which gives unlimited access to the GVB system for as many days as you need, up to a maximum of nine. Prices start at ƒ10 for one day and ƒ15 for two, going up in multiples of four to ƒ43 for nine days. For long-term stays, you might consider a season ticket, valid for a month or a year. For further details and advice visit the GVB office, whose operatives usually speak English.

Finally, note that the city has been cracking down on fare dodgers (known as *zwartrijders* – "black riders"), and wherever you're travelling, and at whatever time of day, there's a reasonable chance you'll have your ticket checked. If caught riding "black", you're liable for a ƒ60 fine (plus the price of the ticket you should have bought), payable on the spot.

Bikes

One of the most agreeable ways to explore pancake-flat Amsterdam is by **bicycle**. The city has an excellent network of designated bicycle lanes (*fietspaden*) and for once cycling isn't a fringe activity – there are cyclists everywhere. Much to the chagrin of the city's taxi drivers, the needs of the cyclist often take precedence over those of the motorist and if there's a collision, by law it's always the driver's fault. Despite this, no one blames the taxi drivers for the high incidence of **bike theft** in the city – this is a real problem, and you should lock up your bike thoroughly whenever it's not in use.

Bike **rental** is straightforward. There are lots of rental companies (*fietsenverhuur*) but the benchmark is set by NS railways, who have outlets at over eighty stations, including Amsterdam Centraal – current rates are ƒ9,50 per day and ƒ38 per week, with substantial discounts for most rail ticket holders. For a list of other outlets see the "Listings", p.36. Before renting, make sure you check the return time, the bike's age and condition, and any special discounts offered for longer rental periods. All firms, including NS, ask for some type of security, in the form of a cash deposit (some will take credit card imprints) and/or passport. Remember that you are legally obliged to have reflector bands on both wheels.

Taxis and cars

Taxis are plentiful in Amsterdam; they can be found in ranks on the main squares or by phoning the 24-hour radio-controlled central office on ☎677 7777 – you can't hail them on the street. Most drivers know their way around fairly well, though rates are pricey by any standards – a ƒ5,80 flat fee, plus ƒ2,85 per kilometre during the day, ƒ3,25 between midnight and 6am.

The centre of Amsterdam is geared up for trams and bicycles rather than **cars** as a matter of municipal policy. While pedestrianized zones as such are not extensive, motorists still have to negotiate a convoluted one-way system, not to mention herds of cyclists and fast-moving trams. It's also official policy to limit parking spaces in favour of bicycle racks, and zealous traffic police roam the city ready to clamp or tow away any vehicle that breaks the rules; it costs ƒ130 to have a clamp removed and a minimum of ƒ300 to reclaim an impounded car. What's more, the limited street spaces available are expensive: a fixed tariff applied across the city centre of ƒ4,75 per hour (Mon–Sat 9am–7pm) or ƒ2,75 per hour (Mon–Sat 7–11pm & Sun noon–11pm) – between 11pm and 9am it's free. City-centre car parks charge similar rates, the idea being to encourage drivers to use the free **"Park and Ride"** (P&R)

service – watch for the signs as you approach the city. Otherwise, **parking permits** can be bought in person from the Parking Control offices (Dienst Stadstoezicht) detailed in the the "Listings" (see p.36) for ƒ28,50 per day (9am–7pm), or ƒ142,50 for a week (9am–7pm). Note also that a number of the better hotels offer guests special parking permits for up to three days at ƒ30 a day.

Canal transport

Apart from choosing one of the many organized boat cruises available (see box on p.63), the best way to get around Amsterdam's canals is to take the **Canal Bus** (☎623 9886). The bus operates on three circular routes, which meet once, at the jetty opposite Centraal Station beside Prins Hendrikkade. There are eleven stops in all and together they give easy access to all the major sights. Boats leave from opposite Centraal Station (every 10–20min; 10am–5pm) and at least every half hour from any other jetty. A day ticket for all three routes, allowing you to hop on and off as many times as you like, costs ƒ22 per adult, ƒ15 for children (4–12 years old); it's valid until noon the following day and entitles the bearer to significant discounts at several museums. A similar boat service, **Museumboot** (☎530 1090) calls at six jetties located at or near eighteen of the city's major attractions, departing from opposite Centraal Station (every 30–45min; 10am–5.30pm). A come-and-go-as-you-please day ticket costs ƒ25.

Another waterborne "travel" option is **Canal Bikes**, four-person pedaloes which seem to take a lifetime to get anywhere, but are nevertheless good fun, particularly in the summer. Canal Bike (☎626 5574) rent their pedaloes out at four central locations: on the Singelgracht opposite the Rijksmuseum; the Prinsengracht outside the Anne Frank House; on Keizersgracht at Leidsestraat; and near the *American* hotel beside Leidseplein. Rental prices per hour, each, are ƒ10 (3–4 people) or ƒ12,50 (1–2 people), and there's a refundable deposit of ƒ50. The Canal Bikes can be picked up at one location and left at any of the others; a map showing five possible routes between the jetties costs ƒ3,50.

Organized tours

No one could say that the Amsterdam tourist industry doesn't make the most of its canals; **cruises** are its staple diet. Right throughout the year, and especially in the summer, an armada of glass-topped **boats** powers along the waterways, offering everything from a quick hour-long excursion to a fully fledged dinner cruise. There are dozens of operators, several of which crowd the dock beside the Damrak, near Centraal Station. Excursion **prices** vary according to the season, but the boat companies keep to a similar tariff: for the one-hour tour reckon on ƒ15 per adult, ƒ7,50 per child (4–12 years old); ƒ50 (ƒ25) for a two-hour candlelit cruise – we've given a selection in the box opposite. Bear in mind that boat rides are popular and long queues commonplace in the summer. Many visitors find canal trips delightful, but the commentary can sometimes be tedious, and the views disappointing. That said, it's certainly true that Amsterdam can look enchanting at night when the bridges are illuminated.

As for **land-based tours**, as you might expect there's a wide choice, from a quick zip round the city by tram through to leisurely bus and boat tours out into the Dutch countryside. Again, we've given a selection in the box opposite, but the Amsterdam VVV also issues a comprehensive brochure detailing all the various guided tours on offer. More unusual options include guided tours of the city's museums, walks and city-centre cycle tours; the VVV will make the necessary

CANAL CRUISES AND GUIDED TOURS

Canal Bus, opposite Centraal Station ☎623 9886. A "Canals and All That Jazz" cruise (April–Oct Sat 8–10pm), with a live jazz band and unlimited drinks and snacks. Tickets cost *f*57 for adults, *f*37 for children (4–12 year olds). Departs from the jetty opposite the Rijksmuseum; advance booking required.

Holland International, Damrak 90 ☎625 3035. Large tour operator running a wide range of bus trips from city sightseeing tours (1 daily; 3hr 30min; *f*48) to a gallop through Holland on their "Grand Holland Tour" (1 daily except Sat; 9hr; *f*75). The same company also does canal cruises, beginning with the basic one-hour sightseeing trip round the city centre for *f*15 per adult. Boats leave every 15min (9am–6pm) and every 30min (6–10pm) from the jetty at the northern end of Damrak, facing Centraal Station.

Mee in Mokum, Hartenstraat 18 ☎625 1390. Two- to three-hour guided

walking tours of the older parts of the city provided by long-time Amsterdam residents. Tours once daily; *f*5 per person.

P. Kooij, on the Rokin, opposite the east end of Spui ☎623 3810. Arguably the best of the major boat tour operators, this company offers hour-long canal cruises for *f*15 with live commentary (daily: April–Oct 9.30am–10pm; Nov–March 10am–5pm; every 30min). Also two-hour "Cheese and Wine" canal cruises daily at 9pm for *f*50.

Yellow Bike Tours, Nieuwezijds Kolk 29, off Nieuwezijds Voorburgwal ☎620 6940. This efficient company organizes three-hour guided cycling tours around the city centre (1 or 2 daily; April–Oct). Tours cost *f*30 per person, including the bike. They also do a full-day bike tour of the Waterland (see p.108) to the north of Amsterdam for *f*45 per person. In both cases, advance reservations are required.

bookings on your behalf for free. They also have an extensive list of recommended guides, some of whom have tempting specialities in such subjects as Dutch architecture and art.

Accommodation

Accommodation in Amsterdam can be extremely difficult to find, and is a major expense: even hostels are pricey for what you get, and hotels are among the most expensive in Europe. The city's compactness means that you're pretty much bound to end up somewhere within easy reach of the centre, but if you arrive without a reservation, you'll need to search hard to find a decent place to stay. At peak periods throughout the year – July and August, Easter, Christmas – you're strongly advised to **book well ahead**; hotel rooms and even hostel beds can be swallowed up remarkably quickly, and if you leave finding a room to chance, you may well be disappointed (and/or out of pocket). The VVV will make advance bookings, and book rooms on the spot for a *f*6 fee, or sell you a comprehensive leaflet on hotels in the city (*f*5). You can also reserve rooms in advance by contacting the **Netherlands Reservation Centre** (☎+31-70/419 5500), who coordinate three Web sites where you can view availability and prices and make hotel and apartment bookings. The three sites are *www.hotelres.nl*, *www.amsterdam.nl* and *www.visitholland.com*. You'll also find an online reservation service for hotels

ACCOMMODATION PRICE CODES

All the **hotels** detailed in this chapter have been graded according to the following categories. The codes are based on the price of the cheapest double room – without private bath, etc – during high season. In the case of **hostels** we've given the code if they have double rooms, otherwise we've stated the actual price per dorm bed per night.

① up to ƒ100/€45
② ƒ100–150/€45–67.50
③ ƒ150–200/€67.50–90
④ ƒ200–250/€90–112.5

⑤ ƒ250–300/€112.50–135
⑥ ƒ300–400/€135–180
⑦ ƒ400–500/€180–225
⑧ ƒ500/€225+

at *www.hotels-holland.com*. Something to bear in mind when choosing a hotel is the fact that many of Amsterdam's buildings have narrow, very steep **staircases**, and not all hotels have installed lifts. If this is a consideration for you, check before you book.

If you arrive at Centraal Station, you'll probably be approached by **touts** offering rooms or beds in hostels and cheap hotels. Despite the fact that most of them are genuine enough, our advice is to steer clear. If the place they're offering is in our listings you can phone it directly yourself, and if it isn't, it's probably been left out for a reason.

Hotels

In the main, Amsterdam's hotel prices start at around ƒ90 for a double, and although some form of **breakfast** – "Dutch" (bread and jam) or "English" (bacon and eggs) – is normally included at all but the cheapest and the most expensive hotels, some places can give the barest value for money. There are a huge number of what might be called comfortable **family hotels**, with basic, en-suite double rooms hovering more or less around the ƒ150 mark: the ones listed here have something particular to recommend them over the rest – location, value for money or ambience. Don't be afraid to ask to see the room first, and to refuse it if you don't like it. Incidentally, it is illegal for a hotel to refuse entry to anyone on the grounds of sexual orientation.

For gay hotels see p.128. All accommodation is marked on the map on pp.66–67.

The Old Centre

Centrum, Warmoesstraat 15 (☎624 3535, fax 420 1666, *centrum@xs4all.nl*). On a tatty street in the Red Light District, just five minutes' walk from Centraal Station, but, considering the location, some rooms (high up and at the back) are very quiet and light – in contrast to the bar. Choice of large and small rooms, with or without bath/shower. Friendly and accommodating. ②.

Cok City, Nieuwezijds Voorburgwal 50 (☎422 0011, fax 420 0357). A three-star chain hotel, which is sparklingly clean and popular with tour groups. En-suite rooms with TV, plus a kitchenette on each floor. Has a non-smoking floor. A ten-minute walk southwest of Centraal Station. ⑤.

De Gerstekorrel, Damstraat 22 (☎624 1367, fax 623 2640, *gersteko@euronet.nl*). Tram #4, #9, #16, #24 or #25 from Centraal Station to Dam square. Small, simple hotel, steps away from the Dam, with large, brightly decorated and well-lit rooms. Pleasant staff and good breakfast. On a noisy, bustling street (ask for a back room). Recommended. ④.

Grand, Oudezijds Voorburgwal 197 (☎555 3111, fax 555 3222, *hotel@degrandwestin.nl*). Tram #4, #9, #16, #24 or #25 from Centraal Station to Dam square. Originally a Royal Inn dating from 1578, and after that the Amsterdam Town Hall, this extraordinary building is a centrepiece of the city's medieval district. It claims to offer "a sublime combination of luxury, warm hospitality and unrivalled grandeur" – and comes pretty close. *f*650 or so for a double. ⑧.

Nes, Kloveniersburgwal 137 (☎624 4773, fax 620 9842, *hotel.nes@wxs.nl*). Tram #4, #9, #16, #24 or #25 from Centraal Station to Muntplein. Extremely pleasant and quiet, with a lift; well-positioned away from noise but close to shops and nightlife. Prices vary, depending on the view. ⑥.

Nova, Nieuwezijds Voorburgwal 276 (☎623 0066, fax 627 2026, *novahtl@pi.net*). Tram #1, #2 or #5 from Centraal Station to Spui. Spotless rooms, all en suite and with fridge and TV. Lift and secure access. Perfect, quiet location. ⑥.

Rho, Nes 5 (☎620 7371, fax 7826). Tram #4, #9, #16, #24 or #25 from Centraal Station to Dam square. A very comfortable hotel in a quiet alley off Dam square, with an extraordinary high-ceilinged lounge, originally built as a theatre in 1908. The place looks a bit run-down from the outside, but it's still a fine city-centre option, with helpful and welcoming staff. ④.

St Nicolaas, Spuistraat 1a (☎626 1384, fax 623 0979, *www.hotelnicolaas.nl*). Very pleasant, well-run little hotel housed in a former mattress factory (with a king-size lift to prove it). All-wood decor throughout, all rooms are en suite, comfortable and scrupulously clean; the only minus is the traffic noise. Recommended. Five minutes' walk from Centraal Station. ③.

Victoria, Damrak 1 (☎623 4255, fax 625 2997, *victoria@euronet.nl*). Opposite Centraal Station, the *Victoria* is one of the landmarks of the city – a tall, elegant building, wonderfully decorated throughout – and one of the classiest hotels, with every possible amenity. ⑧.

Winston, Warmoesstraat 123 (☎623 1380, fax 639 2308, *www.winston.nl*). A ten-minute walk from Centraal Station. Hotel designed for an arty crowd, which is safe and affordable, but popular (and noisy). Light and airy rooms (sleeping from one to six), some en suite, some with a communal balcony, twenty of which are specially commissioned "art" rooms, including the Durex Room and Heineken Room – the management plans to refurbish all the rooms in this way over the next few years. Lift and full disabled access. Recommended. ②.

West of the Old Centre

Ambassade, Herengracht 341 (☎626 2333, fax 624 5321, *www.ambassade-hotel.nl*). Tram #1, #2 or #5 from Centraal Station to Spui. Elegant canalside hotel made up of ten seventeenth-century houses, with antique-furnished lounges and comfortable en-suite rooms. Banquet-like breakfasts are an extra *f*22,50 but well worth it. A good middle-of-the-range option. ⑥.

Blakes, Keizersgracht 384 (☎530 2010, fax 530 3020, *hotel@blakes.nl*). Tram #1, #2 or #5 from Centraal Station to Keizersgracht. The latest Anouchka Hempel hotel (there are already two in London), housed in a seventeenth-century building, centred on a beautiful courtyard and terrace. Both the decor and the restaurant menu combine Oriental and European styles. ⑦–⑧.

De Bloeiende Ramenas, Haarlemmerdijk 61 ☎624 6030, fax 420 2261, *myhotel@ibn.net*). Welcoming and friendly hotel with comfortable rooms at sensible prices, in a peaceful location to the west of the centre, away from the nightlife, but with good access to the city's markets. A fifteen-minute walk from Centraal Station. ②.

Canal House, Keizersgracht 148 (☎622 5182, fax 624 1317, *canalhousehotel@compuserve.com*). Tram #13, #14 or #17 from Centraal Station to Westermarkt. Magnificently restored seventeenth-century building, centrally located on one of the principal canals. American family-run hotel with a friendly bar and cosy rooms, towards the top of this price bracket. ⑤.

Clemens, Raadhuisstraat 39 (☎626 9658, fax 624 6089). Tram #13, #14 or #17 from Centraal Station to Westermarkt. Just one of the options on this hotel strip. Clean, neat and good value for money. This is one of the city's busiest streets, so ask for a room at the back. ②.

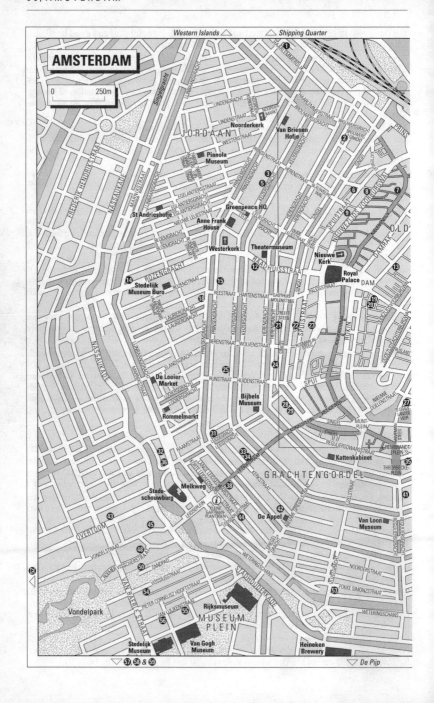

Western Islands △   △ Shipping Quarter

AMSTERDAM

0   250m

JORDAAN

Noorderkerk

Van Brienen Hofje

Pianola Museum

Greenpeace HQ

St Andrieshofje

Anne Frank House

Westerkerk

Theatermuseum

Nieuwe Kerk

Royal Palace

DAM

Stedelijk Museum Buro

ROZENGRACHT

OLD

De Looier Market

Bijbels Museum

Rommelmarkt

Kattenkabinet

GRACHTENGORDEL

Stads-schouwburg

Melkweg

De Appel

Van Loon Museum

Vondelpark

Rijksmuseum

MUSEUM PLEIN

Stedelijk Museum

Van Gogh Museum

Heineken Brewery

▽ 57, 58 & 59   ▽ De Pijp

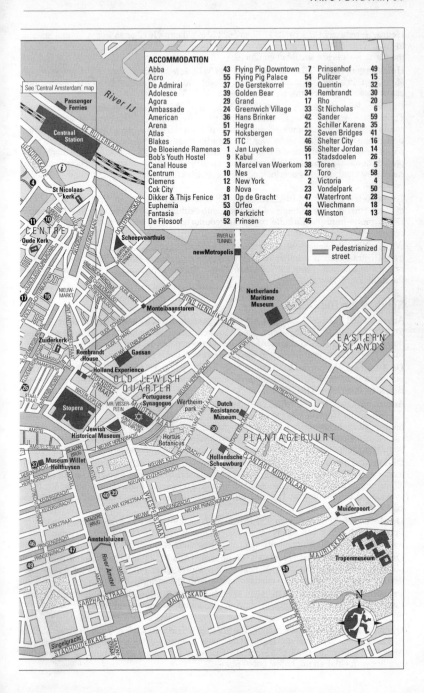

See 'Central Amsterdam' map

ACCOMMODATION

Abba	43	Flying Pig Downtown	7	Prinsenhof	49
Acro	55	Flying Pig Palace	54	Pulitzer	15
De Admiral	37	De Gerstekorrel	19	Quentin	32
Adolesce	39	Golden Bear	34	Rembrandt	30
Agora	29	Grand	17	Rho	20
Ambassade	24	Greenwich Village	33	St Nicholas	6
American	36	Hans Brinker	42	Sander	59
Arena	51	Hegra	21	Schiller Karena	35
Atlas	57	Hoksbergen	22	Seven Bridges	41
Blakes	57	ITC	46	Shelter City	16
De Bloeiende Ramenas	1	Jan Luycken	56	Shelter Jordan	14
Bob's Youth Hostel	9	Kabul	11	Stadsdoelen	26
Canal House	3	Marcel van Woerkom	38	Toren	5
Centrum	10	Nes	27	Toro	58
Clemens	12	New York	2	Victoria	4
Cok City	8	Nova	23	Vondelpark	50
Dikker & Thijs Fenice	31	Op de Gracht	47	Waterfront	28
Euphemia	53	Orfeo	44	Wiechmann	18
Fantasia	40	Parkzicht	48	Winston	13
De Filosoof	52	Prinsen	45		

Pedestrianized street

Hegra, Herengracht 269 (☎623 7877, fax 623 8159). Tram #1, #2 or #5 from Centraal Station to Spui. Welcoming atmosphere and relatively cheap for the location, on a beautiful stretch of the canal. Rooms are small but comfortable. ②.

Hoksbergen, Singel 301 (☎626 6043, fax 638 3479, *hotelhoksbergen@wxs.nl*). Tram #1, #2 or #5 to Spui. Friendly, standard hotel, with a light and open breakfast room overlooking the canal. Basic en-suite rooms, all with telephone and TV. ③.

Pulitzer, Prinsengracht 315 (☎523 5235, fax 627 6753, *sales_amsterdam@sheraton.com*). Tram #13, #14 or #17 from Centraal Station to Westermarkt. An entire row of seventeenth-century canal houses converted into a determinedly luxurious hotel that's often rated the best in Amsterdam. Subsidence over the centuries means that the inside of the hotel is a war-ren of steep stairs and crooked corridors, which only adds to its character. Individually dec-orated rooms are delightful and some have lift access; you're also spoilt for choice between canal views and windows overlooking the sumptuous internal courtyard. Around ƒ500 for a double. ⑧.

Toren, Keizersgracht 164 (☎622 6352, fax 626 9705, *hotel.toren@tip.nl*). Tram #13, #14 or #17 to Westermarkt. Fine example of a seventeenth-century canal house, once the home of a Dutch prime minister. En-suite rooms are comfortable and well-furnished, and the hotel retains a good deal of grace. ④.

Wiechmann, Prinsengracht 328 (☎626 3321, fax 8962). Tram #13, #14 or #17 to Westermarkt from Centraal Station. Another canal-house restoration, family-run for fifty years, with dark wooden beams and restrained style throughout. Rooms kept in perfect condition. Close to the Anne Frank House. ③–④.

South of the Old Centre

Agora, Singel 462 (☎627 2200, fax 627 2202, *agora@worldonline.nl*). Tram #1, #2 or #5 from Centraal Station to Koningsplein. Nicely located, small and amiable hotel right near the flower market; doubles cost upwards of ƒ150, three- and four-bed rooms proportionally less. Many rooms have canal views, and the wood-beam decor is delightful. ③.

De Admiraal, Herengracht 563 (☎626 2150, fax 623 4625). Tram #4, #9 or #14 from Centraal Station to Rembrandtplein. Friendly hotel close to the nightlife, with wonderful canal views. Breakfast is an extra ƒ10. ②.

American, Leidsekade 97 (☎556 3000, fax 556 3001). Tram #1, #2 or #5 from Centraal Station to Leidseplein. Landmark Art Deco hotel dating from 1902 (and in pristine, renovated condi-tion), right on Leidseplein. Large, double-glazed, modern doubles from around ƒ500. If you can't afford to stay, don't leave Amsterdam without soaking up some of the atmosphere at the popular and superbly decorated *Café Americain* overlooking the square. ⑧.

Dikker & Thijs Fenice, Prinsengracht 444 (☎626 7721, fax 625 8986). Tram #1, #2 or #5 from Centraal Station to Prinsengracht. Small and stylish hotel on a beautiful canal close to all the shops. Rooms vary in decor but all include a telephone and TV; those on the top floor give a good view of the city. There's a lift, but it's small and antiquated. Breakfast not includ-ed. ⑥.

Op de Gracht, Prinsengracht 826 (☎626 1937, no fax). Tram #4 from Centraal Station to Prinsengracht. B&B in a stately canalhouse on one of the main canals. Just two rooms taste-fully decorated, both with en-suite bathroom. Minimum stay two nights. ③.

Orfeo, Leidsekruisstraat (14 ☎623 1347, no fax). Tram #1, #2 or #5 to Prinsengracht. Very pleasant hotel round the back of Leidseplein, with a small Finnish sauna for guests and decent breakfasts served until midday. Popular with gay visitors. ②–③.

Prinsenhof, Prinsengracht 810 (☎623 1772, fax 638 3368, *prinsof@xs4all.nl*). Tram #4 from Centraal Station to Prinsengracht. Artfully decorated, this is one of the city's top budget options; the best rooms are at the back. ②.

Quentin, Leidsekade 89 (☎626 2187, fax 622 0121). Tram #1, #2 or #5 from Centraal Station to Leidseplein. Very friendly small hotel, often a stopover for artists performing at the Melkweg. Welcoming to all, and especially well-regarded among gay and lesbian visitors, but families with children might feel out of place. ②.

Schiller Karena, Rembrandtplein 26 (☎554 0700, fax 624 0098, *sales@gtschiller.goldentulip.nl*). Tram #4, #9 or #14 from Centraal Station to Rembrandtplein. Once something of a hangout for Amsterdam's intellectuals, this chain hotel still has one of the city's best-known and most atmospheric bars on its ground floor. Named after the painter and architect Schiller, whose works are liberally sprinkled throughout the hotel. Wonderful Art Deco furnishings in all the public areas. The drawback is its location on tacky Rembrandtplein. ⑤.

Seven Bridges, Reguliersgracht 31 (☎623 1329). Tram #4 from Centraal Station to Prinsengracht. Perhaps the city's most charming hotel – and certainly one of its better-value ones – so-called because its canalside location affords a view of seven bridges in a row. Beautifully decorated, spotless rooms, which are regularly upgraded. Small and popular, so often booked solid. Breakfast is served in your room. ④–⑤.

Marcel van Woerkom, Leidsestraat 87 (☎ & fax 622 9834, *www.marcelamsterdam.nl*). Tram #1, #2 or #5 from Centraal Station to Prinsengracht. Well-known, popular B&B run by an English-speaking graphic designer and artist, in a stylish restored house, with four en-suite doubles available for two, three or four people sharing. A haven of peace surrounded by the buzz of the city, with regulars returning year after year, so you'll need to ring well in advance in high season. Breakfast not included, but there are tea- and coffee-making facilities. ④.

East of the Old Centre

Adolesce, Nieuwe Keizersgracht 26 (☎626 3959, fax 627 4249). Tram #9 or #14 to Waterlooplein. Large, popular and welcoming hotel, with neat if unspectacular rooms and a large dining room and bar. ②.

Fantasia, Nieuwe Keizersgracht 16 (☎623 8259, fax 622 3913, *reservation@ fantasia_hotel.com*). Tram #9 or #14 to Waterlooplein. Nicely situated hotel on a broad, quiet canal just off the Amstel; the rooms are well maintained, connected by quaint, narrow corridors, and there are also some very attractive attic rooms for *f*135. ②–③.

Rembrandt, Plantage Middenlaan 17 (☎627 2714, fax 638 0293). Tram #9 to the Artis Zoo. Elegant hotel with a dining room dating from the sixteenth century, though the building itself is nowhere near as old. The plain rooms pale somewhat by comparison, but are clean enough. ②.

The Museum Quarter and the Vondelpark

Abba, Overtoom 122 (☎618 3058, fax 685 3477). Tram #1 from Centraal Station to 1e Constantijn Huygensstraat. Recently renovated rooms, each with TV and telephone. Friendly, helpful staff; winter discounts. Busy street location, though. ②.

Acro, Jan Luyckenstraat 44 (☎662 0526, fax 675 0811). Tram #2 or #5 from Centraal Station to Van Baerlestraat. Excellent, modern hotel with stylish rooms, a plush bar and self-service restaurant (breakfast only). Well worth the money. ③.

Atlas, Van Eeghenstraat 64 (☎676 6336, fax 671 7633). Tram #2 from Centraal Station to Jacob Obrechtstraat. Situated just to one side of the Vondelpark, this Art Nouveau building houses a personable modern hotel with every convenience and comfort, plus an à la carte restaurant. Small, tranquil and very welcoming. ④.

De Filosoof, Anna van den Vondelstraat 6 (☎683 3013, fax 685 3750, *filosoof@xs4all.nl*). Tram #1 from Centraal Station to Jan Pieter Heijestraat. Hospitable hotel on a charming little street off the Vondelpark. The owner has a passion for philosophy: each room, small but comfortable, is named after a different philosopher, and furnished with relevant period pieces, paintings and, of course, their books. There's a small library too. Unique and attractive. ③.

Jan Luycken, Jan Luyckenstraat 58 (☎573 0730, fax 676 3841, *info@janluycken.nl*). Tram #2 or #5 from Centraal Station to Van Baerlestraat. Elegant, privately-run hotel in imposing nineteenth-century townhouses. Stylish and comfortable. ⑥–⑦.

Parkzicht, Roemer Visscherstraat 33 (☎618 1954, fax 618 0897). Tram #1 from Centraal Station to 1e Constantijn Huygensstraat. Quiet unassuming little hotel on a pretty backstreet near the Vondelpark and museums, with an appealingly lived-in look – clean and characterful. ②.

Prinsen, Vondelstraat 38 (☎616 2323, fax 6112, *manager@prinsnenhotel.demon.nl*). Tram #1 to 1e Constantijn Huygensstraat from Centraal Station. Family-style hotel on the edge of the Vondelpark; quiet and with a large, secluded garden at the back. ④.

Toro, Koningslaan 64 (☎673 7223, fax 675 0031). Tram #2 from Centraal Station to Emmastraat. Lovely hotel in two very comfortably furnished turn-of-the-century townhouses on a peaceful residential street by the southern reaches of the Vondelpark. Has its own garden and terrace overlooking a lake in the park. ⑤.

Hostels

The bottom line for most travellers is taking a dormitory bed in a **hostel**, and there are plenty to choose from: official Hostelling International places, unofficial private hostels, even Christian hostels; in fact, you'll probably be accosted outside the train station with numerous offers of beds. Most hostels will either provide (relatively) clean bed linen or charge a few guilders for it – so your own sleeping bag may be a better option. Many hostels also lock guests out for a short period each day, both for security reasons and to clean the place; some set a nightly curfew, though these are usually late enough not to cause too much of a problem. Many hostels don't accept reservations from June to August.

The cheapest deal you'll find is around ƒ25 per person per night; at better-furnished and/or more central hostels the average is closer to ƒ35. Much more and you might as well be in a hotel room. Note that any place that won't allow you to see the dorm before you pay is worth avoiding. If you want a little extra privacy, many hostels also offer triples, doubles and singles for much less than you'd pay in a regular hotel, though the quality and size of rooms can leave a lot to be desired.

The Old Centre

Bob's Youth Hostel, Nieuwezijds Voorburgwal 92 (☎623 0063, fax 675 6446). An old favourite of backpackers and a grungy crowd, *Bob's* is lively and smoky. Small dorms at ƒ26 per person, including breakfast in the coffeeshop on the ground floor (which also does cheap dinners). A ten-minute walk from Centraal Station.

Flying Pig Downtown, Nieuwendijk 100 (☎420 6822, fax 624 9516, *www.flyingpig.nl*). A five-minute walk from Centraal Station, this clean and large hostel is well run by ex-travellers familiar with the needs of backpackers. Free use of kitchen facilities, no curfew, all-night bar and there's a late-night coffeeshop, *Twin Pigs*, next door. Justifiably popular, with a dorm bed priced between ƒ26,50 and ƒ38,50 depending on the size of the dorm. During the peak season you'll need to book well in advance.

Kabul, Warmoesstraat 38 (☎623 7158, fax 620 0869). A couple of minutes' from Centraal Station. Huge, famous and bustling, with an international clientele and multilingual staff. Rooms sleep between one and sixteen people. Higher dorm rates than usual – ƒ40 in peak season, including use of all facilities. Given the extra cost, it's not always as clean as it should be, but it's safe, there's no lockout or curfew, and there's a late bar next door. Groups are no problem, and you can book in advance.

The Shelter City, Barndesteeg 21 (☎625 3230, fax 623 2282, *www.shelter.nl*). Metro Nieuwmarkt. A non-evangelical Christian youth hostel smack in the middle of the Red Light District. At ƒ28 these are some of the best-value beds in Amsterdam, with bed linen, shower and sizeable breakfast included. Dorms are single-sex, lockers require a ƒ10 deposit and there's a midnight curfew (1am at weekends). You might be handed a booklet on Jesus when you check in, but you'll get a quiet night's sleep and the sheets are clean.

Stadsdoelen, Kloveniersburgwal 97 (☎624 6832, fax 639 1035). Metro Nieuwmarkt, or tram #4, #9, #16, #24 or #25 from Centraal Station to Muntplein. The closer to the station of the two official HI hostels, with clean, semi-private dorms at ƒ30,50 for members, who get priority in high season; non-members pay a ƒ5 supplement. Sheets cost a steep ƒ6,50. Guests get a range of discounts on activities in the city. The bar serves good-value if basic food, and there's a 2am curfew.

West of the Old Centre

The Shelter Jordaan, Bloemstraat 179 (☎624 4717, fax 627 6137, *www.shelter.nl*). Tram #13, #14 or #17 from Centraal Station to Marnixstraat. The second of Amsterdam's two Christian youth hostels, again great value at ƒ28 per bed, with breakfast and bed linen included. Dorms are single-sex, lockers require a ƒ10 deposit and there's a 2am curfew. Friendly and helpful staff, plus a decent café. Sited in a particularly beautiful part of the Jordaan.

South of the Old Centre

Hans Brinker, Kerkstraat 136 (☎622 0687, fax 638 2060). Tram #1, #2 or #5 from Centraal Station to Prinsengracht. Well-established and raucously popular Amsterdam cheapie, with dorm beds going for around ƒ40. Singles and doubles (②) also available. The facilities are good, dorms are basic and clean, and it's very close to the Leidseplein buzz. One to head for if you're out for a good time (and not too bothered about getting a good night's sleep), though be prepared to change dorms several times during any extended stay.

Euphemia, Fokke Simonszstraat 1 (☎622 9045, fax 622 9045, *euphjm@pi.net*). Tram #16, #24 or #25 from Centraal Station to Weteringcircuit. Situated a shortish walk from Leidseplein and the major museums, with a likeable laid-back atmosphere and big, basic rooms with TVs. They're pricey though: doubles (②–③), plus three- and four-bed rooms for a very steep ƒ85 per person in high season and at weekends, dropping to half that during low season. Breakfast not included.

East of the Old Centre

Hotel Arena, 's-Gravesandestraat 51 (☎694 7444, fax 663 2649, *www.hotelarena.nl*). Metro Weesperplein, then a ten-minute walk. A renovated old convent on the edge of the Oosterpark which is a major centre for youth culture. Simply furnished attic dorms provide some of the best hostel accommodation in the city, which, from ƒ37,50 per person, is relatively expensive but worth it: the atmosphere more than compensates. It also has en-suite doubles (②). Breakfast isn't included. Women-only dorms at peak times. Lockers available. Facilities include an excellent and varied programme of live music and dance nights, a great bar and restaurant, the convent gardens, and even parking facilities. Open year-round; no curfew; wheelchair access.

The Museum Quarter and the Vondelpark

Flying Pig Palace, Vossiusstraat 46 (☎400 4187, fax 400 4105, *www.flyingpig.nl*). Tram #1, #2 or #5 from Centraal Station to Leidseplein, then a five-minute walk. The better of the two *Flying Pig* hostels, facing the Vondelpark and close to the most important museums. Immaculately clean and well maintained by a staff of travellers, who well understand their backpacking guests. Free use of kitchen facilities, no curfew and good tourist information. Dorms start at ƒ26,50 per person, with double rooms (①–②) available too. Great value.

Vondelpark, Zandpad 5 (☎589 8996, fax 589 8955, *fit.vondelpark@njhc.org*). Tram #1, #2 or #5 from Centraal Station to Leidseplein, then a five-minute walk. Well located and, for facilities, the better of the two HI hostels, with a bar, restaurant, TV lounge, free Internet access and bicycle shed, plus various discount facilities for tours and museums. HI members have priority in high season; non-HI members pay an extra ƒ5. Rates are ƒ38 per person in the dorms, including use of all facilities, shower, sheets and breakfast. Singles, doubles (②) and rooms sleeping up to six are available. Secure lockers; lift; no curfew. Book well in advance.

Campsites

There are several **campsites** in and around Amsterdam, most of them easily accessible by car or public transport. The four listed below are recommended by the VVV, divided into "youth campsites", which are self-explanatory, and "family campsites", which are more suitable for those seeking some quiet, or touring with a caravan or camper. For information on city campsites throughout the Netherlands take a look at *www.stadscampings.nl*.

Youth Campsites

Vliegenbos, Meeuwenlaan 138 (☎636 8855, fax 632 2723). Bus #32, #36 or nightbus #73 from Centraal Station. April–Sept. A relaxed and friendly site, just a 10min bus ride into Amsterdam North from the station. Facilities include a general shop, bar and restaurant. Rates are ƒ14,75 per night per person, with tent-rental at ƒ5 per person; hot showers are included. There are also huts with bunk beds and basic cooking facilities, for ƒ85 per night for four people; phone ahead to check availability. Under-18s need to be accompanied by an adult; no pets.

Zeeburg, Zuiderzeeweg 29 (☎694 4430, fax 694 6238, *camping@xs4all.nl*). Train from Centraal Station (or tram #10 from Leidseplein) to Muiderpoort Station, then bus #37. Open all year. Slightly better equipped than the *Vliegenbos*, but more difficult to get to. Rates are ƒ7,50 per person, plus ƒ5 for a tent, ƒ5 for a motorbike and ƒ7,50 for a car. Hot showers are an extra ƒ1,50. Cabins sleeping two and four are ƒ25 per person per night, including bedlinen. A sleep-in tent, which includes several bunkbeds, costs ƒ17,50.

Family Campsites

Amsterdamse Bos, Kleine Noorddijk 1, Aalsmeer (☎641 6868, fax 640 2378). Take yellow NZH bus #171 from Centraal Station. April–Oct. Facilities include a bar, shop and restaurant, but this is a long way out, on the southern reaches of the Amsterdamse Bos. Rates are ƒ8,75 per night (ƒ4,50 for four- to twelve-year-olds), hot showers included, plus ƒ4,75 for a car, ƒ11 for a camper and ƒ6,75 for a caravan. Huts sleeping up to four cost ƒ65 a night, which includes a gas stove.

Gaasper Camping, Loosdrechtdreef 7 (☎696 7326, fax 696 9369). Metro Gaasperplas. Mid-March to December. Campsite just the other side of the Bijlmermeer housing complex in Amsterdam Zuidoost (southeast), and easily reached from Centraal Station by metro. Very close to the Gaasperplas park, which has facilities for all sorts of outdoor activities. Rates are ƒ6,50, plus ƒ7,25 per tent, ƒ6,25 for a car, ƒ9,25 for a caravan. Hot showers ƒ1.50.

The City

Amsterdam's **compact centre**, confined by the Singelgracht, contains almost all the city's leading attractions and takes only about forty minutes to stroll from one end to the other. Centraal Station, where you're likely to arrive, lies on the centre's northern edge, its back to the River IJ: from the station, the city fans south in a web of concentric canals, surrounded by suburbs. The centre is short of landmarks and does not readily divide into distinct neighbourhoods, so the ordering of the sections that follow is to a certain extent arbitrary, though it does follow the city's historic development. Bear in mind, however, that just wandering around to get the flavour of Amsterdam is often the most enjoyable way to experience this unusual place.

At the heart of the city is Amsterdam's most vivacious district, the **Old Centre**, an oval-shaped affair whose jumble of antique streets and narrow canals are confined to the north by the River IJ and in the south by the Singel. This was where

Amsterdam began, starting out as a fishing village at the mouth of the River Amstel and then, when the river was dammed in 1270 (leading to the name Amstelredam), flourishing as a trading centre, receiving its municipal charter from a new feudal overlord, the Count of Holland, in about 1300. Thereafter, the city developed in stages, each of which was marked by the digging of new canals and, after a particularly severe fire in 1452, by the abandonment of timber for stone as the main building material. Today, it's the handsome stone buildings of subsequent centuries, especially the seventeenth, which provide the district with most of its architectural highlights. Strolling across the bridge from **Centraal Station** brings you onto the Damrak, the spine of the Old Centre and the thoroughfare that once divided the "Old Side" of the medieval city to the east from the "New Side" to the west. The Damrak culminates in **Dam square**, flanked by two of the city's most impressive buildings, the Koninklijk Paleis (Royal Palace) and the Nieuwe Kerk. To the east of Damrak is the **Red Light District**, which stretches up to Nieuwmarkt. It's here you'll find many of the city's finest buildings, though the seediness of the tentacular red-light zone dulls many charms. That said, be sure to spare time for the district's two delightful churches – the Amstelkring and the Oude Kerk. Just beyond the reach of the Red Light district is druggy **Nieuwmarkt**, an unappetizing start to the **Kloveniersburgwal**, which forms one of the most beguiling parts of the Old Centre, with a medley of handsome old houses lining the prettiest of canals. From here, it's a short walk west to the **Rokin**, a shopping boulevard running north to the Dam and at the bottom of which is Muntplein, a busy square where you'll find the floating flower market.

The Old Centre is bordered by the first of the major canals, the Singel, followed closely by the Herengracht, Keizersgracht and Prinsengracht – collectively known as the **Grachtengordel**, or "Girdle of Canals". These canals were part of a major seventeenth-century urban extension and, with the interconnecting radial streets, form the city's distinctive web shape. This is the Amsterdam you see in the brochures: still, dreamy canals, crisp reflections of seventeenth-century town houses, cobbled streets, railings with chained bicycles – an image which, although a little too familiar, is still utterly authentic. Here also are several of Amsterdam's most appealing museums, including two opulent canalhouses in the form of the Museum Willet-Holthuysen and the Van Loon Museum, not to mention the free beer you get on a tour of the Heineken Brewery. Even more popular, however, is the world-famous Anne Frank House, on Prinsengracht.

Beyond the Grachtengordel, the **Jordaan** to the west grew up as a slum and immigrant quarter and remains the traditional heart of working-class Amsterdam, though in recent years it has experienced a measure of gentrification. The area boasts few specific sights, but its mazy streets and narrow canals make it a charming area to wander. On the other side of the centre is the **Old Jewish Quarter**, which, along with the adjacent **Plantagebuurt** was once home to the city's large Jewish community. Since the German occupation during World War II, this area has changed more than any other – its population gone and landscape altered through the construction of the Town Hall – but there are several poignant reminders of earlier times, most notably the old Portuguese Synagogue and the first-rate Jewish Historical Museum. Just to the north of the Plantagebuurt lie the **Eastern Islands**, once an expanse of grimy dockland but now an up-and-coming residential area that holds the ambitious Dutch Maritime Museum.

Finally, Amsterdam's three leading museums are clustered together in what is sometimes known as the **Museum Quarter**, on the edge of Museumplein, just beyond the southern boundary of the Grachtengordel. The trio – the **Rijksmuseum**, the **Van Gogh Museum** and the **Stedelijk Museum** – between them possess a quite outstanding assortment of paintings, and they also form a cultural prelude to the sprawling greenery of the nearby **Vondelpark**, Amsterdam's loveliest park.

Centraal Station to Dam Square

With its high gables and cheerful brickwork, the neo-Renaissance **Centraal Station** is an imposing prelude to the city. At the time of its construction in the 1880s, it aroused much controversy because it was seen to separate the centre from the River IJ, source of the city's wealth, for the first time in Amsterdam's long history. There was controversy about the choice of architect too. The man chosen, Petrus J.H. Cuypers, was a Catholic, and in powerful Protestant circles there were mutterings about the vanity of his designs (he had recently completed the Rijksmuseum – see p.101) and their unsuitability for Amsterdam. In the event, the station was built to Cuypers' design, but it was to be his last major commission; thereafter he spent most of his time building parish churches.

Outside the station, **Stationsplein** is a messy open space, edged by ovals of water, packed with trams and dotted with barrel organs and chip stands – in the summer street performers vying for attention complete the picture. Across the water, to the southeast on Prins Hendrikkade, rise the whopping twin towers and dome of **St Nicolaaskerk** (Mon–Sat 11am–4pm; free), the city's foremost Catholic church. Dating back to the 1880s, the cavernous interior holds some pretty dire religious murals, mawkish concoctions only partly relieved by swathes of coloured brickwork. Above the high altar is the crown of the Habsburg Emperor Maximilian, very much a symbol of the city and one you'll see again and again. Amsterdam had close ties with Maximilian: in the late fifteenth century he came here as a pilgrim and stayed on to recover from an illness. The burghers funded many of his military expeditions and, in return, he let the city use his crown in its coat of arms – a practice which, rather surprisingly, survived the seventeenth-century revolt against Spain.

From Stationsplein, **Damrak**, a wide but unenticing avenue lined with tacky restaurants, bars and bureaux de change, storms south into Dam square. After passing an inner harbour crammed with the bobbing canal boats of Amsterdam's considerable tourist industry, you'll come, on the left hand side, to the old Stock Exchange, or **Beurs** (Tues–Sun 10am–4pm; ƒ6) – known as the "Beurs van Berlage" – a seminal work designed at the turn of the century by the leading light of the Dutch Modern movement, Hendrik Petrus Berlage (1856–1934). Berlage re-routed Dutch architecture with the building, forsaking the historicism that had dominated the nineteenth century, and whose prime practitioner had been Petrus Cuypers. Instead he opted for a style with cleaner, heavier lines, inspired by the Romanesque and the Renaissance, but with a minimum of ornamentation – and in so doing anticipated the Expressionism that swept northern Europe from 1905 to 1925. The Beurs has long since lost its commercial function and nowadays holds a modest exhibition on the history of the exchange, but the building is the main event, from the graceful exposed ironwork and shallow-arched arcades of the main hall through to a fanciful frieze celebrating the stockbroker's trade. Slightly further along, the enormous and long-established **De Bijenkorf** – literally "beehive" – department store extends south as far as the Dam. Amsterdam's answer to Harrods, De Bijenkorf posed all sorts of problems for the Germans when they occupied the city in World War II.

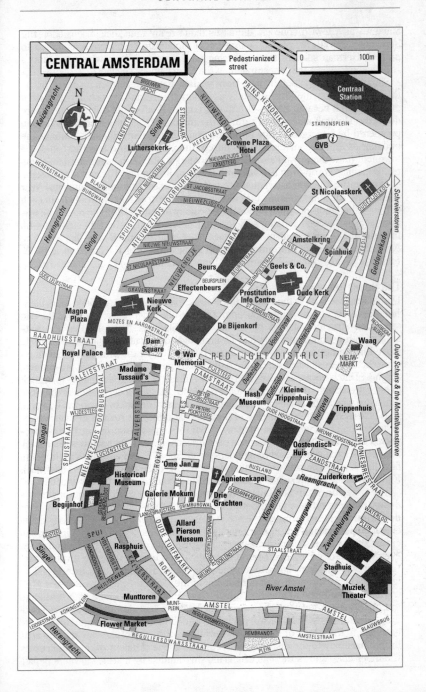

Since it was a Jewish concern, the Nazis didn't really want their troops shopping here, but it was just too popular to implement a total ban; the bizarre solution was to prohibit German soldiers from shopping on the ground floor, where the store's Jewish employees were concentrated, in the luxury goods section.

Situated at the heart of the city, **Dam square** gave Amsterdam its name: in the thirteenth century the River Amstel was dammed here, and the fishing village that grew around it became known as "Amstelredam". Boats could sail into the square down the Damrak and unload right in the middle of the settlement, which soon prospered by trading herrings for Baltic grain. In the early fifteenth century, the building of Amsterdam's principal church, the Nieuwe Kerk, and thereafter the town hall (now the Royal Palace), formally marked the Dam as Amsterdam's centre, but since World War II it has lost much of its dignity. Today it's as much a choked traffic junction as a square, but it does possess the main municipal **War Memorial**, a prominent stone tusk alongside twelve urns filled with soil from each of the Netherlands' provinces (plus the ex-colony of Indonesia). The memorial was designed by Jacobus Johannes Pieter Oud (1890–1963), a De Stijl stalwart who thought the Expressionism of Berlage (see above) much too flippant. The Amsterdam branch of **Madame Tussaud's** waxworks is on the Dam too, at no. 20 (daily: July–Aug 9.30am–7.30pm; Sept–June 10am–5.30pm; ƒ19,50, children ƒ16).

The Royal Palace

Dominating the Dam is the **Koninklijk Paleis**, the Royal Palace (guided tours daily: June & July 10am–6pm; Aug 12.30–5pm; ƒ7). The title is deceptive, given that the vast sandstone structure started out as the city's Stadhuis (town hall) in the mid-seventeenth century, and only had its first royal occupant when Louis Bonaparte moved in during the French occupation (1795–1813). At the time of the building's construction, Amsterdam was at the height of its powers. The city was pre-eminent amongst Dutch towns, and had just resisted William of Orange's attempts to bring it to heel; predictably, the council craved a residence that was a declaration of the city's municipal power and opted for a startlingly progressive design by Jacob van Campen, who proposed a Dutch rendering of the classical principles revived in Renaissance Italy. Work started in 1648 on what was then the largest town hall in Europe, supported by no less than 13,659 wooden piles driven into the Dam's sandy soil – a number every Dutch schoolchild remembers by adding a "1" and a "9" to the number of days in the year. The poet Constantijn Huygens called the new building "The world's Eighth Wonder / With so much stone raised high and so much timber under".

The **exterior** of the Stadhuis is very much to the allegorical point: pediments depict Amsterdam as a port adored by maritime gods on one side and by river deities on the other, while above are representations of the values the city council espoused – Prudence, Justice and Peace, plus Temperance and Vigilance to either side of a muscular, globe-carrying Atlas. One deliberate precaution, however, was the omission of a central doorway – just in case the mob turned nasty (as they were wont to do) and stormed the place. The building's **interior** similarly proclaims the pride and confidence of the Golden Age; the **Citizen's Hall** contains the enthroned figure of Amsterdam, sumptuously inlaid with brass and marble, looking down on the world and heavens laid out at her feet. A good-natured and witty symbolism pervades the building: cocks fight above the entrance to the Court of Petty Affairs, while Apollo, god of the sun and the arts, brings harmony to the disputes; and a plaque above the door of the Bankruptcy Chamber aptly shows the Fall of Icarus, surrounded by marble carvings depicting hungry rats scurrying around an empty chest and unpaid bills. Among the **paintings** dotted around the building, most are large-scale historical canvases of little distinction, with the exception of Ferdinand Bol's glossy *Moses the Lawgiver*.

The Nieuwe Kerk

Vying for importance with the Royal Palace is the adjacent **Nieuwe Kerk** (usually daily 10am–5pm; free, but admission charged during exhibitions; recorded information ☎638 6909). Despite its name (literally "new church"), it's an early fifteenth-century structure built in a late flourish of the Gothic style, with a forest of pinnacles and high, slender gables. Badly damaged by fire on several occasions and unceremoniously stripped of most of its fittings by the Calvinists, the **interior** is a hangar-like affair of dour demeanour, whose sturdy compound pillars soar up to support the wooden vaulting of the ceiling. Amongst a scattering of decorative highlights, look out for an extravagant, finely carved mahogany **pulpit** that was fifteen years in the making, a cleverly worked copper **chancel screen** and a flashily Baroque **organ case**. Behind the high altar there's also the spectacularly vulgar tomb of Admiral **Michiel de Ruyter** (1607–1676), complete with trumpeting angels, conch-blowing Neptunes and cherubs all in a tizzy. In a long and illustrious naval career Ruyter trounced in succession the Spaniards, the Swedes, the English and the French, and his rise from deck hand to Admiral-in-Chief is the stuff of national legend. His most famous exploit was a raid up the River Thames to Medway in 1667 and the seizure of the Royal Navy's flagship, *The Royal Charles*; the subsequent Dutch crowing almost drove Charles II to distraction. Ruyter was buried here with full military honours and the church is still used for state occasions – the coronations of queens Wilhelmina, Juliana and, in 1980, Beatrix, were all held here.

The Red Light District

The whole area to the east of Damrak, between Warmoesstraat, Nieuwmarkt and Damstraat, is the **Red Light District**, known locally as the "De Walletjes" – since this was where the old city walls ran. It stretches across the two canals that marked the eastern edge of medieval Amsterdam, Oudezijds Voorburgwal and Oudezijds Achterburgwal, both of which are now seedy and seamy, though the legalized prostitution here is world renowned and has long been one of the city's most distinctive and popular draws. The two canals, with their narrow connecting passages, are thronged with "window brothels" and at busy times the crass, on-street haggling over the price of various sex acts is drowned out by a surprisingly festive atmosphere. Interspersing the shabbiness are the handsome facades of old merchants' houses, most notably along **Oudezijds Voorburgwal**, once one of the wealthiest parts of the city, and nicknamed the "Velvet Canal". The canal's northern reaches are overlooked by the **Oude Kerk** (April–Nov Mon–Sat 11am–5pm, Sun 1–5pm; Dec–March Mon–Fri & Sun 1–5pm, Sat 11am–5pm; *f*5), an attractive Gothic structure with high-pitched gables and finely worked lancet windows. There's been a church on this site since the mid-thirteenth century, but most of the present building dates from the mid-fourteenth. The Protestants cleared the church of almost all of its ecclesiastical tackle during the Reformation, but its largely bare **interior** does hold several interesting features. These include some fruity and folksy misericords, a few faded vault paintings recovered from beneath layers of whitewash in the 1950s and the unadorned memorial tablet of Rembrandt's first wife, Saskia van Uylenburg. Better still are the three beautifully coloured **stained-glass windows**

COMMERCIAL SEX IN AMSTERDAM

Developed in the 1960s, Amsterdam's liberal approach to social policy has had several unforeseen consequences, the most dramatic being its international reputation as a centre for both drugs (see p.81) and **prostitution**. However, the tackiness of the Red Light District is just the surface sheen on what is a serious attempt to address the reality of sex-for-sale, and to integrate this within a normal, ordered society. In Dutch law, prostituting oneself has long been legal, but the state has always drawn the line at brothels. The difficulties this created for the police were legion, so finally, in 1999, brothels were legalized in the hope that it would bring a degree of stability to the sex industry. The authorities, in particular, wanted to first get a grip on the use of illegal immigrants as prostitutes, and second alleviate the problem of numbers; the amount of "window brothels" is limited, so a significant group of women have begun to ply their trade illicitly in bars and hotels. This new legislation is partly the result of a long and determined campaign by the prostitutes' trade union, **De Rode Draad** ("The Red Thread"), which has also improved the lot of its members by setting up health insurance and pension schemes.

One of the strongest features of the Dutch approach to commercial sex is its lack of prudery. The **Prostitution Information Centre**, at Enge Kerksteeg 3 (between Warmoesstraat and the Oude Kerk; Tues, Wed, Fri & Sat 11.30am–7.30pm; ☎420 7328), is a legally recognized *stichting*, or charitable foundation, set up to provide prostitutes, their clients and general visitors with clear, dispassionate information about prostitution. In addition to selling books and pamphlets, the PIC runs courses in prostitution at beginner and advanced level, provides support groups for clients and their partners, and publishes the *Pleasure Guide* in Dutch and English, which bills itself as "an informative magazine about having a paid love-life". By positioning itself on the commercial interface between the Red Light District and the rest of the city – and devoting itself to aiding communication between the two – the PIC has done much to subvert the old exploitative dominance of underworld pimps.

You can read about the city government's regulations and attitude towards prostitution online at *www.amsterdam.nl*.

beside the ambulatory in the Lady Chapel. Dating from the 1550s, two of the three depict Biblical scenes, while the third is both a later and – as a sign of the changing times – secular work, celebrating the Treaty of Munster of 1648, which wrapped up the Thirty Years' War and recognized Dutch independence from the Habsburgs. All the windows show their characters in classical gear with togas and sandals, but for different reasons: Biblical figures were usually clad in Greco-Roman clothes because this was thought to be accurate, whereas, a century later, the point was to emphasize the dignity of the treaty signers and their symbolic significance.

The Amstelkring and Zeedijk

A short walk from the Oude Kerk, towards the top end of Oudezijds Voorburgwal at no. 40, the clandestine **Amstelkring** (Mon–Sat 10am–5pm, Sun 1–5pm; ƒ7,50) was once the principal Catholic place of worship in the city and is now one of Amsterdam's most enjoyable museums. In 1578, the city finally forsook the Catholic Habsburgs and declared for the Protestant rebels in what was known as the Alteratie (Alteration). Broadly speaking, the new regime treated its Catholics well – commercial pragmatism has always outweighed religious zeal here – but there was a degree of discrimination; Catholic churches were recycled for

Protestant use and their members no longer allowed to practise openly. The result was an eccentric compromise: Catholics were allowed to hold services in any private building providing that the exterior revealed no sign of their activities – hence the development of the city's clandestine churches (*schuilkerken*), amongst which the Amstelkring is the only one to have survived intact.

The Amstelkring, more properly Ons Lieve Heer Op Solder ("Our Dear Lord in the Attic"), occupies the loft of a wealthy merchant's house and is a pleasure to investigate, with a narrow nave skilfully shoehorned into the available space. Flanked by elegant balconies, the nave has an ornately carved organ at one end and a mock-marble high altar, decorated with Jacob de Wit's mawkish *Baptism of Christ*, at the other. Even the patron of the church, one Jan Hartman, clearly had doubts about de Wit's efforts – the two spares he procured just in case are now displayed behind the altar. The rest of the house has been left untouched, its original furnishings reminiscent of interiors by Vermeer or De Hooch. Amstelkring, meaning "Amstel Circle", is the name of the group of nineteenth-century historians who saved the building from demolition.

Curving southeast from the northern end of Oudezijds Voorburgwal, **Zeedijk** was originally just that – a dike to hold back the sea – and the wooden house at no. 1 is one of the oldest in the city, built as sailors' lodgings around 1550. As in other such places, sailors could pay their bill by barter here (having usually whored or gambled away their money), and for some unknown reason, trading in pet monkeys was particularly popular – hence the name *In't Aepjen* ("In the Monkeys"), retained by the café currently occupying the premises. As for the rest of Zeedijk, it begins promisingly with a huddle of antique buildings, but soon descends into seediness, with junkies and dealers hanging about in ramshackle doorways, altogether threatening enough to make you hurry on to the open spaces of Nieuwmarkt.

Nieuwmarkt, Kloveniersburgwal and around

Nieuwmarkt was long one of the city's most important markets and the place where Jews (from the nearby Jewish Quarter – see p.94) and Gentiles traded. However, during World War II the Germans cordoned it off with barbed wire and turned the square into a holding pen, after which its old exuberance never returned. These days the market has all but vanished, though there are small markets for organic food on Saturdays (9am–5pm) and for antiques on Sundays (May–Sept 9am–5pm), with a few stalls selling fish, fruit and vegetables during the week.

The focus of the square, the sprawling multi-turreted **Waag**, dating from the 1480s, has had a chequered history. Built as one of the city's fortified gates, Sint Antoniespoort, Amsterdam's expansion soon made it obsolete and the ground floor was turned into a municipal weighing-house (*waag*), with the rooms upstairs taken over by the surgeons' guild. It was here that the surgeons held lectures on anatomy and public dissections, the inspiration for Rembrandt's *Anatomy Lesson of Dr Tulp*, displayed in the Mauritshuis Collection in The Hague. Abandoned by the surgeons and the weigh-masters in the nineteenth century, the building served as a furniture store and fire station before falling into disuse, though it has recently been renovated to house an excellent café-bar and restaurant, *In de Waag* (see p.113 for further details).

Strolling along Rechtboomssloot from the northeast corner of Nieuwmarkt, it takes only a couple of minutes to reach the **Montelbaanstoren**, a sturdy tower dating from 1512 that overlooks the **Oude Schans**, a canal dug around the same time to improve the city's shipping facilities. The tower was built to protect the city's eastern flank but its decorative spire was added later, when the city felt more secure, by Hendrik de Keyser (1565–1621), the architect who did much to create Amsterdam's prickly skyline.

At the top of the canal, turning left along busy Prins Hendrikkade takes you to the unusual **Scheepvaarthuis** ("Shipping Building"), on the left at no. 108, next to tiny Buiten Bantammerstraat. Completed in 1917, this is the flashiest of the buildings designed by the Amsterdam School of architecture, the work of Johann Melchior van der Mey (1878–1949). An almost neurotic edifice, covered with a welter of decoration celebrating the city's marine connections, the facade is shaped like a prow and is surmounted by statues of Poseidon, Amphitrite, his wife, and female representations of the four points of the compass. Slender turrets and Expressionistic carving add to the effect and inside there's more nautical playfulness with sea horses and dolphins, ships and anchors decorating everything from the skylights to the doors.

Along Kloveniersburgwal

Heading south from Nieuwmarkt it's a pleasant walk along **Kloveniersburgwal** to the **Trippenhuis**, at no. 29, a huge overblown mansion complete with Corinthian pilasters and a grand frieze built for the Trip family in 1662. One of the richest families in Amsterdam, the Trips were a powerful force among the **Magnificat**, the clique of families (Six, Trip, Hooft and Pauw) who shared power during the Golden Age. One part of the Trip family dealt with the Baltic trade, another with the manufacture of munitions (in which they had the municipal monopoly), but in addition to this they also had trade interests in Russia and the Middle East, much like the multinationals of today. In the nineteenth century, the Rijksmuseum collection was displayed here, but the house now contains the Dutch Academy of Sciences.

Directly opposite, on the right bank of the canal, there's a very different house that gives an idea of the sort of resentment such ostentatious displays of wealth engendered. Legend asserts that Mr Trip's coachman was so taken aback by the size of the new family residence that he exclaimed he would be happy with a home no wider than the Trips' front door – which is exactly what he got. At a metre or so across the **Kleine Trippenhuis**, Kloveniersburgwal 26, is one of the narrowest houses in Amsterdam.

Further along the canal, on the corner of Oude Hoogstraat, is the former headquarters of the Dutch East India Company, the **Oostindisch Huis**, a monumental red-brick structure built in 1605 shortly after the founding of the company. It was from here that the Company organized and regulated its immensely lucrative trading interests in the Far East, importing shiploads of spices, perfumes and exotic woods. This trade underpinned Amsterdam's Golden Age, but predictably the people of what is now Indonesia, the source of most of the raw materials, received little in return. However, despite the building's historic significance, it's of little interest today, being occupied by offices and the university.

From the Oostindisch Huis, you can either proceed up Oude Hoogstraat to the Hash Museum (see below) or keep straight for the huddle of narrow streets and picturesque drawbridges edging the south end of Kloveniersburgwal. This is one of the prettiest corners of the Old Centre, especially among the old facades of **Staalstraat**, along the narrow **Groenburgwal** canal and amidst the Victorian pomp of Nieuwe Doelenstraat. Also here is **Oudemanhuispoort**, a passage leading through to Oudezijds Achterburgwal which was once part of an almshouse for elderly men (hence the strange name), but is now lined by secondhand bookstalls.

Around the Oostindisch Huis

At the other end of tiny Oude Hoogstraat, close to the Oostindisch Huis at Oudezijds Achterburgwal 148, the **Hash Marihuana Hemp Museum** (daily 11am–10pm; *f*8) is still going strong despite intermittent battles with the police. As well as featuring displays on the various types of dope and numerous ways to smoke it, the museum has a live indoor marijuana garden, samples of textiles and paper made with hemp, and pamphlets explaining the medicinal properties of

---

DRUGS IN AMSTERDAM

Amsterdam's liberal policies on commercial sex (see p.78) are similarly extended to **soft drugs**, and the city has an international reputation as a haven for the dope-smoker, though, in fact, this confuses toleration with approval. Many visitors are surprised to find that all drugs, hard and soft, are technically illegal in Amsterdam, the caveat being that since 1976 the possession of small amounts of cannabis (up to 30g/1oz) has been ignored by the police. This pragmatic approach has led to the rise of "smoking" **coffeeshops**, selling bags of dope much in the same way as bars sell glasses of beer.

From its inception, there have been problems with this policy. In part, this is because the Dutch have never legalized the cannabis supply chain – or more specifically that section of it within their national borders – and partly because the 30g-rule has proved difficult to enforce. Inevitably, the relative laxity of the Dutch has made the country in general and Amsterdam in particular attractive to soft (and arguably hard) **drug dealers**. The Dutch authorities have tried hard to keep organized crime out of the soft drug market, but drug dealing and drug tourism – of which there is an awful lot – irritate many Amsterdammers no end.

In recent years, the French and German governments have put pressure on the Dutch to bring their drug policy into line with the rest of Europe – one recent concession obliged coffeeshops to choose between selling dope or alcohol, and many chose the latter. Overall however, while emphasizing their credentials in the fight against hard drugs (justifiably so – the country's figures for hard-drug addiction are among the lowest in Europe) the Dutch have stuck to their liberal guns on cannabis. Furthermore, by treating drugs as a medical rather than criminal problem, Amsterdam's authorities have been able to pioneer positive responses to **drugs' issues**. The council operates a system of free needle exchanges and – more unusually – has even set up tables at nightclubs for the purpose of chemically analyzing Ecstasy for clubbers. It also runs a wide range of rehabilitation programmes, although it recently decided to overhaul the methadone programme it introduced for heroine addicts in 1979; methadone is now largely discredited as a means of weaning addicts off the drug so the Dutch began issuing free heroin in tightly controlled quantities to users in 1998, a nationwide trial whose results are eagerly anticipated.

Nevertheless, for the casual visitor the main blot on the Amsterdam landscape is the groups of **hang-around junkies** who gather in and near the Red Light District, especially amongst the narrow streets and canals immediately to the east of the Oude Kerk (see p.77). The police estimate that there are around a thousand hard-drug users who, as they put it, "cause nuisance", and although the addicts are unlikely to molest strangers, they are a threatening presence, especially if you're travelling alone. In fairness, however, the police have done their best to clean things up, dramatically improving the situation on the Zeedijk and Nieuwmarkt, which were once notorious for hard drugs. You can read about the city government's regulations and attitude towards cannabis online at the Honest Cannabis information site, *www.thc.nl*.

cannabis. There's also a shop selling pipes, books, videos and plenty of souvenirs. Amsterdam's reliance on imported dope ended in the late 1980s when it was discovered that a reddish weed bred in America – "skunk" – was able to flourish under artificial lights; over half the dope sold in the coffeeshops is now grown in Holland, a change that has helped minimize the role of organized crime in the supply chain. For more information on drugs in Amsterdam see the box on p.81.

The triangular parcel of land at the southern end of Oudezijds Achterburgwal (which you can also reach through the Oudemanhuispoort – see above) is packed with university buildings, together forming a pleasant urban ensemble, but the red-shuttered, seventeenth-century **Huis op de Drie Grachten**, the "House on the Three Canals", stands out in particular, sitting prettily on the corner of Oudezijds Achterburgwal and Oudezijds Voorburgwal. Close by, through an ornate gateway at Oudezijds Voorburgwal 231, is the **Agnietenkapel** (St Agnes Chapel; Mon–Fri 9am–5pm; *f*2,50), originally part of a Catholic convent, but now owned by the university. Upstairs the chapel has a good-looking, first-floor auditorium dating from the fifteenth century; it's used for temporary exhibitions mainly devoted to the university's history. Roughly opposite, the building at no. 300 has been known for years as **ome Jan** ("Uncle John's") for its former function as central Amsterdam's pawn shop, though now it's the back of a bank. The poet Vondel ended his days working here, and a short verse above the entrance extols the virtues of the pawn shop and the evils of usury. From ome Jan it's just a few yards to the trams and traffic of Rokin.

The Rokin and around

The **Rokin** picks up where the Damrak (see p.74) leaves off, cutting south in an elegant sweep following the former course of the River Amstel. This wide boulevard was the business centre of the nineteenth-century city and although it has lost much of its prestige, grandiose old mansions like Sotheby's, at no. 102, and the elaborate *fin-de-siècle* Maison de Bonneterie clothes store, at no. 140, are reminders of more elegant times. The Rokin hits the city's canal system at Lange Brugsteeg and close by, beside the water at Oude Turfmarkt 127, the **Allard Pierson Museum** (Tues–Fri 10am–5pm, Sat & Sun 1–5pm; *f*9,50) holds Amsterdam's archeological collection. Highlights of this small and modest museum include a remarkably well-preserved assortment of Coptic clothes, plus Etruscan sculpture, Greek pottery and jewellery and a number of scale models – the Egyptian pyramids and such like – as well as a life-size model of a Greek chariot.

Rokin ends at Muntplein, where the **Munttoren** ("Mint Tower") was originally a mint that formed part of the old city walls, a plain brick structure to which Hendrik de Keyser, in one of his last commissions, added a flashy spire in 1620. A few metres away, the floating **Bloemenmarkt**, or flower market (daily 9am–6pm), extends along the southern bank of the Singel west as far as Koningsplein. Popular with locals and tourists alike, the market is the main supplier of flowers to central Amsterdam, its thousands of blooms now sharing stall space with souvenir clogs, garden gnomes and delftware.

The Amsterdam Historical Museum and Begijnhof

Running parallel to, and just to the west of Rokin, pedestrianized **Kalverstraat** has been a commercial centre since it was used to host a calf market in medieval times. It's now a run-of-the-mill shopping street, but halfway down, a lopsided gateway at no. 92 forms an unexpected entrance to the **Amsterdams Historisch Museum** (Amsterdam Historical Museum; Mon–Fri 10am–5pm, Sat & Sun 11am–5pm; ƒ8), the main entrance being on St Luciensteeg, a sidestreet off Kalverstraat. Housed in the restored seventeenth-century buildings of the municipal orphanage, the museum attempts to survey the city's development with a scattering of artefacts and lots of paintings from the thirteenth century onwards. It's a garbled collection, lacking continuity and poorly labelled, but a reorganization is underway and in the meantime highlights include several rooms, each containing **paintings** that illustrate a particular civic theme. One room has works relating to the surgeons' guild – notably Rembrandt's wonderful *Anatomy Lesson of Dr Jan Deijman* – while another depicts the regents of several orphanages, self-contented bourgeoisie in the company of the grateful poor. The orphanage's own Regents' Room, or office, dating from the seventeenth century, has survived too, but the most diverting part of the museum is the (free) **Schuttersgalerij**, the Civic Guard Gallery, occupying the glassed-in passageway immediately outside the museum. Exhibited here are a group of huge militia portraits, from serious-minded paintings of the 1540s through to lighter affairs from the seventeenth century.

Close to the Historical Museum along narrow Gedempte Begijnensloot, the **Begijnhof** (daily 10am–5pm; free) was founded in the fourteenth century as a home for the *beguines* – members of a Catholic sisterhood living as nuns, but without vows and with the right of return to the secular world. The original medieval complex comprised a series of humble brick cottages looking onto a central green, their backs to the outside world. These cottages were mostly replaced by larger, grander houses after the Reformation, but the secretive, enclosed design survived, totally removed from the bustle of the surrounding city. However a couple of pre-Reformation buildings do remain, including the **Houten Huys**, which, constructed in 1477, is the oldest house in Amsterdam, erected before the city forbade the construction of wooden houses as an essential precaution against fire. The **English Reformed Church**, which takes up one side of the Begijnhof, is of medieval construction too, but it was taken from the *beguines* and given to Amsterdam's English community during the Reformation. Plain and unadorned, the church is of interest for its pulpit panels, several of which were designed by a youthful Piet Mondrian (1872–1944) the leading De Stijl artist. After they had lost their church, and in keeping with the terms of the Alteratie (see p.78), the *beguines* were allowed to celebrate Mass inconspicuously in the clandestine **Catholic chapel** (Mon 1–6pm, Tues–Sun 9am–6pm; free), a homely little place with some terribly sentimental religious paintings which they established in the house opposite their old church.

Spui

Emerging from the south side of the Begijnhof, you hit the **Spui** (rhymes with "cow"), a long and slender open space flanked by bookshops and fashionable café-bars. In the middle is a cloying statue of a young boy, known as **'t Lieverdje** ("Little Darling" or "Loveable Scamp"), a gift to the city from a cigarette company in 1960. It was here in the mid-1960s, with the statue seen as a symbol of the addicted consumer, that the playful **Provos** (see box) organized some of their most successful *ludiek* ("pranks").

One block south of the Spui, Heiligeweg, or "Holy Way", now an uninspiring extension to Kalverstraat, was once part of a much longer route used by pilgrims

THE PROVOS AND THE KABOUTERS

Amsterdam's reputation as a wacky, offbeat city rests largely on its experiences in the 1960s, when social and political discontent began to coalesce into opposition to the city council's redevelopment plans. In common with similar movements in Paris and the US, these Amsterdam protests developed a playful aspect, and, as a consequence, garnered substantial public support. One of the popular groupings that emerged, led by Roel van Duyn and called the **Provos** (a name derived from "provocation"), took to holding small "happenings" around the 't Lieverdje statue on the Spui. In 1965, a clumsy attempt by the police to break up one of these happenings provoked a riot, but this disturbance was nothing compared with the scenes a few months later when, in March 1966, Princess (now Queen) Beatrix married an ex-Nazi, Claus von Amsberg. The Provos objected to the massive cost of the event as well as the Fascist connection and while the wedding procession was passing through the city, rioters clashed with police amidst smoke bombs and tear gas. Amsberg himself was jeered with the refrain "Give us back the bikes," a reference to the commandeering of hundreds of bikes by the retreating German army in 1945. The rioting continued throughout the summer, prompting Amsterdam's police chief to resign, followed by the mayor.

In 1966, the Provos won over two percent of the vote in municipal elections, and gained a seat on the city council. They brought with them their wide-ranging and imaginative **White Plans**, whose most famous proposal was to ban cars from the centre of Amsterdam and provide 20,000 white bicycles instead. The bicycles were to be distributed for people to use free of charge, who would leave them at their journey's end for someone else, but trials didn't really work and the plan was never implemented. By 1967, the Provos' plans for the rejuvenation of Amsterdam had become over-idealistic and unmanageable, and the group split. Van Duyn promptly founded a group called the **Kabouters**, after a helpful gnome in Dutch folklore. The Kabouters' manifesto described their form of socialism as "not of the clenched fist, but of the intertwined fingers, the erect penis, the escaping butterfly . . ." In the local elections of 1970, they met with some success, taking five council seats, but again implementation of the White Plans proved problematic. The Kabouters modified the White Bicycle Plan into a similar idea involving small, economical white cars, but trials in 1974 received poor public support and the plan was abandoned. In 1981, after ten years or so on the margins of Amsterdam politics, the Kabouters finally disintegrated; Van Duyn, though, has continued his involvement in local politics, and is still on the council as a member of the Green Party.

heading into Amsterdam. Every other religious reference disappeared centuries ago, but there is one interesting edifice here, the fanciful gateway of the old **Rasphuis** ("House of Correction") that now fronts a shopping mall near the corner with Kalverstraat. The gateway is surmounted by a sculpture of a woman punishing two criminals chained at her sides above the single word *Castigatio* ("punishment"). Beneath is a carving by Hendrik de Keyser showing wolves and lions cringing before the whip; the inscription reads "It is a virtue to subdue those before whom all go in dread".

The Grachtengordel

Medieval Amsterdam was enclosed by the Singel, part of the city's protective moat, but this is now just the first of five canals that reach right around the city centre, extending anti-clockwise from Brouwersgracht to the River Amstel in a "girdle of canals" or **Grachtengordel**. These were dug in the early years of the seventeenth century as part of a comprehensive plan to extend the boundaries of a city no longer able to accommodate its burgeoning population. Increasing the area of the city from 450 to 1800 acres was a monumental task, and the conditions imposed by the council were strict. The three main waterways, Herengracht, Keizersgracht and Prinsengracht, were set aside for the residences and businesses of Amsterdam merchants, while the radial canals were reserved for more modest artisans' homes. Everyone, even the wealthiest merchant, had to comply with a set of rules when building their house. In particular, the council prescribed the size of each building plot – the frontage was set at thirty feet, the depth two hundred – and although there was a degree of tinkering, the end result was the loose conformity you can see today: tall, narrow residences, whose individualism is mainly restricted to decorative gables and the occasional facade stone to denote name and occupation. It was almost the end of the century before the scheme was finished – a time when, ironically, Amsterdam's decline had already begun – but it remains to the council's credit that it was executed with such success.

Of the three main canals, **Herengracht**, the "Gentlemen's Canal", was the first to be dug, followed by the **Keizersgracht**, the "Emperor's Canal" named after the Holy Roman Emperor and fifteenth-century patron of the city, Maximilian. Further out still, the **Prinsengracht**, the "Princes' Canal", was named in honour of the princes of the House of Orange. The merchants who dominated Amsterdam soon lined the three with their mansions, the grandest concentrated on Herengracht, where the stretch of water between Leidsegracht and the Amstel was soon nicknamed the "**Golden Bend**" (De Gouden Bocht).

The Grachtengordel is the most charming part of Amsterdam, its lattice of olive-green waterways and small humpback bridges overlooked by street upon street of handsome seventeenth-century houses. It's a subtle cityscape too – full of surprises, with an unusual facade stone here, a bizarre carving there – and one whose overall atmosphere appeals rather than any specific sight (with the exception of the Anne Frank House).

Brouwersgracht to Leliegracht

Running west to east along the northern edge of the three main canals is leafy **Brouwersgracht**, one of the most peaceful and picturesque waterways in the city. In the seventeenth century, Brouwersgracht lay at the edge of Amsterdam's great harbour. This was where many of the ships returning from the East unloaded their silks and spices, and as one of the major arteries linking the open sea with the city centre, it was lined with storage depots and warehouses. Breweries flourished here too, capitalizing on their ready access to shipments of fresh water. Today, the harbour bustle has moved elsewhere, and the warehouses have been converted into apartments, their functional architecture interrupting the long ranks of residential facades. Look down any of the major canals from here and you'll see why visitors admire the city for its gentle interplay of water, brick, and stone. Indeed, picking any of the three main canals to head down means missing the other two, unless you're prepared to weave a circuitous, but rewarding, route.

Strolling south along **Prinsengracht** from Brouwersgracht, past handsome canal houses and tumbledown houseboats, it only takes a minute or two to reach the **Van Brienen Hofje**, at Prinsengracht 89–133, which you can walk around for free. This is one of the prettiest of the city's *hofjes*, or courtyard almshouses, built in 1804, according to the entrance tablet, "for the relief and shelter of those in need." Continue walking for a few metres more and you'll come to the first cross-street connecting the main canals, **Prinsenstraat**, which quickly runs into **Herenstraat**, an appealing little street of flower shops and cafés, greengroceries and secondhand clothes shops. At the east end of Herenstraat, turn right onto Herengracht and it's a short walk to the **Leliegracht**, one of the tiny radial canals that cut across the Grachtengordel, and home to a number of bookshops and canal-side bars. Though there are precious few extant examples of Art Nouveau and Art Deco architecture in Amsterdam, one of the finest is the tall and striking building at the Leliegracht–Keizersgracht junction. The building was designed by Gerrit van Arkel in 1905, and added to in the late 1960s; it is now **Greenpeace's world headquarters**.

The Anne Frank House

In 1957, the Anne Frank Foundation set up the **Anne Frank House** (daily: April–Aug 9am–9pm; Sept–March 9am–7pm; closed Yom Kippur; ƒ10) in the house at Prinsengracht 263, close to the Leliegracht, where the young diarist used to listen to the Westerkerk bells until they were taken away to be melted down for the German war effort. Since the posthumous publication of her diaries, Anne Frank has become extraordinarily famous, in the first instance for recording the iniquities of the Holocaust, and latterly as a symbol of the fight against oppression and, in particular, racism. The house is now one of the most popular attractions in town, so try to go early (or late) to avoid the crowds.

The story of Anne, her family and friends, is well known. Anne's father, **Otto Frank**, was a well-to-do Jewish businessman who ran a successful spice-trading business and lived in the southern part of the city. After the German occupation of the Netherlands, he felt – along with many other Jews – that he could avoid trouble by keeping his head down, but by 1942 this was clearly not going to be possible: Amsterdam's Jews were isolated and conspicuous, being confined to certain parts of the city and forced to wear a yellow star. Roundups, too, were becoming increasingly common. In desperation, Otto Frank decided – on the advice of two Dutch friends, Mr Koophuis and Mr Kraler – to move the family into the unused back of their warehouse on the Prinsengracht. The Franks went into hiding in July 1942, along with a Jewish business partner and his family, the Van Daans. They were separated from the eyes of the outside world by a bookcase that doubled as a door. As far as everyone else was concerned, they had fled to Switzerland.

So began the two-year occupation of the *achterhuis*, or back annexe. The two families were joined in November 1942 by a Mr Dussel, a dentist friend. Koophuis and Kraler, who continued working in the front office, regularly brought supplies and news of the outside world. In her diary Anne Frank describes the day-to-day lives of the inhabitants of the annexe: the quarrels, frequent in such a claustrophobic environment; celebrations of birthdays, or of a piece of good news from the Allied Front; and her own, slightly unreal, growing up (much of which, it's been claimed, was later deleted by her father).

Two years later, the atmosphere was optimistic: the Allies were clearly winning the war and liberation seemed within reach. It wasn't to be. One day in the summer of 1944 the Franks were betrayed by a Dutch collaborator and the Gestapo arrived and forced Mr Kraler to open up the bookcase. Thereafter, the occupants of the annexe were all arrested and quickly sent to Westerbork – the transit camp in the north of the country where all Dutch Jews were processed before being moved to Belsen or Auschwitz. Of the eight from the annexe, only Otto Frank survived; Anne and her sister died of typhus within a short time of each other in Belsen, just one week before the German surrender.

Anne Frank's **diary** was among the few things left behind in the annexe. It was retrieved by one of the people who had helped the Franks and handed to Anne's father on his return from Auschwitz; he later decided to publish it. Since its appearance in 1947, it has been constantly in print, translated into 54 languages, and has sold millions of copies worldwide. The rooms the Franks lived in for two years are left much the same as they were during the war, even down to the movie star pin-ups in Anne's bedroom and the marks on the wall recording the children's heights. A number of other rooms offer background detail on the war and occupation: one presents a video biography of Anne, from her frustrated hopes in hiding up until her death in 1945; another details the gruesome atrocities of the Holocaust, and gives some up-to-date examples of fascism and anti-Semitism in Europe, drawing pertinent parallels with the war years. Anne Frank was only one of about 100,000 Dutch Jews who died during World War II, but this, her final home, provides one of the most enduring testaments to its horrors. Her diary has been a source of inspiration to many, including Nelson Mandela.

The Westerkerk and around

Just to the south of the Anne Frank House, the **Westerkerk** (Mon–Fri 10am–4pm; Sat 10am–1pm; free) dominates the district, its 85-metre tower (April–Sept Mon–Sat 10am–4pm; *f*3) – without question Amsterdam's finest – soaring graciously above the gables of Prinsengracht. On its top perches the crown of Emperor Maximilian, a constantly recurring symbol of Amsterdam (see p.343) and the finishing touch to what was only the city's second place of worship built expressly for Protestants. The church was designed by Hendrik de Keyser and completed in 1631 as part of the general enlargement of the city, but whereas the exterior is all studied elegance, the interior – as required by the Calvinist congregation – is bare and plain. The church is also the reputed resting place of **Rembrandt**, though the location of his pauper's tomb is not known. Instead, the painter is commemorated by a small memorial in the north aisle, close to which his son Titus is buried. Rembrandt adored his son – as evinced by numerous portraits – and the boy's death dealt a final crushing blow to the ageing and embittered artist, who died just over a year later.

Westermarkt, an open square in the shadow of the Westerkerk, possesses two evocative statues. At the back of the church, beside Keizersgracht, are the three pink granite triangles (one each for the past, present and future) of the **Homo-Monument**. The world's first memorial to persecuted gays and lesbians, commemorating all those who died at the hands of the Nazis, it was designed by Karin Daan and recalls the pink triangles the Germans made homosexuals sew into and display on their clothes during World War II. The monument has now become a focus for the city's gay community and the site of ceremonies and wreath-laying throughout the year, most notably on Queen's Day (April 30), Coming-Out Day (Sept 5) and World AIDS Day (Dec 1). The monument's inscription, by the Dutch writer Jacob Israel de Haan, translates as "Such an infinite desire for friendship". Nearby, on the south side of the church by Prinsengracht, is a small but beautifully crafted **statue of Anne Frank** by the gifted Dutch sculptor Mari Andriessen (1897–1979), who is also the creator of the dockworker statue outside Amsterdam's Portuguese Synagogue (see p.97).

A few metres from the Westermarkt at Herengracht 168, the **Theatermuseum** (Theatre Museum: Tues–Fri 11am–5pm, Sat–Sun 1–5pm; *f*7,50) holds an enjoyable collection of theatrical bygones, from props through to stage sets, with a particularly good selection of costumes and posters. Occupying a pair of fine old mansions – the restrained neoclassicism of no. 168 contrasting with the ostentatious neo-Renaissance facade of the (Hendrik de Keyser-designed) house next door – the museum runs a lively programme of temporary exhibitions. At times however, the sumptuousness of the interior decoration almost overwhelms the displays, not least with the eighteenth-century ceiling paintings by Jacob de Wit, the extravagant stucco work and, most dramatic of all, the slender and ornate spiral staircase.

Raadhuisstraat to Leidsegracht – and the Biblical Museum

Westermarkt adjoins **Raadhuisstraat**, the principal thoroughfare into the Old Centre, which runs east to the Dam (see p.76). South of here the main canals are less appealing than the narrow **cross-streets**, many of which are named after animals whose pelts were used in the local tanning industry – there's Reestraat ("Deer Street"), Hartenstraat (Hart) and Berenstraat (Bear), to name but three. The tanners are (thankfully) long gone, but they've been replaced by some of the most pleasant shopping streets in the city – the shops here sell everything from carpets to handmade chocolates, toothbrushes to beeswax candles. The area's southern boundary is marked by **Leidsegracht**, a mostly residential canal, lined with chic town houses and a medley of handsome gables. This section of the Grachtengordel offers one notable attraction, the **Bijbels Museum** (Biblical Museum; Mon–Sat 10am–5pm, Sun 1–5pm; *f*5), which occupies a pair of splendid seventeenth-century stone mansions frilled with tendrils, carved fruit and scrollwork at Herengracht 366, near the corner with Leidsegracht. Built for one of Amsterdam's wealthy merchant families, the Cromhouts, the houses were designed by Philips Vingboons, arguably the most inventive of the architects who worked on the Grachtengordel during the city's expansion. The **interior** is comparatively plain, but the main hall does sport an extravagant painted ceiling portraying classical gods and goddesses – the work of Jacob de Wit – and at the back of the building is a fine, old Dutch kitchen. In these proud premises are exhibited the **bibles** gathered together over a lifetime by a nineteenth-century vicar, one Leendert Schouten. Amongst them is the first Dutch-language bible ever printed, dating from 1477, and several exquisite illuminated bibles from as early as the tenth century. There's also a scattering of archeological items from Palestine and Egypt and several models of the temples of Solomon and Herod. Attempts to reconstruct these Biblical temples were something of a cottage industry in Holland, with scores of Dutch antiquarians beavering away, bible in one hand and modelling equipment in the other, but Schouten himself went one step further and made his own version of the Tabernacle, on display here too.

The Golden Bend and Rembrandtplein

Strolling east from Leidsegracht, the elegant sweep of **Herengracht** unravels in the so-called **"Golden Bend"** (De Gouden Bocht), where the canal is overlooked by a long sequence of double-fronted mansions, some of the most opulent dwellings in the city. Most of the houses here date from the eighteenth century, with double stairways leading to the entrance, underneath which the small door was for the servants, and the lightly ornamented cornices that were fashionable at the time. Classical references are common too, both in form – pediments, columns and pilasters – and decoration, from scrolls and vases through to geometric patterns inspired by ancient Greece. One of the first buildings to look out for on the north side of the canal is **no. 475**, an extravagant edifice surmounted by a slender French-style balustrade and a coat of arms, whilst the owners of the comparable residence at **no. 493** opted to finish off their house with a grandly carved pediment. A couple of doors on at no. 497 a rather more modest mansion is home to the peculiar **Kattenkabinet** (Cats' Cabinet; Mon–Fri 10am–2pm, Sat & Sun 1–5pm; ƒ10), an enormous collection of art and artefacts relating to cats installed by a Dutch financier, whose own cherished moggy, John Pierpont Morgan, died in 1984; feline fanatics will be delighted. The house also contains a number of paintings by Jacob de Wit.

Across the canal, the facades of nos. **458–462** are soft and finely decorated affairs, typical of such double-fronted mansions, whereas those at nos. **504–508** are big and blowsy, their balustrades decorated by dolphins and an imperious Neptune (the two columned portal next door at no. **502** indicates the mayor's official residence). Finally, take a look at **no. 507**, just opposite: an imposing building, all neoclassical pilasters and slender windows, it was once the home of Jacob Boreel, the one-time major whose attempt to impose a burial tax prompted a riot during which the mob ransacked his house.

Strolling east, it's a few metres more to pedestrianized Thorbeckeplein, a scrawny adjunct to **Rembrandtplein**, itself a dishevelled bit of greenery that was formerly Amsterdam's butter market, renamed in 1876; today it claims to be one of the city's nightlife centres, though the crowded restaurants are firmly tourist-targeted. Rembrandt's pigeon-spattered statue stands in the middle, his back wisely turned against the square's worst excesses, which include live (but deadly) outdoor muzak. Of the prodigious number of cafés and bars here, only the bar of the **Schiller Hotel** at no. 26 stands out, with an original Art Deco interior reminiscent of an ocean liner. Tacky Reguliersbreestraat, leading off the northwest corner of Rembrandtplein, is notable only for the city's most extraordinary cinema, the **Tuschinski** (guided tours July & Aug daily 10.30am; ƒ10), at nos. 26–28, which also has a marvellously well-preserved Art Deco interior. Opened in 1921 by a Polish Jew, Abram Tuschinski, the cinema boasts Expressionist paintings, coloured marbles and a wonderful carpet, handwoven in Marrakesh to an original design.

Back on the Herengracht, near the Amstel, the **Museum Willet-Holthuysen** (Mon–Fri 10am–5pm, Sat & Sun 11am–5pm; ƒ7,50), at no. 605, is billed as "a peep behind the curtains into an historic Amsterdam canal house" which just about sums it up. The house itself dates from 1685, but the interior was remodelled by successive members of the coal-trading Holthuysen family until the last of the line, Sandra Willet-Holthuysen, gifted her home and its contents to the city in 1895. Renovated a number of years ago, most of the public rooms, notably the **Blue Room** and the **Dining Room**, have now been returned to their original eighteenth-century rococo appearance – a flashy and ornate style copied from France, which the Dutch merchants held to be the epitome of refinement and good taste. The chandeliers are gilded, heavy affairs, the plasterwork neat and fancy, and graceful drapes hang to either side of long and slender windows. The museum's collection of fine and applied arts belongs to Sandra's husband, Abraham Willet; its forte is glass, silver and ceramics, including a charming selection of Chinese porcelain exhibited in the Blue Room.

The Amstel to the Van Loon Museum

Herengracht comes to an abrupt halt beside the wide and windy **River Amstel**, which was long the main route into the interior, with goods arriving downstream to be traded for the imported materials held in Amsterdam's many warehouses. Turning left here takes you to the Blauwbrug ("Blue Bridge") and the Old Jewish Quarter (see p.94), whilst in the opposite direction the **Magere Brug** ("Skinny Bridge") is arguably the cutest of the city's many swing bridges. From here, it's a few metres further south along the Amstel to the **Amstelsluizen**, the Amstel Locks. Every night, the municipal water department closes these locks to begin the process of sluicing out the canals. A huge pumping station on an island out to the east of the city then starts to pump fresh water from the IJsselmeer (see p.149) into the canal system; similar locks on the west side of the city are left open for the surplus to flow into the IJ and, from there, out to sea via the North Sea Canal. The watery contents of the canals is thus refreshed every three nights – though, what with three centuries of algae, prams, shopping trolleys and a few hundred rusty bikes, the water is appealing just as long as you're not in it.

Doubling back along the Amstel, turn down **Keizersgracht** and you'll soon reach **Reguliersgracht** at a point where its humpback bridges are overlooked by several fine facades: nos. 37 and 39 have the classic neck gables popular with the merchants of the day, as do the slightly more ornate nos. 17–21. Numbers 11 and 13 are different again, these two buildings possessed of the plain spout gables, external pulleys and shuttered windows used in the construction of the city's seventeenth-century warehouses. From the junction, it's just a few metres more to the **Van Loon Museum** at no. 672 (Fri–Mon 11am–5pm; ƒ7,50), which has perhaps the finest accessible canal house interior in Amsterdam. Built in 1672, the first tenant of the property was the artist Ferdinand Bol, who seems to have been one of the few occupants to have avoided some sort of scandal. The Van Loons, who bought the house in 1884 and stayed until 1945, are a case in point. The last member of the family to live here was Willem van Loon, a banker whose wife, Thora van Loon-Egidius, was *dame du paleis* to Queen Wilhelmina. Of German extraction, Thora was proud of her roots and allegedly entertained high-ranking Nazi officials here during the occupation – a charge of collaboration that led to the Van Loons being shunned by polite society. Recently renovated, the **interior** of the house has been returned to its eighteenth-century appearance, a bright and breezy rococo style of stucco, colourful wallpaper and rich wood panelling. The top-floor landing has several pleasant Grisaille **paintings** sporting Roman figures and one of the bedrooms – the "painted room" – is decorated with a Romantic painting of Italy, depicting the overgrown classical ruins and diligent peasants that were a favourite theme in Amsterdam from around 1750 to 1820. The oddest items are the fake bedroom doors: the eighteenth-century owners were so keen to avoid any lack of symmetry that they camouflaged the real bedroom doors and created imitation, decorative doors in the "correct" position instead.

Vijzelstraat and the Heineken Brewery

A short walk west along Keizersgracht from the Van Loon Museum brings you to **Vijzelstraat**. From here, continue west along Keizersgracht for Leidsestraat and Leidseplein (see below) or turn down Vijzelstraat for the ten-minute walk south to the **Heineken Brouwerij** (Heineken Brewery; tours Mon–Fri 9.30am & 11am; June–Sept also at 1pm & 2.30pm; July & Aug also Sat noon & 2pm; over-18s only; ƒ2). One of the city's best-known attractions, looming on the far side of the

Singelgracht canal, this was Heineken's headquarters from 1864 to 1988, when the company was restructured and brewing was moved to a more efficient location out of town. Since then, Heineken has developed the site as a tourist attraction with displays on the history of beer-making in general and Heineken in particular. The old brewing facilities are included on the tour, but the main draw is the snacks and **free beer**; as you'd imagine, the atmosphere is highly convivial when there are 200 people downing as much beer as they can reasonably stomach. Note that tours are often sold out so try and get tickets in advance.

To get to Leidseplein (see below) from the brewery you can either take the more pleasant route, by doubling back along Vijzelgracht and heading west along Prinsengracht, or the direct route, by hauling along busy and unappealing Weteringschans.

Leidseplein and around

Leidseplein is the bustling hub of Amsterdam's nightlife, a rather cluttered and disorderly open space that has never had much character. The square once marked the end of the road in from Leiden and, as horse-drawn traffic was banned from the centre long ago, it was here that the Dutch left their horses and carts – a sort of equine car park. Today, it's quite the opposite: continual traffic made up of trams, bikes, cars and pedestrians gives the place a frenetic feel. This is supplemented by the dozens of bars, restaurants and clubs on the square and surrounding sidestreets – a bright jumble of jutting signs and neon lights – which include the famous Melkweg venue, housed in a converted dairy, and the Boom Chicago café-theatre. Given the proximity of these places to one another, it's not surprising that on a good night Leidseplein can be Amsterdam at its carefree, exuberant best.

Leidseplein also contains two buildings of some architectural note. The first is the grandiose **Stadsschouwburg**, a neo-Renaissance edifice dating from 1894 which was so widely criticized for its clumsy vulgarity that the city council of the day withheld the money for decorating the exterior. Home to the National Ballet and Opera until the Muziektheater (see p.96) was completed on Waterlooplein in 1986 it is now used for theatre, dance and music performances. However, its most popular function is as the place where the Ajax football team (see p.24) gather on the balcony to wave to the crowds whenever they win anything – as they often do.

Close by, just beside the square at Leidsekade 97, is the four-star **American Hotel**. One of the city's oddest buildings, it's a monumental and slightly disconcerting rendering of Art Nouveau, with angular turrets, chunky dormer windows and fancy brickwork. Completed in 1902, the present structure takes its name from its demolished predecessor, which was – as the stylistic peccadillo of its architect, W. Steinigeweg – decorated with statues and murals of North American scenes. Inside the present hotel is the *Café Americain*, once the fashionable haunt of Amsterdam's literati, but now more a mainstream location for high tea. The Art Nouveau decor is well worth a look – an array of stained glass, shallow brick arches and heavy-duty chandeliers.

Leidseplein is something of a crossroads. From here, it's a short walk west across the Singelgracht to Amsterdam's main park, the Vondelpark (see p.107), or you can head south to the Rijksmuseum (see p.101). Alternatively, **Leidsestraat**, one of Amsterdam's principal shopping streets, leads northeast, but it's a long gauntlet of fashion and shoe shops of little distinction and you're better off going one block east to Nieuwe Spiegelstraat, an appealing mixture of bookshops and corner cafés that extends south into Spiegelgracht to form the **Spiegelkwartier**. The district is home to the pricey end of Amsterdam's antiques trade and **De Appel**, a lively centre for contemporary art at Nieuwe Spiegelstraat 10 (Tues–Sun noon–5pm; ƒ2,50).

The Jordaan

Lying to the west of the city centre, bordered by Prinsengracht on one side and Lijnbaansgracht on the other, the **Jordaan** is a likeable and easily explored area of slender canals, narrow streets and simple but architecturally varied houses. In all probability the **Jordaan** takes its name from the French word *jardin* ("garden"), since the area's earliest settlers were French Protestant Huguenots, who fled here to escape persecution in the sixteenth and seventeenth centuries. Traditionally the home of Amsterdam's working class, it has recently experienced a transformation into one of the city's most attractive and sought-after residential neighbourhoods. However, well into the twentieth century the Jordaan's inhabitants were primarily stevedores and factory workers, earning a crust amongst the docks, warehouses and boatyards that extended north beyond Brouwersgracht, the Jordaan's northern boundary. Specific sights hereabouts are few and far between – the best you'll do is the contemporary arts of the Jordaan's **Stedelijk Museum Buro** – but it's still a delightful area to wander, its cobweb of narrow streets following the lines of the original polder drainage ditches rather than any municipal outline. This gives the district its distinctive, mazy layout – and much of its present appeal.

Leidsegracht to Rozengracht

The southern boundary of the Jordaan is generally held to be the **Leidsegracht**, though it's open to debate; according to dyed-in-the-wool locals the true Jordaaner is born within earshot of the Westerkerk bells – and you'd be hard pushed to hear the chimes this far south. The narrow streets and canals just to the north of the Leidsegracht are mostly modern affairs, but **Looiersgracht** (pronounced "lawyers-gracht") retains a cluster of tumbledown cottages and, at no. 38, the indoor **Rommelmarket** (daily except Fri 11am–5pm), a vast, permanent flea market and jumble sale. Slightly further up, at Elandsgracht 109, is the rather more sophisticated **De Looier antiques market** (daily except Fri 11am–5pm, Thurs till 9pm), which is good for picking up Dutch bygones such as tiles and ceramics, with a few stalls dealing in particular items or styles such as silver trinkets or delftware.

The streets heading north from Elandsgracht are unremarkable, and easily the most agreeable route is along **Lijnbaansgracht** (literally "Ropewalk Canal"). This slender canal threads its way round most of the city centre and here – in between Looiersgracht and Rozenstraat – it's quiet, cobbled and leafy, the sleepy waters flanked by old brick buildings. On Rozenstraat itself, at no. 59, is an annexe of the Stedelijk Museum (see p.106), the **Stedelijk Museum Buro Amsterdam** (Tues–Sun 11am–5pm; free), which provides space for up-and-coming Amsterdam artists, with exhibitions, installations and occasional lectures and readings.

One block further north, **Rozengracht** lost its canal years ago and is now a busy main road of no particular merit. Rembrandt spent the last ten years of his life here at no. 184, but his old home is long gone too, and today only a plaque marks the spot. Rembrandt's last years were scarred by the death of his wife Hendrickje in 1663 and his son Titus five years later.

Rozengracht to Westerstraat

The streets and canals extending north from Rozengracht form the heart of the Jordaan. Beyond Rozengracht, the first canal is the **Bloemgracht** ("Flower Canal"), a small and leafy waterway lined with houseboats. With its maze of cross-streets, the Bloemgracht, along with **Egelantiersgracht** ("Rose-Hip Canal") immediately to the north, exemplifies the new-found fashionableness of the Jordaan. Tiny streets filled with cafés, bars and odd little shops generate a warm, relaxed community atmosphere and murals have been painted onto blank walls with care. There are several attractive old houses on Bloemgracht too, especially nos. 87–91 with their dinky step gables and distinctive facade stones, depicting a *steeman* ("city-dweller"), *landman* ("farmer") and *seeman* ("sailor") living side by side.

A couple of streets up, tucked away down an alley on Egelantiersgracht between nos. 107 and 114, is one of the Jordaan's hidden hofjes – the **St Andrieshofje**, a small, quiet courtyard surrounded by antique houses, its entranceway lined with delft tiles. Not far away, at no. 12, **Café 't Smalle** is one of Amsterdam's oldest cafés, opened in 1786 as a *proeflokaal*, a tasting house for the adjacent gin distillery. In the eighteenth century, when there were no quality controls, each batch of *jenever* (Dutch gin) could turn out differently, so customers were loth to part with their money until they had tasted the gin. As a result, each distillery ran a *proeflokaal* offering free samples. The *'t Smalle*'s waterside terrace is one of the most pleasant spots in the city to take a tipple – though nowadays it's not for free. It only takes a couple of minutes to walk from Egelantiersgracht to **2e Tuindwarsstraat** and its continuation **2e Anjeliersdwarsstraat**, which together hold many of the Jordaan's trendier stores and clothing shops as well as some of its liveliest bars and cafés.

At the end of 2e Anjeliersdwarsstraat is workaday **Westerstraat**, one of the district's main thoroughfares. The street has little going for it except for the small but fascinating **Pianola Museum** (Sun 1–5pm; *f*7,50) at no. 106, whose collection of pianolas and automatic music-machines date from the beginning of the twentieth century. Fifteen have been restored to working order. These machines, which work on rolls of perforated paper, were the jukeboxes of their day, and the museum has a vast collection of 14,000 rolls of music, some of which were "recorded" by famous pianists and composers – Gershwin, Debussy, Scott Joplin, Art Tatum and others. The museum runs a regular programme of pianola music concerts, where the rolls are played back on restored machines.

The Noorderkerk and around

At the east end of Westerstraat, by Prinsengracht, is Hendrik de Keyser's **Noorderkerk** (March–Nov Sat 11am–1pm; free). This church, finished in 1623, was the architect's last creation, and probably his least successful. A bulky, over-bearing building of brown and grey, it represented a radical departure from the conventional church designs of the time, having a symmetrical Greek cross floor plan, with four equally proportioned arms radiating out from a steepled centre. Uncompromisingly dour, it proclaimed the serious intent of the Calvinists who worshipped here, but this is the kindest thing to be said about it – and it's hard to understand quite how Keyser, who designed such elegant structures as the Westerkerk (see p.87), could have ended up building this.

The **Noordermarkt**, the forlorn square outside the church, holds a **statue** of three figures clinging to each other, a poignant tribute to the bloody Jordaanoproer riot of 1934, part of a successful campaign to stop the government cutting unemployment benefit during the Depression. The inscription reads "The strongest chains are those of unity". The square also hosts two of Amsterdam's best open-air markets: an antiques and general household goods market on Monday mornings (9am–1pm), and the popular Saturday farmers' market, the **Boerenmarkt** (9am–3pm), a lively affair selling organic fruit and vegetables, as well as freshly baked breads and a plethora of oils and spices. Cross an unmarked border though and you'll find yourself in the middle of the bird market, which operates on an adjacent patch at much the same time, and, if you're at all squeamish, is best avoided – brightly coloured birds squeezed into tiny cages are not for everyone.

The Old Jewish Quarter and the East

Originally one of the marshiest parts of Amsterdam, prone to regular flooding, the narrow slice of land sandwiched between the curve of the Amstel, Kloveniersburgwal and the Nieuwe Herengracht was the home of Amsterdam's Jews from the sixteenth century up until World War II. By the 1920s, this **Old Jewish Quarter**, focusing on Waterlooplein and Jodenbreestraat and often called the Jodenhoek ("Jews' Corner"), was crowded with tenement buildings and smoking factories, but in 1945 it lay derelict – and neither has post-war redevelopment treated it kindly. Picking your way round the numerous modern-day obstacles isn't much fun, but persevere – amongst all the cars and concrete are several moving reminders of the Jewish community that perished in the war. Beyond lies the eastern section of Amsterdam's centre, made up of the **Plantagebuurt** and the **Eastern Islands**. The backbone of Plantagebuurt is Plantage Middenlaan, a wide boulevard stretching east from the Old Jewish Quarter and constructed in the mid-nineteenth century as part of the creation of a smart, leafy suburb – one of Amsterdam's first. The artificial Eastern Islands, dredged out of the River IJ to accommodate warehouses and docks, once formed part of a vast maritime complex that spread right along the River IJ. Industrial decline set in during the 1880s, but the area is currently being redefined as a residential district.

St Antoniesbreestraat, Jodenbreestraat and the Rembrandt House

Stretching southwest from Nieuwmarkt, **St Antoniesbreestraat** once linked the city centre with the Jewish quarter, but its huddle of shops and houses was mostly demolished in the 1980s to make way for a main road. The plan was subsequently abandoned, but the modern buildings that now line most of the street hardly fire the soul. Two structures that lighten the architectural gloom however are the **Pintohuis** at no. 69, easily spotted by its creamy Italianate facade, and the **Zuiderkerk** (centre: Mon–Wed & Fri 9.30am–5pm, Thurs noon–8pm, free; tower: June–Sept only Wed–Sat 2–4pm; *f*3), accessible through an old archway on the right hand side. The latter dates from 1611 and was the first church built in the city specifically for the Protestants. It was designed by Amsterdam's flashy architect and sculptor, Hendrik de Keyser (1565–1621), whose distinctive – and very

THE JEWS IN AMSTERDAM

From the late sixteenth century onwards, Amsterdam was the refuge of **Jews** escaping persecution throughout the rest of Europe. The **Union of Utrecht**, ratified in 1579, signalled the start of the influx. Drawn up by the largely Protestant northern Dutch provinces in response to the invading Spanish army, the treaty combined the United Provinces (later to become the Netherlands) in a loose federation, whose wheels could only be greased by a degree of religious toleration then unknown elsewhere across the continent. Whatever the Protestants may have wanted, they knew that the Catholic minority (around 35 percent) would only continue to support the rebellion against the Spanish Habsburgs if they were treated well – the Jews benefited by osmosis and consequently immigrated here in their hundreds.

The toleration, however, did have its limits: Jewish immigrants were forced to buy citizenship; Christian-Jewish marriages were illegal; and, as with the Catholics, they were only allowed to practise their religion discreetly behind closed doors. A proclamation in 1632 also excluded from them from most guilds – effectively withdrawing their right to own and run businesses. This forced them either to excel in those trades not governed by the guilds or introduce new non-guild ones into the city, the result being that by the middle of the eighteenth century the city's Jewish community was active in almost every aspect of the economy, with particular strongholds in bookselling, tobacco, banking and commodity futures.

The first major Jewish influx was of **Sephardic** Jews from Spain and Portugal, where persecution had begun in earnest in 1492 and continued throughout the sixteenth century. In the 1630s, the Sephardim were joined in Amsterdam by hundreds of (much poorer) **Ashkenazi** Jews from German-speaking central Europe. The two groups established separate synagogues and, although there was no ghetto as such, the vast majority settled on and around what is now Waterlooplein, then a distinctly unhealthy tract of marshland subject to regular flooding by the River Amstel. Initially known as **Vlooyenburg**, this district was usually referred to as the **Jodenhoek** (pronounced "yo-den-hook"), or "Jews' Corner", though this was not, generally speaking, a pejorative term – Rembrandt, for instance, was quite happy to live here and frequently painted his Jewish neighbours. Indeed, given the time, the most extraordinary feature of Jewish settlement in Amsterdam was that it occasioned mild curiosity rather than outright hate, as evinced by contemporary prints of Jewish religious customs, where there is neither any hint of stereotype nor discernible demonisation.

The restrictions affecting both Jews and Catholics were removed during Napoleon's occupation of the United Provinces, when the country was temporarily renamed the Batavian Republic (1795-1806). Freed from official discrimination, Amsterdam's Jewish community flourished and the Jewish Quarter expanded, nudging northwest towards Nieuwmarkt and east across Nieuwe Herengracht, though this was just the focus of a community whose members lived in every part of the city. In 1882, the dilapidated houses of the Vlooyenburg were razed and several minor canals filled in to make way for **Waterlooplein**, which became a largely Jewish marketplace, a bustling affair that sprawled out along St Antoniesbreestraat and Jodenbreestraat. At the turn of the twentieth century, there were around 60,000 Jews living in Amsterdam, but refugees from Hitler's Germany swelled this figure to around 120,000 in the 1930s. The disaster that befell this community during the German occupation in World War II is hard to conceive, but the bald facts speak for themselves: when Amsterdam was liberated, there were only 5000 Jews left and the Jodenhoek was, to all intents and purposes, a ghost town. At present, there are about 25,000 Jews resident in the city, but while Jewish life in Amsterdam has survived, its heyday is gone forever.

popular – style extrapolated elements of traditional Flemish design, with fanciful detail and frilly towers added wherever possible. The basic design of the Zuiderkerk is firmly Gothic, but the soaring tower, which you can climb up during the summer, is typical of his work, complete with balconies and balustrades, arches and columns. Now deconsecrated, the church has been turned into a municipal information centre with displays on housing and the environment, plus temporary exhibitions revealing the city council's plans for future development.

St Antoniesbreestraat runs into **Jodenbreestraat**, the "Broad Street of the Jews", at one time the Jodenhoek's principal market and centre of Jewish activity. Badly served by post-war development, this ancient thoroughfare is now short on charm, with the exception of the modern symmetries – and cubist, coloured panels – of the apartment blocks that spill along part of the street. In these unlikely surroundings stands **Het Rembrandthuis**, at no. 6 (Rembrandt House; Mon–Sat 10am–5pm, Sun 1–5pm; *f*7,50, more during exhibitions), its slender facade decorated by pretty wooden shutters and a tiny pediment. Rembrandt bought this house at the height of his fame and popularity, living here for over twenty years and spending a fortune on furnishings – an expense that ultimately contributed to his bankruptcy. An inventory made at the time details a huge collection of paintings, sculptures and art treasures he'd amassed, almost all of which was confiscated after he was declared insolvent and forced to move to a more modest house on Rozengracht in the Jordaan in 1658. The city bought the artist's Jodenbreestraat house in 1907 and then had it renovated. It now holds an extensive collection of Rembrandt's **etchings** as well as several of the original copper plates on which he worked. The biblical illustrations attract the most attention, though the studies of tramps and vagabonds are equally appealing. An accompanying exhibit explains Rembrandt's engraving techniques and there are temporary exhibitions focusing on various aspects of Rembrandt's life and times.

Next door, the multimedia **Holland Experience** (daily 10am–6pm; *f*17,50, under-16s *f*15) is a kind of sensory-bombardment movie about Holland and Amsterdam, with synchronized smells, a moving floor and a simulation of a violent thunder storm. From here, it's a couple of minutes' walk to **Gassan Diamonds** (daily 9am–5pm; free), which occupies a large and imposing brick building dating from 1897 on Nieuwe Uilenburgerstraat. Before World War II, many local Jews worked as diamond cutters and polishers, though there's little sign of the industry here today, this factory being an exception.

Waterlooplein

Jodenbreestraat runs parallel to the **Stadhuis en Muziektheater** (Town Hall and Concert Hall), a sprawling complex whose indeterminate modernity dominates **Waterlooplein**, a rectangular parcel of land that was originally swampy marsh. This was the site of the first Jewish Quarter, but by the late nineteenth century it had become an insanitary slum, home to the poorest of the Ashkenazi Jews. The slums were cleared in the 1880s and thereafter the open spaces of the Waterlooplein hosted the largest and liveliest marketplace in the city, the place where Jews and Gentiles met to trade. In the war, the Germans used the square to round up their victims, but despite these ugly connotations the Waterlooplein was revived in the 1950s as the site of the city's main **flea market**. Unfortunately though it was only a stopgap as far as the city council was concerned; a depopulated Jodenhoek was, they felt, ideal for redevelopment. For starters whole streets were demolished to make way for the motorist – with Mr Visserplein, for example, becoming little more than a traffic intersection (see below) – and then, warming to their theme in the late 1970s, the council announced the building of a massive new concert-and-city-hall complex on Waterlooplein. Opposition was immediate and widespread, but attempts to prevent the building failed, and the Muziektheater opened in 1986, since when it has established a reputation for artistic excellence. One of the story's abiding ironies is that the title of the protest campaign – "**Stopera**" – has passed into common usage to describe the complex.

Mr Visserplein and the Portuguese Synagogue

Just behind the Muziektheater is **Mr Visserplein**, a busy junction for traffic speeding towards the IJ tunnel. It takes its name from Mr Visser, President of the Supreme Court of the Netherlands in 1939. He was dismissed the following year when the Germans occupied the country, and became an active member of the Jewish resistance, working for the illegal underground newspaper *Het Parool* ("The Password") and refusing to wear the yellow Star of David. He died in 1942, a few days after publicly – and famously – denouncing all forms of collaboration.

Unmissable on the corner of Mr Visserplein is the brown and bulky brickwork of the **Esnoga** or **Portugees synagoge** (Portuguese Synagogue; April–Oct Mon–Fri & Sun 10am–4pm; Nov–March Mon–Thurs 10am–4pm, Fri 10am–3pm, Sun 10am–noon; closed Yom Kippur; *f*7,50), completed in 1675 for the city's Sephardic Jews. One of Amsterdam's most imposing buildings, the central structure, with its grand pilasters and blind balustrade, was built in the broadly neoclassical style that was then fashionable in Holland. It is surrounded by a courtyard complex of small outhouses, where the city's Sephardim have fraternized for centuries. Barely altered since its construction, the synagogue's lofty interior follows the Sephardic tradition in having the Hechal (the Ark of the Covenant) and *tebah* (from where services are led) at opposite ends. Also traditional is the seating, with two sets of wooden benches (for the men) facing each other across the central aisle – the women have separate galleries up above. A set of superb brass chandeliers holds the candles that remain the only source of artificial light. When it was completed, the synagogue was one of the largest in the world, its congregation almost certainly the richest; today, the Sephardic community has dwindled to just sixty members, most of whom live outside the city centre. In one of the outhouses, a video sheds light on the history of the synagogue and Amsterdam's Sephardim; the mystery is why the Germans left it alone, and no one knows for sure, but it seems likely that they intended to turn it into a museum once all the Jews had been eradicated.

Jonas Daniel Meijerplein and the Jewish Historical Museum

Next to the synagogue, on the south side of its retaining wall, is **Jonas Daniel Meijerplein**, a scrawny triangle of lawn named after the eponymous lawyer, who in 1796, at the remarkable age of sixteen, was the first Jew to be admitted to the Amsterdam Bar. It was here in February 1941 that around 400 Jewish men were forcibly loaded up on trucks and taken to their deaths at Mauthausen concentration camp, in reprisal for the killing of a Dutch Nazi during a street fight. The arrests sparked off the **February Strike** (Februaristaking), a general strike in protest against the Germans' treatment of the Jews. It was organized by the outlawed Communist Party and spearheaded by Amsterdam's transport workers and dockers – a rare demonstration of solidarity with the Jews in occupied Europe and the Netherlands, where the majority of people had done little to protest against the actions of the SS. The strike was quickly suppressed, but is still commemorated by an annual wreath-laying ceremony on February 25, as well as by Mari Andriessen's statue of the **Dokwerker** ("dockworker") here on the square.

Across the square, on the far side of the main road, the **Joods Historisch Museum** (Jewish Historical Museum; daily 11am–5pm; closed Yom Kippur; *f*8) is cleverly housed in four Ashkenazi synagogues dating from the late seventeenth century. For years after the war these buildings lay abandoned, but they were finally refurbished – and connected by walkways – in the 1980s to accommodate a wide-ranging collection that covers most aspects of Dutch Jewish life and beliefs. The Nieuwe Synagoge of 1752 is the starting point of the self-guided tour and displays memorabilia from the long history of the Jews in the Netherlands as well as a poignant section on the war, complete with several especially moving photographs. In addition, there's a display of the powerful autobiographical paintings of Charlotte Salomon, who was killed in the Auschwitz concentration camp at the age of 26. Further on, the ground floor of the capacious Grote Synagoge of 1671 focuses on religious practice and beliefs, while the upper level holds a finely judged social history of the city's Jews, tracing their prominent role in a wide variety of industries, both as employers and employees.

Plantage Middenlaan and the Dutch Resistance Museum

From Mr Visserplein, it's a short walk east along Muiderstraat to the lush **Hortus Botanicus** (April–Sept Mon–Fri 9am–5pm, Sat & Sun 11am–5pm; Oct–March Mon–Fri 9am–4pm, Sat & Sun 11am–4pm; *f*7,50), a pocket-sized botanical garden at the corner of Plantage Middenlaan and Plantage Parklaan. Founded in 1682, the gardens contain six thousand plant species (including various carnivorous varieties) on display both outside and in a series of hothouses, including a Three-Climates Glasshouse, where the plants are arranged according to their geographical origins. The garden makes a relaxing break on any tour of central Amsterdam and you can stop off for coffee and cakes in the orangery. Across the street, in the small **Wertheimpark** beside the Nieuwe Herengracht canal, is the **Auschwitz monument**, designed by the Dutch writer Jan Wolkers. It's a simple affair with symbolically broken mirrors and a cracked urn containing the ashes of some of the Jews who died in Buchenwald. The inscription reads *Nooit meer Auschwitz* ("Auschwitz – Never Again").

Continue down the right-hand side of Plantage Middenlaan to reach another sad relic of the war at no. 24, **De Hollandsche Schouwburg** (daily 11am–4pm except Yom Kippur; free), a predominantly Jewish theatre that became the main assembly point for Dutch Jews prior to their deportation. Inside, there was no daylight and families were interned in conditions that foreshadowed those of the camps they would soon be taken to. The building has recently been refurbished to house a small exhibition on the plight of Amsterdam's Jews, but the old auditorium out at the back has been left as an empty, roofless shell. A memorial column of basalt on a Star of David base stands where the stage once was, an intensely mournful monument to suffering of unfathomable proportions.

From De Hollandsche Schouwburg, it's a brief walk northeast along Plantage Kerklaan to the excellent **Verzetsmuseum**, at no.61 (Dutch Resistance Museum; Tues–Fri 10am–5pm, Sat & Sun noon–5pm; *f*8). The museum outlines the development of the Dutch Resistance from the German invasion of the Netherlands in May 1940 to the country's liberation in 1945. Thoughtfully presented, the main gangway examines the experience of the majority of the population, dealing honestly with the fine balance between co-operation and collaboration. Side rooms are devoted to aspects of the movement, from the brave determination of the Communist Party, who went underground as soon as the Germans arrived, to more ad hoc responses like the so-called Milk Strike of 1943, when hundreds of milk producers refused to deliver. In English and Dutch, the text to all the exhibits is illustrated by fascinating old photographs and a host of original arte-facts, from examples of illegal newsletters to signed German death warrants. Apart from their treatment of the Jews, which is also detailed here, perhaps the most chilling feature of the occupation was the use of indiscriminate reprisals to terrify the population. For the most part it worked, though there were always a minority courageous enough to resist. The museum has dozens of little metal sheets providing biographical sketches of the members of the Resistance – and it's this mixture of the general and the personal that is its real strength.

From the museum, there's a choice of routes: you can continue northeast along Plantage Kerklaan to the Eastern Islands (see below) or return to Plantage Middenlaan, at the east end of which is the Muiderpoort gateway and the Tropenmuseum (the Tropical Museum; see p.100).

The Eastern Islands

At the northern end of Plantage Kerklaan, just beyond the Dutch Resistance Museum, a footpath and bridge lead over to the **Eastern Islands**, the first of which – **Entrepotdok** – is, conveniently enough, the most interesting. On the far side of the bridge old brick warehouses stretch right along the quayside, distin-guished by their spout gables, multiple doorways and overhead pulleys. Built by the **Dutch East India Company** in the eighteenth century, they were once part of the largest warehouse complex in continental Europe, a gigantic customs-free zone established for goods in transit. On the ground floor, above the main entrance, each warehouse sports the name of a town or island; goods for onward transportation were stored in the appropriate warehouse until there were enough to fill a boat or barge. The warehouses have been tastefully converted into offices and apartments, a fate that must surely befall the central East India Company **compound**, whose grand neoclassical entrance is at the west end of Entrepotdok on Kadijksplein. Founded in 1602, the Dutch East India Company was the chief pillar of Amsterdam's wealth for nearly two hundred years. Its high-percentage profits came from importing spices into Europe and to secure them the compa-ny's ships ventured far and wide, establishing trading links with India, Ceylon (modern-day Sri Lanka), Indo-China, Malaya, China and Japan, though modern-day Indonesia was always the main event. In the 1750s, the Dutch East India Company went into decline, partly because the British expelled them from most of the best trading stations, but mainly because the company over-borrowed. The Dutch government took it over in 1795.

From Kadijksplein, it's a couple of minutes' walk to the **Nederlands Scheepvaartmuseum** (Dutch Maritime Museum; Tues–Sun 10am–5pm; mid-July to mid-Sept also Mon 10am–5pm; *f*14,50), which occupies the old arse-nal of the Dutch navy, a vast sandstone structure built on the edge of the Oosterdok on Kattenburgerplein, with four symmetrical, and dour, facades sur-rounding a central, cobbled courtyard. It's the perfect location for a Maritime Museum – or at least it would be if the museum's collection, spread over three floors, was larger – in the event it seems a little forlorn, rattling around a build-ing that's just too big.

The ground floor displays a flashy gilded barge built for King William I in 1818 and is used to host temporary exhibitions. The next floor up, devoted to shipping in the seventeenth and eighteenth centuries, is the most diverting. It includes garish ships' figureheads, examples of early atlases and navigational equipment, and finely detailed models of the clippers of the East India Company, then the fastest ships in the world. There are oodles of nautical paintings too, some devoted to the achievements of Dutch trading ships, others showing heavy seas and shipwrecks and yet more celebrating the successes of the Dutch Navy. **Willem van de Velde II** (1633–1707) was the most successful of the Dutch marine painters of the period and there's a good sample of his work here – canvases that emphasize the strength and power of the Dutch warship, often depicted in battle. The final floor is devoted to the nineteenth and twentieth centuries and, compared with the one below, fails to excite, though the minutely precise ships' models are of some passing interest. Outside, moored at the museum jetty, is a full-scale replica of an East Indiaman, the *Amsterdam*. It's crewed by actors, and plenty more will be needed when the 78-metre *Stad Amsterdam* clipper is completed in the next couple of years.

Strolling west along the waterfront from the Maritime Museum along Prins Hendrikkade, the foreground is dominated by a massive elevated hood that rears up above the entrance to the IJ tunnel. This hood is occupied by the large and lavish **newMetropolis Science and Technology Centre** (Tues–Sun 10am–6pm; *f*24) – follow the signs for the ground-floor entrance and on your way, along the quayside, you'll pass a long line of retired canal boats, low, wide and powerful-looking. Billing itself as the "centre for human creativity" the newMetropolis is geared towards kids, and has five interrelated exhibition areas – Technology, Energy, The Lab, Humanity and Science – spread over six floors. The focus is very much on interactive displays, the idea being to make learning fun, with exhibits along the lines of huge soap bubbles you have to get into and boats and planes you can set in motion using a light beam. In addition there's a Glass Hall for temporary exhibitions, a cinema, a theatre and a Children's World. The centre is very popular with school groups.

The Tropenmuseum and around

Overlooking the canal at the far end of Plantage Middenlaan, the **Muiderpoort** (pronounced "mao-der-port"), Amsterdam's old east gate, dates from medieval times, though the present structure was built in the 1770s, a pompous neoclassical structure complete with a flashy cupola and grandiosely carved pediment. Napoleon staged a triumphal entry into the city through the Muiderpoort in 1811, but his imperial pleasure was tempered by his half-starved troops, who could barely be restrained from helping themselves in a city of (what was to them) amazing luxury.

Beyond the gate, across the Singelgracht canal on Mauritskade, rises the gabled and turreted **Royal Tropen Instituut** – formerly the Royal Colonial Institute – a sprawling complex which contains the **Tropenmuseum** (Museum of the Tropics: Mon–Fri 10am–5pm, Sat & Sun noon–5pm; *f*12,50), whose entrance is round the side at Linnaeusstraat 2. With its cavernous central hall and three floors of gallery space, the museum has room to focus on all the world's tropical and sub-tropical zones and impresses with its applied art. Amongst many artefacts, there are Javanese stone friezes, fancy carved wooden boats from the Pacific, a whole room of masks and, perhaps strangest of all, ritual totem poles cut from giant New Guinea mangroves. The collection is imaginatively presented through a variety of media – slides, videos and sound recordings – and there are creative and engaging displays devoted to such subjects as music-making and puppetry, as well as traditional storytelling. There are also reconstructions, down to sounds and smells, of typical streets in India, China or Africa, plus candid expositions on the problems besetting the developing world, both urban – the ever-expanding slum dwellings of cities like Bombay – and rural, examining such issues as the destruction of the world's tropical rainforests. The permanent collection is enhanced by an ambitious programme of temporary exhibitions.

Part of the Tropenmuseum is geared up for children under the age of twelve. This section, the **Kindermuseum** (Children's Museum), takes a hands-on approach to the same themes as the main museum but operates restricted opening hours; call ☎568 8233 for details.

The Museum Quarter and Vondelpark

Amsterdam's three main museums lie on the edge of **Museumplein**, the city's largest open space, whose wide lawns, extending south from the Singelgracht to Van Baerlestraat, are used for a variety of outdoor activities, from visiting circuses to political demonstrations. The largest of the museums is the **Rijksmuseum**, which occupies a huge late nineteenth-century edifice built in an inventive historic style by Petrus Josephus Hubertus Cuypers, also the creator of Centraal Station (see p.74), in the early 1880s. The museum possesses one of the most comprehensive collections of seventeenth-century **Dutch paintings** in the world, with twenty or so of Rembrandt's works, plus a healthy sample of canvases by Steen, Hals, Vermeer and their leading contemporaries. There are also representative displays of every other pre-twentieth-century period of Dutch and Flemish painting, along with an outstanding medieval Sculpture and Decorative Arts section. Close by, the **Van Gogh Museum** boasts the finest assortment of Van Gogh paintings in the world, whilst the **Stedelijk Museum** focuses on modern and contemporary art. Together the three museums comprise one of Amsterdam's biggest pulls.

A few minutes' walk to the northwest of Museumplein lies the sprawling greenery of the **Vondelpark**, Amsterdam's loveliest park, while its south side is overlooked by the **Concertgebouw**, the city's most prestigious classical music concert hall.

The Rijksmuseum
The **Rijksmuseum** (daily 10am–5pm; ƒ15) is labyrinthine, so although the sections are clearly labelled be sure to pick up a free **floor plan** at the entrance. The other problem is that the collection's organization leaves something to be desired: works by the same artist can be distributed in several different rooms, which is frustrating, though more helpfully, the **labelling** is in both Dutch and English. The collection is too large to absorb in one visit, so if time is limited it's best to be content with the core paintings supplemented by a few selective forays into other sections. All the major works are described in detail in the *Treasures of the Rijksmuseum* (ƒ35), on sale at the museum shop, while the much more affordable – and very useful – *A Walk featuring highlights of the Dutch Golden Age*, a pamphlet costing just ƒ1, is sold at the first-floor information desks. It is worth bearing in mind that, since the museum's paintings are on a rotation system, some of the works mentioned in the account below may not always be on display.

FIFTEENTH AND SIXTEENTH CENTURY

Beginning beside the top-floor shop, the Rijksmuseum's collection of early Flemish – or more properly Netherlandish – paintings runs chronologically through the eastern wing. First off are the highly stylized works of the pre-Renaissance painters, traditionally known as the "**Flemish Primitives**", whose preoccupations were exclusively religious. Depicting biblical figures or saints, these paintings are devotional snapshots, dotted with symbols that provided a readily-understood lexicon for the medieval onlooker. Thus, in the *Madonna Surrounded by Female Saints*, painted by an unknown artist referred to thereafter as the **Master of the Virgin Among Virgins**, each of the saints wears a necklace that contains her particular symbol – St Barbara the tower of her imprisonment and so on. However, the most striking paintings in this section are by **Geertgen tot Sint Jans**. His *Holy Kindred*, painted around 1485 and displayed in Room 201, is a skilfully structured portrait of the family of Anna, Mary's mother, in which the Romanesque nave represents the Old Testament, the Gothic choir the New. Mary and Joseph in the foreground parallel the figures of Adam and Eve behind by the altar and Joseph holds a lily, emblem of purity, over Mary's head. The collection moves into the sixteenth century with the work of **Jan van Scorel**, represented here by a voluptuous *Mary Magdalen*, next to which is his pupil **Maerten van Heemskerck**'s portrait of the master of the Mint *Pieter Bicker*, shiftily counting out the cash. There's also a memorable *Carrying of the Cross* by **Quinten Matsys**, long Antwerp's leading painter and a transitional figure in so far as he was one of the first Netherlandish artists to be influenced by the Italian Renaissance.

THE GOLDEN AGE

Beyond the early Netherlandish works lie the classic paintings of the **Dutch Golden Age**, beginning in Rooms 208 and 209 with several wonderful canvases by **Frans Hals**, most notably his expansive *Marriage Portrait of Isaac Massa and Beatrix Laen*. Relaxing beneath a tree, a portly Isaac glows with contentment as his new wife sits beside him in a suitably demure manner. Here also is **Dirck van Baburen**'s sensational *Prometheus in Chains* – a work from the Utrecht School, which used the paintings of Caravaggio as its model – and in the small circular gallery (Room 207) are displayed the miniatures of **Hendrick Avercamp**, noted for their folksy and finely detailed skating scenes. Moving on, there are more thoroughly Dutch works in, for instance, the soft, tonal river scenes of the Haarlem artist **Salomon van Ruysdael** and the cool church interiors of **Pieter Saenredam**. Beyond this is a mixed selection of canvases by some of Rembrandt's better-known pupils, including **Ferdinand Bol**'s *Portrait of Elizabeth Bas* (Room 215). Perhaps the most talented of the master's pupils was **Carel Fabritius**, who was killed in 1654 at the age of thirty-two, when Delft's powder magazine exploded. His *Portrait of Abraham Potter* (Room 215), a restrained, skilful work of soft, delicate hues, contrasts heavily with the same artist's grisly *The Beheading of St John the Baptist* (Room 222). Mingling with these works are several paintings by **Rembrandt** himself – from the artist's mature period, for the most part, notably a late *Self-Portrait*, caught in mid-shrug as the Apostle Paul, a self-aware and defeated old man. There's also the finely detailed *Portrait of Maria Trip*, a wonderfully expressive portrait of his first wife *Saskia* and the emotional subtlety of *The Staalmeesters*.

The next rooms (Rooms 216–220) take you into the latter half of the seventeenth century, and include works ranging from **Gerrit Berckheyde**'s crisp depictions of Amsterdam and Haarlem to the carousing peasants of **Jan Steen**. Steen's *Feast of St Nicholas*, with its squabbling children, makes the festival a celebration of disorderly greed, while the drunken waywardness of his *Merry Family* and *The Drunken Couple* verge on the anarchic. Steen was also capable of more subtle works, a famous example being his *Morning Toilet*, which is full of associations, referring either to sexual pleasures just had or about to be taken. Room 221A focuses on **Vermeer**, whose *Love Letter* reveals a tension between servant and mistress – the lute on the woman's lap was a well-known sexual symbol – and *The Kitchen Maid*, an exquisitely observed domestic scene, literally right down to the nail – and its shadow – on the background wall. Similarly, in the precise *Young Woman Reading a Letter,* the map behind her hints at the far-flung places her loved one is writing from.

THE GALLERY OF HONOUR

Room 223, a small side room at the end of this part of the museum introduces one of the Rijksmuseum's greatest treasures, Rembrandt's **The Night Watch** of 1642. This is undoubtedly the most famous and probably the most valuable of all the artist's pictures, restored after being slashed in 1975, and hung – as architect Cuypers intended – at the end of the so-called **Gallery of Honour**, the museum's stately, top-floor centrepiece. The painting is of a Militia Company and as such celebrates one of the companies formed in the sixteenth century to defend the United Provinces against Spain. As the Habsburg threat receded, so the militias became social clubs for the well-heeled, who were eager to commission their own group portraits as signs of their prestige. *The Night Watch* depicts Amsterdam's Kloveniersdoelen company, but the title is actually inaccurate – it got its tag in the eighteenth century when the background darkness was misinterpreted. Though not as subtle as much of the artist's later work, the painting is an adept piece, full of movement and carefully arranged. Paintings of this kind were collections of individual portraits as much as group pictures, and for the artist their difficulty lay in including each single face while simultaneously producing a coherent group scene. Rembrandt opted to show the company preparing to march off, a snapshot of military activity in which banners are unfurled, muskets primed and drums rolled. There are a couple of allegorical figures as well, most prominently a young, spotlit woman who has a bird hanging from her belt, a reference to the Kloveniersdoelen's traditional emblem of a claw. *The Night Watch* is surrounded by several other militia paintings, two of which are by **Bartholomeus van der Helst**: the one on the left of *The Night Watch* is perhaps the best of them – it's lively and colourful, but its arrangement and lighting are static.

Elsewhere, the Gallery of Honour houses a healthy sample of large-scale Dutch paintings, though admittedly some are notable only for their size. Two of Rembrandt's better-known pupils crop up here: **Nicholas Maes**, with one of his typically intimate scenes in *An Old Woman at Prayer*, and **Ferdinand Bol**, with his flashy and fleshy *Venus and Adonis*. Nearby is Rembrandt's touching depiction of his cowled son, *Titus*, and *The Jewish Bride*, one of his very last pictures, finished in 1667. No one knows who the people are, nor whether they are actually married (the title came later), but the painting is one of Rembrandt's most telling, the paint dashed on freely and the hands touching lovingly, as Kenneth Clark wrote, in a "marvellous amalgam of richness, tenderness and trust".

APPLIED ART

The Rijksmuseum owns a vast hoard of **applied art**, but unless your stamina is limitless, it's wise to restrict yourself to a single period. The most impressive section is the top-floor **Medieval and Renaissance** collection, which occupies Rooms 238 to 261 on the other (west) side of the Gallery of Honour. Room 238 kicks off with a handful of Byzantine trinkets and a glass case crammed with beautiful Limoges enamels, whilst Room 239 holds the magnificent *Ten Mourners*, sensitive and finely detailed fifteenth-century carvings taken from the Antwerp tomb of Isabelle de Bourbon, wife of Charles the Bold. Contemporaneous with these is a whole raft of religious carvings amongst which are a number of wonderful altarpieces, or **retables**. Thousands of these were produced in the Low Countries from the end of the fourteenth century up until the Reformation, the standard format being the creation of a series of mini-tableaux illustrating biblical scenes with medieval characters and landscapes, though it's the extraordinary detail that impresses most. Few of the wood carvers of the period are known by name, but one exception is **Adriaen van Wesel** of Utrecht, several of whose works are displayed here (for example, the *Meeting of the Magi*) in all their lively, crowded dynamism.

Room 248 marks the start of the Renaissance section, whose wide-ranging exhibits include everything from tapestries and cabinets to beds and porcelain. In particular there are three rooms (Rooms 255–257) devoted to **delftware**, the blue-and-white ceramics to which Delft gave its name in the seventeenth century. The original designs were stylized copies of Chinese ceramics imported by the Dutch East India Company, but the patterns soon changed to depict more traditional Dutch landscapes, animals and comic figures. By the early years of the eighteenth century, Delft's craftsmen had become confident enough to create vases, jars and even musical instruments in polychrome as well as the traditional blue and white – and examples of each and every period are on display. There's another Sculpture and Applied Art section below on the ground floor, this time focusing on the seventeenth and eighteenth centuries, and yet another in the basement, where there's more Dutch porcelain and a couple of rooms devoted to Art Nouveau.

THE SOUTH WING

Recently remodelled, the **South Wing** is reached through a passageway from the main building, or via its own entrance at Hobbemastraat 19 – round the back of the museum. There are two floors. On the ground floor is the **Asiatic Art** section, where pride of place goes to the Chinese and Japanese statues, paintings, ceramics and lacquerwork. The top floor up above is primarily devoted to **eighteenth- and nineteenth-century Dutch paintings**, picking up chronologically where the Gallery of Honour leaves off. Here you'll find the chief proponents of Dutch Impressionism amongst the work of the **Hague School**, a label that covers a variety of styles and painters who shared a clarity and sensitivity in their depiction of the Dutch landscape. Of the major Hague School painters, the Rijksmuseum collection is strongest on the work of **Jan Weissenbruch**, whose land- and seascapes, such as *View near the Geestbrug*, hark back to the compositional techniques of Van Ruysdael and the Maris brothers. **Jacob Maris**'s sultry landscapes are the most representative of the School, while the works of the younger **Willem Maris** are more direct and approachable – his *Ducks* is a good example. **Anton Mauve**'s work is similar, his *Morning Ride on the Beach* filled with shimmering gradations of tone that belie the initial simplicity of the scene. While members of the Hague School were creating gentle landscapes, a younger generation of Impressionist painters working in Amsterdam – the **Amsterdam School** – was using a darker palette to capture city scenes. By far the most important work from this turn-of-the-century group is **G.H. Breitner's** *Singelbrug near Paleisstraat in Amsterdam*, a random moment in the street recorded and framed with photographic dispassion. Breitner worked best when turning his attention to rough, shadowy depictions of the city, as in *Rokin* and *Damrak*. **Josef Israëls'** work is lighter in tone and mood, with canvases like *Donkey Rides on the Beach* showing his affinities with the French Impressionists of the period.

The Van Gogh Museum

Vincent van Gogh (1853–1890) is arguably the most popular, most reproduced and most talked about of all modern artists, so it's not surprising that the **Van Gogh Museum** (daily 10am–6pm; *f*12,50) comprising a fabulous collection of the artist's work, is one of Amsterdam's top tourist attractions. Housed in an angular building designed by a leading light of the De Stijl movement, Gerritt Rietveld, and opened to the public in 1973, it's a well-conceived and beautifully presented introduction to the man and his art, with the kernel of the collection inherited from Vincent's art-dealer brother Theo. It's located a brief walk west of the Rijksmuseum on the north edge of Museumplein.

The museum starts on the ground floor with a group of works by some of Van Gogh's well-known friends and contemporaries, many of whom influenced his work – Gauguin, Millet, Adolph Monticelli and others. It then moves on to the works of the man himself, presented for the most part chronologically on the first floor. The first paintings go back to the artist's **early years** in Nuenen, southern Holland, where he was born: dark, sombre works in the main, ranging from an assortment of drab grey and brown still-lifes to the gnarled faces and haunting, flickering light of *The Potato Eaters* – one of Van Gogh's best-known paintings, and the culmination of hundreds of studies of the local peasantry.

Across the hall, the sobriety of these early works is easily transposed onto the **Parisian** urban landscape, particularly in the *View of Paris*, where the city's domes and rooftops hover below Montmartre under a glowering, blustery sky. But before long, under the sway of fellow painters and – after the bleak countryside of North Brabant – the sheer colour of the city itself, his approach began to change. This is most noticeable in the views of Montmartre windmills, a couple of self-portraits, and the pictures from Asnières just outside Paris, where the artist used to travel regularly to paint. Look out also for *A Pair of Shoes*, a painting that used to hang in the house Van Gogh shared with Gauguin in Arles, the dazzling movement of *Wheatfield with a Lark* and the almost neurotic precision of his *Flowerpot with Chives*.

In February 1888, Van Gogh moved to **Arles**, inviting Gauguin to join him a little later. With the change of scenery came a heightened interest in colour, and the predominance of yellow as a recurring motif: it's represented best in such paintings as *Van Gogh's Bedroom* and the *Harvest at La Crau*, and most vividly in *The Yellow House*. A canvas from the artist's *Sunflowers* series is justly one of his most lauded works, intensely, almost obsessively, rendered in the deepest oranges, golds and ochres he could find. Gauguin told of Van Gogh painting these flowers in a near trance; there were usually sunflowers in jars all over their house.

At the asylum in **St Rémy**, where Van Gogh committed himself in 1889 after snipping off part of his ear and offering it to a local prostitute, his approach to nature became more abstract: trees bent into cruel, sinister shapes and skies coloured purple and yellow, as in the *Garden of St Paul's Hospital*. Van Gogh is at his most expressionistic here, the paint applied thickly, often with a palette knife, especially in the final, tortured paintings done at **Auvers**, where Van Gogh lodged for the last three months of his life. It was at Auvers that he painted the frantic *Ears of Wheat* and *Wheatfield with a Reaper*, in which the fields swirl and writhe under weird, light-green, moving skies. It was a few weeks after completing these last paintings that Van Gogh shot and fatally wounded himself.

The two floors above provide a back-up to the main collection: the second floor has a study area with PC access to an excessively detailed computerized account of Van Gogh's life and times, and the third features a changing selection from the museum's vast stock of Van Gogh **drawings** and less familiar paintings, plus notebooks and letters. This floor also affords space to relevant temporary exhibitions illustrating Van Gogh's artistic influences, or his own influence on other artists. There's much more temporary exhibition space in the new, ultra-modern annexe reached via the first-floor escalator. Completed in 1998 and partly underground, the annexe was financed by a Japanese insurance company – the same conglomerate that paid $35 million for one of Van Gogh's *Sunflowers* canvases in 1987. The museum also has a shop and café, both located on the ground floor beside the main entrance.

The Stedelijk Museum

Amsterdam's number one venue for modern art, the **Stedelijk Museum** (daily: April–Sept 10am–6pm; Oct–March 11am–5pm; *f*9), next door to the Van Gogh Museum, is still at the cutting edge after a hundred years or more. Its permanent collection is wide-ranging and its temporary exhibitions – based both on its own acquisitions and on loaned pieces, and regularly extending to photography and installations – are usually of international standard. It's housed in a grand neo-Renaissance building dating from 1895, but the interior is very modern and a new wing was added in the 1950s.

The museum's ground floor is usually given over to **temporary exhibitions**, often by living European artists. Contemporary Dutch art is a particular favourite, so keep an eye out for the work of such painters as Jan Dibbets, Rob Scholte and Marlene Dumas. Also on the ground floor are a couple of large-scale permanent attractions – **Karel Appel**'s *Bar* in the foyer, installed in the 1950s, and the same artist's wild daubings in the restaurant. But perhaps the most interesting permanent exhibit is **Ed Kienholz**'s *Beanery* (1965), in the basement: modelled on his local bar in Los Angeles, the tableau's clock-faced figures, combined with the music and hum of conversation, create a nervous, claustrophobic background to the horror of the newspaper headline in the vending machine – "Children Kill Children in Vietnam Riots". For Kienholz, this is *real* time, and time inside the bar is "surrealist time. . . where people waste time, lose time, escape time, ignore time".

Upstairs, the first floor is given over to a changing selection drawn from the museum's **permanent collection**. Broadly speaking, this starts off with drawings by Picasso, Matisse and their contemporaries, and moves on to paintings by major Impressionists (Manet, Monet, Bonnard) and Post-Impressionists (Ensor, Van Gogh, Cézanne). Further on, Mondrian holds sway among the De Stijl group, from his early, muddy-coloured abstractions to the cool, boldly coloured rectangular blocks for which he's most famous. Kasimir Malevich is similarly well represented, his dense attempts at Cubism leading to the dynamism and bold, primary tones of his "Suprematist" paintings – slices, blocks and bolts of colour that shift around as if about to resolve themselves into some complex computer graphic. Elsewhere, depending on what's on show, you may come across some of the Stedelijk's wide collection of Marc Chagall paintings, and a number of pictures by American Abstract Expressionists Mark Rothko, Ellsworth Kelly and Barnett Newman, in addition to the odd work by Lichtenstein or Warhol. Jean Dubuffet, too, with his swipes at the art establishment, may well have a profile, and you might catch Matisse's large cutout, *The Parakeet and the Mermaid*.

The Vondelpark and the Concertgebouw

Amsterdam is desperately short of green spaces, which makes the leafy expanses of the **Vondelpark**, just northwest of Museumplein, doubly welcome. This is easily the largest and most popular of the city's parks, its network of footpaths used by a healthy slice of the city's population. The park dates back to 1864, when a group of leading Amsterdammers clubbed together to transform the soggy marshland that lay beyond the Leidsepoort into a landscaped park. The group, who were impressed by the contemporary English fashion for natural (as distinct from formal) landscaping, gave the task of developing the new style of park to the Zocher family, big-time gardeners who set about their task with gusto, completing their work in 1865. Named after the seventeenth-century poet Joost van den Vondel, the park proved an immediate success and was expanded to its present size (45 hectares) in 1877. It now possesses over 100 species of tree, a wide variety of local and imported plants, and – amongst many incidental features – a **bandstand** and excellent **rose garden**. Neither did the Zochers forget their Dutch roots: the park is latticed with ponds and narrow waterways, home to many sorts of wildfowl. There are other animals too: cows, sheep, hundreds of squirrels plus, bizarrely enough, a large colony of bright-green parakeets. The Vondelpark has several different children's **play areas** and during the summer regularly hosts free **concerts** and theatrical performances, mostly in its own specially designed open-air theatre.

A ten-minute walk from the Vondelpark's northern edge, along Van Baerlestraat, will bring you to the **Concertgebouw** (Concert Hall), home of the famed – and much recorded – Royal Concertgebouw Orchestra. When the German composer Brahms visited Amsterdam in the 1870s he was scathing about the locals' lack of culture and, in particular, their lack of an even halfway suitable venue for his music. In the face of such ridicule, a consortium of Amsterdam businessmen got together to fund the construction of a brand-new concert hall and the result was the Concertgebouw, completed in 1888. An attractive structure with a pleasingly grand neoclassical facade, the Concertgebouw has become renowned among musicians and concert-goers for its marvellous acoustics, though it did have to undergo major repairs when it was discovered that the wooden piles on which it rested were rotting away. The overhaul included the addition of a new, largely glass wing that contrasts nicely with the red brick and stone of the rest of the building. Although the Concertgebouw attracts the world's best orchestras and musicians, ticket prices can be surprisingly inexpensive – the venue operates an arts-for-all policy – and from September to May there are often free walk-in concerts at lunchtime.

CYCLING IN THE WATERLAND

Amsterdam North, on the far side of the River IJ, has flourished since the construction of the IJ tunnel in the 1960s linked it with the city centre. Today, a solid wedge of modern housing crowds the river bank, but beyond, to the northeast of the built-up area, is the **Waterland**, an open expanse of peat meadows, lakes, polders and marshland. Until the turn of the twentieth century, this parcel of land was a marshy fen, whose scattered population made a healthy living raising and grazing cattle to be sold in Amsterdam. The Waterland was then made much more tractable by the digging of drainage canals, prompting wealthy Amsterdammers to build their summer residences here. These myriad waterways still pattern the district today and are home to a wide range of waterfowl, as are the many lakes, the largest of which – abutting the Markermeer – is the **Kinselmeer**.

Easily the best way to explore the Waterland is by **bike** – the cycle paths are excellent, buses are few and far between and some of the more secluded spots can't be reached by car. Before you catch the ferry (see below), visit the Amsterdam VVV and pick up their Waterland leaflet (*f*3,50), which outlines a circular, 38km-long bike tour. The recommended route begins at the **Adelaarswegveer ferry dock** on the north side of the IJ, from where you follow Meeuwenlaan to the big roundabout at the start of Nieuwendammerdijk. This long thin lane leads east, running parallel to the river, before it meets Schellingwoudedijk and then Durger Dammerdijk at the southern tip of the long dike stretching up the coast, with the polders and a scattering of tiny villages just inland. The route's compulsory stop is the village of **Broek-in-Waterland** whose oldest streets are lined with charming wooden mansions painted in the so-called *Broeker* grey, and the most obvious detour is out along the causeway to the pretty island village of Marken (see p.148) – an extra 3km or so each way – and the ride can be made in either direction, clockwise or anti-clockwise.

GVB operates two **ferries** across the IJ from Pier 8 behind Centraal Station. Neither ferry (*veer*) takes cars but both carry foot passengers, bicycles and motorbikes for free. Of the two, the Buiksloterwegveer – like a huge mobile air-traffic control tower – shuttles back and forth every ten minutes or so, 24 hours a day, running to the foot of Buiksloterweg. The smaller Adelaarswegveer (Mon–Sat 6.20am–8.50pm) connects with the southern end of Meeuwenlaan, the starting point of the Waterland bike tour. For details of **bike rental** companies in Amsterdam, see p.61.

Eating

Amsterdam may not be Europe's culinary capital – Dutch cuisine is firmly rooted in the meat, potato and cabbage school of cooking – but as a recompense, the country's colonial past ensures that there's a wide range of non-Dutch **restaurants**. Amsterdam is acclaimed for the best Indonesian food outside Indonesia, at hard-to-beat prices – and an always worthwhile choice is *rijsttafel*, a selection of six or eight different dishes and hot sauces. Other cuisines are also well-represented; aside from French, Iberian and Italian places, there are several fine Thai restaurants, as well as Middle Eastern and Indian establishments. Amsterdam also excels in the quantity and variety of its *eetcafés* and **bars** (see p.115), which serve increasingly adventurous food, quite cheaply, in a relaxed and unpretentious setting.

BUDGET EATING

At all the following, you can get a decent meal for less than ƒ15:

Bojo, Lange Leidsedwarsstraat 51. Also round the corner at Leidsekruisstraat 12. Both near Leidseplein. Possibly the best-value – though certainly not the best – Indonesian place in town. Recommended for the young, lively atmosphere, but the food is very much a hit-and-miss affair, and you'll have to wait a long time both for a table and service. Mon–Wed 4pm–2am, Thurs & Sun noon–2am, Fri & Sat noon–4am.

Het Beeren, Koningsstraat 15. Huge portions of the simplest Dutch fare – cabbage, mashed potato and steaming stew. Off Nieuwmarkt. Daily 5.30–9.30pm.

La Place, part of *Vroom & Dreesman* department store, Kalverstraat 201. City centre, self-service buffet-style restaurant, where it's possible to fill up for under ƒ12. Daily 10am–9pm.

Maoz Falafel, Reguliersbreestraat 45, off Rembrandtplein. The best street-food in the city – mashed chickpea balls deep-fried and served in Middle Eastern bread, with as much salad as you can eat, for the grand sum of ƒ6. Other branches at Leidsestraat and Ferdinand Bolstraat. Mon–Thurs & Sun 11am–2am, Fri & Sat 11am–3am.

Mensa Agora, Roeterstraat 11, near Plantage Kerklaan. Self-service student cafeteria, with all that that entails. In the Plantagebuurt district. Mon–Fri noon–2pm & 5–7pm.

Mensa Atrium, Oudezijds Achterburgwal 237. City centre self-service cafeteria attached to the University of Amsterdam (but open to all); full meals for under ƒ10, though the quality leaves a little to be desired. Mon–Fri noon–2pm & 5–7pm.

Mr Hot Potato, Leidsestraat 44. The only place in the city centre for baked potatoes – nothing fancy, but cheap (average ƒ5). Daily 10am–8pm.

Toko Sari, Kerkstraat 161, near Leidseplein. Fabulous Indonesian takeaway. Tues–Sat 11am–6pm.

Amsterdam's **tearooms** (see p.114) – calling themselves this to steer clear of druggy "coffeeshop" connotations – correspond roughly to the normal concept of a café: places that are generally open all day, might serve alcohol but definitely aren't bars, don't allow dope-smoking, but which have good coffee, sandwiches, light snacks and cakes. The pick make great places to stop off for lunch or a snack.

Restaurants

Unless otherwise stated, all the places listed below serve food daily from 5 or 6pm until 10 or 11pm. Some will stay open later for customers who are already installed, and times may vary depending on the time of year and how busy things are.

African, Middle Eastern and Turkish

Artist, 2e Jan Steenstraat 1 (☎671 4264). A small Lebanese restaurant just off Albert Cuypstraat, in the De Pijp district east of Sarphatipark – and south of the Rijksmuseum. Inexpensive.

Indaba, Utrechtsestraat 96 (☎421 3852). Authentic South African interior, and, with the likes of zebra, ostrich and kudu on the menu, authentic flavours too; the cook brings the food to your table. Popular so make a reservation. South of Rembrandtplein. Moderate.

RESTAURANT PRICES

As a guideline, the following categories indicate the average cost per person for a main course without drinks.

Budget: Under ƒ20/€9
Inexpensive: ƒ20–30/€9–13.50

Moderate: ƒ30–40/€13.50–18
Expensive: Over ƒ40/€18

Izmir, Kerkstraat 66, south of Leidsestraat (☎627 8239). Cosy, family-run little Turkish place in the Grachtengordel; a welcoming atmosphere and fine kebabs. Daily 5pm–midnight. Inexpensive.

Pygmalion, Nieuwe Spiegelstraat 5a (☎420 7022) Good spot for both lunch and dinner, popular among local workers. South African dishes include crocodile steaks, and there's a good selection of sandwiches. Near the Rijksmuseum. Moderate.

Turquoise, Wolvenstraat 22 (☎624 2026). Good Turkish restaurant in the Grachtengordel with a beautiful long bar, giving it a café-like atmosphere. Inexpensive.

The Americas

Iguazu, Prinsengracht 703, at Leidsestraat (☎420 3910). For carnivores only: a superb Argentinian–Brazilian restaurant, with some of the finest fillet steak in town. Daily noon–midnight. Moderate.

Café Pacifico, Warmoesstraat 31 (☎624 2911). Quality array of Mexican (and Mexican–Californian) food, in a cramped and crowded little joint only minutes from Centraal Station. Moderate.

Poco Loco, Nieuwmarkt 24 (☎624 2937). Cajun split-level restaurant with a friendly, cheerful atmosphere, and a menu including burritos, steaks and jambalaya. Inexpensive.

Rose's Cantina, Reguliersdwarsstraat 38, near Rembrandtplein (☎625 9797). Mexican restaurant in the heart of Amsterdam, near Rembrandtplein, qualifying as possibly the city's most crowded, which includes the garden terrace at the back. Moderate.

Rosen & Tortilla's, Prinsengracht 126, at Leliegracht (☎620 6525). Atmospheric Mexican restaurant serving the usual main courses, as well as a good range of tapas. Its location right by the water in the Grachtengordel makes it a good place to eat in the summer. Open 10am–1am. Inexpensive.

Chinese, Thai and Filipino

Cambodja City, Albert Cuypstraat 58–60 (☎671 4930). Thai and Vietnamese restaurant serving delicious meat fondues, soups and prawn dishes, with friendly, but no-nonsense, service. In the De Pijp district south of the Singelgracht and east of the Rijksmuseum. Inexpensive–Moderate.

Dynasty, Reguliersdwarsstraat 30 (☎626 8400). Festive choice of Indo-Chinese food, with Vietnamese and Thai options; not for the shoestring traveller. Subdued atmosphere suits the prices (average ƒ75). Near Rembrandtplein. Closed Tues. Expensive.

Lana Thai, Warmoesstraat 10 (☎624 2179). Among the best Thai restaurants in town, with seating overlooking the Damrak. Quality food, chic surroundings but high prices (ƒ40–50). Closed Tues. Expensive.

Mango Bay, Westerstraat 91 (☎638 1039). Small intimate Filipino restaurant with laid-back service and fairly reasonable prices – there's a set three-course menu for just over ƒ40. In the Jordaan. Moderate.

Top Thai, Herenstraat 22 (☎623 4463). A popular restaurant that boasts some of the best Thai food in Amsterdam, with spicy, authentic dishes at a good price, and a friendly atmosphere. For complete burn-out try one of their chilli salads. North end of the Grachtengordel. Inexpensive.

Dutch

De Blauwe Hollander, Leidsekruisstraat 28 (☎623 3014). Dutch food in generous quantities – something of a boon in an otherwise touristy, unappealing part of town, near Leidseplein. Expect to share a table. Inexpensive.

Claes Claesz, Egelantiersstraat 24 (☎625 5306). Exceptionally friendly Jordaan restaurant that attracts a good mixed crowd and serves excellent Dutch food. Live music from Thursday to Saturday, and Sunday's "theatre-dinner" sees various Dutch theatrical/musical acts between the courses. Closed Mon. Moderate.

De Eettuin, 2e Tuindwarsstraat 10 (☎623 7706). Hefty portions of Dutch food, with salad from a serve-yourself bar. Non-meat eaters can content themselves with the large, if dull, vegetarian plate, or the delicious fish casserole. In the Jordaan. Inexpensive.

Haesje Claes, Spuistraat 275 (☎624 9998). Dutch cuisine at its best. Extremely popular – go early to get a table. In the city centre. Daily noon–10pm. Moderate.

Keuken van 1870, Spuistraat 4 (☎624 8965). Former soup kitchen in the heart of the city, still serving Dutch meat-and-potato staples. Frill-free. Mon–Fri 12.30–8pm, Sat & Sun 4–9pm. Budget.

Koevoet, Lindenstraat 17 (☎624 0846). The "Cow's Foot" – or, alternatively, the "Crowbar" – is a traditional Jordaan *eetcafé* serving unpretentious food at good prices. Closed Mon. Budget.

Piet de Leeuw, Noorderstraat 11 (☎623 7181). Amsterdam's best steakhouse, dating from the Forties. Excellent steaks, and a mouthwatering Dame Blanche dessert. Mon–Fri noon–11pm, Sat & Sun 5–11pm. South of Rembrandtplein, off Vijzelgracht. Inexpensive.

De Silveren Spiegel, Kattengat 4, off Spuistraat (☎624 6589). There's been a restaurant in this location – off the northern end of Spuistraat – since 1614, and "The Silver Mirror" is one of the best in the city, with a delicately balanced menu of Dutch cuisine. The proprietor lives on the coast and brings in the fish himself. Spectacular food, with a cellar of 350 wines to complement it. Four-course dinner for two at a table set with silver is a cool *f*200, though you can get away with around *f*77,50 each. Closed Sun. Expensive.

't Zwaantje, Berenstraat 12 (☎623 2373). Old-fashioned Dutch restaurant with a nice atmosphere and well-cooked, reasonably priced food. In the Grachtengordel, a five-minute walk southwest of the Dam. Moderate.

PANCAKES

In the tradition of simple cooking, **pancakes** are a Dutch speciality – for fillers and light meals, you'd be hard pushed to find better. Although there are plenty of places dotted around town, those listed below are recommended. Expect to pay between *f*8 and *f*15.

Bredero, Oudezijds Voorburgwal 244 (☎622 9461). On the edge of the Red Light District, one of the city's best-value pancake places. June–Sept daily noon–10pm, Oct–May times vary, often only open at weekends.

Le Soleil, Nieuwe Spiegelstraat 56 (☎622 7147). Pretty little restaurant (once visited by the Queen) which makes some great pancakes – try one with ginger and raisins. Open until 6pm.

The Pancake Bakery, Prinsengracht 191, just south of Prinsenstraat (☎625 1333). Open all day, in a beautiful old house on the canal. A large selection of filled pancakes from *f*10, many big enough to count as a meal. Daily noon–9.30pm.

Pannekoekhuis Upstairs, Grimburgwal 2 (☎626 5603). Minuscule place in a tumbledown house, in the city centre opposite the university buildings, with sweet and savoury pancakes at low prices. Student discount. Wed–Fri noon–7pm, Sat & Sun noon–6pm.

Fish

Albatros, Westerstraat 264 (☎627 9932). Family-run restaurant in the Jordaan serving some mouth-wateringly imaginative fish dishes. A place to splash out and linger over a meal. Closed Wed. Expensive.

Le Pêcheur, Reguliersdwarsstraat 32 (☎624 3121). Beautiful restaurant with a well-balanced menu (the four-course set menu is good value at around *f*70). Lovely garden terrace in the summer. Near Rembrandtplein. Open for lunch. Closed Sun. Moderate.

Lucius, Spuistraat 247 (☎624 1831). Pricey at around *f*60 for two courses, but one of the best fish restaurants in town. Their speciality is fresh seafood, but the diverse menu includes wonderful smoked salmon and a vast array of all kinds of shellfish, delicately prepared. Very popular. Closed Sun. Expensive.

Werkendam, St Nicolaasstraat 43 (☎428 7744). Stylish, affordable seafood restaurant in one of the alleys running from Nieuwezijds Voorburgwal to Nieuwendijk, largely frequented by local professionals. Efficient and friendly staff. Inexpensive.

Indian

Akbar, Korte Leidsedwarsstraat 33 (☎624 2211). Fabulous South Indian food, especially strong on tandoori, with a fine choice across the board. Plenty for vegetarians. Friendly service. Near Leidseplein. Daily 5–11.30pm. Moderate.

Shiva, Reguliersdwarsstraat 72 (☎624 8713). The city's outstanding Indian restaurant in terms of quality and price, with a wide selection of dishes, all expertly prepared. Vegetarians well catered for. Highly recommended. Near Rembrandtplein. Inexpensive.

Tandoor, Leidseplein 19 (☎623 4415). Doesn't quite live up to its excellent reputation perhaps, but pretty good nonetheless. The tandoori dishes are highly recommended, and won't break the bank. Inexpensive.

Indonesian

Cilubang, Runstraat 10 (☎626 9755). Small, Grachtengordel restaurant, with a friendly atmosphere, serving well presented spicy dishes. Moderate.

Kantjil en de Tijger, Spuistraat 291 (☎620 0994). High-quality food averaging around *f*55 per person, served in a stylish wood-panelled grand café. Moderate–Expensive.

Puri Mas, Lange Leidsedwarsstraat 37 (☎627 7627). Exceptionally good value for money, on a street better known for rip-offs. Friendly and informed service preludes spectacular *rijsttafels*, both meat and vegetarian. Near Leidseplein. Recommended. Moderate.

Sahid Jaya, Reguliersdwarsstraat 26 (☎626 3727). Excellent restaurant where you can eat outside surrounded by a beautiful flower garden. Near Rembrandtplein. Helpful and friendly staff. Moderate.

Sama Sebo, Pieter C. Hooftstraat 27 (☎662 8146). Amsterdam's best-known Indonesian restaurant, especially for its *rijsttafel* – and good value if you choose à la carte dishes. The food is magnificent. Closed Sun. Over Singelgracht from Leidseplein. Inexpensive–Moderate.

Sie Joe, Gravenstraat 24 (☎624 1830). Small café-restaurant at the back of Nieuwe Kerk which is great value for money. The menu is far from extensive, but comprises well-prepared simple dishes such as *gado gado*, *sateh* and *rendang*. Mon–Sat 11am–7pm, Thurs till 8pm. Budget.

Japanese

Bento, Kerkstraat 148, at Nieuwe Spiegelstraat (☎422 4248). Superbly prepared vegetarian and vegan macrobiotic dishes, with fish options. Choice of authentic *tatami* seating (cross-legged at a low table) or a more usual table-and-chair. In the Grachtengordel. Closed Mon. Moderate–Expensive.

Hotel Okura, Ferdinand Bolstraat 333 (☎678 7111). The two restaurants in this five-star hotel – the sushi restaurant *Yamazato*, and the grill-plate restaurant *Teppan-Yaki Sazanka* –

serve the finest Japanese cuisine in the city. Just south of the Heineken brewery. Reckon on at least *f*95 per person. Both are also open for lunch from noon–2.30pm. Expensive.

Zushi, Amstel 20, near Rembrandtplein (☎330 6882). High-tech, city centre sushi bar, serving colour-coded dishes on a conveyor belt running along the bar. Daily noon–midnight. Inexpensive.

Other European

Bonjour, Keizersgracht 770, east of Utrechtsestraat (☎626 6040). Classy French cuisine in a romantic setting; particularly good charcoal-grilled dishes. Set menus from *f*45. Closed Mon & Tues. In the Grachtengordel. Moderate.

Casa di David, Singel 426, north of Koningsplein (☎624 5093). Solid-value dark wood Italian restaurant with a long-standing reputation. Pizzas from wood-fired ovens, fresh hand-made pasta, and more substantial fare. Best seats are by the window. Moderate.

Centra, Lange Niezel 29 (☎622 3050). City centre cantina, near Oude Kerk, with a wonderful selection of Spanish food, masterfully cooked and genially served. One of Amsterdam's best restaurants. Daily 1–11pm. Inexpensive.

Christophe, Leliegracht 46 (☎625 0807). Classic Michelin-starred restaurant on a quiet and beautiful canal in the Grachtengordel, drawing inspiration from the olive-oil-and-basil flavours of southern France and the chef's early years in North Africa. His aubergine terrine with cumin has been dubbed the best vegetarian dish in the world. Reservations far outstrip capacity. Expect to pay *f*50–60 for two courses. Closed Sun. Expensive.

Dionysos, Overtoom 176 (☎689 4441). Good Greek restaurant a little to the south of Leidseplein, with the distinct added advantage of serving until 1am. Phone ahead if you're going to turn up after midnight. Daily 5pm–1am. Inexpensive.

Duende, Lindengracht 62 (☎420 6692). Wonderful little tapas bar up in the Jordaan, with good, cheap tapas (*f*3–8 each). Includes a small venue in the back for live dance and music performances. Mon–Thurs 4pm–1am, Fri 4pm–2am, Sat 2pm–2am, Sun 2pm–1am. Budget.

Hemelse Modder, Oude Waal 9, in the centre off Oude Schans (☎624 3203). Tasty meat, fish and vegetarian food in French–Italian style at reasonable prices in an informal atmosphere. Highly popular (especially among the gay community). Closed Mon. Moderate.

In de Waag, Nieuwmarkt (☎422 7772). Comfortable and stylish Belgian café-restaurant with uniformed staff. Daily 10am–12am. Moderate.

L'Angoletto, Hemonystraat 2. Everyone's favourite Italian, always packed out – as you'll see from the condensation on the two big windows; the long wooden tables and benches create a very sociable atmosphere. No bookings, so just turn up and hope for the best. About ten minutes' walk south of Rembrandtplein. Closed Sat. Inexpensive.

La Pipa, Gerard Doustraat 50 (☎679 2318). A great favourite with the Spanish community in Amsterdam with good food, sometimes accompanied by spontaneous flamenco performances. A short walk south of the Heineken brewery. Moderate.

Le Zinc. . . et les Dames, Prinsengracht 999, just west of Reguliersgracht (☎622 9044). Wonderfully atmospheric little place serving good quality, simple French fare for an average of *f*45; there's a particularly good wine list. In the Grachtengordel. Closed Mon & Sun. Expensive.

Prego, Herenstraat 25 (☎638 0148). Small Grachtengordel restaurant serving exceptionally high-quality Mediterranean cuisine from *f*65 or so for two courses. Polite and friendly staff. Daily 6–10pm. Expensive.

Vegetarian

Bolhoed, Prinsengracht 60, just south of Prinsenstraat (☎626 1803). Something of an Amsterdam institution. Familiar vegan and vegetarian options from the daily changing menu, with organic beer to wash it down. More expensive than you might imagine. In the Grachtengordel. Daily noon–10pm. Moderate.

Golden Temple, Utrechtsestraat 126 (☎626 8560). Laid-back place with a little more soul than the average Amsterdam veggie joint. Well-prepared, lacto-vegetarian food (without sugar and milk) and pleasant, attentive service. No alcohol and non-smoking throughout. South of Rembrandtplein. Inexpensive.

Oininio, Prins Hendrikkade 20 (☎553 9328). Vegetarian restaurant in a new-age centre near Centraal Station, serving dishes made of fresh ingredients brought in daily. The menu changes according to season. Inexpensive–Moderate.

De Vliegende Schotel, Nieuwe Leliestraat 162 (☎625 2041). Perhaps the best of the city's cheap and wholesome vegetarian restaurants, the "Flying Saucer" serves delicious food in large portions. Lots of space, a peaceful ambience and a good noticeboard. In the Jordaan. Budget.

De Vrolijke Abrikoos, Weteringschans 76 (☎624 4672). All ingredients, produce and processes are organic or environmentally friendly in this restaurant that serves fish and meat as well as vegetarian dishes. Near Leidseplein. Closed Tues. Inexpensive–Moderate.

Tearooms

Bagels & Beans, Keizersgracht 504, near Leidsestraat. The latest bagel eatery, *B&B* makes some of the most creative and delicious snacks, attracting a young public: their version of strawberries and cream cheese is a big favourite in the summer. The "Beans" part of the name refers to the coffee you can have to accompany your bagel.

Café Esprit, Spui 10a. Swish modern café, with great sandwiches, rolls and superb salads.

Dialoog, Prinsengracht 261a. A few doors down from the Anne Frank House, one long room filled with paintings, restrained classical music, and downstairs, a gallery of Latin American art. A good choice of sandwiches and salads, too.

Gary's Muffins, Reguliersdwarsstraat 53, near Rembrandtplein. The best, and most authentic, New York bagels in town, with American-style cups of coffee (and half-price refills) and fresh-baked muffins. Open until 3am.

Jordino, Haarlemmerdijk 25, near Brouwersgracht. Small tearoom with an enormous variety of chocolates, pastries and ice cream – heaven for anyone with a sweet tooth.

Lunchcafé Winkel, Noordermarkt 43. A popular café on the corner with Westerstraat; something of a rendezvous on Saturday mornings, with the farmers' market in full flow, and some of the most delicious apple-cake in the city going like, well, like hot apple-cake.

Metz, Keizersgracht 455, near Leidseplein. Wonderful café on the top floor of the Metz department store, giving panoramic views over the canals of Amsterdam. Pricey, but then if you're shopping in Metz, you're not supposed to care.

Puccini, Staalstraat 21. Lovely cake- and chocolate-shop and café, with wonderful handmade cakes, pastries and good coffee. Close to Waterlooplein.

Villa Zeezicht, Torensteeg 3, north of Raadhuisstraat. Small, centrally located place, serving excellent rolls and sandwiches; also some of the best apple-cake in the city, fresh-baked every 10 minutes or so.

Drinking

Amsterdam is well known for its drinking, and with good reason: the selection of **bars** and **café-bars** is one of the real pleasures of the city. There are, in essence, two kinds of Amsterdam bar. The traditional, old-style bar is the **brown café** – a *bruin café* or *bruine kroeg*; these are cosy places so called because of the dingy colour of their walls, stained by years of tobacco smoke. As a backlash, slick, self-consciously modern **designer bars** have sprung up, many of them known as "grand cafés", which tend to be as un-brown as possible and geared towards a largely young crowd. We've included details of the more established ones, although these places come and go – something like seventy percent are said to close down within a year of opening. Most café-bars (often called *eetcafés*) and some bars sell food – anything from snacks to an extensive menu. Another type of drinking spot – though there are very few of them left – are the **tasting houses** (*proeflokalen*), originally the sampling rooms of small private distillers, now tiny, stand-up places that sell only spirits and close around 8pm

Bars

Bars, of either kind, open at around 10am or 5pm; those that open in the morning do not close at lunchtime, and both stay open until around 1am during the week, 2am at weekends (sometimes until 3am). **Prices** are fairly standard everywhere, and the only time you'll pay through the nose is when there's music, or if you're foolish (or desperate) enough to step into the obvious tourist traps around Leidseplein and along Damrak. Reckon on paying roughly *f*2,75 for a standard-measure small beer, called a *pils* (or, if you get it in a straight glass, a *fluitje*). A tiny beer chaser, called a *kleintje pils*, costs the same.

For listings of gay bars, see p.129.

The Old Centre

De Buurvrouw, St Pieterspoortsteeg 29. Dark, noisy bar with a wildly eclectic crowd. Near the Allard Pierson Museum.

Cul de Sac, Oudezijds Achterburgwal 99. Down a long alley in what used to be a seventeenth-century spice warehouse, this is a handy retreat from the Red Light District. Small, quiet and friendly.

Dantzig, Zwanenburgwal 15. Easy-going grand café, right on the water just to the west of Waterlooplein, with comfortable chairs, friendly service and a low-key, chic atmosphere. Food served at lunchtime and in the evenings.

De Drie Fleschjes, Gravenstraat 16. Tasting house for spirits and liqueurs, which would originally have been made on the premises. No beer, and no seats either; its clients tend to be well heeled or well soused (often both). Behind the Nieuwe Kerk. Closes 8pm.

Droesem, Nes 41. On a thin, theatre-packed alley behind the Dam, this is a highly recommended wine-bar, with your selection arriving in a carafe filled from a barrel, along with a high-quality choice of cheeses and other titbits to help it on its way.

De Engelbewaarder, Kloveniersburgwal 59. Once the meeting place of Amsterdam's bookish types, this is still known as a literary café. Relaxed and informal, it has live jazz on Sunday afternoons.

Frascati, Nes 59, east of Rokin. Theatre bar, elegantly brown with mirrors and a pink marble bar, popular with a young, media-type crowd. Good, too, for both lunchtime and informal evening eating, with full meals for around *f*20, snacks and soups for less. Recommended.

Gaeper, Staalstraat 4. Convivial brown café packed during the school year with students from the university across the canal. Good food and outside seating. Just west of Waterlooplein.

't Gasthuis, Grimburgwal 7, west of Waterlooplein. Another brown café popular with students. Both this place and *Gaeper* are run by brothers, so it's in more or less the same style.

De Hoogte, Nieuwe Hoogstraat 2a. Small alternative bar on the edge of the Red Light District, just south of the Nieuwmarkt. Good music, engaging atmosphere, and beers a little cheaper than usual.

Hoppe, Spui 18. One of Amsterdam's longest-established and best-known bars, and one of its most likeable, frequented by the city's dark-suited office crowd on their wayward way home. Summer is especially good, when throngs of drinkers spill out on to the street.

De Jaren, Nieuwe Doelenstraat 20. One of the grandest of the grand cafés: overlooking the Amstel next to the university, with three floors and two terraces, this place oozes elegance. All kinds of English reading material, too – this is one of the best places to nurse the Sunday paper. Also serves reasonably priced food and has a great salad bar. A short walk west of Waterlooplein. Daily from 10am.

Vrankrijk, Spuistraat 216. The best and most central of Amsterdam's few remaining squat bars. Cheap drinks, hardcore noise, and almost as many dogs-on-strings as people. Buzz to enter – from 10pm onwards.

West of the Old Centre

Aas van Bokalen, Keizersgracht 335, at Huidenstraat. Unpretentious local bar with good food. Great collection of Motown tapes. Very small, so go either early or late.

De Admiraal, Herengracht 319, at Wolvenstraat. Large and uniquely comfortable *proef-lokaal*, with a vast range of liqueurs and spirits to explore.

De Beiaard, Herengracht 90, south of Herenstraat. Light and airy 1950s-style bar for genuine beer aficionados. There's a wide selection of bottled and draught beers, selected with true dedication by the owner, who delights in filling you in on the relative properties of each.

Belhamel, Brouwersgracht 60. Kitschy bar/restaurant with an Art Nouveau-style interior and excellent, though costly, French food. The main attraction in summer is one of the most picturesque views in Amsterdam.

Hegeraad, Noordermarkt 34. Lovingly maintained old-fashioned brown café with a fiercely loyal clientele. The back room, furnished with red plush and paintings, is the perfect place to relax with a hot chocolate.

Kalkhoven, Prinsengracht 283, at Raadhuisstraat. One of the city's most characteristic brown cafés. Nothing out of the ordinary, but warm and welcoming.

Het Molenpad, Prinsengracht 653, just north of Leidsegracht. This is one of the most appealing brown cafés in the city: long, dark and dusty. Also serves remarkably good food. Fills up with a young, professional crowd after 6pm. Recommended.

De Prins, Prinsengracht 124, at Leliegracht. Boisterous student bar, with a wide range of drinks and a well-priced menu. A great place to drink in a nice part of town. Food served from 10am to 10pm.

Sjaalman, Prinsengracht 178, just north of Raadhuisstraat. Small bar with a pool table and Thai food. Good in the summer when the church tower is lit up.

't Smackzeyl, Brouwersgracht 101. Uninhibited drinking hole on the fringes of the Jordaan (corner of Prinsengracht). One of the few brown cafés to have Guinness on tap; also an inexpensive menu of light dishes.

Spanjer & van Twist, Leliegracht 60. A gentle place, which comes into its own on summer afternoons, with chairs lining the most peaceful stretch of water in the city centre.

De Twee Zwaantjes, Prinsengracht 114, just north of Leliegracht. Tiny Jordaan bar whose live accordion music and raucous singing to either love or hate. Oompah-pah all the way.

South of the Old Centre

Café Americain, *American Hotel*, Leidseplein 28. The terrace bar here was the gathering place for Amsterdam media people for years, and it's worth coming at least once, if only for the decor: Art Nouveau frills coordinated down to the doorknobs. A place to be seen, with prices not surprisingly above average. Good fast lunches, though.

De Duivel, Reguliersdwarsstraat 87. Tucked away on a street of bars and coffeeshops near Rembrandtplein, this is the only hip-hop café in Amsterdam, with continuous beats and a clientele to match. Opposite the hip-hop coffeeshop *Free I*.

Het Land van Walem, Keizersgracht 449, just north of Leidsestraat. One of Amsterdam's nouveau-chic cafés: cool, light, and vehemently un-brown. The clientele is stylish, and the food is a kind of hybrid French–Dutch; there's also a wide selection of newspapers and magazines, including some in English. Breakfast in the garden during the summer is a highlight. Usually packed.

Huyschkaemer, Utrechtsestraat 137. Attractive small local bar-restaurant on a street renowned for its eateries, just south of Rembrandtplein. A favourite watering-hole of arty students. At weekends the restaurant space is turned into a dance floor.

Café Klein Wiener Wad, Utrechtsestraat 135. Small, self-consciously modern café; trendy and unavoidably intimate. South of Rembrandtplein.

De Koe, Marnixstraat 381. A fine, popular café amidst the many in this area, and, being slightly further out from the Leidseplein, one of the less busy options, too.

Mulligan's, Amstel 100, near Rembrandtplein. By far the best Irish pub in the city, with an authentic atmosphere, superb Gaelic music and good service.

Oosterling, Utrechtsestraat 140. Stone-floored local bar-cum-off-licence that's been in the same family since the middle of the last century. Very quiet – home to some serious drinkers. South of Rembrandtplein.

Café Schiller, Rembrandtplein 26. Art Deco bar of the upstairs hotel, authentic in both feel and decor, and offering a genteel escape from the tackiness of Rembrandtplein.

Vive la Vie, Amstelstraat 7, near Rembrandtplein. Small, campy bar, patronized mostly, but not exclusively, by women and transvestites.

Café de Wetering, Weteringstraat 37. Tucked away out of sight off the Spiegelgracht, this is a wonderfully atmospheric local brown café, complete with wood beams, sleeping cat and, during the winter, an open fire.

De Zotte Proeflokaal, Raamstraat 29, just north of Leidseplein. Belgian hangout – food, liqueurs and hundreds of different types of beer.

Coffeeshops

In Amsterdam a **"coffeeshop"** is advertising just one thing – **cannabis**. You might also be able to get coffee and cake, but the main activity in a coffeeshop is smoking. There are almost as many different kinds of coffeeshop as there are bar: some are neon-lit, with loud music and day-glo decor, but there are plenty of others that are quiet, comfortable places to take it easy.

The first thing you should know about the city's coffeeshops is that locals use them too; the second thing is that they only use ones outside the Red Light District. Practically all the coffeeshops you'll run into in the centre are worth avoiding, either for their decor, their deals or their clientele. Plasticky, neon-lit dives abound, pumping out mainstream varieties of house, rock or reggae at ear-splitting level; the dope on offer is usually limited and of poor quality – and, since they're mostly serving tourists, they can rig the deals without fear of comeback. A short time exploring the city will turn up plenty of more congenial, high-quality outlets for buying and enjoying cannabis, light years away from the tack of the city centre.

When you first walk into a coffeeshop, how you **buy the stuff** isn't immediately apparent – it's illegal to advertise cannabis in any way, which includes calling attention to the fact that it's available at all. What you have to do is ask to see the **menu**, which is normally kept behind the counter. This will list all the different hashes and grasses on offer, along with (if it's a reputable place) exactly how many grammes you get for your money. **Hash** you may come across originates in various countries and is pretty self-explanatory, apart from *Pollem*, which is compressed resin and stronger than normal. **Marijuana** is a different story, and the old days of imported Colombian, Thai and sensimelia are fading away; taking their place are limitless varieties of Nederwiet, Dutch-grown under UV lights and more potent than anything you're likely to have come across. Skunk, Haze and Northern Lights are all popular types of Dutch weed, and should be treated with caution – a smoker of low-grade British draw will be laid low (or high) for hours by a single spliff of Skunk. You would be equally well advised to take care with **space-cakes** (see p.81), which tend to have a delayed reaction (up to two hours before you notice anything strange – don't get impatient and gobble down another one!) and, once they kick in, they can bring on an extremely intense, bewildering high – 10–12 hours is common. Some large coffeeshops, such as the Bulldog, refuse to sell them, and advise you against buying elsewhere.

The coffeeshops we list are better than average; most of them open around 10am or 11am and close around midnight.

Borderline, Amstelstraat 37, off Rembrandtplein. Opposite the *iT* club (see p.127), with gently bouncing house beats. Open until 2.30am Fri & Sat.

The Bulldog, Leidseplein 15; Korte Leidsedwarsstraat 49. The biggest and most famous of the coffeeshop chains, and a long way from its pokey Red Light District dive origins. The main Leidseplein branch (the Palace), housed in a former police station, has a large cocktail bar, coffeeshop, juice bar and souvenir shop, all with separate entrances. It's big and brash, not at all the place for a quiet smoke, though the dope they sell (packaged up in neat little brand-labelled bags) is reliably good.

Dampkring, Handboogstraat 29 off Spui. Colourful coffeeshop with loud music and laid-back atmosphere, known for its good-quality hash.

Global Chillage, Kerkstraat 51, just south of Leidsestraat. Celebrated slice of Amsterdam dope culture, always comfortably filled with tie-dyed stone-heads propped up against the walls, so chilled they're horizontal.

Grey Area, Oude Leliestraat 2, north of Raadhuisstraat. High-class coffeeshop with menu (and prices) to match.

Homegrown Fantasy, Nieuwezijds Voorburgwal 87a. Attached to the Dutch Passion seed company, this sells the widest selection of marijuana in Amsterdam, most of it local.

Kadinsky, Rosmarijnsteeg 9, north of Spui. Strictly accurate deals weighed out to a background of jazz dance. Chocolate chip cookies to die for.

't Kruydenhuysje, Keizersgracht 665. One of the best general coffeeshops in the city – in an old canal house on a quiet stretch of the Keizersgracht near Rembrandtplein, with a welcoming atmosphere, good dope and a wonderful little terrace. Highly recommended.

The Otherside, Reguliersdwarsstraat 6, near Rembrandtplein. Gay coffeeshop, (in Dutch, "from the other side" is a euphemism for gay). Despite stiff competition from its more established neighbours, it's managed to find a niche. Mostly men, but women welcome.

Paradox, 1e Bloemdwarsstraat 2. If you're fed up with the usual coffeeshop food offerings of burgers, cheeseburgers or double cheeseburgers, *Paradox* satisfies the munchies with outstanding natural food, including spectacular fresh fruit concoctions. In the Jordaan. Closes 8pm.

Pie in the Sky, 2e Laurierdwarsstraat 64. Beautiful canal-corner setting in the Jordaan, great for outside summer lounging.

Rusland, Rusland 16, west of Waterlooplein. One of the first Amsterdam coffeeshops, a cramped but vibrant place that's a favourite with both dope fans and tea addicts (it has 43 different kinds). A cut above the rest.

Siberië, Brouwersgracht 11. Set up by the former staff of *Rusland* and notable for the way it's avoided the over-commercialization of the larger chains. Very relaxed, very friendly, and worth a visit whether you want to smoke or not.

Entertainment and nightlife

The quality of music, theatre and film on offer in Amsterdam is high and benefits from substantial government subsidies. Classical music is a particular forte – the city possesses two excellent orchestras – and although the rock-pop scene is not a patch on, say, New York or London, Amsterdam's unusually youthful population ensures that you're almost bound to stumble across fringe events and an inventive variety of affordable entertainment. Good venues to start are the major multimedia centres, which offer a taste of everything (see box below).

Information and Tickets

For information about **what's on**, a good place to start is the **Amsterdam Uitburo**, or **AUB**, the cultural office of the city council, which is housed in a corner of the Stadsschouwburg theatre on Leidseplein (daily 10am–6pm, Thurs until 9pm; ☎0900/0191). They offer advice on anything remotely cultural, sell tickets and have **listings magazines**, though the best you'll do is either the AUB's own monthly *Uitkrant*, which is comprehensive and free, but in Dutch, or the VVV's bland and uncontroversial English-language *What's On In Amsterdam* (*f*4). Take a look, too, at the AUB's *Uitlijst* noticeboards, which include a weekly update on pop music events, or grab a copy of the *Camel uitlijst* from any café for the latest

---

MULTIMEDIA CENTRES

Three major venues in Amsterdam offer a vast range of entertainment, covering all bases. If you're unsure where to start your foray into **night-time Amsterdam**, check out the following.

Arena, 's-Gravensandestraat 51 (☎694 7444, *www.hotelarena.nl*) Part of the major reorganization of what used to be the *Sleep-In* hostel, the Arena is a multimedia centre featuring live music and cultural events, with a bar, coffeeshop and restaurant. Awkwardly located out to the east of the centre (trams #6 and #10), the Arena's intimate hall tends to feature underground bands from around the world. Start time around 9.30pm.

Melkweg ("Milky Way"), Lijnbaansgracht 234a (☎624 1777, *www.melkweg.nl*) Probably Amsterdam's most famous entertainment venue, and these days one of the city's prime arts centres, with a young, hip clientele. A former dairy (hence the name) just round the corner from Leidseplein, it has two separate halls for live music, putting on a broad range of bands covering everything from reggae to rock, all of which lean towards the "alternative". Late on Friday and Saturday nights, excellent offbeat disco sessions go on well into the small hours, sometimes featuring the best DJs in town. As well as the gigs, there's also a fine monthly film programme, a theatre, gallery, and bar and restaurant (Marnixstraat entrance) open Wed–Sun 2–9pm (dinner from 5.30pm). Concerts start between 9pm and 11pm.

Paradiso, Weteringschans 6–8 (☎626 4521, *www.paradiso.nl*). A converted church near the Leidseplein, with bags of atmosphere, featuring bands ranging from the up-and-coming to the Rolling Stones. It has been known to host classical concerts, as well as debates and multimedia events (often in conjunction with the nearby Balie centre). Bands usually get started around 9pm.

live music gigs. Also in Dutch is the newspaper *Het Parool*'s Wednesday entertainment supplement, *Uit en Thuis*. In addition, any cinema can provide the long,
thin, fold-out "Week Agenda", which gives details of all films showing in the city
that week (Thursday to Wednesday). The English magazine *Time Out* has a
weekly updated entertainment pages on the net at *www.timeout.nl*.

Tickets for most performances can be bought at the Uitburo (for a *f*3 fee) and
VVV offices, or reserved by phone through the AUB Uitlijn (☎0900/0191) for a
one-percent booking fee. You can also buy tickets for any live music event in the
country at the GWK bureau de change offices at the Leidseplein and the post
office at Singel 250, again for around a one-percent fee. Obviously the cheapest
way to obtain tickets is to ask at the venue itself. If you're under 26, the AUB is
the place to go for a **Cultureel Jongeren Passport (CJP)**, which costs *f*22,50
and gets you reductions on entry to theatres, concerts and *filmhuizen*. Generally
the only people eligible for **discounts** at cultural events are students, over-65s
(though most places will only take Dutch ID) and CJP card-holders.

Rock music

As far as live music goes, Amsterdam is a regular tour stop for many major artists,
and something of a testing ground for current rock bands. Until recently, **Dutch
rock** was almost uniformly dire, but Dutch groups nowadays can lay claim to both
quality and originality. Look out for the celebrated Urban Dance Squad, the
Osdorp Posse and other members of the dance/hip-hop scene, or try to catch
rock bands like Bettie Serveert. Mathilde Santing is a popular draw whenever she
plays. Bear in mind, too, that Amsterdam is often on the tour circuit of up-and-
coming British bands – keep a sharp eye on the listings.

With the construction of the brand-new 50,000-seat ArenA out in the southeastern suburbs of the city, Amsterdam has finally gained the stadium **rock
venue** it has craved for years. However, the ArenA is taking some time to catch
on, and, aside from the Tina Turner/Michael Jackson brand of superstar, most
major touring acts still choose to play at Rotterdam's Ahoy sports hall. The
three dedicated music venues in Amsterdam city centre – the **Paradiso**, the
Melkweg and the **Arena** (not to be confused with the ArenA) – are all much
smaller, and supply a constantly changing seven-days-a-week programme of
music to suit all tastes and budgets – see box on p.119 for details. Alongside the
main venues, the city's clubs, bars and multimedia centres sporadically host
performances by live bands. As far as **prices** go, for big names you'll pay anything between *f*40 and *f*60 a ticket; ordinary gigs cost *f*10–25, although some
places charge a membership (*lidmaatschap*) fee on top. If no price is listed,
entrance is usually free.

Smaller venues

De Buurvrouw, Pieterspoortsteeg 29, east of the Dam (☎625 9654). Eclectic alternative bar
featuring loud local bands.

Cruise Inn, Zeeburgerdijk 271, northeast of the Tropenmuseum (☎692 7188). Off the beat-
en track, but with great music from the 1950s and 1960s. Saturday is R&B night.

Last Waterhole, Oudezijds Armsteeg 12 (☎624 4814). In the depths of the Red Light
District, just north of the Oude Kerk, this is the favoured spot for Amsterdam's biker set.
However, the Dutch variety lacks bark as well as bite, and travellers from the hostel upstairs
are welcome at the pool tables or to join the jam sessions onstage.

Maloe Melo, Lijnbaansgracht 163 (☎420 4592). A dark, low-ceilinged bar, with a small back room featuring local bluesy acts.

Meander Café, Voetboogstraat 5, south of Spui (☎625 8430). Daily live music of the soul, funk and blues variety.

OCCII, Amstelveenseweg 134 (☎671 7778). Cosy former squat bar at the far end of the Vondelpark, with occasional live alternative music.

Winston Kingdom, Warmoesstraat 123 (☎623 1380). Adventurous small venue, next to the hotel, featuring everything from live Ghanean percussion and symphonic rock to R&B, punk/noise and club nights. Poetry night once a month on Monday.

Folk and World Music

The Dutch **folk music** tradition in Amsterdam is virtually extinct, although interest has been revived of late by the duo Acda and de Munnik, and there are still one or two touring folk singers who perform traditional Jordaan *smartlappen* (torchsongs) at the Carré theatre. More accessible is **world music**, for which there are a couple of good venues: the Utrecht-based Network for Non-Western Music (☎030/231 9676) is an organization that regularly brings world music performers to Amsterdam, to play at the Tropenmuseum theatre; and music from around the world is also a regular feature of the Melkweg's programme.

Venues

Akhnaton, Nieuwezijds Kolk 25, off Nieuwendijk (☎624 3396). A "Centre for World Culture", specializing in African and Latin American music and dance parties. On a good night, the place heaves with people.

Mulligans, Amstel 100, near Rembrandtplein (☎622 1330). Irish bar head and shoulders above the rest for atmosphere and authenticity, with Gaelic musicians and storytellers most nights for free.

Tropen Instituut Theater, Linnaeusstraat 2 (☎568 8500, *www.kit.nl/theater*). Part of the Tropical Institute, this formal theatre specializes in the drama, dance, film and music of the developing world.

Winston Kingdom, Warmoestraat 123 (☎623 1380). See listing above.

Jazz

For **jazz** fans, Amsterdam can be a treat. Since the 1940s and 1950s, when American jazz musicians began moving to Europe to escape discrimination back home, the city has had a soft spot for jazz. There's an excellent range of jazz venues for such a small city, varying from tiny bars staging everything from Dixieland to avant-garde, to the Bimhuis – the city's major jazz venue – which plays host to both international names and homegrown talent. Saxophonists Hans Dulfer, Willem Breuker and Theo Loevendie, and percussionist Martin van Duynhoven, are among the **Dutch musicians** you might come across – and they're well worth catching if you get the chance. If your Dutch is up to it, you can get **information** on jazz events all over Holland by phoning the Jazzline on ☎626 7764.

Venues

Café Alto, Korte Leidsedwarsstraat 115 (☎626 3249). It's worth hunting out this legendary little jazz bar just off Leidseplein for the quality modern jazz every night from 10pm until 3am (and often much later). It's big on atmosphere, though slightly cramped, but entry is free, and you don't have to buy a (pricey) beer to hang out and watch the band.

Bamboo Bar, Lange Leidsedwarsstraat 66, near Leidseplein (☎624 3993). Legend has it Chet Baker used to live upstairs and jam onstage to pay his rent. These days the *Bamboo* is an unpretentious, friendly bar with blues and jazz, plus occasional salsa nights. Free entry, but you need to buy a drink. Open from 9pm.

Bimhuis, Oude Schans 73–77 (☎623 1361). The city's premier jazz venue for almost thirty years, with an excellent auditorium and ultra-modern bar. Concerts Thurs–Sat, free sessions Mon–Wed. There's also free live music in the bar on Sun at 4pm. Concert tickets are for sale on the day only.

Bourbon Street, Leidsekruisstraat 6, near Leidseplein (☎623 3440). Friendly bar with a relaxed atmosphere and quality blues and jazz nightly until 3am.

De Engelbewaarder, Kloveniersburgwal 59 (☎625 3772). Excellent live jazz sessions on Sunday afternoon and evening.

IJsbreker, Weesperzijde 23, south of Mauritskade (☎693 9093). Principally a venue for contemporary music (see below), but with occasional avant-garde and free-jazz evenings.

Le Maxim, Leidsekruisstraat 35, near Leidseplein (☎624 1920). Intimate piano bar that's been going since the Sixties, with live music nightly.

Classical music, opera and contemporary music

There's no shortage of **classical music** concerts in Amsterdam, with two major orchestras based in the city, plus regular visits by other Dutch orchestras. Amsterdam's **Royal Concertgebouw Orchestra** remains one of the most dynamic in the world, and occupies one of the finest concert halls to boot. The other resident orchestra is the **Netherlands Philharmonic**, based at the Beurs van Berlage concert hall, which has a wide symphonic repertoire and also performs with the Netherlands Opera at the Muziektheater. As far as **smaller classical ensembles** go, Dutch musicians pioneered the use of period instruments in the 1970s, and Ton Koopman's Amsterdam Baroque Orchestra and Frans Brüggen's Orchestra of the 18th Century are two internationally renowned exponents. Koopman's Amsterdam Baroque Choir and the Amsterdam Bach Soloists are also pre-eminent. As well as the main concert halls, a number of Amsterdam's churches (and former churches) host regular performances of classical and chamber music; both types of venue are listed below.

The most prestigious venue for **opera** is the Muziektheater (otherwise known as the Stopera) on Waterlooplein, which is home to the Netherlands Opera company – going from strength to strength under the guidance of Pierre Audi – as well as the National Ballet. Visiting companies sometimes perform here, but more often at the Stadsschouwburg and the Carré theatre.

As far as **contemporary music** goes, the IJsbreker centre on the Amstel is a leading showcase for musicians from all over the world. Local talent is headed by the Asko and Schoenberg Ensembles, as well as the Nieuw Ensemble and the Volharding Orchestra. Look out also for Willem Breuker and Maarten Altena, two popular musicians who successfully combine improvised jazz with composed new music.

The most prestigious multi-venue Dutch festival by far is the annual **Holland Festival** every June (info ☎530 7111), which attracts the best domestic mainstream and fringe performers in all areas of the arts, as well as an exciting international line-up. Otherwise, one of the more interesting music-oriented events is the **piano recital** held towards the end of August on a floating stage outside the *Pulitzer Hotel* on the Prinsengracht – with the whole area floodlit and filled with small boats, and every available spot on the banks and bridges taken up, this can be a wonderfully atmospheric evening. Also around this time, Amsterdam holds the **International Gaudeamus Music Week**, a forum for debate and première performance of cutting-edge contemporary music.

Venues

Beurs van Berlage, Damrak 213 (☎627 0466). The splendid interior of the former stock exchange (see p.74) has been put to use as a venue for theatre and music. The resident Netherlands Philharmonic and Netherlands Chamber Orchestra perform in the huge but comfortable Yakult Zaal and the AGA Zaal, the latter a very strange, glassed-in room-within-a-room.

Carré Theatre, Amstel 115–125, near Rembrandtplein (☎622 5225). A splendid hundred-year-old structure (originally built for a circus) which represents the ultimate venue for Dutch folk artists, and hosts all kinds of top international acts: anything from Russian folk dance to *La Cage aux Folles*, with reputable touring orchestras and opera companies squeezed in between.

Concertgebouw, Concertgebouwplein 2–6 (☎671 8345). After a facelift and the replacement of its crumbling foundations in the early 1990s, the Concertgebouw is now looking – and sounding – better than ever. The acoustics of the Grote Zaal (Large Hall) are unparalleled, and a concert here is a wonderful experience. The smaller Kleine Zaal regularly hosts chamber concerts, often by the resident Borodin Quartet. Though both halls boast a star-studded international programme, prices are on the whole very reasonable, rarely over *f*35, and *f*20 for Sunday morning events. Free Wednesday lunchtime concerts are held from Sept to May (doors open 12.15pm, arrive early), and in July and August there's a heavily subsidized series of summer concerts. Look out also for occasional swing/jazz nights.

Engelse Kerk, Begijnhof 48 (☎624 9665). The church with the biggest programme – three to four performances a week, lunchtime, afternoon and evening, with the emphasis on period instruments.

IJsbreker, Weesperzijde 23, south of Mauritskade (☎668 1805). Out of the town centre by the Amstel, with a delightful terrace on the water. Has a large, varied programme of international modern, chamber and experimental music, as well as featuring obscure, avant-garde local performers. Concerts are occasionally held in the Planetarium of the Artis Zoo.

Muziektheater, Waterlooplein (☎625 5455). Part of the *f*306 million complex that includes the city hall. The theatre's resident company, Netherlands Opera, offers the fullest, and most reasonably priced, programme of opera in Amsterdam. Tickets go very quickly. Look out for free lunchtime concerts Sept–May.

Oude Kerk, Oudekerksplein 23 (☎625 8284). Hosts organ and carillon recitals, as well as occasional choral events. In summer, in conjunction with the Amstelkring Museum, the church organizes a series of "walking" concert evenings, consisting of three separate concerts at different venues, with time for coffee and a stroll between each.

Stadsschouwburg, Leidseplein 26 (☎624 2311). These days somewhat overshadowed by the Muziektheater, but still staging significant opera and dance (it's the home theatre of The Hague's innovative company, the Netherlands Dance Theatre), as well as visiting English-language theatre companies.

Waalse Kerk, Oudezijds Achterburgwal 157 (Information from the Old Music Society on ☎030/236 2236). Weekend afternoon and evening concerts of early music and chamber music.

Dance

Of the major **dance companies** based in Amsterdam, the largest and most prestigious is the Muziektheater's National Ballet, under Wayne Eagling – though their critics say they lack verve and imagination. Also working regularly in Amsterdam are the noted Dutch choreographers Toer van Schayk and Rudi van Dantzig, while for **folk dance** fans the excellent Folkloristisch Danstheater is based in the city. However, a constant feature of dance in Holland is the prevalence of non-Dutch choreographers and dancers, and the work of William Forsyth, Lloyd Newson, Saburo Teshigawara and others is regularly on show. On a smaller scale, Amsterdam is particularly receptive to the latest trends in **modern dance**, and has many experimental dance groups, often incorporating other media into their productions. Look out for performances by the Dans Werkplaats Amsterdam and the extraordinary Cloud Chamber company.

Venues

Cosmic Theater, Nes 75, east of Rokin (☎622 8858). A modern dance and theatre company featuring young professionals with a multicultural background.

Folkloristisch Danstheater, Kloveniersburgwal 87 (☎623 9112). Original folk dance from around the world, with international choreographers brought in to work with the dancers.

Former Storkfabriek, Csaar Peterstraat 213, northeast of the Tropenmuseum (☎419 3088). Old factory featuring dance, mime and various theatre groups.

Muziektheater, Waterlooplein (☎625 5455). Home of the National Ballet, but with a third of its dance schedule given over to international companies.

Theatre and cabaret

Surprisingly for a city that functions so much in English, there is next to no **English-language theatre** to be seen in Amsterdam. The Stalhouderij is the only company working in English, performing in a broom-cupboard of a theatre in the Jordaan, though English-language touring companies do regularly visit. English-language **comedy** and **cabaret**, on the other hand, has become a big thing in Amsterdam, spearheaded by the resident and extremely successful Boom Chicago comedy company. During the summer in particular, a number of small venues host mini-seasons of English-language stand-up comedy and cabaret featuring touring British performers.

Venues

De Balie, Kleine Gartmanplantsoen 10 (☎623 2904). A multimedia centre for culture and the arts, located off the Leidseplein, which often plays host to drama, debates, international symposia and the like, sometimes in conjunction with the Paradiso (see p.119) next door.

Badhuis-Theater de Bochel, Andreas Bonnstraat 28 (☎668 5102). A former bath house out near the Oosterpark, this is now a low-profile forum for all kinds of visiting productions and guest directors.

Boom Chicago, Korte Leidsedwarsstraat 12, near Leidseplein (☎423 0101). Something of a phenomenon in Amsterdam in recent years, this rapid-fire improv comedy troupe performs nightly to crowds of both tourists and locals, and has received rave reviews. With inexpensive food and the cheapest beer in town (in pitchers, no less!), the comedy need not be funny – but it is.

Marionette Theatre, Nieuwe Jonkerstraat 8, near Centraal Station (☎620 8027). Continues an old European tradition with its performances of operas by Mozart and Offenbach. Although they're touring Holland and the rest of Europe for most of the year, the wooden marionettes return to Amsterdam around May, October and Christmas. Call for details of performances, and to find out about their opera dinners.

Melkweg, Lijnbaansgracht 234a, near Leidseplein (☎624 1777 after 1pm). At the centre of the city's cultural scene, this is often the first-choice venue for foreign touring companies.

Stadsschouwburg, Leidseplein 26 (☎624 2311). Often hosts productions on tour from London or New York.

Stalhouderij, Bloemgracht 57/1 (☎626 4088). Amsterdam's only non-subsidized English-language theatre company, mounting new productions every six weeks or so in one of the city's smallest, most intimate theatre spaces. Contemporary and modern works, Shakespeare, readings, classes and workshops.

Film

Most of Amsterdam's commercial **cinemas** are huge multiplexes showing a selection of general releases. There's also a scattering of film houses (*filmhuizen*) showing **revival and art films** and occasional retrospectives. Pick up a copy of the "**Week Agenda**" from any cinema for details of all films showing in the city. Weekly programmes change on Thursdays. Almost all foreign movies playing in Amsterdam are shown in their **original language** and subtitled in Dutch. Films are rarely dubbed in Dutch, but if they are, *Nederlands Gesproken* will be printed in the listings.

As a guide, **tickets** cost around *f*15 for an evening show on the weekend at mainstream cinemas, a few guilders less during the week. Prices at the *filmhuizen* are a bit lower still, and can drop to as little as *f*6 for a Sunday morning showing. Amsterdam's only regular cinematic event is the fascinating **International Documentary Film Festival** in December (info ☎627 3329).

Filmhuizen and arthouse cinemas

Cavia, Van Hallstraat 52 (☎681 1419). Incongruously sited above a martial arts centre, this is one of the best of the small *filmhuizen*, with an eclectic and non-commercial programme of international movies. West of the Jordaan. Tram #10.

Desmet, Plantage Middenlaan 4a (☎627 3434). *Filmhuis* on the border between mainstream and arthouse cinema, and still showing a lot of European films, which tend to have a long run in Amsterdam. Tram #7, #9, or #14.

Kriterion, Roetersstraat 170 (☎623 1708). Stylish duplex cinema close to Weesperplein metro. Shows arthouse and quality commercial films, with late-night cult favourites. Friendly bar attached. Tram #6, #7, #10.

Melkweg, Lijnbaansgracht 234a (☎624 1777 after 1pm). As well as music, art and dance, the Melkweg manages to maintain a consistently good monthly film and video programme, ranging from mainstream fodder through to obscure imports. Near Leidseplein.

The Movies, Haarlemmerdijk 161, near Browersgracht (☎624 5790). A beautiful Art Deco cinema, and a charming setting for independent films. Worth visiting for the bar and restaurant alone, fully restored to their original sumptuousness. Late shows at the weekend. Tram #3.

Rialto, Ceintuurbaan 338 (☎675 3994). The only fully authentic arthouse cinema in Amsterdam, showing an enormously varied programme of European and World movies, supplemented by themed series and classics. South of the centre in the De Pijp area. Tram #3, #24 or #25.

De Uitkijk, Prinsengracht 452, near Berenstraat (☎623 7460). The oldest cinema in the city (pronounced "out-kike"), in a converted canal house with no bar, no ice cream and no pop-corn – but low prices. Shows popular movies for months on end.

Clubs

Clubbing in Amsterdam is not the style-conscious business it is in many other capitals: most Amsterdam clubs – even the hip ones – aren't very expensive or dif-ficult to get into. As for the music itself, Amsterdam is not at the cutting edge of experimentation: **house** is definitely the thing backed up by hip-hop, modern and retro funk, jazz and underground trance and trip-hop, but unless you go looking for something special, a random dip into a club will probably turn up mellow, undemanding house beats.

That said, the late '90s saw a craze for pumped-up, 200bpm+ **"gabber"** (pro-nounced the Dutch way, with a throaty "kh" at the beginning), laid on at vast arenas for thousands of shaven-headed speed-freaks. If you can find a gabber event (check for flyers at Midtown Records, Nieuwendijk 104; ☎638 4252), expect to pay a hefty ƒ60 or more for entry, although it'll go on until dawn. Incidentally, there are now practically no illegal raves or parties in and around Amsterdam, and the last squat venues have finally made way for apartment buildings.

Most clubs have very reasonable **entry prices**, hovering between ƒ15 and ƒ20 at weekends and then dropping to between ƒ7,50 and ƒ10 during the week, some-times going as low as ƒ5, especially in the gay scene. A singular feature of Amsterdam clubbing however is that you tip the bouncer: if you want to get back into the same place next week, ƒ2 or ƒ5 in the palm of his hand will do very nice-ly thank you. Drinks prices are just slightly more expensive than in cafés at around ƒ4–5 but not excessively hiked up, and, as in the rest of the city, toilets cost money (25c or 50c). **Dress codes** are minimal or nonexistent, except where we've noted in the listings below.

For listings of gay clubs, see p.129.

Although all the places listed below **open** at either 10pm or 11pm, there's not much point turning up anywhere before midnight; unless stated otherwise, everywhere stays open until 5am on Friday and Saturday nights, 4am on other nights.

For **news** and flyers about clubs, upcoming parties and raves, drop in to places like Clubwear House, at Herengracht 265 (☎622 8766), and the Hair Police and Conscious Dreams, next door to each other at Kerkstraat 115 and 117. Alternatively, pick up the *Camel uitlijst* in any café, which gives a pretty definitive listing of live music venues and clubs.

Selected clubs

Club 114, Herengracht 114, north of Leliegracht (☎622 7685). One of the longest estab-lished club locations in Amsterdam, recently reborn and playing all kinds of non-housey music, from hip-hop to R&B, with heavy trance nights. Nightly; prices vary.

Escape, Rembrandtplein 11 (☎622 3542). What once used to be a tacky disco is now h.
to Amsterdam's hottest Saturday night, "Chemistry", every so often featuring Holland's tc
DJ, Dimitri. A vast hangar, with room for 2000 people (although you may still have to queue).
Closed Sun.

iT, Amstelstraat 24, near Rembrandtplein (☎625 0111). Large disco with a superb sound system, often featuring well-known live acts. Has popular and glamorous gay nights (see below),
but Thursday, Friday and Sunday are mixed gay/straight and attract a dressed up, uninhibited crowd.

Mazzo, Rozengracht 114 (☎626 7500). One of the city's hippest and most laid-back clubs, with
a choice of music to appeal to all tastes. Perhaps the easiest-going bouncers in town. Open
nightly.

Melkweg, Lijnbaansgracht 234a, near Leidseplein (☎624 1777 after 1pm). After the bands
have finished, this multimedia centre plays host to some of the most enjoyable theme nights
around, everything from African dance parties to experimental jazz-trance.

The Ministry, Reguliersdwarsstraat 12, near Rembrandtplein (☎623 3981). A new club trying to catch a wide brand of party people and featuring quality DJs. Speed garage, house and
R&B. Monday night jam session with the local jazz talent. Open late.

Paradiso, Weteringschans 6–8, near Leidseplein (☎623 7348). One of the principal venues in
the city, which on Fridays turns into the unmissable VIP (Vrijdag In Paradiso) Club, from
midnight onwards. Also hosts one-off events – check listings.

Soul Kitchen, Amstelstraat 32a, near Rembrandtplein (☎620 2333). Relaxed club that's
refreshingly oriented towards 1960s and 1970s soul and funk rather than the usual housey
stuff.

West Pacific, Westergasfabriek, Haarlemmerweg 8–10 (☎597 4458). After playing host to
many an acid rave in the late 1980s, this converted gas factory is now *the* up-and-coming location in the city. An on-site café with an open fireplace attracts a trendy crowd of young
Amsterdammers, who stay late to party. West of the Jordaan.

Gay Amsterdam

No other city in Europe accepts **gay people** quite as readily as Amsterdam. Here,
more than anywhere, it's possible to be openly gay and accepted by the straight
community. Furthermore, Amsterdam has become a magnet for the international gay scene and boasts a dense sprinkling of advice centres, bars and clubs. The
COC (pronounced "say-oh-say"), the national gay and lesbian pressure group, celebrated its fiftieth birthday in 1996 – one of the longest-lived, and largest, groups
of its kind in the world.

Amsterdam has four recognized **gay areas**: the most famous and lively centres
are on **Kerkstraat** and **Reguliersdwarsstraat**, with the latter having a more out-
going, international scene. The streets just north of **Rembrandtplein** are a camp
focus, as well as being home to several rent-boy bars, while **Warmoesstraat**, in
the Red Light District, is cruisy and mainly leather- and denim-oriented. Many
bars and clubs have **darkrooms**, which are legally obliged to provide safe-sex

condoms. The **clubs** listed below cater either predominantly or ... **gay** clientele. Some venues have both gay only and mixed ...ghts, as noted. **Lesbian**-only nights are on the increase and many ... nights for both men and women.

...more information than is listed below, get hold of a copy of the wide-...**Columbia Fun Map** of Amsterdam produced by the SAD-Schorer... ...ting (see below). You could also invest in a copy of the *Best Guide to Amsterdam*, a comprehensive gay **guidebook** (in English) available from most gay bookshops around the world. Among the many local gay newspapers and magazines, the fortnightly *Gay Krant* has all the details you could conceivably need, including up-to-the-minute listings, though it is in Dutch only; their Web site is at *www.gaykrant.nl*. There's also the **Gay and Lesbian Switchboard** (☎623 6565; daily 10am–10pm; *www.dds.nl/~glswitch*), an English-speaking service which provides help and advice, and **MVS Radio**, Amsterdam's gay and lesbian radio station (office ☎620 0247). This broadcasts daily from 6pm to 9pm on 106.8FM (or 103.8 via cable) – try and catch the English-language talk show *Aliens*, on Sunday.

Advice centres and bookshops

American Book Centre, Kalverstraat 185 (☎625 5537). Large general bookstore, with a fine gay and lesbian section.

COC, Rozenstraat 14; office ☎626 3087 (Mon–Fri 9am–5pm), information ☎623 4079 (till 10pm). Amsterdam branch of the national gay and lesbian organization, offering advice, contacts and social activities (including an English-speaking group; info ☎420 3068), plus a coffeeshop (Mon–Sat 1–5pm) and a large noticeboard. The general COC café (Wed 8pm–midnight, Fri 10pm–3am) is also the venue for more specific "themed" nights: an HIV café (Thurs 8pm–midnight), a youth café (Wed 8pm–midnight) and multicultural night (Sun 8pm–midnight). One of the most popular women-only nights in Amsterdam is held regularly on Saturday in both the café (10pm–3am) and the nightclub (10pm–3am).

Intermale, Spuistraat 251 (☎625 0009). Well-stocked gay bookshop, with a wide selection of English, French, German and Dutch literature, as well as cards, newspapers and magazines. They have a worldwide mail order service.

SAD Schorerstichting, P.C. Hooftstraat 5 (☎662 4206, *info@sadschorer.nl*; Mon–Fri 9am–5.30pm). Gay and lesbian counselling centre near the Rijksmuseum, offering professional and politically conscious advice on identity, sexuality and lifestyle.

Vrolijk, Paleisstraat 135, off the Dam (☎623 5142, *www.xs4all.nl/~vrolijk*). "The largest gay and lesbian bookstore on the continent", with a vast stock of new and secondhand books and magazines, as well as music and videos.

Hotels

For details of the accommodation **price codes** used below see p.64. All the hotels listed are marked on the map on pp.66–67.

Golden Bear, Kerkstraat 37 (☎624 4785, fax 627 0164, *www.goldenbear.nl*). Tram #1, #2 or #5 to Prinsengracht. Solid budget option, recently given a modern-style makeover, with a good range of clean, comfortable rooms, some en suite. ②.

Greenwich Village, Kerkstraat 25 (☎626 9746, fax 625 4081). Tram #1, #2 or #5 to Prinsengracht. A well-kept, if slightly down-at-heel hotel surrounded by gay bars and clubs on Amsterdam's main gay street. Rooms sleeping from one to six people, all ƒ75 per person. Helpful and friendly staff. ②.

ITC (International Travel Club), Prinsengracht 1051 (☎623 0230, fax 624 5846, *office@itc-hotel.com*). Tram #4 to Prinsengracht. A little way away from the major gay areas, close to the Amstelveld on a tranquil section of canal, and perhaps the least expensive gay hotel of this quality. Off-season discounts. ③.

New York, Herengracht 13 (☎624 3066, fax 620 3230). Five minutes' from Centraal Station. Recently renovated, this is a popular, two-star, exclusively gay hotel, consisting of three modernized seventeenth-century houses. High standards throughout, with a good Dutch breakfast. No lift. ④.

Orfeo, Leidsekruisstraat 14 (☎623 1347, no fax). Tram #1, #2 or #5 to Prinsengracht. Very pleasant hotel round the back of Leidseplein, with a small Finnish sauna for guests and decent breakfasts served until midday. ②–③.

Waterfront, Singel 458 (☎623 9775, fax 620 7491). Tram #1, #2 or #5 to Koningsplein. Smart value-for-money hotel on a major canal, close to the shopping and nightlife, with decent rooms and service. ③.

Sander, Jacob Obrechtstraat 69 (☎662 7574, fax 679 6067, *htlsandr@xs4all.nl*). Tram #16 from Centraal Station to Jacob Obrechtstraat. Right behind the Concertgebouw, a spacious, pleasant hotel, especially welcoming to gay men and women – though heteros are welcome too. ④.

Bars

Amstel Taveerne, Amstel 54, near Rembrandtplein. Well-established, traditional gay bar with regular singalongs. Always packed, and at its most vivacious in summer when the crowds spill out onto the street.

April, Reguliersdwarsstraat 37, off Rembrandtplein. On the itinerary of almost every gay visitor to Amsterdam. Lively and cosmopolitan, with a good selection of foreign newspapers, cakes and coffee, as well as booze.

Camp Café, Kerkstraat 45, south of Leidsestraat. Pleasant mix of friendly regulars and foreign visitors. Worth a visit for the ceiling alone, which is covered with a collection of beer mugs from around the world.

Downtown, Reguliersdwarsstraat 31, off Rembrandtplein. A favourite with visitors. Relaxed and friendly, with inexpensive meals.

Fellows, Amstel 50, near Rembrandtplein. Civilized and immaculately clean bar on the river. An ideal location in summer.

Gaiety, Amstel 14, near Rembrandtplein. Small gay bar with a warm welcome. One of the most popular young gay haunts in Amsterdam.

Havana, Reguliersdwarsstraat 17, off Rembrandtplein. Stylish and would-be sophisticated hangout patronized by those who like to be seen out on the town.

Mankind, Weteringstraat 60, southeast of Leidseplein. Quiet, non-scene bar with its own terrace and landing stage. Lovely in summer.

Shako's, 's Gravelandseveer 2, near Rembrandtplein. Friendly, studentish bar in a quiet street on the Amstel.

De Steeg, Halvemaansteeg 10, off Rembrandtplein. Camp and often outrageous small bar. Can be packed at peak times, when everyone joins in the singalongs.

Clubs

COC, Rozenstraat 14 (☎626 3087). Very popular women-only disco and café in the Jordaan every Sat from 8pm called "Just Girlsz", popular with younger lesbians. Pumping on Friday nights too (mixed men/women).

Cockring, Warmoesstraat 96 (☎623 9604). Currently Amsterdam's most popular – and very cruisey – gay men's disco. Light show and bars on two levels. Get there early at the weekend to avoid queuing. Nightly; free.

Exit, Reguliersdwarsstraat 42, off Rembrandtplein (☎625 8788). Along with *iT* (see below), the city's most popular gay club. Current sounds play nightly to an upbeat, cruisey crowd. Predominantly male, though women are admitted. Free.

Getto Girls, Warmoestraat 51 (☎421 5151). Women-only night on Tuesdays at the *Getto* with plenty of music, plus a bar serving vegetarian food and cocktails. Transforms into a dance club later on in the evening.

Havana, Reguliersdwarsstraat 17, off Rembrandtplein (☎620 6788). Small dance floor above a bar slap in the middle of a buzzing gay area. Very popular with a mixed clientele (gay, yuppie, art crowd); mostly men, but women admitted. Also perhaps the only place in town to cater for people who want to dance but still get up for work the next day. Mon–Thurs & Sun 11pm–1am, Fri & Sat 11pm–2am; free.

De Huyschkaemer, Utrechtsestraat 137, south of Rembrandtplein (☎627 0575). More like a local café shifting its dinner tables at night to make space for a dance floor, but a fun night all the same, run by a gay man and attracting a somewhat serious, but nevertheless cheerful clientele. Not exclusively gay.

iT, Amstelstraat 24, near Rembrandtplein (☎625 0111). Saturday night here really is IT, as the city's most glamorous transvestites come out to play and the place gets packed out (men only). Thursday night is free if you're gay, and Sunday is a popular gay/straight night.

Liplickers Club, at *Sinners in Heaven*, Wagenstraat 3, near Rembrandtplein (☎620 1375). Female-only dance night every first Sunday of the month, with changing themes and music.

You II, Amstel 178, near Rembrandtplein (☎421 0900). Amsterdam's first and long awaited official lesbian dance club, which opened its doors in the summer of 1999. Men are in fact welcome, as long as they're accompanied by a woman.

Vive la Vie, Amstelstraat 7, near Rembrandtplein (☎624 0114). Café mainly for women, which shifts its tables at the weekend to make room for a dance space.

Shopping

Where Amsterdam scores in the shopping stakes is in some excellent, unusual **speciality shops** (beads, clogs and condoms, to name just three), a handful of great **street-markets** and its shopping convenience – the city centre concentrates most of what's interesting within its tight borders. What's more, the majority of shops are still individual businesses rather than chains, which makes a refreshing change from most big cities.

Shopping in Amsterdam can be divided roughly by area. Broadly, the **Nieuwendijk/Kalverstraat** strip is where you'll find mostly dull, high-street fashion and mainstream department stores. Here too, just off Dam square, is **Magna Plaza**, a massive shopping mall spread over five floors and complete with a Virgin Megastore, espresso bars and teenagers joy-riding on the escalators. Elsewhere, **Koningsplein** and **Leidsestraat** used to be home to the most exclusive shops, but many of them have fled south, though there is still a surprisingly good selection of affordable designer shoe and clothes stores. The **Jordaan** is where many local artists ply their wares; you can find individual items of genuine interest here, as well as more specialized, adventurous clothes shops and some affordable antiques. Less affordable antiques – the cream of Amsterdam's renowned trade – can be found in the Spiegelkwartier, centred on **Nieuwe Spiegelstraat**, while to the south, **P.C. Hooftstraat** and **Van Baerlestraat** play host to designer clothiers, upmarket ceramics stores, confectioners and delicatessens.

As for **opening hours**, the majority of shops take Monday morning off, not opening up until noon or 1pm and closing again at 6pm. On Tuesday, Wednesday and Friday, hours are the standard 9am to 6pm, while Thursday is late-opening night (*koopavond*), with most places staying open from 9am until 9pm. Saturday hours are normally 8.30 or 9am to 5 or 5.30pm, and all except the larger shops on the main streets are closed on Sunday.

Most small and medium-sized shops – and even some of the larger ones – won't accept **payment** by credit card: don't take it for granted in anywhere but the biggest or most expensive places. Shops that do will accept the usual range of major cards (American Express, Visa, Mastercard, etc.), but never travellers' cheques. Practically everywhere, however, takes Eurocheques, with the appropriate card as guarantee.

Books and magazines

Virtually all Amsterdam bookshops stock at least a small selection of **English-language books**, though prices are always inflated (sometimes dramatically). In the city centre it's possible to pick up most English **newspapers** the day they come out, and English-language **magazines** are available, too, from both newsstands and bookshops. The **secondhand** and **antiquarian** booksellers listed below are only the most accessible; for a comprehensive list, pick up from any of them the leaflet *Antiquarian & Secondhand Bookshops of Amsterdam*.

General bookstores

American Book Center, Kalverstraat 185 (☎625 5537). Vast stock, all in English, with lots of imported US magazines and books. Especially good gay section. Students get ten percent discount.

Athenaeum, Spui 14 (☎623 3933). Excellent all-round bookshop with an adventurous stock. Also the best source of international newspapers and magazines.

The English Bookshop, Lauriergracht 71 (☎626 4230). A small but quirky collection of titles, many of which you won't find elsewhere. In the Jordaan.

Milieuboek, Plantage Middenlaan 2H (☎624 4989). Right next to the Hortus Botanicus, and specializing in books on green and environmental issues.

Scheltema Holkema Vermeulen, Koningsplein 20, just south of Spui (☎523 1411). Amsterdam's biggest and best bookshop. Six floors of absolutely everything. Open late and on Sundays.

Stadsboekwinkel, Waterlooplein 18 (☎622 4537). The shop for all books on Amsterdam: architecture, transport, history, urban planning, geography, etc.

Waterstone's, Kalverstraat 152 (☎638 3821). Dutch branch of the UK high-street chain, with four floors of books and magazines. A predictable selection, but prices are sometimes cheaper here than elsewhere.

Zwart op Wit, Utrechtsestraat 149, south of Rembrandtplein (☎622 8174). Small but well-stocked store. Open on Sunday afternoons and until 7pm during the week.

Secondhand and antiquarian

Book Traffic, Leliegracht 50 (☎620 4690). An excellent and well-organized selection, run by an American.

Brinkman, Singel 319, near Spui (☎623 8353). Stalwart of the Amsterdam book trade, Brinkman has occupied the same premises for forty years. Worldwide mail order service.

Egidius, Haarlemmerstraat 87, near Brouwersgracht (☎624 3255). A good selection of literature, art, poetry, plus a gallery selling lithographs.

De Kloof, Kloveniersburgwal 44 (☎622 3828). Enormous higgledy-piggledy used bookshop on four floors. Great for a rummage.

Vrouwen In Druk, Westermarkt 5 (☎624 5003). Secondhand books, all by women authors.

Specialist bookstores

Art Book, Van Baerlestraat 126 (☎644 0925). The city's best source of high-gloss art books, situated near the Van Gogh Museum. Check out also the shops of the main museums, particularly the Stedelijk.

Boekie Woekie, Berenstraat 16 (☎639 0507). Books by and on Dutch artists and graphic designers.

Lambiek, Kerkstraat 78, near Leidsestraat (☎626 7543). Amsterdam's largest and oldest comic bookshop and gallery, with an international stock.

Jacob van Wijngaarden, Overtoom 97 (☎612 1901). The city's best travel bookshop, with knowledgeable staff and a huge selection of books and maps. West across the Singelgracht from Leidseplein

Pegasus, Singel 367, near Spui (☎623 1138). The best politics collection in the city.

Scheltema Holkema Vermeulen, Koningsplein 20, south of Spui (☎523 1411). A multi-storey general bookshop with a comprehensive travel section, including hiking maps for Holland and beyond, mostly in English.

Clothes

When it comes to **clothes**, good-value, if uninspiring, mainstream styles are to be found amongst the shops and stores of Kalverstraat and Nieuwendijk. Classier stuff is on sale along Rokin and Leidsestraat, and the really top-range designer shops are clustered in the south of the city on P.C. Hooftstraat and Van Baerlestraat. More interestingly, a reasonable range of one-off youth-oriented and **secondhand clothing** shops are dotted around the Jordaan, on Oude and Nieuwe Hoogstraat, and along the narrow streets that connect the major canals west of the Old Centre. In addition, the Waterlooplein flea market (see p.96) is a marvellous hunting ground for secondhand bargains. What follows is a brief run-down of some of the more exciting outlets.

Antonia, Gasthuismolensteeg 12, just south of Raadhuisstraat (☎627 2433). A gathering of adventurous Dutch designers under one roof. Good on shoes and bags too.

Clubwear House, Herengracht 265 (☎622 8766). The place for everything to do with clubbing in Amsterdam, from flyers to fabulous clothes. DJs play in-store on Saturdays.

Daffodil, Jacob Obrechtstraat 41 (☎679 5634). Designer labels only in this posh secondhand shop down by the Vondelpark.

Exota, Nieuwe Leliestraat 32 (☎420 6884); also at Hartenstraat 10. Good, fairly priced selection of simple new and used clothing, in the Jordaan and Grachtengordel respectively.

Hair Police, Kerkstraat 113 (☎620 8567). Well-known for its colourful, dreadlocked hair-dresser at the back (and now also its all-female team of tattooists), this shop has a selection of eclectic, interesting styles from both sides of the Atlantic.

Jojo, Huidenstraat 23 (☎623 3476); also at Runstraat 9. Decent secondhand clothes from all eras. Particularly good for trench coats and 1950s jackets.

Laura Dols, Wolvenstraat 7 (☎624 9066). Vintage clothing and lots of hats.

Local Service, Keizersgracht 400, near Spui (☎626 6840). Men's and women's fashions. Ultra-trendy and expensive.

Kelere Kelder, Prinsengracht 285, at Raadhuisstraat (no phone). Goldmine for used alternative clothing. Fri–Sun 1–6pm.

Leidsestraat, Amsterdam

Amsterdam mural

Singel canal, Amsterdam

ANTONY CASSIDY

Royal Palace, Amsterdam

ANTONY CASSIDY

Amsterdam Gay Pride

ANTONY CASSIDY

Amsterdam canal houses

n Jeanette, Centraal Station (☎421 5194). Organic, handmade, additive-free, preser-
ee, low-sugar chocolates – surprisingly delicious.

den Broek, Heinekenplein 25 (☎611 0812). Beats Albert Heijn hands down in
g except image. Cheaper across the board; bigger too. Trams #16, #24 or #25.
roughly 9am–9pm. More branches dotted around the suburbs.

urwinkel, Weteringschans 133 (☎638 4083). Main branch of a chain selling only
od (thus a little more expensive). Much better tasting fruit and vegetables than any-
e, also grains, pulses and Bon Bon Jeanette chocolates. Superb bread. Smaller
round town. Mon–Sat 7am–8pm, Thurs till 9pm, Sun 11am–6pm.

uffins, Prinsengracht 454, near Rembrandtplein (☎420 1452). The best, most
ew York bagels (and muffins) in town. Branches at Marnixstraat 121 and at
arsstraat 53, the latter open until 3am.

idenstraat 19 (☎624 8087). Very central, with a good selection of fruit and veg-
excellent bread, a short walk west of Spui.

m, Reguliersbreestraat 36, by Rembrandtplein (☎623 1205). One of the city's
pastry shops, showered with awards. Not cheap, but you're paying for the
equivalent of Gucci. Also at Ferdinand Bolstraat 119 and Linnaeusstraat 80.

Haarlemmerdijk 184, near Brouwersgracht (☎620 3550). Famous for their
North African pastries, French bread, etc.

unstraat 25 (☎623 5322). The best wholegrain and sourdough breads in town,
ade from organic grains.

ngracht 32 (☎624 4093). Majestic selection of cheeses and expert advice,
ssibilities.

---

terdam's markets are more diverting than its shops. There's a fine
ket on Waterlooplein, vibrant **street markets** such as the Albert
hasizing food and cheap clothing, and smaller **weekly markets**
thing from stamps to flowers.

t, Albert Cuypstraat, between Ferdinand Bolstraat and Van Woustraat.
general goods and food market, with some great bargains to be had –
all partway down on the right for the best deals on vegetables. Mon–Sat
he city centre.

gracht, near Utrechtsestraat. Flowers and plants, but much less of a
nenmarkt. Friendly advice on what to buy, and the location is a perfect
. Mon 10am–3pm.

el, between Koningsplein and Muntplein. Flowers and plants, ostensi-
ularly frequented by locals. Bulbs for export (with health certificate).
nday as well. Mon–Sat 9am–5pm.

Wonderful rambling collection of secondhand books, with many a
the unsorted boxes. Fri 10am–3pm.

markt, next to the Noorderkerk. Organic farmers' market selling all
n produce, plus amazing fresh breads, exotic fungi, fresh herbs and
t 9am–5pm.

perstraat, south of Mauritskade. Covers about the same ground as
not a tourist in sight. Bags of atmosphere, exotic snacks on offer,
s. Mon–Sat 9am–5pm.

Thorbeckeplein, south of Rembrandtplein. Low-key but high-
locations, with much lower prices than you'll find in the gal-
al books as well. Neither operates during the winter. Both Sun

Centraal Station clocktower, Amsterdam

Amsterdam flea market

Amsterdam coffeeshop

Brown café interior, Amsterdam

Canal scene, Zaanse Schans

Clogs, Zaanse Schans

Alkmaar cheese market

Reflections, P.C. Hooftstraat 66 (☎664 0040). The absolute *crème de*
to match. Near the Rijksmuseum.

Stilett, Damstraat 14 (☎625 2854). A cut above the regular T-shirt
tective owner – no pictures!

Zipper, Huidenstraat 7 (☎623 7302); also at Nieuwe Hoogstraa
Used clothes selected for style and quality – strong on jeans an
it's very popular, and everything is in good condition.

Department stores

Amsterdam's **department stores**, like many of the
of safety. Venture inside only if you have an unfulfi
save them for specifics. Slightly more exciting is
office building at Nieuwezijds Voorburgwal 182, be
a department store but a covered mall shelterin
tionery to underwear. Alternatively, try the **Kal**
on Kalverstraat, close to the Munt, with a range

De Bijenkorf, Dam 1 (☎621 8080). Dominating the
the city's biggest and most diverse shop, a huge bust
range and little snobbishness. Departments to head
and kidswear; there's also a good range of newspap

HEMA, Nieuwendijk 174 (☎623 4176); also in the
tre. A kind of Dutch Woolworth's, but of a better
and other essentials, and occasional designer del
can sometimes find the same items at knockdow
in the back of the shop.

Metz & Co., Keizersgracht 455 (☎624 8810).
on Liberty prints (it used to be owned by Libe
er furniture of the kind that's exhibited in m
Rietveld chair. If your funds won't stretch q
floor Rietveld restaurant, which gives great

Vroom & Dreesmann, Kalverstraat 203 –
Amsterdam branch of a middle-of-the-road
unadventurous, but check out the listeni
best place for a free Mozart recital with

Food, drink and superm

As you might expect, Amsterdam
They supplement a more predic

Albert Heijn, Koningsplein 4, just
currently Mon–Sat 10am–10pm, S
supermarket chain but still sm
Nieuwmarkt 18 and Waterloople
tre: Haarlemmerdijk 1, Overtoo

De Belly, Nieuwe Leliestraat
ing all things organic.

De Bierkoning, Paleisstraat
850 different beers, with ma

Bonbon Atelier Lawenda
chocolates. In the Jordaan.

Bon B
vative-fr

Dirk va
everythi
Mon–Sat

De Natu
organic fo
where els
branches a

Gary's M
authentic
Reguliersd

Gimsel, Hu
etables and

Kwekkeboo
most famous
chocolatier's

Mediterrané
croissants; also

Paul Année,
bar none – all

Wegewijs, Roze
with sampling p

Markets

In general, Ams
central **flea ma**
Cuypmarkt, emp
devoted to every

Albert Cuypmark
The city's principal
check out Hilten's s
9am–5pm. South of

Amstelveld, Prinser
scrum than the Bloe
spot to enjoy the cana

Bloemenmarkt, Sing
bly for tourists, but reg
Some stalls open on Su

Boekenmarkt, Spui.
priceless gem lurking i

Boerenmarkt, Noorder
kinds of organically grow
home-made mustards. S

Dapperstraatmarkt, Da
the Albert Cuyp, but with
and generally better price

Kunstmarkt, Spui, and
quality art market in two
leries; prints and occasio
10am–3pm.

De Looier, Elandsgracht 109. Indoor antiques market, with a whole variety of dealers selling everything from 1950s radios to sixteenth-century delftware. Generally good quality. Daily except Fri 11am–5pm, Thurs till 9pm.

Nieuwmarkt. One of the last remnants of the Nieuwmarkt's ancient market history, and a rival to the more popular and better-stocked Boerenmarkt, with organic produce, breads, cheeses, and arts and crafts. Sat 9am–5pm.

Noordermarkt, Noordermarkt, next to the Noorderkerk. Junk-lover's goldmine, with a general market on Mondays full of all kinds of bargains, tucked away beneath piles of useless rubbish. Get there early. There's also a farmers' produce market (Sat 9am–3pm) and a bird market (Sat 8am–1pm), though the latter is best avoided. General market Mon 9am–1pm, Sat 8am–3pm.

Oudemanhuispoort, off O.Z. Achterburgwal. Charming little book market held in a university corridor since 1876, with new and used books of all kinds, many in Dutch but some in English. You can sit and read your purchases in the university hall, with a coffee and sandwich. Mon–Sat 10am–4pm.

Rommelmarkt, Looiersgracht 38. A vast, permanent indoor flea market and jumble sale, with things turning up here that were left unsold at the city's other street markets. Mon–Thurs, Sat & Sun 11am–5pm.

Stamp and Coin Market, N.Z. Voorburgwal, south of Dam square. Organized by the specialist shops crowded in the nearby alleys. Wed & Sat 11am–4pm.

Waterlooplein, behind the Stadhuis. A real Amsterdam institution, and the city's best flea market by far. Sprawling and chaotic, it's the final resting place for many a pair of yellow corduroy flares; but there are more wearable clothes to be found, and some wonderful antique/junk stalls to root through. Secondhand vinyl too. Mon–Sat 9am–5pm.

Miscellaneous shops

Perhaps more than any other city in Europe, Amsterdam is a great source of odd little shops, **speciality shops** devoted to one particular product or interest. What follows is a selection of favourites.

Condomerie Het Gulden Vlies, Warmoesstraat 141 (☎627 4174). Condoms of every shape, size and flavour imaginable. All in the best possible taste.

Couzijn Simon, Prinsengracht 578 (☎624 7691). Antique toys and dolls.

Elisabeth Hendriks, Nieuwe Spiegelstraat 61 (☎623 0085). A whole place devoted to snuff-bottles.

D. Eberhardt, Damstraat 16 (☎624 0724). Chinese and southeast Asian crafts, ceramics, clothes and jewellery.

Donald E. Jongejans, Noorderkerkstraat 18 (☎624 6888). Hundreds of old spectacle frames, all of them without a previous owner. Supplied the specs for Bertolucci's *The Last Emperor*.

Gerda's, Runstraat 16 (☎624 2912). Amsterdam is full of flower shops, but this one is the most imaginative and sensual. An aesthetic experience.

The Head Shop, Kloveniersburgwal 39 (☎624 9061). Every dope-smoking accessory you could possibly need, along with assorted marijuana memorabilia.

't Klompenhuisje, Nieuwe Hoogstraat 9a, south of Nieuwmarkt (☎622 8100). Amsterdam's best and brightest array of clogs.

Knopenwinkel, Wolvenstraat 14 (☎624 0479). Buttons in every conceivable shape and size.

Nieuws Innoventions, Prinsengracht 297 (☎627 9540). Specialists in modern designer items for the home – projector clocks, remote control lamps, Philippe Starck vases, etc. Also round dice, chocolate body-paint and shark laundry pegs.

1001 Kralen, Rozengracht 54 (☎624 3681). "Kralen" means beads, and 1001 would seem a conservative estimate in this place in the Jordaan, which sells nothing but.

P.G.C. Hajenius, Rokin 92 (☎623 7494). Old established tobacconist selling its own and other brands of cigars, tobacco, smoking accessories, and every make of cigarette you can think of.

Peter Doeswijk, Vijzelgracht 11 (☎420 3133). Phones – hundreds of identical, old rotary-dial phones, each painted with a different design (and they all work). It's chutzpah, if nothing else.

Santa Jet, Prinsenstraat 7 (☎427 2070). Hand-made Latin American items, from collectibles to humorous knick-knacks, and plenty of religious icons. You can visit a palm-reader by appointment after the shop has closed.

't Winkeltje, Prinsengracht 228 (☎625 1352). Jumble of cheap glassware and crockery, candlesticks, antique tin toys, kitsch souvenirs, old apothecaries' jars and flasks. Perfect for browsing.

Witte Tandenwinkel, Runstraat 5 (☎623 3443). The "White Teeth Shop" sells wacky toothbrushes and just about every dental hygiene accoutrement you could ever need.

Listings

AIRLINES at Schiphol airport: Aer Lingus (☎601 0265); Alitalia (☎577 7444); British Airways (☎601 0245); British Midland (☎604 1075); Delta Airlines (☎316 1676); Easyjet (☎653 2598); KLM (☎649 9123); KLM uk (☎474 7747); United Airlines (☎653 4620).

BANKS AND BUREAUX DE CHANGE Amsterdam's banks usually offer the best deals. Hours are Monday to Friday 9am to 4pm, with a few banks also open Thursday until 9pm or on Saturday morning; all are closed on public holidays (see p.45). Central locations include ABN-Amro at Dam 2, Leideseplein 25, Rozengracht 88 and Rokin 80; and the ING Bank at Damrak 80 and Herengracht 580 (near Amstel). Outside these times, you'll need to go to one of the many bureaux de change scattered around town. GWK, whose main 24-hour branches are at Centraal Station and Schiphol Airport, offers competitive rates, as does Thomas Cook at Dam 23 (daily 9am–6pm; ☎625 0922), Damrak 1–5 (daily 8am–8pm; ☎620 3236) and Leidseplein 31 (daily 9am–6pm; ☎626 7000). Beware of other agencies though, as some offer great rates but then slap on an extortionate commission, or, conversely, charge no commission but give bad rates. The VVV tourist office also changes money as does American Express at Damrak 66 (Mon–Fri 9am–5pm, Sat 9am–noon; ☎504 8777).

BIKE RENTAL You can rent bikes at the following outlets: Bike City, Bloemgracht 70 (☎626 3721); Holland Rent-a-Bike, Damrak 247 (☎622 3207); Koenders Take-a-Bike, Stationsplein 12 (☎624 8391); MacBike, Mr Visserplein 2 (☎620 0985); Macbike Too, Marnixstraat 220 (☎626 6964); Zijwind, Van Ostadestraat 108 (☎673 7026).

CAR PARKS The following are all 24hr city-centre car parks: De Bijenkorf, Beursplein, off Damrak; Byzantium, Tesselschadestraat 1, near Leidseplein; De Kolk, Nieuwezijds Kolk 20; Muziektheater, Waterlooplein (under City Hall); Parking Plus Amsterdam Centraal, Prins Hendrikkade 20, east of Centraal Station.

CAR RENTAL Selected car rental agencies (*auto-verhuur*): Adams, Nassaukade 346 (☎685 0111); Avis, Nassaukade 380 (☎683 6061); Budget, Overtoom 121 (☎612 6066); Diks, Van Ostadestraat 278 (☎662 3366); Europcar, Overtoom 51 (☎683 2123); Hertz, Overtoom 333 (☎612 2441); Ouke Baas, van Ostadestraat 366 (☎679 4842).

CONSULATES UK, Koningslaan 44 (☎676 4343); USA, Museumplein 19 (☎575 5309).

EMERGENCIES For all emergencies (Police, Ambulance, Fire), dial ☎112.

FREE AMSTERDAM Larger branches of Albert Heijn supermarkets often have free **coffee** for shoppers (and occasionally nibbles of this and that too), and many bakeries around town offer bite-sized bits of fresh gourmet **bread** or pastries (although generally as an incentive to buy at least something). The **markets** on Albert Cuypstraat and Dapperstraat close at 5pm, when over-juicy tomatoes and bruised apples go begging. Fine wines and cheeses can be found on offer at the opening of a new exhibition at one of Amsterdam's many **galleries**; just try and look interested in the art as well. There are no restrictions on listening to your favourite **CDs** all day long on the top floor of Vroom and Dreesman (Kalverstraat) or in the Virgin Megastore, where you can also play the latest **video games** to your heart's content. Many larger cafés trust you with today's English **newspapers**, so long as you leave them behind for the next freeloader. The café in De Bijenkorf is next to their magazine department; they allow you to pick any magazine off the shelf, peruse it at your leisure over a (paid-for) cup of coffee, then put it back. There is also free **art** (the Schuttersgallerij outside the Amsterdam Historical Museum on Kalverstraat), a free **boat-ride** across the IJ to Amsterdam North and back (the "IJveer" boats leave Pier 8 behind Centraal Station roughly every 10min), free lunchtime **concerts** at the Concertgebouw (October to June only), free **jazz** nightly at Bourbon Street, Café Alto and the Bamboo Bar (all near Leidseplein), even free **postcards** in café racks that are sometimes worth sending.

INTERNET A good central Internet Café is at Martelaarsgracht 11, and you can use the facilities at the *In de Waag* café-restaurant at Nieuwmarkt 4 (which are supplied by the Society for Old and New Media housed in the same building) for the price of a drink.

KIDS Apart from parks (see below) there are a number of places in Amsterdam where you can take kids, which include: the Artis Zoo, Plantage Kerklaan 40 (☎523 3400; tram #7, #9 or #14), taking in aquariums, a planetarium and a Children's Farm; the Kindermuseum, part of the Tropenmuseum (see p.100) which aims to promote understanding of other cultures through lively and entertaining exhibits; the Museum Tramlijn (☎673 7538), a set of working antique trams which run from Haarlemmermeer Station down to the Amsterdamse Bos; and the newMetropolis centre (see p.100). The only café in Amsterdam intended for families is *Enfant Terrible*, De Genestetstraat 1 (☎612 2032), which has great food and a supervised play area.

LAUNDRY (*wassalons*) The Clean Brothers, Kerkstraat 56 (daily 7am–9pm) is the best self-service launderette, with a sizeable load currently ƒ8 to wash, 25c per five minutes in the drier; they also do service-washes, dry-cleaning, ironing, etc; branches at Jacob van Lennepkade 179 and Westerstraat 26. Other launderettes are to be found at: Oudebrugsteeg 22 (off Damrak), Elandsgracht 59 (Jordaan), Warmoesstraat 30, Monnikenstraat 8 and Oude Doelenstraat 12 (Red Light District) and Herenstraat 24.

LEFT LUGGAGE Centraal Station has coin-operated lockers and a staffed left luggage office.

LOST PROPERTY For items lost on the trams, buses or metro, contact GVB Head Office, Prins Hendrikkade 108–114 (Mon–Fri 9am–4pm; ☎460 5858). For property lost on a train, go to the Gevonden Voorwerpen office at the nearest station; Amsterdam's is at Centraal Station, near the left luggage lockers (☎557 8544; 24hr). If you collect your property within two days there is no charge, but after two days each item costs ƒ5, and after three days all unclaimed property goes to the Central Lost Property Office at 2e Daalsedijk 4, Utrecht (☎030/235 3923), and costs ƒ7,50 per item to pick up. If you lose something in the street or a park, try the police lost property at Stephensonstraat 18 (Mon–Fri noon–3.30pm; ☎559 3005). Schiphol Airport's lost and found number is ☎601 2325.

MOPED RENTAL Moped Rental Service, Marnixstraat 208 (☎422 0266).

PARKS Amstelpark, beyond ring road to the south (bus #69 or #169 from Amstel station); Amsterdamse Bos (bus #170, #171 or #172 from Raadhuisstraat); Beatrixpark, next to RAI exhibition centre (tram #5); Oosterpark (tram #3, #6, #9, #10 or #14); Sarphatipark, De Pijp (tram #3); and Westerpark (tram #3 or #10).

POLICE Headquarters are at Elandsgracht 117 (☎559 9111).

POST OFFICE The main post office (Mon–Fri 9am–6pm, Thurs till 8pm, Sat 10am–1.30pm) is at Singel 250, on the corner with Raadhuisstraat; a second major post office (Mon–Fri 9am–9pm, Sat 9am–noon) is at Oosterdokskade 5, a couple of hundred metres east of Centraal Station

PUBLIC TRANSPORT Information on ☎0900/9292.

WINDMILLS The most central windmill in Amsterdam is the De Gooyer in the Eastern Islands, and the best preserved one is in the south of the Amstelpark.

WOMEN'S CONTACTS Amsterdam has an impressive feminist infrastructure: there are support groups, health centres and businesses run by and for women. A good starting point to find out what's going on in the city is Het Vrouwenhuis, Nieuwe Herengracht 95 (☎625 2066; Mon–Fri 11am–4pm), an organizing centre for women's activities and cultural events. Xantippe, Prinsengracht 290 (☎623 5854), is a women's bookshop with a wide selection of feminist titles in English.

travel details

Trains

Amsterdam CS to: Alkmaar (every 15–20min; 30min); Amersfoort (every 30min; 35min); Apeldoorn (every 30min; 1hr); Arnhem (every 30min; 1hr 10min); Den Helder (every 30min; 1hr 10min); Dordrecht (every 30min; 1hr 30min); Eindhoven (every 30min; 1hr 30min); Enkhuizen (every 30min; 1hr); Groningen (every 30min; 2hr 20min); Haarlem (every 10min; 15min); The Hague/Den Haag (every 15–20min; 50min); Hoorn (every 30min; 40min); Leeuwarden (hourly; 2hr 25min); Leiden (every 15–20min; 35min); Maastricht (hourly; 2hr 30min); Middelburg (hourly; 2hr 35min); Nijmegen (every 30min; 1hr 30min); Rotterdam (every 30min; 1hr 10min); Schiphol Airport (every 15min; 20min); Utrecht (every 30min; 30min); Vlissingen (hourly; 2hr 45min); Zwolle (hourly; 1hr 20min).

Buses

Amsterdam St Nicolaaskerk to: Edam (#110; every 30min; 40min); Marken (#111; every 30min; 30min); Monnickendam (#111; every 30min; 20min); Volendam (#110; every 30min; 30min).

Amsterdam Weesperplein to: Muiden (#136; every 30min; 40min); Naarden (#136; every 30min; 55min).

Ferries

Amsterdam (behind CS) to: Amsterdam North (every 10–15min; 10–15min).

CHAPTER TWO

NORTH HOLLAND

Stretching north from Amsterdam to the island of Texel, the province of **North Holland** is one of the country's most explored regions. Though not as densely populated as its sister province to the south (see Chapter 3), it's still a populous area, and holds some of Holland's prime tourist attractions. The landscape is typically Dutch, the countryside for the most part a familiar polder scene of flat fields, cut by trenches and canals, stretching far into the distance, the wide horizons broken only by the odd farmhouse or windmill. Lining most of the western coast are rugged areas of dune and long, broad sandy beaches, while on the other side the coast of the Markermeer and IJsselmeer, formerly the Zuider Zee (see box on p.149), is home to old seaports-turned-yachting communities, which sport the vestiges of a glorious past in picturesquely preserved town centres.

> North Holland has its own tourist Web site at *www.noord-holland-tourist.nl* with extensive information in English.

The majority of North Holland is easily visited by means of day-trips from Amsterdam, but such cursory explorations do the province few favours. The urban highlight is undoubtedly **Haarlem**, an easy day-trip west from Amsterdam but in itself definitely worth treating as an overnight stop. Haarlem also gives ready access to some wild stretches of dune and beach – at their prettiest amidst the **Nationaalpark de Kennemerduinen** – and one of the country's largest coastal resorts in **Zandvoort**. For investigating the bulk of the province however there are two obvious routes: along the east coast bordering the Markermeer and IJsselmeer, or, inland, from Zaandam through to the island of Texel, with various resorts on the west coast along the way. The former starts with the villages nearest Amsterdam – **Marken** and **Volendam** – kitsch places full of tourists in search of clogs and windmills during summer, but with considerable charm if you can visit off-season, whilst neighbouring **Edam** is one of the country's most appealing little villages, which has somehow managed to escape the tourist hordes. Further north, **Hoorn** and **Enkhuizen** were once major Zuider Zee ports, whose historic wealth, based on shipbuilding and the Baltic trade, is reflected in a liberal scattering of handsome old buildings. Modern development has hacked Hoorn around, but Enkhuizen remains a fascinating town and the possessor of one of the country's best open-air museums, the Zuiderzeemuseum. The inland route starts a short train ride from Amsterdam in the Zaanstad conurbation, whose chief attraction is the antique windmills and canals of the recreated Dutch village of **Zaanse Schans**. Further up the line, **Alkmaar** is usually visited as a day-trip for its ceremonial Friday cheese market but is worth a longer sojourn if you're keen to experience small-town provincial Holland – it also makes a good base for visiting the resorts stretching along the western coast, especially **Bergen-aan-Zee**. Beyond, in the far north of the province, the island of **Texel** is the most accessible

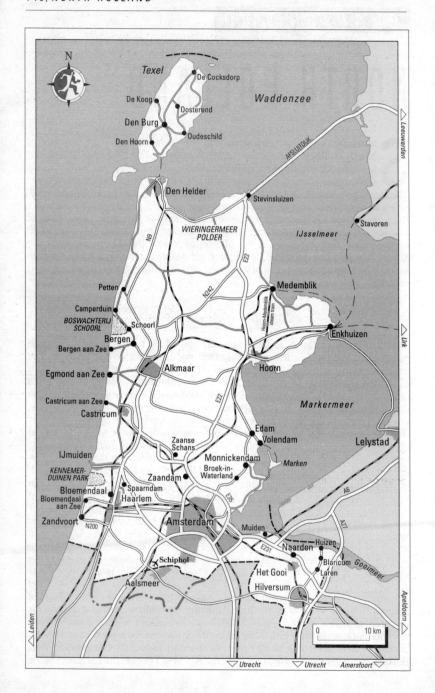

N

Texel
De Cocksdorp
De Koog
Oosterend
Den Burg
Oudeschild
Den Hoorn

Waddenzee

AFSLUITDIJK

Leeuwarden

Den Helder
Stevinsluizen

WIERINGERMEER
POLDER

IJsselmeer

Stavoren

N9

N242

E22

Urk

Petten
Camperduin
BOSWACHTERIJ
SCHOORL
Schoorl
Bergen
Bergen aan Zee
Egmond aan Zee

Medemblik

Hoorn-Medemblik
stoom tram

Enkhuizen

Alkmaar

E22

Hoorn

Markermeer

Castricum aan Zee
Castricum

Lelystad

Edam
Volendam

Zaanse
Schans

Marken

IJmuiden
KENNEMER-
DUINEN PARK

Monnickendam
Broek-in-
Waterland

Zaandam

A6

Bloemendaal
Spaarndam
Bloemendaal
aan Zee
Haarlem

Zandvoort
N200

Amsterdam
Muiden

Naarden

Huizen

E231

A27

Gooimeer

Schiphol

Blaricum
Laren

Aalsmeer

Het Gooi
Hilversum

E35

Apeldoorn

0   10 km

Leiden

Utrecht   Utrecht   Amersfoort

ACCOMMODATION PRICE CODES

All the **hotels** detailed in this chapter have been graded according to the following categories. The codes are based on the price of the cheapest double room – without private bath, etc – during high season. In the case of **hostels** we've given the code if they have double rooms, otherwise we've stated the actual price per dorm bed per night.

① up to ƒ100/€45
② ƒ100–150/€45–67.50
③ ƒ150–200/€67.50–90
④ ƒ200–250/€90–112.50

⑤ ƒ250–300/€112.50–135
⑥ ƒ300–400/€135–180
⑦ ƒ400–500/€180–225
⑧ ƒ500/€225+

and busiest of the Wadden Sea islands. It's very crowded during summer, but don't be put off by the numbers: with a bit of walking you can find places well off the beaten tourist track – and far away from the hustle and bustle of Amsterdam.

Most of North Holland is located, logically enough, north of Amsterdam, but the borders of the province also dip down south of the capital, taking in Schiphol airport and parts of the bulb-growing areas around Aalsmeer (covered in Chapter 3). Southeast from Amsterdam the steady sprawl of leafy suburbs collectively known as **Het Gooi** is included in the province too, the highlight of which is the old fortified town of **Naarden**.

Getting around North Holland by **public transport** is easy enough with **trains** linking all the major settlements and **buses** filling in the gaps. If you want to continue north out of the province, the two **dikes** that enclose the Markermeer and the IJsselmeer carry handy road links: the former connecting Enkhuizen with Lelystad on the reclaimed Flevoland polders (see p.272) and the latter, the Afsluitdijk, making the thirty-kilometre trip from Den Oever to the province of Friesland (see Chapter 4).

Haarlem and around

Though only fifteen minutes from Amsterdam by train, **HAARLEM** has a quite different pace and feel from the capital. Founded on the banks of the River Spaarne in the tenth century, the town first prospered through its use by the counts of Holland as a place to levy tolls on local shipping, but later developed as a clothmaking centre. In 1572, the town sided with the Protestant rebels against the Habsburgs, a decision they came to regret when a large Spanish army led by Frederick of Toledo besieged them in December of the same year; it was a desperate affair that lasted for eight months, but finally the town surrendered after receiving various assurances of good treatment – assurances which Frederick promptly broke, massacring over two thousand of the Protestant garrison and all their Calvinist ministers. Recaptured in 1577 by the Protestants under William the Silent, Haarlem went on to enjoy its greatest prosperity in the seventeenth century, becoming a centre for the arts and home to a flourishing school of painters. Nowadays, it's an easily absorbed town of around 150,000 people, with a good-looking centre studded with fine old buildings and containing the outstanding **Frans Hals Museum**, located in the almshouse where the artist spent his last, and for some his most brilliant, years.

Well worth an afternoon in itself – maybe even an overnight stay if you're tired of the crowds and grime of Amsterdam – Haarlem is also a short train ride from two coastal resorts: the clumsy modern town of **Zandvoort-aan-Zee**, redeemed by its long sandy beach, and the **Bloemendaal-aan-Zee** beach resort, both of which allow easy access to the undeveloped dunes and seashore of the nearby **Nationaalpark de Kennemerduinen**.

Arrival, information and accommodation

With fast and frequent services from Amsterdam, Haarlem's splendid **train station**, an example of the Amsterdam School of architecture, is located on the north side of the city centre, about ten minutes' walk from the main square, the Grote Markt. The **bus station** is in front of the train station and the **VVV** is next door (April–Sept Mon–Sat 9am–5.30pm; Oct–March Mon–Fri 9am–5.30pm, Sat 9am–4pm; ☎0900/616 1600, ƒ1 per min). The latter issues free city maps and brochures and has a small supply of **private rooms**, which cost around ƒ35 per person per night plus a ƒ10 room reservation fee, but note that they are mostly on the outskirts of town. Haarlem has three central **hotels**, the pick of which is the homely *Amadeus*, a low-key spot with plain but perfectly comfortable, en-suite rooms at Grote Markt 10 (☎023/532 4530, fax 532 2328; ②). The front bedrooms here provide enjoyable views over the main square, their only drawback being the pigeons thrashing around on the window sill. Also on the Grote Markt, at no. 27, is the *Carillon*, another inexpensive place with frugal rooms (☎023/531 0591, fax 531 4909; ②), while the four-star *Golden Tulip Lion d'Or* is a smart chain hotel housed in a sturdy nineteenth-century building close to the train station at Kruisweg 34 (☎023/532 1750, fax 532 9543; ③). There's a **youth hostel** near the sports stadium a couple of kilometres to the north of the town centre, at Jan Gijzenpad 3 (April–Dec; ☎023/537 3793, fax 537 1176; ƒ25); bus #2 or #6 runs frequently from the station – a ten-minute journey. **Campsites** are dotted along the coast in and around Zandvoort – see p.147.

The Town

At the heart of **HAARLEM** is the **Grote Markt**, a wide and attractive open space flanked by an appealing ensemble of Gothic and Renaissance architecture, including an intriguing if exceptionally garbled **Stadhuis**, whose turrets and towers, balconies and galleries were put together in piecemeal fashion between the fourteenth and the seventeenth centuries. At the other end of the Grote Markt stands a **statue** of a certain Laurens Coster (1370–1440), who, Haarlemmers insist, is the true inventor of printing. Legend tells of him cutting a letter "A" from the bark of a tree, dropping it into the sand by accident, and, hey presto, realising how to create the printed word. The statue shows him holding the wooden letter up

EXCURSIONS FROM HAARLEM

Woltheus Cruises, by the river at Spaarne 11 (☎023/535 7723), operate several **boat trips** from Haarlem, the most interesting of which is a twice-weekly excursion to Zaanse Schans (July–Aug; 7hr; ƒ25; see p.160). Haarlem is also just a quick bus ride from the Keukenhof Gardens (see p.180), about 13km south of town.

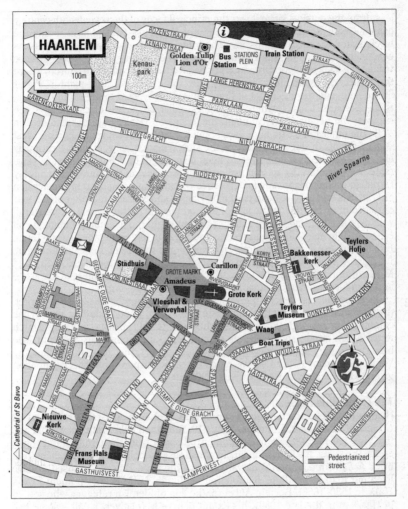

triumphantly, but most historians agree that it was actually the German Johannes Gutenberg who invented printing, in the early 1440s.

The statue stands in the shadow of the **Grote Kerk** or **Sint Bavokerk** (Mon–Sat 10am–4pm; *f*2,50), a mighty Gothic structure supported by heavy buttresses. The church is surmounted by a good-looking lantern tower directly above the transept crossing, which is actually made of wood, but clad in lead – the original stone version had to be dismantled when, in 1514, it proved too heavy for its supports and was about to crash down. Finally finished in 1538, after 150 years of work, the church dwarfs the surrounding clutter of streets and houses, and serves as a landmark from almost anywhere in the town. If you've been to the Rijksmuseum in Amsterdam (see p.101), the Grote Kerk may seem familiar, at least from the outside, since it was the principal focus of the seventeenth-century painter Gerrit Berckheyde's many views of Haarlem's Grote Markt – only the black-coated burghers are missing. The **interior** is breathtakingly cavernous, its beauty enhanced by the stark, white power of the vaulting. The present entrance (round the back on Oude Groenmarkt) leads to the east end of the church, where the southern ambulatory contains the tombstone of the painter Pieter Saenredam, and the choir that of Frans Hals. Nearby, next to the south transept, is the Brewers' Chapel, where the central pillar bears two black marks – one showing the height of a local giant, the 2.64m-tall Daniel Cajanus, who died in 1749, the other the 0.84m-high dwarf Simon Paap from Zandvoort. Further west still, on the north side of the nave, is the Dog Whippers' Chapel, built – curiously enough – for the men employed to keep dogs out of the church, and now separated from the nave by an iron grille. At the west end of the church, the mighty Christian Müller **organ** was four years in the making, completed in Amsterdam in 1738. It is said to have been played by Handel and Mozart (the latter on his tour of the country in 1766, at the age of ten) and is one of the biggest in the world, with over five thousand pipes and loads of snazzy Baroque embellishment; if you can make it to one of the organ recitals (mid-May to mid-September Tues 8.15pm, July & Aug also Thurs 3pm; free), it's well worth the effort. Beneath the organ, Jan Baptist Xavery's lovely group of draped marble figures represent Poetry and Music offering thanks to the town, which is depicted as a patroness of the arts – in return for its generous support in the purchase of the organ.

Back outside, just beyond the western end of the church, the old meat market, the **Vleeshal** (Mon–Sat 11am–5pm, Sun noon–5pm; ƒ7,50, including Verweyhal; combined ticket with Frans Hals Museum ƒ12,50) boasts a flashy Dutch Renaissance facade and serves as an annexe to the Frans Hals Museum (see below), holding temporary exhibitions of modern art. Just along the square, the **Verweyhal** (same details) serves much the same purpose, with special attention given to the local artist Kees Verwey (1900–1995).

The Frans Hals Museum

Haarlem's chief attraction, the **Frans Hals Museum** at Groot Heiligland 62 (Mon–Sat 11am–5pm, Sun noon–5pm; ƒ10, combined ticket with Verweyhal and the Vleeshal ƒ12,50), is a five-minute stroll south from the Grote Markt – just follow the signs. It's housed in an old almshouse complex, a much modified redbrick *hofje* with a central courtyard, where the aged Hals is supposed to have lived out his last destitute years on public funds. Little is known about **Frans Hals** (c.1580–1666). Born in Antwerp, the son of Flemish refugees who settled in Haarlem in the late 1580s, his extant oeuvre is relatively small – some two hundred paintings and nothing like the number of sketches and studies left behind by Rembrandt. This is largely because Hals wasn't fashionable until the nineteenth century, and a lot of his work was lost before it became collectable. His outstanding gift was as a portraitist, showing a sympathy with his subjects and an ability to capture fleeting expression that some say even Rembrandt lacked. Seemingly quick and careless flashes of colour characterize his work, blended into a coherent whole to leave us a set of marvellously animated seventeenth-century figures.

The museum begins with the work of other artists: first a small group of sixteenth-century paintings, the most prominent a triptych by Gerard David and a polished *Adam and Eve* by Jan van Scorel. Afterwards, Room 10 features a good group of paintings by the **Haarlem mannerists**, including works by **Carel van Mander** (1548–1606), leading light of the Haarlem School and mentor of many of the other painters represented here. There's also a curious painting by Haarlem-born **Jan Mostaert** (1475–1555), his *West Indian Scene* depicting a band of naked, poorly armed natives trying to defend themselves against the cannon and sword of their Spanish invaders; the comparison with the Dutch Protestants is obvious. Moving on to Room 11, **Cornelis Cornelisz van Haarlem** (1562–1638) best followed van Mander's guidelines: his *Wedding of Peleus and Thetis* is an appealing rendition of what was then a popular subject, though Cornelisz gives as much attention to the arrangement of his elegant nudes as to the subject. This marriage precipitated civil war amongst the gods and was used by the Dutch as a warning against discord, a call for unity during the long war with Spain. Similarly, the same artist's *Massacre of the Innocents* connects the biblical story with the Spanish siege of Haarlem in 1572.

Frans Hals was a pupil of van Mander too, though he seems to have learned little more than the barest rudiments from him. The Hals paintings begin in earnest in Room 21 with a set of "Civic Guard" portraits – group portraits of the militia companies initially formed to defend the country from the Spanish, but which later became social clubs for the gentry. Getting a commission to paint one of these portraits was a well-paid privilege – Hals got his first in 1616 – but their composition was a tricky affair and often the end result was dull and flat. With great flair and originality, Hals made the group portrait a unified whole instead of a static collection of individual portraits, his figures carefully arranged, but so cleverly as not to appear contrived. For a time, Hals himself was a member of the Company of St George, and in the *Officers of the Militia Company of St George* he appears in the top left-hand corner – one of his few self-portraits.

Further on in the museum, Hals' later paintings are darker, more contemplative works, closer to Rembrandt in their lighting. In Room 26, the *Governors* and *Governesses of St Elizabeth Gasthui*, painted in 1641, are good examples, as are the portraits of the *Regents* and *Regentesses of the Oudemannenhuis*, in Room 28. The latter were commissioned when Hals was in his eighties, a poor man despite a successful painting career, hounded for money by the town's tradesmen and by the mothers of his illegitimate children. As a result he was dependent on the charity of people like those depicted here: their cold, self-satisfied faces staring out of the gloom, the women reproachful, the men only slightly more affable. The character just right of centre in the *Regents* painting has been labelled (and indeed looks) drunk, although it is inconceivable that Hals would have depicted him in this condition; it's more likely that he was suffering from some kind of facial paralysis, and his jauntily cocked hat was simply a popular fashion of the time. There are those who claim Hals had lost his touch by the time he painted these pictures, yet their sinister, almost ghostly power as they face each other across the room, suggests quite the opposite. Van Gogh's remark that "Frans Hals had no fewer than 27 blacks" suddenly makes perfect sense.

Haarlem's other sights

Beyond the Frans Hals Museum, at the end of Groot Heiligland, turn left along the canal and it's a short walk east to the River Spaarne, whose gentle curves mark the eastern periphery of the town centre. Turn left again, along Turfmarkt and its continuation Spaarne, to reach the surly stonework of the **Waag** (Weigh House) and then the country's oldest museum, the **Teylers Museum**, located in a grand old building at Spaarne 16 (Tues–Sat 10am–5pm, Sun noon–5pm; ƒ10). Founded in 1774 by a wealthy local philanthropist, one Pieter Teyler van der Hulst, the museum should appeal to scientific and artistic tastes alike. It contains everything from fossils, bones and crystals, to weird, H.G. Wells-type technology (including an enormous eighteenth-century electrostatic generator) and sketches and line drawings by Michelangelo, Raphael, Rembrandt and Claude, among others. The drawings are covered to protect them from the light, but don't be afraid to pull back the curtains and peek. Look in, too, on the rooms beyond, filled with work by eighteenth- and nineteenth-century Dutch painters, principally Breitner, Israëls, Weissenbruch and, not least, Wijbrand Hendriks, who was once the keeper of the art collection here. Teyler also bestowed his charity on the riverside **Teylers Hofje**, a little way east around the bend of the Spaarne at Koudenhorn 64. With none of the cosy familiarity of the town's other *hofjes,* this is a grandiose affair, a neoclassical edifice dating from 1787 and featuring solid columns and cupolas. Nearby, the elegant fifteenth-century tower of the **Bakenesserkerk** (no public access), on Vrouwestraat, is a flamboyant, vaguely oriental protrusion on the Haarlem skyline.

Two other sights that may help structure your wanderings are on the opposite side of town. Van Campen's **Nieuwe Kerk**, just west of Grote Houtstraat, was added – rather unsuccessfully – onto Lieven de Key's bulbed, typically Dutch tower in 1649, though the interior possesses a crisp soberness that acts as an antidote to the soaring heights of the Grote Kerk. Just beyond, and much less self-effacing, the Roman Catholic **Cathedral of St Bavo** (April–Oct Mon–Sat 10am–noon & 2–4.30pm; free) is one of the largest ecclesiastical structures in Holland. Designed by Joseph Cuypers, son of P.J. Cuypers (see p.74 and p.101), and built on the west bank of the Leidsevaart canal between 1895 and 1906, it is broad and spacious inside, with cupolas and turrets crowding around an apse reminiscent of Byzantine churches, the whole surmounted by a distinctive copper dome.

Eating and drinking

Haarlem's best **restaurants** are conveniently clustered around the Grote Markt and on Oude Groenmarkt. Excellent options include the *Applause,* a chic little place at Grote Markt 23a (☎023/531 1425), where main courses hover around the ƒ35 mark, and the slightly more expensive and equally smart *De Componist,* at Korte Veerstraat 1 (☎023/532 8853); both serve Dutch cuisine. The moderately priced *Quatre Mains,* Grote Markt 4 (☎023/542 4258) specializes in fondues and the eccentric *Haarlem aan Zee,* Oude Groenmarkt 10 (☎023/531 4884), whose interior is done out like a Dutch beach, serves a splendid range of seafood, with main dishes averaging between ƒ30 and ƒ40. The very popular and inexpensive *Restaurant La Plume,* Lange Veerstraat 1 (☎023/531 3202), offers a range of tasty dishes from pastas through to traditional Dutch. For a **drink**, *In Den Uiver,* just off the Grote Markt at Riviervismarkt 13, is a lively and extremely appealing bar offering occasional live music, while the *Grand Café Fortuyn,* Grote Markt 21, is a quieter, cosier spot, as is the laidback and typically Dutch *'t Ouwe Proef,* an intimate bar at Lange Veerstraat 7. Alternatively, there's the long-established and boisterous *Café Mephisto,* Grote Markt 29, and *Café 1900,* Barteljorisstraat 10, a fashionable locals' hangout serving drinks and light meals in a pleasant turn-of-the-century interior. Finally, *Ze Crack,* at the junction of Lange Veerstraat and Kleine Houtstraat, is a dim, smoky bar with good sounds.

Around Haarlem

Haarlem is just 7km from the coast at **ZANDVOORT**, a major seaside resort whose agglomeration of modern apartment blocks strings along the seashore behind a wide and sandy beach. As resorts go it's pretty standard – packed in summer, dead and gusty in winter – but the **beach** is excellent and the place also musters a casino and a car racing circuit. What's more, Zandvoort is one of the few places on the Dutch coast with its own train station (see below): the journey from Amsterdam to Zandvoort only takes twenty-five minutes, which makes it an easy day-trip – ideal for a spot of sunbathing.

Some 3km north along the coast from Zandvoort are the beachside shacks, dunes and ice cream stalls of **BLOEMENDAAL-AAN-ZEE**, a pocket-sized resort (not to be confused with Bloemendaal) which possesses several campsites (see below). It is also located on the southern edge of the **NATIONAALPARK DE KENNEMERDUINEN**, whose pine woods and dunes cover 1250 hectares of coastline. Maps of the park are widely available – petrol stations and local VVVs will, for example, oblige – and are useful if you intend to negotiate its network of footpaths and cycle trails. Bike rental is available in Zandvoort. The park's **visitor centre** is in its southeast corner, just off the N200. To the north of the park is the gritty ferry port and eminently missable industrial town of IJmuiden.

Just north of Haarlem is the village of **SPAARNDAM**, which has little to recommend it other than a well-known statue of Hans Brinker, the young lad who supposedly saved the district from disaster by sticking his finger in a hole in the dike. However, although the tale has the ring of truth about it, it is all fictitious – invented by the American writer Mary Mapes Dodge in her children's book *The Silver Skates* of 1873. The monument to the heroic little chap was unveiled in 1950 – more, it seems, as a tribute to the opportunistic Dutch tourist industry than anything else.

Practicalities

Zandvoort is well served by train: from June to August there are five trains hourly from Haarlem and three from Amsterdam Centraal, as well as one every half hour from Haarlem the rest of the year – the **train station** is only a five-minute walk (if that) from the beach. There are buses from Haarlem too – the **bus station** is in the centre of the resort on Louis Davidsstraat. There's no real reason to stay overnight in Zandvoort, but the **VVV** (April to mid-July & mid-Aug to Sept Mon–Sat 9am–5pm; mid-July to mid-Aug Mon–Sat 9am–7pm; Oct Mon–Sat 10am–12.30pm & 1.30–5pm; Nov–March Tues–Sat 10am–12.30pm & 1.30–4.30pm; ☎023/571 7947), a short, signposted walk west of the train station at Schoolplein 1, has a full list of local accommodation. This includes several four-star tower-block **hotels** dotted along the seashore, amongst which the slick 120-room *Gran Dorado Strandhotel*, Trompstraat 2 (☎023/572 0000, fax 573 0000; ④) is probably the most appealing. At the other end of the market, the VVV books **private rooms** for ƒ30 per person per night, but in summer these fill up fast – so ask early or telephone ahead. **Bike rental** is available at the Rent-a-bike centre, Passage 20, in Zandvoort (May–Aug; ☎023/571 3343), and at several local campsites.

Bloemendaal-aan-Zee has two good **campsites**, both among the dunes within comfortable reach of the beach: the sprawling De Lakens, at Zeeweg 60 (☎023/573 2266, fax 573 2288; April–Oct), and Bloemendaal at Zeeweg 72 (☎023/573 2178, fax 573 2174; April to late Sept). Bus #81 runs from Haarlem train station to Bloemendaal-aan-Zee – and Zandvoort – along the N200; both campsites are just to the north of, and within easy walking distance of, this road.

The east coast

The turbulent waters of the **Zuider Zee** were once busy with Dutch trading ships plying to and from the Baltic. This Baltic trade was the linchpin of Holland's prosperity in the Golden Age, revolving around the import of huge quantities of grain, the supply of which was municipally controlled to guarantee against famine. The business was immensely profitable and its proceeds built a string of prosperous seaports – including Volendam, Hoorn and Enkhuizen – and nourished market towns like Edam, while the Zuider Zee itself supported numerous fishing villages such as Marken. In the eighteenth century the Baltic trade declined, leaving the ports economically stranded, and, with the rapid increase in the Dutch population during the nineteenth century, plans were made to reclaim the Zuider Zee and turn it into farmland. The first part of the scheme was the completion of a dam, the Afsluitdijk, across the mouth of the Zuider Zee in 1932, but by the time a second, complementary barrier linking Enkhuizen with Lelystad was finished in 1976, the steam had gone out of the project. The old Zuider Zee was never completely drained and most has remained water, with the two dams creating a pair of freshwater lakes – the **Markermeer** and **IJsselmeer**.

These placid, steel-grey lakes are popular with day-tripping Amsterdammers, who come here in their hundreds to sail boats and visit a string of pretty little towns and villages. These begin on the coast just a few kilometres north of Amsterdam with the picturesque old fishing village of **Marken** and the former seaport of **Volendam**. In the summer, it's possible to travel between these two by boat, but the trip can also be made – if a little less conveniently – by bus via **Monnickendam**, another historic place (but of less interest) that has now become a sailing centre. Buses also link Volendam with **Edam**, a far prettier proposition and much less swamped by tourists. You don't necessarily need to make a choice though, since all three places can comfortably be visited in a day. A little way north of Edam, the Markermeer shore curves east to form a jutting claw of land at the base of which is **Hoorn**, an old Zuider Zee port whose compact centre, with its slender harbour and narrow streets, boasts a diverting assortment of Golden Age buildings. Though worth an hour or two of anyone's time, Hoorn is best viewed as a stop on the way to **Enkhuizen**, arguably the region's prettiest town, an engaging ensemble of narrow cobbled streets and slender waterways. Enkhuizen was once a flourishing Zuider Zee port and its heritage is celebrated in the excellent, open-air **Zuiderzeemuseum**. It's also within easy striking distance of another old seaport, **Medemblik**, as well as to the Afsluitdijk over to Friesland (see Chapter 4).

Marken, Monnickendam and Volendam

Once an island in the Zuider Zee, **Marken** was, until its road connection to the mainland in 1957, pretty much a closed community, supported by a small fishing industry. Despite its proximity to Amsterdam, its biggest problem was the genetic defects caused by close and constant intermarrying; now it's how to contain the tourists, whose numbers increase yearly. That said, there's no denying the

THE CLOSING OF THE ZUIDER ZEE

The towns and villages that string along the east coast of North Holland flourished during Amsterdam's Golden Age (see p.346), their economies buoyed up by ship-building, the Baltic sea trade and the demand for herring. They had access to the open sea via the waters of the **Zuider Zee** ("Southern Sea") and, to the north, the connecting **Waddenzee** ("Mud Sea"). Both seas were comparatively new, created when the North Sea broke through from the coast in the thirteenth century – the original coastline is marked by Texel (see p.165) and the Frisian Islands (see Chapter 000). However, the Zuider Zee was shallow and tidal, part salt and part freshwater, and accumulations of silt began to strangle its ports – notably Hoorn and Enkhuizen – from the end of the seventeenth century. Indeed, by the 1750s the Zuider Zee ports were effectively marooned and the only maritime activity was fish-ing – just enough to keep a cluster of tiny hamlets ticking over, from Volendam and Marken on the sea's western coast, to Stavoren (see p.242) and Urk (see p.274) on the eastern side.

The Zuider Zee may have provided a livelihood for local fishermen, but most of Holland was more concerned by the danger of flooding it posed, as time and again storms and high tides combined to breach the coastal defences. The first plan to seal off and reclaim the Zuider Zee was proposed in 1667, but the rotating-turret windmills that then provided the most efficient way of drying the land were insuf-ficient for the task and matters were delayed until suitable technology arrived – in the form of the steam-driven pump. In 1891, **Cornelis Lely** (1854–1929), after whom Lelystad (see p.274) was named, proposed a retaining dike and his plans were finally put into effect after devastating floods hit the area in 1916. Work began on this dike, the **Afsluitdijk**, in 1920 despite some uncertainty among the engi-neers, who worried about a possible rise in sea-level around the islands of the Waddenzee. In the event, their concerns proved groundless and, on May 28, 1932, the last gap in the dike was closed and the Zuider Zee simply ceased to exist, replaced by the freshwater **IJsselmeer**.

The original plan was to reclaim all the land protected by the Afsluitdijk, and three large-scale land reclamation schemes were completed over the next forty years: **Noordoostpolder** in 1942 (48,000 hectares), **Oostelijk Flevoland** in 1957 (54,000 hectares) and **Zuidelijk Flevoland** in 1968 (44,000 hectares). In addition, a complementary dike linking Enkhuizen with Lelystad was finished in 1976, thereby creating lake **Markermeer** – a necessary prelude to the draining of anoth-er vast stretch of the IJsselmeer. The engineers licked their contractual lips, but they were out of sync with the majority of the population, who were now opposed to any further draining of the lake. Partly as a result, the grand plan was abandoned and, after much governmental huffing and puffing, the Markermeer was left alone.

There were many economic benefits to be had in the closing of the Zuider Zee. The threat of flooding was removed, the country gained great chunks of new and fertile farmland and the roads that were built along the top of the two main retain-ing dikes brought North Holland within twenty minutes' drive of Friesland. The price was the demise of the old Zuider Zee **fishing fleet**. Without access to the open sea, it was inevitable that most of the fleet would go down the pan, though some skippers wisely transferred to the north coast before the Afsluitdijk was completed. Others learnt to fish the freshwater species that soon colonized the Markermeer and IJsselmeer, but in 1970 falling stocks prompted the government to ban trawling. This was a bitter blow for many fishermen and there were several violent demon-strations before they bowed to the inevitable. Today, villages such as Marken and Urk are shadows of their former selves, forced to rely on tourist kitsch to survive.

picturesque charms of the island's one and only village – also called **MARKEN** – where the immaculately maintained houses, mostly painted in deep green with white trimmings, cluster on top of artificial mounds raised to protect them from the sea. There are two main parts to the village, **Havenbuurt**, behind the harbour, and **Kerkbuurt** around the **church** (mid-May to Oct Mon–Sat 10am–5pm; free), an ugly 1904 replacement for its longstanding predecessor. Of the two Kerkbuurt is the less touristy, its narrow lanes lined by ancient dwellings and a row of old eel-smoking houses, now the **Marken Museum**, Kerkbuurt 44 (April–Oct Mon–Sat 10am–4.30pm, Sun noon–4.30pm; free), devoted to the history of the former island and its fishing industry. Across in the Havenbuurt, one or two of the houses are open for tourists, proclaiming themselves to be "typical" of Marken, and the waterfront is lined by snack bars and souvenir shops, often staffed by locals in traditional costume. It's all a tad prosaic, but now and again you get a hint of how hard life used to be – most of the houses on the waterfront are raised on stilts, allowing the sea to roll under the floors in bad weather, enough to terrify most people half to death.

Known as the **Waterland**, the marshy fenland stretching along and behind the coast of the Markermeer between Amsterdam and the beginning of the Marken causeway, is best explored by bike from Amsterdam – see box on on p.108.

If you are travelling from Marken to Volendam by bus (see below), you have to change at **MONNICKENDAM** – so while you're here you may as well spend a few minutes nosing around. Once an important Zuider Zee port, Monnickendam has reinvented itself as a sailing centre and its large harbour heaves with hundreds of yachts. Reminders of its Golden Age heyday do, however, crop up here and there – nothing dramatic, but the long and spindly main street is adorned by an attractive **Waag** (weighing house) and the **Speeltoren**, the conspicuous brick tower of the old town hall, which comes complete with a sixteenth-century carillon. The local speciality is **smoked eel**, something of an acquired taste perhaps, but still worth a try – either from a shop or down at a harbour stall.

Larger but not nearly as quaint as Marken, the old fishing village of **VOLENDAM** has had, by comparison with its neighbour, some rip-roaring cosmopolitan times. In the early years of the twentieth century it became something of an artists' retreat, with both Picasso and Renoir spending time here. The artists are, however, long gone and nowadays Volendam is crammed with day-tripping tourists bobbing in and out of the souvenir stalls that run the length of the main street. Quiet places, never mind pretty ones, are hard to find, but narrow **Meerzijde**, one street back from the harbour, does have its moments in its mazy alleys and mini-canals. One curiosity to look out for is a plaque at the corner of Berend Demmerstraat and Josefstraat marking how high the floodwaters of 1916 rose here.

Practicalities

Marken is accessible direct from Amsterdam on **bus** #111. This departs from the bus stop across the street from St Nicolaaskerk, close to Centraal Station (every 15–30min; 30min) and drops you beside the car park on the edge of Marken village, from where it's a five-minute walk to the centre. Marken does not have a **VVV** and neither is there anywhere **to stay**. In season, a passenger **ferry** links Marken with Volendam (March–Oct daily every 30min 11am–6pm; 30min; *f*10; information ☎0299/363331), but at other times it's a fiddly **bus** trip: take bus #111 back towards Amsterdam, but get off at the Swaensborch stop on the edge of Monnickendam village. At Swaensborch, change to bus #110, which runs from Amsterdam to Volendam and Edam; or it's a five- to ten-minute walk to Monnickendam harbour.

In **Volendam** bus #110 from Monnickendam drops passengers on Zeestraat, just along the street from the **VVV**, at no. 37 (April–Sept daily 10am–5pm; Oct–March Mon–Sat 10am–3pm; ☎0299/363747). From the VVV, it's a couple of minutes' walk to the waterfront. With Amsterdam just a short bus ride away and Edam even nearer (see below), there's absolutely no reason to stay overnight here, but if you do, the long-established *Best Western Spaander* on the waterfront at Haven 15 (☎0299/363595, fax 369615; ③) is the most attractive option. In the summertime, there is a regular **passenger ferry** to Marken (see above).

If you're planning to use more than a bus or two, buy a timetable in Amsterdam before you set out.

Edam

Further on down the #110 bus route from Amsterdam, just 3km from Volendam, you might expect **EDAM** to be jammed with tourists considering the international fame of the rubbery red balls of cheese that bear its name. In fact, Edam generally lacks the crowds and is a delightful, good-looking and prosperous little town of neat brick houses, swing bridges and slender canals. Founded by farmers in the twelfth century it boomed in the seventeenth as a shipbuilding centre with river access to the Zuider Zee. The excellent pasture land surrounding the town is still grazed by large herds of cows, but nowadays most Edam cheese is produced elsewhere, even in Germany; "Edam" is the name of a type of cheese and not its place of origin. This does, of course, rather undermine the authenticity of Edam's open-air **cheese market**, held every Wednesday in July and August on the Kaasmarkt (10.30am–12.30pm), but it's still a popular attraction and the only time the town heaves with tourists. Edam's cheese market is a good deal more humble than Alkmaar's (see p.161), but it follows the same format, with the cheeses laid out in rows before the buyers sample them. Once a cheese has been purchased, the cheese porters, dressed in the traditional white costumes and straw boaters, spring into action, carrying them off on their gondola-like trays.

The Town

At the heart of Edam is the **Damplein**, a pint-sized main square where an elongated humpbacked bridge has long vaulted in the Voorhaven canal, which once used to flood the town with depressing regularity. Also on the square is Edam's eighteenth-century **Stadhuis**, a severe Louis XIV-style structure whose plain symmetries culminate in a squat little tower, and the **Edams Museum** (April–Oct Tues–Sat 10am–4.30pm, Sun 1.30–4.30pm; *f*3,50), housed in an attractive building whose crow-stepped gables date from 1530. Inside, a modest assortment of local bygones is redeemed by the curious floating cellar, supposedly built by a retired sea captain who could not bear the thought of sleeping on dry land. From Damplein, it's a short walk along Grote Kerkstraat to the rambling **Grote Kerk** (April–Oct daily 2–4.30pm; free), on the edge of the fields to the north of the village. This is the largest three-ridged church in Europe, with a huge organ built in 1663 and a vaulted ceiling constructed in wood in an attempt to limit the subsidence caused by the building's massive weight. A handsome, largely Gothic structure, it contains several magnificent **stained-glass windows** dating from 1606 to 1620, mostly heraldic but including historical scenes too. Unfortunately, the church's strong lines are disturbed by the almost comically stubby spire, which was shortened to its present height after a lightning strike started a fire in 1602.

Strolling back from the church, take Matthijs Tinxgracht – one street west of Grote Kerkstraat – along the canal and you'll soon reach the Kaasmarkt, site of both the cheese market and the **Kaaswaag** (Cheese Weighing House), whose decorative panels celebrate – you guessed it – cheese-making and bear the town's coat-of-arms, a bull on a red field with three stars. From here, it's a couple of hundred metres to the sixteenth-century **Speeltoren**, the elegant tower visible from all over town, and roughly the same distance again – south along Lingerzijde – to the impossibly picturesque bridge of **Kwakelbrug**. This leads over to one of Edam's most charming streets, **Schepenmakersdijk**, a cobbled, canalside lane flanked by immaculate gardens and the quaintest of houses.

To explore Edam's every architectural nook and cranny, pop into the VVV, in the Stadhuis (see below), and buy their *A Stroll through Edam* (*f*4,95).

Practicalities

Leaving Amsterdam every half hour from near St Nicolaaskerk, **bus #110** takes thirty-five minutes to reach Volendam and ten minutes more to get to Edam. Edam's **bus station** is on the southwest edge of town, on Singelweg, a five-minute walk from Damplein. There are no signs, but aim for the easily spotted Speeltoren tower: cross the distinctive swing-bridge, turn right and follow Lingerzijde as it jinks left and right. From the Speeltoren, it's a few metres east to the Damplein, where the **VVV** (April–Oct Mon–Sat 10am–5pm; Nov–March Mon–Sat 10am–2pm; ☎0299/315125) issues town maps and has the details of **boat trips** both along the local canals and out into the Markermeer. **Bike rental** is available at Ronald Schot, in the town centre by the Speeltoren at Kleine Kerkstraat 9 (☎0299/372155); a one-day rental costs *f*10.

The VVV also has a selection of **private rooms** (*f*30–40 per person including breakfast), which they will book on your behalf for free. Otherwise, there are three **hotels**, the pick being the charming *De Fortuna*, just round the corner from the Damplein at Spuistraat 7 (☎0299/371671, fax 371469; ③). This three-star hotel, with its immaculate garden flowing down to a canal, has just thirty comfortable rooms distributed amongst six cosy little houses. An appealing second choice is the *Damhotel*, which occupies a modernized old inn opposite the VVV (☎0299/371766, fax 374031; ②). The third hotel is the rather more modest, one-star *Harmonie*, in a plain but pleasant canalside house a couple of hundred metres east of the VVV at Voorhaven 92 (☎0299/371664; ②). The nearest **campsite** is east of town near the lakeshore at Zeevangszeedijk 7 (☎0299/371994) – a twenty-minute walk east along the canal from Damplein.

For **eating**, *De Fortuna* has the best restaurant in town, but eating at the *Damhotel* is barely a hardship – and it's a good deal cheaper; both serve Dutch cuisine.

Hoorn

The old Zuider Zee port of **HOORN**, some 17km north of Edam, "rises from the sea like an enchanted city of the east, with its spires and its harbour tower beautifully unreal". So wrote the English travel writer E.V. Lucas in 1905, and the town is still very much a place you should either arrive at or leave by sea – though you probably won't get the chance to do either. During the seventeenth century this was one of the richest of the Dutch ports, referred to by the poet Vondel as the "trumpet" of the Zuider Zee, handling the important Baltic trade and that of the Dutch colonies. The Dutch East India Company (see p.346) had one of its centres of operation here; *The Tasman* left its harbour to "discover" Tasmania and New Zealand, and in 1616 William Schouten sailed away to navigate a passage around South America, calling its tip "Cape Hoorn" after his native town. The harbour silted up in the early eighteenth century, however, stemming trade and gradually turning Hoorn into one of the so-called "dead cities" of the Zuider Zee – a process completed with the creation of the IJsselmeer (see box on p.149).

The Town

Perhaps surprisingly, Hoorn's former glories are hard to detect in what is today a busy modern town: the harbour is a yacht marina and the elegant streets and buildings that evince the town's heyday have too often been defaced by modern development. That said, the convoluted streets bordering the harbour boast a fine ensemble of old merchants' houses whose tall and slender gables can, on occasion, rival those of Amsterdam. At the centre is **Roode Steen**, literally "red stone", an unassuming square that used to hold the town scaffold and now focuses on the swashbuckling statue of **Jan Pieterszoon Coen** (1587–1629), founder of the Dutch East Indies Empire and one of the bright lights of the seventeenth century. Coen was a headstrong and determined leader of the Dutch imperial effort, under whom the Far East colonies were consolidated and rivals, like the English, were kept at bay. His settling of places like the Moluccas and Batavia was something of a personal crusade, and his austere, almost puritanical way of life was in sharp contrast to the wild and unprincipled behaviour of many of his compatriots on the islands.

On one side of Roode Steen stands the early-seventeenth-century **Waag**, designed by Hendrik de Keyser (see p.80) and now a café-bar more enjoyable for its setting, amidst the ponderous wooden appliances that helped the weighing, than its food. On the other side, and dominating the square, the **Westfries Museum** (Mon–Fri 11am–5pm, Sat & Sun 2–5pm; *f*5) is Hoorn's most prominent sight, housed in the elaborately gabled former West Friesland government building of 1632. The gable is decorated with the coats of arms of the house of Orange-Nassau and the region's towns. Now a district within the province of North Holland, West Friesland incorporates the chunk of land between Alkmaar, Hoorn and Enkhuizen, but its origins are much grander. Speaking a distinctive German dialect, the Frisians once controlled a narrow sliver of seaboard stretching west from Bremerhaven in Germany to Belgium. Charlemagne conquered them in the 780s and incorporated their territory into his empire, chopping it down in size and dividing the remainder into seven regions, two of which – West Friesland and Friesland (see Chapter 000) are now in the Netherlands.

Inside, the museum convincingly re-creates the interiors of the time when Hoorn's power was at its height. Along with any number of unascribed portraits, furniture and ceramics, the walls of the council chamber (Room 7) are covered with militia portraits by Jan Rotius, who portrays himself in the painting by the window (he's the figure by the flag on the left) and employs some crafty effects in the other canvases. Walk past the figure in the far right of the central painting and watch his foot change position from left to right as you pass. On the second floor, in Room 16, there's a painting of 1632 by Jan van Goyen (*Landscape with a Peasant Cart*) and a wooden fireplace carved with tiny scenes showing a whaling expedition – Hoorn was once a whaling port of some importance. Other items of interest include a view of Hoorn painted in 1622, a room containing portraits of various East India Company dignitaries, including one of a severe-looking Coen, while on the top floor are mock-ups of seventeenth-century trades and shops – even a prison cell.

Strolling east from Roode Steen, **Grote Oost** is shadowed by fine old mansions, many of which sport neat rococo balustrades. But the most appealing house of all is the **Bossuhuizen**, on the right at the corner with Slapershaven, its facade decorated with a long and slender frieze depicting a sea battle of 1573 – which Admiral Bossu actually lost. Continuing down Slapershaven, past some of the most comfortable houseboats imaginable – some have garages, others are even thatched – you soon reach the inner harbour, the **Binnenhaven**, with its clutter of sailing boats and antique barges. Overlooking the harbour, on Oude Doelenkade, is a long row of old warehouses, with their prim shutters and crow-stepped gables, whilst, just over the swing bridge and also beside the Binnenhaven, Veermanskade is fringed by elegant merchants' houses mostly dating to the seventeenth century. In particular, look out for the birthplace of **Willem Ysbrantzoon Bontekoe** (1587–1657), at Veermanskade 15 – the facade stone shows a particularly ugly spotted cow, as in *bonte* ("spotted") and *koe* ("cow"). A sea captain with the East India Company, Bontekoe published his journal in 1646, a hair-raising account of his adventures that proved immensely popular. Portraying himself as astute and brave in equal measure, Bontekoe's most eventful voyage included the snapping of the mainmast, an epidemic of scurvy and an explosion that forced the crew to abandon ship, all en route from Hoorn to Jakarta. At the end of Veermanskade rises the solid brickwork of the **Hoofdtoren**, a defensive watchtower from 1532, and at its base you'll find a friendly bronze sculpture of 1968 entitled *Three Ships' Boys*, by Jan van Druten.

Doubling back along Veermanskade, turn left at the swing bridge along Nieuwendam and it's a couple of minutes' walk round the canal to Appelhaven and the **Museum Van De Twintigste Eeuw** (Museum of the Twentieth Century; Tues–Sun 10am–5pm; *f*5), housed in two former cheese warehouses at Bierkade 4. Its permanent displays of daily life during this century, though not exactly gripping, are supplemented by changing exhibits with titles such as "Travel Posters – A Nostalgic Journey" and "100 Years of Blokker" (Blokker is the Dutch equivalent of Woolworth's). A scale model of Hoorn in 1650 and an audio-visual display describing the role of the town in the Dutch Golden Age, are more diverting, but not much more. From the museum, it's a couple of minutes' walk back to Roode Steen – take narrow Grote Havensteeg from Appelhaven.

Practicalities

If you're coming from Amsterdam, the easiest way to reach Hoorn is by train (every 30min; 40min); from Edam, take bus #114 from the bus station (every 30min; 30min). Both leave you at Hoorn **train station**, on the northern edge of town about ten minutes' walk from the centre – just follow the signs to the Westfries Museum. It isn't immediately obvious where the **VVV** is – it's located in between the train station and the Westfries Museum (but nearer the train station) at Veemarkt 4 (June–Aug Mon 1–6pm, Tues–Fri 9.30am–6pm, Thurs also 7–9pm,

EXCURSIONS FROM HOORN

Hoorn is the starting point for **steam train services** (April–Oct Tues–Sun 11am–2.20pm, July & Aug also Mon same times; 1hr; ƒ14,50 one-way, ƒ20 return; information ☎0229/219231) to Medemblik (see p.159), which can make an agreeable day out, especially if you're travelling with young children – there are between one and four departures per day. At Medemblik, a **ferry** runs on to Enkhuizen (April–Oct 1–2 daily; 1hr 30min; ƒ14,50 one-way, ƒ20 return); rather than buying separate tickets though, you should buy a combination round-trip ticket in Hoorn, which gets you to Medemblik by steam train, Enkhuizen by ferry and back to Hoorn by a normal train – these cost ƒ20. Outside the summer season, if you want to get from Hoorn to Medemblik, catch bus #39 (hourly; 30min).

Sat 9.30am–5pm & Sun 1–5pm; Sept–May Mon 1–5pm, Tues–Sat 9.30am–5pm; ☎0900/403 1055). Veemarkt runs parallel to, and one block east of, Kleine Noord, which is – along with its continuation Grote Noord – the main shopping street.

With Enkhuizen and Edam so near, there's no real reason to stay in Hoorn, but there are four recommendable **hotels** in the centre and the VVV has a small number of **private rooms** (at around ƒ30 per person per night). The cheapest of the hotels is the small and plain, family-run *De Posthoorn*, with the rooms above a café, off Kleine Noord at Breed 27 (☎0229/214057, fax 219057; ②). Close by, in a modern building at Breed 31, is the comfortable, three-star *De Keizerskroon* (☎0229/212717, fax 211022; ②), and there's the *Petit Nord*, a smart four-star hotel in a boring location on the main shopping street at Kleine Noord 53 (☎0229/212750, fax 215745; ③). Last but not least, the three-star *De Magneet*, Kleine Oost 5 (☎0229/215021, fax 237044; ②), occupies a pleasant location close to the harbour.

For **food**, *Sweet Dreams*, metres from the Waag at Kerkstraat 1, is an excellent café offering delicious omelettes and Mexican dishes – and it's open until midnight. Another café, *Het Witte Paard*, off Kerkstraat opposite the Grote Kerk at Lange Kerkstraat 27, serves Dutch food and vegetarian dishes daily until 11pm, whilst *De Eethoorn*, beside the Grote Kerk at Kerkplein 7, is an appealingly inexpensive *eetcafé* and a good spot for a **drink** – as are the handful of bars down by the Binnenhaven. Amongst Hoorn's **restaurants**, the *Isola Bella*, Grote Oost 65 (☎0229/217171), is a first-class, cosy and reasonably priced Italian place, while the more formal *Alpino*, Breed 32 (☎0229/218567), serves tasty French specialities.

Enkhuizen

The beguiling little town of **ENKHUIZEN**, just 16km east along the coast from Hoorn and twenty-five minutes by train, was once one of the country's most important seaports. From the fourteenth to the early eighteenth century, when its harbour silted up, it prospered from the Baltic sea trade and North Sea herring fishing industry and indeed its maritime credentials were second to none: it was home to Holland's largest fishing fleet and its citizens were renowned for their seamanship, with the Dutch East India Company always keen to recruit here. It was also the first town in North Holland to rise against Spain, in 1572, but, unlike many of its Protestant allies, it was never besieged – its northerly location kept it safely out of reach of the Habsburg army. Subsequently, Enkhuizen slipped into a long-lasting economic reverie, becoming a remote and solitary backwater until, in recent years, tourism has revived its fortunes. About twenty minutes' walk from end to end, the town centre, with its ancient streets and slender canals, has preserved its medieval shape, a rough circle with a ring of bastions and moat on one side, and the old sea dike on the other. Enkhuizen also possesses no less than three pretty harbours and a major attraction in the extensive **Zuiderzeemuseum**, which details the history and cultural significance of the sea to the region. It divides into two parts: the indoor **Binnenmuseum** and the rather more interesting **Buitenmuseum**, a well conceived recreation of life in the old Zuider Zee ports between 1880 and 1932. The town is also a good place to visit for its summer **ferry** connections to Stavoren and Urk across the IJsselmeer.

Arrival, information and accommodation

Trains to Enkhuizen, which is at the end of the line, stop right opposite the head of the main harbour – the Buitenhaven, at the southeastern corner of the town centre. **Buses** stop on one side of the train station, while on the other, about 200m to the east, is the **VVV**, at Tussen Twee Havens 1 (April–Oct daily 9am–5pm; Nov–March Mon–Fri 9am–5pm & Sat 9am–2pm; ☎0228/313164). The VVV has a small supply of **private rooms**, at around ƒ35 per person per night, issues free maps and has a list of all the town's accommodation.

Of the places **to stay** the guesthouse *Het Gastenhuis*, Westerstraat 158 (☎0228/318217, fax 317517; ③) certainly has the town's most unusual lodgings, with just one suite for two in a meticulously refurbished and tastefully remodelled old merchant's house, including a fine Renaissance facade. It's popular, so advance booking is pretty much essential. **Hotels** include the three-star *Die Port van Cleve*, Dijk 74 (☎0228/312510, fax 318765; ③), which occupies a good-looking old building overlooking one of the town's three harbours, a short walk from the train station – their comfortable rooms, however, are fairly characterless; *Villa Oud Enkhuizen*, Westerstraat 217 (☎0228/314266, fax 318171; ③), a delightful hotel housed in an immaculate Victorian residence on the west side of the centre, with cosy rooms and an outside terrace and garden; and *Het Wapen van Enkhuizen*, Breedstraat 59 (☎0228/313434, fax 320020; ②) an unassuming three-star hotel located right in the centre of town by the Stadhuis, with spick and span, comfortable rooms. In addition, there are two summer-only **campsites** handily located on the edge of the centre. The nearest is the Enkhuizer Zand on the far side of the Zuider Zee Museum at Kooizandweg 4 (☎0228/317289, fax 312211; April–Sept). The other is De Vest, Noorderweg 31 (☎0228/321221, no fax; April–Sept), which fits snugly onto one of the old bastions. To get there, follow Vijzelstraat north off Westerstraat, continue down Noorderweg, and turn left by the old town ramparts; from the train station to the campground is about 1.5km.

FERRIES FROM ENKHUIZEN

During the summer you can travel from Enkhuizen **by passenger ferry** east to the other side of the IJsselmeer, either to **Stavoren** (May–Sept 3 daily; April & Oct twice daily; 1hr 20min; ƒ12 one-way, ƒ17,50 return; see p.242) or **Urk** (July & Aug 3 daily; 1hr 45min; ƒ12,50 one-way, ƒ18,50 return; see p.274). Alternatively you can travel north to the village of **Medemblik** (April–Oct twice daily; 1hr 30min; ƒ14,50 one-way, ƒ20 return; see p.159). All ferries leave from behind the train station, and you can buy tickets from the VVV, who will also have details of departure times.

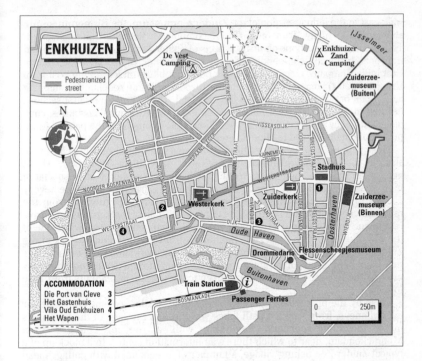

The Town

A good place to start an exploration of Enkhuizen's compact centre is **Westerstraat**, the town's spine, a busy pedestrianized street that is home to most of its shops and stores. At one end stands the **Westerkerk**, an early fifteenth-century Gothic church whose free-standing wooden tower is painted in violently incongruous colours – orangey-beige and green. The interior of the church, with its three naves of equal height, is distinguished by its rood-screen, a mid-sixteenth century extravagance whose six subtly carved panels show biblical figures – Moses, Joshua and the Evangelists. From the Westerkerk, it's a couple of minutes' walk south to the **Oude Haven** ("old harbour") and its jangle of sailing boats and low-slung barges. The harbour stretches east in a gentle curve that leads round to the conspicuous **Drommedaris**, a heavy-duty brick watchtower built in 1540 to guard the enclosure. Immediately to the east is the oldest part of town, a narrow lattice of ancient alleys amongst which, in a wonderful tiny old house at Zuiderspui 1, is the pocket-sized **Flessenscheepjesmuseum** (daily: Oct–May 10am–6pm; June–Sept 10am–8pm; ƒ5), an establishment devoted to that ubiquitous maritime curiosity, the ship-in-bottle. Well presented and labelled, the exhibits are fascinating, with vessels ranging from East Indiamen to steamboats, and containers from a tiny scent bottle to a thirty-litre wine flagon.

Take Zuider Havendijk north from here along the canal and turn left at the end for the **Zuiderkerk**, a hulking Gothic pile with a massive tower. Close by, just to the east, is the solid, classically styled mid-seventeenth-century **Stadhuis**, a dour-looking edifice that still houses the city council. From the Stadhuis, it's a short walk east to the indoor section of the **Zuiderzeemuseum**, the **Binnenmuseum**, at Wierdijk 18 (daily 10am–5pm; *f*8, *f*18 combined ticket with Buitenmuseum). This has separate sections on many aspects of Zuider Zee life, including trade and transport, boats and shipbuilding, fishing and whaling, land reclamation and the East India Company. One of the more curious exhibits is an ice-cutting boat from Urk (see p.274), once charged with the responsibility of keeping the shipping lanes open between the island and the mainland. There are also several sections devoted to applied art, most notably some extravagant regional costumes, complete with fancy Dutch caps, and several beautiful examples of the painted furniture traditionally carved in Hindeloopen (see p.240).

Most people, however, give the indoor museum a miss and instead make straight for the **Buitenmuseum** (April–Oct daily 10am–5pm; *f*18), whose nearest entrance is about 250m to the north along Wierdijk. Note also that in high season – usually July and August – there's a free ferry service (every 15min) to the open-air museum from the train station, as there is from the museum car park to the south of the centre; just follow the signs as you drive into town. The Buitenmuseum itself stretches north along the seaward side of the old dike that once protected Enkhuizen from the turbulent waters of the Zuider Zee. It contains over 130 dwellings, stores, workshops and even streets that have been transported here from every part of the region; together they provide the flavour – albeit rather antiseptically – of life hereabouts from 1880 to 1932.

Close by the boat wharf, there's a series of lime kilns, conspicuous by their tall chimneys, from which a path takes you through the best of the museum's many intriguing corners, beginning with a row of cottages from Monnickendam, near to which there's an information centre. In a mock-up of a typical Zuider Zee fishing village, a number of streets lined with cottages lead off from here, with examples of buildings from Urk among other places – their modest, precisely furnished interiors open to visitors and sometimes inhabited by characters in traditional dress, hamming it up for the tourists. Further on, a number of buildings sit along and around a central canal. There's a post office from Den Oever; a grocery from Harderwijk; an old laundry, thick with the smell of washing; a chemist and a bakery from Hoorn, the latter selling pastries and chocolate; while a cottage from Hindeloopen doubles up as a restaurant. It all sounds rather kitsch, and in a way it is: there are regular demonstrations of the old ways and crafts; goats and sheep roam the stretches of meadow, and the exhibition is mounted in such an earnest way as to almost beg criticism. But the attention to detail is very impressive, and the whole thing is never overdone, with the result that many parts of the museum are genuinely picturesque. Even if you see nothing else in Enkhuizen (and many people don't), you really shouldn't miss it.

Eating and drinking

For a small town, Enkhuizen has a good supply of **restaurants**. Handy, town-centre options include the cosy *De Smederij*, Breedstraat 158 (☎0228/314604), which offers a wide-ranging menu – from mussels to meat – all at reasonable prices, and the equally inexpensive Dutch food of the *Het Wapen Hotel Restaurant*, Breedstraat 59 (☎0228/313434). More upmarket is the French cuisine of the first-rate *Restaurant d'Alsace*, Westerstraat 116 (☎0228/313434), but the outstanding place in town is *Die Drie Haringhe*, Dijk 28 (☎0228/318610; closed Tues), which serves imaginative dishes that often feature local ingredients. Housed in a seventeenth-century building, the atmosphere is restrained but the food is quite magnificent, if a little pricey. This is *the* place to try IJsselmeer pike (*snoek*), a white fish and local delicacy. A good place for a **drink** is the *'t Ankertje* pub at Dijk 4, an atmospheric, old-fashioned kind of place with nautical knick-knacks hanging on the walls.

Medemblik to the Afsluitdijk

Just a few kilometres north along the coast from Enkhuizen, **MEDEMBLIK** is one of the most ancient towns in Holland, a seat of pagan kings until the seventh century, though there's not a great deal to entice you here nowadays, unless you're madly into yachts. The only sign visible today of Medemblik's ancient beginnings is the **Kasteel Radboud**, perched by the harbour at Oudevaartsgat 8 (mid-May to mid-Sept Mon–Sat 10am–5pm & Sun 2–5pm, mid-Sept to mid-May Sun only 2–5pm; *f*5). It is named after the eighth-century baron who first fortified this spot, though the structure that survives is not his at all, but a much-restored thirteenth-century fortress built by Count Floris V, who was murdered in Muiden (see p.168) and buried in Alkmaar (see p.161). The restoration was planned by Petrus J.H. Cuypers, the architect responsible for Amsterdam's Centraal Station and Rijksmuseum. Inside the castle, exhibits outline the fort's history and there's a ragbag of archeological finds from local sites. The old train station, where the summer steam train draws in (see p.155), houses the **VVV** (April–Oct Mon–Sat 10am–5pm, July & Aug also Sun same times; Nov–March Mon–Sat 10am–noon & 2–4pm; ☎0227/542852), while at Oosterdijk 4 there's the **Nederlands Stoommachinemuseum** (Dutch Steam Engine Museum; April–Oct Tues–Sun 10am–5pm; *f*7), an assembly of thirty ancient steam engines in a former pumping station. Otherwise most people come to Medemblik to sail: the harbour is busy throughout summer with the masts of visiting and resident yachters and there is a ferry linking it with Enkhuizen (see p.155).

North of Medemblik, the **Wieringermeer Polder** was reclaimed in the 1920s, filling in the gap between the former Zuider Zee island of Wieringen and the mainland. Towards the end of World War II, just three weeks before their surrender, the Germans flooded the area, boasting they could return Holland to the sea if they wished. After the war, it was drained again, leaving a barren, treeless terrain that had to be totally replanted. Almost sixty years later, it's indistinguishable from its surroundings, a familiar polder landscape of flat, geometric fields, highlighted by neat and trim farmhouses leading north to the **Afsluitdijk** highway over to Friesland (see Chapter 4). The sluices on this side of the Afsluitdijk are known as the **Stevinsluizen**, after Hendrick Stevin, the seventeenth-century engineer who first had the idea of reclaiming the Zuider Zee. At the time, his grand plan was impracticable – the technology was unavailable – but his vision lived on, to be realized by Cornelis Lely (see box on p.149), though he too died before the structure was completed. At the North Holland end of the dike, there's a statue of Lely by the modern Dutch sculptor Mari Andriessen – for other examples of Andriessen's work, see p.87 and p.98, in Chapter 1. Further along the dike, at the point where the barrier was finally closed, there's an observation point on which an inscription reads "A nation that lives is building for its future" – a linking of progress with construction that read well in the 1930s, but, given the disrepute into which redevelopment has often fallen, reads strangely today.

The inland route: Zaandam to Texel

The inland route north through the province begins with the build-up of settlements collectively known as Zaanstad, which trails northwest of Amsterdam on the far side of the River IJ. Two places here in particular are worth visiting – **Zaandam**, the urban core of Zaanstad, and the museum-village of **Zaanse Schans**, complete with its old wooden cottages and windmills. Stay on the train and it's another thirty minutes or so to **Alkmaar**, a pleasant old town with a clutch of handsome Golden Age buildings and a traditional open-air cheese market that is much admired by tourists. Nearby is the good-looking village of **Bergen**, home to the enjoyable Museum Kranenburgh of fine art, which itself lies close to the woods and dunes of the Boswachterij Schoorl nature reserve. The latter rolls down to the coast near the seaside resort of **Bergen-aan-Zee**. It's another short haul to **Den Helder**, a humdrum port at the province's northern tip that is useful for the ferry over to the island of **Texel** (see p.165).

As for public transport, a fast and frequent **train** service runs north from Amsterdam linking Zaandam, Koog-Zaandijk (for Zaanse Schans), Alkmaar and Den Helder. From each train station, **buses** run to the smaller communities that are not on the rail line, usually every hour or half-hour.

Zaandam and Zaanse Schans

From the train as it heads north from Amsterdam it's not an especially enticing prospect, but unassuming **ZAANDAM** is an amiable, largely modern town that merits a brief stop. It was a popular tourist hangout in the nineteenth century, when it was known as "La Chine d'Hollande" for the faintly oriental appearance of its windmills, canals, masts, and row upon row of brightly painted houses. Claude Monet spent some time here in the 1870s, and, despite being suspected of spying and under constant police surveillance, immortalized the place in a series of paintings. Follow the main street, Gedempte Gracht, from the train station for five minutes (the **VVV** is at no. 76; Mon–Fri 9am–5.30pm, Sat 9am–4pm; ☎075/616 2221), turn right down Damstraat, right again, and left down Krimp, and you can see something of Monet's Zaandam, the harbour spiked with masts beyond a little grouping of wooden houses. On Krimp itself, at no. 23, is the town's main modern claim to fame, the **Czaar Petershuisje** (Tues–Fri 10am–1pm & 2–5pm, Sat & Sun 1–5pm; ƒ3,50), a house in which the Russian Tsar Peter the Great stayed when he came to study shipbuilding here. In those days Zaandam was an important shipbuilding centre, and the tsar made four visits to the town, the first in 1697 when he arrived incognito and stayed in the simple home of one Gerrit Kist, who had formerly served with him. A tottering wooden structure enclosed within a brick shelter, the house is little more than two tiny rooms, decorated with a handful of portraits of a benign-looking emperor and the graffiti of tourists going back to the mid-nineteenth century. Among the few things to see is the cupboard bed in which Peter is supposed to have slept, together with the calling cards and pennants of various visiting Russian delegations; around the outside of the house is an exhibition on the shipbuilding industry in Zaandam. Napoleon is said to have remarked on visiting the house, "Nothing is too small for great men."

Most visitors to Zaanstad are, however, here to visit the recreated Dutch village of **ZAANSE SCHANS**. The village is made up of cottages, windmills and workshops assembled from all over the region, in an energetic and endearing attempt to reproduce a Dutch village as it would have looked in the eighteenth and early nineteenth century. Spread over a network of narrow canals beside the River Zaan, it's a pretty spot and deservedly popular, with the particular highlight being the working **windmills**, giant industrial affairs used – amongst other things – to cut wood, grind mustard seeds and produce oil. This is the closest place to Amsterdam to see working windmills and there's a scattering of other attractions too, notably a **Kaasmakerij** (Cheese-making workshop) and a **Klompenmakerij** (Clog-making workshop), where you can watch the village's employees practising traditional skills. You can walk round the village at any time, but the windmills and workshops are only open during the day, mostly from 9am to 5pm in winter, 6pm in summer; admission is around *f*2 per person per attraction. There are also enjoyable hour-long **boat trips** on the River Zaan from the jetty near the De Huisman mustard windmill (April–Sept daily 10am–5pm, every hour; *f*8).

It's about 1km to Zaanse Schans from the nearest train station, **Koog-Zaandijk**, two stops up the line from Zaandam. To get there directly from Zaandam, take bus #88 (every 30min; 10min) from the train station.

Alkmaar

Forty minutes from Amsterdam by train and thirty from Koog-Zaandijk, the little town of **ALKMAAR** was founded in the tenth century in the middle of a marsh, and takes its name from the auk diving bird which lived here, as in *alkeen meer*, or auk lake. Just like Haarlem, the town was besieged by Frederick of Toledo, but heavy rain flooded its surroundings and forced the Spaniards to withdraw in 1573, an early Dutch success in the Eighty Years' War. Alkmaar's agreeable, partially canalized centre is still surrounded by its medieval moat, part of which has been incorporated into the Noordhollandskanaal, itself part of a longer network of waterways running north from Amsterdam to the Waddenzee, beyond the Afsluitdijk.

Alkmaar has a cluster of impressive medieval buildings, but is best known for its much-touted **cheese market** (mid-April to mid-Sept Fri 10am–noon), an ancient affair that these days ranks as one of the most extravagant tourist spectacles in Holland. Cheese has been sold on the main square here since the 1300s, and although it's no longer a serious commercial concern, the market remains popular and continues to draw the crowds. If you want to see it be sure to get there early, as by opening time the crowds are already thick on the ground. The ceremony starts with the buyers sniffing, crumbling, and finally tasting each cheese, followed by intensive bartering. Once a deal has been concluded, the cheeses – golden discs of Gouda mainly, laid out in rows and piles on the square – are borne away on ornamental carriers by four groups of porters (*kaasdragers*) for weighing. The porters wear white trousers and shirt plus a black hat whose coloured bands – green, blue, red or yellow – represent the four companies that comprise the cheese porters' guild. Payment for the cheeses, tradition has it, takes place in the cafés around the square.

The Town

Even if you've only come for the cheese market, it's worth seeing something of the rest of the town before you leave. On the main square, the **Waag** (Weighing House) was originally a chapel dedicated to the Holy Ghost, but was converted

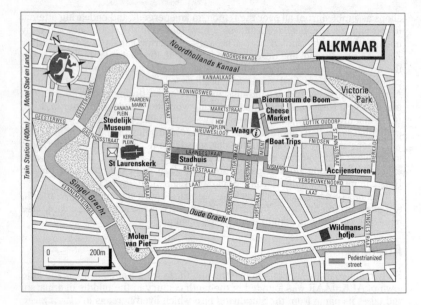

and given its delightful east gable – an ostentatious Dutch Renaissance affair
bedecked with allegorical figures – shortly after the town's famous victory against
the Spanish. Nowadays the Waag houses the **VVV** (see below) and the
Kaasmuseum (Cheese Museum; April–Oct Mon–Thurs & Sat 10am–4pm, Fri
9am–4pm; f5), with displays on the history of cheese, cheese-making equipment
and suchlike. Just off the north side of the square, the **Biermuseum de Boom**,
housed in the old De Boom brewery at Houttil 1 (Tues–Sat 10am–4pm, Sun
1–4pm; f4), has displays tracing the brewing process from the malting to the bot-
tling stage, aided by authentic props from this and other breweries the world over.
There's lots of technical equipment, enlivened by mannequins and empty bottles
from once innumerable Dutch brewers – though few, curiously, from De Boom
itself. It's an engaging museum, lovingly put together by enthusiasts, and there's
a shop upstairs where you can buy a huge range of beers and associated mer-
chandise, as well as a downstairs bar serving some eighty varieties of Dutch beer.

Heading south from the Waag along Mient, it's a few metres to the jetty from
where boat trips (see below) leave for a quick zip round the town's central canals
– an enjoyable way to spend forty-five minutes. At the south end of Mient, the
open-air **Vismarkt** (Fish Market; Fri 9am–noon) marks the start of the
Verdronkenoord canal, whose dignified facades lead down to the spindly
Accijnstoren (Excise Tower), part harbour master's office, part fortification
built during the long struggle with Spain in 1622. Turn left at the tower along
Bierkade and you'll soon reach **Luttik Oudorp**, another attractive corner of the
old centre, a slender canal leading back to the Waag.

One block south of the Waag, pedestrianized **Langestraat** is Alkmaar's main,
mundane, shopping street, whose only notable building is the **Stadhuis**, a florid
affair, half of which (the eastern side and tower) dates from the early sixteenth
century. At the west end of Langestraat lurks **St Laurenskerk** (mid-April to mid-

Sept Fri 9am–5pm; June–Aug also Tues–Thurs & Sat noon–5pm), a Gothic church of the late fifteenth century whose pride and joy is its huge **organ**, commissioned at the suggestion of the diplomat and political big-wheel Constantijn Huygens in 1645. The case was designed by Jacob van Campen, the architect who was later to design Amsterdam's town hall (see p.76), and decorated with paintings illustrating the triumph of David by Caesar van Everdingen (1617–1678). The artist's seamless brushstrokes and willingness to kow-tow to the tastes of the burgeoning middle class were to make him a wealthy man. In the apse is the tomb of Count Floris V, penultimate in the line of medieval counts of North Holland, who did much to establish the independence of the towns hereabouts and was murdered for his trouble by jealous nobles in 1296.

Across from the church, in the newly enlarged cultural centre, the **Stedelijk Museum** (Municipal Museum; Tues–Fri 10am–5pm, Sat & Sun 1–5pm; *f*3), displays pictures and plans of the siege of 1573, along with an assortment of seventeenth-century paintings. Amongst the latter is a striking *Holy Family* by Gerard van Honthorst (1590–1656), a Mannerist who specialized in glossy portraits of high officials. There's also work by Pieter Saenredam and Maerten van Heemskerck (1498–1574), a transitional figure who was tutored in the Dutch Mannerist style before a visit to Italy in 1532 changed the direction of his work. Greatly impressed by the Italians, Heemskerck returned home to paint in the style of Michelangelo, populating his large canvases with muscular men-of-action and buxom women.

Practicalities

From Alkmaar's **train** and **bus station**, it's about ten minutes' walk to the centre of town: keep straight outside the station, turn right down Snaarmanslaan and then left at busy Geesterweg, which leads over the old city moat to St Laurenskerk. From the church, it's another five minutes' walk east along Langestraat to the **VVV**, housed in the Waag on Waagplein (Mon 10am–5.30pm, Tues & Wed 9am–5.30pm, Thurs 9am–9pm, Fri 9am–6pm & Sat 9.30am–5pm; ☎072/511 4284). Alkmaar only takes an hour or two to explore, but if you decide to stay the VVV has plenty of **private rooms** for about *f*30 per person per night, including breakfast, though most places are on the outskirts of town and en-suite rooms are rare. Failing that, Alkmaar has one recommendable central **hotel**, the *Motel Stad en Land*, a plain and simple two-star establishment near the train station at Stationsweg 92 (☎072/512 3911, fax 511 8440; ③).

Boat trips leave from the jetty on Mient (May–Aug daily hourly 11am–5pm; April, Sept & Oct Mon–Sat only same times; during the cheese market every 20min; 25min; *f*6). There are also longer trips to Zaanse Schans (mid-May to late Oct 2–3 weekly; 6hr; *f*17,50 one-way, *f*27,50 return) and even to Amsterdam (mid-June to mid-Sept weekly; 9hr; *f*22,50 one-way, *f*37,50 return); ask at the VVV for further details or contact the operators, Woltheus Cruises, at the Kanaalkade jetty, on the north side of the centre (☎072/511 4840).

For **food**, Alkmaar is well served by *'t Waegh-Stuck*, just off the Waagplein at Fnidsen 101, a smart restaurant serving tasty and traditional Dutch cuisine at reasonable prices. Otherwise, *'t Gulden Vlies*, Koorstraat 30, is a recommendable grand café with a good line in light meals, and *Porto Fino*, close to the Waag at Mient 5, is a traditional Italian place serving delicious pizzas from *f*10. **Drinking**, too, is also well catered for. There are two groups of bars, one on Waagplein, the other around the Vismarkt, at the end of the Verdronkenoord canal. Among the former, the pick is *Proeflokaal 't Apothekertje*, an old-style bar, open until 2am, with an antique-cluttered interior and a laid-back atmosphere. Metres away, *Café Corridor* is younger and plays loud music late into the night. On Verdronkenoord, *De Pilaren* is another noisy place, though catering to a rather cooler crowd, some of whom take refuge in the *Café Stapper* next door, if the music gets too much.

Bergen and the coast

Bus #160 leaves Alkmaar train station every fifteen minutes or so – hourly on Sunday – for the ten-minute ride to **BERGEN**, a cheerful village whose main square, the **Plein**, is an amiable affair flanked by good-looking, vaguely rustic buildings. Bus #160 stops on the Plein (before pressing on to the coast – see below) and from here it's a couple of minutes' walk south along Breelaan to the **Sterkenhuis Museum** at Oude Prinsweg 21 (Tues–Sat 1–5pm, July & Aug also Sun 1–5pm; ƒ3). Occupying a seventeenth-century mansion, the museum holds regular exhibitions of work by contemporary Dutch artists and usually has a section on a largely forgotten episode in the Napoleonic Wars, when a combined army of 30,000 English and Russian soldiers were defeated by a Franco-Dutch force here in 1799. From the Sterkenhuis, it's a short walk west to the **Museum Kranenburgh**, a fine arts museum housed in a handsome neoclassical villa at Hoflaan 26 (Tues–Sun 1–5pm; ƒ7,50). Bergen has been something of a retreat for artists since the late nineteenth century and the museum features the work of the Expressionist Bergen School, which was founded here in 1915. Greatly influenced by the Post-Impressionists, especially Cézanne, none of the group is original enough to stand out, but taken as a whole it's a delightful collection and one that is supported by an imaginative programme of temporary exhibitions. These often focus on the two contemporaneous Dutch schools that were to have much more artistic impact – De Ploeg and De Stijl (see p.358). In addition, and warming to this artistic past, the local council organizes all sorts of cultural events in Bergen, including open-air sculpture displays and concerts, whilst the village also boasts a scattering of chichi art-for-sale galleries.

From Bergen's Plein, bus #162 (hourly; 15min) makes the trip northwest to the hamlet of **SCHOORL**, travelling along the eastern border of the **Boswachterij Schoorl**, a nature reserve whose wooded dunes stretch 5km west to the sea – one of the widest undeveloped portions of the whole Dutch coastline. The reserve is criss-crossed by cycling and walking trails and for all but the briefest of visits, you should pick up a map from the Bergen **VVV**, at Plein 1 (Mon–Fri 10am–5.30pm & Sat 10am–1pm; ☎072/581 3100). If you take a shine to Bergen, there are two good **hotels**, the smart, four-star *HCR Marijke*, just five minutes' walk south of Plein at Dorpsstraat 23 (☎072/581 2381, fax 589 7771; ③), and the rather more intimate, three-star *Russenweg*, right in the centre at Breelaan 26 (☎072/589 8484, fax 589 5830; ②). Another option is to push on north from Schoorl, taking bus #150, which links Alkmaar with Den Helder (see p.165) via the coast, weaving through a string of small-scale resorts, the most agreeable of which are **CAMPERDUIN** and **PETTEN**.

The coast

Heading west from Bergen, bus #160 takes ten minutes to travel the 5km to the coast at **BERGEN-AAN-ZEE**, a seaside resort where the main event is the long sandy beach with its thick border of grassy dunes. The resort also has a large

Marine aquarium at Van der Wijckplein 16 (daily: April–Oct 10am–6pm; Nov–March 11am–5pm; ƒ11,50). If you fancy a night by the sea, the *Hotel Nassau-Bergen*, at Van der Wijckplein 4 (☎072/589 7541, fax 589 7044; ④), has every convenience – from an outdoor swimming pool to tennis courts – and is situated just 50m from the beach.

Another coastal option – take half-hourly bus #165 from Alkmaar train station – is **EGMOND-AAN-ZEE**, a slightly larger resort but not as engaging, though it does have a splendid beach. It is also within striking distance of another stretch of protected coastline, the **Noordhollands Duinreservaat**, whose woods and dunes (cycling and walking trails) here stretch south for more than 10km to **CASTRICUM-AAN-ZEE** and beyond.

Den Helder

Forty minutes north from Alkmaar by train, **DEN HELDER** is a town of around sixty thousand, though it was little more than a fishing village until 1811, when Napoleon, capitalizing on its strategic position at the very tip of North Holland, fortified it as a naval base. It's still the principal home of the Dutch navy, and national fleet days (Vlootdagen) are held here on one weekend during the summer – usually in July – when, should you desire it, you can check out a huge portion of the Dutch navy. For further details, contact the Den Helder **VVV**, at Bernhardplein 18 (☎0223/625544). Otherwise, the place holds little of interest: its centre is an uninspiring muddle of modern architecture prefacing a seedier old quarter down near the harbour and the only real reason to come here is to take one of the plentiful ferries across the water to the island of Texel. If this is your plan, take NZH bus #3 (direction: Veerboot Texel) direct from the train station to the harbour and miss out the town altogether. If you want to make the twenty-minute walk to the ferry through the town centre, follow Spoorstraat from the station and turn left at the end; should you have time to spare, be sure to pop into Den Helder's **Marine Museum**, 200m from the dock at Hoofdgracht 3 (Tues–Fri 10am–5pm, Sat & Sun noon–5pm; May–Oct also Mon 10am–5pm; ƒ7,50). The museum makes a gallant attempt to conjure interest in what is, for most people, hardly a riveting subject, and the sections tracking through the history of the Dutch navy are well presented and entertaining. In particular, look out for the stuff on the naval heroes of yesteryear, especially Admiral Michiel de Ruyter (1607–1676), who trounced in succession the Spaniards, the Swedes, the English and the French. His most daring exploit was a raid up the River Thames to Medway in 1667 and the seizure of the Royal Navy's flagship, *The Royal Charles*, a raid that drove Charles II almost to distraction. There's lots of technical information too – on shipbuilding techniques and the like – and two decommissioned **vessels**, the 1960s submarine *Tonijn* and the veteran World War II minesweeper the *Abraham Crijnssen*; both are open for inspection.

Texel

The largest of the islands of the Waddenzee – and the easiest to get to – **TEXEL** (pronounced "tessel") is a lush, green thumb of land, speckled with small villages and lined on its western side by large areas of dune and extensive beaches. Now 24km long and 9km wide, much of it has actually been reclaimed from the sea, and, until the draining of its main polder on the northeastern side of the island

during the nineteenth century, it was shaped quite differently, the dunes protecting a much smaller expanse of farmland. It's an incredibly diverse and pretty island – something borne out by the crowds that congregate here during the summer months.

Ferries from the mainland (see below) drop you in the middle of nowhere – near a tiny hamlet called 't Horntje – but buses connect with ferry arrivals to take you to **DEN BURG**, the main settlement – no more than a large village, but home to the island's VVV (details below). As for sights, there's precious little to see in Den Burg beyond a small **museum** of local history, at Kogerstraat 1 (April–Oct Mon–Fri 10am–12.30pm & 1.30–3.30pm; *f*3,50), but it does make a decent base for seeing the rest of the island. The VVV has booklets detailing good **cycling routes**, as well as the best places to view the island's many **bird colonies**, protected in sanctuaries right across Texel (the island is one of the most important breeding grounds in Europe). Though you can see them well enough from a distance, you may want to get closer – in which case you need to seek permission at EcoMare in De Koog (see below).

As regards other villages, **OUDESCHILD**, on the coast about 3km southeast of Den Burg, is worth a quick look for its **Beachcombers Museum**, at Barentszstraat 21 (Maritiem en Juttersmuseum; Tues–Sat 10am–5pm; *f*8), a fascinating collection of marine junk recovered from offshore wrecks – everything from aeroplane engines to messages-in-bottles. Otherwise, in the opposite direction, **DE KOOG**, halfway up the western coast of Texel, is the island's main resort. It's a busy, popular spot equipped with a good, sandy beach, which gives easy access to the circuitous streams, dunes and marshes of the delightful **De Slufter nature reserve**. De Koog also possesses lots of restaurants and hotels, a small army of campsites and a nature centre, **EcoMare**, at Ruyslaan 92 (daily 9am–5pm; *f*12,50), with a small natural history museum and a refuge for lost birds and seals, which you can watch being fed at 11am and 3pm. Moving on, the northern tip of Texel is occupied by the solitary hamlet of **DE COCKSDORP**, definitely worth visiting if you like to feel a long way from civilization, its wedge of lonely little houses trailing along a slender inlet. In the southern part of the island, **DEN HOORN** is another tiny place, surrounded by bulbfields and a handy base for exploring the thick mass of dunes that constitutes Texel's southern tip.

Practicalities

Ferries (daily 6.30am–9.30pm) leave Den Helder for Texel roughly hourly, though the early-morning ferries don't run on Sundays or in the off-season (Sept–April). The journey takes twenty minutes, and costs *f*10 return (*f*8,25 in the off-season); a bike adds another *f*6 (*f*5), and a car *f*48,50 (*f*40,50). For more information call ☎0222/369691. If you want to use public **transport** while you're on Texel, ask about the *f*6 day-ticket (June–Sept only) when you buy your ferry ticket. If you know where you want to go, you can also arrange for a Telekomtaxi to take you anywhere on the island; again ask at the ferry dock. The best way to get around the island, though, is by **bike**: there are a couple of **rental** outfits in Den Burg – F. Zegel, Parkstraat 16, or A. Kievit, Jonkerstraat 2.

The island's **VVV** is in Den Burg at Emmalaan 66 (Mon–Fri 9am–6pm, Sat 9am–5pm; April–Oct also Fri till 9pm; July & Aug also Sun 10am–1.30pm; ☎0222/314741), where you can book **private accommodation** throughout the island. The cheapest **hotel** in Den Burg is *'t Koogerend*, Kogerstraat 94 (☎0222/313301, fax 315902; ②); it's a friendly place, but you pay over the odds for the location. There are also two **youth hostels** on either side of Den Burg on the roads to Oudeschild and De Koog – respectively called *Panorama* at Schansweg 7 (☎0222/315441, fax 313889; *f*26,50), and *De Eyercoogh*, at Pontweg 106 (same details as *Panorama*; July & Aug only). To get to the *Panorama*, take bus #29 from the ferry dock; for *De Eyercoogh* it's bus #28.

If you're **camping**, you're spoilt for choice. In and around Den Burg are four sites: best are the small, well-run De Koorn Aar at Grensweg 388 (☎0222/312931, fax 322208; April–Oct), which has easy bus connections all over the island, and 't Woutershok at Rozendijk 38 (☎0222/313080; April–Oct), which is run by Nivon, a nationwide organization devoted to culture, nature and recreation. Other sites dotted across the island include, in De Koog, Kogerstrand, Badweg 33 (☎0222/317208; April–Oct), scattered among the dunes two minutes from the beach, and Euroase Texel, Bosrandweg 395 (☎0222/317290, fax 317 194;

April–Oct), which also has bungalows on the beach. In De Cocksdorp, De Krim, Roggeslootweg 6 (☎0222/390111, fax 390121; all year) is quite upmarket, with luxury bungalows and a pool. Finally, in Den Hoorn, Loodsmansduin, Rommelpot 19 (☎0222/319203; April–Oct), is a large, isolated site with plenty of space for caravans.

One of the best of a small range of places to **eat and drink** in Den Burg is the café *De Worsteltent* at Smitsweg 6; and in De Koog, you'll be spoilt for choice. If you make it as far as De Cocksdorp, you can refresh yourself with a drink, a pancake or a full meal at the *Paviljoen Vliezicht Restaurant* (☎0222/316340; mid-March to Oct) on the beach.

Het Gooi

Known collectively as **Het Gooi**, the sprawling suburbs that spread southeast from Amsterdam towards Amersfoort (see p.218) are interrupted by open heaths, canals and woods, reminders of the time when this was a sparsely inhabited area largely devoted to sheep-farming. This changed after the Amsterdam–Amersfoort railway was constructed in 1874, when hundreds of prosperous Amsterdammers built their country homes here. Today, Het Gooi's low-key rural attractions remain popular with Dutch holidaymakers, but by and large the area is hardly essential viewing. That said, **Naarden**, encrusted by its star-shaped fortifications, is an agreeable little town, whilst both **Muiden** and **Hilversum**, the other two major places of interest, have some architectural interest – the first for its old castle, the second for the strikingly modern designs of Willem Dudok.

Getting around Het Gooi by **public transport** is straightforward. Only Hilversum is on the rail network, but bus #136 weaves a circuitous route through the area, beginning in Amsterdam and ending in Hilversum.

Muiden

The first town you reach, **MUIDEN** (pronounced "mao-dn"), is squashed around the Vecht, a river usually crammed with pleasure boats and dinghies primed to sail out into the Markermeer. It's the most famous sailing harbour in the Het Gooi area, not least because the royal yacht, *De Groene Draek*, is often moored here. Most of the sightseeing is done by weekend admirals eyeing up each other's boats, but an extra spark of interest is provided by the **Muiderslot** at Herengracht 1 (April–Oct Mon–Fri 10am–4pm, Sat & Sun 1–4pm; Nov–March Sat & Sun 1–3pm; guided tours only – call ahead to arrange one in English; ☎0294/261325; *f*7,50). In the thirteenth century this was the home of Count Floris V, a sort of aristocratic Robin Hood who favoured the common people at the nobles' expense. They replied by kidnapping the count, imprisoning him in his own castle and stabbing him to death. Ransacked in the fourteenth century, Muiderslot's interior has now been returned to its seventeenth-century appearance in honour of a slightly more recent occupant, the poet Pieter Hooft. He was chatelain here from 1609 to 1647, a sinecure that allowed him to entertain a group of artistic and literary friends who became known as the Muiden Circle, and included Grotius, Vondel, Huygens and other Amsterdam intellectuals. The obligatory guided tour centres on this clique, in a restoration that is both believable and likeable – two things period rooms often aren't.

From the jetty outside the Muiderslot, boats leave regularly for the fortress island of **Pampus** (April–Oct Tues–Fri 10.30am & 2pm, Sat & Sun 1 & 3pm; *f*17,50, including entry to the fortress; bookings on ☎0294/480999 or via the VVV – see below), a few kilometres out to sea. It was built at the end of the nineteenth century as part of Amsterdam's defence system, but has now fallen into ruin.

Practicalities

There are no trains to Muiden, but a fast and frequent **bus** service links the town with Amsterdam: take bus #136 (every 30min; 30min) from Amsterdam's Weesperplein metro station, in the vicinity of the Skinny Bridge (see p.90), or Amstelstation; the same service continues on to Naarden and Hilversum. Be warned that once you break free of Amsterdam, signs telling you where you are are few and far between and you can easily sail past Muiden without noticing – ask the driver to give you a shout.

In Muiden, the bus drops you on the edge of town, a short, signposted walk from the Muiderslot and the **VVV** at Kazernestraat 10 (April to late Oct Mon–Fri 10am–5pm, Sat 10am–2pm; ☎0294/261389). Once you've done the sights, there's no real reason to hang around unless, that is, you fancy pottering around in a **boat** – the Muiden Jachtverhuur Station (MYCS), at Naarderstraat 10 (☎0294/261413) rents out sailboats. As far as eating and drinking goes, there are a couple of obvious places but you'd do far better to carry on to Naarden, where there's a better choice.

Naarden

Look at a postcard of **NAARDEN**, about 8km east of Muiden, and it seems as if the town was formed by a giant pastry-cutter: the double rings of ramparts and moats, rare in Europe, were engineered between 1675 and 1685 to defend the eastern approaches to Amsterdam. They were still used in the 1920s, and one of the fortified spurs is now the wonderfully explorable **Vestingmuseum** (Fortification Museum; April–Oct Tues–Fri 10.30am–5pm, Sat & Sun noon–5pm; mid-June to Aug also Mon 10.30am–5pm; Nov–March Sun noon–5pm only; *f*10) at Westwalstraat 6, whose claustrophobic underground passages demonstrate how the garrison defended the town for 250 years. For an extra *f*4, you can also take a boat-trip around the fortress.

The rest of Naarden's tiny centre is peaceful and attractive. The small, low houses mostly date from after 1572 when the Spanish sacked the town and massacred the inhabitants, an act designed to warn other settlements in the area against insurrection. Fortunately they spared the late Gothic **Grote Kerk** (June to mid-Sept daily 2–4pm; free) and its superb vault paintings. Based on drawings by Dürer, these twenty wooden panels were painted between 1510 and 1518 and show an Old Testament story on the south side, paralleled by one from the New Testament on the north. To study the paintings without breaking your neck, borrow a mirror at the entrance. The church is also noted for its wonderful acoustics: every year there are several acclaimed performances of Bach's *St Matthew Passion* in the Grote Kerk in the days leading up to Easter – details from the VVV (see below). A haul up the 235 steps of the Grote Kerk's landmark square **tower** (tours July–Aug Tues–Sun 1, 2, 3 & 4pm; *f*4) gives the best view of the fortress, and, less attractively, of Hilversum's TV tower. The elaborately step-gabled building opposite the church is the **Stadhuis**, built in 1601 and still in use today; if the door's open, you're free to wander round inside.

Naarden also possesses the mildly absorbing **Comeniusmuseum** at Kloosterstraat 33 (April–Oct Tues–Sat 10am–5pm, Sun noon–5pm; Nov–March Tues–Sun 1–4pm; ƒ4,50). Jan Amos Komenski (1592–1670), known as Comenius, was a philosopher, cartographer and educational reformer who was born in Moravia, then part of the Holy Roman Empire and today part of the Czech Republic. A Protestant, he was expelled from the empire for his religious beliefs in 1621 and spent the next 36 years wandering round Europe preaching and teaching before finally settling in Amsterdam. The museum outlines Comenius' life and times and takes a stab at explaining his work, notably his government-commissioned plan to improve the Swedish educational system and his 1658 *Orbis Pictus* ("The World in Pictures"), the first-ever picture-book for children. Further sections relate his work to that of other philosophers of the day, principally the Frenchman René Descartes, who also lived in Amsterdam (from 1629 to 1649). After his death, Comenius was, for some unexplained reason, buried here in Naarden – hence the museum and the adjoining **mausoleum**, the last remnant of a medieval convent built on the site in 1438. In the 1930s the Dutch authorities refused the Czechoslovak government's request for the repatriation of the philosopher's remains, and instead sold them the building (and the land it stood on) for the symbolic price of one guilder: the mausoleum remains a tiny slice of Czech territory to this day. The museum-mausoleum is popular with Czech and Slovak tourists and Bratislava's Comenius University is named after the philosopher.

Practicalities

Naarden is on the same **bus** #136 route as Muiden (see above), with the journey from Amsterdam taking fifty minutes. The bus drops you off within sight of the Grote Kerk's tower – and within easy walking distance of all the sights. Everything is clearly signposted, including the **VVV**, about ten minutes' walk away at Adriaan Dortsmanplein 1b (May–Oct Mon–Fri 10am–5pm, Sat 10am–3pm, Sun noon–3pm; Nov–April Mon–Sat 10am–2pm; ☎035/694 2836). There are no central **hotels**, but the modern *Tulip Inn Naarden* (☎035/695 1514, fax 6951089; ④), is a reliable chain hotel on the edge of town by the A1 motorway.

For **food**, there's a concentration of places along the main shopping street, Marktstraat; from the bus stop, take Cattenhagestraat and you'll soon reach it. Café options include the *Salon de Thé Sans Doute* at no. 33, great for sandwiches and coffee, and the *Café De Doelen*, next to the Grote Kerk on the south side at no. 7, perfect for an inexpensive meal. On Cattenhagestraat itself, there's a first-rate Chinese–Indonesian restaurant, *Good Dates* at no. 34 (☎035/694 4836), but the best place in town is the pricey *Het Arsenaal* (☎035/694 9148), a smart restaurant occupying the old arsenal, which dates from 1688, and offering an à la carte menu of French–Dutch cuisine for around ƒ70 a head.

Hilversum

The main town of Het Gooi is **HILVERSUM**, a leafy nineteenth-century commuter suburb built just 7km south of Naarden for wealthy Amsterdammers, who created a well-heeled smugness that survives to this day. In recent years, many of the old villas have been flashily modernized and some have been converted into studios for Dutch broadcasting companies – the town is the centre of the Dutch broadcasting network. Behind the neatly trimmed hedges and lace curtains live some of the country's most comfortably-off bourgeoisie.

Hilversum's main sight is the **Raadhuis** (town hall), about 800m west of the train station at Dudopark 1. Dating from 1931, the building is the work of Willem Marinus Dudok (1884–1974), an architect who was influenced by the innovative American Frank Lloyd Wright. The structure's design is based on a deceptively simple progression of straw-coloured blocks rising to a clock tower, with long, slender bricks giving it a strong horizontal emphasis. The interior is well worth seeing too: essentially a series of lines and boxes, its marble walls are margined with black, like a monochrome Mondrian painting all coolly and immaculately proportioned. Dudok also designed the interior decorations, and though some have been altered, his style confidently prevails, right down to the ashtrays and lights. Long-time resident of Hilversum, Dudok worked for the city council for over thirty years, first as the director of public works and then as the city architect. If the Raadhuis whets your appetite, the VVV (see below) sells a guide (*f*3) to several of the other buildings he designed in town.

Other than that there's not much to see, but Hilversum does have several mildly diverting museums, the pick being the central **Goois Museum** (Tues–Sun 1–5pm; *f*3), in the old town hall at Kerkbrink 6 and devoted to local history. Outside the town centre, the **Omroepmuseum**, at Oude Amersfoortseweg 121–131 (Tues–Fri 10am–5pm, Sat & Sun noon–5pm; *f*8,50), has displays and videos on Dutch broadcasting history; to get there, take bus #134 to the Hilversum Sportpark stop; ask the driver to put you off.

Practicalities

Trains leave Amsterdam's Centraal Station twice an hour for Hilversum, and take about thirty minutes to get there. **Bus** #136 also runs to Hilversum from Amsterdam, departing from both the Weesperplein metro station, not far from the Skinny Bridge (see p.90), and the Amstelstation; departures are every half hour, but the bus follows a meandering route and the journey takes all of two hours. Hilversum's train and bus stations are next door to each other and a short walk from the **VVV**, at Noordse Bosje 1 (Mon–Fri 9.30am–6pm, Thurs till 9pm, & Sat 10am–4pm; mid-Sept to mid-May Mon–Fri 9am–5pm, Sat 9.30am–5pm; ☎035/624 1751). They have a small supply of **private rooms** (②), but with Amsterdam so close, and connections to more interesting towns so easy, there's little reason to stay here.

For **eating and drinking**, the pick of several inexpensive options near the train station is the *Grand Café Gooiland* at Emmastraat 2 (☎035/628 1926); they have a good range of Dutch and French dishes. Alternatively, the excellent *Nusantara*, is a well established Indonesian restaurant at Vaartweg 15a (☎035/623 2367).

If you're using Hilversum for further explorations into Het Gooi (see below), you can **rent bikes** at the train station.

Around Hilversum: exploring Het Gooi

Hilversum makes a good base for seeing the best of **Het Gooi** (which you can easily do in a day), and the VVV (see above) sells an excellent walking and cycling map of the area, the *Wandel- en fietskaart Gooi en Vechtstreek* (*f*9,50). The text isn't in English, but the map is pretty easy to understand and on the ground the routes are well-signposted. In particular, consider embarking on the **"Gooiroute"** – a scenic thirty-kilometre-long cycle route that leads across the heather to Laren, then via Blaricum to Huizen on the shore of the Gooimeer, and back via the woods to Hilversum. To get to the route from Hilversum train station, cross the rail line and continue along this road until just after you've crossed a roundabout, where you'll find the first "Gooiroute" signpost at a small road to the right. If you don't fancy the idea of cycling, bus #136 (every 30min between Amsterdam and Hilversum) is almost like a guided tour, taking the most circuitous route possible through every town and village along the way.

The most attractive village in Het Gooi is **LAREN**, halfway between Hilversum and the Gooimeer, if only because of its excellent **Singer Museum** of modern art at Oude Drift 1 (Tues–Sat 11am–5pm, Sun noon–5pm; ƒ8,50); bus #136 stops outside. Once a drowsy sheep-farming community, Laren became fashionable with artists in the 1870s, notably those of the Impressionist Hague School, and the surrounding landscape, as well as the village's farmers and weavers, and even the interiors of their farmhouses, all appear in their paintings. In later years, Expressionist and Modernist painters also came to the Laren area, and their works were gathered together by the Singers, an American couple who moved from Pittsburgh to Laren in 1901. The museum, which is based on their collection, opened in 1956 and, as well as paintings by Laren artists, contains works from France and America. As for the rest of the town, its shady streets and diminutive houses centre around the **Brink**, the main square, which has several pleasant bars, an outdoor pancake restaurant and **St Jans Basiliek** (Mon–Thurs 9am–noon; free), a good-looking church built in 1925.

travel details

Trains

Alkmaar to: Haarlem (every 30min; 25min); Hoorn (every 30min; 25min).

Amsterdam CS to: Alkmaar (every 30min; 30min); Den Helder (every 30min; 1hr); Enkhuizen (every 30min; 55min); Haarlem (every 15min; 15min); Hilversum (hourly; 30min); Hoorn (every 30min; 35min); Zaandam (every 15min; 10min).

Haarlem to: Alkmaar (every 30min; 25min); Hoorn (every 30min; 25min); Zandvoort (every 30min; 10min).

Hilversum to: Amersfoort (every 30min; 15min); Utrecht (every 20min; 20min).

Buses

Alkmaar to: Bergen (every 15min; 15min); Harlingen (hourly; 1hr 45min); Leeuwarden (hourly; 2hr 15min).

Amsterdam to: Edam (every 30min; 40min); Marken (every 30min; 30min); Muiden (every 30min; 40min); Naarden (every 30min; 55min); Volendam (every 30min; 30min); Zaandam (every 30min; 40min); Zaanse Schans (every 30min; 1hr).

Edam to: Hoorn (every 30min; 25min).

Enkhuizen to: Lelystad (every 2hr; 45min).

Haarlem to: Bloemendaal (every 30min; 15min); Zandvoort (every 15min; 20min).

Hoorn to: Medemblik (every 30min; 30–40min).

Marken to: Monnickendam (every 30min; 15min).

Monnickendam to: Volendam (hourly; 20min).

Muiden to: Hilversum (every 30min; 1hr 15min); Naarden (every 30min; 15min).

Ferries

Den Helder to: Texel (hourly; 20min).

Enkhuizen to: Medemblik (April–Oct 1–2 daily; 1hr 30min); Stavoren (April–Oct 2–3 daily; 1hr 20min); Urk (July & Aug Mon–Sat 3 daily; 1hr 45min).

Marken to: Volendam (March–Oct daily every 30min; 20min).

CHAPTER THREE

SOUTH HOLLAND AND UTRECHT

S outh Holland is the most densely populated province of the Netherlands, with a string of towns and cities that make up most of the **Randstad**, or rim-town. Careful urban planning has succeeded in stopping this from becoming an amorphous conurbation, however, and each town has a pronounced identity. A short hop from Amsterdam, **Leiden** is a university town par excellence, its antique centre latticed by canals and packed with fine old buildings. **The Hague**, once a dull government town, is now a likeable city with more than a sniff of affluence, and **Delft**, a smaller place with just 100,000 inhabitants and arguably the prettiest town centre of all, is flushed with handsome seventeenth-century buildings. Next it's on to the rough and tumble of big-city **Rotterdam**, the world's biggest port, from where it's a short journey inland to both **Gouda**, a good-looking country town historically famed for its cheese market, and the tranquil charms of rural **Oudewater**. Back on the coast, **Dordrecht** marks the southern end of the Randstad and is of interest as an ancient port and for its location, within easy striking distance of the windmills of the **Kinderdijk** and the creeks and marshes of the **Biesbosch**. The sprawling industrial complex of **Utrecht** remains – at least at heart – a university town benefiting from a lively, youthful atmosphere.

Historically, South Holland is part of what was once simply **Holland**, the richest and most influential province in the country. Throughout the Golden Age, Holland was far and away the most dominant province in the political, social and cultural life of the Republic, overshadowing its neighbours whose economies were dwarfed by Holland's success. There are constant reminders of this pre-eminence in the buildings of this region: elaborate town halls proclaim civic importance and even the usually sombre Calvinist churches allow themselves decorative excesses – the later windows of Gouda's Janskerk being a case in point. Many of the great painters either came from or worked here, too – Rembrandt, Vermeer, Jan Steen – a tradition that continued into the nineteenth century with the paintings of the Hague School. All the towns offer good museums and galleries, most notably The Hague's **Mauritshuis** and Rotterdam's **Boijmans-Van Beuningen**. The coastal cities – especially Leiden and The Hague – are only a short bus or tram ride from the wide sandy beaches of the North Sea coast, while the pancake-flat Randstad landscape is at least brightened by rainbow flashes of bulbfields in spring – the **Keukenhof Gardens**, near Leiden, have the finest display.

A fast and efficient rail network makes travelling around South Holland extraordinarily easy, and where the trains fizzle out, buses take over.

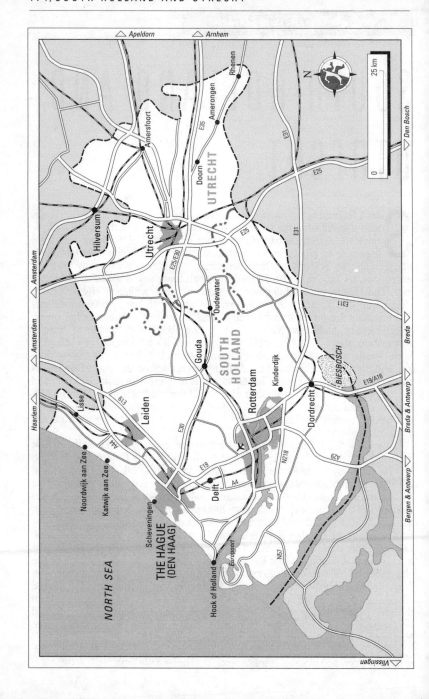

ACCOMMODATION PRICE CODES

All the **hotels** detailed in this chapter have been graded according to the following price categories. The codes are based on the price of the cheapest double room – without private bath, etc – during high season. In the case of **hostels** we've given the code if they have double rooms, otherwise we've stated the actual price per dorm bed per night.

① up to ƒ100/€45
② ƒ100–150/€45–67.50
③ ƒ150–200/€67.50–90
④ ƒ200–250/€90–112.50

⑤ ƒ250–300/€112.50–135
⑥ ƒ300–400/€135–180
⑦ ƒ400–500/€180–225
⑧ ƒ500/€225+

Leiden

Situated 30km southwest of Amsterdam, **LEIDEN** may well have been founded by the Romans as a forward base on an important trade route running behind the dunes; it was certainly fortified in the ninth century when the local lords added a castle, among the marshes on an artificial mound. After Flemish weavers migrated here in the fourteenth century the town prospered as a cloth-making centre, though it really became famous for its **university**, a gift from William the Silent as a reward for enduring a year-long siege by the Spanish. The town emerged victorious on October 3, 1574, when William cut through the dykes around the town and sailed in with his fleet for a dramatic rescue. The event is still commemorated with an annual fair, fireworks, and the consumption of two traditional dishes: herring and white bread, which the fleet was supposed to have brought with them, and *hutspot*, a vegetable and potato stew, a cauldron of which was apparently found simmering in the abandoned Spanish camp outside the town walls.

Ideal for a day-trip from Amsterdam, from where there are fast and frequent trains, Leiden possesses a string of good museums – too many in fact to see in one day, so be selective – and lots of good bars and restaurants. A lively and energetic place (largely due to its students), the town centre has real charm, its maze of narrow lanes and ancient buildings webbed with a complicated network of canals.

The Town

A good place to start an exploration of the town centre is the **Rapenburg**, a slender canal lined by some of Leiden's grandest mansions. In one of the largest, at no. 28, is the town's best-known attraction, the **Rijksmuseum Van Oudheden** (National Museum of Antiquities; Tues–Fri 10am–5pm, Sat & Sun noon–5pm; ƒ7). This is also Holland's principal archeological museum, boasting Egyptian and classical collections. You can see one of its major exhibits, the *Temple of Taffeh*, for free: situated in a courtyard near the museum entrance, this was a gift from the Egyptian government, in gratitude for Dutch help with the 1960s UNESCO excavations which uncovered a number of Nubian monuments. Dating back to the first century AD, the temple was adapted in the fourth century to the worship of Isis, eventually being sanctified as a Christian church four hundred years later.

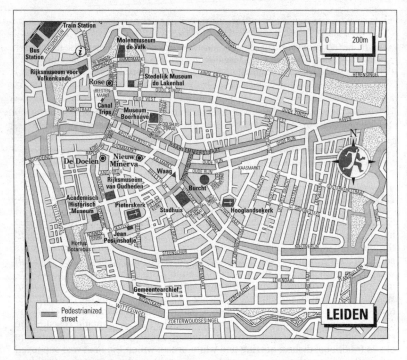

The Egyptians placed firm conditions on their legacy: no one should have to pay to see it, and the temperature and humidity must be carefully regulated, with the lights overhead simulating the passage of the sun.

Inside the museum proper, the first exhibit is the remains of a temple dedicated to Nehellania – a goddess of sailors – which was uncovered in Zeeland. Next comes classical Greek and Roman sculpture, leading chronologically through Hellenistic works to busts, statues and friezes from Imperial Rome. The most enjoyable collection, though, is the Egyptian one, beginning with wall reliefs, statues and sarcophagi from tombs and temples, and continuing in the rooms immediately above with a set of mummies and sarcophagi as complete as you're likely to see outside Egypt; the *Three Figures of Maya* are exceptionally well preserved. The third floor is devoted to the Netherlands: an archeological history of the country from prehistoric, Roman and medieval times, which is, perhaps inevitably, less interesting than the rest of the museum.

Further along Rapenburg, at no. 73, parts of the medieval monastery that became the university's first home still stand and hold the **Academisch Historisch Museum** (Sept–June Wed–Fri 1–5pm; free), detailing the university's history. Through the courtyard, the **Hortus Botanicus** gardens (Mon–Fri 9am–5pm, Sun 10am–5pm; April–Sept also Sat 9am–5pm; *f*5) is a lovely spot, lushly planted and subtly landscaped across to the Witte Singel canal. Planted in 1587, this is one of the oldest botanical gardens in Europe, a mixture of carefully tended beds of shrubs and hothouses full of tropical foliage.

Pieterskerk, the Stadhuis and the Waag

Cross Rapenburg from the Academisch Historisch Museum, and you're in the network of narrow streets that constitutes the medieval town, converging on a central square and the Gothic **Pieterskerk** (daily 1.30–4pm), Leiden's principal church. Deconsecrated now, it has an empty warehouse-like feel, but among the fixtures that remain are a simple and beautiful Renaissance rood screen and a host of memorials to the sundry notables buried here – including one to **John Robinson** (1575–1625), leader of the Pilgrim Fathers. Robinson lived in a house on the site of what is now the **Jean Pesijnshofje** at Kloksteeg 21, right beside the church. A curate in England at the turn of the seventeenth century, he was suspended from preaching in 1604, later fleeing with his congregation to pursue his Puritan form of worship in the more amenable atmosphere of Calvinist Holland. Settling in Leiden, Robinson acted as pastor to growing numbers, but still found himself at odds with the establishment. In 1620, one hundred of his followers – "The Pilgrim Fathers" – sailed via Plymouth for the untrammelled wilderness of America, though Robinson died before he could join them; he's buried in the church.

If you want to find out more about the Pilgrim Fathers, stroll down to Leiden's municipal archives, the **Gemeentearchief** (Mon–Fri 9.30am–5pm, Sat 9am–12.15pm; free) at Boisotkade 2a, which has an outstanding collection of documents relating to the settlers (the best of these can be viewed on-line at *www. leiden.nl/gemeentearchief*). Alternatively, head east to **Breestraat**, which marks the edge of Leiden's commercial centre, but is undistinguished except for the **Stadhuis**, an imposing edifice whose Renaissance facade is a copy of the late six-teenth-century original destroyed by fire in 1929. Behind the Stadhuis, the canals that cut Leiden's centre into pocket-sized islands converge at the busiest point in town, the site of a vigorous general **market** on Wednesdays and Saturdays. Here, a tangle of narrow bridges is flanked by a number of buildings, from overblown Art Nouveau department stores to modest terrace houses. On the south side is the **Waag** (Weigh House), a replacement for a previous Gothic structure, built to a design by Pieter Post (1608–1669) and fronted with a naturalistic frieze showing a merchant watching straining labourers. Pieter Post was a successful architect, but his artist brother, Frans, was even better known for his major contribution to the *Historia Naturalis Brasiliae*, an influential ethnographic study of eastern Brazil, a Dutch colony from 1630 to 1654.

The Hooglandsekerk and the Burcht

The general market sprawls right over the bridges and extends southeast along one of the town's prettiest canals, the **Nieuwe Rijn**. Strolling along its north bank, take the first left, Burgsteeg, and turn right at the end for the **Hooglandsekerk**, on Nieuwstraat (mid-May to mid-Sept Mon 1–5pm, Tues–Fri 11am–3.30pm, Sat 11am–4pm; free). A light and lofty Gothic structure built in stages over a couple of hundred years, the church holds a monument to Pieter van der Werff, the heroic burgomaster of Leiden at the time of the 1573–74 siege. When the situation became so desperate that the people were all for giving up, the burgomaster, no doubt remembering the massacre of Haarlem, offered up his own body to be eaten. The invitation was declined, but it inspired new determination in the town's flagging citizens.

Doubling back to the end of Burgsteeg, follow the alley and you'll soon reach the **Burcht** (daily 10am–10pm; free), the heavily restored stone shell of a medieval fortress perched high above the town on an artificial mound. This is where Leiden began, as an isolated ninth-century stronghold amongst the marshes; it's worth climbing up to the fort for a panoramic view of Leiden's roofs and towers. At the far end of the alley is the **Oude Rijn** canal, on the other side of which lies the blandly pedestrian **Haarlemmerstraat**, the town's main shopping street.

Museum Boerhaave and the Municipal Museum

A few metres to the north of Haarlemmerstraat, the **Museum Boerhaave** – the National Museum of the History of Science and Medicine – at Lange Agnietenstraat 10 (Tues–Sat 10am–5pm, Sun noon–5pm; f5) is named after a seventeenth-century Leiden surgeon, Herman Boerhaave. It gives a brief but fairly absorbing overview of scientific and medical developments over the last five centuries, with particular reference to Dutch achievements, including some gruesome surgical implements, pickled brains and suchlike.

Five minutes' walk north from here, Leiden's municipal museum, the **Stedelijk Museum de Lakenhal** (Tues–Sat 10am–5pm, Sun noon–5pm; f8), housed in the old Cloth Hall at Oude Singel 32, has a similarly engaging exhibition. On the ground floor amongst a healthy sample of local sixteenth- and seventeenth-century paintings are examples of the work of Jacob van Swanenburgh (first teacher of the young Rembrandt), Jan Lievens (with whom Rembrandt shared a studio), and **Gerrit Dou** (1613–1675), whose exquisite *Astrologer* is in Room 8. Rembrandt's first pupil, Dou began by imitating his master, but soon developed his own style, pioneering the Leiden tradition of small, minutely detailed pictures of enamel-like smoothness. There's also Lucas van Leyden's (1494–1533) alarming and spectacularly unsuccessful *Last Judgement* triptych in Room 6, several paintings devoted to the siege of 1574 and the heroics of burgomaster Werff, plus mixed rooms of furniture, silver, tiles, glass and ceramics. **Rembrandt** himself, despite being born in Leiden, is poorly represented; he left his home town at the tender age of fourteen, and, although he returned in 1625, it was only for six years, after which he settled permanently in Amsterdam. Only a handful of his Leiden paintings survive, but there's one here, *Agamemnon before Palamedes*, a stilted and rather unsuccessful rendition of the classical tale, painted in 1626. The other floors of the museum are of cursory interest only: the first floor holds several old guild rooms moved here from other parts of Leiden, the second floor is used for temporary exhibitions and the top floor has a series of modest displays on the town's history.

The Windmill and Ethnology Museums

At the west end of Oude Singel turn right and it's a couple of hundred metres to the **Molenmuseum De Valk** (Valk Windmill Museum; Tues–Sat 10am–5pm, Sun 1–5pm; f5), a restored grain mill and the last survivor of the twenty-odd windmills built on the town's outer fortifications in the eighteenth century. On the ground floor are the millers' living quarters, furnished in simple period style, while upstairs are several different displays, the most interesting of which is a slide show and exhibition recounting the history of Dutch windmills.

From the windmill, it's a five-minute walk west along Binnenvestgracht to the **Rijksmuseum voor Volkenkunde** at Steenstraat 1 (National Museum of Ethnology; Tues–Fri & Sun 10am–5pm, Sat noon–5pm; f10). This museum has comprehensive sections dealing with Indonesia and the Dutch colonies and decent ones on the South Pacific and Far East. However, it gives most other parts of the world a less than thorough showing, and it's far from being an essential stop.

Practicalities

Leiden's ultra-modern **train station** is next to the **bus station** on the northwest edge of town, a five- to ten-minute walk from the centre along Stationsweg. Halfway, at no. 210, is the VVV (Mon–Fri 11am–7pm & Sat 11am–3pm; ☎0900/222 2333), which has useful maps and brochures detailing walking tours of the town as well as a wide range of regional information. Of the town's **hotels**, the most appealing is the excellent *Nieuw Minerva*, which occupies several old canalside houses in the centre at Boommarkt 23 (☎071/512 6358, fax 514 2674, *www.nieuwminerva.nl*; ②), and whose "honeymoon room" (⑤) boasts a four-poster bed and fancy drapes. A good second choice is the three-star, fifteen-room *De Doelen*, by another of the town's canals at Rapenburg 2 (☎071/512 0527, fax 512 8453; ②). Finally, there's the bargain-basement *Hotel Rose*, at Beestenmarkt 14 (☎071/514 6630, fax 521 7096; ①). **Canal trips** around the town centre depart between three and five times daily from the Beestenmarkt, between April and September; tickets cost *f*9 per person and the trip lasts forty minutes.

Many of Leiden's choicest **cafés and restaurants** are concentrated around Pieterskerk. It's here you'll find *M'n Broer*, Kloksteeg 7, an agreeable, low-key café-bar offering a tasty range of light meals, and the rather more polished *Bistro La Cloche*, a French restaurant just up the street at no. 3 (☎071/512 3053). Nearby, *La Bota*, at Herensteeg 9, has some of the best-value local food in town as well as an excellent array of beers, while *Koetshuis de Burcht*, at Burgsteeg 13 (☎071/512 1688), is a fashionable French/Dutch bistro working to an imaginative menu. Another good choice is the smart, bistro-style *Restaurant de Gouvernante*, Kort Rapenburg 17 (☎071/514 8818; closed Mon), which serves such delicacies as steak with truffles – for a reasonable *f*40; reservations are advisable. There's no shortage of places to **drink**. *Hebes*, Oude Rijn 1, is a traditional neighbourhood bar with a low-key atmosphere, and quite the opposite of the lively *North End English Pub* at Noordeinde 55, on the corner with Rapenburg. Close by, opposite the old university building, *Barrera* is a fashionable café-bar, a student favourite which has light meals and a range of beers. Otherwise, *Jazzcafé The Duke*, on the corner of Oude Singel and Nieuwe Beestenmarkt, has a friendly bar and live jazz most nights, and *Café Jazzmatazz*, round the corner on Lange Scheistraat, also features live music and attracts an expat crowd.

Around Leiden: the bulbfields

The pancake-flat fields extending north from Leiden towards Haarlem are the heart of the Dutch **bulbfields**, whose bulbs and blooms support a billion-guilder industry and some ten thousand growers, as well as attracting tourists in their droves. Bulbs have flourished here since the late sixteenth century, when one Carolus Clusius, a Dutch botanist and one-time gardener to the Habsburg emperor, brought the first tulip bulb over from Vienna, where it had – in its turn – been brought from Asia Minor by an Austrian aristocrat. The tulip flourished in Holland's sandy soil and was so highly prized that it became the subject of irrational speculation. At the height of the boom – in the mid-1630s – bulbs were commanding extraordinary prices: the artist Jan van Goyen paid *f*1900 and two paintings for ten rare bulbs, while a group of one hundred bulbs was swapped for a coach and horses. When the government finally intervened in 1636, the industry returned to the real world, leaving hundreds of investors ruined – much to the satisfaction of the country's Calvinist ministers who had railed against the excesses.

Other types of bulbs were also introduced, and today the **spring flowering season** begins in mid-March with crocuses, followed by daffodils and yellow narcissi in late March, hyacinths and tulips from mid-April through to May, while gladioli flower in August. The view from any train in the region immediately north of Leiden takes in glorious fields divided into geometric blocks of pure colour. With your own transport, you can take in the full beauty of the bulbfields by way of special routes marked by hexagonal signposts – local VVVs sell pamphlets listing the best vantage points – or you can visit the bulb growers' showpiece, the **Keukenhof Gardens**, easily enough by bus from Leiden or Haarlem. Bear in mind also that there are any number of local **flower festivals** and **parades** in mid- to late April – every local VVV has details of these.

The Keukenhof Gardens
The small town of **Lisse**, halfway between Leiden and Haarlem, is home to the **Keukenhof Gardens** (late March to late May daily 8am–7.30pm; *f*18), the largest flower gardens in the world. The Keukenhof was set up in 1949 by a group of prominent bulb growers to inspire people to the joys of growing flowers from bulbs in their own gardens. Literally the "kitchen garden", its site is the former estate of a fifteenth-century countess, who used to grow herbs and vegetables for her dining table here – hence the name. Some seven million flowers are on show for their full flowering period, complemented, in case of especially harsh winters, by 5000 square metres of glasshouses holding indoor displays. You could easily spend a whole day here, swooning among the sheer abundance of it all, but to get the best of it you need to come early, before the tour buses pack the place. There are several restaurants in the 28 hectares of grounds, and well-marked paths take you all the way through the gardens, which specialize in daffodils, narcissi, hyacinths and tulips. To get to the Keukenhof by public transport from Leiden, take **bus** #54 from the bus station (every 30min; 30min). There are no direct bus services from Haarlem – you have to change in Lisse; details at the Haarlem VVV or bus station.

Aalsmeer
You can see the flower industry in action in **AALSMEER**, 23km northeast of Leiden, towards Amsterdam. The **flower auction** here, again the largest in the world, is held daily in a building the size of 75 football fields (Mon–Fri 7.30–11am; *f*5). The dealing is fast and furious (fortunately recorded information in English is available, via headphones at various locations within the building) and the turnover staggering. In an average year around *f*2.5 billion worth of plants and flowers are traded, many of them arriving in florists' shops throughout Europe on the same day. Be sure to arrive well before 10am or you won't see a single flower.

Around Leiden: the coast – Katwijk and Noordwijk

Like several of its neighbours, Leiden has easy access to some fine **beaches**, and although the nearest seaside resorts aren't in themselves much to write home about, in good weather a trip out to the coast is quite enticing. The best local option is **KATWIJK-AAN-ZEE**, a thirty-minute ride west from Leiden station on bus #31 (every 15min, half-hourly on Sunday). There is something very civil about this unassuming resort, its low-slung houses strung along behind a wide sandy beach. Here and there, a row of cottages recalls the time when Katwijk was a busy fishing village, but there are no real sights as such with the possible exception of a chunky **lighthouse**, dating from 1610. The bus #31 terminus is next to the lighthouse, and close to an undeveloped expanse of dunes that extends south along the shore toward The Hague – an ideal stretch for secluded sunbathing. If you decide to spend the night here, the **VVV** (April–Aug Mon–Sat 9am–6pm, July–Aug also Sun 11am–3pm; Sept–March Mon–Fri 9am–5pm & Sat 9am–1pm; ☎071/407 5444), a few metres from the lighthouse at Vuurbaakplein 11, will do their best to help you out. They have a supply of **private rooms** (①) as well as a list of hotels and pensions, but they may struggle to find a vacancy in July and August. The *Noordzee*, on the seafront at Boulevard 72 (☎071/401 5742, fax 407 5165; ②), is a well-kept three-star **hotel** whose rooms have small balconies and sea views, and the building itself sports some charming Art Deco flourishes. On the northern edge of the resort, beside the main bus route, are the **Katwijk Sluices**. Completed in 1807, this chain of gates regulates the flow of the Oude Rijn as it approaches the sea. Around high tide, the gates are closed and when they are re-opened, the pressure of the accumulated water brushes aside the sand deposited at the mouth of the river – a simple system that effectively fixed the course of the Oude Rijn, which for centuries had been continually diverted by the sand deposits, flooding the surrounding area.

NOORDWIJK-AAN-ZEE, some 4km up the coast and reachable by half-hourly bus #40 and #42 from Leiden station in thirty minutes, is larger and of less appeal than Katwijk. Indeed, it's not much more than a sequence of hotel developments built across the undulating sand dunes behind the coast. The one time it's worth coming to see the town is the last weekend in April, when a flower parade from Haarlem arrives and makes an illuminated tour of Noordwijk. The next morning the floats are displayed in the village.

The Hague and Scheveningen

THE HAGUE (Den Haag) is different from any other Dutch city. Since the sixteenth century it's been the political capital and the focus of national institutions, in a country built on civic independence and munificence. Frequently disregarded until the development of central government in the nineteenth century, The Hague's older buildings are a rather subdued and modest collection with little of Amsterdam's flamboyance. Most of the city's canal houses are demurely classical and exude a sense of sedate prosperity. In 1859 English poet Matthew Arnold wrote: "I never saw a city where the well-to-do classes seemed to have given the whole place so much of their own air of wealth, finished cleanliness, and comfort; but I never saw one, either, in which my heart would so have sunk at the thought of living." In some ways, things haven't changed much: today's "well-to-do classes" – mostly diplomats in dark Mercedes and executives of multinationals – ensure that most of the city's hotels and restaurants remain firmly in the expense account category, and the nightlife is similarly packaged. But, away from the mediocrity of wealth, The Hague does have cheaper and livelier bars and restaurants – even its share of restless adolescents hanging around the pizza joints – and has in recent years done much to jazz itself up.

Furthermore, there is compensation in the city's excellent museums, princi-pally the famed royal collection of old Dutch masters at the **Mauritshuis**, and more modern works of art at the **Gemeentemuseum**.

Arrival, information and accommodation

The Hague has two **train stations** – Den Haag HS (Hollands Spoor) and Den Haag CS (Centraal Station). Of the two, Den Haag CS is the more convenient, sited five minutes' walk east of the town centre. Many of the city's trams and buses stop here too. The adjacent complex houses the **VVV** (Mon–Fri 8.30am–5.30pm, Sat 10am–5pm; July–Aug also Sun 11am–3pm; ☎0900/340 3505, 75c per min). They provide a wide range of information on the city and its sur-roundings, will help with accommodation (see below), and publish a comprehen-sive and free monthly listings magazine, **The Hague Agenda**. Den Haag HS, the other station, is 1km to the south. There are frequent rail services between the two as well as trams from Den Haag HS to the centre – several services make the five-minute journey, so check the destination sign before hopping on. The Hague is the country's third largest city, but almost everything worth seeing is within easy walking distance of Den Haag CS. If you intend to use the city's buses and trams, the standard *strippenkaart* is widely available – coin-operated machines at the train stations dispense them and the VVV sells them too. The VVV and coun-ters at the train station also sell the *dagkaart* (day-card; ƒ10), the best bet if you're only here for the day and plan to shuttle around the city's peripheries.

Accommodation

The Hague has a good supply of central **hotels**, with many of the more comfort-able (and sometimes luxurious) dotted near the Binnenhof, just to the west of Den Haag CS. There is also a cluster of plainer, less expensive hotels around Den Haag HS; the **HI hostel** is here as well. The Hague can get very busy, so advance reservations are a good idea especially during the week when business folk visit in numbers – and push up hotel prices: weekend rates are usually around 33 per-cent cheaper. If necessary, the VVV will help you find a hotel room in either The Hague or the neighbouring resort of Scheveningen (see p.193) for a small charge.

Aristo, Stationsweg 164–166 (☎ & fax 070/389 0847). Clean and tidy hotel metres from Den Haag HS station; some of the rooms are bigger and brighter than the others, so ask to see before you register. ①.

Astoria, Stationsweg 139 (☎070/384 0401). Well-cared for, two-star hotel in a simple little building a couple of minutes' walk from Den Haag HS station. One of the city's better budget options, but the rooms are small and there's no breakfast. ①.

't Centrum, Veenkade 6 (☎070/346 3657, fax 310 6460). Small, unassuming but cosy two-star hotel by the canal just west of the Palais Noordeinde. ②.

City Hostel Den Haag, Scheepmakersstraat 25 (☎070/315 7888, fax 315 7877). This large and extremely comfortable HI hostel is located just 400m east of – and across the canal from – Den Haag HS. A good range of facilities includes laundry, luggage storage, a café, Internet terminals, and a small library. Smart family rooms plus 6- to 24-bed dorms; ƒ32.30–37.

Corona, Buitenhof 39 (☎070/363 7930, fax 361 5785). In a great location just across the street from the Binnenhof, this smart chain hotel – a Golden Tulip – has large and extremely com-fortable rooms from ƒ320 in the week, ƒ210 at the weekend. ④.

des Indes Intercontinental Den Haag, Lange Voorhout 54 (☎070/361 2345, fax 345 1721). Luxurious five-star hotel that has long been – and still is – a favourite with visiting bigwigs. It was built in the 1850s as a private residence for a Dutch aristocrat, but became a hotel thirty years later. The interior is rich and ornate and comes complete with gilded scrollwork, columns and thick carpets. Rooms begin at around ƒ400, but some reach stratospheric rates four or five times more than that. ⑦.

Novotel Den Haag Centrum, Hofweg 5 (☎070/364 8846, fax 356 2889). Efficient, four-star chain hotel with very comfortable rooms right in the centre of things, across the street from the Binnenhof. ④.

Parkhotel, Molenstraat 53 (☎070/362 4371, fax 361 4525). This spick and span chain hotel has over one hundred pleasant rooms decorated in brisk modern style, some of which overlook the Palais Noordeinde gardens next door. ⑥.

The city centre

Best viewed from the front, where the **Hofvijver** (court pond) mirrors the attractive symmetry of the front façade, the extensive **Binnenhof** ("inner court") is right in the centre of the city, both its oldest quarter and home to Holland's bicameral parliament. Count William II built a castle here in the thirteenth century, and the settlement that grew up around it became known as the "Count's Domain" – *'s Gravenhage*, literally "Count's Hedge" – which is still the city's official name. William's descendants became the region's most powerful family, simultaneously acting as Stadholders (effectively provincial governors) of most of the seven United Provinces, which rebelled against the Habsburgs in the sixteenth century. In due course, one of the family, Prince Maurice of Orange-Nassau (1567–1625), established his main residence in The Hague, which had become, to all intents and purposes, the political capital of the country. As the embodiment of central rather than municipal power, the Binnenhof was at times fêted, at others virtually ignored, until the nineteenth century when The Hague officially shared political capital status with Brussels during the uneasy times of the United Kingdom of the Netherlands (1815–1830). Thereafter it became the seat of government and home to a functioning legislature.

The lack of prestige in the modest brick buildings of the Binnenhof irked Dutch parliamentarians until 1992, when they moved in to a flashy new extension next door. Much of the original Binnenhof – a broadly rectangular complex built around two connecting courtyards – is used for government offices and there's not that much to see. The exception is the **Ridderzaal** (Knights' Hall), a slender-turreted structure that looks distinctly church-like, but was in fact built as a banqueting hall for Count William in the thirteenth century. Now used for state occasions, it's been a courtroom, market and stable, and so often renovated that little of the original remains. An uninspiring guided tour of the Ridderzaal and the chambers of parliament (often closed Mon & Tues) starts regularly from the information office at Binnenhof 8a (Mon–Sat 10am–4pm, last tour 3.45pm; ƒ5).

The Mauritshuis Collection

To the immediate east of the Binnenhof, the **Mauritshuis**, Korte Vijverberg 8 (Tues–Sat 10am–5pm, Sun 11am–5pm; ƒ12.50), is located in an elegant seventeenth-century mansion. Generally considered to be one of the best galleries in Europe, it's famous for its extensive range of Flemish and Dutch paintings from the fifteenth to the eighteenth century, based on the collection accumulated by Prince William V of Orange (1748–1806). All the major Dutch artists are represented and it's well laid out, with multilingual cards in each room providing background notes on all the major canvases. At present the rooms are not

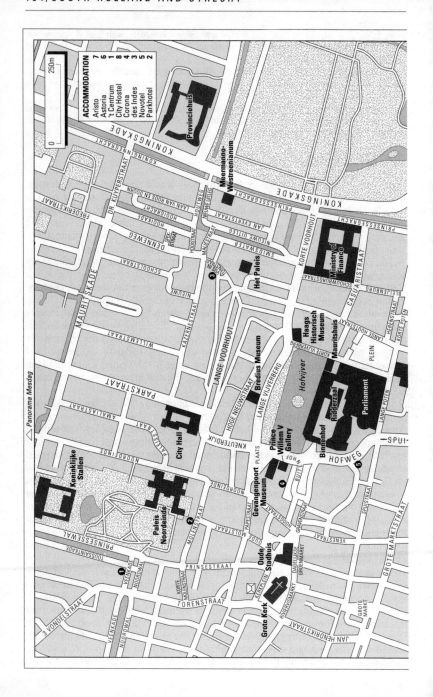

ACCOMMODATION

Aristo	7
Astoria	6
't Centrum	1
City Hostel	8
Corona	4
des Indes	3
Novotel	5
Parkhotel	2

Provinciehuis

Meermanno-
Westreenianum

Ministry of
Finance

Het Paleis

Haags
Historisch
Museum

Mauritshuis

PLEIN

Bredius Museum

Hofvijver

Ridderzaal

Parliament

City Hall

Koninklijke
Stallen

Prince
Willem V
Gallery

Binnenhof

HOFWEG

SPUI

Gevangenpoort
Museum

Paleis
Noordeinde

△ Panorama Mesdag

Oude
Stadhuis

Grote Kerk

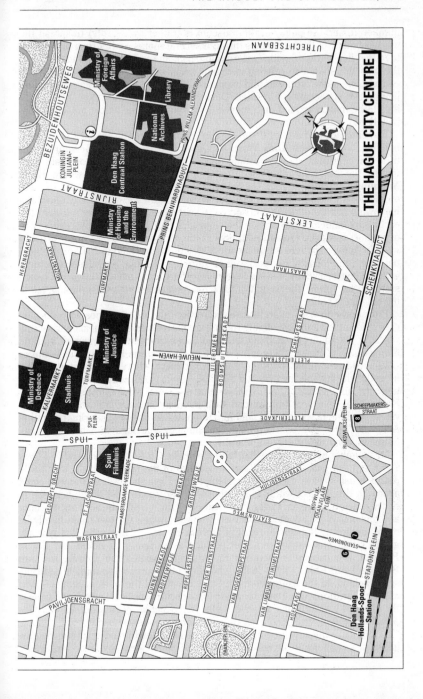

THE HAGUE CITY CENTRE

numbered, and the policy of the museum is (rather awkwardly) to spread the works of many of the key artists through several rooms, rather than place them together. For further detailed information, pick up the free plan at the entrance; the museum shop also sells an excellent guidebook for *f*25. Alternatively you can join one of the irregular and expensive conducted tours – prices depend on length; ask at reception for times. During major exhibitions, expect the paintings to be moved around or removed from show and the whole museum completely reorganized.

The entrance and museum shop are in the **basement** on the east side of the building, together with **Andy Warhol**'s *Queen Beatrix*, a twentieth-century aperitif to the collection above. Heading up the stairs to the **first floor**, walk back toward the old front doors and enter the room on the left, where **Hans Memling**'s *Portrait of a Man* is a typically observant work, right down to the scar on the nose. Close by, **Rogier van der Weyden**'s *The Lamentation of Christ* is a harrowing picture of death and sorrow, Christ's head hanging down toward the earth, surrounded by the faces of the mourners, each with a particular expression of anguish and pain. **Quentin Matsys** (1465–1530) was the first major artist to work in Antwerp, where he was made a Master of the Guild in 1519. An influential figure, the focus of his work was the attempt to imbue his religious pictures with spiritual sensitivity, and his *Descent from the Cross* is a fine example – Christ's suffering face under the weight of the Cross contrasted with the grinning, taunting onlookers behind.

Proceeding in a counterclockwise direction, through a series of rooms on either side of the Italianate dining room, exhibits include two giant allegorical canvases by Jan Sanders van Hemessen and Lucas Cranach the Younger's spirited *Man with a Red Beard*. There are also two works by **Hans Holbein the Younger** (1497–1543), a striking *Portrait of Robert Cheeseman*, where all the materials – the fur collar, the falcon's feathers and the cape – seem to take on the appropriate texture, and his *Portrait of Jane Seymour*, one of several pictures commissioned by Henry VIII, who sent him abroad to paint matrimonial candidates. Holbein's vibrant technique was later to land him in hot water: an over-flattering portrait of Anne of Cleves swayed Henry into an unhappy marriage with his "Flanders' Mare" that was to last only six months.

Of a number of paintings by **Adriaen Brouwer** (1605–1638), *Quarrel at a Card Table* and *Inn with Drunken Peasants* are two of the better known, with thick, rough brush-strokes recording contemporary Flemish lowlife. Brouwer could approach this subject with some authority, as he spent most of his brief life in either a tavern or prison. **Peter Paul Rubens** (1577–1640), the acclaimed painter and diplomat, was a contemporary of Brouwer, though the two could hardly be more dissimilar: Rubens' *Portrait of Isabella Brant*, his first wife, is a typically grand, rather statuesque work, not perhaps as intriguing as *Adam and Eve in Paradise*, a collaboration between Rubens, who painted the figures, and **Jan Brueghel the Elder** (1568–1625), who filled in the dreamlike animals and landscape behind. In the same room are two examples of the work of Rubens' chief assistant, **Anthony van Dyck** (1599–1641), a portrait specialist who found fame at the court of English King Charles I. His *Pieter Stevens of Antwerp* and *Quinton Simons of Antwerp* are good early examples of his tendency to flatter and ennoble – no doubt this helped his career prospects no end. Nearby, and again showing the influence of Rubens, is the robust *Adoration of the Shepherds* by Jacob Jordaens.

On the **second-floor** landing, the broad brush-strokes of **Frans Hals'** *Laughing Boy* are far removed from the restrained style he was forced to adopt in his more familiar paintings of the burghers of Haarlem. **Carel Fabritius** (1622–1654), pupil of Rembrandt and (possibly) teacher of Vermeer, was killed in a gunpowder explosion at Delft when he was only twenty-two. Few canvases of his survive but an exquisite exception is *The Goldfinch*, a curious, almost impressionistic work, with the bird reduced to a blur of colour. One of his Delft contemporaries was **Gerard Houckgeest**, who specialized in church interiors, like *The Tomb of William of Orange*, a minutely observed study of architectural lines lightened by expanses of white marble.

Off the second-floor landing, on the left at the front of the museum, is the Mauritshuis' most famous painting, **Jan Vermeer's** *View of Delft*, a superb townscape of 1658, with the fine lines of the city drawn beneath a cloudy sky, a patchwork of varying light and shade – though the dispassionate, photographic quality the painting has in reproduction is oddly lacking in the large canvas. In the same room, **Gerard Ter Borch's** *Lice Hunt* is in striking contrast to Vermeer's detachment, a vignette of seventeenth-century domestic life.

Heading in a counterclockwise direction, other highlights include the busy, stick-like figures of the *Winter Scene* by **Hendrik Avercamp** (1585–1634), the deaf and dumb artist from Kampen, and **Paulus Potter's** lifelike *Young Bull*, a massive canvas complete with dung and a pair of quite frightening testicles. Best known of the **Rembrandt**s is the *Anatomy Lesson of Dr Tulp*, from 1632, the artist's first commission in Amsterdam. The peering pose of the "students" who lean over the corpse solved the problem of emphasis falling on the body rather than the subjects of the portrait, who were in fact members of the surgeons' guild. Hopefully Tulp's skills as an anatomist were better than his medical advice, which included the recommendation that his patients drink fifty cups of tea a day.

Dotted throughout the museum are no fewer than thirteen paintings by **Jan Steen** (1625–1679), including a wonderfully riotous picture carrying the legend "The way you hear it, is the way you sing it" – a parable on the young learning bad habits from the old – and a typically salacious *Girl Eating Oysters*.

Around the Hofvijver

A few metres to the north of the Mauritshuis, the **Haags Historisch Museum**, Korte Vijverberg 7 (Tues–Fri 11am–5pm, Sat & Sun noon–5pm; *f*7), occupies a handsome Neo-Classical mansion that was originally home to the city's leading militia company, the so-called Archers of St Sebastian. The museum traces the convoluted history of the city with a wide range of displays – everything from a hotch potch of archeological finds to an intricate doll's house of 1910 – and is strong on medieval church silver and antique furniture. Best of all, however, are the assorted paintings of the city, notably those by Jan Steen and his father-in-law, Jan van Goyen (1596–1656), a pioneer of realistic landscape painting who is well represented by his enormous and finely detailed *View of The Hague*.

Across the street from the Historical Museum are the trees and cobble-stones of **Lange Voorhout**, a wide L-shaped street-cum-square that is overlooked by a string of stately mansions, whose neo-classical pretensions span the seventeenth and eighteenth centuries and now accommodate most of the major embassies. Most conspicuous is the **Hotel des Indes**, an opulent hotel at the northeast corner of the square, where the ballerina Anna Pavlova died in 1931 and where today you stand a fair chance of being flattened by a chauffeur-driven limousine. Opposite, at number 74, the **Het Paleis Museum** (open during exhibitions only, Tues–Sun 11am–5pm; *f*10) occupies another of these grand mansions and was a favourite royal residence from 1901 to 1934. Nowadays, it's used for displays of fine and applied art.

The narrow streets and canals just to the east of Lange Voorhout comprise one of the prettiest corners of the city centre, a jumble of intimate old buildings that extends to the busy Prinsessegracht boulevard. There are several good bars and restaurants here and one specific sight, the **Museum Meermanno-Westreenianum**, Prinsessegracht 30 (Tues–Fri 11am–5pm, Sat & Sun noon–5pm; *f*5), which possesses a small collection of remarkably well-preserved medieval illuminated manuscripts and bibles.

Doubling back to the north side of Hofvijver, allow half an hour or so to visit the delightful **Bredius Museum**, Lange Vijverberg 14 (Tues–Sun noon–5pm; *f*6), which displays the eclectic collection of paintings bequeathed to the city by a one-time director of the Mauritshuis, Abraham Bredius in 1946. Packed together in this fine old house, with its stucco work and splendid staircase, are some exquisite works, notably several mini-canvases by Rembrandt including a *Christ's Head*, and an *Erection of the Cross* whose glutinous paintwork forms one of the artist's darkest, most melancholic works. Amongst the genre paintings is a characteristic *Boar Hunt* by Roelandt Savery (1576–1639), all green foliage and fighting beasts, and the careful draughtsmanship of Aert van de Neer's (1603–1677) *Festivities on the Ice*. There are also two noteworthy paintings by Jan Steen, the salacious *Couple in a Bedchamber* and the curious *Satyr and the Peasant*, a representation of a well-known Aesop fable in which the satyr, sat at the table with his hosts, is bemused by human behaviour. The creature's confusion is symbolically represented by two contrasting figures, one of whom blows on his soup to cool it down, while the other blows into his hands to keep them warm.

The Gevangenpoort and the Prince Willem V Gallery

A short walk from the Bredius Museum, on the west side of the Hofvijver, the **Museum Gevangenpoort**, Buitenhof 33 (Prisoner's Gate Museum; Tues–Fri 11am–4pm, Sat & Sun noon–4pm; hourly tours, last tour 4pm; *f*6), was originally part of the city fortifications. Used as a prison until the nineteenth century, it now contains an array of instruments of torture and punishment centred around its Chamber of Horrors. As well as the guillotine blades, racks and gallows, the old cells are in a good state of preservation – including the *ridderkamer* for the more privileged captives. Here Cornelis de Witt, Burgomaster of Dordrecht, was imprisoned before he and his brother Johan, another staunch Republican and leader of the States of Holland, were dragged out and murdered by an Orangist mob in 1672. The brothers were shot, beheaded and cut into pieces that were then auctioned to the crowd; Johan's tongue is preserved for a macabre posterity in the storerooms of the Gemeentemuseum. The Gevangenpoort is popular; join the line about fifteen minutes before the tour begins to guarantee a place.

Down the street at Buitenhof 35, the **Galerij Prins Willem V** (Tues–Sun 11am–4pm; *f*2.50, or free with Mauritshuis ticket) was created in 1773 as the private picture gallery of the eponymous prince and Stadtholder of the United Provinces. On display is a diverting collection of seventeenth-century paintings including examples of the work of the prolific Jan Steen as well as Jacob Jordaens and Paulus Potter. There's also the folksy *Girl with a Lamp* by Gerard Dou, a pupil and companion of the young Rembrandt, and one of Willem van de Velde the Younger's (1633–1707) most successful maritime paintings, the *Warship at Sunset*. However, the gallery is perhaps more interesting as an example of an eighteenth-century "cabinet" picture gallery. The fashion then was to sandwich paintings together in a cramped patchwork from floor to ceiling, and though it's faithful to the period, this does make viewing difficult for eyes more used to spacious modern museums.

The Grote Kerk and the Noordeinde Palace

The lattice of narrow, sometimes seedy, streets and squares stretching west of the Buitenhof zero in on the crow-stepped gables of the sixteenth-century **Oude Stadhuis** (the Old City Hall) and St Jacobskerk or the **Grote Kerk** next door (July–Aug Mon–Fri 11am–4pm; free; otherwise closed except during exhibitions). Dating from the middle of the fifteenth century and easily the best of The Hague's old churches, the building's cavernous interior, with its three naves of equal height, has an exhilarating sense of breadth and handsome timber vaulting. Like most Dutch churches, it's short on decoration, but there are one or two highlights, notably the **stained-glass windows** in the choir ambulatory. Two are particularly exquisite and may well be the work of Dirk Crabeth, one of the craftsmen responsible for the windows in Gouda's St Janskerk (see p.206). Of the two, one depicts the Annunciation, the other shows the Virgin descending from heaven to show the infant Jesus to a kneeling Emperor Charles V, who footed the bill. Nearby, in the choir, stands a memorial to Admiral Jacob van Opdam, who was blown up with his ship during the little-remembered naval battle of Lowestoft in 1665. Also look out for the Renaissance pulpit: similar to the one in Delft's Oude Kerk (see p.196), it has carved panels framing the apostles in false perspective.

From the Grote Kerk, it's a short walk northeast to the sixteenth- and seventeenth-century **Paleis Noordeinde** (no admission), the grandest of several royal buildings that lure tourists onto the expensive "Royal Tours" of The Hague and its surroundings. Outside the palace's main entrance, on Noordeinde, is a jaunty equestrian **statue** of William the Silent and just beyond is the clumping modern architecture of today's city hall.

North of the city centre

Ten minutes' walk north of the Paleis Noordeinde, and accessible by tram #7 from Centraal Station, the **Panorama Mesdag**, Zeestraat 65 (Mon–Sat 10am–5pm, Sun noon–5pm; ƒ7.50), was designed in the late nineteenth century by Hendrik Mesdag, banker turned painter and local citizen become Hague School luminary. For the most part, Mesdag painted unremarkable seascapes tinged with an unlikeable bourgeois sentimentality, but there's no denying the achievement of his panorama, a depiction of Scheveningen as it would have appeared in 1881. Completed in four months with help from his wife and the young George Hendrik Breitner, the painting is so naturalistic that it takes a few moments for the skills of lighting and perspective to become apparent. Ten minutes' walk north from the Panorama at Laan van Meerdervoort 7f is the house Mesdag bought as a home and gallery. At the time it overlooked one of his favourite subjects, the dunes, the inspiration for much of his work, and today it contains the **Mesdag Museum** (Tues–Sun noon–5pm; ƒ5). His collection includes a number of Hague School paintings which, like his own work, take the seascapes of the nearby coast as their

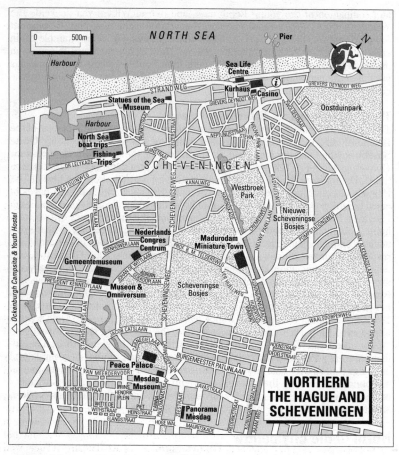

The map shows the following labels:

NORTH SEA

Pier

Harbour

Sea Life Centre

GREVERS DEYNOOT WEG

STRANDWEG

Kürhaus   Casino

Statues of the Sea Museum

GREVERS DEYNOOT WEG

Oostduinpark

Harbour

NEPTUNUSSTRAAT

STEVIN

NIEUWE PARK LAAN

North Sea boat trips

DUINSTRAAT

KEIZERSTRAAT

Fishing Trips

DR LELYKADE

S C H E V E N I N G E N

BADHUISWEG

KANALWEG

Westbroek Park

WESTDUINWEG

SCHEVENINGSEWEG

HARTING ALLEE

Nieuwe Scheveningse Bosjes

CHIMEERWEG

POMPSTATIONSWEG

STATENLAAN

SCREENHOWER LAAN

Nederlands Congres Centrum

JOHAN DE WITTLAAN

ADRIAN GOEKOOPLAAN

PROF B. M. TELDERSWEG

Madurodam Miniature Town

NIEUWE PARKLAAN

VAN ALKEMADELAAN

Gemeentemuseum

PRESIDENT KENNEDYLAAN

Museon & Omniversum

Scheveningse Bosjes

PROF TRUELIWEG

KONINGINNEGRACHT

STADHOUDERSLAAN

SCHEVENINGSEWEG

WAALSDORPERWEG

JACOB CATSLAAN

CARNEGIELAAN

HOENSTRAAT

DEDELSTRAAT

VAN ALKEMADELAAN

LAAN VAN MEERDERVOORT

Peace Palace

BURGEMEESTER PATIJNLAAN

Mesdag Museum

PRINS HENDRIKSTRAAT

HENDRIK PLEIN

PAULWINSTRAAT

JAVASTRAAT

WITTE DE WITHSTRAAT

PIET HEINSTRAAT

ZEESTRAAT

FREDERIKSTRAAT

KONINGINNEGRACHT

ELANDSTRAAT

Panorama Mesdag

HOGE WAL

MAURITSKADE

PRINS

NORTHERN THE HAGUE AND SCHEVENINGEN

0   500m

N

Ockenburgh Campsite & Youth Hostel

subject. There are also paintings by Corot, Rousseau, Delacroix and Millet, though none of them represents the artists' best achievements. Perhaps the most interesting exhibits are the florid and distinctive paintings of Antonio Mancini, whose oddly disquieting subjects are reminiscent of Klimt.

The Peace Palace

Round the corner from the Mesdag Museum, framing the Carnegieplein, the **Peace Palace** or Vredespaleis (usually Mon–Fri hourly guided tours at 10am, 11am, 2pm & 3pm, June–Sept also at 4pm; ƒ5; check with the VVV for times of tours in English) is home to the Court of International Justice, and, for all the wrong reasons, a monument to the futility of war. Toward the end of the nineteenth century, Tsar Nicholas II called an international conference for the peaceful reconciliation of national problems. The result was the First Hague Peace Conference of 1899, whose purpose was to "help find a lasting peace and, above all, a way of limiting the progressive development of existing arms". This in turn led to the formation of a Permanent Court of Arbitration housed obscurely in The Hague until the American industrialist Andrew Carnegie gave $1.5 million for a large new building – the Peace Palace. These honourable aims came to nothing with the onset of World War I: just as the donations of tapestries, urns, marble and stained glass were arriving from all over the world, so Europe's military commanders were preparing their offensives. Backed by a massive law library, fifteen judges are still sit today, conducting trade matters in English and diplomatic affairs in French. Widely respected and generally considered neutral, their judgements are nevertheless not binding.

The Gemeentemuseum, Museon and Omniversum

About 1.5km northwest of the Peace Palace, the **Gemeentemuseum**, Stadhouderslaan 41 (Tues–Sun 11am–5pm; ƒ10; tram #7 from Centraal Station), is easily the most diverse of The Hague's many museums. Designed by Hendrik Petrus Berlage (1856–1934) and completed in 1935, the building itself is often regarded as his masterpiece, an austere but particularly appealing structure with brick facings superimposed upon a concrete shell. Unfortunately, the museum can be confusing and the labelling inconsistent, but there are some superb collections such as the musical instruments – especially the harpsichords and early pianos – and the Islamic ceramics. The manageable delft collection is among the world's finest and the large Fashion Gallery hosts an ambitious range of temporary exhibitions on fashion and associated subjects. The modern art section outlines the development of Dutch painting since the 1860s, through the Romantic, Hague and Expressionist schools to the De Stijl movement. **Piet Mondrian**, the most famous member of the De Stijl group, dominates this part of the gallery and pride of place goes to the recently acquired *Victory Boogie Woogie*, his last and some would say finest work. In fact, the museum has the world's largest collection of Mondrian paintings, though much of it consists of (deservedly) unfamiliar early works painted before he evolved the abstraction of form into geometry and pure colour for which he's best known.

Adjoining the Gemeentemuseum is a modern building that houses the **Museon** (Tues–Fri 10am–5pm, Sat & Sun noon–5pm; ƒ10), a sequence of non-specialist exhibitions dealing with human activities and the history of the earth – everything from rock formations to the use of tools. Self-consciously internationalist, it's aimed at school parties, as is the adjoining **Omniversum** or "Space Theatre" (Tues–Wed 10am–5pm, Thurs–Sun 10am–9pm; ƒ17.50; call ☎070/354 7479 for programme). A planetarium in all but name, it possesses all the technical gadgetry you'd expect.

The Madurodam Miniature Town

Halfway between The Hague and Scheveningen, the **Madurodam Miniature Town** (daily: April–June 9am–8pm; July–Aug 9am–10pm; Sept–March 9am–5pm; ƒ19.50), reachable on tram #1 or #9, is heavily plugged by the tourist authorities, though its origins are more interesting than the rather trite and expensive present, a stylised version of a Dutch town constructed on a 1:25 scale. The money was put up by one J.M.L. Maduro, who wished to establish a memorial to his son, George, who had distinguished himself during the German invasion of 1940 and died in Dachau concentration camp five years later. There's a memorial to him just by the entrance, and profits from the Miniature Town are still used for general Dutch social and cultural activities. The replica town itself is extremely popular – so be prepared to queue.

Eating and drinking

The Hague has an excellent range of **restaurants** and although some are aimed squarely at the city's fat-cat crowd, many more are very affordable. There is a cluster of first-rate places just north and east of Lange Voorhout along Denneweg, Frederikstraat and amongst the surrounding sidestreets – frankly you need look no further. The pick of the city's **bars** and **café-bars** are concentrated on and around the busy Grote Markt, south of the Grote Kerk. The more expensive establishments charge around ƒ40 for a main course, mid-range places ƒ20–30.

Restaurants

Chez Pierrette, Frederikstraat 56 (☎070/360 6167). Chic and busy French brasserie serving delicious food in an informal atmosphere and at reasonable prices.

De Dageraad, Hooikade 4 (☎070/364 5666). Justifiably popular, unassuming and well-established vegetarian restaurant offering tasty and inexpensive meals. Occupies a pleasant canalside location in the tangle of narrow streets just to the east of Lange Voorhout. Closed Mon.

De Dennetuin, Denneweg 130 (☎070/365 9788). Amiable restaurant serving from a wideranging menu featuring international and Dutch dishes.

Limón, Denneweg 39a (☎070/356 1465). Atmospheric Spanish tapas restaurant catering to a chic, youngish crowd. Great food; a popular spot.

Luden, Frederikstraat 36 (☎070/360 1733). Classy little restaurant offering a Dutch/French menu which shows flair and imagination. Moderately expensive.

Malienkolder, Maliestraat 9 (☎070/364 5542). Stylish and inexpensive bistro-style restaurant with French and Dutch dishes. A few metres from the foot of Denneweg.

Pinelli, Dagelijkse Groenmarkt 31 (☎070/365 6368). A few metres from the Grote Kerk, this well-established Italian restaurant serves up delicious pizza and pasta at affordable prices.

Plato, Frederikstraat 32 (☎070/363 6744). Smart and cosy restaurant offering tasty and reasonably priced French/Dutch cuisine.

Saur, Lange Voorhout 47 (☎070/346 2565). Across the street from the Historical Museum, this old-fashioned place, with its Art Deco flourishes and French menu, serves some of the best steaks in town. Moderately expensive and quite formal. Closed Sun.

Café-bars and bars

De Boterwaag, Grote Markt 8a. Immensely appealing café-bar housed in an old and cavernous brick-vaulted weigh house. Very popular with a youthful crowd and offers a wide range of beers as well as inexpensive bar food, though this hardly inspires the palate.

De Landeman, Denneweg 48. Mellow bar near the southern end of Denneweg.

Le Café Hathor, Maliestraat 22. Just 100m or so from the foot of Denneweg, this agreeable, laid-back café-bar occupies charming old premises and has a lovely canalside terrace to boot.

Plein 19, Plein 19. A young(ish) professional crowd are drawn to this smart little bar on the square immediately to the east of the Binnenhof.

The **North Sea Jazz Festival**, held every year in mid-July at the Nederlands Congres Centrum, Churchillplein 10, is The Hague's most prestigious jazz event, attracting international media coverage and many of the world's most famous musicians. Details of performances are available from the VVV, which will also reserve accommodation, virtually impossible to find after the festival has begun. Various kinds of tickets can be purchased; a *dagkaart*, for example, valid for an entire day, costs around ƒ80.

De Zwarte Ruiter, Grote Markt 27. This fashionable bar boasts a good selection of beers and ales, and positively heaves on the weekend.

Listings

Bikes Can be rented from either of The Hague's train stations at standard rates.

Car rental Achilles Europcar, Prinses Marijkestraat 5 (☎070/381 1811); Avis, Theresiastraat 216 (☎070/385 0698); Budget, 1e van der Kunstraat 282 (☎070/397 2239).

Doctor General medical care: day ☎070/345 5300; night ☎070/346 9669.

Embassies/consulates Australia, Carnegielaan 4 (☎070/310 8200); Canada, Sophialaan 7 (☎070/311 1600); Ireland, Dr Kuyperstraat 9 (☎070/363 0993); UK, Lange Voorhout 10 (☎070/427 0427); US, Lange Voorhout 102 (☎070/310 9209).

Emergencies Fire, Police, Ambulance ☎112.

Information A free monthly magazine with details of concerts, theatre performances, special events and entertainments in The Hague and environs is available from the VVV. It's called *the hague agenda*.

Markets Food: Markthof, Gedempte Gracht/Spui (Mon 11am–6pm, Tues–Sat 9am–5pm, Thurs till 9pm). Antiques, books and curios: Lange Voorhout (May–Sept Thurs 11am–7pm & Sun 11am-5pm); Plein (Oct–May Thurs 11am–7pm).

Pharmacy Central pharmacy at Korte Poten 7a (☎070/346 4748). For information on night services, call ☎070/345 1000.

Post office Main post office on Kerkplein (Mon–Fri 9am–6pm, Thurs till 8pm, Sat 9am–4pm).

Public transport enquiries Domestic ☎0900/9292; International ☎0900/9296.

Taxi HTMC ☎070/390 7722; HCT City Taxi ☎070/383 0830.

Scheveningen

Situated on the coast about 4km from the centre of The Hague, the old fishing port of **SCHEVENINGEN** is now the country's biggest coastal resort, a sometimes tacky, often breezy place that attracts more than nine million visitors a year. It also has one curious claim to fame: during World War II, resistance groups tested suspected Nazi infiltrators by getting them to say "Scheveningen" – an impossible feat for Germans, apparently, and not much easier for English-speakers either. The Hague and Scheveningen were once separated by a thick strip of forested dune, but nowadays it's hard to know where one ends and the other begins. There is, however, no mistaking Scheveningen's principal attraction, its **beach**, a long expanse of golden sand that is hard to resist on a warm day, especially as it only takes about ten minutes to get there by **tram** from The Hague's Centraal Station (#1 or #9), and just a few minutes more from Den Haag HS (tram #8).

Scheveningen's main tram stop is a couple of hundred metres from its most impressive building, the **Kurhaus**, a grand hotel of 1885, built when this was one of the most fashionable resorts in Europe. Pop inside for a peek at its central hall, a richly decorated affair with pendulous chandeliers and rich frescoes bearing mermaids and semi-clad maidens cavorting high above the diners – though you can enjoy the atmosphere for just the price of a coffee. Most of Scheveningen's other attractions are within easy walking distance of the Kurhaus: the **casino** is next door; it's east along the seashore to the cement **pier** and its amusement arcades; and west to the **Sea Life Centre**, Strandweg 13 (daily 10am–6pm, July & Aug till 8pm; *f*15.50), a glorified aquarium complete with a seabed walkway and coral reef. About 250m further west is the much more original **Museum Beelden-aan-Zee**, at Harteveltstraat 1 (Tues–Sun 11am–5pm; *f*7.50). Opened in 1994, this features an intriguing assortment of modern sculptures arranged around a pavilion built by King William I for his ailing wife, Wilhelmina, in 1826. There are examples of the work of many leading sculptors, including Karel Appel and Wim Quist, Man Ray and Fritz Koenig, and although there is supposed to be a unifying theme – the human experience – it's the variety of forms and materials that impresses most.

Set apart at the west end of the resort, about 2km from the Kurhaus, is Scheveningen's sprawling **harbour** (haven), the focus of an industrial complex that incorporates a busy container depot and fish docks. The local trawler fleet is a shadow of its former self, but there are still several excellent **seafood restaurants** hereabouts – try the excellent *Ducdalf*, at Dr Lelykade 5 (☎070/355 7692), or the more straightforward and less expensive *Havenrestaurant* at Treilerdwarsweg 2 (☎070/354 5783). If you fancy trying to catch a meal yourself, there are also North Sea **fishing trips** during the summer – both the Scheveningen VVV (see below) and The Hague VVV have the details. Most fishing trips depart from Dr Lelykade, the southern dock of the inner harbour – tram #8 from Den Haag HS. Other ocean-going excursions are possible too – again details from either VVV. Scheveningen also has an ambitious programme of **special events**, including an international **sand sculpture** competition in early May and a massive international **kite festival** that takes over the beach and much of the town in early June.

Scheveningen is best visited as a day-trip from The Hague, but if you do decide to stay, the **VVV**, by the seafront just east of the Kurhaus at Gevers Deynootweg 1134 (July–Aug Mon–Sat 9am–7pm, Sun 11am–3pm; rest of year Mon–Sat 9am–5.30pm; ☎0900/340 3505, 75c per min), issues a free brochure listing all the resort's hotels and pensions. Out-of-season, there are oodles of vacant rooms, but in the summer it's best to use the VVV's accommodation booking service.

Delft

Despite its desultory surroundings, the compact centre of **DELFT** has considerable charm: gabled red-roofed houses stand beside tree-lined canals, and the pastel colours of the brickwork and bridges give the place a faded, placid tranquillity. It's one of the most visited spots in Holland, but although the tourist crowds can be oppressive in the height of the summer, there's no gainsaying the town centre's good looks or the appeal of its ancient buildings, several of which date from its medieval heyday. Delft is also famous for the **Jan Vermeer** (1632–1675) connection. The artist was born in the town and died here, too – leaving a wife, eleven children and a huge debt to the local baker. He had given the man two pictures as security, and his wife bankrupted herself trying to retrieve them. Vermeer's most celebrated painting is his 1661 *View of Delft*, now displayed in the Mauritshuis in The Hague (see p.183), but if you're after a townscape that even vaguely resembles the picture, you'll be disappointed – it doesn't exist and in a sense it never did. Vermeer made no claim to be a realist and his *View* accorded with the landscape traditions of his day in presenting an idealised Delft framed by a broad expanse of water and dappled by a cloudy sky.

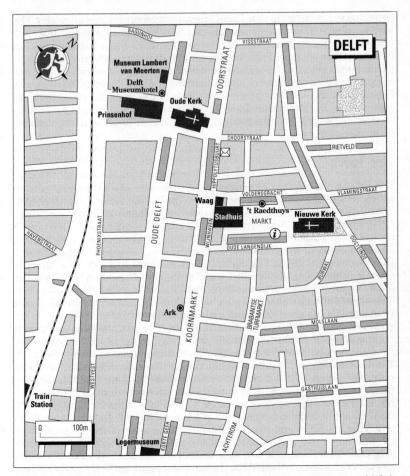

The town's other claim to fame is **delftware**, the clunky ceramics to which it gave its name in the seventeenth century. Delftware actually traces its origins to Mallorca, where craftsmen developed **majolica**, a type of porous pottery that was glazed with bright metallic oxides. During the Renaissance, these techniques were exported to Italy from where they spread north, first to Antwerp and then to the United Provinces. Initially, delft pottery designs featured Dutch and Italian landscapes, portraits and biblical scenes, but the East India Company's profitable import of Chinese ceramics transformed the industry. Delft factories freely copied Chinese designs and by the middle of the seventeenth century they were churning out blue-and-white tiles, plates, panels, jars and vases – even exporting to China, where they undercut Chinese producers. The delft factories were themselves undercut in the middle of the eighteenth century by the British and the Germans and by the time Napoleon arrived they had all but closed down. There was a modest revival of the delft industry in the 1870s and there are several local producers today, but it's mostly cheap mass-produced stuff of little originality. The town's many souvenir shops are jam-packed with delftware, but if that isn't enough, head for the factory of **Porceleyne Fles** (Mon–Sat 9am–5pm; April–Oct also Sun 9.30am–5pm; ƒ5), the leading local manufacturer, which still produces handpainted ceramics. The factory is located on the south side of Delft, a ten-minute bus ride from the train station (bus #63 or #129); a visit includes a multi-lingual video presentation and demonstrations of the production process. More conveniently, **De Porcelijne Lampetkan**, just behind the Nieuwe Kerk, is an appealing little shop selling a good range of antique delftware at (comparatively) reasonable rates.

The Town

The obvious place to start an exploration of Delft is the **Markt**, a central point of reference with the Stadhuis at one end and the Nieuwe Kerk at the other, with cafés and restaurants lined up in between and a **statue** of Delft's own Hugo Grotius in the middle. A well-known scholar and statesman, Grotius (1583–1645) was sentenced to life imprisonment by Maurice of Orange-Nassau during the political turmoil of the 1610s, but was subsequently rescued by his wife who smuggled him out of goal in a chest. Grotius still came to a sticky end, dying of exposure after being shipwrecked near Danzig. The **Nieuwe Kerk** (April–Oct Mon–Sat 9am–6pm, Sun noon–6pm; Nov–March Mon–Sat 11am–4pm, Sun noon–4pm; ƒ4) is new only in comparison with the Oude Kerk, as there's been a church on this site since 1381. Most of the original structure was destroyed in the great fire that swept through Delft in 1536, and the remainder in an explosion a century later – a disaster, incidentally, which claimed the life of the artist Carel Fabritius, Rembrandt's greatest pupil and (debatably) the teacher of Vermeer. The most striking part of the restoration is in fact the most recent – the 100-metre spire, replaced in 1872 and from whose summit there's a great view of the town (same hours as the church). Unless you're a Dutch monarchist, the church's interior is rather uninspiring: it contains the burial vaults of the Dutch royal family, the most recent addition being Queen Wilhelmina, in 1962. Only the mausoleum of William the Silent grabs your attention, a hodgepodge of styles concocted by Hendrik de Keyser. Keyser also designed the **Stadhuis** opposite, though its delightful facade, equipped with small dormer windows, shutters, fluted pilasters and shell decoration, is dwarfed by the sulky stonework of the old medieval keep that he incorporated into the newer building.

Just behind the Stadhuis, beside the canal, is the **Wijnhaven**, one of Delft's prettiest streets, leading north along Hippolytusbuurt to the Gothic **Oude Kerk** (April–Oct Mon–Sat 9am–6pm, Sun noon–6pm; Nov–March Mon–Sat 11am–4pm, Sun noon–4pm; ƒ4), arguably the town's finest building. Simple and well-propor-tioned, despite its unhealthily leaning tower, the present edifice is the result of a succession of churches constructed here between the thirteenth and the seven-teenth centuries. Inside, the unadorned vaulting proves interiors don't have to be elaborate to avoid being sombre. The pride of the church is its pulpit of 1548, intri-cately carved with figures emphasized in false perspective, but also notable is the modern stained glass, depicting and symbolizing the history of the Netherlands – particularly the 1945 liberation – in the north transept. If you're curious about the tombs – including that of Admiral Maarten van Tromp, famed for hoisting a broom at his masthead to "sweep the seas clear of the English" – take a look at the free *Striking Points* pamphlet available at the entrance. Incidentally, the English had the last laugh on Tromp, who was killed during a sea battle off Texel in 1653.

Opposite the Oude Kerk, in the former Convent of St Agatha, is the **Prinsenhof** (Tues–Sat 10am–5pm, Sun 1–5pm; *f*5), which served as the main residence of William the Silent of Orange-Nassau from 1572 to 1584. A rambling, somewhat confusing building with two floors, the Prinsenhof holds the municipal art collection, an immensely appealing jumble of works whose highlights begin in the old refectory (Room 7) with the curious *Wretched State of the Netherlands*. This inflammatory canvas by an unknown seventeenth-century Protestant depicts the Habsburg commander, the Duke of Alva, in cahoots with the Devil and the Pope, enslaving the Low Countries with each province represented by one of the seventeen chained women before him. Meanwhile, in the background, Margaret of Parma, the region's Habsburg governor, can be seen fishing in a pool of blood. Just beyond Room 7, the bottom of the old stone staircase marks the spot where **William the Silent** was assassinated on July 10, 1584. A former army commander of both Charles V and Philip II, William turned against the Habsburgs during Alva's persecution of the Protestants in 1567. William went on to lead the Protestant revolt against Philip, mustering a series of armies and organizing the *Watergeuzen*, a guerrilla unit that played a key role in driving back the imperial army. In return, Philip put a bounty of 25,000 gold crowns on William's head, but in the event the man who shot him was not a professional assassin but a fanatical Catholic, Balthazar Gerard, who did the deed for his religion. Two bullets passed right through William and the **bullet holes** are now protected by a glass sheet, put there to stop visitors sticking their fingers in the holes. Moving on, there's more fine and applied art upstairs, most notably a room full of anatomy paintings – *The Anatomy Lesson* of 1681 by Cornelis de Man is especially striking – and another of militia paintings. During the long war with Spain, every Dutch city had its own Militia, but as the Habsburg threat diminished the militias devolved into social clubs, each of them keen to immortalize their particular company in a group portrait. The most famous of these is Rembrandt's *Night Watch* in Amsterdam's Rijkmuseum (see p.101), but there are several good examples here, particularly Michiel van Miereveld's *Banquet of the Delft Militia*.

A few metres to the north of the Prinsenhof, the canalside **Museum Lambert van Meerten**, at Oude Delft 199 (Tues–Sat 10am–5pm, Sun 1–5pm; *f*3.50), exhibits the town's best collection of delftware. There are jars and vases, plates and panels, but the museum's speciality is its tiles – a fabulous hoard collected by the nineteenth-century industrialist after whom the museum is named. In particular, look out for the vibrant tile picture of the Battle of La Hogue – in which an Anglo-Dutch fleet worsted the French in 1692 – displayed on the staircase.

Heading south from the Museum Meerten along Oude Delft, it's about 1km to the **Legermuseum**, housed in a pair of old arsenals and a warehouse at Korte Geer 1 (Tues–Sat 10am–5pm, Sun noon–5pm; *f*6). Here you'll find a display of weaponry, uniforms and military accoutrements labelled only in Dutch – which may sound supremely dull, but isn't, even if you're not an enthusiast. The military history of the Netherlands is outlined from Roman times onwards, including detailed sections on the Spanish wars and the ill-advised colonialist enterprises of the 1950s – shown in surprisingly candid detail.

Practicalities

From either of The Hague's train stations, it only takes a few minutes to reach Delft, where it's a ten-minute walk east from the train station to the town centre – just follow the signs. You can also make the journey on tram #1 from Den Haag Centraal Station; in Delft the tram rattles along along Phoenixstraat/Westvest between the train station and the centre. Delft **VVV** is bang in the centre of town at Markt 85 (April–Sept Mon–Fri 9am–6pm, Sat 9am–5pm, Sun 10am–3pm; Oct–March Mon–Fri 9am–5.30pm, Sat 9am–5pm; ☎015/212 6100).

Delft is probably best visited as a day-trip, but there are several good **hotels**, beginning with the *Ark*, an attractive four-star place occupying three tastefully restored seventeenth-century canal houses at Koornmarkt 65 (☎015/215 7999, fax 214 4997, *www.deark.nl*; ④). Another appealing option is the *Delft Museumhotel*, which also has a canalside location, in sprucely converted premises close to the Prinsenhof at Oude Delft 189 (☎015/214 0930, fax 214 0935; ④). Several inexpensive and rather more rudimentary hotels overlook the Markt, the pick being the plain *'t Raedthuys*, whose rooms come with or without shower and are above the café at no. 38 (☎015/212 5115; ①).

Many of Delft's **cafés** and **restaurants** are geared up for day trippers and serve routine stuff at inflated prices, but there are also several excellent places, most notably the *De Klikspaan*, Koornmarkt 85 (closed Mon & Tues; ☎015/214 1562), a smart, polished restaurant with main courses around ƒ40. Similar prices apply at the equally chic *Restaurant Français*, near the Oude Kerk at Heilige Geestraat 3 (closed Sun & Mon). Alternatively, *La Fontanella*, near the Stadhuis at Voldersgracht 8, has tasty pizzas from ƒ12, and just along the street at no.4 is the pleasant, pocket-sized *Voldersvier*, great for snacks and cakes. For a **drink**, try *Locus Publicus*, Brabantse Turfmarkt 67, a popular hangout which serves a staggering array of beers and also bar food.

Rotterdam

ROTTERDAM lies at the heart of a maze of rivers and artificial waterways that form the seaward outlet of the rivers Rijn (Rhine) and Maas (Meuse). An important port as early as the fourteenth century, it was one of the major cities of the Dutch Republic and shared its periods of fortune and decline until the nineteenth century when it was caught unawares. The city was ill-prepared for the industrial expansion of the Ruhr, the development of larger ships and the silting up of the Maas, but prosperity returned in a big way with the digging of an entirely new ship canal (the "Nieuwe Waterweg") between 1866 and 1872. Indeed, the economic upturn was interrupted only by the Depression and World War II – the Germans bombing the city centre in 1940, and the Allies completing the demolition in 1943.

The post-war period saw the rapid reconstruction of the docks and the town centre, and great efforts were made to keep Rotterdam ahead of its rivals. Consequently, when huge container ships and oil tankers made many port facilities obsolete, the Rotterdammers were equal to the challenge and built an entirely new deep-sea port some 25km to the west of the old town. Completed in 1968, the **Europoort** juts out into the North Sea and can accommodate the largest of ships, contributing to Rotterdam's handling of 300 million tonnes of fuel, grain and materials needed or sold by western Europe each year.

Rapid post-war rebuilding transformed Rotterdam's town centre into a giant covered shopping area, a sterile and formless assembly of concrete and glass. This prospect of docks and shops probably sounds unalluring, but Rotterdam has its moments: in the **Boijmans-Van Beuningen Museum** it has one of the best – and most overlooked – galleries in the country, and between the central modernity and dockland sleaze is **Delfshaven**, an old area that survived the bombs. By way of contrast, there's **Oudehaven**, the city's oldest harbour. Bombed during the war, it was dazzlingly redeveloped and is now home to a host of popular bars and cafés. There's not much else, but redevelopment hasn't obliterated Rotterdam's earthy character: the prostitution and dope peddling are for real. If you want to avoid the high spots of the low life, stick to the centre.

Arrival, information and accommodation

Rotterdam has a large and confusing centre edged by its main rail terminus, **Centraal Station**, that serves as the hub of a useful tram and metro system for the city and its suburbs – though it's a seamy, hostile place late at night. The **VVV**, ten minutes' walk away at Coolsingel 67 (Mon–Thurs & Sat 9am–7pm, Fri 9am–9pm, Sun 10am–5pm; ☎010/414 0000), has all the usual tourist information as well as details and tickets for forthcoming concerts and events. They also sell a useful brochure incorporating a city map (*f*4), supply free copies of *Simply the Best*, an excellent **listings** booklet aimed at young budget travellers, and also maps of the tram, bus and **underground system**. The latter is divided into zones for the calculation of fares (two sections of a *strippenkaart* for a single trip in the central zone).

The VVV's **accommodation** booking service can be handy as the city's cheaper hotels tend to fill up fast. There are a clutch of reasonably priced hotels a kilometre or so to the southwest of the station, easily accessible by tram. These include the small *Roxane*, 's-Gravendijkwal 14 (☎010/436 6109, fax 436 2944; tram #1, #7 or #9; ①), and the larger and more comfortable *Wilgenhof*, overlooking the canal on the corner at Heemraadssingel 92–94 (☎010/425 4892, fax 477 2611; tram #1 or #7; ②). More central options include the *Bazar* at Witte de Withstraat 16 (☎010/206 5151, fax 206 5159; ②), with only seven rooms but great, modernistic décor and bathtubs in all rooms, plus an adjoining restaurant which is a pleasant place to hang out. Alternatively, the modern and trim *Hotel Emma*, Nieuwe Binneweg 6 (☎010/436 5533, fax 436 7658; ③), is in the same area and has street parking nearby for guests, whilst the *Breitner* is another good option, close to the Boijmans Museum at Breitnerstraat 23 (☎010/436 0262, fax 436 4091; metro Dijkzigt or tram #4 or #5; ③); it has a garden terrace. Beside the south bank of the Nieuwe Maas is the excellent *Hotel New York* (☎010/439 0500, fax 484 2701; ③), where most of the extremely comfortable rooms have river views. You can get there by water taxi or on the metro – it's a five-minute walk from Wilhelminaplein station. The **youth hostel** is 3km from the station at Rochussenstraat 107 (☎010/436 5763, fax 436 5569; tram #4 or metro Dijkzigt & bus #39; *f*26.50).

The City

From Centraal Station, Kruisplein leads south onto Westersingel/Mauritsweg, cutting this part of the city into two sections – to the west is the deteriorated housing of many of the city's migrant workers, and to the east is the **Lijnbaan**,

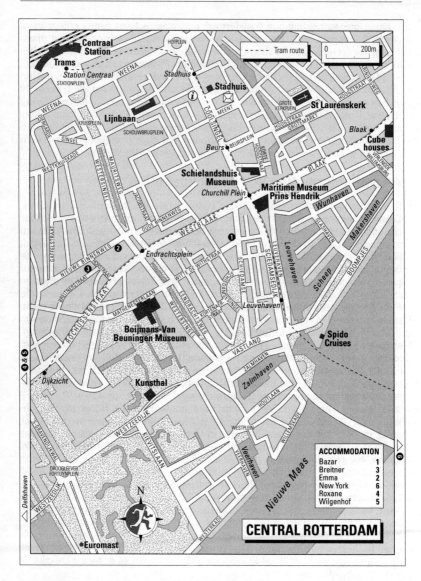

CENTRAL ROTTERDAM

ACCOMMODATION	
Bazar	1
Breitner	3
Emma	2
New York	6
Roxane	4
Wilgenhof	5

Europe's first pedestrianized shopping precinct, completed in 1953. The Lijnbaan connects into a baffling series of apparently endless shopping areas hemmed in by Weena, Coolsingel, Westblaak and Mauritsweg. To the east of Coolsingel, just off Beursplein, the fifteenth-century **St Laurenskerk** (Grote Kerk; Tues–Sat 10am–4pm; Oct–May closed Thurs; free) suffered a clumsy renovation which has left it cold and soulless. You can climb the tower the third Saturday of the month from May to September. Nearby, and marginally more exciting, is the redevelopment of the **Blaak** area (metro Blaak, tram #1, #3 or #13, bus #32 or #49) with a new central library adjoining a remarkable series of cubist houses, replacing a part of the old city centre destroyed by the bombing. The curious **Kijk-Kubus** (Cube House; March–Oct daily 11am–5pm; Jan–Feb Fri–Sun 11am–5pm; ƒ3.50) is at Overblaak 70, near Blaak train station; it's a somewhat disorientating tour of an upside-down house, where you're likely to bang your head on a beam and feel dizzy if you peer out of the windows.

Heading west, the **Maritime Museum Prins Hendrik** (Tues–Sat 10am–5pm, Sun 11am–5pm; ƒ6) is situated in the old harbour area beside the Leuvehaven. Apart from an enterprising programme of temporary nautical exhibitions, the outside area has been spruced up for the museum's prime exhibit – an immaculately restored mid-nineteenth-century ironclad, the *Buffel*, complete with communal sinks shaped to match the angle of the bows, a couple of ships' figureheads and a string of luxurious officers' cabins.

Across the boulevard to the north, surrounded by high-rise apartment buildings, the **Schielandshuis Museum** (Tues–Fri 10am–5pm, Sat & Sun 11am–5pm; ƒ6) is housed in a seventeenth-century mansion at Korte Hoogstraat 31, and has a variety of very good displays on the history of Rotterdam, including original footage of the bombing of the city in World War II and incorporating the *Atlas van Stolk* collection of drawings and prints, which includes fascinating sketches of pre-colonial Indonesia.

Doubling back to the south, the shape and feel of the Leuvehaven Harbour has been transformed by the freeway that now scoots along the top of the old enclosing sea dyke, the Boompjes. This busy road leads southwest past the **Kunsthal**, Westzeedijk 41 (Tues–Sat 10am–5pm, Sun 11am–5pm; ƒ10), which showcases first-rate exhibitions of contemporary art, photography and design. Pushing on west, the **Euromast** perches on a rather lonely park corner beside the Nieuwe Maas. Originally just a drab, grey observation platform thrown up in 1960, the **Spacetower** (April–Sept daily 10am–7pm; Oct–March daily 10am–5pm; ƒ15) was added later, its revolving elevator rising on the outside of the 185-metre tower. The view is spectacular, but no less than you'd expect considering the price of entry.

Delfshaven

If nothing in the city centre can be called exactly picturesque, **DELFSHAVEN** goes part of the way to make up for it. It's a 45-minute walk southwest of Centraal Station – fifteen minutes by tram #4 or #6 (direction Schiedam, tram stop Spanjaardstraat), or a couple of minutes on foot from Delfshaven metro. Once the harbour that served Delft, it was from here that the Pilgrim Fathers set sail in 1620, changing to the more reliable *Mayflower* in Plymouth before continuing onward to the New World. Delfshaven was only incorporated into Rotterdam in 1886 and managed to survive World War II virtually intact. Long a neglected area, the town council finally recognized its tourist potential and has set about conserving and restoring the whole locality. Most of the buildings lining the canals are eighteenth- and nineteenth-century warehouses, seen today as "desirable residences" by the upwardly mobile, who look set to turn Delfshaven into an upmarket suburb. The **Dubbelde Palmboom Museum**, Voorhaven 12 (Tues–Fri 10am–5pm; ƒ6), once a jenever distillery, is now an historical museum, with a wide-ranging, if unexceptional collection of objects representing work and leisure in the Maas delta. Nearby, the **Zakkendragershuisje**, Voorstraat 13 (Tues–Sat 10am–5pm, Sun 1–5pm; free), was originally the guild room of the Grain Sack Carriers, who decided the allocation of duties by dice. Today, it's a privately owned, fully operational tin foundry, selling a variety of items made in the old moulds.

The Boijmans-Van Beuningen Museum

To the northeast of Delfshaven, back toward the centre, the **Boijmans-Van Beuningen Museum**, Mathenesserlaan 18–20 (Tues–Sat 10am–5pm, Sun 11am–5pm; *f*10, more during special exhibitions), is Rotterdam's one great attraction, a fifteen-minute walk from Centraal Station or accessible by tram #5 or Eendrachtsplein metro. Amid the enormous collection of paintings – from Flemish Masters to Pop Art – you're sure to find something to your liking, though the sheer size of the displays can be overpowering, while the constant rotation of exhibits tends to make guidebooks redundant. The information desk provides an updated and simplified diagrammatic outline of the museum, but in general terms pre-nineteenth-century paintings are in the old wing, modern paintings in the new wing and both wings are divided into two interconnecting floors.

The main entrance leads into the new wing where the first floor is packed with modern paintings, best known of which are the **Surrealists**. De rigueur for students' bedrooms in the 1970s, it's difficult to appreciate Salvador Dali's *Spain* as anything more than the painting of the poster. Other works by René Magritte, Max Ernst and Giorgio de Chirico provide a representative sample of a movement whose images seem to have lost much of their power since. Surrealism was never adopted by Dutch artists, though the Magic Realism of **Carel Willink** has its similarities in the precise, hallucinatory technique he uses to distance the viewer in *Self Portrait with a Pen*. **Charley Toorop**'s *Three Generations* is also realism with an aim to disconcert – the huge bust of her father, Jan, looms in the background and dominates the painting. Look out also for the **Van der Vorm Collection**, which has paintings from many of Europe's most famous artists, including Monet, Van Gogh, Picasso, Gauguin, Cézanne and Munch, as well as a representative sample of the Barbizon and Hague schools, notably **J.H. Weissenbruch**'s *Strandgezicht*, a beautiful gradation of radiant tones.

Also on the first floor, but in the old wing and arranged in chronological order, are the museum's earlier paintings, beginning with an excellent **Flemish and Netherlandish religious art section**, whose sumptuous *Christ in the House of Martha and Mary* by Pieter Aertsen is outstanding. **Hieronymus Bosch**, famed for his nightmarish visions, is represented by four of his more mainstream works. Usually considered a macabre fantasist, Bosch was actually working to the limits of oral and religious tradition, where biblical themes were depicted as iconographical representations, laden with explicit symbols. In his *St Christopher*, the dragon, the hanged bear and the broken pitcher lurk in the background, representations of danger and uncertainty, whereas the Prodigal Son's attitude to the brothel behind him in *The Wanderer* is deliberately ambivalent. Bosch's technique never absorbed the influences of Renaissance Italy, and his figures in the *Marriage Feast at Cana* are static and unbelievable, uncomfortably arranged around a distorted table. Other works in this section include paintings by **Jan van Scorel**, who was more willing to absorb Italianate styles as in his *Scholar in a Red Cap*; the Bruges artist **Hans Memling**, whose capacity for detail can be seen in his *Two Houses in a Landscape*; **Pieter Brueghel the Elder**'s mysterious, hazy *Tower of Babel*; and **Geertgen tot Sint Jans**' beautiful, delicate *Glorification of the Virgin*.

Further on, a small selection of **Dutch Genre** paintings reflects the tastes of the emergent seventeenth-century middle class. The idea was to depict real-life situations overlaid with a symbolic moral content. Jan Steen's *Extracting the Stone* and his *Physician's Visit* are good humorous examples, while Gerrit Dou's *The Quack*, ostensibly just a passing scene, is full of small cameos of deception – a boy catching a bird, the trapped hare – that refer back to the quack's sham cures. In this section also are a number of **Rembrandts**, including two contrasting canvases: an analytic *Portrait of Alotta Adriaensdr*, her ageing illuminated but softened by her white ruff, and a gloomy, indistinct *Blind Tobias and his Wife* painted twenty years later. His intimate *Titus at his Desk* is also in marked contrast to the more formal portrait commissions common to his day. Most of the work of Rembrandt's pupil **Carel Fabritius** was destroyed when he was killed in a Delft gunpowder explosion in 1654; an exception is his *Self-Portrait*, reversing his master's usual technique by lighting the background and placing the subject in shadow.

Finally, the ground floor of the old wing is devoted to a roughly chronological series of galleries exhibiting applied, decorative art and design, from the jewellery and household items of the Middle Ages, through Dutch silverware, tiles and glass, to the latest industrial design.

Waterway excursions

One way of exploring the waterways you can see from the Euromast is on the **Spido cruises** that leave from beside the Boompjes at the south end of the Leuvehaven, a quick tram or metro ride south from Centraal Station (tram #5, #6, #20 or Leuvehaven metro).

Between April and September tours run every 45 minutes between 9.30am and 5pm, less frequently at other times of year, and take an hour and fifteen minutes; prices start at *f*16 per person. They head off past the wharfs, landings, docks and silos of this, the largest port in the world, though it's actually more impressive at night, when the illuminated ships and refineries gleam like Spielberg spaceships. In season, there are also longer, less frequent trips to Dordrecht, the windmills of Kinderdijk, the Europoort and the Delta Project (see below), from between *f*25 and *f*50 per person. Further details are available from the VVV, or the boat operators at Leuvehoofd 25 (☎010/275 9988).

The Spido excursion to the series of colossal dams that make up the **Delta Project**, along the seaboard southwest of Rotterdam, only provides the briefest of glances, and it's better to visit by bus, which takes two hours. To get there, take the underground to Spijkenisse (30min) and catch bus #104 for Vlissingen (Mon–Sat hourly, Sun every 2hr), which travels along the road that crosses the top of the three dams that restrain the Haringvliet, Grevelingen and Oosterschelde estuaries. For more on the Delta Project and Delta Expo, see Chapter 6, pp.309–310.

Eating and drinking

The best bet for a cheap sit-down **meal** during the day is around the Lijnbaan shopping centre. Dozens of cafés, snack bars and fast-food outlets line the streets, with *dagschotels* generally around ƒ15. For lunch or dinner, there are many places serving Dutch food on Mauritsweg, between the station and the Boijmans Museum. On Witte de Withstraat *The Bazar*, at no.16 (☎010/206 5151; evenings only), does excellent kebabs and vegetarian meals, but it's a popular spot and reservations are a good idea at weekends. Alternatively, there's a decent café at the Boijmans Museum, while *De Pijp*, Gaffelstraat 90 (☎010/436 6896), is a good international restaurant five minutes' walk north of the museum. Oude and Nieuwe Binneweg are lined with **cafés and bars** – try *De Vijgeboon* at Oude Binneweg 146a, *Sijf* at Oude Binnenweg 115, on the corner with Jacobstraat (☎010/433 2610), or *Rotown* at Nieuwe Binneweg 19: all have affordable dinner menus featuring tasty Dutch staples; *Rotown* offers regular **live music** too. Also in the centre is *Dudok*, at Meent 8 (☎010/433 3102), a brasserie with an extensive menu (available in English on request) and lots of space. The *Consulat*, Westersingel 28 (☎010/436 3323), is a long established student café-bar with very good, cheap food; again it is popular at weekends, so reservations are a good idea. There are lots of **smokers' coffeeshops** around the centre, but two to start with are *Le Pool* upstairs on Eendrachtsweg by Eendrachtsplein and *Witte de With* at Witte de Withstraat 92.

Listings

Airport enquiries Rotterdam Airport, Airportplein 60 (☎010/446 3444; bus #33).

Bureau de change At most banks (Mon–Fri 9am–4pm) or Centraal Station (Mon–Sat 7.30am–10pm, Sun 9am–10pm).

Car rental Avis, Rotterdam Airport (☎010/415 8842) and Kruisplein 21 (☎010/433 2233); Hertz, Schiekade 986 (☎010/404 6088); Europcar, Pompenburg 646 (☎010/411 4860).

Dentist ☎010/455 2155.

Emergencies Police, Ambulance & Fire ☎112.

Football At *Feyenoord* stadium – bus #49 or Stadion train from Centraal Station. Game details from the VVV; most games are on Sundays.

Internet access *Internet Corner* – located upstairs in the Virgin Megastore (☎010/411 1752).

Left Luggage Coin-operated lockers at the train station.

Markets General, including antiques, on Mariniersweg (Tues & Sat 9am–5pm). Stamps, coins and books on Grotekerkplein (Tues & Sat 9.30am–4pm).

Medical assistance Doctor ☎010/420 1100; Ambulance ☎112.

Pharmacies 24-hr service details ☎010/411 0370.

Police Doelwater 5 (☎010/274 9911).

Post office Coolsingel 42 (Mon 11am–6pm, Tues–Thurs 9am–6pm, Fri 8.30am–8.30pm, Sat 9.30am–3pm); Delftseplein 31 (Mon–Fri 8.30am–6pm).

Public Transport enquiries ☎0900/9292

Taxi Rotterdamse Taxi Centrale ☎010/462 6060.

Gouda

A pretty little place some 25km northeast of Rotterdam, **GOUDA** is almost everything you'd expect of a Dutch country town: a ring of quiet canals that encircle ancient buildings and old docks. More surprisingly, its **Markt**, a ten-minute walk from the train station, is the largest in Holland – a reminder of the town's

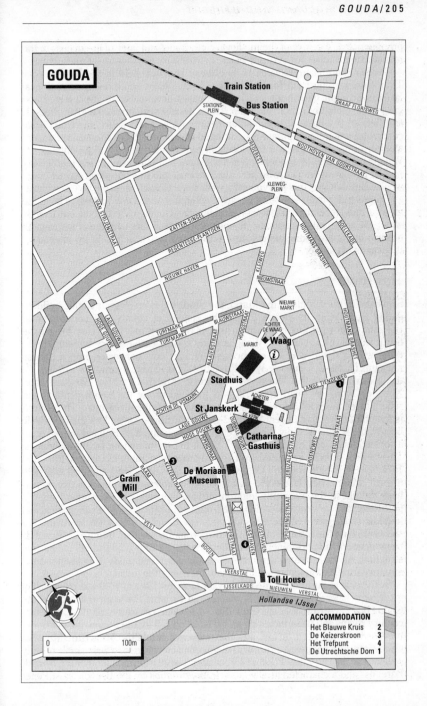

GOUDA

Train Station

Bus Station

GRAAF FLORISWEG

STATIONS-
PLEIN

VREDEBEST

NOOTHOVEN VAN GOORSTRAAT

KLEIWEG-
PLEIN

KATTEN-SINGEL

REGENTESSE-PLANTOEN

NIEUWE HAVEN

VAN STRIJENSTRAAT

LAGE GOUWE

HOGE GOUWE

RAAM

TURFMARKT

TURFMARKT

MAAERSTRAAT

BLAUWSTRAAT

HOOGSTRAAT

KLEIWEG

NIEUWSTRAAT

NIEUWE
MARKT

ACHTER
DE WAAG

HOUTMANS GRASHET

BOELEKADE

MARKT ◆ **Waag**

i

Stadhuis

LANGE TIENDEWEG ●1

ACHTER DE VISMARKT

St Janskerk

ACHTER
DE KERK

GEUZENSTRAAT

LAGE GOUWE

HOGE GOUWE

DUBBELE BUURT

PEPERSTRAAT

●2

**Catharina
Gasthuis**

JERUZALEMSTRAAT

GROENEWEG

HOUTMANS GRASHET

●3

**Grain
Mill**

RAAM

KEIZERSTRAAT

NAAIERSTRAAT

**De Moriaan
Museum**

VEST

PEPERSTRAAT

WESTHAVEN

OOSTHAVEN

SPOERINGSTRAAT

✉

BOGEN

●4

VEERSTAL

IJSSELKADE

Toll House

NIEUWEN VERSTAL

Hollandse IJssel

N

0   100m

ACCOMMODATION

Het Blauwe Kruis	**2**
De Keizerskroon	**3**
Het Trefpunt	**4**
De Utrechtsche Dom	**1**

prominence as a centre of the medieval cloth trade, and later of its success in the manufacture of cheeses and clay pipes.

Gouda's main claim to fame is its **cheese market**, held in the Markt every Thursday morning from June to August. Traditionally, some one thousand local farmers brought their home-produced cheeses here to be weighed, tested and graded for moisture, smell and taste. These details were marked on the cheeses, and formed the basis for negotiation between buyer and seller, the exact price confirmed using an elaborate code of hand-claps. Today, the cheese market is a shadow of its former self, a few locals in traditional dress standing outside the Waag, surrounded by modern open-air stands. Not surprisingly, it's mercilessly milked by tour operators, who herd their victims into this humdrum scene every week – but don't let this put you off a visit, since Gouda's charms lie elsewhere.

There's a jazz festival in town in early September and, if you happen to be in the area in mid-December, it's worth phoning the Gouda VVV to find out exactly when the town will be holding its splendid candlelit pre-Christmas festival. All electric lights are extinguished on the main square, which is lit up instead by thousands of candles.

The Town

Slap-bang in the middle of the Markt, the **Stadhuis** is an elegant Gothic building dating from 1450, its facade fringed by statues of counts and countesses of Burgundy above a tinkling carillon that plays every half-hour. Nearby, on the north side of the square, the **Waag** is a tidy seventeenth-century building, decorated with a detailed relief of cheese-weighing, now converted into a cheese museum (April–Oct Tues & Wed, Fri–Sun 1–5pm, Thurs 10am–5pm; *f*3.50). To the south, just off the Markt, **St Janskerk** (March–Oct Mon–Sat 9am–5pm; Nov–Feb Mon–Sat 10am–4pm; *f*3) was founded in the thirteenth century and rebuilt three times after fires, most recently in the sixteenth century. The church is famous for its magnificent **stained-glass windows**; as well as their intrinsic beauty, the windows show the way religious art changed as Holland moved from a society dominated by the Catholic Church to one influenced by the Calvinists. The biblical themes executed by Dirk and Wouter Crabeth between 1555 and 1571, when Holland was still Catholic, have an amazing clarity of detail and richness of colour. Their last work, *Judith Slaying Holofernes* (Window no. 6), is perhaps the finest, the story unfolding in intricate perspective. By comparison, the post-Reformation windows, which date from 1572 to 1603, adopt an allegorical and heraldic style typical of more secular art. *The Relief of Leiden* (Window no. 25) shows William the Silent retaking the town from the Spanish, though Delft and its burgomasters take prominence – no doubt because they paid the bill for its construction. All the windows are numbered and a detailed guide is available at the entrance for *f*10; binoculars will help you make out the detail.

By the side of the church, the flamboyant **Lazarus Gate** of 1609 was once part of the town's leper hospital, until it was moved to form the back entrance to the **Catharina Gasthuis**, a hospice till 1910. A likeable conglomeration of sixteenth-century rooms and halls, including an old isolation cell for the insane, the interior of the Gasthuis has been turned into the municipal **Stedelijk Museum** (Mon–Sat 10am–5pm, Sun noon–5pm; *f*4.25). The collection incorporates a fine sample of early religious art in The Chapel (Room 13), notably a large triptych, *Life of Mary*, by Dirk Barendsz and a characteristically austere *Annunciation* by the Bruges artist Pieter

Pourbus. Other highlights include a spacious hall, *Het Ruim* (Room 10), that was once a sort of medieval hostel, but is now dominated by paintings of the Civic Guard, principally two group portraits by Ferdinand Bol; the intricate silver-gilt *Chalice and Eucharist Dish* was presented to the Guard in the early fifteenth century. Two later rooms have a modest selection of Hague and Barbizon School canvases, notably work by Anton Mauve and Charles Daubigny. Downstairs, beside the isolation cell, there is a chilling collection of torture instruments from the old city jail. The English guide costs *f*1 and lists exhibits here and in De Moriaan (see below).

Gouda's other museum, **De Moriaan** (Mon–Sat 10am–5pm, Sun noon–5pm; *f*4.25, or free with Stedelijk Museum ticket), is in a cosy old merchant's house at Westhaven 29, with a mixed bag of exhibits from clay pipes to ceramics and tiles. Westhaven itself is a winsome jumble of old buildings that head off toward the old toll house and a dilapidated mill beside the Hollandse IJssel river, on the southern edge of the town centre. There's a restored, fully operational **grain mill** (Sat 9am–4pm, Thurs 9am–2pm; *f*2.50) five minutes' walk west of the Markt, at Vest 65.

Practicalities

Gouda's **train** and **bus stations** are to the immediate north of the town centre, ten minutes' walk from the VVV, Markt 27 (Mon–Fri 9am–5pm, Sat 10am–4pm; ☎0182/513666), which has a limited supply of **private rooms**, and will make reservations for a small charge. The most reasonably priced **hotel** is the plain and simple *Het Blauwe Kruis*, Westhaven 4 (☎0182/512677; ①). There are three other, more agreeable hotels in the town centre: the excellent value *De Utrechtsche Dom*, in an airy and pleasantly renovated old building five minutes' walk from the station at Geuzenstraat 6 (☎0182/528833, fax 549534, *www.rsnet.nl/hotel*; ②); the *De Keizerskroon*, to the west of Westhaven at Keizerstraat 11–13 (☎0182/528096; ②); and the *Het Trefpunt* at Westhaven 46 (☎0182/512879; ②).

For **food**, Gouda has literally dozens of cafés and snack bars geared up for the day-trippers who descend on the town in droves during the summer. Among them, *'t Groot Stedelijk*, Markt 44, has a variety of cheap Dutch dishes, and there are pancakes at *'t Goudse Winkeltje*, Achter de Kerk 9a. Alternatively, you might go for pizza at the *Rimini*, Markt 28 (☎0182/522993), or decent Indonesian food at *Warung Srikandi*, Lange Groenendaal 108 (☎0182/519412). For a **drink**, *Café Central*, Markt 23, is a pleasant place to nurse a beer, while the most popular spot is the excellent *Eetcafé Vidocq*, Koster Gijzensteeg 8 – turn left out of the market past *Café Central* and take the first on the right.

Around Gouda: Oudewater

Eleven kilometres east of Gouda and easily accessible by bike (rent one from the train station) or bus #180 (every half hour), **OUDEWATER** is a compact and delightful little town that holds a unique place in the history of Dutch witchcraft. It's estimated that over a million women across Europe were burned or otherwise murdered in the widespread **witch-hunts** of the sixteenth century, and not only from fear and superstition: anonymous accusation to the authorities was an easy way of removing a wife, at a time when there was no divorce. Underlying it all was a virulent misogyny and an accompanying desire to terrorize women into submission. There were three main methods for investigating accusations of witchcraft: in the first, **trial by fire**, the suspect had to walk barefoot over hot cinders or have a hot iron pressed into the back or hands. If the burns blistered, the accused was innocent as witches were supposed to burn less easily than others; naturally, the (variable) temperature of the iron was crucial. **Trial by water** was still more hazardous: dropped into water, if you floated you were a witch, if you sank you were innocent – though very probably drowned. The third method, **trial by weight**, presupposed that a witch would have to be unduly light to fly on a broomstick, so many towns – including Oudewater – used the Waag (town weighhouse) to weigh the accused. If the weight didn't accord with a notional figure derived from the height, the woman was burned. The last Dutch woman to be burnt as a witch was a certain Marrigje Ariens, a herbalist from Schoonhaven, whose medical efforts, not untypically, inspired mistrust and subsequent persecution. She died in 1597.

Oudewater's Waag gained its fame from the actions of Charles V (1516–52), who saw a woman accused of witchcraft in a nearby village. The weighmaster, who'd been bribed, stated that the woman weighed only a few pounds, but Charles was dubious and ordered the woman to be weighed again in Oudewater, where the officials proved unbribable, pronouncing a normal weight and acquitting her. The probity of Oudewater's weighmaster impressed Charles, and he granted the town the privilege of issuing certificates, valid throughout the empire, stating that "The accused's weight is in accordance with the natural proportions of the body". Once in possession of the certificate, one could never be brought to trial for witchcraft again. Not surprisingly, thousands of people came from all over Europe for this life-saving piece of paper, and to Oudewater's credit no one was ever condemned.

Oudewater's sixteenth-century Waag has survived, converted into the **Heksenwaag** (Witches' Weigh House; April–Oct Tues–Sat 10am–5pm, Sun noon–5pm; *f*3), a family-run affair, where you can be weighed on the original rope and wood balance. The owners dress up in national costume and issue a certificate in olde-worlde English that states nothing, but does so very prettily. There's not much else to see here, but it's a pleasant little place, whose traditional stepped gables spread out along the River Hollandse IJssel as it twists its way through town.

If you decide to **stay**, the **VVV**, Markt-Oostzyde 8 (April–Sept Tues–Sat 10.30am–4.30pm, Sun 1–4.30pm; Oct–March Tues 10am–noon, Thurs 1.30–3.30pm, Sat 11am–3pm; ☎0348/564636), has details of several inexpensive (①) **private rooms**, and there is one central **hotel**, the *Abrona* at Broekerstraat 20 (☎0348/567466; ③). For **food**, café *'t Bactertje*, at Markt-Oostzyde 14, does decent snacks. and *Joia* is a quality brasserie serving Dutch cuisine at Havenstraat 1–2 (☎0348/567150).

Dordrecht and around

Some 15km southeast of Rotterdam, the ancient port of **DORDRECHT**, or "Dordt" as it's often called, is a likeable town beside one of the busiest waterway junctions in the world, where tankers and containers from the north pass the waterborne traffic of the Maas and Rijn. Eclipsed by the expansion of Rotterdam and left relatively intact by World War II, Dordrecht has also been spared the worst excesses of postwar development to emerge with a particularly beguiling centre adorned by a confusion of ancient buildings. Within easy reach is some of the province's prettiest countryside, including the windmills of the **Kinderdijk** and the **Biesbosch** nature reserve.

Granted a town charter in 1220, Dordrecht was the most important and powerful town in Holland until well into the sixteenth century. One of the first cities to declare against the Habsburgs in 1572, it was the obvious site for the first meeting of the Free Assembly of the Seven Provinces, and for a series of doctrinal conferences that tried to solve a whole range of theological differences among the various Protestant sects. The Protestants may have hated the Catholics, but they inherited the medieval church's enthusiasm for theological debate; in 1618, at the Synod of Dordt, the Remonstrants argued with the Calvinists over the definition of predestination – pretty weighty stuff compared to the Synod of 1574, when one of the main rulings demanded the dismantling of church organs.

From the seventeenth century, Dordrecht lost ground to its great rivals to the north, slipping into comparative insignificance, its economy sustained by trade and shipbuilding.

Arrival, information and accommodation

Well connected by train to all the Randstad's major cities, Dordrecht's adjoining **train** and **bus** stations are a ten-minute walk from the town centre, straight down Stationsweg/Johan de Wittstraat and left at the end along Bagijnhof/Visstraat. A couple of minutes from the station, the **VVV**, Stationsweg 1 (Mon–Fri 9am–5.30pm, Sat 9.30am–1pm, May–Aug open Sat until 5.30pm; ☎078/613 2800), has a superb booklet describing a **walking tour** of the city, worth the ƒ5 if you've got an hour or two to spare.

The VVV also has a list of cheap **private rooms**, which it will reserve for ƒ3.50 per person. There are three central **hotels**: the *Klarenbeek*, near the VVV at Johan de Wittstraat 35 (☎078/614 4133, fax 614 0861; ②); the *Dordrecht*, by the river near the west end of Spuiboulevard at Achterhakkers 12 (☎078/613 6011, fax 613 7470; ③); and the excellent *Bellevue*, Boomstraat 37 (☎078/613 7900, fax 613 7921; ③), overlooking the Maas from the northern tip of the old town by the Groothoofdspoort. There are cheaper alternatives approximately 4km east of town along Baanhoekweg, the road that forms the northern perimeter of the Biesbosch (bus #5 from the station, then a 20min walk from the last stop), in a complex that includes *De Hollandse Biesbosch* at no. 25 (☎078/621 2167, fax 621 2163; ②), a campsite of the same name (April–Oct) and a **HI hostel** (☎078/621 2167, fax 621 2163; ƒ28). If you call ahead, the hostel will have a taxi collect you from the bus stop for a minimal charge.

The most agreeable **campsite**, *De Kleine Rug* (☎078/616 3555; April–Oct, advance bookings essential July & Aug), is about 1km south of Baanhoekweg on a sandspit at Loswalweg 1: take bus #3 to Stadspolder, walk fifteen minutes down to the end of Loswalweg and ask the people at *Camping 't Vissertje*, Loswalweg 3 (☎078/616 2751; April–Sept) to ring across for the boat to ferry you over, or call from the bank.

The Town

The old part of Dordrecht juts out into the Maas, divided by three concentric waterways that once protected it from attack. From the train station, the second canal is the heart of the town, flowing beside the **Voorstraat**, today's main

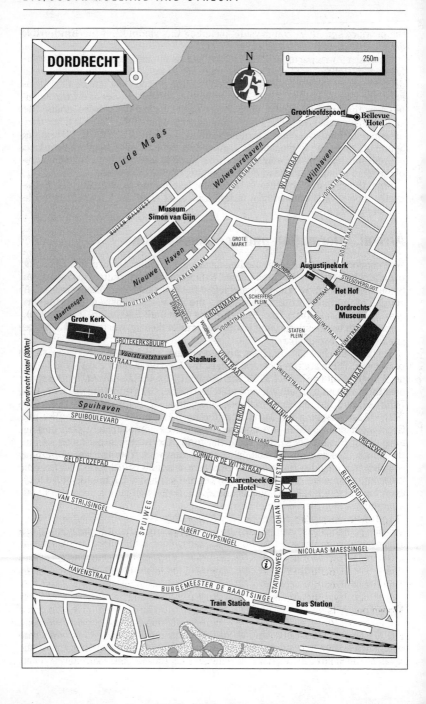

shopping street. At the junction of Voorstraat and Visstraat, the Visbrug spans the canal with a heavy-handed **monument** to the de Witt brothers, Johan and Cornelius, prominent Dutch Republicans who paid for their principles when they were torn to pieces by an Orangist mob in The Hague in 1672. To the right, Voorstraat bends its way northeast, a chaotic mixture of the old, the new and the restored, intersected by a series of tiny alleys that once served as the town's docks. Cutting off Voorstraat at Wijnbrug, the **Wijnhaven** was used by the city's merchants to control the import and export of wine when they held the state monopoly from the fourteenth to the seventeenth centuries. To the right of the Nieuwebrug, just past the Augustijnekerk, a handful of buildings around the courtyard of **Het Hof** mark the remains of the Augustine monastery founded here in 1275. Largely rebuilt after a fire in 1512, the complex houses the **Statenzaal** (Tues–Sat 1–5pm; free), where the free states held their first assembly in 1572; a little of the atmosphere of those heady times still lingers, with grand tapestries hanging on the walls and the coats of arms of the participating provinces proudly engraved on the windows.

At the end of Voorstraat, the **Groothoofdspoort** was once the main city gate and has a grand facade dating from 1618, pushed up against the *Hotel Bellevue*, with its fine views over the surrounding waterways. The town's innermost canal is just along the waterfront from here, divided into two harbours and home to the cruisers, barges and sailing boats that ply up and down the Maas. Fringed by stately buildings and criss-crossed by rickety footbridges, it's an attractive setting for the **Museum Simon van Gijn**, Nieuwe Haven 29 (Tues–Sun 11–5pm; *f*6.50, but closed for renovation till 2001), whose collection of local memorabilia and period rooms is of moderate interest, best of all the eighteenth-century Brussels tapestries and a fine Renaissance chimneypiece of 1550, transferred from the old guild house of the arquebusiers.

Near the southwest end of Nieuwe Haven, the **Grote Kerk** (April–Oct Tues–Sat 10.30am–4.30pm, Sun noon–4pm; Nov & Dec first & third Sat of the month 2–4pm; guided tour at 2.15pm; free) is visible from all over town, its fourteenth-century **tower** (April–Oct same times; Nov–March Sat 1–4pm if the weather's fine; *f*2) topped with incongruous seventeenth-century clocks. One of the largest churches in Holland, it was built to emphasize Dordrecht's wealth and importance, but it's heavy and dull, despite its attractive environs, and there's only an elaborately carved choir inside to hold your interest. Climb the tower for a great view over the town and its surrounding waters. From beside the church, Grotekerksbuurt leads to the stolid classicism of the **Stadhuis**, back on the Voorstraat.

The Dordrechts Museum

To the southeast of the town centre, the **Dordrechts Museum**, Museumstraat 40 (Tues–Sun 11am–5pm; *f*8), is a ten-minute walk from the train station: turn right off Johan de Wittstraat on the far side of the first canal as you head into town, and follow the signs. Well presented and clearly labelled (in Dutch), the museum concentrates on the work of local artists, both in its permanent and temporary displays. Highlights of the permanent collection include a couple of finely drawn portraits by Jacob Cuyp (on the wall of the staircase as you leave), and a whole room (Room 5) devoted to the work of his son, Albert. Born in Dordrecht, **Albert Cuyp** (1620–1691) was influenced by those of his contemporaries who had visited Italy, modulating his work with the soft, yellowish tones of the Mediterranean. Noted for his Italianate landscapes, seascapes and town scenes, his *Resting Riders in a Landscape* is representative of his work, in contrast to the muted tones of traditional Dutch landscape painting, as illustrated by Jan van Goyen's *View of Dordrecht*, the city's bustle restricted to the bottom section of the canvas, beneath a wide sky and flattened horizon.

A student of Rembrandt, **Nicolaes Maes** (1632–1693) first specialized in informal domestic scenes, as in *The Eavesdropper* (Room 6), turning his skills to portrait painting after his visit to Antwerp in 1670. A good example of his later work is his flattering picture of *Jacob de Witt the Elder* (Room 7). More curiously, *De Dordtse Vierling* (the Dordt quadruplets) is an odd, unattributed seventeenth-century painting of a dead child and her three swaddled siblings, a simple, moving tribute to a lost daughter; and high on the wall of the staircase nearby, the massive *Gezicht op Dordt* (View of Dordt) is a masterpiece of minutely observed naturalist detail by Adam Willaertz (1577–1644).

On the second floor, there's a selection of work by the later and lesser Ary Scheffer (1795–1858), who was born in Dordrecht, but lived in Paris from 1811. His much-reproduced *Mignon Pining for her Native Land* struck a chord in the sentimental hearts of the nineteenth century. Jozef Israels' *Midday Meal at the Inn* and G.H. Breitner's *Lauriergracht 1891* (Room 14) are among a small collection of Amsterdam and Hague School paintings, though the collage style of their Italian associate, Antonio Mancini (Room 13), is of more immediate appeal.

Eating and drinking

Voorstraat is lined with good **restaurants**. *Costa d'Oro*, near the Grote Kerk at Voorstraat 444, (☎078/613 6875), has tasty Italian dishes from ƒ18 and there is another good Italian place nearby, *Piccolo Italia*, at no. 259 (☎078/614 4950). Otherwise, *Pablos Canteena* on Huoffuin (☎078/614 2126), serves very good Mexican food and is next door to *Dappen*, a good bar that's lively at weekends. Near Visbrug, *Crimpet Salm* at Visstraat 7 (☎078/614 5557), occupies a gorgeous old building that once housed the fish merchants' guild; it still serves fine seafood in the evening. *Visser's Poffertjessalon* has very good pancakes, does a mean "meatloaf in a bun" and is a good place to mix with locals. It's next door to *Pat O'Brien's*, at Groenmarkt 1, which does pub food and has live music every Sunday afternoon. The cavernous café-restaurant *de Pontonnier* (☎078/631 6369), Grote Kerksplein 13, is another decent spot for typical Dutch food, whilst *De Stroper* (☎078/613 0094), at Wijnbrug 1, specializes in fish and vegetarian meals.

For **drinking**, *'t Avontuur*, Voorstraat 193, is about the cheapest bar in town, with a reasonable selection of beers. Other good bars include the nearby *Café de Tijd* at Voorstraat 170, the lively *Taverne in de Klandermeulen* at Statenplein 86 and the *Centre Ville* on Visbrug. There's **live music** at the *Jazzpodium*, Grotekerkplein 1, usually on Wednesday, Friday and Saturday (☎078/614 0815). For gigs, concerts and theatre, consult the VVV's listings sheet. There are a number of **smokers' coffeeshops** in town, *Ashila* on Bagijnhoffstraat (near Vest on the map) being a friendly place to start. *Groothoofd*, at the harbour, has the best terraces for summer and sometimes has live music.

Around Dordrecht: the Biesbosch and the Kinderdijk

On November 18, 1421, South Holland's sea defences gave way and the "St Elizabeth Day flood" formed what is now the Hollands Diep sea channel and the

Harbour in winter, Volendam

Centre of Edam

Kinderdijk windmill

Cheese relief, Gouda

Tulips, Keukenhof Gardens

Wooden cottage, Marken

RONALD BADKIN/TRAVEL INK

COLIN MARSHALL/TRAVEL INK

MIKE MCQUEEN/IMPACT

BARRY STACEY/TRAVEL INK

Scheveningen beach

Bulbfields, Lisse

View of Rotterdam from Willems Bridge

Fish market stall, Middelburg

Onze Lieve Vrouwe Basiliek, Maastricht

Biesbosch (reed forest) – an expanse of river, creek, marsh and reed covering around fifteen square kilometres to the south and east of Dordrecht. It was a disaster of major proportions, with seventy towns and villages destroyed, and a death toll of around 100,000. The effect on the region's economy was catastrophic too, with the fracturing of links between South Holland and Flanders accelerating the shift in commercial power to the north. Those villages that did survive took generations to recover, subjected, as they were, to raids by the wretched refugees of the flood.

Inundated twice daily by the tide, the Biesbosch produced a particular **reed culture**, its inhabitants using the plant for every item of daily life, from houses to baskets and boats, selling excess cuttings at the local markets. It was a harsh existence that lasted well into the nineteenth century, when the reeds were replaced by machine-manufactured goods. Today, the Biesbosch is a **nature reserve** whose delicate eco-system is threatened by the very scheme that aims to protect the province from further flooding. The Delta Project dams (see Chapter Six p.309–310) have controlled the rivers' flow and restricted the tides' strength, forcing the reeds to give ground to other forms of vegetation incompatible with the area's bird and plant life. Large areas of reed have disappeared, and no one seems to know how to reconcile the nature reserve's needs with those of the seaboard cities.

The park divides into two main sections, north and south of the Nieuwe Merwede channel, which marks the provincial boundary between South Holland and North Brabant. The undeveloped heart of the nature reserve is the **Brabantse Biesbosch**, the chunk of land to the south, whereas tourist facilities have been carefully confined to the north, on a strip just east of Dordrecht, along the park's perimeter. Here, the **Bezoekerscentrum De Hollandsche Biesbosch**, Baanhoekweg 53 (Tues–Sun 9am–5pm; May & June also Mon noon–5pm; free), accessible by bus #5 from Dordrecht train station, has displays on the flora and fauna of the region, a beaver observatory and an hourly audiovisual show (ƒ4). **Boat trips** for the Brabantse Biesbosch leave from the jetty beside the Bezoekerscentrum (July–Aug daily; Sept–Oct Wed & Sun). Prices vary according to the itinerary, but start at ƒ25.50 for the day ("Dagtochten") and at ƒ18 for a two-hour excursion ("Rondvaarten"); ask Dordrecht VVV for times and further details. Some of the longer excursions visit the **Biesboschmuseum**, on the southern shore of the Nieuwe Merwede at Spieringsluis 4 (Tues–Sat 10am–5pm, Sun noon–5pm; ƒ5.50), where there are further details on the ecology of the Biesbosch and the origins of its distinctive reed culture. Further details of boat trips are available at the Dordrecht VVV and direct from both visitors' centres.

The other way of visiting the nature reserve is by **bike**, for rent at standard rates from Dordrecht train station and the VVV, which also sells detailed maps of the district and brochures on suggested cycle routes. The ride from town to the Biesbosch takes about half an hour, via the shuttle passenger boat service that runs from the dock by Kop van 't Land, 5km southeast of the town centre, to a point about 1km northeast of the Biesboschmuseum.

The Kinderdijk

Some 12km north of Dordrecht, the **Kinderdijk** (child's dyke) sits at the end of a long drainage channel which feeds into the River Lek, whose turbulent waters it keeps from flooding the polders around Alblasserdam. Sixteenth-century legend suggests it takes its name from the time when a cradle, complete with cat and kicking baby, was found at the precise spot where the dyke had just held during a particularly bad storm. A mixture of symbols – rebirth, innocence and survival – the story encapsulates the determination and optimism with which the Dutch fought the floods for hundreds of years.

Today, the Kinderdijk is famous for its picturesque, quintessentially Dutch **windmills**, all eighteen lining the main channel and its tributary beside the Molenkade for some 3km. Built around 1740 to drive water from the Alblasserwaard polders, the windmills are put into operation every Saturday afternoon in July and August plus the first Saturday of the month from May to December. In addition, one of the windmills is open to visitors from April to September (Mon–Sat 9.30am–5.30pm; *f*3.50) and they all swing into action on National Windmill day, April 30. Without a car, the easiest way to explore the district from Dordrecht is by **bike**; alternatively, take bus #252 to Alblassendam, then #154 (direction Utrecht) to the mills. If you decide to **stay**, the tiny village of Kinderdijk is to the immediate west of the dyke, on the banks of the Lek. There's just one **hotel**, *Kinderdijk*, West Kinderdijk 361 (☎078/691 2425, fax 691 5071; ②). Advance booking is essential from June to August.

Utrecht

"I groaned with the idea of living all winter in so shocking a place", wrote Boswell in 1763, and **UTRECHT** still promises little as you approach: surrounded by shopping centres and industrial developments, the town only begins to reveal itself in the old area around the Domkerk, roughly enclosed by the Oude and Nieuwe Gracht – sunken canals dating from the fourteenth century. It is this area that has most appeal, partly on account of its scattering of historical sights, but also its lively atmosphere, thanks to the student population. Indeed, although Utrecht seems a tad provincial when compared to Amsterdam, just half an hour away by train, there's enough youthful spirit here to keep you overnight – though the sights themselves can easily be explored in a day.

Founded by the Romans in the first century AD, the city of Utrecht became home to a wealthy and powerful medieval bishopric, which controlled the surrounding region under the auspices of the German emperors. In 1527, the bishop sold off his secular rights and shortly afterwards the town council enthusiastically joined the revolt against Spain. Indeed, the **Union of Utrecht**, the agreement that formalized the opposition to the Habsburgs, was signed here in 1579. Some two hundred years later, the **Treaty of Utrecht** brought to an end some of Louis IV of France's grand imperial ambitions. In between, in 1636, Utrecht University was founded, making it the second oldest university in the country after Leiden.

Arrival, information and accommodation

Train and bus stations both lead into the Hoog Catharijne shopping centre, on the edge of the city centre; the main **VVV** office is at Vredenburg 90 (Mon–Fri 9am–6pm, Sat 9am–4pm; ☎0900/414 1414, 50c per min), a seven-minute walk away. They have a range of information on the city and surroundings, and provide city maps as well as the comprehensive listings magazine *Uit Lopper*. Though the city is compact enough to explore on foot, touring the canals, either by boat or by

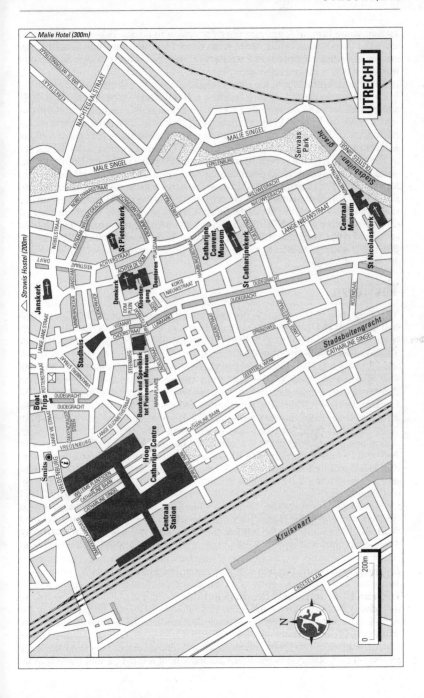

cycling along towpaths, adds another dimension to a visit. **Bikes** can be rented from the train station, while **canal trips** depart hourly from Oude Gracht at the corner of Lange Viestraat and Potterstraat near the Viebrug bridge, behind the main post office (daily 11am–5pm; *f*11).

As for **accommodation**, the most ambient place is the *Strowis*, a budget hostel housed in a seventeenth-century building at Boothstraat 8 (☎ & fax 030/238 0280, *www.strowishostel.nl*; dorm beds *f*20; ①) – a 15min walk east from the station or take bus #3, #4, #8 or #11 to the Janskerkhof stop. The hostel has pleasant rooms and dorms with (limited) access for travellers with disabilities, plus guest cooking facilities and free email. It is linked to the ACU Culture Centre around the corner at Voorstraat 71, which serves cheap, veggie meals in the evenings. Both have lots of info on what's happening, especially cultural events. The official **HI hostel** is in an old country manorhouse at Rhijnauwenselaan 14, Bunnik (☎030/656 1277, fax 657 1065; *f*25), 5km southeast of Utrecht – take bus #40 or #41 from the train station. Two good hotels are the *Hotel Smits*, a smart modern place right in the centre at Vredenburg 14 (☎030/233 1232, fax 232 8451, *www.smits.nl*; ④), and the small and attractive *Malie*, east of the centre at Maliestraat 2 (☎030/231 6424, fax 234 0661, *www.maliehotel.nl*; ③), where all the rooms are air-conditioned and recently refurbished.

The Town

The focal point of the centre is the **Domtoren**, at over 112m the highest church bell tower in the country. It's one of the most beautiful, too, its soaring, un-buttressed lines rising to a delicate, octagonal lantern, added in 1380. Hourly guided tours (April–Oct Mon–Fri 10am–5pm, Sat & Sun noon–5pm; Nov–March Sat 11am–5pm & Sun noon–5pm; last entry one hour before closing; *f*7.50) take you unnervingly near to the top, from where you can see Rotterdam and Amsterdam on a clear day. Below, only the eastern part of the great cathedral – the **Domkerk** – remains, the nave having collapsed (with what must have been an apocalyptic crash) during a storm in 1674. It's worth peering inside (May–Sept Mon–Fri 10am–5pm, Sat 10am–5pm & Sun noon–5pm; Oct–April Sat 10am–5pm & Sun noon–5pm; free) to get a sense of the hangar-like space the building once had, and to wander through the **Kloostergang**, the fourteenth-century cloisters that link the cathedral to the chapterhouse. The Kloostertuin, or cloister gardens, are reckoned to be the best place in town to listen to the carillon concerts from the Domtoren.

Heading northwest from here, the grandiose nineteenth-century **Stadhuis** overlooks a bend in the Oude Gracht, and nearby is an unusual little museum, the **Nationaal Museum van Speelklok tot Pierement**, Buurkerkhof 10 (Tues–Sat 10am–5pm, Sun 1–5pm; *f*9), a collection of burping fairground organs and inge-nious musical boxes worth an hour of anyone's time. The museum is housed in the **Buurkerk**, once the home of one sister Bertken, who was so ashamed of being the illegitimate daughter of a cathedral priest that she hid away in a small cell here for 57 years, until her death in 1514.

The city has two other good museums, though they are a little way from the centre. The national collection of ecclesiastical art, the **Catharijne Convent Museum** (Tues–Fri 10am–5pm, Sat & Sun 11am–5pm; *f*10), at Nieuwe Gracht 63, has a mass of paintings, manuscripts and church ornaments from the ninth century on, brilliantly exhibited in a complex built around the old convent. This excellent collection of paintings includes work by Geertgen tot Sint Jans, Rembrandt, Hals and, best of all, a luminously beautiful *Virgin and Child* by van Cleve (Room 15). The convent incorporates the late Gothic **St Catharijnekerk**, whose radiant white interior is enhanced by floral decoration.

Keep walking down along Nieuwe Gracht and you reach the **Centraal Museum** at Agnietenstraat 1 (Tues–Sat 11am–5pm, Sun noon–5pm; *f*10). Its claim to hold "25,000 curiosities" may be exaggerated, but it does have a good collection of paintings by Utrecht artists of the sixteenth and seventeenth centuries. **Jan van Scorel** (1495–1562) lived in Utrecht before and after he visited Rome, and he brought the influence of Italian humanism north. His paintings, like the vividly individual portraits of the *Jerusalem Brotherhood*, combine High Renaissance style with native Dutch observation. The central figure in white is van Scorel himself: he made a trip to Jerusalem around 1520, which accounts for his unusually accurate drawing of the city in *Christ's Entry into Jerusalem*. A group of painters influenced by another Italian, Caravaggio, became known as the **Utrecht School**. Such paintings as **Honthorst**'s *The Procuress* adapt his chiaroscuro technique to genre subjects, and develop an erotic content that would itself influence later genre painters like Jan Steen and Gerrit Dou. Even more skilled and realistic is **Terbrugghen**'s *The Calling of St Matthew*, a beautiful balance of gestures dramatizing the tax collector's being summoned by Christ to become one of the twelve disciples.

Gerrit Rietveld, the De Stijl designer, was most famous for his brightly coloured geometrical chairs, displayed in the applied art section. Part of the **De Stijl** philosophy (see Contexts, p.358) was that the approach could be used in any area of design, though Rietveld's angular furniture is probably better to look at than to sit on. There are more pieces of his furniture housed out of town, in the **Schröderhuis** at Prins Hendriklaan 50 (organized tours only, Wed–Sat 11am–5pm; call first on ☎030/236 2310; *f*9), accessible on bus #4 from the train station. He designed and built the house in 1924 for one Truus Schröder and her family. It's hailed as one of the most influential pieces of modern architecture in Europe, demonstrating the organic union of lines and rectangles that was the hallmark of the De Stijl movement. The ground floor is the most conventional part of the building, since its design had to meet the rigours of the building licence; however, Rietveld was able to let his imagination run riot with the top floor living space, creating an utterly flexible environment where only the outer walls are solid – indeed the entire top floor can be subdivided in any way, simply by sliding the modular walls.

Eating and drinking

There are masses of decent places to **eat** along Oude Gracht, both on the street and below, where the brick cellars, used as warehouses when Utrecht was a river port, have been converted to busy cafés, bars and restaurants. Options here include the cheap waterside pancake bakery *De Oude Muntkelder* at no. 112, the vegetarian *De Werfkring* at no. 123 (☎030/231 1752), and the pricier but popular *Tantes Bistro* at no. 61 (☎030/231 2191). Also check out *Grand Café Polman's Huis* (☎030/231 3368), on the corner of Jansdam and Keistraat, if only for its turn-of-the-century interior, and another, more fashionable and exotic vegetarian place, *Milky*, at Zakkendragersteeg 22 (☎030/231 9616). For breakfast or coffee there's the media hang-out *Café Orloff*, by the junction of Oude Gracht and Wed, just south of the Dom.

There are several good **bars** on and around Oude Gracht, including *Winkel van Sinkel*, at no. 158, a large and often crowded bar fronted by a group of caryatids and offering dance music on Fridays and Saturdays – plus a chill-out room downstairs in the vaulted cellars. There's also the *Stadkasteel Oudaen*, Oude Gracht 99, with beer brewed on the premises and reasonable Dutch food, while *De Witte Ballons* is a very friendly spot at Lijnmarkt 10–12.

Most of Utrecht's thirty or so **smokers' coffeeshops** are on the outskirts of town, but two city-centre options are *Andersom* at Vismarkt 23 and *Headshop* at Oudegracht 208.

East of Utrecht

The Utrechtse Heuvelrug (Utrecht Ridge) stretches across the eastern edge of the province of Utrecht, a wooded region that attracts many local visitors for its gentle walking and cycling. **Amersfoort**, twenty minutes from Utrecht by train, is the main town in the area – an attractive and easy-going place with a handful of decent museums, and certainly worthy of a detour if you're passing. The countryside south of here is dotted with the remains of medieval castles, most of them subsequently converted into grand chateaux. The castles at **Doorn** and **Amerongen**, in particular, warrant a brief excursion if you're heading east towards Arnhem, while the little town of **Rhenen**, prettily set beside the Rhine, pulls in tourists aplenty to view the fifteenth-century church of St Cunera.

Amersfoort

Near the border between the provinces of Utrecht and Gelderland, the town of **AMERSFOORT** was first fortified in the eleventh century and received its charter in 1259. Surprisingly, it managed to avoid the attentions of the rival armies during the Revolt of the Netherlands, and some of today's centre dates from the fifteenth century, lying at the heart of a series of twisting canals that once served to protect the town from attack. The main square, the Hof, where the market is held on Friday and Saturday, is edged by the giant hulk of the **St Joriskerk** (June–Aug daily 9.30am–6.30pm; free), an unusual, predominantly Gothic edifice finished in 1534. The nave and aisles are of equal height, and only the south porch stops the exterior from resembling an aircraft hangar. Like most churches of the period, it was an enlargement of an earlier building, but here the original Romanesque tower was left inside the later fifteenth-century construction.

A few minutes' walk northeast along Langestraat, the **Kamperbinnenpoort** is a turreted thirteenth-century gate, extensively renovated in the 1930s. From here, north and south of Langestraat, Muurhuizen follows the line of the old city moat, and is named for its **"wallhouses"**, built into the city walls. At the northern end of Muurhuizen, the **Museum Flehite**, Westsingel 50 (Tues–Fri 10am–5pm, Sat & Sun 2–5pm; ƒ7.50), is located in one of these wallhouses, a fancifully gabled building of Neo-Renaissance design. This is the town's main museum, but it's packed with a dreary assortment of items of strictly local interest. The museum also has a bizarre annexe across the road, the chapel and male ward of a medieval hospice, the **St Pieters-en-Bloklands Gasthuis** (Tues–Fri 10–5pm, Sat & Sun 2–5pm; same ticket). Close by, spanning the canal, is the ridiculously picturesque **Koppelpoort**, a fifteenth-century town gate, which defended Amersfoort's northern approach by dropping down a wooden panel and sealing off the canal.

Back on Westsingel, 500m past the museum, all that remains of Amersfoort's other main church, the **Onze Lieve Vrouwekerk** (June–Aug Tues–Fri 10am–5pm, Sat & Sun noon–5pm; free) also known as Langejan, is the fifteenth-century tower: the rest was accidentally blown up in 1797. The original building was paid for by pilgrims visiting the *Amersfoort Madonna*, a small wooden figure that had been thrown into the town canal by a young girl in 1444. Legend has it that the girl was on her way to enter one of Amersfoort's convents when she became ashamed of her simple figurine, so she decided to throw it away. In the manner of such things, a dream commanded her to retrieve the statuette, which subsequently demonstrated miraculous powers. Part morality play, part miracle, the story fulfilled all the necessary criteria to turn the figure into a revered object, and the town into a major centre of medieval pilgrimage. Otherwise, art lovers may troop into town to visit the **Mondriaanhuis**, near the tower at Kortegracht 11 (Tues–Fri 10am–5pm, Sat & Sun 1–5pm; *f* 6), birthplace of Piet Mondrian, with a small exhibition about his life and reproductions of many of his paintings, but the final port of call should be the **Brewery de Drie Ringen**, Kleine Spui 18 (Thurs–Sat noon–6pm; free), in whose adjoining bar you can sample the local brew.

Practicalities

Amersfoort **train station** is 400m from the VVV at Stationsplein 9 (Oct–April Mon–Fri 9am–5.30pm, Sat 9am–1pm; May–Sept Mon–Fri 9am–6pm, Sat 9am–2pm; ☎0900/112 2364) – turn left out of the station and follow the road. From the train station, it's a good ten minutes' walk east to the town centre. In the unlikely event you decide to stay, the VVV has a good supply of private **rooms** (①) and will call ahead to make a booking, though most of them are way out of the town centre. There are also a couple of convenient and reasonably priced **hotels**, the cheapest being *De Tabaksplant* at Conickstraat 15 (☎033/472 9797, fax 470 0756; ①) – go out of the town centre through the Kamperbinnenpoort and take the first major left turn. The slightly larger *De Witte* is just to the southwest of the Onze Lieve Vrouwekerk at Utrechtseweg 2 (☎033/461 4142, fax 463 5821; ②).

For **food**, there are a number of snack-bars along the main shopping street, Langestraat, and outdoor cafés around Hof and Groenmarkt, including *Onder de Linde* at Groenmarkt 15. Two other good spots for light meals, both on Hof, are *'t Geweten*, a Belgian bar, and *Café de Blauwe Engel*. In the evening, *De Kluif*, at Groenmarkt 3 (☎033/463 3729; closed Mon) is one of the most popular spots in town for decent Dutch food. Alternatively, there's the Mexican restaurant *Gringo*, by the old Catholic church at 't Zand 16 (☎033/472 8225), and the excellent Italian *San Giorgio*, Krommestraat 44 (☎033/461 5685).

There are some first-rate **bars** in town, among them the ever-buzzing *'t Nonnetje* on Groenmarkt 3, the ancient *In den Grooten Slock* on the corner of Hof and Langestraat at Zevenhuisen, and the atmospheric *Mariposa*, off Langestraat at Valkestraat 10. The last has the best beer selection in town and live music on Fridays. Finally, *Trenchtown* at Krommestraat 41 is a **smokers' coffeeshop** right in the centre.

Doorn

Just south of the A12 motorway between Utrecht and Arnhem, **DOORN**, reachable by bus #51 from Utrecht or #55 and #56 from Amersfoort, holds one of the more awkward skeletons in Holland's historical cupboard. The **Kasteel Huis Doorn** (mid-March to Oct Tues–Sat 10am–5pm, Sun 1–5pm, guided tours only every 20min; f7.50; last tickets sold one hour before closing), a medieval castle converted into a classical manorhouse in 1792, was home to Kaiser Wilhelm II from 1920 to 1941, following his flight from Germany at the end of World War I. At a time when the British government was mounting a "Hang the Kaiser" campaign, the Dutch, who had been neutral during the war, allowed Wilhelm to live in their country; although he was supposedly under house arrest, you won't feel much sympathy when you see the comfortable rooms and extensive grounds of the manor. The guided tour takes in the usual trappings of a stately home – elegantly decorated rooms, furnished here in the style of the 1920s – and, among Wilhelm's personal souvenirs, an extraordinary collection of snuffboxes from the era of Frederick the Great. There's a bust of the Kaiser in the gardens and House of Hohenzollern tea-cloths in the souvenir shop.

There is no real reason to hang around Doorn after visiting the castle, but the **VVV**, nearby at Dorpsstraat 4 (April–Sept Mon–Fri 9.30am–5pm, Sat 9am–2pm; Oct–March Mon–Fri 9.30am–12.30pm & 1.30–5pm; ☎0343/412015), has a small supply of **private rooms**. There's also one reasonably priced **hotel**, the *Rodestein*, at Sitiopark 10 (☎0343/412409; ②).

Amerongen and Rhenen

Eight kilometres east of Doorn, the most interesting feature of **AMERONGEN** is its thirteenth-century **castle** (April–Oct Tues–Fri 10am–5pm, Sat & Sun 1–5pm; f7), the present structure largely dating from the 1680s, when it was rebuilt by Godard Van Reede after the French wars. Like many Dutch aristocrats, the Van Reedes did well when William of Orange became king of England in 1688 – in this case one of them became Earl of Athlone after he helped defeat the Irish at the Battle of the Boyne in 1690. The Amerongen castle stayed in the family's hands until 1879, when it was inherited by the German Count van Aldenburg – first host to Kaiser Wilhelm after he left Germany in November 1918 – and is now owned by the state. It's rather a stuffy place, awash with tedious family portraiture, but redeems itself with a handful of interesting features from the seventeenth-century restoration. The splendid painted ceilings in the state room and the hall include a cheerful white elephant (Van Reede belonged to the Danish Order of the Elephant, a sort of ambassadorial post), there are some Flemish tapestries scattered throughout the house, and the giant eighteenth-century backgammon set in the master bedroom contrasts nicely with the tiny furniture of earlier, physically smaller generations. The **VVV** office (same hours as the castle plus Oct–March Tues & Thurs 1.30–4pm; ☎0343/452020) adjoins the entrance to the castle at Drostestraat 20.

Eleven kilometres further on, **RHENEN**'s strategic position on the north bank of the Rhine made it one of the first places in the area to be settled, and the **Streekmuseum** at Het Rondeelkerkstraat 1 (Tues–Fri noon–5pm, Sat 1–5pm; July & Aug also Sun 1–5pm; f2.50) has an engaging collection of historical finds, including Merovingian weapons, jewellery and pottery and a bronze burial urn, the largest found in Holland. The museum also holds a collection of gargoyles, statues of saints and other relics from **Sint Cunerakerk** (July to mid-Sept 2–3.30pm; free), a late Gothic church, with an attractive 84-metre **tower** (climbable July and Aug at 2pm & 3pm), from the top of which there are panoramic views. According to legend, St Cunera, a fifth-century English princess on a pilgrimage to Rome, was attacked by the Huns and had to be rescued by Radboud, king of Rhenen, who brought her here to his castle. Cunera became hugely popular with the locals because of her work with the poor and the sick, but was murdered by Radboud's jealous queen; thereafter, her spirit supposedly carried out dozens of miracles. The legend brought so many pilgrims to Rhenen that the town acquired the funds to build its tower, started in 1492 and completed 31 years later.

There's little reason to **stay** over in Rhenen but, if you do get stuck, the cheapest place in town is *Pension Rhenen*, Herenstraat 75 (☎0317/617214; ①). The **VVV** office is in a kiosk at Frederik van de Paltshof 46 (July–Aug Mon–Fri 9am–1pm & 1.30–5.30pm, Sat 9am–noon; Sept–June Mon–Fri 9am–5pm, Sat 10am–noon; ☎0317/612333).

travel details

Trains

Amersfoort to: Amsterdam CS (every 15min; 35min); Utrecht (every 15min; 20min); Zwolle (every 30min; 35min).

Leiden to: Amsterdam CS (every 30min; 35min); The Hague CS (every 30min; 35min).

The Hague to: Amersfoort (every 20min; 1hr); Delft (every 15min; 12min); Dordrecht (every 30min; 40min); Gouda (every 20min; 20min); Rotterdam (every 15min; 25min); Utrecht (every 20min; 40min).

Rotterdam to: Dordrecht (every 10min; 20min); Gouda (every 20min; 20min); Utrecht (every 20min; 45min).

Utrecht to: Amersfoort (every 15min; 20min); Arnhem (every 15min; 30min); Leeuwarden (hourly; 2hr); Zwolle (every 30min; 1hr).

Buses

Amersfoort to: Doorn (hourly; 30min).

Gouda to: Oudewater (hourly; 20min).

The Hague to: Katwijk (every 30min; 25min).

Leiden to: Katwijk (every 10min; 25min); Noordwijk (every 30min; 40min).

Utrecht to: Doorn (hourly; 25min).

CHAPTER FOUR

THE NORTH AND THE FRISIAN ISLANDS

U ntil the opening of the Afsluitdijk in 1932, which bridged the mouth of the Zuider Zee, the **north** of Holland was a relatively remote area, a distinct region of small provincial towns that was far from the mainstream life of the Randstad, further south. Since the completion of the dyke, the gap between north and west Holland has narrowed, and fashion and custom seem almost identical. The main exception is linguistic: Friesland has its own language, more akin to Low German than Dutch, and its citizens are keen to use it.

Three provinces make up the north of the country – **Drenthe**, **Groningen** and **Friesland** – though for a long time the Frisians occupied the entire area. Charlemagne recognized three parts of Friesland: West Frisia, equivalent to today's West Friesland, across the IJsselmeer; Central Frisia (today's Friesland); and East Frisia – now Groningen province. At that time much of the region was prey to inundation by the sea, and houses and sometimes entire settlements would be built on artificial mounds or *terpen* (known as *wierden* in Groningen), which brought them high above the water level. It was a miserable sort of existence, and not surprisingly the Frisians soon got around to building dykes to keep the water out permanently. You can still see what's left of some of the mounds in Friesland, though in large settlements they're mostly obscured.

During the Middle Ages the area that is now Friesland proper remained independent of the rest of Holland, asserting its separateness regularly until it was absorbed into the Habsburg empire by Charles V in 1523. It's still something of a maverick among Dutch provinces, although the landscape is familiar enough – dead flat and very green, dotted with black- and-white cattle and long thatched farmhouses crowned with white gable finials or *uleburden*, in the form of a double-swan motif, which were originally meant to deter evil spirits. Of the towns, **Leeuwarden**, the provincial capital of Friesland, is pleasant, if sedate, with two outstanding museums, one of which has the largest collection of tiles in the world. However, many visitors prefer the west coast of the province, where a chain of small towns prospered during the sixteenth-century trading heyday of the Zuider Zee. Each coastal town has its own distinct charm and character, from the splendid merchant houses of **Harlingen** to the painted furniture and antique neatness of **Hindeloopen** and the tile manufacturers of **Makkum**. Inland, southwest Friesland is a tangle of lake and canal that's been transformed into one of the busiest water sports areas in the country, centring on the town of **Sneek**.

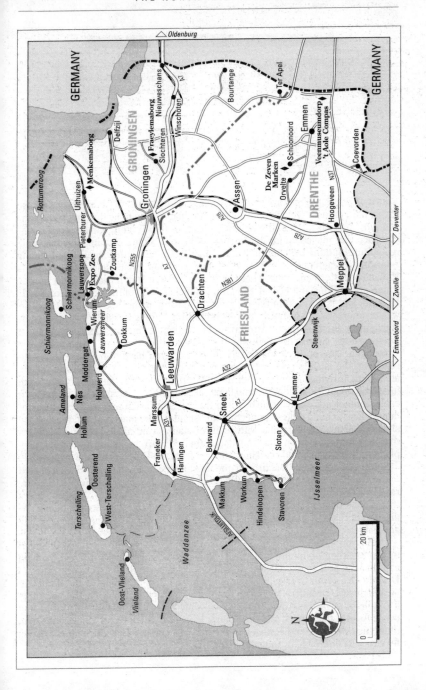

East of Friesland, the province of Groningen, equivalent to Charlemagne's East
Frisia, has comparatively few attractions. Its villages tend to be dull and suburban,
and most tourists stick to the university town of **Groningen**, a lively, cosmopolitan place that makes up for its shortage of historic sights with its busy bars and
restaurants and the best nightlife in the north. Off the north coast lie the **Frisian
Islands**, a fragmented extension of the sandbank that runs the length of
Holland's western coastline. There are five populated Dutch islands in all, four of
which are in Friesland (Texel, the fifth, is officially part of the province of North
Holland, and is covered in the chapter of the same name; see pp.165–168). The
westernmost two, **Vlieland** and **Terschelling**, are accessible by boat from
Harlingen; further east, **Ameland** is reachable by bus and ferry from
Leeuwarden, **Schiermonnikoog** by bus and boat from Leeuwarden or
Groningen. One of the few areas of the country you have to put any effort into
reaching, the islands preserve a rare peace and constitute an important nature
area, with thriving colonies of birds and a rich flora and fauna. They're also,
inevitably, popular holiday destinations, although the tourists who arrive here
each summer are easily absorbed into the miles of beach and wide expanses of
dune. Plans to build dykes connecting the islands to the mainland and reclaim the
shallows all around were met with such resistance from naturalists and islanders
that they have now been abandoned, and there's a strong feeling among the people here that they should remain as distinct from the Dutch mainland as possible.

South of Groningen, **Drenthe** is the most sparsely populated and least visited
of the Dutch provinces, and it's not hard to see why. Though the Hondsdrug, the
range of low hills that spreads northeast of Emmen towards Groningen,
bears traces of settlement dating back to around 2500 BC – the earliest sign of any civilization in Holland – for most of its history Drenthe was little more than peat bog
and barren moor, of little military or economic significance.

During the nineteenth century, the face of much of the province was changed
by the founding of innumerable peat colonies, whose labourers drained the land
and dug the peat to expose the subsoil below. As a result of their work, parts of
Drenthe are given over to prosperous farmland, with agriculture the dominant
local industry. Drenthe's two main towns are of no special interest and have only
a couple of attractions that could conceivably bring you this far off the beaten
track: **Assen**, the capital, has the Drents Museum, which has a superb collection
of prehistoric finds, and **Emmen** is the best place to see Drenthe's most original
feature – its *hunebeds*, or megalithic tombs.

Leeuwarden and around

An old market town at the heart of an agricultural district, **LEEUWARDEN** was formed from the amalgamation of three *terpen* that originally stood on an expanse of water known as the Middelzee. Later it was the residence of the powerful Frisian Stadholders, who vied with those of Holland for control of the United Provinces. These days it's the neat and distinctly cosy capital of Friesland, with an air of provincial prosperity and a smug sense of independence. It lacks the concentrated historic charm of many other Dutch towns, but it has a number of grand buildings and two outstanding museums, not to mention an appealingly compact town centre that is almost entirely surrounded and dissected by water.

Arrival, information and accommodation

Leeuwarden's **train and bus stations** virtually adjoin each other, five minutes' walk south of the town centre. The **VVV** at the train station (Mon–Fri 9am–5.30pm, Sat 10am–3pm, June–Aug Sat until 4pm; ☎0900/202 4060 at *f*1 per min) publishes a leaflet in English detailing a brick-by-brick walking tour of the centre and has a short list of private **rooms** that covers the whole of Friesland, including the town itself. There are only two reasonably priced **hotels** in town: the *De Pauw*, near the train station at Stationsweg 10 (☎058/212 3651, fax 216 0793; ②), is convenient and comfortable enough; the *Hotel 't Anker*, on the north side of the centre at Eewal 69–75 (☎058/212 5216, fax 212 8293; ②), is a good and more central alternative, though it does sometimes get full – book in advance if you can. The *Bastion* is a reliable fallback if the others are full, though it's a good walk out of town at Legedijk 6 (☎058/289 0112, fax 289 0512; ①). The plushest option is *Bilderberg Oranje*, across from the train station at Stationsweg 4 (☎058/212 6241, fax 212 1441; ④). **Camping** *Kleine Wielen* (☎0511/431 660; April–Sept) is about 6km out toward Dokkum, nicely sited by a lake; take bus #10, #13, #51 or #62 from the station.

The Town

If you've swallowed all the tourist office myths about Friesland being a land of historic beauty, rural charm and the like, Leeuwarden is initially a bit of a disappointment, with the southern part of the town centre near the station an indeterminate, rather careless mixture of the old and new. Heading north, high-rise blocks and shopping centres line Wirdumerdijk into the centre of town at **Waagplein**, a long, narrowing open space cut by a canal and flanked by cafés and large department stores. The **Waag** itself dates from 1598, but it's been converted into a restaurant and bank. Walking west, **Nieuwestad** is Leeuwarden's main shopping street, from where Kleine Kerkstraat, a turn on the right, leads to the **Oldehoofster Kerkhof** – a large square-cum-car park near the old city walls. At the end of the square stands the precariously leaning **Oldehove**. Something of a symbol for the city, this is part of a cathedral started in 1529 but never finished because of subsidence, a lugubrious mass of disproportion that defies all laws of gravity and geometry. To the right stands a statue of the Frisian politician and trade unionist P.J. Troelstra, who looks on impassively, no

doubt admonishing the city fathers for their choice of architects. Those brave enough can climb the forty-metre-high tower (May–Sept Mon–Sat 2–5pm; *f*2.50).

A little further west is the **Prinsentium**, a small park that was once the pleasure garden of the ruling Nassaus and which is still a quiet place to wander by the river and admire, on the other side, the bronze and rather thoughtful Frisian cow, donated to the city by the Frisian Cattle Syndicate.

Along Grote Kerkstraat

Grote Kerkstraat leads east from the square, following the line of the track that connected two of Leeuwarden's original *terpen*, Oldehove and Nijehove. Close by, at Grote Kerkstraat 11, is **Het Princessehof** (Mon–Sat 10am–5pm, Sun 2–5pm; *f*6.50), a house from 1650 that was once the residence of the Stadholder William Friso and also the birthplace of graphic artist M. C. Escher. It's now a ceramics museum, with the largest collection of tiles in the world, though the layout is a little confusing and there are no English-language guidebooks available. If you're really interested in ceramics you could spend days here; if not, be selective, as the sheer quantity of material is overwhelming.

Of the many displays, two are outstanding. The first, through the ornamental arch at the reception desk and up the stairs to the third floor, is the collection of **Chinese**, **Japanese** and **Vietnamese ceramics**, which outlines the rise and fall of Far Eastern "china" production. In the sixteenth century Portuguese traders first began to bring back Chinese porcelain for sale in Europe. It proved tremendously popular, and by the seventeenth century the Dutch, among others, had begun to muscle in. Ships crammed with plates and dishes shuttled back and forth to the China coast, where European merchants bargained with local warlords for trade and territorial concessions or "hongs" – hence Hong Kong. The benefits of the trade were inevitably weighted in favour of Western interests, and the Chinese could only watch with dismay as the bottom fell out of the market when European factories began to reproduce their goods. The Dutch soon modified the original, highly stylized designs to more naturalistic patterns with a lighter, plainer effect, with the result that Chinese producers were forced to make desperate attempts to change their designs to fit Western tastes.

The earliest pieces on display in this section date from the sixteenth century, notably several large blue and white plates of naive delicacy, decorated with swirling borders and surrealistic dragons. Although Chinese producers began to work to European designs in the early eighteenth century, it was many years before the general deterioration in manufacture became apparent, and some of the most exquisite examples of Chinaware date from as late as the middle of the eighteenth century – not least those from the Dutch merchantman *Geldermalsen*, which sank in the waters of the South China Sea in 1752 and was salvaged in 1983. Some 150,000 items of cargo were retrieved, and there's a small sample here, including a magnificent dish of bright-blue entwined fish bordered by a design of flowers and stems – in stark contrast to the crude, sad-looking Chinese imitations of Western landscapes and coats of arms across the room.

On the second floor, to the left of the stairs, you'll find another room devoted to the development of **Chinese porcelain** from prehistory onward, with representative examples illustrating major trends. The finest work dates from the Ming Dynasty (1368–1644), with powerful open-mouthed dragons, billowing clouds, and sharply drawn plant tendrils. This room leads to the other section you shouldn't miss, a magnificent array of **Dutch tiles**, with good examples of all the classic designs – soldiers, flowers, ships, and so forth – framed by uncomplicated borders. Well documented and clearly laid out, the earliest tiles date from the late fifteenth century, the work of Italians based in Antwerp who used a colourful and expensive tin-glazing process. By the seventeenth century, tiles were no longer exclusive to the wealthy, and the demands of a mass market transformed the industry. Popular as a wall covering – the precursor of wallpaper – thousands of identical tiles were churned out by dozens of Dutch factories (there were seven in Friesland alone). The emphasis was on very simple designs, characteristically blue-on-white, the top end of the market distinguished by extra colours or the size of the design: the more tiles it took to make the "picture", the more expensive the tile.

The collection of **European ceramics and porcelain** slots awkwardly around the other exhibits: best are the Art Deco and Art Nouveau pieces on the second floor, and the modern work in the basement. More interesting, if you're not too exhausted, is the small collection of **Middle Eastern tiles** in the basement, including thirteenth-century pieces from Persia and a few flamboyant Iznik tiles from the sixteenth century.

East of the museum along Grote Kerkstraat, the mildly diverting **Frisian Literary Museum** (Mon–Fri 9am–12.30pm & 1.30–5pm; *f*1), is housed in the building (no. 212) where Mata Hari, something of a local heroine, spent her early years. Her old home has become a repository for a whole range of Frisian documents and a handful of pamphlets in English on the Frisian language. A permanent display details P.J. Troelstra, the Frisian socialist politician and poet, who set up the Dutch Social Democratic party in 1890 and headed the Dutch labour movement until 1924.

At the far end of Grote Kerkstraat, the **Grote** or **Jacobijner Kerk** (June–Sept Tues–Fri 2–4pm), though restored in recent years, remains an unremarkable Gothic construction. Another victim of subsidence, the whole place tilts slightly toward the newer south aisle, where you can see some fragmentary remnants of sixteenth-century frescoes. In front of the church a modernistic **monument** remembers Leeuwarden's wartime Jewish community, based on the classroom registers of 1942; it's an imaginative and harsh reminder of suffering and persecution. Three minutes' walk west of the church, the **Frisian Nature Museum** at Schoenmakersperk 2 (Tues–Sat 10am–5pm & Sun 1–5pm; *f*6) has exhibitions on the flora and fauna of Friesland.

The Fries Museum and around

South of here, on Turfmarkt, the **Fries Museum** (Mon–Sat 11am–6pm, Sun 1–5pm; *f*7.50) is one of Holland's best regional museums. Founded by a society that was established in the nineteenth century to develop interest in the language and history of Friesland, the museum traces the development of Frisian culture from prehistoric times up until the present day. It also incorporates the Frisian Resistance Museum, with its story of the local resistance to Nazi occupation, and an exhibition on the infamous Mata Hari.

The museum's extensive collection of silver is concentrated on the ground floor of the main building. Silversmithing was a flourishing Frisian industry throughout the seventeenth and eighteenth centuries, most of the work commissioned by the local gentry, who were influenced by the fashions of the Frisian Stadholder and his court. The earliest piece is an elegant drinking horn of 1397, and there are some particularly fine examples of chased silver in Baroque style, where each representation is framed by a fanciful border or transition. This distinctive "Kwabornament" design flourished in Friesland long after it had declined in the rest of Holland. Some of the more curious exhibits date from the mid-seventeenth century when it was fashionable to frame exotic objects in silver: a certain Lenert Danckert turned a coconut into a cup, while Minne Sikkes fitted silver handles to a porcelain bowl to create a brandy cup. Most of the later exhibits are ornate, French-style tableware.

Upstairs, on the first floor, there's a selection of early majolica, many examples of different sorts of porcelain and a mundane collection of seventeenth-century Frisian painting. Rather more interesting are the rooms devoted to the island of Ameland and the painted furniture of Hindeloopen – rich, gaudy and intense, patterned with tendrils and flowers on a red, green or white background. Most peculiar of all are examples of the bizarre headgear of eighteenth-century Hindeloopen women – large cartwheel-shaped hats known as *Deutsche muts* and (the less specifically Frisian) *oorijzers*, gold or silver helmets that were an elaborate development of the hat clip or brooch. As well as an indication of social standing, a young girl's first *oorijzer* symbolized the transition to womanhood.

The top floor of the main building has a chronological exhibition tracing the early days of the Nazi invasion, through collaboration and resistance on to the Allied liberation. A variety of photographs, Nazi militaria, Allied propaganda and tragic personal stories illustrate the text, but the emphasis is very much on the local struggle rather than the general war effort.

Back by the ticket desk downstairs, a passage leads through to the museum's second building where you'll find the exhibition on **Mata Hari**. A native of Leeuwarden, Mata Hari's name has become synonymous with the image of the "femme fatale". A renowned dancer, she was arrested in 1917 by the French on charges of espionage and subsequently shot, though what she actually did remains a matter of some debate. In retrospect it seems likely that she acted as a double agent, gathering information for the Allies while giving snippets to the Germans. Photographs, letters and other mementoes illustrate the rather pathetic story.

Near the Fries Museum stands one of the most striking buildings in Leeuwarden – the **Kanselarij**, a superb gabled Renaissance structure of 1571, which hosts art exhibitions in the summer. The original plan placed the gable and the corresponding double stairway in the centre of the facade, but they are in fact slightly to the right because the money ran out before the work was finished. Just south of the Fries Museum, at Turfmarkt 48, the weirdly wonderful 1930s **Utrecht Building** today contains a restoration workshop. A little way north of Turfmarkt is the Catholic church of **St Boniface**, a belated apology to an English missionary killed by the pagan Frisians in 754, along with 52 other Christians, at nearby Dokkum. It's a neo-Gothic building of 1894 designed by P.J.H. Cuypers, its ornamented spire imposing itself on what is otherwise a rather flat skyline. The spire was almost totally destroyed in a storm of 1976 and many people wanted to take the opportunity to pull the place down altogether – even to replace it with a supermarket. Fortunately the steeple was replaced at great expense and with such enormous ingenuity that its future seems secure, making it one of the few Cuypers churches left in Holland.

Eating and drinking

One of the most popular places to **eat** in Leeuwarden is *Eetcafé Spinoza* at Eewal 50–52, a youthful, reasonably priced restaurant with a range of vegetarian dishes. Groente Markt nearby (and Uniabuurt which runs off it) offer a reasonable choice of restaurants including *Pizzeria Antonio* and the Dutch-French *Eetcafe De Linde*, with early evening *dagschotels* at *f*14.75, and *Eetcafe Havana*. There is Mexican food at the *Yucatan* on St Jacobsstraat or, further east, the rather smart *Café Het Leven*, at Druifstreek 57/A. If you're splashing out, the *l'Oranje Hotel*, Stationsweg 4, has two excellent restaurants; expect to pay around *f*45 for three courses at the bistro and the same for one course at the main restaurant. Next door, and much cheaper, *Onder de Luifel* has a long though not particularly thrilling menu.

For **drinking** in a quiet atmosphere, settle down in the delightful old furniture at the bar of the *Hotel De Pauw*, Stationsweg 10; boisterous types prefer the *Herberg De Stee*, next door. In the centre of town, the *Fire Palace*, at Nieuwestad N.Z. 49, overlooking the canal, is a big bar that doubles as the town's main disco at weekends. There's a series of lively bars on Doelesteeg, most with loud music, and quieter drinking spots across the bridge on Nieuwesteeg, including *de Bottelier* and *de Twee Gezusters*.

Listings

Boat tours For information on guided boat trips to the Frisian lakes contact the VVV.
Books Van der Velde, Nieuwestad 90, has a good stock of English-language titles.
Car parking Behind the train station (*f*5 per day).
Car rental Budget, Valeriusstraat 2 (☎058/213 5626).
Cinemas Nieuwestad 42 and 85.
Emergencies ☎112.
Internet Access At the Bibliotheek, Wirdumerdijk 34 (☎058/234 7777).
Left luggage Lockers (*f*4 per day) at the station (daily 6am–midnight).
Markets General market on Mon & Fri, Wilhelminaplein.
Pharmacy Details of nearest (emergency) pharmacy on ☎058/213 5295.
Police Holstmeerweg 1 (☎058/213 2423).
Post office Oldehoofster Kerkhof 4 (Mon–Fri 9am–6pm, Sat 10am–1.30pm).
Taxi Leeuwarder Taxicentrale (☎058/212 2222).

Around Leeuwarden: Popta Slot

On the western outskirts of Leeuwarden, the tiny village of **MARSSUM** incorporates **Popta Slot** (guided tours only: April–May & Sept–Oct Mon–Fri 2.30pm; June Mon–Fri 11am, 2pm & 3pm; July & Aug Mon–Sat hourly 11am–5pm; *f*6). This trim, onion-domed eighteenth-century manor house sits prettily behind its ancient moat; inside, the period rooms are furnished in the style of the local gentry. Doctor Popta was an affluent lawyer and farmer who spent some of his excess wealth on the neighbouring **Popta Gasthuis**, neat almshouses cloistered behind an elaborate portal of 1712. Buses #71 and #91 leave Leeuwarden bus station for the ten-minute trip to Marssum approximately every thirty minutes during the week, hourly on Sunday.

West of Leeuwarden: Franeker, Harlingen and the islands

Seventeen kilometres west of Leeuwarden, **FRANEKER** was the cultural hub of northern Holland until Napoleon closed the university in 1810. Nowadays it's a quiet country town with a spruce old centre of somewhat over-restored old buildings. The train station is five minutes' walk to the southeast of town – follow Stationsweg round to the left and over the bridge, first left over the second bridge onto Zuiderkade and second right along Dijkstraat. Buses from Leeuwarden drop off passengers on Kleijenburg, at the northwest corner of the old town centre.

All the town's key sights are beside or near the main street, **Voorstraat**, a continuation of Dijkstraat, which runs from east to west to end in a park, **Sternse Slotland** – the site of the medieval castle. Near the park at Voorstraat 51, the VVV is housed in the **Waag** of 1657, which also serves as the entrance to the **Museum 't Coopmanshus** (Tues–Sat 10am–5pm; May–Sept also Sun 1–5pm; *f*2.75) next door, whose ground floor has bits and pieces relating to the university and its obscure alumni. In the old senate room, there is a pile of slim boxes carved to resemble books that contain dried samples of local flora and fauna, the gift of Louis Bonaparte.

Heading east along Voorstraat, past the stolid **Martenahuis** of 1498, the Raadhuisplein branches off to the left; opposite, above the Friesland Bank, is the **Kaatsmuseum** (May–Sept Tues–Sat 1–5pm; *f*2.50), devoted to the Frisian sport of *Kaatsen* or Dutch tennis. The nearby **Stadhuis** (Mon–Fri 1.30–5pm; free), with its twin gables and octagonal tower, is rather more interesting. It's a magnificent mixture of Gothic and Renaissance styles built in 1591 and worth a peek upstairs for the leather-clad walls – all the rage until French notions of wallpaper took hold in the eighteenth century. Opposite, at Eise Eisingastraat 3, there's a curious, primitive eighteenth-century **Planetarium** (Tues–Sat 10am–5pm; mid-April to mid-Sept also Sun & Mon 1–5pm; *f*5) built by a local woolcomber, Eise Eisinga, and now the oldest working planetarium in the world. Born in 1744, Eisinga was something of a prodigy: he taught himself mathematics and astronomy, and published a weighty arithmetic book when aged only seventeen. In 1774, the unusual conjunction of Mercury, Venus, Mars and Jupiter under the sign of Aries prompted a local paper to predict the end of the world. There was panic in the countryside, and an appalled Eisinga embarked upon the construction of his planetarium, in order to dispel superstition by demystifying the workings of the cosmos. It took him seven years, almost as long as he had to enjoy it before his disdain for the autocratic Frisian Stadholder caused his imprisonment and exile. His return signalled a change of fortunes. In 1816 he was presented with the order of the Lion of the Netherlands, and, two years later, a royal visit persuaded King Willem I to buy the planetarium for the state, granting Eisinga a free tenancy and a generous annual stipend until his death in 1828.

The planetarium isn't of the familiar domed variety but was built as a false ceiling in the family's living room, a series of rotating dials and clocks indicating the movement of the planets and associated phenomena, from tides to star signs. The whole apparatus is regulated by a clock, driven by a series of weights hung in a tiny alcove beside the cupboard-bed. Above the face of the main dials, the mechanisms – hundreds of hand-made nails driven into moving slats – are open for inspection. A detailed guidebook explains every aspect and every dial and there's an explanatory video in English, shown on request.

Practicalities

Franeker's **VVV** is at Voorstraat 51 (Tues–Sat 9am–5pm; ☎0900/9222), five minutes' walk northwest of the train station. Of the town's **hotels**, your first choice should be the friendly *De Stadsherberg*, on the continuation of Stationsweg at Oude Kaatsveld 8 (☎0517/392686, fax 398095; ②), or failing that *De Bogt Fen Gune*, on the left turn at the west end of Voorstraat, Vijverstraat 1 (☎0517/392416, fax 393111; ②) or the more basic *De Bleek*, near the station at Stationsweg 1 (☎0517/392124, fax 392124; ①).

The town **campsite**, *Bloemketerp* (☎0517/395099, fax 395150, *bloemketerp @wxs.nl*; April–Sept) is ten minutes' walk north of the train station at Burg J Dijkstraweg 3 – up Stationsweg, Oud Kaatsveld and Leeuwarderweg, then left. For **food**, try *La Terraz*, Zilverstraat 7 or *De Grillerije* at Groenmarkt 14, both good for a sandwich or croissant at lunchtime. *Amicitia*, Voorstraat 9, is a reasonably priced cafe; *Grillerije*, Zilverstraat 14, is nice in the evening. The hotel *De Bogt Fen Gune* has the oldest student **bar** in the country and it's still worth dropping in for a drink.

Harlingen

Just north of the Afsluitdijk, 30km west of Leeuwarden, **HARLINGEN** is more compelling than Franeker. An ancient and historic port that serves as the ferry terminus for the islands of Terschelling and Vlieland, Harlingen is something of a centre for traditional Dutch sailing barges, a number of which are usually moored in the harbour. A naval base from the seventeenth century, the town straddles the **Vliestroom** channel, once the easiest way for shipping to pass from the North Sea through the shallows that surround the Frisian islands and on into the Zuider Zee. Before trade moved west, this was Holland's lifeline, where cereals, fish and other foodstuffs were brought in from the Baltic to feed the expanding Dutch cities.

Harlingen has two **train stations**: one on the southern edge of town for trains from Leeuwarden, the other, Harlingen Haven, right next to the docks, handling trains connecting with boats to the islands. From Harlingen Haven the old town spreads east, sandwiched between the pretty Noorderhaven and more functional Zuiderhaven canals, a mass of sixteenth- to eighteenth-century houses that reflect the prosperity and importance of earlier times. However, Harlingen is too busy to be just another cosy tourist town: there's a fishing fleet, a small container depot, a shipbuilding yard and a resurgent ceramics industry. The heart of town is the **Voorstraat**, a long, tree-lined avenue that's home to an elegant eighteenth-century **Stadhuis**, the VVV and the **Hannemahuis Museum** at no. 56 (July to mid-Sept Tues–Sat 10am–5pm & Sun 1.30–5pm; mid-Sept to Oct & April–June Mon–Fri 1.30–5pm; ƒ2.50). Sited in an eighteenth-century merchant's house, the museum concentrates on the history of the town and includes some interesting displays on shipping and some lovely, locally produced tiles – for once in manageable quantities.

REACHING THE ISLANDS

Ferries leave Harlingen for the crossings (1hr 45min) to the islands of Terschelling and Vlieland at least three times daily throughout the summer and twice daily during the winter. The return fares are currently ƒ35.45 for either island (not including tourist and port taxes), plus ƒ17.45 for bikes. The ferries dock at West Terschelling and Oost-Vlieland, the islands' main settlements. From May to the end of September there's an additional ferry service connecting Terschelling and Vlieland (ƒ8 one-way). There's also a fast **hydrofoil** service: from May to September it runs three times a day to Terschelling, twice daily to Vlieland and from September to May twice a day to Terschelling only. The hydrofoil costs an extra ƒ20 return, and saves you an hour each way in travelling time, so it's worth it if you're going for a day trip.

Visitors' cars are not allowed on Vlieland, but in any case the best way of exploring any of the Frisian islands is by **bike**. There are rental companies near the ferry terminals on both islands, charging a uniform rate of ƒ8 per day, ƒ35 per week, for a basic bike – although given the steep, stony hills, it's worth shelling out a few extra guilders for a machine with decent gears.

Harlingen was once a tile-making centre, and the industry flourished here until it was undermined by the rise of cheap wallpaper. The last of the old factories closed in 1933, but the demand for traditional crafts later led to something of a recovery, and the opening of new workshops during the 1970s. If you like the look of Dutch tiles, this is a good place to buy. The **Harlinger Aardewerk en Tegelfabriek** at Voorstraat 84 sells an outstanding range of contemporary and traditional styles, if you've got the money – Dutch handicrafts don't come cheap. Finally, the **Galerie de Vis** at Noordehaven 40 (Wed–Sat 1–5pm) has occasional displays of local art and merits a brief detour.

Practicalities

No great bargains on the **accommodation** front in Harlingen. The *Heerenlogement* is on the eastern continuation of Voorstraat at Franekereind 23 (☎0517/415846, fax 412762; ①), while the slightly more expensive *Anna Casparii* (☎0517/412065, fax 414540; ②) is more central, on the canal at Noorderhaven 6. Third choice is the *Zeezicht*, by the harbour at Zuiderhaven 1 (☎0517/412536, fax 419001; ③), which, despite its higher rates, isn't in such a nice location. If you're looking for an even better deal, the **VVV** at Voorstraat 34 (May–Aug Mon–Fri 9am–6pm, Sat 9am–12.30pm & 1.30–5pm; Sept–April Mon–Fri 9am–5pm, Sat 10am–3pm; ☎0900/919 1999 at ƒ1 per min) has a list of **rooms** and **pensions**, many of which you'll spot by walking down Noordehaven. The nearest **campsite**, *De Zeehoeve* (☎0517/413465, fax 416971; April–Sept), is a twenty-minute walk along the sea dyke to the south of town at Westerzeedijk 45 – follow the signs from Voorstraat.

As you'd expect, Harlingen's speciality is fresh **fish**, and there are fish stands, fish restaurants and snack bars dotted around the centre of town. Best is *De Tjotter* on the edge of the Noorderhaven at Rommelhaven 2, a combined snack bar and restaurant with a wide range of North Sea delicacies. Alternatives are the *de Gastronoom* next to the VVV, *de Noordepoort* at Noorderhaven 17, which has good-value daily specials, and the hotel restaurants. **Nightlife** is quiet but there are several decent **bars**, including *'t Skutsje*, on the corner of Frankereind and Heiligeweg.

Terschelling

Of all the Frisian islands, **Terschelling** is the easiest to reach – which is both an attraction and a problem. If you just want a taste of the islands without making too much effort, this is the place to head for; but, if you're looking for tranquillity, Vlieland, Ameland or Schiermonnikoog are a better bet. A major tourist resort in its own right, the town of **WEST TERSCHELLING** is a rather unappealing sprawl of chalets, bungalows and holiday complexes that spreads out from what remains of the old village – a mediocre modernity that belies West Terschelling's past importance as a port and safe anchorage on the edge of the Vliestroom channel, the main shipping lane from the Zuider Zee.

Strategically positioned, West Terschelling boomed throughout the seventeenth century, as a centre for supply and repair of ships and with its own fishing and whaling fleets – it paid the price for its prominence when the British razed the town in 1666. The islanders were renowned sailors, much sought after by ships' captains who also needed them to guide vessels through the treacherous shallows and shifting sandbanks that lay off the Vliestroom. Shipwrecks were common all along the island's northern and western shores – the VVV sells a sketch of the island marked

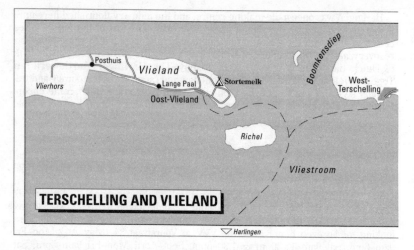

Posthuis
Vlieland
Vlierhors
Lange Paal
Stortemelk
West-
Terschelling
Oost-Vlieland
Boomkensdiep
Richel
Vliestroom
TERSCHELLING AND VLIELAND
▽ Harlingen

with all the known disasters. The most famous victim was the *Lutine*, which sank while carrying gold and silver to British troops stationed here during the Napoleonic wars. The remains are still at the bottom of the sea, and only the ship's bell was recovered – now in Lloyd's of London, it's still rung whenever a big ship goes down.

The best place to bone up on Terschelling's past is the excellent **Museum 't Behouden Huys**, near the ferry terminus at Commandeurstraat 30 (April–Oct Mon–Fri 10am–5pm, mid-June to Sept also Sat 1–5pm; *f*6). Prime exhibits here include maps of the old coastline illustrating Terschelling's crucial position, various items from the whaling fleet, lots of sepia photos of bearded islanders and a shipwreck diving room. There's also a rather desultory tribute to the local explorer Willem Barents, who hit disaster when pack ice trapped his ship in the Arctic in 1595. Undaunted, he and his crew managed to survive the whole winter on the ice and sailed back in the spring. Barents mounted other, more successful expeditions into the Arctic regions, discovering Spitzbergen and naming the Barents Sea – all in the fruitless search for the northwest passage to China. He died in the Arctic in 1597. If you're extra keen on things aquatic, there's a tiny **Fishing Museum** at the back of a shop on Raadhuisstraat (Mon–Sat 10am–12.30pm & 2–5pm; *f*1.75) and, just east of town, the **Centre for Nature and Landscape**, Burg Reedekerstraat 11 (April–Oct Mon–Fri 9am–5pm, Sat & Sun 2–5pm; Nov–March Mon–Sat 2–6pm; *f*8), which contains a decent aquarium.

Throughout the summer West Terschelling is packed with tourists sampling the restaurants and bars that line the main streets, Torenstraat in particular, while others cycle off across the island to the beach at **WEST-AAN-ZEE** where there's a café, *Zilver Meeuw*, and as much empty beach as you're prepared to look for. The more northerly of the two cycling routes passes through an odd cemetery in a wood, with a small Commonwealth forces graveyard – as ever the inscriptions make sad reading, with few of the downed bombardiers aged more than 25.

West Terschelling practicalities

Accommodation is hard to come by in July and August when all the cheaper places tend to be booked up months in advance. At other times you have a wide

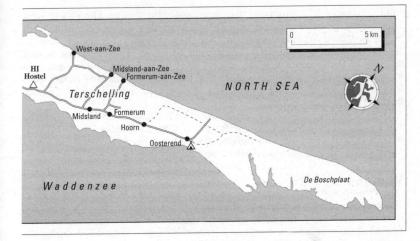

choice – try the *Hotel Buren*, Burg Mentzstraat 20 (☎0562/442226, fax 444020; ②) or the slightly cheaper *Hotel Aletha*, Trompstraat 6 (☎0562/442050; ②), both not far from the ferry terminus. There's a pleasant **HI hostel** at Burgmeester van Heusdenweg 39 (☎0562/442338, fax 443312; April–Sept; ƒ30). It's a 1.5km walk eastwards along the coast, or you can take the bus to the Dellewal stop. There are also a number of **campsites** east of town along the southern shore.

The **VVV** (Mon–Sat 9.30am–5.30pm; ☎0562/443000, *vvvter@euronet.nl*), near the ferry port, provides a full list of pensions and **rooms** and operates a booking service. They also take bookings for the rest of the island, offer a variety of **walking tours**, and can give information on seal viewing excursions and details of cycling routes. For somewhere to **eat**, try *Strandpaviljoen De Walvis* at Groene Strand on the western edge of West Terschelling, where you can buy snacks and drinks while taking in the sea view.

Around the island
From West Terschelling the other villages stretch out along the southern part of the island, sheltered from winter storms by the sand dunes and occasional patches of forest that lie to the immediate north. The island's **bus** service leaves from right next to the ferry terminus and is excellent, connecting all the villages in a matter of minutes; you could also rent a **bike**, for about ƒ8 a day from a number of shops down near the harbour and also at the ferry terminal.

Quite simply, the further east you go the more attractive the island becomes: the two final settlements, **HOORN** and **OOSTEREND**, are particularly pleasant, within easy reach of empty tracts of beach and the nature reserve **De Boschplaat**, where thousands of waterfowl congregate in the marshy shallows of the southeastern shore. To help protect the birds, De Boschplaat is closed during the breeding season (March 15–Aug 15), although the VVV runs guided tours for bird enthusiasts. Oosterend also has a **café**, *De Boschplaat*, one of the best places to eat on the island, and a handful of **campsites.**

If you want to **stay** somewhere other than West Terschelling, and are looking for a bit of peace and quiet, aim for pensions between the villages of Formerum and Oosterend – far enough east to escape most of the crowds. The VVV in West Terschelling (see above) has details. Definitely worth a visit in Formerum itself is the delightful **Wrakkenmuseum "De Broerderijk"**, Formerum Zuid 13 (April–Nov daily 10am–6pm; ƒ2). The ground floor is an atmospheric bar decked out with all things nautical, while upstairs there's a collection of items salvaged from the island's beaches and shipwrecks, including cannons and coins, relics from the British ship *HMS Lutine*, and Holland's largest collection of diving helmets.

Five kilometres before you reach Oosterend is the *Heartbreak Hotel* (follow the signs), at Strandpaviljoen Tordelenweg 2 (March–Nov daily 10am–2am; ☎0562/448634). This pleasant **pub** overlooking the beach features live Fifties bands nightly during July and August; meal prices range between ƒ20–35.

Vlieland

The complex pattern of sandbank shallows that lies to the south of **Vlieland**, just west of Terschelling, helped to make the island one of the most isolated and neglected parts of nineteenth-century Holland. Of minor importance during the great days of the Zuider Zee trade, Vlieland lost one of its two villages to the sea in the eighteenth century, and there was never enough money to have it rebuilt. Tourism has brought wealth to the thousand or so islanders, but it's all very low key: development has been restrained and the island is popular for family holidays – cycling, windsurfing, beaches and country walks. The quietest of the Frisian islands, no cars are allowed and the only settlement, **OOST-VLIELAND**, is little more than a restaurant-lined main street surrounded by second homes, chalets and bungalows. There's little to see in the village as such, although the Armenhuis in the small square is a particularly attractive seventeenth-century country dwelling. The town's museum, the **Tromps Huys** at Dorpsstraat 99 (Mon–Sat 10am–noon & 2–5pm), has a mundane collection of antiques and Vlieland bygones.

Practicalities

Accommodation is limited, and virtually impossible to find throughout the summer, although the **VVV** at Havenweg 10 (Mon 8.30am–5pm, Tues–Fri 9am–5pm, Sat 9.15–11.45am & 3.30–4.45pm, Sun 10.30–11.45am, also opens for brief periods daily to coincide with ferry arrivals; ☎0562/451111, *info@vlieland.net*) does its best with the few private **rooms**, and will help groups rent apartments and "dune houses". Cheapest of the hotels and pensions is the *Duin en Dal* on the main street at Dorpsstraat 163 (☎0562/451684; ②); you'll find more for around the same price along the road, as well as the more comfortable *Badhotel Bruin*, Dorpsstraat 88 (☎0562/451301, fax 451227, *badhotel-bruin@wxs.nl*; ③) and the smart *De Wadden*, Dorpsstraat 61 (☎0562/452626, fax 452623, *info@hoteldewadden.nl*; ③). The most convenient **campsite**, *De Stortemelk* (☎0562/451225, fax 451259), is on the sand dunes behind the beach, about half an hour's walk or a ten-minute bike ride northeast of Oost-Vlieland, at Kampweg 1.

The best way of seeing the island is by bike, though there's also a limited **bus** service that travels along the southern shore from near the ferry terminus. For **excursions**, the VVV has information on birdwatching expeditions, and private operators organize day-trips to the northern tip of Texel (ƒ25 return) by means of a tractor-like lorry, which crosses the great expanse of sand ("Vliehors") that forms Vlieland's western extremity to connect with a boat.

South of Leeuwarden: Sneek, the lakes, and the IJsselmeer ports

The Leeuwarden–Stavoren train line passes through a series of small Frisian towns with a speed that gainsays their earlier isolation. Until well into the nineteenth century, the lakes, canals and peat diggings south and east of Sneek made land communications difficult, and the only significant settlements were built close to the sea or on major waterways. Dependent on water-borne commerce, these communities declined with the collapse of the Zuider Zee trade, but, because of their insularity, some maintained particular artistic and cultural traditions – from the painted furniture and distinctive dialect of Hindeloopen to the style and design of many of Makkum's tiles. Passing through by train, the small settlements resemble what in fact they once were – islands in the shallow marshes. Nowadays, all the tiny old towns are popular holiday destinations, of which **Sneek**, the centre of a booming pleasure-boat industry, is by far the busiest.

Sneek

Twenty minutes by train from Leeuwarden, **SNEEK** (pronounced "snake") was an important shipbuilding centre as early as the fifteenth century, a prosperous maritime town protected by an extensive system of walls and moats. Clumsy postwar development has robbed the place of most of its charm – its centre has one of the most interminable shopping precincts in western Europe – but there are still some buildings of mild interest.

Sneek's **train** and **bus** stations are five minutes' walk from the old centre, directly east down Stationsstraat. This leads to the scruffy main square, **Martiniplein**, whose ponderous sixteenth-century **Martinikerk** (mid-June to Aug Mon–Sat 2.30–5pm, Tues–Fri also 7.30–9pm; free) is edged by an old wooden belfry. Around the corner at the end of Grote Kerkstraat, the **Stadhuis**, Marktstraat 15 (mid-July to mid-Aug Mon–Thur 2–4pm), is all extravagance, from the Rococo facade to the fanciful outside staircase; inside there's an indifferent display of ancient weapons in the former guardroom. Heading east along Marktstraat, veer right after the VVV and follow the signs to the nearby **Scheepvart Museum en Oudheidkamer**, Kleinzand 14 (Mon–Sat 10am–5pm, Sun noon–5pm; ƒ4), a well-displayed collection of maritime models, paintings, and related miscellany. There's also a room devoted to the Visser family, who made a fortune during the eighteenth century by transporting eels to London. A little further along, at Kleinzand 32, the **Weduwe Joustra** off-licence has an original nineteenth-century interior, worth glancing in for its old barrels and till, even if you decide not to indulge in a bottle of *Beerenburg*, a herb-flavoured gin that's a local speciality. Similarly worth a passing look is **De Tovebal**, an old sweetshop directly south of the Martiniplein at Oude Koemarkt 17. Turn right at the end of Koemarkt and you reach the grandiose **Waterpoort** – all that remains of the seventeenth-century town walls.

If you want to see more of the lakes, there are **boat trips** in July and August leaving from the Oosterkade, over the bridge by the east end of Kleinzand. Itineraries and prices vary and there's no fixed schedule of sailings: you can do anything from a quick tour of the town's canals to venturing out into the open sea. Contact the VVV or the boat owners at the dock for up-to-date details.

Practicalities

Sneek gets exceptionally busy and accommodation is impossible to find during **Sneek Week**, the annual regatta held at the beginning of August, when the flat green expanses around town are thick with the white of slowly moving sails. At other times, if you want to stay in Sneek, the **VVV**, right in the centre of town near the Stadhuis at Marktstraat 18 (Mon–Sat 9am–5pm; ☎0515/414096, *vvvs-neek@tref.nl*), will arrange private **rooms** for a small fee. The town's cheapest **hotel** is the down-at-heel *Ozinga*, immediately south of the Waterpoort at Lemmerweg 8 (☎0515/412216, fax 419212; ①). The *Douldersplaats*, by the train station at Stationsstraat 64 (☎0515/413175, fax 425455; ②), is more comfortable, while *De Wijnberg*, Marktstraat 23 (☎0515/412421, fax 413369; ②) is good value and central. The *Wigledam* **HI hostel**, (☎0515/412132, fax 412188; April–Oct; *f*30), is some 2km southeast of the town centre at Oude Oppenhuizerweg 20 – head east to the end of Kleinzand, turn right down Oppenhuizerweg, and it's the first major road on the left. If you're heavily laden, take VEONN bus #99 from the station. The nearest **campsite** is *De Domp*, Domp 4 (☎0515/412559; no buses), a couple of kilometres northeast of the centre on Sytsingawiersterleane, a right turn off the main road to Leeuwarden. *Camping De Potten*, Paviljoenweg (☎0515/415205; April–Oct), lies some 5km east of town beside the pretty **Sneekemeer**, the nearest of the Frisian lakes, and a bus runs to the campsite from the town in July and August (check at the station for details). De Potten rents a good range of watersports equipment at reasonable prices and the VVV can give you a list of other rental options.

Sneek has a large number of **restaurants**, few of which have much character: Leeuwenburg, behind the VVV, is the best place to look for reasonably priced *dagschotels* – try *Van der Wal* – while *'t Stoofje*, Oude Koemarkt 11, has a variety of tasty pancakes. *Hinderlooper Kamer*, Oosterdijk 10, is a smart, cheerful bistro with reasonably priced Dutch food; *Klein Java*, Wijde Noorderhorne 18, offers Indonesian meals. The best **bars** are on Leeuwenburg too, including *Amicitia*, with a cinema next door providing distraction from the quiet night-life.

Bolsward

Some 10km west of Sneek, **BOLSWARD** (pronounced "Bozwut" in the local dialect) is the archetypal Frisian country town, with tractors on the roads and geese in the streets. Founded in the seventh century, this was a bustling and important textile centre in the Middle Ages, though its subsequent decline has left a population of around ten thousand and only a handful of worthwhile sights. Your first stop should be the **Stadhuis**, at Jongemastraat 2 – a magnificent red-brick, stone-trimmed Renaissance edifice of 1613. The facade is topped by a lion holding a coat of arms over the head of a terrified Turk, and below a mass of twisting, curling carved stone frames a series of finely cut cameos, all balanced by an extravagant external staircase. Inside there's a small **museum** of local archeological/historical bits and pieces (April–Oct Thurs & Fri 9am–noon & 2–4pm; July

& Aug Mon–Fri 10am–5pm; f2). Ten minutes' walk away, the fifteenth-century **Martinikerk** at Groot Kerkhof (Mon–Fri 10am–noon & 2–4pm; July & Aug also Sat 2–4pm; f2.50) is Bolsward's other major sight, originally built on an earthen mound for protection from flooding. Some of the wood carving inside is quite superb: the choir with its rare misericords from 1470 and, particularly, the seventeenth-century pulpit, carved by two local men from a single oak tree. The panels depict the four seasons: the Frisian baptism dress above the young eagle symbolizes spring, while the carved ice skates (winter) on the other side are thought to be unique. The Reformation was a little less iconoclastic here than elsewhere, and the only visible damage is the odd smashed nose on some of the figures. The stone font dates from around 1000, while the stained-glass windows at the back depict occupation by the Nazis and subsequent liberation by the Canadians.

Bolsward is also home of the **Frisian Brewery**, Snekerstraat 43 (Mon, Tues, Thurs & Fri 3–6pm, guided tour at 4pm; Sat 10am–6pm, guided tour hourly; ☎0515/577449; f7.50). The smallest brewery in Holland, it produces eight different kinds of *Us Heit* beer, and you can learn all about the production process before sampling the product.

Practicalities

Buses #98 and #99 connect Sneek train station with Bolsward (Mon–Sat every 20min, Sun hourly; 15min), and, should you decide to stay, the **VVV**, Marktplein 1 (Mon 1.30–5.30pm, Tues–Fri 9am–12.30pm & 1.30–5.30pm, July & Aug also Sat 9.30am–1.30pm; ☎0515/572727), has a handful of private **rooms**. There are two convenient **hotels**, the *Stads Herberg Heeremastate*, Heeremastraat 8 (☎0515/573063, fax 573974; ②), and *De Wijnberg*, Marktplein 5 (☎0515/572220, fax 572665, *de.wijnberg@tricat.nl*; ②), and a couple of **pensions** by the Martinikerk.

Workum

Ten minutes southwest of Sneek by train, **WORKUM**, a long, straggly town with an attractive main street, has the appearance of a comfortable city suburb, protected by several kilometres of sea defences. In fact, until the early eighteenth century it was a seaport, though nowadays indications of a more adventurous past are confined to the central square, 3km from the train station, with its seventeenth-century **Waag** at Merk 4, which contains a standard nautical-historical collection (April–Oct Tues–Fri 10am–5pm, Sat–Mon 1–5pm; f3). Immediately behind, the **St Gertrudskerk** (Mon–Sat 11am–5pm; f1.50), the largest medieval church in Friesland, contains a small collection of mostly eighteenth-century odds and ends. Far more absorbing, if you're into religious art, is the **Museum Kerkelijke Kunst** in the neo-Gothic St Werenfridus Kerk at Noard 175 (June to mid-Sept Mon–Sat 1.30–5pm; f3). Just down the road at Noard 6, the likeable **Jopie Huisman Museum** (April–Oct Mon–Sat 10am–5pm & Sun 1–5pm; Nov & March daily 1–5pm; f5) is devoted to paintings by a contemporary artist, most of which have an appealingly unpretentious focus on Frisian life.

If you want to **stay over**, the **VVV** (Mon–Fri 9.30am–12.30pm & 1.30–5pm, Sat 9.30am–4pm; ☎0515/541300, *vvvijsselmeergeb@tref.nl*) across from the Merk at Noard 5, has a limited number of **private rooms**. Alternatively, head for the *Gulden Leeuw*, Merk 2 (☎0515/542341, fax 543127; ①) where facilities include a decent **restaurant**, or the *Herberg van Oom Lammert en Tante Klaasje*, next door at Merk 3 (☎ & fax 0515/541370; ②). There's a **campsite**, *Camping It Soal* (☎0515/541443, fax 543640; April–Oct) located on the IJsselmeer, 3km south of the centre.

Makkum

From Workum train station a minibus service (#102, Mon–Sat every 2–3hr; 30min) heads south to Hindeloopen (see below) or north to the agreeable town of **MAKKUM** – in fact more easily accessible from Bolsward by bus #98 (Mon–Sat hourly, Sun afternoon every 2hr; 20min; ☎0900/1961 in advance as it's only a regular service on request, and must be ordered much like a taxi). Though saved from postcard prettiness by a working harbour, Makkum's popularity as a centre of traditional Dutch ceramics manufacture means it can be overwhelmed by summer tourists. The local product rivals the more famous delftware in quality, varying from the bright and colourful to more delicate pieces. The **VVV**, Pruikmakershoek 2 (Jan–April & Nov–Dec Mon–Fri 10am–noon & 1–4pm; May–June & Sept–Oct Mon–Sat 10am–4pm & Sun 1.30–5pm; July–Aug Mon–Sat 10am–5.30pm & Sun 1.30–5pm; ☎0515/231422, *vvvijsselmeergeb@tref.nl*) is sited in the old Waag beneath the **Fries Aardewerkmuseum** (same opening times as the VVV; *f3*), which features, predictably enough, representative samples of local work. If you haven't seen enough tiles here to satisfy your curiosity, there's plenty more, notably in the Tichelaar family **workshops** at Turfmarkt 65 (Mon–Fri 9am–5.30pm, Sat 10am–5pm; *f4*), or you can visit their factory shop for free. There are no bargains, though, and most of the modern tiles have either staid traditional motifs or ooze an unappealing domestic cosiness; the vases and larger plates are more exciting but also more expensive.

If you decide to **stay**, the **VVV** has a few **private rooms**; otherwise try *Hotel de Prins* at Kerkstraat 1 (☎0515/231510; ①), or the more pleasantly located *De Waag*, two minutes around the corner at Markt 13 (☎0515/231447, fax 232737; ②). Both hotels have basic, low-priced **restaurants** while *It Posthus*, in the old post office building at Plein 15, has main courses averaging around *f34*; otherwise you could try *De Maitak* at Markt 25–27, which does a good range of sandwiches and light lunches.

Hindeloopen

Next stop down the rail line, the village of **HINDELOOPEN** juts into the IJsselmeer twenty minutes' walk west of the train station, its primness extreme even by Dutch standards. Until the seventeenth-century Hindeloopen prospered as a Zuider Zee port, concentrating on trade with the Baltic and Amsterdam. A tightly knit community, the combination of rural isolation and trade created a specific culture, with a distinctive dialect – *Hylper*, Frisian with Scandinavian influences – a sumptuous costume and, most famous of all, an elaborate style of painted furniture. Adopting materials imported into Amsterdam by the East India Company, the women of Hindeloopen dressed in a florid combination of colours where dress was a means of personal identification: caps, casques and trinkets indicated marital status and age, and the quality of the print indicated social standing. Other Dutch villages adopted similar practices, but nowhere were the details of social position so precisely drawn. The development of dress turned out to be a corollary of prosperity, for the decline of Hindeloopen quite

THE ELFSTEDENTOCHT

The **Elfstedentocht** is Friesland's biggest spectacle, a gruelling **ice-skating marathon** around Friesland that dates back to 1890, when one Pim Muller, a local sports journalist, skated his way around the eleven official towns of the province – simply to see whether it was possible. It was, and twenty years later the first official Elfstedentocht or "Eleven Towns Race" was born, contested by 22 skaters. Weather – and ice – permitting, it has taken place just fifteen times in the last 100 years, most recently in 1997, and attracts skaters from all over the world.

The race is organized by the Eleven Towns Association, of which you have to be a member to take part; the high level of interest in the race means that membership is very difficult to obtain. The route of the race, which measures about 200km in total, takes in all the main centres of Friesland, starting in Leeuwarden in the town's Friesland Hall, from where the racers sprint – skates in hand – 1500m to the point where they get onto the ice. The first stop after this is Sneek, taking in Hindeloopen and the other old Zuider Zee towns before finishing in Dokkum in the north of the province. The event is broadcast live on TV across the country, and the route lined with spectators.

Of the seventeen thousand or so who take part in the race, there are usually no more than three hundred professional skaters. Casualties are inevitably numerous, although the worst year was 1963, when ten thousand skaters took part and only seventy finished, the rest beaten by the fierce winds, extreme cold and snowdrifts along the way. Generally, however, something like three-quarters of those who start out make it to the finishing line.

simply finished it off. Similarly, the furniture was an ornate mixture of Scandinavian and Oriental styles superimposed on traditional Dutch carpentry. Each item was covered from head to toe with painted tendrils and flowers on a red, green or white background, though again the town's decline resulted in the lapsing of the craft. Tourism has revived local furniture-making, and countless shops now line the main street selling modern versions, though even the smallest items aren't cheap, and the florid style is something of an acquired taste.

Tradition apart, Hindeloopen is a delightful little village pressed against the sea in a tidy jigsaw of old streets and canals, crossed by wooden footbridges; it's popular – and very busy – in summer with yachting types who keep their boats in the huge marina, and windsurfers who benefit from the shallow, sloping beach to the south of the town. There are no particular sights, but the **church** – a seventeenth-century structure with a medieval tower – has some Royal Air Force graves of airmen who perished in the Zuider Zee, while the small **Schaats Museum**, Kleine Wiede 1 (Mon–Sat 10am–6pm & Sun 1–5pm; ƒ2.50), displays some skating mementoes relating to the great Frisian ice-skating race, "De Friese Elfstedentocht" (see above), as well as plenty of painted Hindeloopen-ware in its shop out-front. You can see original examples of this in the small village museum, the **Hidde Nijland Stichting Museum**, next door to the church (March–Nov Mon–Sat 10am–5pm, Sun 1.30–5pm; ƒ3.50), although there's a wider display at the Fries Museum in Leeuwarden.

Practicalities

Hindeloopen's popularity makes finding **accommodation** a problem during the summer, and the town's hotels – the *Skipskwartier*, Oosterstrand 22 (☎0514/524500, fax 524551, *info@skipsmaritiem.nl*; ②), and the newer *De Stadsboerderij*, Nieuwe Weide 9 (☎0514/521278, fax 523016; ③) – tend to fill up early. Book well in advance if you want to be sure of getting a room. The VVV, on the main street at no. 26 (Mon–Sat 10am–12.30pm & 1.30–5pm; ☎0514/522550) can organize the odd private **room**, and the only other alternative is the **campsite**, *Camping Hindeloopen* (☎0514/521452, fax 523221; April to mid-Oct), 1km or so to the south of town near the coast at Westerdijk 9. For **eating**, try the smart *De Gasterie*, just off the harbour at Kalverstraat 13, a lovely place to dine in the evening, or *De Brabander*, Nieuwe Wiede 7, which has main dishes on offer for under *f*20 and a wide array of excellent pancakes – good for both lunch and dinner. Failing that, the stands on the harbour serve fishy snacks during the day.

Sloten

Close to the southern coast of Friesland, the main problem with **SLOTEN** is getting there. Of the possible permutations, the easiest option is to take bus #42 (Mon–Fri every 30min, Sat & Sun hourly; 35min) from Sneek train station to the bus change-over point on the motorway at Spannenburg, where connecting service #41 continues west to Sloten, and #44 runs on to Sloten and Bolsward. Confirm your destination with the driver as there are connecting buses with the same numbers heading east.

The smallest of Friesland's eleven towns, Sloten was ruined by the demise of the Zuider Zee trade, and, robbed of its importance, it became something of a museum-piece. Little more than a main street on either side of a central canal, Heerenval, it's really not worth going out of your way for, although it *is* undeniably charming, even if there are a lot of other people sharing its cobbled alleys, windmill, old locks and decorated gables. There's a small **museum** in the town hall on Heerenval (Tues–Fri 10am–5pm; *f*3.50) but otherwise nothing at all to see. Accommodation is limited to a **campsite**, the *Lemsterpoort*, Jachthaven 3 (☎0514/531668), and the **pension** *'t Brechje* at Voorstreek 110 (☎0514/531298; ①), so call ahead to make sure of a vacancy. The VVV, at Heerenwal 57 (July–Aug Mon–Sat 9.30am–5pm; rest of year Tues, Thurs & Sat 1–5pm; ☎0514/531583), rarely has rooms to rent. A couple of **restaurants** on the canal by the bridge do good light lunches and more expensive evening meals, and have nice outdoor seating.

Stavoren

At the end of the rail line, **STAVOREN** – the oldest town in Friesland and also once a prosperous port – is now an ungainly combination of modern housing and old harbour, from where **ferries** make the crossing to Enkhuizen (see p.155) for connecting trains to Amsterdam (see North Holland chapter for rough frequencies and prices). Named after the Frisian god Stavo, Stavoren is a popular boating centre and has a large marina. The best place to **stay** is the hotel *De Vrouwe van Stavoren*, Havenweg 1 (☎0514/681202, fax 681205, *info@hotel-vrouwevanstavoren.nl*; Easter to mid-Oct; ①), attractively sited by the harbour and surprisingly good value. The VVV is on the harbour, two minutes' walk from the station (April–Oct Mon–Sat 9.30am–noon, 1–4.30pm & 5.45–6.15pm, Sun 9.45–10.15am, 1.45–2.15pm & 5.45–6.15pm; ☎0514/681616, *stavpro@hetnet.nl*) and has details of pensions and private rooms, but you'll probably want to move straight on.

North of Leeuwarden: Dokkum and the islands

Edged by the Lauwersmeer to the east and protected by interlocking sea-dykes to the north, the strip of Friesland between Leeuwarden and the Waddenzee is dotted with tiny agricultural villages that were once separated from each other by swamp and marsh. Sparsely inhabited, the area's first settlers were forced to confine themselves to whatever higher ground was available, the terpen which kept the treacherous waters at bay.

DOKKUM, the only significant settlement and one of Friesland's oldest towns, is half an hour by bus from Leeuwarden (#50 & 51; Mon–Fri 3 per hour, Sat & Sun hourly; 30–50min). The English missionary St Boniface and 52 of his companions were murdered here in 754 while trying to convert the pagan Frisians to Christianity. In part walled and moated, Dokkum has kept its shape as a fortified town, but it's best by the side of the Het Grootdiep canal, which cuts the town into two distinct sections. This was the commercial centre of the old town and is marked by a series of ancient gables, including the **Admiraliteitshuis** which serves as the town's mediocre **museum** (April–Sept Tues–Sat 10am–5pm; July & Aug also Mon 11am–5pm; Oct–April Tues–Sat 2–5pm; ƒ3.50). There's not much else: a couple of windmills, quiet walks along the old ramparts and all sorts of things named after St Boniface. If you decide to stay, the **VVV** at Op de Fetze 13 (Mon 1–5pm, Tues–Fri 9am–6pm, Fri also 7–9pm, Sat 9am–5pm; ☎0519/293800, *vvvnof@lauwersland.net*) has a supply of private rooms, while the cheapest **hotel** is the *Van der Meer*, Woudweg 1 (☎0519/292380; ①). There's not much choice as far as **eating** goes: at lunchtime *De Waegh*, at Grote Breedstraat 1, serves medieval-style food – big servings of mostly meat, bread and potatoes – and large cups of coffee; *De Broodtrommel*, a few doors further along at no. 13, offers a selection of bread, pancakes and croissants, while in the evening your best bet is *'t Raedhus* on Nauwstraat, or *Pizzeria Romana*, just off the main canal at Koornmarkt 8.

Wierum and Moddergat

Of all the tiny hamlets in north Friesland, two of the most interesting are Wierum and neighbouring Moddergat. **MODDERGAT**, the more easterly of the two, spreads out along the road behind the seawall 10km north of Dokkum, merging with the village of Paesens. At the western edge of the village, a memorial commemorates the 1893 tragedy when seventeen ships sank during a storm with the loss of 83 lives. Opposite, the **'t Fiskerhuske Museum**, Fiskerpad 4–8 (March–Nov Mon–Sat 10am–5pm; ƒ3.50) comprises three restored fishermen's cottages with displays on the history and culture of the village and details of the disaster: as such small museums go, it's pretty good. Huddled behind the sea-dyke 5km to the west, **WIERUM** has one main claim to fame, its twelfth-century church with a saddle-roof tower and (as in Moddergat) a golden ship on the weather vane. The dyke offers views across to the islands and holds a monument of twisted anchors to the fishermen who died in the 1893 storm and the dozen or so claimed in the century since. The Wadloopcentrum here organizes guided walks across the mud flats: times vary with conditions and tides; further details from Dokkum VVV.

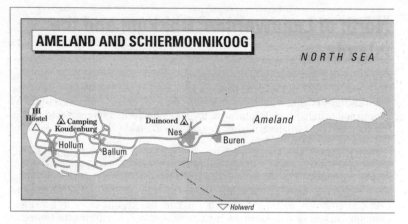

AMELAND AND SCHIERMONNIKOOG

NORTH SEA

HI Hostel
Camping Koudenburg
Hollum
Ballum
Duinoord
Nes
Buren
Ameland

Holwerd

Readily accessible from Dokkum, Moddergat and Wierum are on the same bus route (#52; Mon–Sat 7 daily, Sun 2 daily; ☎0900/1969 at least an hour in advance of the scheduled time to ensure that the bus will arrive at the stop). There are a couple of **places to stay**, the farmhouse pension *Recreatiebedrijf Meinsma*, at Meinsmaweg 5 in Moddergat (☎0519/589396; ②), or the pension *'t Sloepke*, Pastoriestraat 1 (☎0519/589727; ①) in Wierum.

Ameland

Easy to reach from the tiny port of Holwerd, a few kilometres from Wierum, the island of **Ameland** is one of the major tourist resorts of the north Dutch coast, with a population that swells from a mere three thousand to a staggering thirty-five thousand during summer weekends. Boats dock near the main village, **NES**, a tiny place that nestles among the fields behind the dyke. Once a centre of the

REACHING THE ISLANDS

It only takes 35 minutes by bus #66 to get from Leeuwarden to Holwerd, where you can catch the connecting ferry to **Ameland** (Mon–Fri 7.30am, 8.30am [July & Aug only], 9.30am, 11.30am, 1.30pm, 3.30pm [June–Aug only], 5.30pm & 7.30pm; Sat hourly 7.30am–3.30pm during the summer, otherwise 9.30am, 1.30pm, 5.30pm & 7.30pm; Sun 9.30am, 1.30pm, 4.30pm [June–Aug only], 5.30pm, 6.30pm [June–Sept only] & 7.30pm). The trip takes 45 minutes and costs *f*18.80 return. In the other direction, the boat leaves Ameland an hour earlier in each case.

For **Schiermonnikoog**, bus #51 runs from Dokkum (30min) and Leeuwarden (1hr 30min), and bus #63 from Groningen (1hr), for the port of Lauwersoog. Connecting boats take 45 minutes to make the crossing and cost *f*20.85 return (Mon–Sat 6.30am, 9.30am, 11.30am [July & Aug only], 1.30pm [not Sat Nov–Feb] & 5.30pm, Sun 9.30am, 11.30am [June–Aug only] 3.30pm [March–Dec only], 5.30pm & 7.30pm [July–Aug only]). The returning boat leaves from the island one hour later in each case. There are also combined trips direct from Groningen. Taking your bike over will cost extra. Only residents' cars are allowed on Schiermonnikoog.

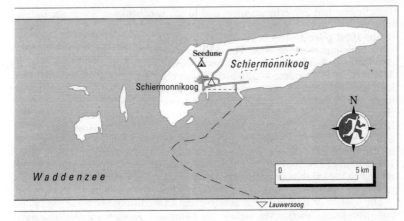

Dutch whaling industry, Nes has its share of cafés, hotels and tourist shops, though quite a bit of the old village survives. High-rise development has been forbidden, and there's a focus instead on the seventeenth- and eighteenth-century captains' houses, known as *Commandeurshuizen*, which line several of the streets. Perhaps surprisingly, the crowds rarely seem to overwhelm the village, but rather to breathe life into it, which is just as well as there's not a lot to do other than wander the streets and linger in cafés. Even if you do hit peak season at Nes, it's fairly easy to escape the crowds on all but the busiest of days, and **bikes** can be rented at a number of shops in the village. If it's raining, you might consider the **Natuurcentrum** at Strandweg 38 (Mon–Fri 10am–5pm & 7–9pm, Sat & Sun 10am–5pm; ƒ6.50), an aquarium and natural history museum with no information in English.

Nes practicalities

Nes has a wide range of **accommodation**, but prices do rise dramatically in summer, when many places are full, peaking at high-season weekends. It's advisable to call ahead if you are visiting in July or August. For a small charge, the **VVV**, Rixvan Doniaweg 2 (Mon–Fri 9am–12.30pm & 1.30–6pm, Sat & Sun 10am–5pm ☎0519/546546, *vvv@ameland.nl*) will fix you up with a pension or private room anywhere on the island. Failing that, you could try the rather basic *Domingo* at De Worteltuin 3 (☎0519/542371; ①), the central *Hotel De Jong* at Reeweg 29 (☎0519/542016; ①) or the cosier *Noordzee*, Strandweg 42 (☎0519/542228, fax 542380; ②). The best-appointed **campsite** is *Duinoord* (☎0519/542070; April–Oct), by the beach about half a mile north of Nes at Jan van Eijckweg 4.

Around the island

Ameland is just 2km wide, 25km long, and its entire northern shore is made up of a fine expanse of sand and dune laced by foot and cycle paths. The east end of the island is the most deserted, and you can cycle by the side of the marshy shallows that once made up the whole southern shore before the construction of the sea-dyke. If you're heavily laden, a summer island **bus** service runs between the principal villages from three to nine times daily, connecting with ferries. There are a variety of **boat** excursions from Nes, including trips to the islands of

Terschelling and Schiermonnikoog, and to the sandbanks to see seals. Details from the VVV or tour operators in Nes. Of the smaller villages that dot the island, the prettiest place to stay is **HOLLUM**, a sedate settlement of old houses and farm buildings west of Nes. The **VVV**, Fabrieksweg 6 (April–Oct Mon–Fri 9am–noon & 2–5.30pm, Sat 10am–noon; Nov–March Mon–Fri 10am–noon & 3–5pm & Sat 10am–noon; ☎0519/546546) can offer the same services as the Nes VVV and is generally less crowded. If you're an aquatic addict or seriously bored there are a couple of small museums here: the **Sorgdragermuseum** at Herenweg 1 (daily 10am–5pm; ƒ4), an old *commandeurshuis*, and the **Reddingsmuseum Abraham Fock**, Oranjeweg 18 (Mon–Fri 10am–5pm, Sat & Sun 1.30pm–5pm; ƒ4), devoted to the local lifeboat teams and the horses that used to drag the boats to the sea. Worthy of a visit is the **lighthouse** near Hollum (daily 10am–5pm; ƒ3.75). You can climb the 170 steps to the viewing platform and on the way catch the exhibits on each level – humorous cartoons, lifeboat service information and shipwreck maps of the Dutch and English coastlines.

The pension *de Welvaart* here, at Burenlaan 4 (☎0519/554634; ①) is good value and convenient. Alternatives include the **campsite**, *Koudenburg Oosterhiemweg* (☎0519/554367), by the heath to the north at Oosterhemweg 2; and to the west, near the lighthouse and the tip of Ameland, there's the *Waddencentrum Ameland* – a good **HI hostel** (☎0519/555353, fax 555355; April–Sept; ƒ37.50 includes compulsory sheet rental) surrounded by sand dunes and forest. You can also rent bikes here from ƒ7.50 a day. To get there take bus #130 to the last stop.

Schiermonnikoog

Until the Reformation, the island of **Schiermonnikoog** belonged to the monastery of Klaarkamp, on the mainland; its name means literally "island of the grey monks". Nothing remains of the monks, however, and these days Schiermonnikoog's only settlement is a prim and busy village bordering on long stretches of muddy beach and sand dune to the north and mud flat and farmland to the south. Schiermonnikoog is the smallest of the Frisian islands at 16km long and 4km wide, and, once you're clear of the weekend homes that fringe the village, it's a wild, uncultivated place, criss-crossed by cycle paths, and, not surprisingly, a popular spot for day-trippers.

Boats from Lauwersoog dock at the island jetty, some 3km from the village; a connecting bus drops you off outside the VVV in the centre. It's even possible to walk to the island across the mud flats from Kloosterburen, a distance of about 8km, but this is not feasible without a guide; see box on p.250 for details.

Accommodation becomes difficult to find in season, when prices rise sharply, and it's essential to ring ahead. The **VVV** (May–Sept Mon–Fri 9am–1pm & 2–6pm, Sat 9.30am–1pm & 2–4.30pm; Oct–April same hours, although closes 30min earlier Mon–Fri; ☎0519/531233) will help by booking private rooms and pensions. The cheapest **hotel** on the island is the *Zonneweelde* (☎0519/531133, fax 531199; ①), in the heart of the village at Langestreek 94; the *Strandhotel Noderstraun* (☎0519/531111, fax 531857; ②), about twenty minutes' walk from the VVV and overlooking the beach at Badweg 32, is a more luxurious alternative; the large *Van der Werff*, Reeweg 2 (☎0519/531203, fax 531748; ②) is a third possibility. Schiermonnikoog's **campsite**, *Seedune* (☎0519/531398), is to the north, in the woods just east of Badweg at Seeduneweg 1. The *Herberg Rijsbergen* – a non-affiliated **hostel,** at Knuppeldam 2 (☎0519/531257, fax 531680; April–Oct; ƒ75 for a bed in peak summer season, otherwise *f*42) is on the east side of the village, fifteen minutes' walk from the VVV. The *Strandhotel* has **windsurfing** equipment for rent; **bikes** are available from several small shops in the village, and the VVV sells good **maps**. For **food and drink** have a wander along Langestreek and Badweg to the north of the VVV.

Groningen and around

Nominally a fiefdom of the bishops of Utrecht from 1040 until 1536, the city of **GRONINGEN** was once an important centre of trade, in reality an autonomous merchant state ruled by a tightly defined oligarchy, whose power was exercised through the city council or *Raad*. In 1536 Charles V forced the town to submit to his authority, but Groningen was nevertheless still hesitant in its support of the Dutch rebellion against his successors. The dilemma for the city fathers was that, although they stood to gain economically from independence, the majority of the town's citizens were Catholic, deeply suspicious of their Protestant neighbours. In the end, the economic argument won the day, and the town became the capital of the Dutch province of Groningen in 1594.

Virtually destroyed during the Allied liberation in 1945, the city is not immediately attractive, with few obvious sights and an eclectic jumble of architectures. However, it does benefit from the presence of its large and prestigious university – one in six of the town's population are students – which gives the place a cosmopolitan and vigorous feel quite unexpected in this part of the country, and keeps prices in its restaurants and bars surprisingly low. This, combined with a superb and innovative museum, a number of good budget places to stay, and a wide range of contemporary arts performances and exhibitions, especially during the academic year, makes Groningen the best urban target in the north Netherlands.

Arrival, information and accommodation

Groningen's **bus** and **train** stations are side by side on the south side of town. The **VVV** is fifteen minutes' walk away at Ged Kattendiep 6 (Mon–Fri 9am–5.30pm, Sat 10am–5pm; ☎0900/202 3050 at *f*1 per min, *info@vvvgroningen .nl*). It offers a range of services, from tourist information (much of it in English) on the town and province to tickets for visiting bands, theatre groups and orchestras. They also have a short list of **private rooms** in both Groningen and the surrounding area, though hardly any are near the city centre.

Groningen has plenty of good, reasonably priced **accommodation**, though it's always wise to call ahead to reserve a room. Straight across the museum bridge from the train station, the third road on the right, Gemempte Zuiderdiep, is a good street to start looking, with the likeable old *Weeva* at no. 8 (☎050/312 9919, fax 312 7904; ②). Two blocks north, the *Garni Friesland*, Kleine Pelsterstraat 4 (☎ & fax 050/312 1307; ①) is another simple choice, while ten minutes' walk east of Gedempte Zuiderdiep, at Damsterdiep 94, the *Garni Groningen* (☎050/313 5435; ①) is friendly if a little spartan, and a good alternative if the more central hotels are full. Two more expensive options are the *Auberge Corps de Garde*, Oude Boteringestraat 72/74 (☎050/314 5437, fax 313 6320, *info@corpsdegarde.nl*; ③) and the *City Hotel Groningen*, Gedempte

---

PEDAL POWER IN GRONINGEN

One of the best things about Groningen is the lack of motor traffic: almost all the centre is **car free**, the result of municipal decisions dating back to the mid-Seventies, when the city suffered some of the worst road congestion in Europe. In typically bold but sensible Dutch fashion, local authorities dismantled a huge motorway intersection in the city centre, closed most of its roads to cars and invested heavily in a network of cycle paths and bus lanes. Today 57 percent of residents travel regularly by **bike**, the highest percentage in the country, and for every car kept out of the city centre, it's reckoned that almost £200 a year is saved in costs to the environment. Groningen is now one of the most popular and appealing cities in the Netherlands, and there are demands for even more restrictions on cars.

Kattendiep 25 (☎050/588 6565, fax 311 5100, *cityhotel@euronet.nl*; ③). If money's tight, head for the *Simplon Jongerenhotel*, Boterdiep 73 (☎050/313 5221, fax 313 3027; *f*50), which boasts clean and well-kept dorms; from the Grote Markt follow Oude Ebbingestraat north over the canal, turn first right and then first left. If you're **camping**, catch bus #2 via Piezerweg from the main square for the ten-minute journey to *Stadspark*, Campinglaan 6 (☎050/525 1624; mid-March to mid-Oct).

The Town

Groningen's effective centre is **Grote Markt**, a wide open space that was badly damaged by wartime bombing and has been reconstructed with little imagination. At its northeast corner is the tiered tower of the **Martinikerk** (June–Aug Tues–Sat noon–5pm; *f*1), a beacon of architectural sanity in the surrounding shambles. Though the oldest parts of the church go back to 1180, most of it dates from the mid-fifteenth century, the nave being a Gothicized rebuilding undertaken to match the added choir. The vault paintings in the nave are beautifully restored, and in the old choir there are two series of frescoes on the walled-up niches of the clerestory. On the right, a series of eight depicts the story of Christmas, beginning with an *Annunciation* and ending with a portrayal of the young Christ in the temple. On the left, six frescoes complete the cycle with the story of Easter. Also in the choir is a maquette of the city centre as it looked before wartime destruction: fifteen years in the making, it's painstakingly accurate. Adjoining the church is the essentially seventeenth-century **Martinitoren** (April–June daily noon–4.30pm; July–Sept daily 11am–4.30pm; Oct–March Sat & Sun noon–4.30pm; *f*3). If you've got the energy, it offers a view that is breathtaking in every sense of the word – fainthearts be warned. Behind the church is the lawn of the **Kerkhof**, an ancient piece of common land that's partly enclosed by the **Provinciehuis**, a rather grand neo-Renaissance building of 1915, seat of the provincial government.

On the opposite side of the Grote Markt, the classical **Stadhuis** dates from 1810, tucked in front of the mid-seventeenth-century **Goudkantoor** (Gold Office); look out for the shell motif above the windows, a characteristic Groningen decoration. From the southwest corner of the Grote Markt, the far side of Vismarkt is framed by the **Korenbeurs** (Corn Exchange) of 1865. The statues on the facade represent, from left to right, Neptune, Mercurius (god of

commerce) and Ceres (goddess of agriculture). Just behind, the **A-kerk** is a fifteenth-century church with a Baroque steeple, attractively restored in tones of
yellow, orange and red. The church's full name is the *Onze Lieve Vrouwekerk
der A*, the A being a small river which forms the moat encircling the town centre. Immediately to the west along A-Kerkhof N.Z., the **Noordelijk
Scheepvaart Museum**, Brugstraat 24 (Tues–Sat 10am–5pm, Sun 1–5pm; *f*6),
is one of the best-equipped and most comprehensive maritime museums in the
country, tracing the history of north Holland shipping from the sixth to the
twentieth centuries. Housed in a warren of steep stairs and timber-beamed
rooms, each of the museum's twenty displays deals with a different aspect of
shipping, including trade with the Indies, the development of peat canals and a
series of reconstructed nautical workshops. The museum's particular appeal is
its imaginative combination of models and original artefacts, which are themselves a mixture of the personal (seamen's chests; quadrants) and the public
(ship figureheads; tile designs of ships). In the same building, the much smaller **Niemeyer Tabaksmuseum** (same times) is devoted to tobacco smoking
from 1600 to the present day. Exhibits include a multitude of pipes and an out-

standing collection of snuff paraphernalia in all sorts of materials, from crystal and ivory to porcelain and silver. The Niemeyer family built their fortune on the tobacco trade, and here you can see the origins of those familiar blue tobacco packets.

To the northwest of here, down a passage off Zwanestraat, the **Groningen University Museum** (Tues–Fri noon–4pm, Sat & Sun 1–4pm; ƒ2.50) gives a taste of the university's history, with exhibits ranging from scientific equipment to photos of derby-hatted students clowning around at the turn of last century. Further north still, up Nieuwe Kijk in 't Jatstraat 104, the **Geraldus van de Leeuw ethnological museum** (Tues–Fri 10am–4pm, Sat & Sun 1–5pm) has collections from Asia, Africa, the Pacific and South America. Alternatively, just south of the Scheepvaart Museum, the **Natuurmuseum** (Tues–Fri 10am–5pm, Sat & Sun 1–5pm; ƒ5), at Praediniussingel 59, has a permanent exhibition (in Dutch) on the ice age, complete with woolly mammoths, and the usual exhibitions on wildlife, geology and land reclamation in the local area.

The town's main draw, though, is the excellent **Groningen Museum** (Tues–Sun 10am–5pm; ƒ12), housed in Alessandro Mendini's spectacular pavilions directly across from the train station. The museum's four main sections take you through a melange of revolving exhibitions on archeology, arts and applied arts, but it is the design of the place almost as much as the contents that impresses. Enter beneath the yellow-gold tower; one floor down via the mosaic-clad staircase, the lower western pavilion holds "The Story of Groningen" – a chronological and well-labelled display on the **archeology and history** of Groningen province, from early terp culture to the local impact of World War II and beyond. Upstairs, and probably the museum's highlight, the **decorative arts** section is beautifully displayed in a circular glass case, with an extensive collection of local silver and Far Eastern ceramics, notably a two hundred-piece sample of porcelain rescued from the *Geldermalsen*, which sank in the South China Sea in 1572. Of the

---

WADLOPEN

Wadlopen, or **mud-flat walking**, is a popular and strenuous Dutch pastime, and the stretch of coast on the northern edge of the provinces of Friesland and Groningen is one of the best places to do it: twice daily, the receding tide uncovers vast expanses of mud flat beneath the Waddenzee. It is, however, a sport to be taken seriously, and far too dangerous to do without an experienced guide – the depth of the mud is variable and the tides inconsistent. In any case, channels of deep water are left even when the tide has receded, and the currents can be perilous. The timing of treks depends on weather and tidal conditions, but most start between 6am and 10am. It's important to be properly equipped; recommended gear includes shorts or a bathing suit, a sweater, wind jacket, knee-high socks, high-top trainers and a complete change of clothes stashed in a watertight pack. In recent years *wadlopen* has become extremely popular, so it's advisable to book at least a month in advance between May and August.

Prices of **organized excursions** are in the region of ƒ30 a head, and include the cost of a return ferry crossing; the VVVs in Dokkum, Leeuwarden and Groningen can provide details, or you could contact one of the *wadlopen* organizations direct: Dijkstras Wadlopencentrum, Hoofdstraat 118, Pieterburen (☎0595/528345), has the most multilingual guides; there's also Stichting Wadlopcentrum Pieterburen, Hoofdstraat 68, Pieterburen (☎0595/528300).

examples on display, several have been "re-sunk" in an aquarium on the museum's floor, still encrusted with accumulated detritus, but others have been cleaned and polished to reveal designs of delicate precision – fine drawings of flowers and stems, and bamboo huts where every stick is distinct.

On the other side of the complex, a series of rooms in the lower east pavilion holds the museum's temporary exhibitions and a fast-revolving selection of contemporary art spreading upstairs to the **visual arts** pavilion, whose deconstructivist design has rendered it the most controversial part of the museum. The collection here includes Rubens' energetic *Adoration of the Magi* among a small selection of seventeenth-century works, Isaac Israels' inviting *Hoedenwinkel* from a modest sample of Hague School paintings, and a number of later works by the Expressionists of the Groningen *De Ploeg* association, principally Jan Wiegers, whose *Portrait of Ludwig Kirchner* is typically earnest. An adventurous acquisition policy has also led the museum to dabble in some of the more unusual trends in modern art, like Carel Visser's 1983 collage *Voor Dali* and the bizarre *Can the Bumpsteers while I Park the Chariot* by Henk Tas. The paintings are regularly revolved, so don't pin your hopes on catching any particular item.

Contemporary art is also displayed at the **Visual Arts Centre** in the Osterpoort, Trompsingel 27 (Tues–Fri 10am–5pm, Sat & Sun 1–5pm) and there are two more specialist museums you might want to see. The **Printing Museum** at Rabenhauptstraat 65 southeast of the train station (Tues–Sun 1–5pm; *f*4), outlines the history of printing with everything from a nineteenth-century steam-driven printing press to word-processors; and lastly, certainly most weirdly, the **Museum of Anatomy and Embryology**, east of the centre at Oostersingel 69 (Mon–Fri 10am–5pm; free), is even nastier than you might imagine.

Groningen's final sight is its **train station**: built in 1896 at enormous cost, it was one of the grandest of its day, decorated with the strong colours and symbolic designs of Art Nouveau tiles from the Rozenburg factory in The Hague. The grandeur of much of the building has disappeared under a welter of concrete, glass and plastic suspended ceilings, but the old first- and second-class waiting rooms have survived pretty much intact, and have been refurbished as restaurants. The epitome of high Gothic style, the oak-panelled walls are edged by extravagantly tiled chimney pieces, while a central pillar in each room supports a papier-mâché fluted ceiling. The third-class waiting room is now a travel agency, but a yellow, blue and white tiled diagram of the Dutch rail system still covers one wall.

Eating, drinking and nightlife

Groningen's nicest places to **eat and drink** are concentrated in three loose areas, each only a couple of minutes' walk from the next. Best of the three is centred on Poelestraat, where an array of open-air cafés pulls in mainly young punters. *Café d'Opera* at no. 17 has good Dutch food and *dagschotels* from *f*12.50; around the corner on Peperstraat, *Het Pakhuis*, down a small alley at no. 8 offers cheapish meals and a lively bar in an atmospheric building; *Andy Warhol*, roughly opposite *Het Pakhuis*, is a cool night café. South of Poelstraat the elegant *Schimmelpennink Huys*, Oosterstraat 53, has excellent and reasonably priced daily specials; there is the Mexican-American *Four Roses* at the junction of Oosterstraat and Gedempte Zuiderdiep; and Dutch food at *Gulzige Kater*, Gedempte Zuiderdiep 33. Across the canal from Poelestraat, the tiny boisterous *Café Kachel* at Schuittendiep 62 is the best of the town's traditional Dutch **bars**, and there are several other decent places to drink nearby.

On the south side of the Grote Markt, the best of a flank of outdoor cafés are the cosy *De Witz* at no. 47, the civilized *De Drie Gezusters* at no. 39, with a great old interior, and the *Café Hooghoudt* in the old Lloyds Insurance building at no. 42; this last also contains a night café serving food until 4am at weekends. Northwest of the Grote Markt, around Zwanestraat, the *Ugly Duck* at no. 28 has fish and Dutch food, including a good-value tourist menu; just to the west, *Soestdijk*, at Grote Kromme Elleboog 6, is pricier and posher; while *Brussels Lof* at A-Kerkstraat 24, is a vegetarian restaurant with good fondues.

For **live music** try *De Vestibule*, Oosterstraat 24; *Vera*, at Oosterstraat 44; or *Troubadour*, Peperstraat 19. The jazz café *De Spieghel* at Peperstraat 11 has live performances (including some reasonably big names) most nights, and there is occasional jazz at *Café de Nimf*, Poelestraat 5, as well as a nightly piano bar, *Café Koster*, at Hoogstraat 7. Most of the more important visiting bands play in the municipal concert hall, the Stadsschouwburg, Turfsingel 86 (☎050/312 5645), and in the De Oosterpoort, Trompsingel 27 (☎050/313 1044), just east of the train station. A good **disco** can be found at the *Palace*, Gelkingestraat 1, which occasionally hosts live bands. The **cinema** with the most varied programme is the Filmcentrum, Poelestraat 30, though the Simplon at Boterdiep 71 shows some good alternative movies and also has live music. **Listings** of all events are contained in *Uitgaanskrant*, available free from the VVV.

Listings

Boat trips Trips along the old town moat around the town centre, *f*7.50 for 75min. Times of sailings and bookings at the VVV.

Books A good range of English-language titles is at *Scholtens-Wristers* on Guldenstraat.

Car rental Budget, Hereweg 36 (☎050/527 2877).

Cinema Filmcentrum Poelestraat, Poelestraat 30 (☎050/312 0433). Simplon Filmhuis (Youth Centre), Boterdiep 71 (☎050/318 4150).

Emergencies ☎112.

Internet Access At the Bibliotheek, Oude Boteringestraat 14 (☎050/368 3683).

Laundry Self or service wash at Handy Wash, Schuitendiep 56 (☎050/318 7587).

Left luggage At the train station (daily 8am–noon & 1–5.30pm); also coin-operated lockers in the ticket hall.

Markets General market, including fruit and vegetables, on the Grote Markt (Tues–Sat from 8am), with curios and miscellaneous antiques on Tues, Fri, and Sat.

Police Herebinnsingel 2 (☎050/513 1313).

Post office On Munnekeholm by the A-kerk (Mon–Fri 8.30am–6.30pm, Sat 10am–1pm) or at Stationsweg 10 (Mon–Fri 9am–5pm, Sat 9am–noon).

Taxi A-Tax, Meerpaal 9 (☎050/542 3040).

Around Groningen

A patchwork of industrial complexes and nondescript villages, the **province of Groningen** has few major attractions; unless you fancy a night in the country near the old monastery at Ter Apel, there's nowhere that really warrants a stay. The easiest trip is to the **botanical gardens** at **HAREN** (April–Oct daily

9am–6pm, Nov–March 9am–5pm; ƒ17.50) a few kilometres to the south via train or bus #51 or #54. From the train station it's a 25min walk – follow the signs. There's a small Chinese garden, English garden and some extensive rose-gardens, although the real highlight is the tropical greenhouse complex, with a vast range of cacti and some wonderful old cycads, as well as the more familiar palms, bananas and ferns. For day-tripping from Groningen city, the most agreeable journey is to the village of **UITHUIZEN**, 25km to the north (hourly trains; 35min), where the moated manor house of **Menkemaborg** (April–Sept daily 10am–noon & 1–5pm; Oct–March Tues–Sun 10am–noon & 1–4pm; closed Mon & Jan; ƒ8) is a marked ten-minute walk from the station. Dating from the fifteenth century and surrounded by formal gardens in the English style, the house has a sturdy compact elegance and is one of the very few mansions, or *borgs*, of the old landowning families to have survived. The interior consists of a sequence of period rooms furnished in the style of the seventeenth century. Something of a specialist interest, the **Museum 1939–1945**, Dingeweg 1 (April–Oct daily 9am–6pm; ƒ10) has an excellent collection of World War II military artefacts – uniforms, weapons and secret radios, etc.

The trip to Uithuizen can be combined with a guided walk across the coastal **mud flats** (*wadlopen* – see box on p.250) to the uninhabited sand-spit island of **Rottumeroog**. Excursions leave from outside Menkemaborg by bus to the coast, between three and four times monthly from June to September. It costs from ƒ25 per person and booking is essential; contact Groningen VVV for details. Without a guide, it's too dangerous to go on the mud flats, but it is easy enough to walk along the enclosing dyke that runs behind the shoreline for the whole length of the province. There's precious little to see as such, but when the weather's clear, the browns, blues and greens of the surrounding land and sea are unusually beautiful. From Uithuizen, it's a good hour's stroll north to the nearest point on the dyke, and you'll need a large-scale map for directions – available from Groningen VVV.

The Lauwersmeer

Some 35km northwest of Groningen, the **Lauwersmeer** is a broken and irregular lake that spreads across the provincial boundary into neighbouring Friesland. Once an arm of the sea, it was turned into a freshwater lake by the construction of the Lauwersoog dam, a controversial Sixties project that was vigorously opposed by local fishermen, who ended up having to move all their tackle to ports on the coast. Spared intensive industrial and agricultural development because of the efforts of conservationists, it's a quiet and peaceful region with a wonderful variety of sea-birds, and increasingly popular with anglers, windsurfers, sailors and cyclists.

The local villages are uniformly dull, however; the most convenient base is **ZOUTKAMP**, near the southeast corner of the lake on the River Reitdiep, accessible by bus from Groningen (#65; hourly; 1hr). The **VVV**, Dorpsplein 1 (April–Sept Mon–Fri 9am–5pm, Sat 10am–noon & 1–4pm, Sun 1–4pm; Oct–March Mon–Fri 9am–noon & 1–4.30pm; ☎0595/401957) has a limited supply of private **rooms**. These can also be reserved at Groningen VVV.

At the mouth of the lake, some 10km north of Zoutkamp, the desultory port of **LAUWERSOOG** is where **ferries** leave for the fifty-minute trip to the island of Schiermonnikoog (see p.246). It's also the home of **Expo Zee** (April–Oct Tues–Sun 11am–5pm; ƒ7.50), 500m south of the harbour, which gives background information on the Lauwersmeer, the Waddenzee and Dutch land reclamation in general. Bus #63 (5 daily; 1hr) connects Groningen with Lauwersoog and the ferries.

Fraeylemaborg and Bourtange

Some 20km east of Groningen on the northern edge of the small town of Slochteren, accessible by bus #78 from the town centre, the typically northern **Fraeylemaborg** (March–Dec Tues–Fri 10am–5pm, Sat & Sun 1–5pm; *f*6) is a well-preserved, seventeenth-century moated mansion, set within extensive parkland. More interesting, some 60km southeast of Groningen, **BOURTANGE** is a superbly restored fortified village which lies close to the German frontier. Founded by William of Orange in 1580 to help protect the eastern approaches to Groningen, Bourtange fell into disrepair during the nineteenth century, only to be entirely refurbished as a tourist attraction in 1964. The design of the village is similar to that of Naarden, outside Amsterdam, and is best appreciated as you walk round the old bastions of the star-shaped fortress. Bus #71 runs from Groningen (Mon–Fri, hourly; 1hr) and drops you by the car-park, from where you enter the village through the **VVV** building and information centre (April–Oct Mon–Fri 9am–5.30pm, Sat & Sun 10.30am–5.30pm; Nov–March Mon–Fri 9am–noon; ☎0599/354600). Entry to the village is free, but there is a charge of *f*8 if you want to see the slide-show which gives a history of Bourtange and to visit the various exhibitions depicting traditional life in the village. There's a **campsite**, *'t Plathuis* (☎0599/354383; mid-March to Oct) at Vlagtwedderstraat 88, and one **hotel**, *De Staakenborgh*, up the road at no. 33 (☎ & fax 0599/354216; ①).

Ter Apel

South from Bourtange, the **Museum Klooster** (Mon–Sat 10am–5pm, Sun 1–5pm, Nov–April closed Mon; *f*5.50), in the small town of **TER APEL** near the German border, is the definite highlight in this part of the country. It's a little difficult to reach without a car, although there's now an hourly bus (#270; 30min) between Bourtange and Ter Apel. This was the monastery of the Crutched Friars, built in 1465, and probably unique among rural monasteries in surviving the Reformation intact, after the enlightened local authorities allowed the monks to remain here during their lifetimes. The chapel, superbly restored, preserves a number of unusual features, including the tripartite sedilia, where the priest and his assistants sat during mass, and a splendid rood-screen that divides the chancel from the nave. Elsewhere, the east wing is a curious hybrid of Gothic and Rococo styles, the cloister has a small herb garden and the other rooms are normally given over to temporary exhibitions of religious art. The monastery is surrounded by extensive beech woods and magnificent old horse-chestnut trees; follow one of the marked walks or simply ramble at your leisure. Opposite, the *Hotel-Restaurant Boschhuis* (☎0599/581208, fax 581906; ①) is ideal for lunch or dinner or for spending a quiet night in the country.

Drenthe

Until the early nineteenth century, the sparsely populated province of **Drenthe** was little more than a flat expanse of empty peat bog, marsh and moor. Today its only conspicuous geographical feature is a ridge of low hills that runs northeast for some 50km from Emmen toward Groningen. This ridge, the **Hondsrug**, was high enough to attract prehistoric settlers whose **hunebeds** (megalithic tombs) have become Drenthe's main tourist attraction. There are few others. **Assen**, the provincial capital, is a dull place with a good museum, and **Emmen**, the other major town, can only be recommended as a convenient base for visiting some of the *hunebeds* and three neighbouring open-air folk culture museums.

Governed by the bishops of Utrecht from the eleventh century, Drenthe was incorporated into the Habsburg empire in 1538. The region sided with the Protestants in the rebellion against Spain, but it had little economic or military muscle and its claim to provincial status was ignored until the days of the Batavian Republic. In the nineteenth century, work began in earnest to convert the province's peat bogs and moors into farmland. *Veenkulunies* (peat colonies) were established over much of the south and east of Drenthe, where the initial purpose of the labourers was to dig drainage canals (*wiels*) and cut the peat for sale as fuel to the cities. Once cleared of the peat, the land could be used to grow crops, and today the region's farms are some of the most profitable in the country.

Assen and around

Some 16km south of Groningen, **ASSEN** is a possible first stop, though not at all a place that you'd wish to get stuck in. Its train and bus station are about five minutes' walk from the centre of town, moving straight ahead across the main road down Stationsstraat. On the eastern side of the central square, Brink is home to both parts of the **Drents Museum** (Tues–Sun 11am–5pm; July & Aug also Mon; *f*10), which, spread over a pleasant group of old houses, is the only thing that makes a stop in town worthwhile. Of the buildings, the *Ontvangershuis*, Brink 1, holds no more than a predictable plod of period rooms, but on the second floor of Brink 5 there's an extraordinary assortment of prehistoric bodies, clothes and other artefacts that have been preserved for thousands of years in the surrounding peat bogs. The bodies are the material remains of those early settlers who built the *hunebeds*, and the museum has a modest display covering their customs and culture. There's also the much vaunted *Pesse Canoe*, the oldest water vessel ever found, dating from about 6800 BC and looking its age. Five kilometres west of the centre of Assen, straight down Torenlaan, the **Automuseum**, Rode Heklaan 3 (April–Oct daily except Sat 9am–6pm; *f*12), has a wide selection of antique and vintage cars. To get there take a bus marked *Verkeerspark* from the train station.

Practicalities

Assen's **VVV** is in the town centre at Brink 42 (Tues–Thurs 9am–6pm, Fri 9am–9pm, Sat 9am–5pm, July & Aug also Mon 11am–6pm; ☎0592/314324, fax 317306). The cheapest place to **stay** is the *Christerus* (☎0592/313517; ②), on the way in from the station at Stationsstraat 17. The *De Nieuwe Brink Hotel*, Brink 13, is a reasonable place to **eat**.

South of Assen: Westerburk Concentration Camp

If you have your own transport, you might want to visit the **Herinneringscentrum Kamp Westerburk** (April–Sept Mon–Fri 10am–5pm, Sat & Sun 1–5pm; *f*7.50) a little south of town, on the road between the villages Amen and Hooghalen. It was here that Dutch Jews were gathered before being transported to the death camps in the east, and, although little remains of the camp itself, the documents and artefacts on display are deeply affecting.

Emmen and around

To all intents and purposes **EMMEN** is a new town, a twentieth-century amalgamation of strip villages that were originally peat colonies. The centre is a modernistic affair, mixing the remnants of the old with boulders, trees and shrubs and a selection of municipal statues that vary enormously in quality.

Emmen is well known for two things: its *hunebeds* and its zoo. The **Zoo** (daily: summer 9am–6pm; winter 9am–4.30pm; *f*26), right in the middle of town at Hoofdstraat 18, boasts an imitation African savanna, where the animals roam "free", a massive sea lion pool – the biggest in Europe – and a giant hippo house. Emmen is also the most convenient place to see *hunebeds*, of which the best is the clearly marked **Emmerdennen Hunebed**, in the woods 1km or so east of the station along Boslaan. This is a so-called passage-grave, with a relatively sophisticated entrance surrounded by a ring of standing stones. The other interesting *hunebed* within easy walking distance is the **Schimmer-Es**, a large enclosure containing two burial chambers and a standing stone; to get there follow Hoofdstraat north from the VVV, take a left down Noorderstraat, right along Noordeinde, left along Broekpad, and first right at Langgrafweg – a distance of about 2km. The **VVV** sells detailed maps of a circular car route along the minor roads to the north of town that covers all the principal remains.

Practicalities

Emmen **train** and **bus** stations adjoin each other, five minutes' walk north of the town centre: head straight down Stationsstraat into Boslaan and turn left down Hoofdstraat, the main drag. The **VVV**, Marktplein 9 (April–Sept Mon 10am–5.30pm, Tues–Fri 9am–5.30pm, Sat 10am–4pm; Oct–March Mon 10am–5pm, Tues–Fri 9am–5pm, Sat 10am–1pm; ☎0591/613000), can arrange **accommodation**. Their list includes pensions, private rooms and hotels. Cheapest pension is *De Wanne* at Stortweg 1 (☎0591/611250, fax 648800; ①), 1.5km southwest of the zoo. For a little more you could stay in the cheapest hotel, the *Boerland* at Hoofdstraat 57 (☎0591/613746, fax 616525; ②), which is immediately behind the train station. For **food**, try the first-floor café of the *Hotel Boerland*.

Around Emmen

BORGER, some 20km northwest of Emmen, has the largest *hunebed* in the country, 25m long on the northeast edge of the village; an adjoining information centre (Mon–Fri 10am–5pm, Sat & Sun 1–5pm; *f*5.50) explains how the dolmens got here. While you're in the area you can also visit the Pfeiffer **glassblowing workshop** and showroom, just west of town at the junction of Rolderstraat and Nuisveen (Mon–Thurs 9am–noon & 12.30–4pm, Fri 9am–noon & 12.30–2.30pm; *f*2). Should you decide to stay, the **VVV** (Easter–Oct Mon–Sat 9.30am–4.30pm; Nov–Easter Mon–Sat 10am–4pm; ☎0599/234855) has a list of private rooms, or you could try the *Hotel Nathalia*, Hoofdstraat 87 (☎0599/234791; ①). Bus #59 runs to Borger on its way between Emmen and Groningen; #24 comes from Assen.

Approximately 11km east of Emmen, toward the German border, the **Veenmuseumdorp 't Aole Compas** (daily: Easter–Oct 10am–5pm; July & Aug

10am–6pm; *f*17.75; bus #45 hourly from Emmen station; 30min) is a massive open-air museum-village that traces the history and development of the peat colonies of the moors of southern Groningen and eastern Drenthe. The colonies were established in the nineteenth century, when labour was imported to cut the thick layers of peat that lay all over the moors. Isolated in small communities, and under the thumb of the traders who sold their product and provided their foodstuffs, the colonists were harshly exploited and lived in abject poverty until well into the 1930s. Built around some old interlocking canals, the museum consists of a series of reconstructed villages that span the history of the colonies. It's inevitably a bit folksy, but very popular, with its own small-gauge railway, a canal barge, and working period bakeries, bars and shops. A thorough exploration takes a full day.

Thirteen kilometres northwest of Emmen, **De Zeven Marken** (April–Oct daily 9am–6pm; *f*5; bus #21 from Emmen), on the northern edge of the village of **SCHOONOORD**, is another open-air museum concerned with life in Drenthe. Exhibits here concentrate on the end of the nineteenth century and cover a wide range of traditional community activities – from sheep farming to education and carpentry. Seven kilometres west, tiny **Orvelte** (April–Oct Mon–Fri 10am–5pm, Sat & Sun 9am–5pm, July & Aug daily 9am–5.30pm; *f*5 for car parking) is another village-museum, fully operational and actually inhabited, though certain buildings may be closed at any time. Owned by a trust which exercises strict control over construction and repair, Orvelte's buildings date from the seventeenth to the nineteenth centuries and include examples of a toll house, a dairy, a farmhouse and a number of craft workshops. Most are open to the public, but you really need a car to get here. The adventurous can try bus #27 from Emmen to Zweeloo (20mins) and then take bus #22 to Orvelte (10mins). Before attempting the journey call for the essential up-to-date information (☎0900/9292) to improve your chances of making successful connections.

travel details

Trains

Emmen to: Zwolle (every 30min; 50–70min).

Groningen to: Amsterdam (every 30min; 2hr 20min); Assen (every 30min; 20min); Leeuwarden (every 30min; 50min); Zwolle (every 30min; 70min).

Leeuwarden to: Amsterdam (every 30min; 2hr 25min); Franeker (every 30min; 15min); Groningen (every 30min; 50min); Harlingen (every 30min; 25min); Hindeloopen (hourly; 35min); Sneek (hourly; 20min); Stavoren (hourly; 50min); Zwolle (every 30min; 1hr).

Buses

Bolsward to: Makkum (Mon–Sat hourly, Sun every 2 hours; 20min).

Groningen to: Emmen (hourly; 1hr 10min); Zoutkamp (hourly; 1hr).

Leeuwarden to: Alkmaar (hourly; 2hr 20min); Dokkum (every 30min–hourly; 30min); Franeker (hourly; 25min).

Sneek to: Bolsward (every 20min; 15min).

Buses and connecting ferries

Groningen to: Lauwersoog (GADO bus #63: 5 daily; 1hr) for boats to Schiermonnikoog (2–6 daily; 50min).

Leeuwarden to: Holwerd (FRAM bus #66: 5–7 daily; 50min) for boats to Ameland (4–8 daily;

45min); Lauwersoog (FRAM bus #51: 4–7 daily; 90min) for boats to Schiermonnikoog (2–6 daily; 50min).

Ferries

Harlingen to: Terschelling (2–3 daily; 1hr 45min); Vlieland (2–3 daily; 1hr 45min).

Stavoren to: Enkhuizen (May–Sept 3 daily; 1hr 20min).

Terschelling to: Vlieland (2–3 daily; 65min).

Vlieland to: Terschelling (2–3 daily; 65min).

Fast Ferries (Hydrofoil)

Harlingen to: Terschelling (3–4 daily; 80min via Vlieland; 50 min otherwise); Vlieland (2–3 daily; 90min via Terschelling; 45min otherwise).

Vlieland to: Harlingen (1 daily; 45min); Terschelling (1–2 daily; 30min).

Terschelling to: Vlieland (1–2 daily; 30min).

International trains

Groningen to: Oldenburg, Germany (2 or 3 daily; 2hr 10 min).

CHAPTER FIVE

OVERIJSSEL, FLEVOLAND AND GELDERLAND

With the eastern provinces of Holland, the flat polder landscapes of the north and west of the country begin to disappear, the countryside growing steadily more undulating as you head toward Germany. Coming from the north, **Overijssel** is the first province you reach, "the land beyond the IJssel", which forms the border with Gelderland to the south. Its more appealing western reaches are a typically Dutch area, in part cut by lakes and waterways around the picturesque water-village of **Giethoorn**, at the heart of a series of towns – **Kampen**, **Deventer**, **Zutphen** and the provincial capital of **Zwolle** – which enjoyed a period of immense prosperity during the heyday of the Zuider Zee trade, from the fourteenth to the sixteenth centuries. At the junction of trade routes from Germany in the east, Scandinavia to the north and South Holland in the west, their future seemed secure and all of them were keen to impress their rivals with the splendour of their municipal buildings. The bubble burst in the seventeenth century, when trade moved west and the great merchant cities of South Holland undercut their prices, but today all are well worth a visit for their ancient centres, splendid churches and extravagant defensive portals. Southeast of here, **Twente** is an industrial region of old textile towns that forms the eastern district of the province, near the German frontier. It's one of the least visited parts of the country and with good reason, only **Enschede**, the main town, providing a spark of interest with an excellent local museum.

The boundary separating Overijssel from the reclaimed lands of Holland's twelfth and newest province, **Flevoland**, runs along the old shoreline of the Zuider Zee. Divided into two halves, the drab **Northeast Polder** in the east and the later **Flevoland Polder** to the west, there's not really much to attract the visitor here, although the fishing village of **Urk** – an island until the land reclamation scheme got under way – is an unusual historical relic. The provincial capital is **Lelystad**, a pretty dire modern town redeemed by some fine museums and an impressive reconstruction of an early-seventeenth-century trading ship.

Gelderland, spreading east from the province of Utrecht to the German frontier, takes its name from the German town of Geldern, its capital until the late

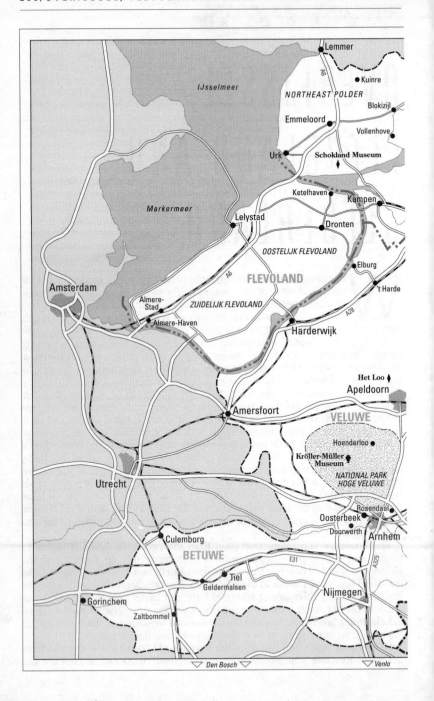

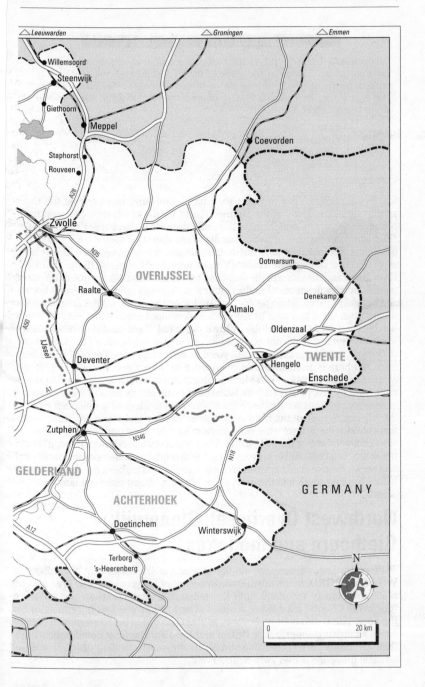

ACCOMMODATION PRICE CODES

All the **hotels** detailed in this chapter have been graded according to the following price categories. The codes are based on the price of the cheapest double room – without private bath, etc – during high season. In the case of **hostels** we've given the code if they have double rooms, otherwise we've stated the actual price per dorm bed per night.

① up to ƒ100/€45
② ƒ100–150/€45–67.50
③ ƒ150–200/€67.50–90
④ ƒ200–250/€90–112.50

⑤ ƒ250–300/€112.50–135
⑥ ƒ300–400/€135–180
⑦ ƒ400–500/€180–225
⑧ ƒ500/€225+

---

fourteenth century. As a province it's a bit of a mixture, varying from the uninspiring agricultural land of the **Betuwe** (Good Land), which stretches west from Nijmegen as far as Gorinchem, to the more distinctive – and appealing – **Veluwe** (Bad Land), an expanse of heath, woodland and dune that sprawls down from the old Zuider Zee coastline to Arnhem. Infertile and sparsely populated, the Veluwe separated two of medieval Holland's most prosperous regions, the ports of the River IJssel and the cities of the Randstad and today it constitutes one of the most popular holiday destinations in the country, strewn with campsites, second homes and bungalow parks. Some people use **Apeldoorn** as a base for the area, but it's a dreary town and if you want to visit the less developed southeastern sector, which has been set aside as the **Hoge Veluwe National Park** (and its Kröller-Müller Museum with a magnificent array of modern art, including one of the largest collections of Van Goghs in the world), you'd be better off basing yourself in Arnhem itself. **Arnhem** is most famous for its bridge, a key objective in the failed Operation Market Garden of 1944 – Field Marshal Montgomery's audacious attempt to shorten the war by dropping parachute battalions behind enemy lines to secure a string of advance positions across the rivers of southeast Gelderland – which left most of the city centre ruined. But it's a lively, agreeable place and a base for other attractions besides the Veluwe – the Netherlands Open-Air Museum, and, of course, the sites commemorating the 1944 battle. The ancient town of **Nijmegen** too, 21km to the south, is a fashionable university city, with a quality contemporary music and arts scene, despite similarly extensive war damage, and makes a good, if brief, stop before heading south into the province of Limburg or east into Germany.

Northwest Overijssel: Steenwijk, Giethoorn and the lakes

Trains from Leeuwarden slip into the province of Overijssel near the village of **WILLEMSOORD**, in the northernmost corner of the province. The area was no more than empty moorland until the nineteenth century, when the so-called "Society of Charity" established a series of agricultural colonies here to cater for the poor. The Dutch bourgeoisie was as apprehensive of the unemployed pauper as its Victorian counterpart in Britain and the 1900 *Baedeker* noted approvingly that "the houses are visited almost daily by the superintending officials and the strictest discipline is everywhere observed".

Trains stop at **STEENWIJK**, on the edge of the old moorlands, an unremarkable settlement that's only really useful as a base for exploring the surrounding lakes of western Overijssel. The town has seen more than its fair share of siege and assault, and, as a result, the towering mass of the Grote Kerk is an inconclusive mixture of styles that's suffered repeatedly from war damage. Otherwise, the centre is still roughly circular, following the lines of the original fortifications whose remains can be seen on the south side of town in a chain of steep, moated earth ramparts.

The town's **train** and **bus stations** are five minutes' walk north of the centre; head straight out of the station and follow the road around until you reach the ring road, cross over onto Doelenstraat, take a right at the T-junction and the Markt is in front of you. The **VVV**, Markt 60 (Mon–Fri 9am–6pm, Sat 9am–4pm; ☎0521/512010), is the place to find out about bus services around the lakes; for up-to-date timetables, ask for the *ARRIVA* bus book, which costs *f*7.95. Steenwijk has one reasonably priced **hotel**, *De Gouden Engel*, at Tukseweg 1 (☎0521/512436; ②), five minutes' walk northwest of the Markt – follow Kerkstraat around into Paardenmarkt and Tukseweg is dead ahead. Only slightly more expensive but more central is *De Hiddingerberg*, Woldmeentherand 15 (☎0521/512311; ②). The VVV also has details of a small number of private **rooms**.

Meppel, Staphorst and Rouveen

South of Steenwijk, the railway tracks from Leeuwarden and Groningen join at **MEPPEL**, a second possible base for travelling on to the lakes, though frankly it's a dull town and its **bus** and **train stations** are a good ten minutes' walk southeast of the centre. The town's **VVV** is at Kromme Elleboog 2 (Mon–Fri 9am–5.30pm, Sat 9am–noon; ☎0522/252888). There are two hotels, the *De Poort van Drente*, at Parallelweg 25 (☎0522/251080; ③) and *De Reisiger*, Dirk Jacobstraat 6 (☎0522/256649, fax 255514; ③). The friendly *Parkhoeve* **HI hostel**, at Leonard Springerlaan 14 (☎0522/251706, fax 262278; May–Aug; *f*27.75) has mixed dorms; it's signposted from the train station and takes about five minutes to reach on foot.

Beyond Meppel lie the elongated villages of **STAPHORST** and **ROUVEEN**, tiny squares of brightly shuttered and neatly thatched farmhouses that line some 10km of road in the shadow of the motorway. Despite significant industrial development in the last decade, both these communities still have strong and strict Calvinist traditions: the majority still observe the Sabbath and many continue to wear traditional costume as a matter of course – and do not wish to be photographed. In any case, apart from the custom of painting their houses in vicious shades of green and sky blue, Staphorst and Rouveen are undistinguished.

Giethoorn and the lakes

Meppel and Steenwijk in the east and the old seaports of Vollenhove and Blokzijl in the west rim an expanse of lake, pond, canal and river that's been formed by centuries of haphazard peat digging. Although it's a favourite holiday spot for watersports enthusiasts, public transport is limited and in any case you really miss the quiet charm of the region if you aren't travelling by **boat**. Fortunately these are available for rent at Giethoorn, in a variety of shapes and sizes, from canoes to motorboats and dinghies. Prices vary, but reckon on *f*100 per day for a motorboat down to *f*35–45 for a canoe. The other alternative is to come on a **boat**

<table>
<tr><td></td></tr>
</table>

BUSES AROUND THE LAKES

From Steenwijk train station #70 to Giethoorn/Zwartsluis (Mon–Fri hourly, Sat 8 daily, Sun 4 daily; 15/30min); change at Zwartsluis for connecting #71 to Vollenhove (Mon–Fri every 30 min, Sat & Sun hourly; 20min); #75 to Blokzijl (Mon–Fri hourly, Sat 4 daily, Sun 3 daily; 15min).

From Meppel train station #73 to Zwartsluis (Mon–Fri 8 daily, Sat 5 daily, Sun 3 daily; 20min); change at Zwartsluis for Vollenhove, as above.
From Zwolle train station #70 or #71 to Zwartsluis & Vollenhove (Mon–Sat every 30 min, Sun every 2hr; 30/50min); #71 continues to Vollenhove; #70 continues to Giethoorn and Steenwijk.

trip from Kampen (see p.269). Itineraries vary, but once or twice weekly, from mid-July to mid-August, boats sail from Kampen to Vollenhove, Blokzijl and Giethoorn. Further details from Kampen VVV.

Giethoorn

The best-known and most picturesque lakeland village is **GIETHOORN**, which flanks a series of interlocking canals that lie some 200m east of the minor N334 road from Steenwijk to Zwolle – not to be confused with the modern village of the same name on the main road itself. Bus #70 from Steenwijk station travels right through modern Giethoorn before reaching the VVV beyond; make sure the driver lets you off at the old village.

Giethoorn's origins are rather odd. The marshy, infertile land here was given to an obscure sect of flagellants in the thirteenth century by the lord of Vollenhove. Isolated and poor, the colonists were dependent on local peat deposits for their livelihood, though their first digs only unearthed the horns of hundreds of goats who had been the victims of prehistoric flooding, leading to the settlement being named "Geytenhoren" (goats' horns). Nowadays Giethoorn's postcard-prettiness of thatched houses and narrow canals criss-crossed by arching footbridges draws tourists in their hundreds, Dutch and German weekenders swarming into the village throughout summer to jam the busy footpaths and clog the waterways in search of some sort of northern Venice. The high prices and water-borne hubbub are certainly similar, although sadly Giethoorn has little else to offer besides.

If you decide to stay, Giethoorn **VVV**, based in a houseboat on Beulakerweg roughly 2km further along the N334 (mid-May to mid-Sept Mon–Sat 9am–6pm & Sun 10am–5pm, mid-Sept to Oct & March to mid-May Mon–Sat 9am–5pm, Nov–March Mon–Fri 9.30am–5pm; ☎0521/361248, *vvv.giethoorn@wxs.nl*), has a list of private **rooms** and **pensions** and will telephone ahead to make a booking; clarify the exact location beforehand, or you could end up walking for miles. Two of the more convenient **hotels** are *'t Centrum* (☎0521/361225, fax 362429; ②) and *De Pergola* (☎0521/361321, fax 362408; ②), both beside Giethoorn's central canal, at Ds. Hylkemaweg 39 and 7. Other alternatives include *Hotel Giethoorn,* Beulakerweg 128 (☎0521/361216, fax 361919; ②), conveniently located near the VVV, and the slightly cheaper *De Jonge* (☎0521/361360, fax 362549; ②), back up the road at Beulakerweg 30. Accommodation is very tight between June and August. On the eastern edge of old Giethoorn, **Lake Bovenwijde** has no fewer than seven **campsites** on its western shore. The two nearest ones, at the end of the main canal, are the *Botel*

Giethoorn, Binnenpad 49 (☎0521/361332, fax 362168) and *De Kragge*, Binnenpad 113 (☎0521/361319); both are open April to October.

For **eating**, most of the hotels have reasonable restaurants. Alternatively, you could try the *Achterhuis*, on the main canal at no. 43, or *Café Fanfare*, further east at Binnenpad 68, which has cheap daily dishes on its wide-ranging menu. **Nightlife** tends to be pretty quiet, although there are jazz and blues festivals over succeeding weekends in August. You're really here, though, for the waterways; most of the campsites and hotels rent **boats**, and the VVV can provide details of more than a dozen other operators. **Water taxis** leave from pretty much everywhere and cost about *f*8 per hour for a trip round the village.

Zwartsluis

South of Giethoorn, bus #70 travels the length of the dyke across Lake Belterwijde before cutting down into **ZWARTSLUIS**, once the site of an important fortress at the junction of waterways from Zwolle and Meppel. There's nothing much to the place today, but a couple of minutes' walk east of the bus station, at the bottom of Dawarsstraat, off Handelskade, is a small Jewish **cemetery** with a touching memorial to those locals who died in the concentration camps.

Vollenhove

At the bus station on the edge of Zwartsluis passengers change for the journey west to **VOLLENHOVE**, one of the most agreeable little towns in northwest Overijssel. Once a maritime fortification guarding the approach to Zwolle, Vollenhove spreads out east from the Vollenhover Kanaal that marks the path of the old Zuider Zee coastline. Buses stop on Clarenberglaan, a five-minute walk away from the main square (straight up Doelenstraat), where the **Onze Lieve Vrouwekerk** is a confusion of towers, spires and gables. The elegant, arcaded **Stadhuis** is attached to the church, and, across Kerkplein, the weathered stone gateposts outside the bank were originally part of the entrance to the **Latin School**. Around the corner from the church is the town's charming ancient **harbour**, a cramped, circular affair encased in steep grass banks.

Vollenhove VVV (April–June & Sept Mon–Sat 10am–noon & 2–4.30pm; July–Aug Mon–Sat 10am–noon & 1.30–5pm; Oct–March Wed 10am–noon & 2–4.30pm; ☎0527/241700) is beside the harbour. It can't offer much help with accommodation, but you can rent bicycles from here (*f*10 per day). There's just the one **hotel**, the *Herberg*, Kerkplein 1 (☎0527/243466; ②). Of the two local **campsites**, the nearest, *'t Akkertien Op De Voorst*, is at Noordwal 3 (☎0527/241452, fax 241378) five minutes' walk southwest of the VVV along the canal. The **restaurant** *De Vollenhof*, Kerkplein 12, serves good fish dishes and has a three-course menu; more appealing – and more expensive – is the *Seidel* restaurant in the old Stadhuis at Kerkplein 3. If you can't afford a meal, pop in for a coffee: the decor is delightfully antique.

Blokzijl

Some 6km to the north, **BLOKZIJL** is more beguiling still, an orange-pantiled cobweb of narrow alleys and slim canals surrounding a trim little harbour. Formerly a seaport, Blokzijl has scores of restored seventeenth-century houses reflecting its mercantile past, and one of the grandest has been converted into the *Hotel Kaatje bij de Sluis*, Zuiderstraat 1 (☎0527/291833, fax 291836, *kaatje@ worldaccess.nl*; ⑤), overlooking the main canal. More basic **accommodation** is available through the **VVV**, Kerkstraat 9a (Easter–May & Oct Mon–Sat 10am–noon & 1.30–4pm; June Mon–Sat 9am–noon & 1.30–4pm; July–Aug Mon–Sat 8.30am–6pm and Sun 10am–noon & 1.30–4.30pm; ☎0527/291414), but it's wise to book in advance in season. *Camping De Sas* is on the south edge of town at Zuiderkade 22 (☎0527/291696; April–Sept).

The town is stuffed with **restaurants**: the *Kaatje bij de Sluis* hotel (see above) has the finest food for miles around, but it is expensive and its restaurant is closed on Monday and Tuesday. Cheaper choices for local food include the *Prins Mauritshuis*, Brouwerstraat 2.

Blokzijl is easily reached in summer by boat from Vollenhove and Zwartsluis, but is a little awkward to reach by bus from Vollenhove: take #71 or #171 heading west and change at **Marknesse** to #75 travelling east. Bus #75 (Mon–Fri hourly, Sat 4 daily, Sun 3 daily) connects Blokzijl direct with Steenwijk – the easier approach – and drops you on the north edge of town, five minutes' walk from the harbour. Blokzijl also makes a good base for exploring the surrounding countryside, in particular the **National Park De Weerribben**, a chunk of protected canal and marshland starting about 3km to the northeast of the town. The VVV can suggest cycle routes through the Weerribben, linking up with any of a number of motorboat trips. The Bezoekerscentrum, at Hoogweg 27 (Tues–Fri 10am–5pm, Sat & Sun noon–5pm), on the north edge of the park, has information on the local flora and fauna.

Bikes can be rented in Blokzijl at Het Keldertje, Zuiderstraat 21 (☎0527/291747), at ƒ10 per day. For the less energetic, **boat trips** leave Blokzijl for Vollenhove and Zwartsluis three times daily in July and August, charging ƒ15 per person. The VVV will have the latest details.

Zwolle

The first major rail junction as you come from the north, **ZWOLLE** is the small and compact capital of Overijssel. An ancient town, it achieved passing international fame when Thomas à Kempis settled here in 1399 and throughout the fifteenth century Zwolle prospered as one of the principal towns of the Hanseatic League, its burghers commissioning an extensive programme of public works designed to protect its citizens and impress their rivals. Within the city walls, German textiles were traded for Baltic fish and grain, or more exotic products from Amsterdam, like coffee, tea and tobacco. The boom lasted for some two hundred years, but by the middle of the seventeenth century the success of Amsterdam and the general movement of trade to the west had undermined its economy – a decline reflected in Zwolle's present-day status as a small market town of no particular significance.

Refortified in successive centuries, today's centre is still in the shape of a star fortress, nine roughly triangular earthen bulwarks encircling both the old town and its harbour, whose waters separate a northern sector off from the rest. Prettily moated and still partly walled, Zwolle is engaging, though the surrounding suburbs, by comparison, are an unattractive modern sprawl.

Arrival, information and accommodation

Well connected by train to many of Holland's major cities and by bus to most of Overijssel's tourist attractions, Zwolle's **train** and **bus** stations are some ten min-

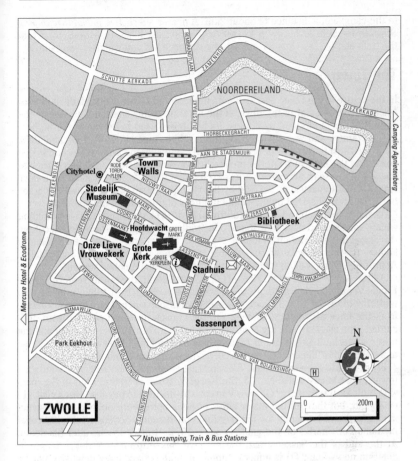

ZWOLLE

NOORDEREILAND

Cityhotel

Town Walls

Stedelijk Museum

Hoofdwacht

Bibliotheek

Onze Lieve Vrouwekerk

Grote Kerk

Stadhuis

Sassenport

Park Eekhout

N

◁ *Camping Agnietenberg*

◁ *Mercure Hotel & Ecodrome*

▽ *Natuurcamping, Train & Bus Stations*

0   200m

utes' walk south of the centre, a little way from the moat down Stationsweg. If you're intending to travel around the lakes and Flevoland by bus, it's well worth buying timetables from the bus station kiosk (Mon–Fri 8am–6pm). The **VVV** is at Grote Kerkplein 14 (Mon 10am–5.30pm, Tues–Fri 9am–5.30pm, Sat 9am–4pm; ☎0900/112 2375, *info@vvv-zwolle.nl*) and can help with finding a **room**. On the accommodation front, the dependable *Cityhotel*, Rode Torenplein 10 (☎038/421 8182, fax 422 0829; ②), is just northwest of the Grote Markt at the end of Melkmarkt. A little out of town the *Mercure Hotel Postiljon Zwolle*, at Hertsenbergweg 1 (☎038/421 6031, fax 422 3069, *h2109@accor-hotels.com*; ②) sometimes offers deals on rooms at weekends. The town's **campsite**, *Camping Agnietenberg*, Haersterveerweg 22 (☎038/453 1530, fax 453 3766; April–Sept), is by the River Vecht on the northeastern outskirts of town and difficult to reach without a car; take the Meppel bus #40 from Zwolle station and ask for the campsite. You'll be let off on the east side of the bridge across the Vecht on the A28. Immediately east of the bus stop, Ordelseweg goes under the A28 and leads north to the campsite, a distance of about 2km. A nearer alternative is *Natuurcamping Schellerberg*, Schellerbergweg 18 (☎038/465 1502, fax 465 6648; May–Sept). From the train station, take bus #5 and ask the driver to tell you which is your stop.

The Town

In the centre of the Grote Markt stands the restored **Grote Kerk**, dedicated to St Michael, patron saint of the town. If the exterior seems spartan it's because the church has been dogged by ill luck. Its bell tower used to be one of the highest in the country and was struck by lightning three times in 1548, 1606 and 1669. After the third time it was never rebuilt and eventually the bells were sold. Inside you'll find the familiar austerity of Dutch Protestantism, with the choir bare and dusty and the seats arranged on a central pulpit plan. The pulpit itself is an intricate piece of Renaissance carving by the German Adam Straes, where the grace of Christ is emphasized by the brutal ugliness of the faces of the sinners.

Attached to the church is the **Hoofdwacht** of 1614, an ornately gabled building which once served as a guardhouse. In front was the place of public execution, the remaining inscription "Vigilate et Orate" (Watch and Pray) a stern piece of advice to the crowds who gathered to witness these bloody spectacles. Appropriately, the building later housed the town's main police station.

A little way west, down an alley off the Grote Markt, the primly restored **Onze Lieve Vrouwekerk** (mid-May to mid-Sept Mon–Sat 1.15–4.15pm; mid-Sept to mid-May Mon–Sat 1.15–3.15pm; tower *f*2) is a discordant mixture of styles dating from the fifteenth century. Once again, the church has been plagued with difficulties – the original building contractor ran off with his advance payment and the tower was rebuilt after a fire in 1815 with an odd-looking turret on top, giving rise to its nickname "Peperbus" (pepperpot), which you can climb if you wish.

From beside the Grote Kerk, Sassenstraat twists and turns its way southeast toward the old city walls. No. 33, the **Karel V Huis**, is all that's left of the mansion built for the Emperor Charles V in case he decided to pay the town a visit. He never did, but then all the major cities of his empire were obliged to construct similarly grand buildings for his possible convenience. Strangely, the bas-relief medallion of Charles on the gable is dated 1571 – thirteen years after his death. At the end of the Sassenstraat, the massive **Sassenpoort** (Wed–Fri 2–5pm & Sat–Sun noon–5pm; *f*1) is a fine example of a fifteenth-century defensive portal, complete with boiling oil and water holes; it gives some idea of just how grand the medieval town must have been.

West of the Grote Markt, at Melkmarkt 41, is the main entrance to the **Stedelijk Museum Zwolle** (Tues–Sat 10am–5pm & Sun 1–5pm; *f*5), which is divided between two houses: the **Drostenhuis** (bailiff's house) on Melkmarkt, a grand sixteenth-century mansion topped with an uncomfortable Rococo pediment and the **Gouden Kroon**, through the garden at the side on Voorstraat. Pride of place in the Drostenhuis goes to the Blokzijl room, a meticulous reconstruction of a wealthy local family's seventeenth-century living quarters. The walnut, leather-upholstered chairs are a good illustration of Dutch furniture making and the mantelpiece holds some examples of Chinese ceramics. There's not much else of note, but of the items displayed on the second floor, there's a bizarre Vollenhove drinking cup in the shape of a bearded man in a doublet and a group of distinctive Art Nouveau Rozenburg vases – all deep strong colours with insects and flowers at the heart of the design – made by the same Hague company that tiled Groningen train station.

North of the Grote Markt, Roggenstraat and subsequently Vispoortenplas lead to a bridge over what was once the city harbour. On its south side much of the old town wall has been restored, including sections with a covered defensive parapet and a couple of fortified towers – principally the **Wijndragerstoren** (wine-porters' tower), which dates from the fourteenth century.

East of the station (15min walk), the **EcoDrome** at Willemsvaart 19 (April–Oct daily 10am–5pm; Nov–March Wed noon–5pm, Sat & Sun 10am–5pm; *f*14.50) is of interest, particularly for children. The park comprises a nature museum, prehistoric animal display including a 150 million-year-old Allosaurus, an aqua tunnel, butterfly garden, plus rides for kids along with exhibitions on all things ecological. Allow about two hours or so for a visit.

Eating and drinking

Zwolle is surprisingly short of interesting places to **eat**. Grote Kerkplein has the inexpensive *Bella Napoli*, offering pizzas from *f*15, and *Eetcafé de Kleine*, with cheap snacks available all day (closed Sun). The *Kota Radja*, Melkmarkt 50 (☎038/421 3534), has reasonable Chinese/Indonesian food; *La Cucaracha*, Sassenstraat 54 (☎038/421 8172), has a standard Mexican selection; while *Thor*, near the Wijndragerstoren, is a resturant-ship with Dutch food on deck starting at around *f*35. Of Zwolle's **bars**, the *Grand Café het Wijnhuis* is the best bet on Grote Kerkplein, while *De Docter* at Voorstraat 3 and *Music Hall X-Ray* at Blijmarkt 15 have live music at the weekend.

Internet access is available at the Bibliotheek, Diezerstraat 80 (☎038/421 7278); Internetzuilen are located on Grote Kerkplein, Gasthuisplein, and the corner of Diezerstraat and Korte Smeden.

Kampen

Just ten minutes from Zwolle by train, the small town of **KAMPEN** strings along the flat flood plain of the IJssel, a bold succession of towers and spires that, together with the other towns along the river, enjoyed a period of real prosperity in the fifteenth century as members of the Hanseatic League. Their success was short-lived, however and by the late sixteenth century they were in decline as trade moved west and Amsterdam mopped up what was left by undercutting their merchants. Indeed, the IJssel towns slipped into obscurity just as Amsterdam rose to the full height of its glory.

The Town

Sidelined by history, Kampen nowadays is little more than four roughly parallel streets edging the river, dotted with the remnants of the town's heyday. A bridge from beside the station spans the IJssel, leading directly into the centre. Clearly visible to the right of the bridge is a leaning tower with a bizarre top that resembles a hollowed-out onion, part of the Stadhuis. Just across the street is a second tower, the seventeenth-century **Nieuwe Toren**, which becomes Kampen's main attraction for one morning each year, usually in mid-July (contact the VVV for the exact date and time), when the **Kampen cow** is pulled up to its top. Insult turned to civic celebration, the cow is a symbol of the alleged stupidity of the inhabitants of Kampen, who are unlucky enough to be the butt of the Dutch equivalent of Irish/Polak jokes. The story goes that when grass began growing at the top of the tower, local farmers asked if they could graze their cattle up there. To commemorate this daft request, an animal has been hoisted up the tower every year ever since, though thankfully it's been replaced by a stuffed model.

The **Stadhuis** itself (Mon–Thurs 10am–noon & 2–4pm, April–Sept also Sat 2–5pm; ƒ1.50) is divided into two parts, the **Oude** and **Nieuwe Raadhuis**: the former was built in 1543, the latter added during the eighteenth century. Of the two, it's the old building which has most of interest, namely the *Schepenzaal* or "Magistrates' Hall", a claustrophobic medieval affair with dark-stained walls capped by a superbly preserved barrel-vault roof and a magnificent stone chimneypiece – a grandiloquent, self-assured work carved by Colijn de Nole in tribute to Charles V in 1545, though the chimney's typically Renaissance representations of Justice, Prudence and Strength speak more of municipal pride than imperial glory. To the right, the magistrate's bench is the work of a more obscure local carpenter, a Master Frederik, who didn't get on with de Nole at all. Angry at not getting the more important job of the chimneypiece, his legacy can be seen on the left-hand pillar, where a minute, malevolent satyr laughs maniacally at the chimney. For further details, pick up the glossy booklet on your way in – entry through the Nieuwe Raadhuis.

Near the Stadhuis, the **Stedelijk Museum**, Oudestraat 158 (Tues–Sat 11am–12.30pm & 1.30–5pm, June–Sept also Sun 1–5pm; ƒ3), is housed in an attractive fifteenth-century merchant's house and merits a brief stop as much for the building as for the collection of local bits and pieces contained within. In the other direction, Oudestraat leads directly south to the **Bovenkerk** (mid-April to mid-Sept Mon & Tues 1–5pm, Wed–Fri 10am–5pm; free), a lovely Gothic church with a light, spacious sandstone interior. Generally regarded as one of the most important Dutch medieval churches, its choir – with thirteen radiating chapels – was the work of Rotger of Cologne, a member of the Parler family of masons who worked on Cologne Cathedral. In the south transept an urn contains the heart of Admiral de Winter, a native of Kampen who fought to rid his country of what he considered to be the yoke of the House of Orange. A staunch Republican, he took part in the successful French invasion of 1795 that created the Batavian Republic; the rest of him lies in the Pantheon in Paris. **Concerts** are held in the church on Thursday evenings around 8pm between May and September, and also on Saturday afternoons in July and August at 3pm (ƒ10).

Beside the Bovenkerk is the earliest of Kampen's three surviving gates, the fourteenth-century **Koornmarktpoort**. The others, the **Cellebroederspoort** and the **Broederpoort**, are of a later, more ornamental design and lie on the west side of town along Ebbingestraat, reached from the Bovenkerk via Schoolstraat.

Finally, it's possible to go on board **De Kanze Kogge** (Mon–Fri 10am–5pm; ƒ3.50), which is a replica of a wrecked medieval ship, of the type used to transport goods to other Hanseatic towns – and which thus played an important role in the history of Kampen. This replica "Kogge" is available for sailing trips, but can otherwise be found moored alongside the quay of the river IJssel, a five-minute walk from the train station.

Practicalities

It takes ten minutes for the twice-hourly train from Zwolle to reach Kampen **station**, five minutes' walk from the town centre. Finding somewhere to **stay** can be difficult as the town has only two **hotels** and these are often full in high season: the *Van Dijk*, IJsselkade 30 (☎038/331 4925, fax 331 6508; ②) and the *De Stadsherberg*, IJsselkade 48 (☎038/331 2645, fax 332 7814; ②), both beside the river. The nearest **campsite** is the *Seveningen* (☎038/331 4891; April–Sept) some 3km northeast of town at Frieseweg 7: heading out of Kampen, cross the bridge and turn left; follow the main road around until it crosses the Ganzendiep canal and the campsite is just beyond – watch out for signs. If you're in difficulties, the Kampen **VVV** is on the main street at Botermarkt 5 (Mon–Fri 9.30am–5.30pm, Sat 9am–4pm; ☎038/331 3500, *vvv@kampen.nl*) and has a very short list of **private rooms**.

If you do manage to get fixed up, Kampen makes a good base for **day-trips** into Flevoland and the Northeast Polder. Throughout July and August **boat trips** leave Kampen to explore the surrounding waterways; there are two- or three-times weekly excursions to Urk, Giethoorn and Enkhuizen. Prices vary according to the itinerary, but the longest trips will cost *f*60–70; up-to-date schedules and bookings are available at the VVV. Alternatively, **bikes** can be rented, as ever, from the train station or from Potkamp, Oudestraat 152 (☎038/331 3495), for *f*10 a day.

For **food**, there's rather stolid Dutch fare at the *De Stadsherberg* hotel, pancakes and snacks at *'t Trappetje*, Oudestraat 25, Chinese/Indonesian meals at *Kota Radja*, Oudestraat 119, or the fish and Dutch specialities of *D'Olde Vismark*, IJsselkade 45.

Elburg

Half an hour from Zwolle by bus, just across the provincial boundary in Gelderland, the tiny coastal town of **ELBURG** once looked out across the Zuider Zee, whose perimeter is now marked by the path of the Veluwemeer as it snakes its way between the mainland and the polders of Flevoland. These days it's one of the most popular day-trip destinations in this part of Holland, awash with visitors throughout the season, here to enjoy the town's seaside flavour and to tour the homeopathic gardens on the outskirts.

Elburg was a successful port with its own fishing fleet from as early as the thirteenth century. However, in 1392 the governor, a certain Arent thoe Boecop, moved the whole town inland as a precaution against flooding. Familiar with the latest developments in town planning, Boecop and his overlord, the Count of Zutphen, laid out the new town as a grid, encircled by a protective wall and moat. Not all of Elburg's citizens were overly impressed – indeed the street by the museum is still called Ledigestede, literally "Empty Way" – but the basic design, with the notable addition of sixteenth-century ramparts and gun emplacements, survived the decline that set in when the harbour silted up and can still be observed today. Elburg's two main streets are Beekstraat, which forms the north–south axis and Jufferenstraat/Vischpoortstraat, which runs east–west; they intersect at right angles to form the main square, the Vischmarkt and all of Elburg's streets radiate from one or the other.

Buses from Zwolle drop visitors just outside the old town, a couple of minutes' walk from the **Gemeentemuseum**, Jufferenstraat 6–8 (April–Sept Mon 2–5pm, Tues–Fri 10am–5pm; Oct–March Tues–Fri 10am–noon & 2–5pm; *f*3), housed in an old convent, with predictable period rooms and objects of local interest. Heading north across Jufferenstraat, the **St Nicolaaskerk** (Mon & Fri 2–5pm,

Tues–Thurs 10am–noon & 2–5pm; *f*1.50) dominates the landscape, even without its spire, which was destroyed by lightning in 1693. West of the church, down Van Kinsbergenstraat, is the old **Stadhuis**, which once served as Boecop's home. At the end of Van Kinsbergenstraat, turn left into Beekstraat for the town's main square, the Vischmarkt, from where Vischpoortstraat leads straight to the best preserved of the medieval town gates, the **Vischpoort**, a much restored brick rampart tower dating from 1594. Inside there's a modest exhibition on the local fishing industry (April–Sept Mon 2–4.30pm, Tues–Fri 10am–noon & 1–4.30pm; *f*3 or same ticket as Gemeetemuseum).

Outside the gate, the pattern of the sixteenth-century defensive works is clear to see – from interior town wall, to dry ditch, to earthen mound and moat. The interior of one of the subterranean artillery **Kazematten** (casements) is open from mid-June to August (Mon 2–5pm, Tues–Fri 10am–5pm, *f*3). Cramped and poorly ventilated, it's easy to see why the Dutch called such emplacements *Moortkuijl*, literally "Pits of Murder". From the Kazematten it's about an hour's stroll right around the ramparts.

Ten minutes' walk northwest from the Vischpoort – turn right along Havenkade and take the second left – lie the **Alfred Vogel Tuinen** (homeopathic gardens) (April–Oct Mon–Fri 9.30am–4.30pm; June–Aug also Sat 10am–3.30pm; guided tours only – see below), six hectares of land that hold a comprehensive collection of homeopathic plants, the life's work of one Alfred Vogel. They form part of a successful business and are in fact Elburg's main tourist attraction. In the summer, free two-hour guided tours begin at the visitors' centre (see below), subject to demand. It's easy to tag onto any of the groups visiting the gardens, although you may want to call ahead (☎0525/687373) to enquire about times for tours in English. The visitors' centre, or **Bezoekerscentrum**, at Industriestraat 15, has a variety of illustrative displays and a mock-up of an old chemist's. However, it's all in Dutch and the surrounding gardens are of far more interest.

Practicalities

Elburg is easily reached from **Zwolle bus station** by service #101 (Mon–Sat every 30min, Sun hourly; 35min). The nearest **train station** is 8km from town at **'T HARDE**, on the Zwolle–Amersfoort line, with trains in both directions every half-hour; be warned, however, that bus #123 from 't Harde station to Elburg runs infrequently (Mon–Fri only 4 daily; 15min), so an easier option may be to get the train to Nunspeet and take the more frequent bus #101.

Elburg's **VVV** is around the corner from the Gemeentemuseum at Ledigestede 31 (May–Aug Mon–Fri 9am–5pm & Sat 10am–4pm; Sept–April Mon noon–5pm, Tues–Fri 9am–5pm, Sat noon–4pm; ☎0525/681520). It has a list of private **rooms** and will phone around to make a booking, but try to get a room in the old centre and come early in the day in high season, when accommodation is tight. The one **hotel**, *Hotel Elburg*, Smedestraat 5 (☎0525/683877, fax 683549; ③), has double rooms for *f*150 and is just off Beekstraat on the southwest side of the centre. The nearest **campsite** is the *Old Putten*, Zuiderzeestraatweg 65 (☎0525/681938; May–Oct), some 500m east of the VVV; head out of the old town along Zwolseweg and Zuiderzeestraatweg is the first on the right.

Of Elburg's many **restaurants** it's difficult to find any of real note. However, *'t Olde Regthuys*, Beekstraat 33, serves a reasonable range of fish dishes beneath fishing nets and ship models suspended above; *da Pietro*, Vischpoorstraat 20, has good pizzas starting at *f*13, and *de Tapperij* at the Hotel Elburg has *dagschotels* for *f*19. If you're after a **drink**, the *Beekzicht*, Beekstraat 39 has a fantastic selection of beers.

For **boat trips**, there are hour-long excursions from Elburg around the Veluwemeer throughout the summer (*f*7 per person). There are also day-trips to Urk (July & Aug 3 weekly) and occasional sailings to Ketelmeer and Harderwijk, among other destinations, which cost around *f*18 per person. The VVV has the latest schedules and will make bookings on your behalf.

The **strip of coast** on both sides of the Veluwemeer around Elburg is popular with Dutch holidaymakers for its watersports, nature reserves and forests. The whole region is dotted with campsites and the best way to explore it all is by **bike**. Cycles are available for rent in Elburg at Rijwiel Cash and Carry, J.P. Broekhovenstraat 3 (☎0525/683939), for about *f*5 a day. The VVV has a comprehensive range of suggested cycle routes.

Flevoland

With the damming of the Zuider Zee and the creation of the IJsselmeer, the coastline north and west of Kampen and Elburg has been transformed, creating two new polder areas, the **Oostelijk** and **Zuidelijk Flevoland polders**, which form an island of reclaimed land in front of the old shoreline and make up the greater part of Holland's twelfth and newest province – **FLEVOLAND**. To the north, the reclaimed land mass of the **Northeast Polder** forms the rest of the new province, the small towns that mark the line of the old coast – Vollenhove, Blokzijl and Kuinre – cut off from open water and now marking the provincial boundary between Flevoland and Overijssel.

The Northeast Polder

The **Northeast Polder** was the first major piece of land to be reclaimed as part of the Zuider Zee reclamation scheme, which began in earnest with the Zuider Zee Reclamation Act of 1918. The key to the project was the completion of the Afsluitdijk between Den Oever in North Holland and Zurich in Friesland in 1932, which separated the open sea from the Zuider Zee and thereby created the freshwater IJsselmeer lake. The draining of the polder was completed in 1936: drained and dried, it provided 119,000 acres of new agricultural pasture, which the government handed out under an incentive scheme to prospective settlers. The original aims of the project were predominantly agricultural and (unlike later polders) little consideration was given to the needs of the settlers, with the result that most of the Northeast Polder is unimaginably boring (the only town of any size, **Emmeloord**, is like a vast housing development) and it's no surprise that, even with the incentives, there were difficulties in attracting settlers. Also, a number of design faults soon became apparent. Without trees the land was subject to soil erosion and the lack of an encircling waterway meant the surrounding mainland dried out and began to sink – problems that have persisted until the present day.

The Schokland Museum

The Northeast Polder incorporates the former Zuider Zee islands of Urk and Schokland, which in Roman times were actually connected as one island.

Schokland, however, was abandoned in the nineteenth century because of the threat of flooding and only the church of 1834 has survived, converted into the **Schokland Museum** (April–Sept daily 10am–5pm, Oct–March Tues–Sun 11am–5pm; f3.50), with displays of all sorts of bits and pieces found during the draining of the polders. From beside the museum, a circular foot- and cycle-path follows the old shoreline of the island, a distance of about 10km. Bikes can sometimes be rented by the hour from the museum; phone ahead (☎0527/251396) to confirm. The museum is a 400-metre walk south of the minor road between Ens and Nagele/Urk – some 3km west of Ens. Buses drop you off on the stretch of road nearest the museum, but it's an awkward journey without a car: take the bus from Zwolle or Kampen station to Ens bus station (Mon–Fri every 30 min, Sun hourly), from where you can either walk or take the connecting bus which passes Schokland on its way to Urk (Mon–Fri 4 daily, none at weekends; 5min).

Urk

The only place really worth a visit in the Northeast Polder is **URK**, a trim harbour and fishing port that was a reluctant addition to the mainland. Centuries of hardship and isolation bred a tight-knit island fishing community here, with its own distinctive dialect and version of the national costume – aspects that have inevitably become diluted by connection to the mainland. However, the island's earlier independence does to some extent live on, rooted in a fishing industry which marks it out from the surrounding agricultural communities.

The damming of the Zuider Zee posed special problems for the islanders and it's hardly surprising that they opposed the IJsselmeer scheme from the beginning (see box on p.149). Some feared that when the Northeast Polder was drained they would simply be overwhelmed by a flood of new settlers, but their biggest concern was that their fishing fleet would lose direct access to the North Sea. After futile negotiations at national level, the islanders decided to take matters into their own hands: the larger ships of the fleet were sent north to fish from ports above the line of the Afsluitdijk, particularly Delfzijl and transport was organized to transfer the catch straight back for sale at the Urk fish auctions. In the meantime, other fishermen decided to continue to fish locally and adapt to the freshwater species of the IJsselmeer. These were not comfortable changes for the islanders and the whole situation deteriorated when the Dutch government passed new legislation banning trawling in the IJsselmeer in 1970. When the inspectors arrived in Urk to enforce the ban, years of resentment exploded in ugly scenes of dockside violence and the government moved fast to sweeten the pill by offering substantial subsidies to compensate those fishermen affected. This arrangement continues today and the focus of conflict has moved to the attempt to impose EU quotas on the catch of the deep-sea fleet.

There's nothing spectacular about Urk but its setting is attractive, its waterfront a pleasant mixture of the functional and the ornamental, and a series of narrow lanes of tiny terraced houses indicate the extent of the old village. A surprising number of the islanders still wear traditional costume and further examples are on display in the **Museum Het Oude Raadhuis**, Wijk 2, no. 2 (April–Oct Mon–Sat 10am–5pm; f4).

The only convenient way of reaching Urk is by **bus** from Kampen and Zwolle (Mon–Sat every 30min, Sun 3 daily after 4pm; 60–80min): ask the driver to drop you off at the stop nearest the centre. From early May to mid-September, Monday to Saturday, **ferries** cross the IJsselmeer between Enkhuizen and Urk two or three times daily and the trip takes around ninety minutes: check with any VVV for times and prices.

Adjoining the museum, Urk **VVV**, Wijk 2 (April–Oct Mon–Fri 10am–5pm, Sat 10am–1pm; Nov–March Wed & Fri 10am–5pm; ☎0527/684040), will help arrange **accommodation**. There are several cheap **pensions** near the harbour: *De Kroon*, Wijk 7, no. 54 (☎0527/681216; ①), *De Kaap*, Wijk 1, no. 5 (☎0527/681509; ①) and the unnamed pension of *Mw. J. Bakker* at Wijk 3, no. 76 (☎0527/685307; ①). The nearest **campsite** is *Recr. Park Hozevreugd*, Wormtweg 9 (☎0527/681785; April–Sept), in the woods some 4km north of Urk along the coastal road. Finally, Urk is a great place to eat **fresh fish** – *De Kaap* (see above), does good lunch specials and all-you-can-eat deals in the evening and has fine views over the IJsselmeer from its window tables; there are also plenty of cheap snack bars along Raadhuisstraat and the more expensive *De Zeebodem*, by the harbour at Wijk 1, no. 67.

The Flevoland polders

The Dutch learned from their mistakes on the Northeast Polder when, in the 1950s and 1960s, they drained the two polders that make up the western portion of the province of Flevoland, ringing the new land with a water channel to stop the surrounding land drying out and sinking. The government also tried hard to make these polders attractive – they're fringed by trees and watersports facilities – but it remains an uphill struggle and people have moved here reluctantly, only persuaded by very cheap housing. **Lelystad**, along with the other new town of **Almere**, 25km to the west, is where most of them end up, and it is here, if anywhere, that you're likely to come, as a handful of attractions on its outer edge repay a short visit.

Lelystad and around

Home to some of Amsterdam's most poorly paid workers, **LELYSTAD** is a largely characterless expanse of glass and concrete surrounded by leafy suburbs. It takes its name from the pioneer engineer who had the original idea for the Zuider Zee scheme but, the epitome of 1960s and early 1970s urban design, the place is something of a disaster. Still, though you certainly won't want to stop here for long, **Batavia Werf** and the adjacent **museums** make it worthy of a look-in.

Just on the outskirts of Lelystad, the shipbuilding yard at **Batavia Werf**, Oostvaardersdijk 1–9 (July–Sept daily 10am–7pm; Oct–June daily 10am–5pm; *f*17.50) pulls in over 300,000 visitors a year. The yard is a working centre for traditional shipbuilding, but its principal attraction is the 56-metre *Batavia*, a reconstruction of a merchant ship – one of the largest of its time – built in 1628 for the Dutch East India Company to bring home exotic cargo from Holland's new colonies in Asia. Heavily armed and loaded with 341 crew and passengers, many of them soldiers employed by the company to ward off pirates, the original *Batavia* sank on its maiden voyage off the west coast of Australia. The reconstruction project began in 1985, but because of the traditional materials and methods used, it was not until April 1995 that the new *Batavia* was officially launched by Queen Beatrix.

There's no guided tour and you're free to clamber all over the ship at will. The hold, down below, has mountains of space for the anticipated freight of wine, coffee, wood and spices, while the orlop deck above demonstrates the suffocatingly cramped living space of the soldiers, in stark contrast with the comfortably proportioned quarters of the captain and officers. Up on the gundeck, replicas of the *Batavia*'s 32 cannon were cast in moulds created to the design of the seventeenth-century originals. Throughout, it is the attention to detail that really catches the eye, particularly in the late-Renaissance style carving, from the bright-red Dutch lion figurehead to the golden heroes on the stern – William of Orange alongside Julius Civilis, leader of the Batavians in their revolt against the Romans in 69 AD.

Once you've finished on board, you can check out the latest work-in-progress, a reconstruction of the man-o'-war *The Seven Provinces* – the seventeenth-century flagship of Admiral Michiel Adriaensz De Ruyter – due for completion in 2005.

While you're in the area there are a few good museums worth catching. The **Nieuw Land Poldermuseum**, opposite Batavia Werf at Oostvaardersdijk 1–13 (Mon–Fri 10am–5pm, Sat & Sun 11.30am–5pm; *f*8.50), is the country's definitive museum on land reclamation. It gives the background on the Zuider Zee plan, with photos, models, films and slides and a worthwhile multimedia show. Most of the information is translated into English and you get a good idea of what's happened and what's scheduled to happen.

The excellent **Museum of Maritime Archeology**, Oostvaardersdijk 1–4 (Mon–Fri 9am–5pm, Sat & Sun 10am–5pm; *f*3.50), has a collection of material retrieved from the extraordinary number of ships that foundered in the treacherous shallows of the Zuider Zee. The museum's centrepiece is the hull of a thirty-metre early seventeenth-century merchant ship, while the contents of the *Lutina*, which went down with its two-man crew in a storm in 1888, are touching in their simplicity – a cargo of clay pipes from Gouda, silver coins and sundry personal effects.

Five minutes' walk back up the main road, the **Nederlands Sport Museum**, Museumweg 10 (Tues–Fri 10am–5pm, Sat & Sun noon–5pm; *f*7.50), is also worth seeing. Photographs and exhibits cover every sport the Dutch have ever been involved in, and interactive displays let you test your skill at fencing and other events. The place is fairly new and, while still finding its feet, has ambitious plans for expansion.

Lelystad can be reached by **train** from Amsterdam CS (every 30min; 40min). A bus runs to Batavia Werf from the station once an hour during the summer, in the absence of which you'll have to pay *f*7 for the train-taxi or hike the 5km on foot. The town can also be reached direct from Kampen on **bus** #143 (Mon–Sat every 30min, Sun hourly; 55min). Coming by car, take the exit to Lelystad from the A6 and follow the signs to Batavia Werf. There is no reason at all to spend a night in Lelystad but, if you have to, the **VVV** is at Stationsplein 186 (☎0320/243444) and can arrange **accommodation**.

Eastern Overijssel: Twente

Southeast of Zwolle, the flat landscape of western Holland is replaced by the lightly undulating, wooded countryside of **Twente**, an industrial region whose principal towns – **Almelo**, **Hengelo** and **Enschede** – were once dependent on the textile industry. Hit hard by cheap Far Eastern imports, they have been forced to diversify their industrial base with mixed success: the largest town, Enschede, still has a serious unemployment problem.

Enschede

If you visit anywhere in Twente it should really be **ENSCHEDE**, the region's main town. Laid waste by fire in 1862, it has a desultory modern centre that's been refashioned as a large shopping precinct, but it's a lively place, with regular festivals, exhibitions and the like and it has a museum with an excellent collection of Dutch art and some interesting 1930s architecture. All in all it's a worthwhile detour if you're heading east into Germany.

The Town

Five minutes' walk south of the train station, **Langestraat** is Enschede's main street. At its northern end, **Markt** is the town's main square, home to the nineteenth-century **Grote Kerk** (July & Aug Sat 2–4pm) in the middle, with its Romanesque tower, and the **St Jacobuskerk** just across the Markt, completed in 1933 on the site of a previous church that burned down in 1862. The severe rectangular shape of the St Jacobuskerk is punctured by angular copper-green roofs, huge circular windows and a series of Gothic arches. The church is built in a beautiful domed and cloistered Neo-Byzantine style, with some good modern sculpture and stained glass. The **Stadhuis**, a couple of minutes away down Langestraat, was finished in the same year and is also something of an architectural landmark, its brown brick tower topped by four eye-catching blue and gold clocks. No expense was spared in its construction and the interior is richly decorated with mosaics and, again, stained glass.

Fifteen minutes' walk north of the centre at Lasondersingel 129 – over the railway tracks at the crossing beside the station, first right, second left and follow the road to the end – the **Rijksmuseum Twente** (Tues–Sun 11am–5pm; ƒ5) is housed in a building of the same era, an Art Deco mansion of 1929, the gift to the nation of a family of mill owners, the Van Heeks, who used the profits they made from their workers to build up one of eastern Holland's finest art collections. The museum contains three main sections: fifteenth- to nineteenth-century art, modern art, primarily Dutch with the emphasis on Expressionism, and applied art, based on exhibits from the region of Twente – prehistoric and medieval artefacts, tiles and porcelain, tapestries and a reconstructed farm.

It's the paintings, inevitably, that provide the most interest, especially the Dutch and Flemish sections. Among a fine sample of early religious art are seven brilliant blue and gold fragments from a French hand-illuminated missal; a primitive twelfth-century wood carving of *Christ on Palm Sunday*; a delightful cartoon strip of contemporary life entitled *De Zeven Werken van Barmhartigheid* (The Seven Acts of Charity); and an extraordinary pair of fifteenth-century altar doors by one Tilman van der Burch, where a deep carved relief of a pastoral scene resembles a modern pop-up book. Of later canvases, Hans Holbein's *Portrait of Richard Mabott* is typical of his work, the stark black of the subject's gown offset by the white cross on his chest and the face so finely observed it's possible to make out the line of his stubble. Pieter Brueghel the Younger's *Winter Landscape* is also fastidiously drawn, down to the last twig, and contrasts with the more loosely contoured bent figures and threatening clouds of his brother Jan's *Landscape*. Lucas Cranach's studies of a bloated *Frederick Grootmoedige* and the spectacularly ugly *Barbara van Saksen* must have done little for the self-confidence of their subjects. Jan Steen's *The Alchemist* is all scurrilous satire, from the skull on the chimneypiece to the lizard suspended from the ceiling and the ogre's whispered advice, and compares with the bulging breasts and flushed countenance of the woman in his *Flute Player*, where the promise of forthcoming sex is emphasized by the vague outline of tussling lovers on the wall in the background. The modern section, too, has a few highlights – Claude Monet's volatile *Falaises près de Pourville*; a characteristically unsettling canvas by Carel Willink, *The Actress Ank van der Moer*; and examples of the work of less well-known Dutch modernists like Theo Kuypers, Jan Roeland and Emo Verkerk.

From beside the Stadhuis, it's a ten-minute walk southwest to Enschede's **Museum Jannink** (Tues–Fri 10am–5pm, Sat & Sun 1–5pm; *f*3), at the junction of Haaksbergerstaat and Industriestraat (head straight down Van Loenshof, turn right at Boulevard 1945 and take the first left), housed in a former mill and devoted to portraying everyday life in Twente from the nineteenth century onward. The most intriguing displays are a series of representative living rooms and a bewildering variety of looms reflecting the development of the textile industry from its origins as a cottage industry to large-scale factory production.

A third museum, the **Natuurmuseum**, De Ruyterlaan 2 (Tues–Fri 10am–5pm, Sat & Sun 1–5pm; *f*3), is also worth a quick look: there's a vivarium on the second floor, some well-presented fossils on the first floor and a mineralogy section in the basement. To get there, turn right leaving the train station along Stationsplein and then down the first major road on the left – a five-minute walk.

Practicalities

The best place to **stay** in Enschede is the unpretentious *Los Ponchos*, right in the centre at Korte Haaksbergerstraat 2 (☎ & fax 053/431 1787; ②). Alternatively, the *Parkhotel*, Hengelosestraat 200 (☎053/435 3855, fax 433 0155; ②) and the *Rodenbach*, Parkweg 39 (☎053/432 3438, fax 430 8402; ②), are a short walk out of the city centre. The **VVV**, in the centre of town at Oude Markt 31 (Mon 10am–5.30pm, Tues–Fri 9am–5.30pm, Sat 9am–2pm; June–Aug also Sat 9–4pm; ☎053/432 3200, *vvv.enschede@tref.nl*), has details of a limited number of private **rooms**.

For **food**, stick to the Markt and the streets around. *Crash*, Markt 6, and *Eetcafe Sam Sam* by the Grote Kerk, both have good daily specials, and popular bars nearby include *De Kater*, *De Geus* and *Poort Van Kleef*. There's also a friendly bar and a varied menu at the *Twente Schouwberg* around the corner from the St Jacobuskerk on Langestraat, the town's principal venue for plays, dance, films and occasional live music.

Around Enschede: Hengelo, Almelo, Oldenzaal, Ootmarsum and Denekamp

Some 10km northwest of Enschede, **HENGELO** has about eighty thousand inhabitants and is Twente's second town, a grim place whose old centre was destroyed during World War II. **ALMELO**, a further 17km northwest, is the region's third largest town, but this too has few attractions: the only buildings of any real interest are the centrally sited **Waag**, whose stepped gables date, surprisingly enough, from 1914, and, in a park east of the Marktplein, a stately seventeenth-century mansion, the **Huize Almelo** (no entry).

Things pick up a little north of Enschede with **OLDENZAAL**, the most agree-able of Twente's other settlements. Founded by the Franks, it was a medieval city of some importance and it was from here, too, that Overijssel's textile industry began its rapid nineteenth-century expansion, spurred on by the introduction of the power loom by Englishman Thomas Ainsworth. The town's principal sight, the **St Plechelmusbasiliek**, is right in the centre (June–Aug Tues & Thurs 2–3pm, Wed 2–4pm; free), an impressive, essentially Romanesque edifice dating from the thirteenth century. Named after St Plechelm, the Irish missionary who brought Christianity here, the interior (visits organized by the VVV – see below) is an exercise in simplicity – strong, sturdy pillars supporting a succession of low semicircular arches. Above, the bell tower is the largest in Europe with a carillon of no less than 46 bells.

Bus #60 leaves Enschede for the twenty-minute trip to Oldenzaal train station every thirty minutes from Monday to Saturday and hourly on Sunday. The approach by **rail** is less convenient as passengers have to change at Hengelo, where it can be up to a thirty-minute wait for the right connection. Oldenzaal's **train station** is ten minutes' walk south of the centre – head down Stationsplein, turn right at the end onto Haerstraat, first left along Wilhelminastraat and it's dead ahead – where the **VVV**, Plechelmusplein 5 (Mon–Fri 9am–5pm, Sat 10am–4pm; ☎0541/514023), has information on private **rooms**. There are sever-al **hotels**: the cheapest is *de Zon*, Bentheimerstraat 1 (☎0541/512413; ②), two minutes from Markt; alternatively, try *de Kroon*, Steenstraat 17 (☎0541/512402; ③). For **eating**, Markt is lined with **bars** and **restaurants** that liven up dramati-cally on weekend evenings: the best bar is *de Engel* at Markt 14, which also serves food; *Las Carretas* at no. 21 has Mexican fare for around *f*20.

Oldenzaal is a good base for visiting the wooded countryside that stretches northeast from near the town to the German border. This is a popular holiday area, littered with campsites, summer cottages, and bungalow parks. The village of **OOTMARSUM** (bus #64 from the station hourly; 15min) is noted for its half-timbered houses and quaint Markt.

By comparison, **DENEKAMP** (bus #52 from the station; hourly; 30min) is rather drab, though the elegant classicism of the **Kasteel Singraven**, some 2km west of the centre, partly makes up for it. Details of guided tours around the cas-tle (mid-April to Sept) are available from the Denekamp VVV, Kerkplein 2 (Mon–Fri 9am–12.30pm & 1.30–5pm, June–Aug also Sat 1–4pm; ☎0541/351205). While you're up at the castle, look out for the **watermill** on the banks of the river, built in 1448 and still functioning.

Deventer and Zutphen

South of Zwolle, the River IJssel twists its way through flat, fertile farmland as it marks out the boundary between Overijssel and Gelderland. For two hundred years the towns of the lower IJssel, **Deventer** and **Zutphen**, shared with Zwolle and Kampen a period of tremendous prosperity as the junction of trade routes from Germany, the Baltic and Amsterdam. Although both towns suffered griev-ously during the wars with Spain, the underlying reasons for their subsequent decline were economic – they could do little to stop the movement of trade to the west and could not compete with the great cities of South Holland. By the eigh-teenth century, they had slipped into provincial insignificance.

Deventer

Twenty-five minutes by train from Zwolle, **DEVENTER** sits calmly on the banks of the IJssel, an intriguing and – in tourist terms – rather neglected place, whose origins can be traced to the missionary work of the eighth-century Saxon monk, Lebuinus. An influential centre of medieval learning, it was here in the late fourteenth century that Gerrit Groot founded the Brotherhood of Common Life, a semi-monastic collective that espoused tolerance and humanism within a philosophy known as *Moderne Devotie* (Modern Devotion). This progressive creed attracted some of the great minds of the time, and Thomas à Kempis and Erasmus both studied here.

The Town

Five minutes from the train station, the centre of town is **Brink**, an elongated marketplace that runs roughly north to south, dividing the old town in two. The **Waag** edges the southern end of the square, a late Gothic edifice that retains an ancient dignity despite its somewhat rickety appearance. Inside, the **Town Museum** (Tues–Sat 10am–5pm, Sun 1–5pm; *f*5, or *f*6 including the Toy Museum – see below) has a thin collection of portrait paintings and a few antique bicycles. More intriguing is the large pan that's nailed to the outside of the Waag's western wall. Apparently, the mintmaster's assistant was found making a tidy profit by debasing the town's coins, so he was put in the pan and boiled alive. The bullet holes weren't an attempt to prolong the agony, but the work of idle French soldiers taking, quite literally, "pot shots".

Behind the Waag, the **Speelgoed en Blikmuseum** (Toy and Tin Museum; Tues–Sat 10am–5pm, Sun 1–5pm; *f*6, including Town Musuem) specializes in mechanical dolls. Walking west from here, Assenstraat's **window cuts** were completed in the early 1980s by a local artist, J. Limburg. Precise and entertaining, each illustrates a particular proverb or belief: at no. 119 the hedgehog's inscription translates as "Thrift yields big revenues" and at no. 81, on a house called *Gevaarlijke Stoffen* (Dangerous Materials), the totem pole is surrounded by slogans including *E pericolose sporcare* (It is dangerous to pollute). Continuing to the west along Assenstraat and veering left down Grote Poot (Big Leg), the **Lebuinuskerk** (Mon–Sat 11am–5pm; free) is one of the most impressive Gothic buildings in eastern Holland and is an expression of Deventer's fifteenth-century wealth and self-confidence. Carefully symmetrical, the massive nave is supported by seven flying buttresses, trimmed by an ornate stone parapet. The interior has been restored and today the expanse of white stone is almost startling, high arched windows and slender pillars reaching up toward a distant timber roof. Below, the church has two magnificent Baroque organs, the delicate remnants of some medieval murals and an eleventh-century crypt with a simple vaulted roof supported by Romanesque, spiral columns.

Back outside, the rear of the Lebuinuskek is joined to the fourteenth-century **Mariakerk**. Services haven't been held here since 1591 and the town council considered demolishing it as early as 1600, but in the event it survived as the town's arsenal and now houses a smart restaurant. Back at Brink, east of the Waag, Rijkmanstraat takes you into the **Bergkwartier**, an area of fairly ancient housing that was tastefully refurbished during the 1960s, one of Holland's first urban renewal projects. Turning left onto Kerksteeg, there's a small piece of iron, the remnants of a ring, embedded in a hole on the right-hand wall. The 1570s were desperate times for the inhabitants of Deventer, fearful of marauding Spanish armies, and, in their efforts to reinforce the town's defences, iron rings were embedded in the walls of many of the streets so that chains could be hung across them. At the end of Kerksteeg, the **Bergkerk** is fronted by two tall towers dating from the thirteenth century, the differences in the colouring of the brick indicating the stages of construction. From the church, Roggestraat leads downhill to the east side of Brink; opposite is a tiny triangle edged by the **Penninckshuis**, whose florid Renaissance frontage is decorated with statuettes of six virtues. The inscription *Alst Godt behaget beter benyt als beclaget* is smug indeed – "If it pleases God it is better to be envied than to be pitied".

Practicalities

Deventer's **bus** and **train** stations are a five-minute walk north of the town centre – left out of the station and first right straight down Keizerstraat and onto the Brink. The **VVV**, Keizerstraat 22 (Mon–Sat 9.30am–5pm, Thurs also until 9pm; ☎0570/613100) is five minutes on foot from the station. For a place of this size, **accommodation** is thin on the ground: there are two central **hotels**, the grimly modern *Royal*, Brink 94 (☎0570/611880; ②) and the slightly more expensive but excellent *Gilde*, housed in an old convent at Nieuwstraat 41 (☎0570/641846, fax 641 819; ②). The other alternative is the **campsite**, *De Worp* (☎0570/613601; May–Sept), west of the centre in the fields across the IJssel. A shuttle boat service crosses the river from the landing stage at the bottom of Vispoort and on the other side it's a five-minute walk down the first turn on the right, Langelaan.

Bars and **restaurants** line both sides of Brink: *de Waagschaal*, no. 77, is a pleasant brown café and there is a varied French and Dutch menu at *La Balance*, no. 72; there are Dutch meals at *De Drie Nissen*, Grote Poot 19, good if pricy Portuguese fare at *Chez Antoinette*, Roggestraat 8, and cheap *dagschotels* at *d'Oude Wijze*, Grote Kerkhof 28. The local speciality is a sort of honey gingerbread, *Deventer koek* and the best place to try it is the antique cake shop, Bussink, at no. 84.

The VVV has information on a walking tour of the city and details of **boat trips** up the IJssel leaving from the jetty near the Vispoort. A weekly programme throughout July and August includes excursions to Enkhuizen, Urk, Kampen, Zwolle and Zutphen, once or twice a week; prices vary according to the itinerary, but for the longer trips reckon on ƒ30 per person return. **Internet** facilities can be found at the Bibliotheek, Brink 70 (☎0570/675700). Finally, on the first day of August the town is the venue for the biggest **book market** held in Europe.

Zutphen

A sleepy little town some 15km south of Deventer, over in Gelderland, **ZUTPHEN** was founded in the eleventh century as a fortified settlement at the junction of the Berkel and IJssel rivers. It took just one hundred years to become an important port and today's tranquillity belies an illustrious and sometimes torrid past. Sacked on numerous occasions, the massacre of its citizens by Spanish forces in 1572 became part of Protestant folklore, strengthening their resolve against Catholic cruelty and absolutism. It was also here that Sir Philip Sidney, the English poet, soldier and courtier, met his death while fighting with the Earl of Leicester's forces against the Spanish in 1586. Sir Philip personified the

"Renaissance man" and even managed to die with some measure of style: mortally wounded in the thigh after having loaned his leg-armour to a friend, Sir Philip offered his last cup of water to yet another wounded comrade, uttering "thy need is greater than mine".

The Town

A five-minute walk from the train station, the effective centre of Zutphen is the **Wijnhuis**, a confused building of pillars and platforms that was begun in the seventeenth century and now houses the VVV. All the old town's main streets radiate from here and although there aren't many specific sights, the place does have charm, a jangle of architectural styles within much of the medieval street plan.

Around the corner from the Wijnhuis, Lange Hofstraat cuts down to the **Grote Kerk** of St Walburga (early May to end-Sept Mon 2–4pm & Tues–Sat 11am–4pm; *f*5), an indifferent, though immense Gothic church. Inside, the most impressive features are an extravagant brass baptismal font and the remarkable medieval **Library**, sited in the sixteenth-century chapterhouse. Established in 1560, the library has a beautiful low-vaulted ceiling that twists around in a confusion of sharp-edged arches rising above the original wooden reading desks. It has all the feel of a medieval monastery, but it was in fact one of the first Dutch libraries to be built for the general public, a conscious effort by the Protestant authorities to dispel ignorance and superstition. The collection is wonderful, ranging from early illuminated manuscripts to later sixteenth-century works, a selection of which are still chained to the lecterns on which they were once read. There are also two manuscript volumes – one a beautiful sixteenth-century illuminated missal, the other an original manuscript attributed to Thomas à Kempis. Curiously, the tiles on one side of the floor are dotted with paw marks, which some contemporaries attributed to the work of the Devil.

Down the alleys east of the church entrance is the fifteenth-century **Drogenapstoren**, one of the old city gates. This is a fine example of a brick rampart tower, taking its name from the time when the town trumpeteer, Thomas Drogenap, lived here.

Heading back toward the Wijnhuis along the Zaadmarkt, you'll come to the **Museum Henriette Polak** at no. 88 (Tues–Fri 11am–5pm, Sat & Sun 1.30–5pm; *f*5) which has a modest collection of twentieth-century Dutch paintings, notably *Landschap* by Wim Oepts, a profusion of strong colours, roughly brushed, that manages a clear impression of a Dutch landscape. The **Stedelijk Museum** (same times, same ticket), on the other side of town toward the station at Rozengracht 3, is housed in the shell of a thirteenth-century Dominican monastery and has a fairly predictable selection of shards, armour and silver. In the old refectory on the second floor there's an altarpiece from around 1400, originally from the Grote Kerk. Finally, the **Graphics Museum**, near the Grote Kerk at Kerkhof 16 (Wed–Fri 1–4.30pm & Sat 11am–3pm; *f*5) merits a quick stop for its collection of printing presses and other paraphernalia relating to the industry.

Practicalities

Zutphen's **VVV**, Stationsplein 39 (Mon 10am–5.30pm, Tues–Fri 9am–5.30pm, Sat 10am–4pm; ☎0900/269 2888), has details of a couple of centrally situated **rooms**, though in July and August it's advisable to arrive early as they disappear fast. Of the **hotels**, the pension-like *Berkhotel* is the best value, at Marschpoortstraat 19 (☎0575/511135, fax 541950, *Berkhotel@tebenet.nl*; ③); alternatively, try the rather more comfortable *Hotel Inntel*, De Stoven 37 (☎0575/525555, fax 529676, *infozutphen@hotelinntel.com*; ③).

There are two good and reasonably priced **restaurants** in Zutphen: *Pizzeria da Enzo*, near the Drogenapstoren at Pelikaanstraat 1a and the *Berkhotel*'s vegetarian café *De Kloostertuin*, Marschpoortstraat 19 (closed Mon). For **bars**, try the lively *Camelot*, Groenmarkt 34, or the quieter *De Korenbeurs*, Zaadmarkt 84. There is occasional live music at *Musiekcafe de Overkat* on Broederen Kerkstraat.

Boat trips run north up the IJssel in July and August (sailing schedules from the VVV). Prices vary according to the route, but a day-trip will cost about ƒ30.

Around Zutphen: the Achterhoek

Extending some 30km southeast from Zutphen to the German border, the **Achterhoek** (Back Corner) is aptly named, a dozy rural backwater whose towns and villages have little to hold your attention. The easy hills have, however, made it a popular spot for cyclists. Small enough to tour from Zutphen, there are no really noteworthy monuments, with the possible exception of the old frontier settlement of **'S-HEERENBERG**, whose tedious, modern centre edges the medieval Raadhuis, church and castle that once belonged to the counts Van de Bergh. Of the three, its the castle, the Huis Bergh, that dominates, its impressive red-brick walls bedecked with shutters, rising abruptly above the moat. Its present appearance was acquired in 1912 when an Enschede industrialist, J.H. van Heek, bought the place and had it restored. Guided tours (March to mid-Dec; call ☎0314/661281 for times; ƒ10) whisk you round an interior littered with sundry late medieval paintings, statues, prayer books and other paraphernalia installed by Heek.

The quickest way to reach 's-Heerenberg is by train from **Prodem** to **Doetinchem**, where you can pick up the bus from the train station for the twenty-minute trip (Mon–Fri every 30min, Sat & Sun hourly). In 's-Heerenberg the bus stops outside the **VVV**, Stadsplein 73 (Mon–Fri 9am–5pm & Sat 10am–1.30pm; ☎0314/663131, *vvvahoek@tref.nl*), which has good suggestions for walking and cycling. If you need to **stay over**, try *The Mill,* Molenstraat 18 (☎0314/661369; ①).

Through the Veluwe: Apeldoorn

Extending west of the River IJssel, the **Veluwe** (literally "Bad Land") of the province of Gelderland is an expanse of heath, woodland and dune edged by Apeldoorn and Amersfoort to the east and west and the Veluwemeer and Arnhem to the north and south. For centuries these infertile lands lay almost deserted, but today they make up Holland's busiest holiday centre, a profusion of campsites, bungalow parks and second homes that extends down to the Hoge Veluwe National Park, a protected zone in the southeast corner that is much the prettiest part and the best place to experience the area – though, unless you're camping, it's more sensibly seen from Arnhem.

Apeldoorn

The administrative capital of the Veluwe, **APELDOORN** was no more than a village at the turn of last century, but it's grown rapidly to become an extensive garden city, a rather characterless modern place that spreads languidly into the surrounding countryside. However, as one-time home of the Dutch royal family, Apeldoorn is a major tourist centre in its own right, popular with those Dutch senior citizens who like an atmosphere of comfortable, rather snobbish privilege. The only sign of life is the annual jazz festival, the **Jazztival**, usually held on the first Friday in June, with jazz musicians performing in the bars and clubs around town. Further details from the VVV.

The Paleis Het Loo

Apeldoorn is most famous for the **Paleis Het Loo** (Tues–Sun 10am–5pm; ƒ12.50, ƒ15 during special exhibitions), situated on the northern edge of town and reachable by half-hourly bus #102 or #104 from the station. Designed in 1685 by Daniel Marot for William III and his Queen Mary, shortly before he acceded to the throne of England and Scotland, the palace was later the favourite residence of Queen Wilhelmina, who lived here until her death in 1962. No longer used by the Dutch royal family – they moved out in 1975 – it was opened as a national museum in the early 1980s, illustrating three hundred years of the history of the House of Orange-Nassau. Inside, seven years of repair work have restored an apparently endless sequence of bedrooms, ballrooms, living rooms and reception halls to their former glory, supplemented by displays of all things royal – from costumes and decorations in the West Wing, to documents, medals and gifts in the East Wing and dozens of royal portraits and miscellaneous memorabilia spread across the main body of the palace. You can view the rooms of William and Mary, including their colourful individual bedchambers, as well as the much later study of Queen Wilhelmina. It's an undeniably complete display, but, unless you've a special interest in the House of Orange, not especially diverting. Better are the formal **gardens** (both William and Mary were apparently keen gardeners), a series of precise and neatly bordered flowerbeds of geometric design that are accessible by long walkways ornamented in the Dutch Baroque style, with fountains, urns, statuettes and portals. The other part of the palace, the **Royal Stables** of 1906, has displays of some of the old cars and carriages of past monarchs, including a baby carriage that's rigged up against gas attack.

Other attractions

The town's second main draw is the **Apenheul** (daily: April–Oct 9.30am–5pm; June–Aug 9.30am–6pm; ƒ19, children ƒ14), just west of town via bus #2. The highlights of this monkey reserve are its gorillas – among the world's largest colonies of the creatures – living on wooded islands that isolate them from the visitors and from the dozen or so species of monkey that roam around the rest of the park. It's best to go early to catch the young gorillas fooling around and antagonising the elders; as the day warms up they all get a bit more slothful. The park is well designed, with a reasonable amount of freedom for most of the animals (at times it's not obvious who is watching who) and you'll see other wildlife including otters, deer and capybara.

If you're staying, it's worth catching the *Lumido* held at the Natuurpark Berg En Bos (July & Aug nightly 10–11.30pm; gates open 7.30pm; ƒ7.50). It's a spectacular **light show** with music, illuminated fountains and gondolas on the water. A **film festival** takes place in the same park during August, and features international films but with only Dutch subtitles; details on the Lumido and film festival are available from the VVV. Finally, in July and August an old **steam train** is put back into service between Apeldoorn and Dieren (a 75-min ride) or you can do a three-legged half-day journey Apeldoorn–Dieren–Zutphen–Apeldoorn by steam train, boat and regular train. Details from the VVV.

Practicalities

The Apeldoorn **VVV** (Jan–April Mon 9.30am–5.30pm, Tues–Fri 9am–5.30pm, Sat 9am–2pm; May–Sept Mon 9.30am–6pm, Tues–Fri 9am–6pm, Sat 9am–5pm; ☎0900/168 1636, *vvvapeld@tref.nl*) is at Stationstraat 72. They have maps of the town and the surrounding area and lists of **rooms** – in season it's advisable to ask them to ring ahead to confirm vacancies. The most reasonably priced **hotel** near the town centre is the *Abbekerk*, Canadalaan 26, a ten-minute walk north of the centre (☎055/522 2433, fax 521 1323; ②), head up Stationstraat and Canadalaan is the fourth left turn after the Marktplein. There's also the *De Grote Beer* **HI hostel**, 4km to the west of town at Asselsestraat 330 (☎ & fax 055/355 3118; *f*30.75), which is open year-round and reachable with bus #4 or #7 to the Chamavenlaan stop. The nearest **campsite**, *De Veldekster* (☎055/542 4711, fax 543 0795), is some 5km southwest of the centre, off Europaweg at Veldekster 25 (bus #110 from the train station).

Don't expect a lot of night-time excitement in Apeldoorn. The main hive of evening activity is the **Caterplein**, where Hoofdstraat meets Nieuwstraat. *Tipico*, an excellent Italian with food for all budgets, is nearby at Kapelstraat 11, while *Old Chap* next door is a decent bar for a pre- or post-prandial drink. *Eetcafé 't Pakhuys*, Beekpark 9, has reasonable Dutch food and there are plenty of cheap shoarma joints nearby. Further south on Hoofdstraat, Raadhuisplein has several good café-bars, including *Brasserie de Kabouter*; the *Blues Café* on Nieuwstraat has occasional live music.

An easy way to see the countryside around town is by **bike**. Details of suggested routes are available from the VVV and bikes can be rented at Harleman, Arnhemseweg 28 (☎055/533 4346; *f*8.50 per day). The VVV can also provide details of walking trails in the forests around the Paleis Het Loo.

Internet access is available at the Bibliotheek, Vosselmanstraat 299 (Mon, Wed & Thurs 11am–8.30pm, Tues & Fri 11am–5.30pm, Sat 11am–4pm; ☎055/526 8400).

Arnhem and around

Around 20km south of Apeldoorn, on the far side of the heathy Hoge Veluwe National Park, **ARNHEM** was once a wealthy resort, a watering-hole to which the merchants of Amsterdam and Rotterdam would flock to idle away their fortunes. Last century it became better known as the place where thousands of British and Polish troops died in the failed Allied airborne operation of September 1944, code-named Operation Market Garden. It's now something of a place of pilgrimage for English visitors, who flock here every summer to pay their respects to the soldiers who died and visit the crucial sites of the battle. Much of the city was destroyed as a result of the operation, and most of what you see today is a post-war reconstruction – and not particularly enticing. However, Arnhem is a lively town that makes a good centre for seeing the numerous attractions scattered around its forested outskirts – the war museums and memorials, the Dutch open-air museum and the Hoge Veluwe Park itself, incorporating the Kröller-Müller Museum and its superb collection of modern art.

Arrival, information and accommodation

Arnhem is a major rail junction, well connected with both Dutch and German cities. The town's **train** and **bus stations**, are only a few minutes' walk from the centre and the **VVV**, Willemsplein 8 (Mon 11am–5.30pm, Tues–Fri 9am–5.30pm & Sat 10am–4pm; ☎0900/202 4075 at 75c per min, *vvvarnh@tref.nl*), which has a good selection of Dutch maps, books on Operation Market Garden, brochures and up-to-date cultural information.

Walking is the best way to **get around** Arnhem town centre, although to see any of the outlying attractions and for some of the accommodation, you'll need at some point to use a **bus**. Arnhem has a rather odd system of trams which describe a figure-of-eight pattern over town. This means there'll often be two buses at the station with the same number and different destinations, so it's important to get the direction as well as the number right.

Accommodation

The VVV operates an **accommodation-booking service** – useful in July and August when Arnhem's handful of reasonably priced **pensions** and **hotels** can fill up early. The cheapest rooms in town are at *Hotel Pension Parkzicht*, Apeldoornsestraat 16 (☎026/442 0698, fax 443 6202; ①) and the nearby and friendly *Hotel Rembrandt*, Paterstraat 1 (☎026/442 0153; ①). Both are a ten-minute walk east from the station: head round the northern edge of Willemsplein onto Jans Buiten Singel; Apeldoornsestraat is at the far end on the left and Paterstraat is just behind the Rembrandt theatre. If money's not too tight, there's the reassuringly comfortable *Hotel Haarhuis* opposite the train station at Stationsplein 1 (☎026/442 7441, fax 442 7449, *haarhuis@bart.nl*; ④) while, if you're on a budget, there's the *Altaveer* **HI hostel** some 5km north of town at Diepenbrocklaan 27 (bus #3, direction Altaveer; ☎026/442 0114, fax 351 4892; *f*30.75). The nearest **campsite** is *Camping Warnsborn*, 6km northwest of the centre at Bakenbergseweg 257 (bus #2 direction Schaarsbergen; ☎026/442 3469, fax 442 1095), although there are many others around the edge of the Hoge Veluwe Park, 5km further north, and one actually in the park itself – an ideal spot for a quiet night's camping.

If you have problems finding something, there's a good alternative outside the city proper: *Hugen's Rozenhoek*, Rozendaalselaan 60 (☎026/364 7290, fax 361 7588; ③), in the leafy suburb of **VELP** (trains every 30min; 10min), is bookable at Arnhem VVV. Untouched by the war, parts of Velp are still much as they were at the beginning of last century – comfortable country mansions and landscaped streets and gardens.

The Town

Predictably, the postwar rebuilding has left Arnhem a patchy place with the usual agglomerations of concrete and glass; however, five minutes' walk southeast from the train station you will find the **Korenmarkt**, a small square which escaped much of the destruction. The streets which lead off the Korenmarkt are pleasantly animated, full of restaurants and bars, while the **Filmhuis**, at Korenmarkt 42, has an excellent programme of international films and late-night showings.

Arnhem deteriorates as you walk southeast from the Korenmarkt and into the area most badly damaged by the fighting. Here you can find the "Bridge too Far",

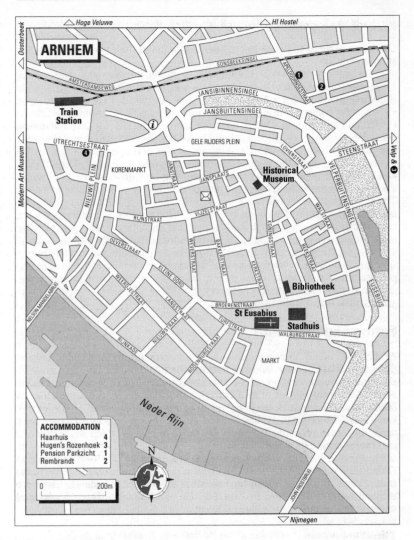

the **John Frostbrug**, named after the commander of the battalion that defended it for four days. It's a plain modern bridge, but it remains a symbol of people's remembrance of the battle, Dutch and British alike. Around its north end you can see the results of the rebuilding – wide boulevards intersect broad open spaces edged by haphazardly placed tower blocks and car parks. Overlooking this rather desolate spot, at the end of the characterless **Markt**, is the church of **St Eusabius** (summer Tues–Sat 10am–5pm & Sun noon–5pm; winter Tues–Sat 11am–4pm Sun noon–4pm; free, ƒ5 for the tower), with the dainty fifteenth-century **Stadhuis** tucked in behind. The church is a fifteenth- to sixteenth-century structure surmounted by a valiantly attempted but rather obvious replacement tower and was extensively renovated for the fiftieth anniversary of Operation Market Garden in September 1994; you can take a lift to the top for fine views around the surrounding area.

From outside the train station, it's a fifteen-minute walk west along Utrechtsestraat and then Utrechtseweg (or take bus #1 direction Oosterbeek) to the **Museum of Modern Art** at no. 87 (Tues–Sat 10am–5pm & Sun 11am–5pm; ƒ5; same-day combined ticket with Historical Museum ƒ7.50), whose speciality is exhibitions of modern Dutch art. The more centrally located **Historical Museum** (Tues–Fri 10am–5pm & Sun 11am–5pm; ƒ5) is located in an old orphanage at Bovenbeekstraat 21. The nucleus of the permanent collection in the Historical Museum is the work of the **Magic Realists**, particularly Carel Willink and Pyke Koch, whose *Vrouwen in de Straat* is a typically disconcerting canvas, the women's eyes looking out of the picture in a medley of contrasting emotions. The paintings of Renier Lucassen, for example *The Kiss* of 1976, establish the stylistic link between the Magic Realism of the 1930s and Dutch contemporary art, the familiar once again given a disturbing and alienating slant. The collection includes numerous archeological finds from the surrounding area; a display of Chinese, Japanese and Delft ceramics from the seventeenth and eighteenth centuries; Dutch silver, notably several guild beakers, whose size and degree of decoration indicated the status of the owner; and a modest selection of paintings from the sixteenth to the nineteenth centuries, with the emphasis on views of the landscape, villages and towns of Gelderland.

Eating and drinking

Arnhem has plenty of decent places for reasonably priced food and a range of good bars. The cheapest food can normally be found on the Jansplein near the post office; *Trocadero* at no. 49 and *Donatellos* at no. 50 offer Mexican and Italian respectively from ƒ10 per head. Carnivores should make for the popular *Eetcafe Mejuffrouw Janssen* at Duizelsteeg 7, just south of Korenmarkt. A little further east *Ceylon*, Looierstraat 11, has an excellent Sri Lankan buffet for ƒ25 per head, while back at Korenmarkt 1, *Pizzeria Da Leone* has pizzas which are particularly good value during its 4–6pm "happy hour".

Most people head for the pavement cafes of Korenmarkt for their **drinking**; *Le Grand Café* is probably the most popular but there are a dozen others to choose from. *Dingos*, Boyenbeekstraat 28, a couple of minutes' walk to the east, is another good bar and has cheap food on Tuesday and Thursday. There is often live music at one or other of the bars on Korenmarkt; get hold of a copy of *Uit Loper* for details of what's on.

Internet access is available at the Bibliotheek, Koningstraat 26 (Mon 1–9pm, Tues, Wed & Fri 10am–6pm, Thurs 10am–9pm, Sat 10am–4pm; ☎026/354 3111).

Around Arnhem

Most people who visit Arnhem in fact do so for the attractions **outside the city** and certainly you could spend several days here visiting the wartime sites of Operation Market Garden, taking in the countryside of the Veluwe park (and its

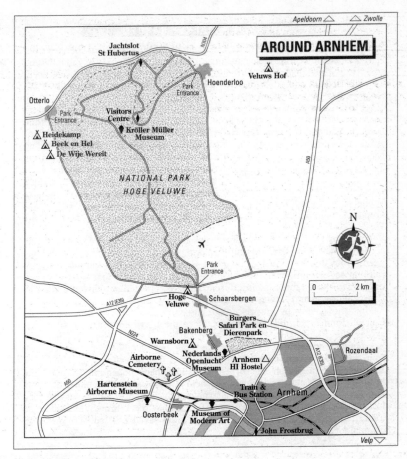

superb modern art museum), not to mention a huge open-air museum of Dutch vernacular archicture – the country's largest – and a castle or two.

Two castles: Doorwerth and Rosendaal

For the most part the banks of the River Rhine near Arnhem are rather dull, though there's an appealing stretch to the west, where you'll find the massive, moated thirteenth-century **Kasteel Doorwerth** (April–Oct Tues–Fri 10am–5pm, Sat & Sun 1–5pm; last entry 4pm; *f*10), carefully reconstructed after war damage. To get there, take bus #88 from the station and ask to be dropped at the stop nearest the Kasteel – from where it's a thirty-minute walk along the river. There's an excellent and pricey **restaurant** there too, which for most people is more of an attraction than the collection of stuffed carcasses and old weapons at the **Nature Museum** (*f*10) which occupies the castle.

OPERATION MARKET GARDEN

By September 1944 most of France and much of Belgium had been liberated from Nazi occupation. Fearing that an orthodox campaign would take many months and cost many lives, Field Marshal Montgomery decided that a pencil thrust north through Holland and subsequently east into the Ruhr, around the back of the Siegfried line, offered a good chance of ending the war early. To speed the advance of his land armies, Montgomery needed to cross several major rivers and canals in a corridor of territory stretching from Eindhoven, a few kilometres north of the front, to Arnhem. The plan, **Operation Market Garden**, was to parachute three airborne Divisions behind enemy lines, each responsible for taking and holding particular bridgeheads until the army could force their way north to join them. On Sunday September 17, the 1st British Airborne Division parachuted into the fields around Oosterbeek, their objective to seize the bridges over the Rhine at Arnhem. Meanwhile, the 101st American Airborne Division was dropped in the area of Veghel to secure the Wilhelmina and Zuid-Willemsvaart canals, and the 82nd was dropped around Grave and Nijmegen, for the crossings over the Maas and the Waal.

The American paratroopers were successful, and by the night of September 20, sections of the main British army, 30 Corps, had reached the American bridge-head across the River Waal at Nijmegen. However, the landings around Arnhem ran into serious problems: Allied Command had estimated that opposition was unlikely to exceed three thousand troops, but as it turned out, the entire 2nd SS Panzer Corps was refitting near Arnhem just when the 1st Division landed. Taking the enemy by surprise, 2nd Parachute Battalion, under Lieutenant-Colonel John Frost, did manage to capture the north end of the road bridge across the Rhine, but it proved impossible to capture the southern end. Surrounded, out-gunned and out-manned, the 2nd Battalion held their position from the 17th to the morning of the 21st, a feat of extraordinary heroism. Meanwhile, othe Polish and British battalions had concentrated around the bridgehead at Oosterbeek, which they held at tremendous cost under the command of General Urquhart. By the morning of the 25th it was apparent that reinforcements in sufficient numbers would not be able to get through in support, so under cover of darkness, a dramatic withdrawal saved 2163 soldiers out of an original force of 10,005.

On the opposite side of Arnhem, lying on the edge of the suburbs of Velp, there's another castle, the **Kasteel Rosendaal** (mid-April to Oct Tues–Sat 10am–5pm & Sun 1–5pm; ƒ8; bus #31 direction Velp Zuid) – an attractive mixture of medieval and eighteenth-century architecture, set in its own parkland. Not far away, on the west side of Velp, the **Museum Bronbeek**, Velperweg 147 (Tues–Sun 10am–5pm; ƒ5; bus #1 direction Velp), occupies a building donated to ex-soldiers by William III in 1859. The collection has all sorts of curious relics left over from the Dutch occupation of Surinam and Indonesia.

World War II memorials: Oosterbeek

The area around Arnhem is scattered with the graveyards of thousands of soldiers who died during **Operation Market Garden**. If you're a devotee of battle grounds and battle plans, Arnhem VVV sells specialist books on the campaign and provides details of organized tours (minimum twenty people). Otherwise, the easiest way to get some idea of the conflict and its effect on this part of Holland is to visit **OOSTERBEEK**, once a small village and now a prosperous suburb of Arnhem. To get here, take the train or bus #1 Oosterbeek.

Following the signs from beside Oosterbeek train station, it's a five-minute walk east to the **Airborne Cemetery**, a neat, symmetrical tribute to nearly two thousand paratroopers, mostly British and Polish, whose bodies were brought here from the surrounding fields. It's a quiet, secluded spot; the personal inscriptions on the gravestones are especially poignant. Ten minutes' walk (or bus #1) south of the station down Stationsweg, the village proper has spruced lawns and walls dotted with details of the battle – who held out where and for how long – as the Allied forces were pinned back within a tighter and tighter perimeter.

The **Airborne Museum** (Mon–Sat 11am–5pm & Sun noon–5pm; *f*6) is just to the west of the village centre along Utrechtseweg, reachable direct from Arnhem on bus #1, housed in the former *Hotel Hartenstein*, where the British forces were besieged by the Germans for a week before retreating across the river. With the use of an English commentary, photographs, dioramas and original military artefacts – from rifles and light artillery to uniforms and personal memorabilia – the museum gives an excellent outline of the battle and, to a lesser extent, aspects of World War II as it affected Holland as a whole. The Army Film and Photographic Unit landed with the British forces, and it's their photographs that stick in the memory – grimly cheerful soldiers hauling in their parachutes, tense tired faces during the fighting, and shattered Dutch villages.

The Nederlands Openluchtmuseum

Immediately north of Arnhem, the **Nederlands Openluchtmuseum** (April–Oct daily 10am–5pm; *f*18, children *f*12.50), reachable by bus #3, direction Alteveer (every 20min), or direct by special bus #13 (July & Aug only; every 20min), is a huge collection of Dutch buildings open to public view. One of the first of its type, the museum was founded in 1912 in order to "present a picture of the daily life of ordinary people in this country as it was in the past and has developed in the course of time". Over the years, original and representative buildings have been taken from all over the country and assembled here in a large chunk of the Veluwe forest. Where possible, buildings have been placed in groups that resemble the traditional villages of the different regions of Holland – from the farmsteads of Friesland to the farming communities of South Holland and the peat colonies of Drenthe. There are about 120 buildings in all, including examples of every type of Dutch windmill, most sorts of farmhouse, a variety of bridges and several working craftshops, demonstrating the traditional skills of papermaking, milling, baking, brewing and bleaching. Other parts of the museum incorporate one of the most extensive regional costume exhibitions in the country and a modest herb garden.

All in all, it's an imaginative attempt to recreate the rural Dutch way of life over the past two centuries. The museum's guidebook costs *f*10 and explains everything with academic attention to detail, although it's by no means essential, as most of the information is repeated on plaques outside each building.

The Hoge Veluwe National Park and Rijksmuseum Kröller-Müller

Spreading north from the Open-Air Museum is the **Hoge Veluwe National Park**, an area of sandy heath and thick woodland that was once the private estate of Anton and Helene Kröller-Müller. Born near Essen in 1869, Helene Müller came from a wealthy family whose money was made in the blast-furnace business. She married Anton Kröller of Rotterdam, whose brother ran the Dutch side of their trading interests and the couple's fortunes were secured when the death of her father and his brother's poor health placed Anton at the head of the company at the age of 27. Apart from extending their business empire and supporting the Boers in South Africa, they had a passionate desire to leave a grand bequest to the nation, a mixture of nature and culture which would, she felt, "be an important lesson when showing the inherent refinement of a merchant's family living at the beginning of the century". She collected the art, he the land, and in the 1930s ownership of both was transferred to the nation on the condition that a museum was built in the park. The museum opened in 1938 and Helene acted as manager until her death in 1939. Today, the park is one of Gelderland's most popular day-trip destinations, although it's large enough to absorb the crowds quite comfortably on all but the sunniest of summer weekends.

Around the park

The Hoge Veluwe Park has three entrances – one near the village of Otterlo on the northwest perimeter, another near Hoenderloo on the northeast edge and a third to the south at Rijzenburg, near the village of Schaarsbergen, only 10km from Arnhem. The **park** is open daily (April–Aug 8am–sunset, Sept–March 9am–sunset; ƒ16, including Rijksmuseum admission; cars ƒ8.50 extra), though in September and early October certain areas are off-limits during the deer rutting season.

There are a number of ways to get to the park by **bus**; easiest is to take the museum special from outside Arnhem train station (June–Sept daily except Mon, bus #12 direction Hoge Veluwe; hourly; ƒ7 return, plus ƒ8 park entrance: pay the driver) to the **Bezoekers Centrum** or visitors' centre (April–Oct daily 10am–5pm; Nov–March Sun 10am–4pm only), in the middle of the park, not far from the museum. The centre has information on the park and the **Museonder** (same hours; free), the world's first underground museum, with displays (including the living roots of a giant beech tree) on all things subterranean. The centre is also one of the places (along with the three entrances) where you can pick up one of over one thousand white bicycles that are left out for everyone's use at no extra charge – definitely the best way of getting around once you're here. When the bus isn't running, you can either rent a bike at Arnhem train station or take bus #107 (direction Lelystad; hourly; 25min) to the entrance at Otterlo. From here it's a four-kilometre cycle ride east to the visitors' centre. Before you enter the park, there is a small **Tile Museum** (Tues–Fri 9am–12.30pm & 1–5pm, Sat & Sun 1–5pm; ƒ6), in Otterlo village, ten minutes' walk from the entrance at Eikenzoom 12 (across from the VVV) and worth an hour of your time. If you are coming to the park from Apeldoorn take bus #110, direction Ede, which runs via the visitors' centre.

Once mobile you can cycle around as you wish, along clearly marked tracks and through stretches of dune and woodland where, particularly in the south of

the park, it's possible to catch sight of some of the park's big game –
red deer, roe and moufflon (Corsican sheep). By comparison, the park's
keep to themselves. Apart from the Kröller-Müller Museum (see below),
thing to see is the **Jachtslot St Hubertus** (guided tours only in Dutch, ~~but~~ you
can ask for English information, every 30min April–Oct Mon–Fri 10–11.30am &
2–4.30pm; Nov–March 2pm & 3pm; closed Jan; free), some 3km north of the visitors' centre, a hunting lodge and country home built for the Kröller-Müllers by
the modernist Dutch architect, H.P. Berlage, in 1920. Dedicated to the patron
saint of hunters, it's an impressive Art Deco monument, with lots of plays on the
hunting theme. The floor plan – in the shape of branching antlers – is representative of the stag bearing a crucifix that appeared to St Hubert, the adopted patron
of hunters, while he was hunting and each room of the sumptuous interior symbolizes an episode in the saint's life – all in all a somewhat unusual commission
for a committed socialist who wrote so caustically about the *haute bourgeoisie*.

The Rijksmuseum Kröller-Müller

Most people who visit the Hoge Veluwe Park come for the **Rijksmuseum
Kröller-Müller** (Tues–Sun 10am–5pm; admission included in park entrance fee
– see previous page), made up of the private art collection of the Kröller-Müllers.
It's one of the country's finest museums, a wide cross-section of modern
European art from Impressionism to Cubism and beyond, housed in a low-slung
building that was built for the collection in 1938 by the Belgian architect Van de
Velde.

The bulk of the collection is in one long wing, starting with the most recent
Dutch painters and working backward. There's a good set of paintings, in particular some revealing *Self-portraits* by Charley Toorop, one of the most skilled and
sensitive of twentieth-century Dutch artists. Her father Jan also gets a good showing throughout the museum, from his pointillist studies to later, turn-of-the-
century works more reminiscent of Aubrey Beardsley and the Art Nouveau
movement. Piet Mondrian is well represented too, his 1909 *Beach near Domburg*
a good example of his more stylized approach to landscape painting, a development from his earlier sombre-coloured scenes in the Dutch tradition. In 1909 he
moved to Paris and his contact with Cubism transformed his work, as illustrated
by his *Composition* of 1917 – simple flat rectangles of colour with the elimination
of the object complete, the epitome of the De Stijl approach. Much admired by
Mondrian and one of the most influential of the Cubists, Fernand Léger's *Soldiers
Playing Cards* is typical of his bold, clear lines and tendency toward the monumental. One surprise is an early Picasso, *Portrait of a Woman*, from 1901, a classic post-Impressionist canvas very dissimilar from his more famous works.

The building as a whole gravitates toward the works of **Vincent Van Gogh**,
with one of the most complete collections of his work in the world, housed in a
large room around a central courtyard and placed in context by accompanying
contemporary pictures. The museum owns no fewer than 278 examples of his
work and doesn't have the space to show them all at any one time; consequently
exhibits are rotated, with the exception of his most important paintings. Of earlier canvases, *The Potato Eaters* and *Head of a Peasant with a Pipe* are outstanding;
rough, unsentimental paintings of labourers from around his parents' home in
Brabant. From February 1886 till early 1888 Van Gogh lived in Paris, where he
came into contact with the Impressionists whose work – and arguments – convinced him of the importance of colour. His penetrating *Self-portrait* is a superb

example of his work of this period, the eyes fixed on the observer, the head and background a swirl of grainy colour and streaky brush-strokes. One of his most famous paintings, *Sunflowers*, dates from this period also, an extraordinary work of alternately thick and thin paintwork in dazzlingly sharp detail and colour.

The move to Arles in 1888 spurred Van Gogh to a frenzy of activity, inspired by the colours and light of the Mediterranean. The joyful *Haystacks in Provence* and *Bridge at Arles*, with its rickety bridge and disturbed circles of water spreading from the washerwomen on the river bank, are from these months, one of the high points of his troubled life. The novelty of the south quickly wore off, however, and Van Gogh's desperate sense of loneliness intensified. At the end of the year he had his first attack of madness – and committed his famous act of self-mutilation. In and out of mental hospital till his suicide in July of the following year, his *Prisoners Exercising* of 1890 is a powerful, sombre painting full of sadness and despair: heads bent, the prisoners walk around in a pointless circle as the walls around them seem to close in.

Finally, outside the museum, behind the main building, there's a **Sculpture Park** (April–Oct Tues–Sun 10am–4.30pm; free), one of the largest in Europe and spaciously laid out with works by Auguste Rodin, Alberto Giacometti, Jacob Epstein and Barbara Hepworth, all appearing at manageable intervals. Notable is Jean Dubuffet's *Jardin d'email*, one of his larger and more elaborate jokes.

Nijmegen

The oldest town in Holland, **NIJMEGEN**, some 20km south of Arnhem, was built on the site of the Roman frontier fortress of *Novio Magus*, from which it derives its name. Situated on the southern bank of the Waal, just to the west of its junction with the Rhine, the town's location has long been strategically important. The Romans used Nijmegen as a buffer against the unruly tribes to the east; Charlemagne, Holy Roman Emperor from 800 to 814, made the town one of the principal seats of his administration, building the Valkhof Palace, an enormous complex of chapels and secular buildings completed in the eighth century. Rebuilt in 1155 by another emperor, Frederick Barbarossa, the complex dominated Nijmegen right up until 1769, when the palace was demolished and the stonework sold; what was left suffered further demolition when the French occupied the town in 1796. In September 1944, the town's bridges were a key objective of Operation Market Garden (see p.290) and although these were captured by the Americans, the disaster at Arnhem put the town on the front line for the rest of the war. The results are clear to see: the old town was largely destroyed and has been replaced by a centre reconstructed to a new plan.

Arrival, information and accommodation

Nijmegen's **train** and **bus stations** are a good fifteen-minute trudge southwest of the town centre; if you can't face the walk, take any bus from the station. The **VVV** is five-minutes' walk from the station at Keizer Karelplein 2 (Mon–Fri 9.30am–5.30pm & Sat 10am–5pm; ☎0900/112 2344 at 75c per min, *info@vvvnijmegen.nl*).

Between July and August, there are a variety of **boat trips** on the Waal. Prices vary according to the itinerary, but excursions range from an hour's river tour (ƒ7.50) to sailings all the way to Rotterdam (ƒ60).

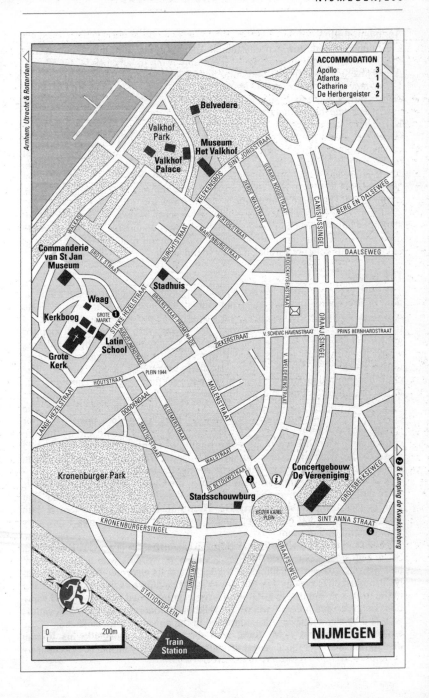

Accommodation

Cheap **accommodation** is pretty thin on the ground in Nijmegen; it's easiest to let the VVV make a booking – preferably well in advance – by phone. Alternatively, there are two **pensions** not far southeast of the train station: the *Catharina*, St Annastraat 64 (☎024/323 1251, fax 360 8534; ①) and *De Herbergierster*, Groesbeekseweg 134 (☎024/322 0922; ①). To reach them head east along one of the southern pair of roads from the station to the Keizer Karelplein; from here St Annastraat is the road heading southeast, with Groesbeekseweg the first turn on the left. The cheaper **hotels** are a little more expensive but tend to be more convenient: the *Apollo* is on the street running east off Keizer Karelplein, at Bisschop Hamerstraat 14 (☎024/322 3594, fax 323 3176; ②). If you're stuck, the *Atlanta*, right in the centre at Grote Markt 38 (☎024/360 3000, fax 360 3210; ②), isn't as pricey as you might imagine, although it can be rather noisy. The nearest **campsite** is *De Kwakkenberg*, Luciaweg 10 (☎024/323 2443, fax 323 4772; April–Oct), a few kilometres south of town, reachable from the station by bus #6, direction Berg en Dal, every twenty minutes. Ask the driver to drop you off at your stop, which will be on the main road, Kwakkenbergweg; Luciaweg runs roughly parallel, a block to the south.

The Town

The town centre is **Grote Markt**, a good fifteen-minute walk from the train station, or five minutes by any bus from immediately outside. Much of the Grote Markt survived the shelling and is surprisingly well preserved, in stark contrast to the modern shops across the road. The **Waag**, with its traditional stepped gables and shuttered windows, stands beside a vaulted passage, the **Kerkboog**, which leads through to the peaceful precincts of the much-renovated Gothic **Grote Kerk of St Stephen** (Mon 10.30am–1.30pm, Sat & Sun 1–4pm). The church is entered around the back to the left, past the attractively carved facade of the old **Latin School** and inside there's some fine Renaissance woodwork. The **tower**, with its vaguely oriental spire, offers a commanding vista over the surrounding countryside (May–Sept Wed & Thurs 2pm & 4pm, opened only for groups of five or more; *f*3.50). The view over the streets beside and behind the church isn't what it used to be – the huddle of medieval houses that sloped down to the Waal was almost totally destroyed during the war and has been replaced by a hopeful but rather sterile residential imitation.

A few metres away, down toward the river, the **Commanderie van St Jan** is more authentic-looking, a reconstruction of a seventeenth-century building that now houses the **Stadsbrouwerij De Hemmel**, Franse Plaats 1 (Sat & Sun noon–5pm; ☎024/360 6167; free; guided tours *f*9), which features a brewery museum and tasting room.

The brand new **Museum Het Valkhof**, Kelfkensbos 59 (Tues–Fri 10am–5pm, Sat & Sun noon–5pm; *f*7.50) houses a variety of exhibits with a local flavour, including innumerable paintings of Nijmegen and its environs – none particularly distinguished except for Jan van Goyen's *Valkhof Nijmegen*, which used to hang in the town hall. Painted in 1641, it's a large, sombre-toned picture – pastel variations on green and brown – where the Valkhof shimmers above the Waal, almost engulfed by sky and river. Also contained in the museum is the collection of the eminent archeologist G.M. Kam, who died in 1922. Alongside his Roman discoveries are other more recent artefacts; together they form a comprehensive picture of the first Roman settlements in the area and elsewhere in the Netherlands.

Returning to the Grote Markt, Burchtstraat heads east roughly parallel to the river, past the dull reddish-brown brick of the **Stadhuis**, a square, rather severe edifice with an onion-domed tower, another reconstruction after extensive war damage. A couple of minutes away, in a park beside the east end of Burchtstraat, lie the scanty remains of the **Valkhof Palace** – a ruined fragment of the Romanesque choir of the twelfth-century palace chapel and, just to the west, a sixteen-sided chapel built around 1045, in a similar style to the palatinate church at Charlemagne's capital, Aachen. These bits and pieces are connected by a footbridge to a **belvedere**, which was originally a seventeenth-century tower built into the city walls; today it's a restaurant and a lookout platform with excellent views over the river.

Nearby museums

Southeast of Nijmegen on the road to Groesbeek, the **Biblical Open-Air Museum**, Profetenlaan 2 (*Heilig Land Stichting*; Easter–Oct daily 9am–5.30pm; ƒ12.50), is accessible by bus #5 (destination Groesbeek; every 30min, 15min), from beside the train station. Ask the driver to indicate your stop on Nijmeegsebaan, from where it's a two-minute walk northeast along Meerwijkselaan to the museum. Here you'll find a series of reconstructions of the ancient Holy Land, including a Galilean fishing village, a complete Palestinian hamlet, a town street lined with Egyptian, Greek, Roman and Jewish houses and, strangely enough, "Bedouin tents of goats' hair as inhabited by the patriarchs". An experience not on any account to be missed.

There's another unusual museum 2km east of here, along Meerwijkselaan – the **Afrika Museum** at Postweg 6, Berg en Dal (April–Oct Mon–Fri 10am–5pm & Sat–Sun 11am–5pm; Nov–March Tues–Fri 10am–5pm & Sat–Sun 1–5pm; ƒ11), where there's a purpose-built West African village, a small animal park and a museum full of totems, carved figurines and musical instruments. You can get here on bus #5 (destination Groesbeek), which runs every twenty minutes to Berg en Dal, though from the bus stop it's still a twenty-minute walk to the museum.

Eating, drinking and nightlife

As you'd expect in a student town, Nijmegen has a wide range of places to eat and drink at sensible prices. For **food**, Kelfkensbos is a good place to start: *'t Circus* at no. 21 has excellent Dutch fare, while the Dutch-French food at *Appels & Peren* at no. 30 is a notch up in price. *Roberto*, Smetiusstraat 7, has good Italian food, and there are several decent places around the Waag, including the popular *Café de Waag*. For drinking, head down Grote Straat to the waterfront; *Kandinsky Café* at Walkade 65 is usually a lively spot, or you could try *Le Figaro* at Walkade 47. If you don't want to be outdoors, *Café in de Blaauwe Hand* is a cosy little bar behind the Grote Kerk and supposedly, the oldest bar in town.

Every inch a fashionable town, Nijmegen attracts some top-name rock **bands**, especially during the academic year. Most perform at the Concertgebouw De Vereeniging, Keizer Karelplein (☎024/322 1100) or the Stadsschouwburg, at Van Schaeck Mathonsingel 2, close to the train station; for latest details see the VVV. For **films**, the Filmcentrum, Marienburg 59 (☎024/322 1612), has good international programmes and some late-night shows.

travel details

Trains

Apeldoorn to: Amersfoort (every 30min; 25min); Deventer (every 30min; 10min); Zutphen (every 30min; 15min).

Arnhem to: Amsterdam (every 30min; 1hr 10min); Cologne (14 daily; 1hr 50min); Nijmegen (every 30min; 20min); Roosendaal (every 30min; 1hr 45min); Velp (every 30min; 10min).

Enschede to: Amsterdam (hourly; 2hr); Zutphen (hourly; 55min).

Zutphen to: Arnhem (every 30min; 30min); Deventer (every 30min; 12min).

Zwolle to: Amersfoort (every 15min; 35–50min); Amsterdam CS (every 30min; 1hr 15min); Arnhem (every 30min; 1hr); Deventer (every 30min; 25min); Emmen (2 hourly; 50min–1hr 10min); Groningen (2 hourly; 1hr 5min); Kampen (2 hourly; 10 min); Leeuwarden (every 30min; 55min); Meppel (every 30min; 15min); Nijmegen (2 hourly; 65–75min); Schiphol (every 30min; 1hr 40min); Steenwijk (2 hourly; 15min); Zutphen (2 hourly; 25–35min).

Buses

Enschede to: Oldenzaal (Mon–Sat every 30min, Sun hourly; 20min).

Kampen to: Lelystad (VAD bus #143 every 30min; 55min); Urk (2 hourly; 60min).

Lelystad to: Enkhuizen (VAD bus #150 every 30min; 35min).

Steenwijk to: Giethoorn (NWH bus #72 Mon–Sat hourly, Sun 5 daily; 15–30min).

Zwolle to: Elburg (VAD bus #101 Mon–Sat every 30min, Sun hourly; 35min); Kampen and Urk (VAD bus #141 hourly; 20min and 1hr 20min respectively).

Ferries

Urk to: Enkhuizen (May, June & Sept 2 daily; July & Aug 3 daily; 1hr 30min).

CHAPTER SIX

ZEELAND, NORTH BRABANT AND LIMBURG

Three widely disparate provinces make up the southern Netherlands: Zeeland, North Brabant and Limburg. **Zeeland** is a scattering of villages and towns whose wealth, survival and sometimes destruction have long depended on the vagaries of the sea. Secured only in 1986, when the dykes and sea walls of the Delta Project were finally completed, once and for all stopping the chance of flooding, at their best – for example in the small wool town of **Veere** or the regional market centre of **Middelburg** – they seem held in suspended animation from a richer past.

As you head across the arc of towns of **North Brabant** the landscape slowly fills out, rolling into a rougher countryside of farmland and forests, unlike the precise rectangles of neighbouring provinces. Though the change is subtle, there's a difference in the people here, too – less formal, less Dutch, and for the most part Catholic, a fact manifest in the magnificent churches of **Breda** and **'s Hertogenbosch**. But it's in solidly Catholic Limburg that a difference in character is really felt.

Continental rather than Dutch, **Limburg** has only been part of Holland since the 1830s, but way before then the presence of Charlemagne's court at Aachen greatly influenced the identity of the region. As Frankish emperor, Charlemagne

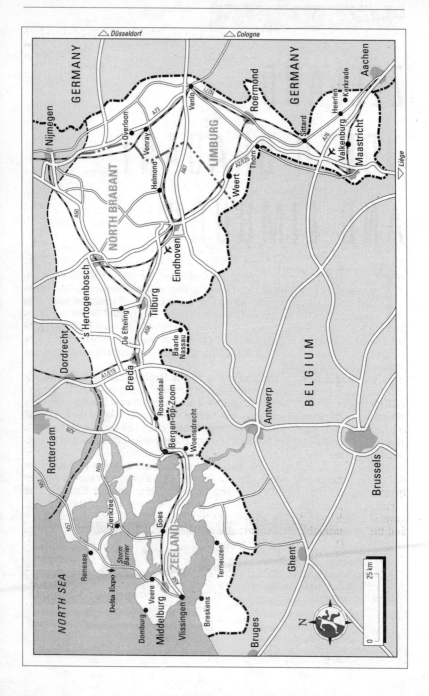

had a profound effect on early medieval Europe, revitalizing Roman traditions and looking to the south for inspiration in art and architecture. Some of these great buildings remain, like **Maastricht**'s St Servaas, and most have a wealth of devotional art that comes as a welcome change after the north. What's more, the landscape steepens sharply and you're within sight of Holland's first and only hills.

ZEELAND

Formed by the delta of three great rivers, the Rijn, the Schelde and the Maas, **Zeeland** comprises three main peninsulas, each consisting of a cluster of islands and semi-islands, linked by dykes, which as well as providing protection from flooding, also form the main lines of communication between each chunk of land. The northernmost landmass, Goeree-Overflakkee, is linked by two dams to Schouwen-Duiveland; the southern cluster is known as Noord and Zuid Beveland, with its western tip, traversed by a narrow canal, known as Walcheren.

Before the Delta Project (see p.309) secured the area, silting up and fear of the sea had prevented any large towns developing and Zeeland remains a condensed area of low dunes and nature reserves, popular with holidaymakers escaping the cramped conurbations nearby. Zeeland also has more sun than anywhere else in Holland: the winds blow the clouds away. Getting around isn't a problem, with bus services making up for the lack of north–south train connections, though undoubtedly the best way to see these islands is to **cycle**, using **Middelburg** as a base and radiating out to the surrounding smaller towns.

Vlissingen (Flushing)

VLISSINGEN is an important ferry terminus, but otherwise there's not really any practical reason to visit. The best thing to do on arrival at the bleak ferry port is leave; a bus takes you to the **train station**, from where there are hourly departures to Amsterdam and intermediate stations. There's also a **ferry service**, leaving from outside the train station, to **BRESKENS** on the southern side of the Westerschelde estuary (Mon–Sat 4.50am–11.50pm every 30min, Sun 6.50am–11.10pm hourly, every 30min in July & Aug), from where buses go on to Bruges.

Perhaps significantly, there are no buses from the ferry dock to the centre of town, although bus #56 plies between the train station and the centre. Here you'll find the unremarkable **St Jacobskerk** on Kleine Markt (July & Aug Mon–Sat 10am–noon; ƒ1.50 donation), the improbably named **Cornelia Quackhofje**, an eighteenth-century almshouse for sailors just north of the Lange Zelke shopping precinct and a **Stedelijk Museum** at Bellamypark 19 (Mon–Fri 10am–5pm, Sat & Sun 1–5pm; ƒ2.50), whose collection includes a room devoted to local naval hero Michiel de Ruyter. Alternatively and rather more fun, you could head for **Het Arsenaal** on Arsenaalplein (Jan–March Wed–Sun 10am–7pm; April–Oct daily 10am–8pm; Nov–Dec Tues–Sun 10am–7pm, last admission 2 hours before closing time; ƒ16, children under 12 ƒ12; ☎0118/415400), a maritime theme park where you can go on a simulated sea voyage, climb an observation tower and walk on a mocked-up seabed among tanks of sharks.

The **VVV** at Oude Markt 13 (Mon 1–6pm, Tues–Thurs 10am–6pm, Fri 10am–9pm, Sat 10am–5pm; ☎0118/422190, *vvvlis@zeelandnet.nl*) has a list of **pensions** including the nearby *Pension Marijke*, Coosje Buskenstraat 88 (☎ & fax 0118/415062; ①) and *Pension El Porto*, Nieuwendijk 5 (☎0118/412807; ①). *Belgische Loodsen Societeit* is on the seafront at Boulevard de Ruyter 4 (☎0118/413608, fax 410427; ②), near the end of Nieuwendijk. More expensive is the *Hotel Truida*, Boulevard Bankert 108 (☎0118/412700, fax 430502, *truida@zeelandnet.nl*; ②).

Middelburg

MIDDELBURG is the largest town in Zeeland and by any reckoning the most likeable. While not crammed with things to see, its streets preserve some snapshots of medieval Holland and a few museums and churches provide targets for your wanderings. Rimmed with the standard shopping precinct, its centre holds a large Thursday market, and, if you can only make it for a day, this is the best time to visit, with local women still wearing traditional costume – to picturesque effect. However Middelburg is best used as a base for exploring the surrounding area, with good regional bus connections and plentiful accommodation.

Arrival, information and accommodation

The **train station** is just a short walk from the centre of town as are the main bus stops, across the bridge on Loskade, opposite the *Hotel Du Commerce*. Head up Segeersstraat and Lange Delft and you find yourself on the Markt. The **VVV** office at Nieuweburg 40 (Mon–Fri 9.30am–5.30pm, Sat 9.30am–5pm, April–Oct also Sun noon–4pm; ☎0118/659900, *vvvmid@zeelandnet.nl*) has details of summer events in the city and a list of **private rooms**. Most of Middelburg's **hotels and pensions** are just minutes away from the Markt: the *Du Commerce*, Loskade 1 (☎0118/636051, fax 626400; ②), just across the bridge from the train station, and the *Beau Rivage*, nearby at Loskade 19 (☎0118/638060, fax 629673; ②), are the most convenient. More central is the *Brasserie De Huifkar*, Markt 19 (☎0118/612998, fax 612386, *huifkar@zeelandnet.nl*; ②), though it only has six rooms. Pensions include *de Koningin van Lombardije*, Blindehoek 12 (☎ & fax 0118/637099; ②) and *Café-Pension Dampoort*, east of the centre at Nederstraat 24 (☎0118/629068; ①). The nearest **campsite**, *Camping Middelburg*, Koninginnelaan 55 (☎ & fax 0118/625395; April–Oct), is about 2km out of town. Head down Zandstraat and Langeviele Weg, south and east of the Koveniersdoelen, or take bus #57 (every 30min) from the station. Further flung is the nearest **HI hostel**, *Kasteel Westhove* (☎0118/ 581254, fax 583342; April–Oct; ƒ31), 13km away, outside Domburg. To get there take bus #53 (Mon–Sat hourly; Sun every 2 hours; 30min) from the station located to the right after crossing the canal bridge.

The Town

Middelburg owed its early growth to the comparative safety of its situation in the centre of Walcheren. The slight elevation gave the settlement protection from the sea and its position on a bend in the River Arne made it reasonably easy to defend. Though its abbey was founded in 1120, the town's isolation meant that it did not

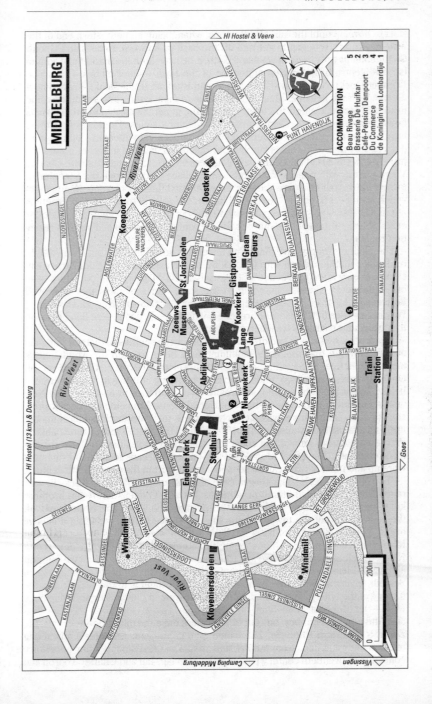

MIDDELBURG

△ *HI Hostel & Veere*

△ *HI Hostel (13 km) & Domburg*

▷ *Goes*

▽ *Camping Middelburg*

▽ *Vlissingen*

ACCOMMODATION

Beau Rivage	5
Brasserie De Huifkar	2
Café-Pension Dampoort	3
Du Commerce	4
de Koningin van Lombardije	1

Koepoort

Oostkerk

St Jorisdoelen

Zeeuws Museum

Graan Beurs

Gistpoort

Koorkerk

Lange Jan

Abdijkerken

Nieuwekerk

Markt

Stadhuis

Engelse Kerk

Kloveniersdoelen

Windmill

Windmill

Train Station

River Vest

River Vest

PUNT HAVENDIJK

200m

0

start to develop until the late Middle Ages, when, being at the western end of the Scheldt estuary, it began to get rich off the back of Antwerp, Bruges and Ghent. Conducting its own trade in wool and cloth, it became both the market and administrative centre of the region and some of the town's street names – Houtkaai (Timber Dock), Korendijk (Grain Dyke) and Bierkaai (Beer Dock) – reveal how diverse its trade became. Most of Middelburg's most interesting buildings come from this period, though the town's **Stadhuis**, generally agreed to be Zeeland's finest, is a wonderfully eclectic mix of architectural styles. The towering Gothic facade is especially magnificent, dating from the mid-fifteenth century and designed by the Keldermans family from Mechelen. Ranged in niches across the front are 25 statues of the counts and countesses of Holland, starting with Charles V and ending with queens Wilhelmina and Juliana placed above the **Vleeshal**, a former meat hall that now houses changing exhibitions of contemporary art which can be visited on conducted tours. Hour-long **tours** of the Stadhuis (April–Oct Mon–Sat 11am–5pm, Sun noon–5pm; check noticeboard outside for exact times; f6) take in the mayor's office, council chambers and various reception rooms.

The Stadhuis' impressive pinnacled tower was added in 1520, but it's as well to remember that this, along with the Stadhuis itself and much of Middelburg's city centre, is only a reconstruction of the original. On May 17, 1940 the city was all but flattened by German bombing in the same series of raids that destroyed Rotterdam. In 1944, in an attempt to isolate German artillery in Vlissingen, Walcheren's sea defences were breached, which resulted in severe flood damage to Middelburg's already treacherous streets.

Restoration was a long and difficult process, but so successful that you can only occasionally tell that the city's buildings have been patched up. Middelburg's most distinctive tower, that of the **Abdijkerken (Abbey Churches)** on Onderdentoren, collapsed under German bombing, destroying the churches below. Today the abbey complex – really three churches in one – is quite bare inside, considering that it's been around since the twelfth century. There's a reason for this: Middelburg was an early convert to Protestantism following the uprising against the Spanish, and in 1574 William the Silent's troops threw out the Premonstratensian monks and converted the abbey to secular use. The abbey's three churches (May–Sept Mon–Fri 10am–5pm; free) were adapted to Protestant worship and most of what can be seen inside dates from the seventeenth century.

The **Nieuwe Kerk** has an organ case of 1692, and the **Wandel Kerk** the outrageously triumphalistic tomb of admirals Jan and Cornelis Evertsen, brothers killed fighting in a naval battle against the English in 1666. The **Koor Kerk**, on the eastern side of the tower, retains the oldest decoration, including a Nicolai organ of 1478. Best fun of all is to climb the 207 steps of the tower (April–Oct Mon–Sat 11am–5pm, Sun noon–5pm; f5), known locally as *Lange Jan* (Long John). In clear weather, there's a tremendous view from its 91-metre summit across Middelburg and over Walcheren as far as the Zeelandbrug and the eastern Scheldt, giving a good sense of how vulnerable Zeeland is to the sea. Finally, the history of the abbey is presented in the **Historama**, in the cloister at Abdijplein 9 (April–Oct Mon–Sat 11am–5pm, Sun noon–5pm, f6).

At the rear of the abbey, housed in what were once the monks' dormitories, the **Zeeuws Museum** (Mon–Sat 11am–5pm, Sun noon–5pm; f9) holds a mixed bag of collections and finds from the Zeeland area. The museum has a tiny but choice collection of twentieth-century paintings by Mesdag, Jan and Charley Toorop and other (local) artists. Downstairs, there's a well-documented assembly of Roman and medieval artefacts, including Nehallenia altar stones. Like those in Leiden's Van Oudheden Museum (see p.175), these seem to have been votive offerings, given by sailors in Roman times in thanks for safe passage across the English Channel. Little more is known about the goddess Nehallenia, though it's possible she was also a goddess of flowers, akin to Flora. Elsewhere in the museum are some lively tapestries, commissioned by the local authorities between 1591 and 1604 to celebrate the naval battles against the Spanish, and a comprehensive display of local costumes.

East of the abbey, **Damplein** was restored to its original breadth by the demolition of a couple of rows of houses. It forms a quieter focus for bars than the Markt and is the site of the **Graanbeurs**, a grain exchange rebuilt in the nineteenth century and today containing some intriguing and humorous stone plaques by international artists – a project known as "Podio del Mondo per l'Arte". To the western side of the square, the **Blauwpoort** (also known as the **Gistpoort** or Yeast Gate) forms a decorative entrance to the abbey complex. Built at the beginning of the sixteenth century from blue limestone, it was virtually destroyed in the last war and what you see today is an indifferent renovation.

Directly north of Damplein on Molenwater, **Miniature Walcheren** (daily: April–Oct 10am–5pm; July–Aug 10am–6pm; ƒ11, children ƒ8) has scaled-down models of Walcheren island's best buildings. It's about as enjoyable as you'd imagine, but might entertain kids for an hour or so. Further east, the distinctive profile of the domed, octagonal **Oostkerk** (May–Oct Thurs 10am–4pm; free) stands high above the surrounding suburbs, near the main road to Veere: built in 1647 to designs by Pieter Post and others, it was one of the first churches in Holland to be built expressly for Protestant use.

While the streets around the Abdijkerken and Stadhuis are the most atmospheric, it's worth walking to the western edge of town to reach the landmark of the **Kloveniersdoelen** at the end of Langeviele. Built in 1607 in exuberant Flemish Renaissance style, this was the home of the city's civic guard, the Arquebusiers, until the end of the eighteenth century, later becoming the local headquarters of the East India Company, and later still a military hospital. Restored in 1969 (as you might have guessed if you spotted the weather vane), it's now a recital hall and is renowned for presenting new and experimental music (there's a festival every year in July; call ☎0118/623650 for details). A short walk north or south of the Kloveniersdoelen, by the edge of Middelburg's old encircling defensive canal, are a couple of eighteenth-century **windmills**: De Hoop mill to the south was once a barley peeling mill; De Seismolen to the north a cereal mill, though it's not possible to enter either today.

The **Roosevelt Study Centre**, Abdij 9 (Mon–Fri 10am–12.30pm & 1.30–4.30pm), a centre for the study of twentieth-century American history (one of the largest in Europe), has a permanent exhibition on presidents Theodore and Franklin Delano Roosevelt and the latter's remarkable wife Eleanor.

The VVV has a guided **walking tour** (April–Oct daily 1.30pm; ƒ7.50) which leaves from their office and lasts one and a half hours, taking in the city's main landmarks. **Horse-drawn carriage rides** also operate from outside the office (June–Sept Mon–Sat 11am–5pm, Sun 1–5pm; 20mins; ƒ4). The VVV can also sell you the *Tourist Pass Middelburg* (ƒ6.50), a booklet which offers information and discounts on museums and boat tours. It's best to calculate first if you're going to use it enough to make any great savings.

Finally, open-top **boats** offer trips on the canals, leaving from the Lange Viele bridge on Achter de Houttuinen (mid-May to mid-Sept Mon–Sat 10am–5pm, Sun noon–4pm; April & Oct Mon–Sat 11am–4pm; ƒ9); the return boat trip to Veere (May–Sept daily departing 10.15am and 2pm; ƒ19.50) leaves from near the train station.

Eating and drinking

Vlasmarkt, running northwest of Markt, has an array of food stuffs, as well as Middelburg's widest selection of **restaurants**, from *La Lupa* at the bottom end of the street which offers cheap pizzas, to *De Mug*, Vlasmarkt 56, with good Dutch–French cooking at moderate prices, an excellent array of beers, and occasional live jazz. A little pricier but still good value, *No 7*, east of Damplein at Rotterdamsekai 7, and *de Cameel*, by the canal at Kinderdijk 82, both have fabulous local food. If your budget is tight, there are a couple of decent shoarma joints in town: *De Nyl*, at St Janstraat 45 and *Cleopatra* at Vlasmarkt 2. Most other restaurants are situated on or around Markt and many are tourist-orientated and pricey for what you get. Elsewhere in town, *Surabaya*, Stationstraat 20, is an Indonesian restaurant with reasonably priced *rijsttafels*. On Thursdays the market stands supply limitless cheap and tasty snacks, especially fresh fishy things.

Bars and cafés are also concentrated on or near the Markt; *De Bommel* is the pick of the bars here, although there's not much to choose between them at the weekends. At the bottom of Vlasmarkt, *Rooie Oortjes* and the popular 't Hof (down the tiny alley) are both excellent and the latter gets occasional live bands. Damplein is another good stretch for drinking: *Rockdesert* at no. 20 is young and raucous while *De Geer*, Lange Viele 55, has the cheapest beer in town.

Listings

Carillon concerts The carillon at Lange Jan plays every 15min and there are year-round concerts Thurs noon–1pm; May to mid-Sept additional concerts Sat 11am–noon; May also Thurs 7–7.30pm; July & Aug also Thurs 7.30–8.30pm.

Cycling Bike rental from the station or Delta Cycle on the Markt (☎0118/639245). If you intend to cycle around, get hold of a copy of the yellow *Zuid-Holland Fietskaart* from the VVV (see p.302) or any bookshop/newsagent; the VVV also sells detailed maps of Walcheren and Zeeland and a book of twenty cycle routes in the region, *Fietsen in Zeeland.*

Internet Access At the Bibliotheek, Kousteensedijk 7 (Mon 5.30–9pm, Tues–Fri 10am–9pm, Sat 10am–1pm; ☎0118/654000).

Markets General market on the Markt Thurs 8.30am–4pm; flower and produce market Sat 8.30am–4pm. Vismarkt has a flea market on the first Sat of the month (except Jan) 9am–4pm; and an antique and curio market from June to Aug Thurs 9am–4pm.

Police Achter de Houttuinen 10 (☎0118/688000).

Post office Lange Noordstraat 48 (Mon 10am–6pm, Tues–Fri 9am–6pm, Thurs till 7pm, Sat 10am–1.30pm).

Ring tilting *Ringrijderij*, a horseback competition where riders try to pick off rings with lances, takes place in August at the Koepoort city gate near Molenwater and in Middelburg's Abbey Square on one day in July, 9am–4pm. Check with the VVV (see p.302) for dates.

Taxi Taxicentrale, ☎0118/612600 or 613200.

The Zeeland coast

The coastline west of Middelburg offers some of the country's finest beaches as well as good walking and cycling country, although on midsummer weekends parts of it virtually disappear beneath the crowds of Dutch and German holiday-makers. Bus #53 from Middelburg station (hourly) runs through **Oostkapelle**, notable for its striking church tower (July–Aug Tues & Fri 7–8pm; *f*1.50), before passing the thirteenth-century Castle Westhove, now a hostel. Next door, the *Zeeuws Biologisch Museum* (April, May, Sept & Oct Sun & Tues–Fri 10am–5pm, Sat & Mon noon–5pm; June–Aug daily 10am–6pm; Nov–March Tues–Sun noon–5pm; *f*8.50) has an aquarium and displays on local flora and fauna.

A couple of kilometres further on, **Domburg**, 14km from Middelburg, is the area's principal resort, a favourite haunt for artists since early last century when Jan Toorop gathered together a group of like-minded painters (including, for a while, Piet Mondrian), inspired by the peaceful scenery and the fine quality of the light. Toorop built a pavilion to exhibit the paintings and the building has been recreated as the **Museum Domburg** (April–Nov Tues–Sun 1–5pm; *f*6) on Ooststraat 10a, near its original location, where revolving exhibitions continue to display works by members of the group. Parts of the Domburg church, including the tower, date from the thirteenth century, although it's off-limits to visitors at present. On the whole, though, you're here to walk on the dunes and through the woods or to cycle the coastpath. An easy seven-kilometre ride west of Domburg is **Westkapelle**, a quieter beach resort with a picturesque lighthouse and a critical spot where the dyke was breached during the 1953 flood.

Practicalities

Domburg's **VVV** is at Schuitvlotstraat 32 (Mon–Fri 9.30am–6pm, Sat 9.30am–6pm, Sun 1–5pm; ☎0118/581342, *vvv@kust-walcheren.nl*); ask the bus driver to drop you nearby. They'll help with accommodation and provide you with a map of the village. The cheapest **hotel** is *De Brouwerij*, Brouwerijweg 6 (☎0118/581285; ①), and the place has dozens of **pensions** starting at around *f*30 per person – *Duinliust* is a safe bet at Badhuisweg 28 (☎0118/582970; ①). The **HI hostel** is at Kasteel Westhove (☎0118/581254, fax 583342; April–Oct; *f*31), a couple of kilometres towards Middelburg on bus #53, and there are several **campsites**, the nearest being *Hof Domburg* at Schelpveg 7 (☎0118/588200, fax 583668; April–Oct), a few minutes' walk west of town. There are plenty of **cafés** to choose from, though don't expect haute cuisine; for something a little different try the great pizzas at *Pizzeria Milano* on Ooststraat. For drinking, *Tramzicht* and *Panache*, both on Stationstraat, are your best bet.

The other resorts also have plenty of pensions and campsites, although you may need to book rooms through one of the VVVs in busy times. The VVV in **Oostkapelle** is at Duinweg 2a (April–Oct Mon–Sat 9am–5pm, July & Aug till 6pm; Nov–March Mon–Fri 9am–5pm, Sat 10am–2pm; ☎0118/582910), while in Westkapelle it is at Markt 69a (same times as Oostkapelle VVV; ☎0118/571281).

Veere

Eight kilometres northeast of Middelburg, **VEERE** is a resolutely picturesque little town by the banks of the Veerse Meer. Today it's a centre for all things maritime, its small harbour jammed with yachts and its cafés packed with weekend
admirals: but a handful of buildings and a large church point to a time when Veere
was rich and quite independent of other, similar towns in Zeeland.

Veere made its wealth through a fortuitous Scottish connection: in 1444 Wolfert
VI van Borssele, the lord of Veere, married Mary, daughter of James I of Scotland.
As part of the dowry, van Borssele was granted a monopoly on trade with Scottish
wool merchants; in return, Scottish merchants living in Veere were granted special privileges. A number of their houses still stand, best of which are those on the
dock facing the harbour: *Het Lammetje* (The Lamb) and *De Struys* (The Ostrich),
dating from the mid-sixteenth century, were combined offices, homes and warehouses for the merchants; they now house the **Museum Schotse Huizen**
(April–Oct Mon–Fri noon–5pm, Sun 1–5pm; *f*5), a rather lifeless collection of
local costumes, old books, atlases and furniture, along with an exhibit devoted to
fishing. Elsewhere there are plenty of Gothic buildings, whose rich decoration
leaves you in no doubt that the Scottish wool trade earned a bundle for the six-
teenth- and seventeenth-century burghers of Veere: many of the buildings (which
are usually step-gabled with distinctive green and white shutters) are embellished
with whimsical details that play on the owners' names or their particular line of
business. The **Stadhuis** at Markt 5 (by arrangement; ☎0118/501253) is similarly
opulent, dating from the 1470s with an out-of-scale, boastful Renaissance tower
added a century later. Its facade is decorated with statues of the lords of Veere and
their wives (Wolfert VI is third from the left), and, inside, a small museum occupies what was formerly the courtroom, pride of place going to a goblet that once
belonged to Maximilian of Burgundy.

Of all Veere's buildings the **Grote Kerk** (April–Oct Mon–Sat 10am–5pm, Sun
1–5pm; *f*5) seems to have suffered most: finished in 1560, it was badly damaged
by fire a century later and restoration removed much of its decoration. In 1808
invading British troops used the church as a hospital and three years later
Napoleon's army converted it into barracks and stables, destroying the stained
glass, bricking up the windows and adding five floors in the nave. Despite all this
damage, the church's blunt 42-metre **tower** (same hours and ticket as church; last
admission 4.30pm) adds a glowering presence to the landscape, especially when
seen across the misty polder fields. According to the original design, the tower
was to have been three times higher, but even as it stands there's a great view
from the top, back to the pinnacled skyline of Middelburg and out across the
breezy Veerse Meer.

Veere fell from importance with the decline of the wool trade. The opening of
the Walcheren Canal in the nineteenth century, linking the town to Middelburg
and Vlissingen, gave it a stay of execution, but the construction of the
Veersegatdam and Zandkreekdam in the 1950s finally sealed the port to seagoing
vessels, and simultaneously created a freshwater lake ideal for watersports. The
VVV office, Oudestraat 28 (July & Aug Mon–Wed, Fri, Sat 10am–5pm, Thurs &
Sun 1–5pm; Sept Mon–Sat 1–5pm; ☎0118/501365), can advise on the rental of all
types of watercraft and has details of **private rooms**. If you prefer to organize
your own accommodation, the cheaper of Veere's two **hotels** is *'t Waepen van*

Veere at Markt 23–27 (☎0118/501231; ②) while the *De Campveerse Toren*, Kade 2, is just slightly more expensive (☎0118/501291, fax 501695; ②). To reach Veere from Middelburg, catch bus #53 (Mon–Sat hourly, Sun every 2hr), or rent a bike from Middelburg train station and take either the main road or the circuitous but picturesque routes from the north of the town.

The Delta Project – and the Delta Expo

On February 1, 1953, a combination of an exceptionally high spring tide and powerful northwesterly winds drove the North Sea over the dykes to flood much of Zeeland. The results were catastrophic: 1855 people drowned, 47,000 homes and 500km of dykes were destroyed and some of the country's most fertile agricultural land was ruined by salt water. Towns as far west as Bergen-op-Zoom and Dordrecht were flooded and Zeeland's road and rail network was wrecked. The government's response was immediate and on a massive scale. After patching up the breached dykes, work was begun on the **Delta Project**, one of the largest engineering schemes the world has ever seen and one of phenomenal complexity and expense.

The plan was to ensure the safety of Zeeland by radically shortening and strengthening its coastline. The major estuaries and inlets would be dammed, thus preventing unusually high tides surging inland to breach the thousands of kilometres of small dykes. Where it was impractical to build a dam – such as across the Westerschelde or Nieuwe Waterweg, which would have closed the seaports of Antwerp and Rotterdam respectively – secondary dykes were to be reinforced. New roads across the top of the dams would improve communications to Zeeland and South Holland and the freshwater lakes that formed behind the dams would enable precise control of the water table of the Zeeland islands.

It took thirty years for the Delta Project to be completed. The smaller, secondary dams – the Veersegat, Haringvliet and Brouwershaven – were built first to provide protection from high tides as quickly as possible, a process that also enabled engineers to learn as they went along. In 1968, work began on the largest dam, intended to close the **Oosterschelde** estuary that forms the outlet of the Maas, Waal and Rijn rivers. It soon ran into intense opposition from environmental groups, who pointed out that the mud flats were an important breeding ground for birds, while the estuary itself was a nursery for plaice, sole and other North Sea fish. Local fishermen too, saw their livelihoods in danger: if the Oosterschelde were closed the oyster, mussel and lobster beds would be destroyed, representing a huge loss to the region's economy.

The environmental and fishing lobbies argued that strengthening the estuary dykes would provide adequate protection; the water board and agricultural groups raised the emotive spectre of the 1953 flood. In the end a compromise was reached, and in 1976 work began on the **Storm Surge Barrier**, a gate that would stay open under normal tidal conditions, allowing water to flow in and out of the estuary, but close ahead of potentially destructive high tides.

The Delta Expo

It's on this barrier, completed in 1986, that the fascinating **Delta Expo** (April–Oct daily 10am–5.30pm; ƒ21.50; Nov–March Wed–Sun 10am–5pm; ƒ14.50) is housed. In spring and summer admission includes a boat trip for a close look at the huge computer-controlled sluice gates. Only once you're inside the Expo itself, though, do you get an idea of the scale of the project. It's best to start with the video presentation before taking in the exhibition itself, which is divided into three areas: the historical background of Holland's water management problems; the technological developments that enabled the country to protect itself; the environmental consequences of applying the technologies and the solutions that followed. The Surge Barrier (and the Delta Project as a whole) has been a triumphant success: computer simulations predict most high tides, but if an unpredicted rise does occur, the sluice gates close automatically in a matter of minutes. On average, a dangerously high tide occurs once every eighteen months.

Reaching the Delta Expo is easy: from Middelburg take the hourly #104 bus from Hof van Tange on the west side of town (10min walk from the VVV near the Kloveniersdoelen building) or allow ninety minutes to cycle; from Rotterdam, take the metro to Spijkenisse and then bus #104; tell the driver you want the Waterland stop.

Brouwershaven and Zierikzee

The Storm Surge Barrier stretches across to the "island" of **Schouwen-Duiveland**. Most of the Dutch tourists who come here head directly west for the vast expanse acres of beach and dune between **HAAMSTEDE** and **RENESSE**, themselves pretty villages but with only the **Slot Moermond** (details of tours of garden from Renesse VVV; mid-June to mid-Aug; ☎0111/460360), a castle built for the local lords just north of Renesse, worth breaking your journey for. You can get to Renesse from Middelburg by bus #104 and from Renesse to **BROUWER-SHAVEN**, in the middle of Schouwen-Duiveland's northern coast, by bus #134, which runs hourly. Until the building of the Nieuwe Waterweg linked Rotterdam to the coast, Brouwershaven was a busy seaport, with boats able to sail right into the centre of town. Other than the pretty gabled houses flanking the harbour and a few narrow streets around the Markt, the **Stadhuis** is the single thing to see, an attractive Flemish Renaissance building of 1599.

Schouwen-Duiveland's most interesting town, though, lies to the south. **ZIERIKZEE**'s position at the intersection of shipping routes between England, Flanders and Holland led to it becoming an important port in the late Middle Ages. It was also famed for its salt and madder – a root that, when dried and ground, produces a brilliant red dye.

Encircled by a defensive canal and preferably entered by one of two sixteenth-century watergates, Zierikzee's centre is small and easily explored, easier still if you arm yourself with a map from the **VVV** at Meelstraat 4 (May–Sept Mon–Fri 9am–5pm, Sat 9am–3pm; Oct–April Mon–Fri 10am–5pm, Sat 10am–1pm; ☎0111/412450). A few minutes' walk from the office, the Gothic **'s Gravensteen** building at Mol 25 (April–Oct Mon–Sat 10am–5pm, Sun noon–5pm; ƒ3.50) was once the jail and is today home to a maritime museum. However, the building is far more interesting than the exhibits: the old cells from the prison are pretty authentic and the removal of plaster walls in 1969 uncovered graffiti and drawings by the prisoners. The basements contain torture chambers and iron cage cells built to contain two prisoners.

Zierikzee's **Stadhuis** is easy enough to find – just head for the tall, fussy spire on Meelstraat 6. Inside, the **Gemeentemuseum** (May–Oct Mon–Fri 10am–5pm;

*f*2) has collections of silver, costumes and a regional history exhibition. Also worth seeing is the **Monstertoren** (April to mid-Sept Mon–Sat 11am–4pm, Sun noon–4pm; *f*2), a tower designed by the Keldermans family on which work was stopped when it reached 97 of its planned 167 metres.

If you need to **stay over**, the VVV has details of **private rooms**; alternatives include the *Pension Beddegoed*, Meelstraat 53 (☎0111/415935, fax 415132; ②), the slightly more expensive *Hotel Monique* at Driekoningenlaan 5 (☎0111/412323; ②), and the *Hotel Van Oppen China Garden*, Verrenieuwstraat 11 (☎0111/412288, fax 417202; ②). Heading to or from Goes from Zierikzee on bus #10 you'll pass over the **Zeelandbrug**, a graceful bridge across the Oosterschelde that, at 5022m, is the longest in Europe.

NORTH BRABANT

North Brabant, Holland's largest province, stretches from the North Sea to the German border. Originally, it was part of the independent Duchy of Brabant, which was taken over by the Spanish, and, eventually, split in two when its northern towns joined the revolt against Spain. This northern part was ceded to the United Provinces under the terms of the 1648 Treaty of Munster; the southern part formed what today are the Belgian provinces of Brabant and Antwerp.

The **Catholic influence** is still strong in North Brabant: it takes its religious festivals seriously and if you're here in March the boozy **carnivals** (especially in the province's capital, **'s Hertogenbosch**) are well worth catching – indeed, it's difficult to miss them. Geographically, woodland and heath form most of the natural scenery, the gently undulating arable land a welcome change in a country whose landscape is ruthlessly featureless.

Bergen-op-Zoom

BERGEN-OP-ZOOM is an untidy town, a jumble of buildings old and new that are the consequence of being shunted between various European powers from the sixteenth century onwards. In 1576 Bergen-op-Zoom sided with the United Provinces against the Spanish and as a result was under near-continuous siege until 1622. The French bombarded the city in 1747 and took it again in 1795, though it managed to withstand a British attack in 1814.

The Town

Walk straight out of the train station and you'll soon find yourself on the **Grote Markt**, an insalubrious square-cum-car park, most cheerful during summer when it's decked out with open-air cafés and the like. The **Stadhuis**, on the north side of the square (by appointment only May–Sept Tues–Sat 1–4.30pm; *f*2), is Bergen's most attractive building, spruced up in recent years and comprising three separate houses: to the left of the gateway an alderman's house of 1397, to the right a merchant's house of 1480 and on the far right a building known as "De Olifant" whose facade dates from 1611. All of this is a lot more appealing than the blunt ugliness of the **Grote Kerk**, a uniquely unlucky building that's been destroyed by siege, fire and neglect innumerable times over the last four hundred years.

CARNIVAL IN BERGEN-OP-ZOOM

In February each year Bergen-op-Zoom hosts one of southern Holland's most vibrant **carnivals**, with virtually every inhabitant joining in its Tuesday procession. It's a great time to be in the town if you can manage it, although you shouldn't expect to find any accommodation – the town gets packed; just do as the locals do and party all night. Contact the VVV for the exact dates.

To the left of the Stadhuis, Fortuinstraat leads to the **Markiezenhof Museum**, Steenbergsestraat 8 (April–Sept Tues–Sun 11am–5pm; Oct–March Tues–Sun 2–5pm; *f*5), a first-rate presentation of an above-average collection that has a little of everything: domestic utensils and samplers from the sixteenth century onward, sumptuous period rooms, architectural drawings, pottery and galleries of modern art. All this is housed in a palace built by Anthonis Keldermans between 1485 and 1522 to a late Gothic style that gives it the feel of an Oxford college. Before reaching the Markiezenhof's main entrance on Steenbergsestraat, you pass the **Zimmer Frei** (Tues–Sun 2–5pm), an exhibition space for twentieth-century artists, worth dropping in on if you're interested in what's on show.

Of the rest of old Bergen-op-Zoom little remains: at the end of Lievevrouwestraat, near the entrance to the Markiezenhof, the **Gevangenpoort** is practically all that's left of the old city defences, a solid-looking fourteenth-century gatehouse that was later converted to a prison.

Practicalities

Outside Carnaval, it's hard to imagine why you'd want to stay over in Bergen, but if you do, the **VVV**, at Stationsstraat 4 (Mon noon–5.30pm, Tues–Fri 9am–5.30pm, Sat 10am–5pm; ☎0900/202 0336, *postbus@vvv-boz.demon.nl*) has details of **private rooms**, along with a map of the centre. The cheapest **hotel** is *De Lantaarn*, Bredasestraat 8 (☎0164/236488, fax 246879; ②) while the **HI hostel**, *Klavervelden,* (April–Oct; *f*27.75) is 4km out of town at Boslustweg 1; take bus #21 or #22 from the station (Ziekenhuis) and it's a ten minute walk from the Lievensberg stop. There are a variety of **restaurants** grouped around the Grote Markt and, while the town's **drinking scene** is not exactly buzzing, *Kunst-en Proeflokaal de Hemel* is a lively spot at Moeregrebstraat 35, just off Steenbergsestraat.

Breda

Though it doesn't boast an awful lot to see, **BREDA**, the prettiest town of North Brabant, is a pleasant, easy-going place. The centre is compact and eminently strollable, with a magnificent church, a reasonable art gallery and a new cultural centre; there's a range of well-priced accommodation, inexpensive restaurants and lively bars; and it's a good springboard for exploring central North Brabant. In short, it's a fine target, whether you're visiting for the day or looking for a base from which to branch out to Zeeland, Dordrecht, 's Hertogenbosch or even Antwerp.

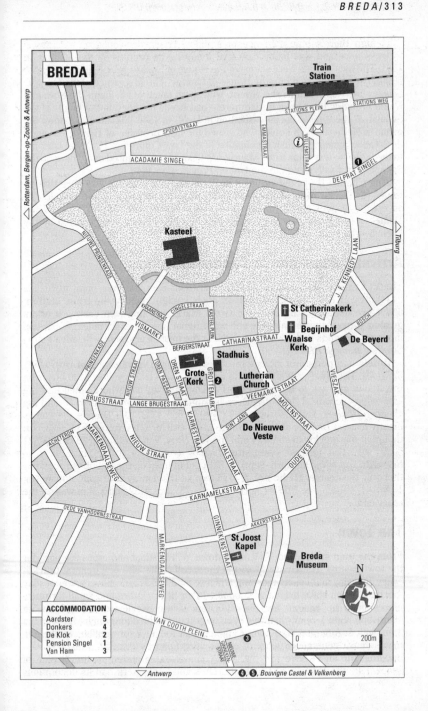

BREDA

Train Station

Rotterdam, Bergen-op-Zoom & Antwerp

STATIONS PLEIN

STATIONS WEG

SPOORSTRAAT

EMMASTRAAT

WILLEMSTRAAT

ACADAMIE SINGEL

DELPRAT SINGEL

❶

Tilburg

J. F KENNEDY LAAN

Kasteel

NIEUWE PRINSENKADE

KRAANSTRAAT

CINGELSTRAAT

KASTEEL PLEIN

✝ **St Catherinakerk**

BOSCH

VISMARKT

BERGERSTRAAT

CATHARINASTRAAT

✝ **Begijnhof**

Waalse Kerk

■ **De Beyerd**

PRINSENKADE

NIEUW STRAAT

TOREN STRAAT

DREN STRAAT

Stadhuis

GROTTEMARKT

VIESZAK

TOREN PASSAGE

Grote Kerk

❷

Lutherian Church

VEEMARKTSTRAAT

MOLENSTRAAT

BRUGSTRAAT

LANGE BRUGESTRAAT

KARRESTRAAT

SINT JANS

De Nieuwe Veste

ACHTEROM

MARKENDAALSEWEG

NIEUW STRAAT

HALSTRAAT

OUDE VEST

OEDE VANHOORNESTRAAT

KARNAMELKSTRAAT

AKKERSTRAAT

MARKENDAALSEWEG

GINNEKENSTRAAT

St Joost Kapel

■ **Breda Museum**

N

VAN COOTH PLEIN

NIEUWE GINNEKEN STRAAT

❸

0   200m

▽ *Antwerp*   ▽ **❹, ❺**, *Bouvigne Castel & Valkenberg*

Though there's little evidence of it today, Breda developed as a strategic fortress town and was badly damaged following its capture by the Spanish in 1581. The local counts were scions of the House of Nassau, which in the early sixteenth century married into the House of Orange. The first prince of the Orange-Nassau line was **William the Silent**, who spent much of his life in the town and would probably have been buried here – had Breda not been in the hands of the Spanish at the time of his assassination in Delft. In 1566 William was among the group of Netherlandish nobles who issued the **Compromise of Breda** – an early declaration against Spanish domination of the Low Countries. The town later fell to the Spanish, was retaken by Maurice, William's son, captured once more by the Spanish, but finally ceded to the United Provinces in 1648.

King Charles II of England lived in the town for a while (it was here that he issued his **Declaration of Breda** in 1660, the terms by which he was prepared to accept the throne), as did (though less reliable historically) Oliver Cromwell and Daniel Defoe. Breda was last fought over in 1793, when it was captured by the French, who hung on to it until 1813.

Arrival, information and accommodation

The **VVV** office, Willemstraat 17 (Mon–Fri 9am–6pm, Sat 9am–5pm; ☎076/522 2444, fax 521 8530, *vvv@bredadigitaal.nl*) is straight outside the **train station**, about five minutes' walk from the Grote Markt and the town centre. It offers **guided tours** between mid-July and mid-August (ask for exact times; *f*7.50) taking in the grounds of the Kasteel as well as the town; it also sells a detailed guide, *Strolling through Breda* (*f*3.50).

Hotels and **pensions** include the *Pension Singel,* Delpratsingel 14 (☎076/521 6271; ①). The others are all too far to reach on foot – take a yellow #130 bus from the station and ask to be dropped off at Duivelsbruglaan, where you'll find the somewhat overpriced *Aard ster*, Duivelsbruglaan 92 (☎076/565 1666; ③) and the cheaper *Donkers*, Duivelsbruglaan 72 (☎076/565 4332; ①). There's the conveniently located *De Klok* at Grote Markt 26–28 (☎076/521 4082, fax 514 3463; ②), though it fills quickly in summer and the *Van Ham*, Van Coothplein 23 (☎076/521 5229; ②). The nearest **campsite**, *Liesbos* (☎076/514 3514, fax 514 6555, *liesbos@worldonline.nl*; April–Sept), is 8km out of town on the #111 bus route; further still, the nearest **HI hostel**, *H et Putven*, is 15km away at Chaam, Putvenweg 1 (☎0161/491323, fax 491756; April–Oct; *f*27.75); bus #132 and a 3km walk at the other end.

The Town

From the train station and VVV, head down Willemstraat and cross the park for the town centre. The **Grote Markt** is the focus of life, site of a general **market** every Tuesday and Friday morning and a second-hand market every Wednesday morning, when stalls loaded with books, bric-a-brac, clothes and small furniture pieces push up against the pocket-Gothic **Grote Kerk** (May–Oct Mon–Sat 10am–5pm, Sun 1–5pm; *f*3; tower open as part of a guided tour only: May–Oct Sat 3pm, July & Aug also Wed 3pm; *f*3.50; contact the VVV for details), whose intimate interior generates a sense of awe you don't usually associate with so small a building, the short nave and high, spacious crossing adding to the illusion of space. Like the majority of Dutch churches, the Grote Kerk had its decorations either removed or obscured after the Reformation, but a few murals have been uncovered and reveal just how colourful the church once was. At the end of the south aisle there's a huge *St Christopher* and other decorations in the south transept embellish the walls and roof bosses. The Grote Kerk's most remarkable feature, though, is the **Mausoleum of Count Engelbrecht II**, a Stadholder and Captain-General of the Netherlands who died in 1504 of tuberculosis – vividly apparent in the drawn features of his intensely realistic face. Four kneeling figures (Caesar, Regulus, Hannibal and Philip of Macedonia) support a canopy that carries his armour, so skilfully sculpted that their shoulders sag slightly under the weight. It's believed that the mausoleum was the work of Tomaso Vincidor of Bologna, but whoever created it imbued the mausoleum with grandeur without resorting to flamboyance: the result is both eerily realistic and oddly moving. During the French occupation the choir was used as a stable, but fortunately the sixteenth-century misericords, showing rustic everyday scenes, survived. A couple of the carvings are modern replacements – as you'll guess from their subject matter.

At the top of Kasteelplein sits the **Kasteel**: too formal to be forbidding and considerably rebuilt since the Compromise of Breda was signed here in 1566. Twenty-five years later the Spanish captured Breda, but it was regained in 1590 thanks to a neat trick by Maurice of Nassau's troops: the Spanish garrison was regularly supplied by barge with peat, so, using the Trojan Horse strategy, seventy troops under Maurice's command hid beneath the peat on the barge and were towed into the castle, jumping out to surprise the Spanish and regain the town. The Spanjaardsgat, an early sixteenth-century watergate with twin defensive bastions that's just west of the Kasteel, is usually (but inaccurately) identified as the spot where this happened. Today the Kasteel is a military academy and there's no admission to its grounds, unless you join one of the VVV tours.

To the east of Kasteelplein on Catherinastraat, the **Begijnhof**, built in 1531, was until quite recently the only *hofje* in Holland still occupied by Beguines. Today it has been given over to elderly women, some of whom look after the dainty nineteenth-century chapel at the rear, the St Catherinakerk, and tend the herb garden that was laid out several hundred years ago. To the right of the Begijnhof entrance, incidentally, is the **Walloon Church**, where Peter Stuyvesant, governor of New York during the 1600s when that city was a Dutch colony, was married.

Catherinastraat, which is lined with stately houses from the seventeenth century, twists around to **De Beyerd**, Boschstraat 22 (Tues–Fri 10am–5pm, Sat & Sun 1–5pm; *f*6), a gallery with changing exhibitions of contemporary art housed in what was once a lunatic asylum. Back in town, **de Nieuwe Veste** is a lively cultural centre at St Janstraat 18; the converted building dates from 1534 and offers regular theatre and concerts, as well as a chance to catch some local art-in-progress during the day. Finally, the **Breda Museum**, at Parade 12 near Oude Vest (Tues–Sun 10am–5pm; *f*5) holds a forgettable collection of ecclesiastical art and oddments, along with exhibits concerning Breda's history.

Eating and drinking

Breda has a decent range of places to **eat**. For cheap, central food, *Da Attilio* is a pizzeria at Grote Markt 35, *Willy's Pizza* on Halstraat is handy for snacks, and *Café de Boulevard* at Grote Markt 10 has a variety of dishes. Less pricey is the popular

Beecker & Wetselaar by the Grote Kerk. Elsewhere, the *Maharajah of India*, Havermarkt 25, has reasonably priced curries, while *Pols*, Halstraat 15, is a small and excellent *eetcafé*. For down-to-earth **drinking**, try *De Groene Sael*, Havermarkt 8, an unpretentious bar serving draft Palm beer and with a small dance floor at the back; *Nickelodeon*, Halstraat 2, is a more upmarket affair, with a swish interior. Connoisseurs of Low Countries beer generally make for *De Beyerd*, Boschstraat 26 while, back in the centre, *Café de Bommel* at Halstraat 3 is a large and lively café-bar with a mix of customers. *De Graanbeurs*, Reigerstraat 20, is a late night disco and bar.

Tilburg

TILBURG is a faceless and unwelcoming industrial town, its streets a maze of nineteenth-century houses and anonymous modern shopping precincts. If you're passing through there are four decent museums within easy walking distance of the train station although, if that's as far as you get into town, you haven't missed much.

Tilburg developed as a textile town, though today most of its mills have closed in the face of cheap competition from India and southeast Asia. The **Nederlands Textielmuseum**, housed in an old mill at Goirkestraat 96 (out of the station, walk west along Spoorlaan, turn right along Gasthuisring and Goirkestraat is the fourth turn on the right; Tues–Fri 10am–5pm, Sat & Sun noon–5pm; *f*7.50), displays aspects of the industry relating to design and textile arts, with a collection of textile designs by Dutch artists and demonstrations of weaving and spinning, as well as a range of looms and weaving machines from around the world. The shiny new **Scryption**, Spoorlaan 434a (Tues–Fri 10am–5pm, Sat & Sun 1–5pm; *f*6), is a fancy name for a collection of writing implements – everything from lumps of chalk to word processors. Particularly interesting are the old, intricate typewriters, some of which you can operate yourself. Next door, the **Noordbrabants Natuurmuseum** (Tues–Fri 10am–5pm, Sat & Sun 1–5pm; *f*7) is basically a load of dead animals and (live) creepy crawlies. The **De Pont** modern art museum (Tues–Sun 11am–5pm; *f*5) is behind the station at Wilheminapark 1.

The **VVV** office is at Stadhuisplein 128 (Mon–Fri 9am–5.30pm, Sat 10am–4pm; ☎013/535 1135, fax 535 3795, *vvvtilb@tref.nl*), ten minutes' walk from the station – cross the main road and keep straight ahead. You'll need their town map to have any chance of finding the **Poppenmuseum** at Telefoonstraat 13–15 (daily 2–4pm; *f*6), a small private collection of dolls. There's little reason to **stay** in Tilburg, but, for the record, the least expensive room in town is at the *Het Wapen van Tilburg* hotel, Spoorlaan 362 (☎013/542 2692; ②). There are several good **cafés** around Korte Heuvel/Piusplein. For **Internet access**, try *Cybergate*, a café at Fabriekstraat 22 (☎013/542 0604), or the Bibliotheek, a short distance across the road from the VVV at Koningsplein 10 (Mon–Wed 11am–8pm, Thurs 11am–9pm, Fri & Sat 10am–5pm).

Around Tilburg: De Efteling

Hidden in the woods fifteen minutes' drive north of Tilburg, the **De Efteling** theme park (April–Oct daily 10am–6pm, July & Aug till 10pm; *f*37.50) is one of the country's principal attractions. Inevitably, the place can't quite match Disney, but it has some excellent rides and, if the weather is reasonable, makes for a great day out, although on summer weekends the queues can be daunting.

The place is attractively landscaped and, especially in spring when the tulips are out, delightful to walk around. Of the rides, *Python* is the most hair-raising, a rollercoaster twister with great views of the park before plunging down the track; *De Bob*, a recreation bob-sleigh run, is almost as exhilarating although over far too quickly, especially if you've queued for ages. *Piranha* takes you through some gentle white-water rapids (expect to get wet). Of the quieter moments, *Villa Volta* is a slightly unsettling room that revolves around you – and just about worth enduring the lengthy introduction in Dutch. For kids, the *Fairy-Tale Wood*, where the park began – a hop from Gingerbread House to Troll King to Cinderella Castle – is still popular. *Carnaval Festival* and *Droomvlucht* are the best of the rides, and there are afternoon shows in the Efteling Theatre. In addition, there are a number of fairground attractions, canoes and paddle-boats, and a great view over the whole shebang and the surrounding woods from the *Pagoda*. A sedate way to check whether you've missed anything is to take the steam train around the park. If you're not up to doing it all, skip the disappointing *Haunted Castle* and the *Fata Morgana*, with its faintly disturbing trawl through a bunch of Moroccan stereotypes.

Practicalities

If you are coming to De Efteling by **train** it is worth buying a *Rail Idee* ticket, which combines the price of the train ticket, the connecting bus service and entry to the park. Bus #136 and #137 run to De Efteling every thirty minutes from Tilburg (15min), and from Den Bosch (40min); in summer, the direct services #182 from Tilburg and #181 from Den Bosch are slightly faster. If you are driving, the park is well-signposted just off the A261 between Tilburg and Waalwijk; parking costs *f*7.50. Though there's little need to **stay**, if you're eager for another day's fun, the *Efteling Hotel* is right by the park (☎0416/282000, fax 281515; ④). There are plenty of **maps** posted around the park, and snack-bars and refreshment stops at every turn.

's Hertogenbosch (Den Bosch)

Capital of North Brabant, **'S HERTOGENBOSCH** is officially known as **Den Bosch**, the name deriving from the words "the Count's Woods" after the hunting lodge established here by Henry I, Duke of Brabant, in the twelfth century. Hieronymous Bosch lived here all his life, but as the town has only two paintings doubtfully attributed to him, the main draws are its cathedral, a number of museums and, not least, an enjoyable nightlife. Consider staying over for a couple of days.

Arrival, information and accommodation

Den Bosch's centre is fifteen minutes' walk from the **train station**. Stop by the VVV office, Markt 77 (Mon 11am–5.30pm, Tues–Fri 9am–5.30pm, Sat 9am–4pm; ☎0900/112 2334 at 75c per min) to pick up a copy of the useful *Wandering around Old Den Bosch* leaflet. The VVV also offers walking tours (*f*3.50).

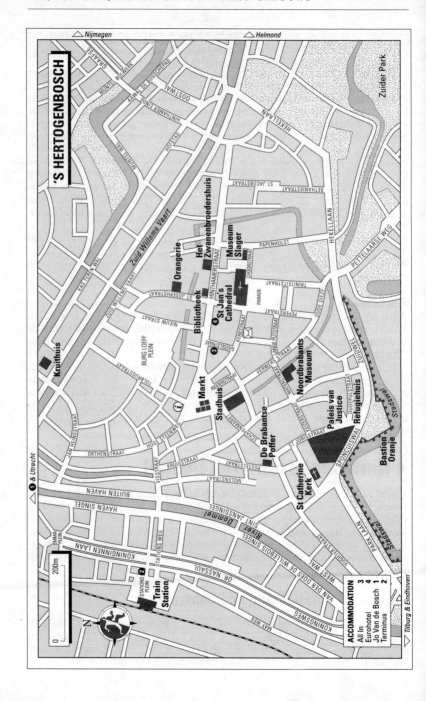

There are three budget **hotels**: most convenient is the *Terminus* at Stationsplein 19 (☎073/613 0666, fax 613 0726; ②); the *Jo van de Bosch*, Boschdijkstraat 39a (☎073/613 8205; ②) is slightly cheaper; and there's the seedy but friendly *All In* (☎073/613 4057; ②), just down the street at Gasselstraat 1, on the corner of Hinthamerpromenade. A little pricier but more central, *Eurohotel* is at Hinthamerstraat 63 (☎073/613 7777, fax 612 8795; ③).

If you want to see a lot of the town, but want to save your legs, there are **boat trips** along the city moat. You've a choice between plying along in a traditional open boat (May–Oct Mon hourly 2–5pm, Tues–Sun hourly 11am–5pm; ☎0900/202 0178 at 75c per min for the necessary reservation; ƒ8.50) from Van Molenstraat (next to *Café van Puffelen*); or a closed boat (May–Sept daily 11am, 12.30pm, 2pm & 3.30pm, ƒ8.50) from St Janssingel near the Wilhelmina bridge, which also takes in the River Dommel and nearby Ertveld Lake. Contact *Rederij Wolthuis*, Sint Lambertusstraat 19 (☎073/631 2048) for information and reservations.

The Town

If you were to draw a picture of the archetypal Dutch Markt it would probably look like the one in Den Bosch. It's broad and cobbled, home to the province's largest market on Wednesday and Saturday and is lined with typical seventeenth-century houses. The sixteenth-century **Stadhuis** (Mon–Thurs 8am–5pm, Fri 8am–noon) has a carillon that's played every Wednesday between 10 and 11am and that chimes the half-hour to the accompaniment of a group of mechanical horsemen.

From just about anywhere in the centre of town it's impossible to miss **St Jan's Cathedral** (daily 10am–5pm; restricted entrance during services). Generally regarded as the finest Gothic church in the country, it was built between 1330 and 1530 and has recently undergone a massive restoration. But if Breda's Grote Kerk is Gothic at its most intimate and exhilarating, then St Jan's is Gothic at its most gloomy, the garish stained glass – nineteenth-century or modern – only adding to the sense of dreariness that hangs over the nave. You enter beneath the oldest and least well-preserved part of the cathedral, the western **tower** (open, if you want to climb it, May–Aug; ƒ6): blunt and brick-clad, it's oddly prominent amid the wild decoration of the rest of the exterior, which includes some nasty-looking creatures scaling the roof – symbols of the forces of evil that attack the church. Inside, there's much of interest. The **Lady Chapel** near the entrance contains a thirteenth-century figure of the Madonna known as *Zoete Lieve Vrouw* (Sweet Dear Lady), famed for its miraculous powers in the Middle Ages and still much venerated today. The brass **font** in the southwest corner was the work of Alard Duhamel, a master mason who worked on the cathedral in the late fifteenth century. It's thought that the stone pinnacle, a weird twisted piece of Gothicism at the eastern end of the nave, was the sample piece that earned him the title of master mason.

Almost filling the west wall of the cathedral is an extravagant **organ case**, assembled in 1602. It was described by a Victorian authority as "certainly the finest in Holland and probably the finest in Europe. . . it would be difficult to conceive a more stately or magnificent design." Equally elaborate, though on a much smaller scale, the south transept holds the **Altar of the Passion**, a retable (a piece placed behind and above the altar to act as a kind of screen) made in Antwerp in around 1500. In the centre is a carved Crucifixion scene, flanked by Christ bearing the Cross on one side and a Lamentation on the other. Though rather difficult to make out, a series of carved scenes of the life of Christ run across the retable, made all the more charming by their attention to period (medieval) costume detail.

Though a few painted sections of the cathedral remain to show how it would have been decorated before the Reformation, most of its paintings were destroyed in the iconoclastic fury of 1566. These included several by **Hieronymus Bosch**, who lived in the town all his life: only two works by Bosch remain (in the north transept) and even their authenticity is doubtful. What is more certain is that Bosch belonged to the town's Brotherhood of Our Lady, a society devoted to the veneration of the Virgin, and that as a working artist he would have been expected to help adorn the cathedral. None of his major works remain in Den Bosch today, but there's a collection of his prints in the Noordbrabants Museum (see below).

Opposite the cathedral at Hinthamerstraat 94, the **Zwanenbroedershuis** (Fri 11am–3pm; free) has an intriguing collection of artefacts, liturgical songbooks and music scores that belonged to the Brotherhood of which Bosch was a member. Founded in 1318, there's nothing sinister about the Brotherhood: membership is open to all and its aim is to promote and popularize religious art and music.

South and east of the cathedral, the **Museum Slager**, Choorstraat 16 (Tues–Fri & Sun 2–5pm; *f*6), contains the works of three generations of the Slager family who lived in Den Bosch. The paintings of the family's doyen, P.M. Slager, such as *Veterans of Waterloo*, have the most authority, but some of the other works are competent, encompassing the major trends in European art as they came and went. Over the hundred and thirty years they have been active (the remaining Slager, Tom, lives in France) the Slager family seems to have spent most of its time painting Den Bosch – or their relatives.

A few minutes' walk southwest of the cathedral, the **Noordbrabants Museum**, Verwersstraat 41 (Tues–Fri 10am–5pm, Sat & Sun noon–5pm; *f*12.50), is housed in an eighteenth-century building that was once the seat of the provincial commissioner and has been enlarged with two new wings. The good-looking collection of local art and artefacts here is uniformly excellent and interesting – unlike many regional museums – and the downstairs galleries often hold superb temporary exhibitions of modern art. The permanent collection includes drawings and prints by Hieronymus Bosch, works by other medieval painters and assorted early torture equipment. There's also a rare *Schandhuik* or "Cloak of Infamy", a wooden cloak carved with adders and toads, symbols of unchastity. In it, women who had been unfaithful to their husbands were paraded on a cart through the city streets in the seventeenth century.

Just down the road from the museum, the **Refugiehuis** at the end of St Jorisstraat (Mon–Fri 9am–5pm), originally a sixteenth-century safe house for those persecuted for their religious beliefs, is today a commercial crafts centre. St Jorisstraat leads down to the site of the old city walls, which still marks the southern limit of Den Bosch. The **Bastion Oranje** once defended the southern section of the city walls, but, like the walls themselves, it has long gone. Still remaining is a large cannon, **De Boze Griet** (The Devil's Woman), cast in 1511 in Cologne and bearing the German inscription "Brute force I am called, Den Bosch I watch over".

For the rest, the backstreets of Den Bosch are a mass of intriguing facades and buildings. To name just one, the **Kruithuis** at Citadellelaan 7 (Tues–Sun 1–5pm; free), northwest of the centre, is an old gunpowder magazine that's been converted into an arts centre, with changing exhibitions of (mostly) contemporary art.

Eating and drinking

Den Bosch's **restaurants** can be pricey: many of those in the centre are geared to expense accounts and are poor value for money. *Da Peppone* at Kerkstraat 77 and *Taormina*, at Verwersstraat 58 are both inexpensive pizzerias. *Bagatelle*, Hinthamerstraat 29, has well-priced Dutch food, as does *Hof van Holland* at Kolperstraat 12. *De Opera*, Hinthamerstraat 115–117, offers a range of wonderful Dutch–French cooking in a relaxed setting: well worth a splurge. *Dry Hamerkens*, Hinthamerstraat 57 (closed Tues), is similarly expensive, though this is hardly surprising, given that you dine in the neatly elegant ambience of a seventeenth-century house that looks as if it's fallen out of a Vermeer. A fairly short distance from the centre of town, *Van Puffelen* at Van Molenstraat 4, is an attractive *eetcafé* above a canal with affordable *dagschotels*.

For **drinking**, it's easy enough to wander up and down Hinthamerstraat or the streets that radiate from the Markt and find somewhere convivial. *Keulse Kar*, Hinthamerstraat 101, is as good a starting point as any, a fairly conservative bar near the cathedral; the nearby *Basilique* on the corner of Torenstraat is also a decent spot. At Hinthamerstraat 97, *'t Bonte Palet* is a tiny, popular and hence often crowded bar that's good for a swift one as you're working your way along the street. Up a few notches on the trendiness scale, *Café Cordes*, Parade 4 (just southwest of the cathedral), is a stylish, aluminium-clad café-bar that brings in Den Bosch's bright young things. *Café Pavlov*, Kerkstraat 38, is also a popular meeting place for the city's youth. *De Blauwe Druif*, at the corner of Markt and Kolperstraat, is a big, boozy pub that takes off on market days and the bar at Kolperstraat 13 is a friendly place to drink and smoke dope. *Duvelke*, Verwersstraat 55, is a deftly decorated drinking den near the Noordbrabants Museum.

Finally, for **Internet access** try the Bibliotheek at Hinthamerstraat 72.

Eindhoven

You might wonder why a town the size of **EINDHOVEN** merits only a page in a guidebook; half an hour there, and a few statistics, will tell you why.

In 1890 Eindhoven's population was 4500. In 1990 it was around 197,000. What happened in between was **Philips**, the multinational electrical firm: the name of Eindhoven's benevolent dictator is everywhere – on bus stops, parks, even the stadium of the famous local football team. The town is basically an extended industrial and research plant for the company, and, save for one impressive art gallery, there's no need to come here unless business (or a football game – PSV Eindhoven, basically the Philips company team, are one of Holland's most consistently successful) forces you.

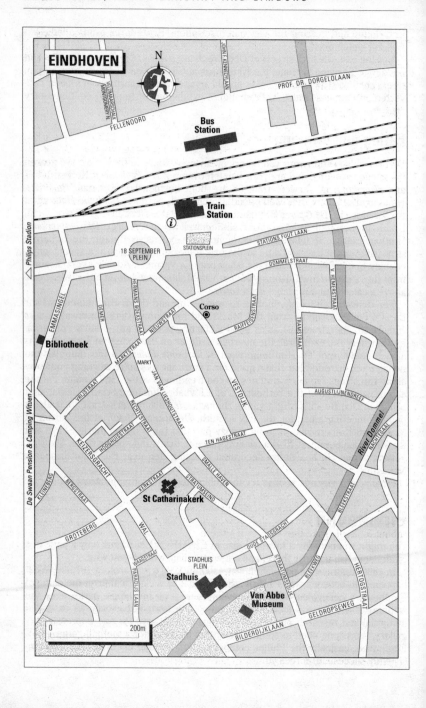

EINDHOVEN

N

VELDMAARSCHAL N
MONTGOMERY N

FELLENOORD

PROF. DR. DORGELOLAAN

JOHN F KENNEDYLAAN

Bus
Station

Train
Station

i

Philips Stadion ◁

STATIONSPLEIN

STATIONS FUUT LAAN

18 SEPTEMBER
PLEIN

DOMMELSTRAAT

V. HEMERSTRAAT

EMMASINGEL

DEMER

HERMANS BOEXSTRAAT

NIEUWSTRAAT

Corso
◉

RAIFFEISENSTRAAT

TRAMSTRAAT

Bibliotheek

MARKTSTRAAT

MARKT

JAN VAN LIESHOUTSTRAAT

VESTDIJK

AUGUSTIJNENDREEF

VRIJSTRAAT

RECHTESTRAAT

TEN HAGESTRAAT

River Dommel

NACHTEGAAL

De Swaan Pension & Camping Witven ◁

KEIZERSGRACHT

HOOGHUISSTRAAT

SMALLE HAVEN

KLEINBERG

BERGSTRAAT

KERKSTRAAT

STRATUMSEIND

St Catharinakerk ✠

BLEEKSTRAAT

GROTEBERG

WAL

OUDE STADSGRACHT

STRATUMSEDIJK

BLEEKWEG

HERTOGSTRAAT

WAAGSTRAAT

PARADIJS LAAN

STADHUIS
PLEIN

Stadhuis

Van Abbe
Museum

GELDROPSEWEG

BILDERDIJKLAAN

0   200m

Eindhoven's only real attraction is **Van Abbe Museum**, Vonderweg 1 (Tues–Sun 11am–5pm; *f*8), with its superb collection of modern paintings that includes works by Picasso, Klein, Chagall, Kandinsky and Bacon. To see this, you need to come between June and September; at other times most of the collection disappears and the place has rotating exhibitions of modern art.

Practicalities

Eindhoven's **VVV** is outside the train station (Mon 10am–5.30pm, Tues–Thurs 9am–5.30pm, Fri 9am–8.30pm, Sat 10am–5pm; ☎0900/112 2363, *vvveindhoven@IAEhv.nl*). It can provide a handy brochure on the city and a list of pensions – only *De Swaan*, Wilhelminaplein 5 (☎040/244 8992; ①), is anywhere near the centre. The one central, affordable **hotel** is the *Corso* at Vestdijk 17 (☎040/244 9131, fax 245 7399; ①). There's a **campsite**, *Camping Witven* (☎040/253 2727, fax 255 4099; April–Oct), 5km outside the city at Runstraat 40 in **VELDHOVEN**; buses #177 and #7 run from the station.

As for eating and drinking, Eindhoven's modern streets contain some stylish **bars** that have sprung up over the last few years to assuage the thirst of the town's affluent youth. Kleine Berg is the best place for food, offering a diverse range of cuisines: *Le Connaisseur* at no. 12 serves cheap Italian food in its bookshelved interior; *Sorman's*, next door, offers reasonable Turkish food; and the *Grand Café Berlage* at no. 16, as slick as anything you'll find in Amsterdam, has a good menu and reasonable prices, while *Café Bommel*, a little further down, is a more old-fashioned traditional bar, good for a quiet drink.

Eindhoven's main strip for drinking is **Stratumseind**, which starts just south of Cuypers' gloomy neo-Gothic **St Catherinakerk**. The *Miller Time* bar at Stratumseind 51 is usually packed with teenagers; *De Krabbedans* at no. 32 is a pricey bar; *Café Bonzo* at no. 49 has a good variety of ales. You can access the **Internet** at the *Trafalgar Pub*, Dommel Straat 2 (daily 4pm–2am; ☎040/244 8820; *f*5 for 30min), or otherwise try the Bibliotheek, Emma Singel 22 (Mon–Fri 11am–8pm, Sat 11am–5pm; ☎040/260 4260) where it's half the price.

Along with Ajax of Amsterdam and Feyenoord of Rotterdam, Eindhoven's football team, **PSV Eindhoven**, is one of Holland's best. Catch games at the **Philips Stadion**, ten minutes' walk west from the train station. For some, the next best thing might be a visit to the **Euro Voetbal Show** at Mathildelaan 85, beside the stadium (Tues–Sun 10am–5pm; ☎0909/300 9979 to make a reservation; *f*17.50, children *f*15). Attractions include a range of the latest football computer games, and you can also view films and test your skills and knowledge about football. Take bus #177 to get there.

East from Eindhoven: Helmond

HELMOND, on the main train line from Eindhoven to Venray, just about merits a stop for its moated late medieval **Kasteel** (Tues–Fri 10am–5pm, Sat & Sun 2–5pm; *f*3.50) that contains a museum with a small historical collection and changing exhibitions of art (though wandering around the castle itself is most fun); and a collection of futuristic houses, **'t Spielhuis**, designed by Piet Blom and opened in 1977. Designed to look like Cubist tree-huts, the buildings most resemble a group of tumbling dice – try and get into the small theatre here (box office open Mon–Fri 10am–1pm) to have a look.

LIMBURG

Limburg is Holland's southernmost province, a finger of land that pushes down into Belgium. The north, around **Venlo**, is mostly farmland and woods; the centre, around **Roermond**, is dominated by the rivers and canals; and in the south, down to Maastricht, rise Holland's only hills. Like North Brabant it's a deeply Catholic area (if anything even more so) and has been influenced both architecturally and socially by the countries it neighbours.

Venlo

Just a few kilometres from the Dutch–German border, **VENLO** has been repeatedly destroyed and recaptured throughout its history, particularly during the last war, when most of its ancient buildings were knocked down during the Allied invasion of Europe. As a result the town is short of sights, and there is little reason to do anything but make a brief stop en route to the National War and Resistance Museum at Overloon.

The cramped streets of Venlo's centre wind medievally around the town's one architectural highlight, the fancily turreted and onion-domed **Stadhuis**, a much-amended building dating from the sixteenth century. Nearby, along Grote Kerkstraat, is the louring pile of **St Martinus Kerk** (Mon–Fri 10am–noon & 2–4pm, Sat & Sun 2–4pm; free), rebuilt after bombing in 1944, but still holding a brilliant golden seventeenth-century reredos. Near the station is the **Limburgs Museum**, Keulsepoort 5 (Tues–Sun 11am–5pm, Thurs 11am–8pm; *f*4.50), the city's historical collection. Best exhibit is the nineteenth-century kitchenware, the largest assortment in western Europe. Venlo's other museum, the **Van Bommel-Van Dam**, Deken van Oppensingel 8 (Tues–Fri 10am–4.30pm, Sat & Sun 2–5pm; *f*3.50), has changing exhibitions of the work of contemporary, mostly local artists. From the train station, take the third right off the roundabout.

Venlo's **VVV**, Koninginneplein 2 (Mon 11am–6pm, Tues–Fri 9am–6pm, Sat 9am–4pm; ☎077/354 3800, *vvvenlo@plex.nl*), opposite the train station, hands out glossy leaflets and can help find accommodation. Otherwise try the nearby *Hotel Wilhelmina*, Kaldenkerkerweg 1 (☎077/351 6251, fax 351 2252; ②), or the convenient *Stationshotel*, Keulsepoort 16 (☎077/351 8230, fax 352 1279; ①). For **eating and drinking**, try the *D'n Dorstigen Haen* at Markt 26, for snacks and a few samples of their huge range of beers. Otherwise, there are cheap light lunches at several cafés around the Stadhuis.

From beside the train station, bus #83 makes the ten-kilometre trip north up along the Maas to the village of Arcen, home to the **Kasteeltuinen** (April–late Oct daily 10am–6pm; *f*19.50), a trim seventeenth-century moated castle surrounded by a fine series of formal gardens set beside narrow canals and a string of tiny lakes.

Venray and the National War and Resistance Museum

A few minutes by train from Venlo, **VENRAY** is a cosy residential town and a stepping stone to **OVERLOON**, site of the **National War and Resistance Museum**.

To reach the museum from Venray, bus #97 leaves the station hourly but your best bet is to take the *treintaxi* (ƒ7 each way) or to rent a bike (ask at the station in Venlo). A six-kilometre ride through fields of wheat brings you to Overloon (which is actually across the provincial border back in North Brabant), an affluent little town that was rebuilt following destruction in the last war during a fierce battle in October 1944 in which 2400 men died. The final stages took place in the woods to the east, where hand-to-hand fighting was needed to secure the area and it's on this site that the museum (daily: Sept–May 10am–5pm; June–Aug 9.30am–6pm; ƒ12.50 plus ƒ3 for essential guidebook) now stands, founded with the military hardware that was left behind after the battle. Its purpose is openly didactic: "Not merely a monument for remembrance, it is intended as an admonition and warning, a denouncement of war and violence." This the museum powerfully achieves, with the machinery of war (which includes tanks, rocket launchers, armoured cars, a Bailey bridge and a V1 flying bomb) a poignant prelude to the excellent collection of documents and posters. To tour the whole museum takes a couple of hours and is a moving experience.

Roermond

ROERMOND, the chief town of central Limburg, is an oddity. Except for a few churches and a museum of fairly specialized interest, there's precious little to see here: its nightlife can't hold a candle to that of Maastricht to the south, cultural happenings are few, and it's not one of Holland's prettier towns either. Yet the town has great personality, caused in part by its long adherence to **Catholicism**. In 1579, seven years after William the Silent had captured Roermond from the Spanish, it fell back into their hands without a struggle and remained under the control of the Spanish (or Austrian) Habsburgs, who actively encouraged Catholic worship, until the town was finally incorporated into the Netherlands in 1839. Reminders of the pre-eminence of the faith are everywhere, most visibly in the innumerable **shrines** to the Virgin built into the sides of houses. Usually high enough off the street to prevent damage, they contain small figures of the Virgin, sometimes decorated with flowers. And it was in Roermond that P.J.H. Cuypers, the architect who crowded the country with Gothic-revival Catholic churches in the nineteenth century, lived and had his workshops. Roermond is also a handy stopover on the way to Maastricht and the south, or Aachen, Düsseldorf and Cologne in Germany, and is useful as a base for visiting nearby **THORN**.

Arrival, information and accommodation

Though it looks straightforward enough on the map, Roermond is a confusing place to walk around, its series of wide streets and broad squares irritatingly similar to the unacquainted. Use the Munsterkerk and river as landmarks, consult our map and you shouldn't get lost for too long.

The **VVV** office, Kranpoort 1, behind Markt (April–Sept Mon–Fri 9am–6pm, Sat 9am–4pm; Oct–March Mon–Fri 9am–5pm, Sat 9am–2pm; ☎0475/335847, *vvv.roer@wxs.nl*), is a fair walk from the train station, so booking your accommodation before you arrive – so that you can go straight to your hotel from the station without visiting the VVV – is worth considering. A good range of inexpensive

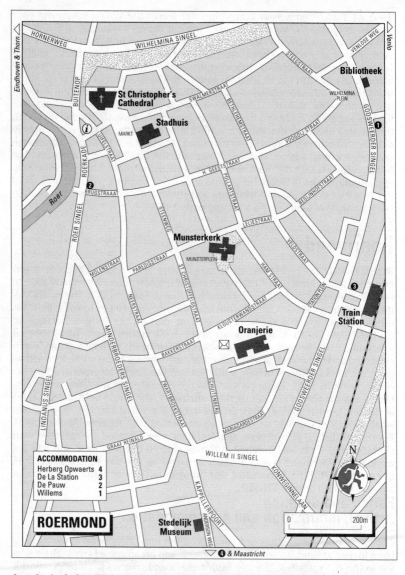

ROERMOND

ACCOMMODATION
Herberg Opwaerts 4
De La Station 3
De Pauw 2
Willems 1

◁ ❹ & *Maastricht*

hotels includes *Willems*, Godsweerdersingel 58 (☎0475/333021; ②); and more expensive *De La Station*, Stationsplein 9 (☎0475/316548, fax 335156; ③). Other possibilities include *De Pauw*, Roerkade 1–2 (☎0475/316597, fax 316400; ②), and a single **pension**, *Herberg Opwaerts*, Hagelkruisweg 7, St Odilienberg (☎ & fax 0475/536540; ①), 5km south of the town. Take bus #79 or #80 from the station.

The Town

Walk into town from the train station and you'll come to the **Munsterkerk** (Fri 10am–noon & 2–5pm, Sat 10am–4pm; free) on Munsterplein, built in Romanesque style in the thirteenth century, but much altered and gothicized by Cuypers in the nineteenth century. Inside, the chief thing to see is the polychrome thirteenth-century **tomb** of Gerhard III and his wife Margaret of Brabant. From here it's a short walk to the **Markt**, a large sloping square that hit the headlines in May 1990, when two Australian tourists were gunned down by members of the **provisional IRA**, who were under the mistaken belief that they were British soldiers. Its proximity to the German border made Roermond an appealing IRA target: soldiers often pass through the town en route to bases along the Rhine, and a quick escape across the border into Germany lessened the likelihood of capture for the assassins.

The town's early eighteenth-century **Stadhuis** stands on the Markt's eastern side, a dull building that's easily overlooked. More noticeable (though not more interesting), **St Christopher's Cathedral** (April–Oct Sat 2–5pm; free) was rebuilt following damage in World War II.

Making your way down the larger streets leading south from the Markt – Marktstraat, Neerstraat and Minderbroeders Singel – you'll come across some later and much more attractive architecture. Wherever you are in town, it's worth keeping an eye open for Roermond's alluring twentieth-century **facades**: the majority are Art Nouveau, often strongly coloured with heavily moulded vegetal patterns and designs, sometimes with stylized animal heads and grotesque characters.

Roermond's principal architectural claim to fame is celebrated at the **Stedelijk Museum**, Andersonweg 2–8 (Tues–Fri 11am–5pm, Sat & Sun 2–5pm; ƒ2.50). **P.J.H. Cuypers** (1827–1921) was Holland's foremost ecclesiastical architect in the nineteenth century, his work paralleling that of the British Gothic revivalist, Augustus Pugin. Almost every large city in the country has a Catholic church by him – those in Eindhoven, Leeuwarden and Hilversum are notable – though his two most famous buildings aren't churches, but the Rijksmuseum and the Centraal Station in Amsterdam. The museum is the building in which Cuypers lived and worked for much of his life and preserves a small private chapel as well as a large extension in which masses of decorative panels, mouldings and fixtures were produced. Other exhibits show his plans and paintings, along with a collection of works by other local artists, chiefly Hendrik Luyten.

Eating and drinking

The three main areas to **eat and drink** are those around the Markt, the Munsterkerk and the train station, although *Il Corso*, an excellent and classily decorated Italian restaurant, is away from all these places at Willem II Singel 16a, the continuation of Godsweerder Singel. On Stationsplein, *Le Journal* and *De Tramhalte*, both at no. 17, are inexpensive café-bars, and the restaurant of the *De La Station* hotel, although pricey for dinner, is worth checking out for its fixed-price lunches. *Le Chapeau* is a croissanterie ideal for breakfast and snacks, just down from Stationsplein at Hamstraat 54; *Tin San* is the best of several Chinese places, just south of the Markt at Varkensmarkt 1.

Roermond lacks first-rate **watering-holes**. The cafés at Stationsplein are often the liveliest nightspots; otherwise try *Preuverie de Sjnats*, Markt 24, for a good range of beers. For a more artistic night out, check out the *Orangerie*, a multicultural centre at Kloosterwandplein 12–16.

Internet access is available at the Bibliotheek at Wilhelminaplein 11.

Thorn

If you do end up staying in Roermond, the village of **THORN** makes for an enjoyable half-day outing. Regular buses link it to the town, but it's more fun to rent a bike from the train station and cycle the 14km through the almost rolling Limburg farmland. If you do cycle, take a map that shows cycle routes – the signs marking the route off the main road are none too good.

Once you get here, it's easy to see why Thorn is a favourite for travel agents' posters. Its houses and farms are all painted white, a tradition for which no one seems to have a credible explanation, but one that distinguishes what would, in any case, be a resolutely picturesque place. The farms intrude right into the village itself, giving Thorn a barnyard friendliness that's enhanced by its cobblestone streets, the closed-shuttered propriety of its houses and, at the centre, the **Abdijkerk** (March–Oct daily 10am–5pm; Nov–Feb Sat & Sun noon–5pm; *f*2.50).

The abbey was founded at the end of the tenth century by a powerful count, Ansfried and his wife Hilsondis, as a sort of religious retirement home after Ansfried had finished his tenure as bishop of Utrecht. Under his control the abbey and the land around it was granted the status of an independent principality under the auspices of the Holy Roman Empire and it was in the environs of the abbey that the village developed. The abbey was unusual in having a double cloister that housed both men and women (usually from local noble families), a situation that carried on right up until the French invasion of 1797, after which the principality of Thorn was dissolved, the monks and nuns dispersed and all the abbey buildings save the church destroyed. Most of what can be seen of the church today dates from the fifteenth century, with some tidying up by P.J.H. Cuypers in the nineteenth. The interior decoration, though, is congenially restrained Baroque of the seventeenth century, with some good memorials and side chapels. If you're into the macabre, the crypt under the chancel has a couple of glass coffins containing conclusively dead members of the abbey from the eighteenth century: this and other highlights are described in the notes that you can pick up on entry (in English) for a self-guided walking tour.

Thorn has one small museum, the **Museum Land of Thorn**, in the historic heart of the village at Wijnguard 14 (March–Nov daily 10am–4.30pm; Nov–March Tues–Sun 11am–4pm; *f*3) which details the history of Thorn, hosts temporary exhibitions of art and houses a 3D painting of the village.

Practicalities

The **VVV**, Wijnguard 14 (March–Nov daily 10am–4.30pm; Nov–March Tues–Sun 11am–4pm; ☎0475/562761) can help with regional information. Thorn makes a great place to stay if you want to get away from it all: the cheaper of two **hotels** is the *Crasborn*, Houtstraat 10 (☎0475/561281, fax 562233; ②), though the atmospheric *Hostellerie La Ville Blanche*, Hoogstraat 2 (☎0475/562341, fax 562828; ③) offers surprisingly affordable luxury. There's also a private **campsite**, *Viverjerbroek*, Kessenicherweg 20 (☎0475/561914, fax 565565; April–Oct), reached by turning right halfway down Hofstraat.

Maastricht

MAASTRICHT made world headlines in 1992, with the signing of the Maastricht Treaty. Up until then, few people outside Holland had heard of this provincial Dutch town, but now everyone at least knows its name, even if they couldn't place it on a map.

Don't, however, let Maastricht's Euro-connections put you off visiting. Far from being the bland, concrete Eurocity you might be expecting, it is one of the most delightful cities in Holland, quite different in feel to the kitsch waterland centres of the north. And it's easy to see why the Eurocrats chose it as the place to sign their united Europe agreement: outward-looking, vibrant and youthful, situated in the corner of the thin finger of land that reaches down between Belgium and Germany and where three languages and currencies coexist, it epitomizes the most positive aspects of European union.

Maastricht is a key industrial centre, with long-established manufacturing companies like Mosa (which produces domestic ceramic products from its plant on the east bank of the river) and Sphinx just north of the city centre, whose name graces toilets nationwide, spearheading Maastricht's prosperity. The town's position in the heart of Europe is also being traded on by the local authorities, keen to draw new money into the region – exemplified in projects like the MECC conference centre to the south of the city, where the treaty business was conducted.

Maastricht is also one of the oldest towns in the country. The first settlers here were Roman and Maastricht became an important stop on their trade route between Cologne and the coast – the town's name derives from the words *Mosae Trajectum* or "Maas Crossing". The Romans left relatively few obvious traces, but the later legacy of Charlemagne – whose capital was at nearby Aachen – is manifest in two churches that are among the best surviving examples of the Romanesque in the Low Countries.

Arrival and information

The centre of Maastricht is on the west bank of the river and most of the town spreads out from here toward the Belgian border. You're likely to arrive, however, on the east bank, in the district known as **Wijk**, a sort of extension to the centre that's home to the train and bus stations and many of the city's hotels. The train station itself is about ten minutes' walk from the St Servaas bridge, which takes you across the river into the centre. All local buses connect with Markt from here, but really, if you have no heavy luggage, it's easy enough to walk. If you're flying direct to Maastricht, the **airport** is north of the city at Beek, a twenty-minute journey away by bus; take bus #61, which runs every thirty minutes to Markt and the train station, or a taxi – a ƒ45 ride.

For local information, the main **VVV** (May–Oct Mon–Sat 9am–6pm; Nov–March Mon–Fri 9am–6pm, Sat 9am–5pm; ☎043/325 2121, *info@vvvmaastricht.nl*) is housed just across the river in the Dinghuis, a tall late fifteenth-century building at

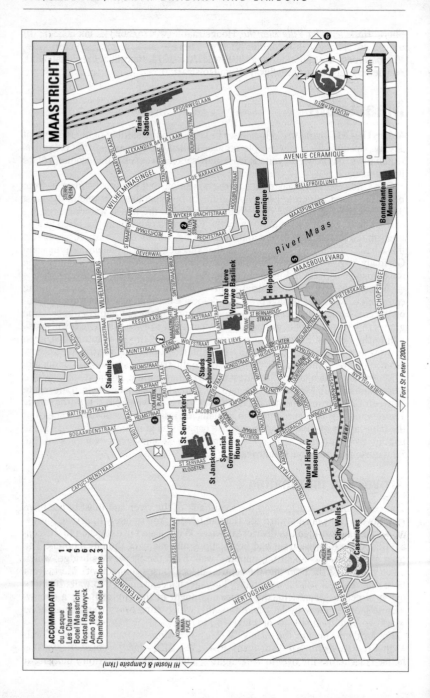

MAASTRICHT

ACCOMMODATION
du Casque 1
Les Charmes 4
Botel Maastricht 5
Hostel Randwyck 6
Anno 1604 2
Chambres d'hote La Cloche 3

Train Station

STERRE PLEIN

SPOORWEGLAAN

ALEXANDER BATA LAAN

WILHELMINASINGEL

ST MAARTENSLAAN

AVENUE CERAMIQUE

LAGE BARAKKEN

Centre Ceramique

BELLEFROIDLUNET

ST MAARTENSLAAN

WYCKER GRACHTSTRAAT

RECHTSTRAAT

MAASPUNTWEG

Bonnefanten Museum

HEUGEMERWEG

OEVERWAL

River Maas

WILHELMINABRUG

Onze Lieve Vrouwe Basiliek

Helpoort

MAASBOULEVARD

ST PIETERSKADE

BISSCHOPSINGEL

KESSELKADE

STOKSTRAAT

ST BERNARDUS STRAAT

Stadhuis

MARKT

MUNTSTRAAT

NIEUWSTRAAT

WOLFSTRAAT

ONZE LIEVE

Stads Schouwburg

SPILSTRAAT

GROTE STAAT

ST JACOBSTRAAT

Spanish Government House

St Servaaskerk

VRIJTHOF

ST SERVAAS KLOOSTER

St Janskerk

Natural History Museum

BATTERIJSTRAAT

HELMSTRAAT

BOGAARDENSTRAAT

CAPUCIJNENSTRAAT

BRUSSELSESTRAAT

CALVARIESTRAAT

TONGERSESTRAAT

City Walls

Casemates

TONGERSE PLEIN

STATENSINGEL

KONINGIN EMMA PLACE

HERTOGSINGEL

TONGERSEWEG

▽ Fort St Peter (200m)

△ HI Hostel & Campsite (1km)

100m

0

Kleine Straat 1, at the end of the main shopping street. As well as information on the city and on film, theatre and music events around town, they have decent maps (f2) and good walking guides. In July and August they organize **city tours** (in English) which leave from the VVV daily at noon (f5.75). You can also buy the Maastricht Guest Card here (f15), which gives discounts in local stores and may be worth buying if you plan to do a lot of shopping.

Getting around, you only really need to use buses to get from the station to the town centre at Markt, or out to St Pietersburg; otherwise it's easy to walk everywhere. Between April and September, Stiphout Cruises runs hourly **cruises** down the Maas (Mon–Sat 10am–3pm, Sun 1–3pm; f10 per person). Stiphout also offers trips taking in the St Pietersberg caves or even as far as Liège (day-trip f32.50). Phone ☎043/351 5300 for details.

Accommodation

For **accommodation**, there's nothing super-cheap. The VVVs have a list of **private rooms** and will either book them for you at the usual fee or sell you the list. There are several good **pensions** including *Anno 1604*, Kattenstraat 11 (☎043/325 0165; ①) and the *Hostel Randwyck,* Endepolsdomein 30 (☎043/361 6835, fax 361 9007; ②). **Hotels** include the *Chambres d'hotes La Cloche*, Bredestraat 41 (☎043/321 2407, fax 321 3059, *rachel@mail.cobweb.nl*; ②), the more comfortable *Les Charmes*, Lenculenstraat 18 (☎043/312 7400, fax 325 8574; ③), and *Botel Maastricht* (☎043/321 9023, fax 325 7998; ①), moored on the river at Maasboulevard, not far from the Helpoort, and with an excellent breakfast. Up a notch in price is the very central *du Casque*, Helmstraat 14 (☎043/321 4343, fax 325 5155; ④). If you're **camping**, the *De Dousberg* site, Dousbergweg 102 (☎043/343 2171, fax 343 0556), almost in Belgium on the far western side of town, is open all year, large and well equipped; take bus #11 from the train station to the campsite. If you arrive at the station after 6.25pm, take bus #28 to Pottenburg and tell the driver where you're heading. From the bus stop it's a 20min walk to the campsite. On Sunday, you can take bus #33, but you have to telephone in advance (☎043/350 5707). The same buses also take you to the *De Dousberg* **HI hostel** at Dousbergweg 4 (☎043/346 6777, fax 346 6755, *dousberghotel@wxs.nl*; f38), which is sited within a sports complex – guests have free use of the swimming pools.

The Town

The busiest of Maastricht's squares is the **Markt**, at its most crowded on Wednesday and Friday mornings, when people hop over the nearby borders for the town's cheap general market. At the centre of the square, which is a car park the rest of the time, the **Stadhuis** (Mon–Fri 8.30am–12.30pm & 2–5.30pm; free) of 1664 was designed by Pieter Post, a square, grey limestone building that is a fairly typical slice of mid-seventeenth-century Dutch civic grandeur. Its double staircase was designed so that the rival rulers of Brabant and nearby Liège didn't have to argue about who should go first on the way in. Inside, the building has an imposing main hall, which gives way to a rear octagonal dome supported by heavy arches.

The second of the town's main central squares, **Vrijthof**, is just west of the Markt, a larger, rather grander open space flanked by a couple of churches on one side and a line of cafés on the other, with tables smothering the wide pavement in summer. During the Middle Ages, Vrijthof was the scene of the so-called "Fair of the Holy Relics", a seven-yearly showing of the bones of St Servaas, the first bishop of Maastricht, which brought plenty of pilgrims into the town but resulted in such civil disorder that it was eventually banned. The church which holds the relics now, the **St Servaaskerk** (April–Oct daily 10am–5pm, July & Aug till 6pm; Nov–March Mon–Sat 10.30am–5pm, Sun 12.30–5pm; ƒ4), dominates the far side of the square. Dating from 950, it's the elaborate amalgamation of an earlier shrine dedicated to St Servaas and the site of his burial in 384. Only the crypt remains of the tenth-century church, containing the tomb of the saint himself, and the rest is mostly of medieval or later construction. You enter on the north side of the church, where a fifteenth-century Gothic cloister leads into the **treasury**, which holds a large collection of reliquaries, goblets and liturgical accessories, including a bust reliquary of St Servaas, decorated with reliefs telling the saint's story, which is carried through the town in Easter processions. There's also a coffin-reliquary of the saint, the so-called "Noodkist", dating from 1160 and bristling with saints, stones and ornate copperwork, as well as a jewelled crucifix from 890 and a twelfth-century Crucifixion in ivory. Beyond the Treasury is the entrance to the rich and imposing interior, the round-arched nave supporting freshly painted Gothic vaulting. Don't miss the mid-thirteenth-century Bergportaal on the south side of the church, the usual entrance during services.

The second most prominent building on the square, next door, is Maastricht's main Protestant church, the fourteenth century **St Janskerk** (April–Oct daily except Sun 11am–4pm), the baptistery of the church of St Servaas when it was a cathedral and nowadays competing for attention with its high and faded, delicate red fifteenth-century Gothic tower, which you can climb for ƒ2.50. The church has some medieval murals, but a climb up the tower is the church's main appeal. On the south side of the square, the sixteenth-century **Spanish Government House** (guided tours only; Wed–Sun 1–5pm; ƒ5) has an attractive Renaissance arcade and a number of period rooms furnished in Dutch, French and the more local Liège–Maastricht style. Among various exhibits are statues and figurines, porcelain and applied arts and a handful of seventeenth-century paintings, though none is exactly essential viewing.

Maastricht's other main church, the **Onze Lieve Vrouwe Basiliek**, is a short walk south of Vrijthof, down Bredestraat, in a small, shady square crammed with café tables in summer. It's unusual for its fortified west front, with barely more than one or two slits for windows. First built around the year 1000, it's a solid, dark and eerily devotional place after the bright Protestant churches of the North – or even the relative sterility of the St Servaaskerk. The Gothic vaulting of the nave springs from a Romanesque base, while the galleried choir is a masterpiece of proportion, raised under a high half-dome, with a series of capitals exquisitely decorated with Old Testament scenes. Off the north aisle, the treasury (Easter to mid-Sept Mon–Sat 11am–5pm, Sun 1–5pm; ƒ3.50) holds the usual array of reliquaries and ecclesiastical garments, most notably the dalmatic of St Lambert – the evangelical bishop of Maastricht who was murdered at Liège in 705, allegedly by a local noble whom he had rebuked for adultery. Entrance to the church is through a side chapel housing the statue of Stella Mare, an object of pilgrimage for centuries and which attracts as many devotees as the church itself.

Around the corner from the square, on Plankstraat, on the edge of a district of narrow streets known as the **Stokstraat Kwartier** after its main gallery- and boutique-lined spine, Stokstraat, is the **Museumkelder Derlon** (Sun noon–4pm; free), in the basement of the hotel of the same name. This contains one of the few remnants of Roman Maastricht – the remains of a temple to Jupiter, a well and several layers of pavement, discovered before the building of the present hotel in the mid-1980s. On the other side of Onze Lieve Vrouweplein lies another of Maastricht's most appealing quarters, narrow streets winding out to the remains of the town battlements alongside the fast-flowing River Jeker, which weaves in and out of the various houses and ancient mills. The best surviving part of the walls is the **Helpoort** of 1229, close to a stretch overlooking the river at the end of St Bernadusstraat; and from here you can walk along the top of the walls almost as far as the **Natural History Museum** at De Bosquetplein 6–7 (Mon–Fri 10am–5pm, Sat & Sun 2–5pm; ƒ6), where there's a small collection on the geology, flora and fauna of the surrounding area, along with a small, lush garden display. A little way south of here, the **Casemates** in the Waldeck Park (tours July–Sept daily 12.30pm & 2pm; Oct–June Sun 2pm; ƒ5.75) are further evidence of Maastricht's once impressive fortifications, a system of galleries created through mining between 1575 and 1825 that were used in times of siege for surprise attacks on the enemy. There used to be many more casemates around the town, but only these survive, making for a fairly draughty way to spend an hour, tours taking you through a small selection of the 10km or so of damp passages. Probably the most interesting thing about them is the fact that the famous fourth "musketeer", d'Artagnan, was killed here, struck down while engaged in an attack on the town as part of forces allied to Louis XIV in 1673.

Ten minutes' walk from the St Servaas bridge, the **Bonnefanten Museum** (Tues–Sun 11am–5pm; ƒ12.50) is one of Maastricht's highlights. Named after the Bonnefanten monastery where it once was housed, the museum now inhabits an impressive modern building on the banks of the Maas. The first floor has a local archeological collection, with relics from pre-history through Roman times to the Middle Ages, much of it dredged up from the river bed, and a modest collection of medieval sculpture and early Italian and Dutch paintings. The rest of the museum is given over to temporary exhibitions of modern and contemporary art, superbly displayed if erratic in quality. Don't miss the lunar capsule-style cupola, usually given over to a single piece of art.

In the neighbourhood of the Bonnefanten Museum is the **Centre Ceramique**, at Avenue Ceramique 50 (☎043/350 5600, *mail@sbm.nl*). This huge modern building is home to the European Journalism Centre, city archives and the library. You can also send emails from here for free, so arrive early as PCs are much in demand. To get here, walk or take bus #1, #56, #57, or #58 to the Avenue Ceramique stop or bus #9 to the Bloemenweg stop.

Outside the centre: St Pietersberg

There are more dank passageways to explore fifteen minutes' walk from the casemates on the southern outskirts of Maastricht, where the flat-topped hill of **St Pietersberg** rises up to a height of about 110m – a popular picnic spot on warm summer weekends. Again these aren't so much caves as galleries created by quarrying, hollowed out of the soft sandstone, or marl, which makes up the hill – an activity which has been going on here since Roman times. Of the two cave systems, the **Zonneberg** is probably the better, situated on the far side of the St Pietersberg hill at Casino Slavante (guided tours in English: July & Aug daily 2.45pm; ƒ5.75). The caves here were intended to be used as air-raid shelters during World War II and were equipped accordingly, though they were only in fact utilized during the last few days before Maastricht's liberation. There is some evidence of wartime occupation, plus what everyone claims is Napoleon's signature on a graffiti-ridden wall. Also on the walls are recent charcoal drawings, usually illustrating a local story and acting as visual aids for the guides, not to mention the ten varieties of bat that inhabit the dark (and cold) corridors.

The other, more northerly system of caves, the **Grotten Noord** (guided tours in English: July–Sept daily at 2.15pm; *f*5.75) is easier to get to (15min walk from the centre of town), but it has less of interest. The entrance is at Chalet Bergrust, on the near side of St Pietersberg close by **Fort St Pieter**, a low brick structure, pentagonal in shape and built in 1702, which nowadays houses a pricey restaurant. The VVV does arrange guided tours (July & Aug by group reservation only; *f*6), which leave from the restaurant, but you'd probably do just as well nursing a drink on the restaurant's terrace, which gives panoramic views over the town and surrounding countryside.

Eating, drinking and nightlife

Maastricht has some of the best cooking in the Netherlands and three or four major breweries, so options abound for good **eating** and **drinking**. There are a number of inexpensive **restaurants** around the Markt, including *Pizzeria Napoli* at no. 71, while elsewhere there's the snackbar *Stap-In*, Kesselkade 61 by the river, and the rather better *de Roeje Knien*, Rechtsraat 76 on the other side, which serves good Dutch food. *Charlemagne* on Onze Lieve Vrouweplein also has reasonably priced steaks, chicken and ribs. Slightly more expensive options include two good Dutch/French restaurants on Tongersestraat, a few minutes from the centre: *'t Orgelke*, at no. 40, and *De Cuyp* at no. 30. *Il Giardino della Mamma*, Onze Lieve Vrouweplein 15, has good pizzas and pasta from *f*15; *L'Hermitage*, St Bernardusstraat 13, around the corner and near the Helpoort, has Mexican food from *f*20; and *In 't Knijpe*, opposite, has a pleasant bar/restaurant and great onion soup.

For drinking, the **bars** on the east side of the Vrijthof have most of the pulling power, particularly in summer when the pavement cafés are packed; *In den Ouden Vogelstruys*, on the corner of Platielstraat, is one of the nicest. Away from the Vrijthof crowds, *de Bobbel*, on Wolfstraat just off Onze Lieve Vrouweplein, is a bare-boards place, lively in the early evening, while *In de Moriaan*, Stokstraat 12, is a delight – possibly the smallest bar in the country and with a cosy terrace in the summer. The no-frills *Café de Stadssleutel*, Kesselkade 60, has the cheapest beer in town, and the student quarter around Tongesestraat has a couple of excellent bars in *Van Sloun* at no.3 and *Tribunal* opposite. On the other side of the river, *De Gijsbrecht*, toward the station on Wycker Brugstraat, is a very busy bar while *Take One*, Rechstraat 28, is a good bet for beer connoisseurs. There's **live music** throughout the year at *d'n Auwestiene*, Kesselkade 43 (Wed–Sun 10pm–5am).

The Lumière Filmhuis, Bogaardenstraat 40b (☎043/321 4080), regularly shows interesting **movies**, often English or American and always subtitled in Dutch.

Listings

Bicycle rental *Aon de Stasie*, Stationsplein (Mon–Fri 6am–midnight, Sat & Sun 6am–1am; ☎043/321 1100; *f*9.50 per day plus *f*38 deposit).

Books There's a branch of De Slegte at Grote Straat 53, good for second-hand English-language paperbacks and much else besides. Try also Bergmans on Nieuwestraat, off Markt, which has a good selection of new English-language titles.

Bureau de change There's a GWK office at the train station, open every day.

Car rental Europcar, Spoorweglaan 18 (☎043/321 6163). The major companies also have desks at the airport.

Post office On Keizer Karelplein, just off the northwest corner of Vrijthof.

Taxi Crals Taxi's B.V., Ankerkade 275 (☎043/363 8484).

Around South Limburg

South Limburg boasts Holland's only true hills and as such is a popular holiday area for the Dutch, many of the villages crammed in summer with walkers from the north taking in the scenery. The countryside is green and rolling, studded with castles (many of which have been converted to hotels), seamed with river valleys and dotted with the timber-framed houses that are unique to the area. Everywhere is within easy reach of Maastricht, though without a car you shouldn't try to cover too much in one day as public transport connections are patchy. **Valkenburg**, the main resort, is perhaps the easiest place to visit, on the main train line from Maastricht to Aachen, though it's packed throughout the summer. Further east down the train line, **Heerlen** and **Kerkrade** are also easily reached, though neither is any great shakes. To the south of the train line, toward the Belgian border, the countryside is wilder and more impressive, the roads snaking over hills and giving long, expansive views all around. It's not at all a Dutch scene and perhaps not what you came to Holland for. But after the grindingly flat landscapes of the northern provinces, it can be excellent therapy – as numerous hotels, at least one for every tiny village, testify.

Cadier-en-Keer, Margraten, Gulpen and Vaals

Five kilometres east of Maastricht, the first stop on the #54 bus route – which eventually goes to Vaals on the German border – **CADIER-EN-KEER** is a small suburb of the city best known for its **Africa Centre** (April–Oct Mon–Fri 1.30–5pm, Sun 2–5pm; otherwise Sun only 2–5pm; ƒ5), ten minutes' walk off to the left of the main road (follow the signs). Housed in the headquarters of the African Missionaries Society, this contains a small museum of mainly West African artefacts, masks, jewellery and statuary arranged by tribe and dating back as far as the thirteenth century – as well as giving details on the contemporary way of life of African peoples. Nearby, the **Maastricht Wine Museum** (Mon–Fri 9am–5pm, Sat 10am–4pm; ƒ6) has displays on production and a free sampler or two.

Bus #54 continues on to **MARGRATEN**, where just before the town proper there's an **American War Cemetery** (daily sunrise–sunset), a peaceful and moving memorial to over eight thousand American servicemen who died in the Dutch and Belgian campaigns of late 1944 and 1945. Buses stop right outside. The centrepiece is a stone quadrangle recording the names of the soldiers, together with a small visitors' room and a pictorial representation and narrative describing the events in this area leading up to the German surrender – while beyond the quadrangle, the white marble crosses that mark the burial places of the soldiers cover a depressingly huge area.

There's not much else to Margraten, nor is there to **GULPEN**, a few kilometres beyond, a nondescript place though with good bus connections all over South Limburg. The town is known for its *Gulpener* beer, the name of which you see all over the province and indeed the rest of Holland, though that aside the only thing that distinguishes Gulpen is the 161-metre-high **Gulpenberg**, which rises roundly behind the town and is home to a **campsite**. If you continue to the end of the #54 route, the pretty village of **VAALS** is notable not only for being the highest point in the country, but also for "Drielandenpunt", where the borders of Belgium, Germany and the Netherlands meet. South of Gulpen, the countryside makes for a pretty route back to Maastricht, either driving yourself or via the # 57 bus route from Gulpen's bus station, taking in the scenically sited villages of **Mechelen**, **Epen** and **Slenaken**.

Valkenburg

Set in the gently wooded valley of the River Geul, **VALKENBURG**, ten minutes east of Maastricht by train, is southern Limburg's major tourist resort, the unloading point for buses full of tourists throughout the summer, with innumerable hotels, restaurants and even a casino. While you wouldn't want to stay here, it's a nice enough place to visit, about as far away from the clogs and canals of the rest of the country as it's possible to get, with a feel more of a Swiss or Austrian alpine resort, its small restaurant-ridden centre sloping up from its fake castle train station to the surrounding green hills, full of grottoes, castles and thermal centres. Valkenburg is also famed for its Christmas-season markets, held in Fluwelengrot and Gemeentegrot, with all manner of special foodstuffs, decorations and street entertainment too.

Theodoor Dorrenplein, five minutes' walk from the train station, is the centre of town, fringed with cafés and home to the VVV, from where the main Grote Straat leads up through the pedestrianized old centre through the old **Grendelpoort** arch to **Grendelplein**, which provides a second focus, the streets which lead off going to Valkenburg's main attractions. A great many of these are directed at children – things like bob-sleigh runs, a fairytale wood, a hopeful reconstruction of Rome's catacombs – and even those that aren't are still the kind of things kids enjoy.

It's worth a walk up to the **Castle** (April–Oct daily 10am–5pm; ƒ5 or combined ticket with Fluwelengrot ƒ10; entrance off Grendelplein), a ruined edifice which overlooks the town from a neatly placed peak above Grote Straat. It was blown up in 1672 on the orders of William III, after he had retrieved it from its French occupiers. Repair and restoration on the castle began in 1921 and continue still, uncovering a series of underground passages that served as an escape route in times of siege. These form part of the **Fluwelengrot** (guided tours only; April–Nov daily 10am–5pm; Dec–March Sat & Sun 11am–4pm; ƒ8 or combined ticket with castle ƒ10), further up the road on the left, a series of caves formed – like those of St Pietersberg in Maastricht – by the quarrying of marl, which has been used for much of the building in this area over the years. Tours leave every hour or so in high summer (much less frequently outside this period), but on the whole they're a damp, cold way to spend an hour, the most interesting features the signatures and silhouettes of American soldiers who wintered here from 1944 to 1945 and a clandestine chapel that was used during the late eighteenth-century French occupation.

If you particularly like caves, or can't be bothered to walk around the Fluwelengrot, the **Gemeentegrot** (same times; *f*6), just off Grendelplein on Cauberg, is similar, but has a train which whips you around its charcoal drawings, memorials to local dignitaries, giant sculptures of dinosaurs and fish hewn out of the rock, and, most engagingly, a weirdly, brightly lit underground lake. The whole tour takes about thirty minutes and costs a guilder extra. Further up the same road as the Fluwelengrot, on the left, the **Steenkolemijn** (guided tours only April–Oct daily 10am–5pm; Nov–March Sat & Sun 2pm & 3pm; *f*11.25) is a reconstruction of a coal mine whose 75-minute tours include a short film on coal-mining, some fake mine-workings and a small fossil museum. Again, good for the kids but not exactly riveting viewing. If the idea of trudging around dank underground passages doesn't appeal to you, you can ascend to the top of the hill above the castle by way of a **cable car** (daily: July & Aug 10am–5pm; rest of year 1–5pm; *f*7.50 return), five minutes' walk down Berkelstraat from the top of Grote Straat – or you can cut through the passage between the castle and the Fluwelengrot. This, a fairly primitive structure of the kind used for ski lifts, with two-person open cars, takes you up to the **Wilhemina Toren**, where you can enjoy the view from the terrace of the inevitable bar-restaurant. If you fancy a trip further afield, you can take a steam or diesel train sightseeing excursion from Valkenburg to Kerkrade (April–Nov Sun & Wed, July & Aug also Thurs; ☎045/544 0018) Finally, if you need a break from the sight-seeing, **Thermae 2000** on Cauberg (daily 9am–11pm; *f*30 for 2hr), the country's first official spa, has saunas, steam rooms and indoor and outdoor pools.

Practicalities

The **VVV** at Theodoor Dorrenplein 5 (Easter–Nov Mon–Fri 9am–6pm, Sat 9am–6pm; Dec–Easter Mon–Fri 9am–5pm, Sat 9am–1pm; ☎043/609 8600, *info@vvvzuidlimburg.nl*) has maps and information on all Valkenburg's attractions, as well as lists of the dozens of **hotels** and **pensions**. Among the cheapest hotels are *de Grendel*, Grendelplein 17 (☎043/601 4868; ②), *the Gaudi*, Grendelplein 14 (☎043/601 5333, fax 601 5334; ②) and *Casa*, Grotestraat 25–27 (☎043/601 2180; ②). Just slightly more expensive are the *De Toerist*, Hovetstraat 3 (☎043/601 2484, fax 609 0060; ②), and *de Uitkijk*, Broekhem 68 (☎043/601 3589, fax 601 4744; ②). **Camping**, the nearest site is *Den Driesch*, a short walk up Dahlemerweg from Grendelplein on the left (☎043/601 2025; April–Nov) and it's popular with young people. An alternative is *Europa Camping*, Cauberg 29 (☎043/601 3097, fax 601 3525; March–Nov). As virtually every second building in Valkenburg is a restaurant, there's little point in listing specific places to **eat**. Suffice to say you can dine cheaply and fairly reasonably at most of the places in the centre – though don't expect haute cuisine.

Heerlen and Kerkrade

HEERLEN, ten minutes further from Valkenburg by train, is quite different, an ugly modern town that sprawls gracelessly over the rolling countryside. But it has one definite attraction in the excellent **Thermen Museum** (daily 10am–5pm; *f*5), which incorporates the excavations of a bath complex from the Roman city of Coriovallum here – a key settlement on the Cologne–Boulogne trade route. These have been enclosed in a gleaming hi-tech purpose-built structure, with walkways leading across the ruins and tapes (in English) explaining what's what. An adjacent room displays finds and artefacts from the site, including glasswork from Cologne, shards of pottery, tombstones and coins, all neatly labelled. To get to the museum, follow Saroleastraat from the station as far as Raadhuisplein and turn right.

Fifteen minutes on from Heerlen lies **KERKRADE**, again an unappealing place, but worthy of a visit for its **Abdij van Rolduc** complex (opening hours vary, call ☎045/546 6888), situated on the far side of town, about a twenty-minute walk from the station. Originally founded by one Ailbert, a young priest who came here in 1104, this is now almost entirely sixteenth-century, used as a seminary and conference centre, but it does preserve a fine twelfth-century church, a model of simplicity and elegance, with contemporary frescoes and a marvellous mosaic floor. The clover leaf-shaped crypt, dark and mysterious after the church and with pillar capitals carved by Italian craftsmen, contains the relics of Ailbert, brought here from Germany where he died. Beside the train station is the **Industrion** (Tues–Sun 10am–5pm; *f*8), an interesting museum which traces the industrial development of the Netherlands, with a focus on paper, graphics, ceramics and coal mining.

travel details

Trains

Breda to: Dordrecht (every 20min; 20min); 's Hertogenbosch (every 30min; 40min); Middelburg (every 30min; 1hr 15min); Maastricht (every 30min; 1hr 45min).

Eindhoven to: Roermond (every 30min; 30min); Venlo (every 30min; 45min).

's Hertogenbosch to: Eindhoven (every 30min; 22min).

Middelburg to: Bergen-op-Zoom (every 30min; 45min); Goes (every 30min; 15min); Roosendaal (every 30min; 55min).

Roermond to: Maastricht (hourly; 30min); Venlo (every 30min; 26min).

Roosendaal to: Breda (every 30min; 18min); Dordrecht (every 30min; 30min).

Tilburg to: Eindhoven (every 30min; 30min); 's Hertogenbosch (every 30min; 15min).

Vlissingen to: Middelburg (every 30min; 7min).

Buses

Middelburg to: Delta Expo (hourly; 30min); Renesse (hourly; 45min); Veere (hourly; 10min).

Renesse to: Brouwershaven (hourly; 1hr 30min).

Zierikzee to: Goes (every 30min; 30min).

Ferries

Vlissingen to: Breskens (Mon–Fri every 30min, Sat & Sun hourly; 20min).

PART THREE

THE

CONTEXTS

THE HISTORICAL FRAMEWORK

The country now known as The Netherlands didn't reach its present delimitations until 1830. Until then the borders of the entire region, formerly known as the Low Countries and including present-day Belgium and Luxembourg, were continually being redrawn following battles, treaties and alliances. Inevitably, then, what follows is, in its early parts at least, an outline of the history of the whole region, rather than a straightforward history of The Netherlands as such. Please note, incidentally, that the term "Holland" refers to the province – not the country – throughout.

BEGINNINGS

Little is known of the **prehistoric** settlers of The Netherlands. Their visible remains are largely confined to the far north of the country, where mounds known as *terpen* were built to keep the sea at bay in Friesland and Groningen, and in Drenthe megalithic tombs, *hunebeds*, stretch scattered across a low ridge of hills, the hondsrug, north of Emmen.

Clearer details of the region begin to emerge at the time of Julius Caesar's conquest of Gaul in 57 BC to 50 BC. He found three tribal groupings living in the region: the mainly Celtic **Belgae** (hence the nineteenth-century term

"Belgium") settled by the Rhine, Maas and Waal to the south; the Germanic **Frisians** living on the marshy coastal strip north of the Scheldt; and the **Batavi**, another Germanic people, inhabiting the swampy river banks of what is now the southern Netherlands. The Belgae were conquered and their lands incorporated into the imperial province of Gallia Belgica, but the territory of the Batavi and Frisians was not considered worthy of colonization. These tribes were granted the status of allies, a source of recruitment for the Roman legions and curiosity for imperial travellers. In 50 AD Pliny observed "Here a wretched race is found, inhabiting either the more elevated spots or artificial mounds… When the waves cover the surrounding area they are like so many mariners on board a ship, and when again the tide recedes their condition is that of so many shipwrecked men."

The **Roman occupation** of Gallia Belgica continued for 500 years until the legions were pulled back to protect the heartlands of their crumbling empire. As the empire collapsed in chaos and confusion, the Germanic **Franks**, who had been settling within Gallia Belgica from the third century, filled the power vacuum, establishing a **Merovingian** kingdom around their capital Tournai (in modern Belgium) with their allies the Belgae. A great swathe of forest extending from the Scheldt to the Ardennes separated this Frankish kingdom from the more confused situation to the north and east, where other tribes of Franks settled along the Scheldt and Leie, Saxons occupied parts of Overijssel and Gelderland, and the Frisians clung to the shore.

Towards the end of the fifth century, the Merovingian king, Clovis, was converted to Christianity and the faith slowly filtered north, spread by energetic missionaries like St Willibrord, first bishop of Utrecht from about 710, and St Boniface, who was killed by the Frisians in 754 in a final act of pagan resistance before they too were converted. Meanwhile, after the death of the last distinguished Merovingian king, Dagobert, in 638, power passed increasingly to the so-called "mayors of the palace", a hereditary position whose most outstanding occupant was **Charles Martel** (c.690–741). Martel dominated a large but all too obviously shambolic kingdom whose military weakness he determined to remedy. Traditionally, the Merovingian (Frankish) army was comprised of a body of infantry led by a small group of cavalry. Martel replaced this with a largely mounted force of highly trained knights, who bore their own military expenses in return for land – the beginnings of the feudal system. These reforms came just in time to save Christendom: in 711 an extraordinary Arab advance, which had begun at the beginning of the seventh century, reached the Pyrenees and a massive Muslim army occupied southern France in preparation for further conquests. In the event, Martel defeated the invaders outside Tours in 732, one of Europe's most crucial engagements and one that saved France from Arab conquest for good. Ten years after Martel's death, his son, Pepin the Short, formally usurped the Merovingian throne with the blessing of the pope, becoming the first of the **Carolingian** dynasty, whose most famous member was **Charlemagne**, son of Pepin and king of the west Franks from 768. In a dazzling series of campaigns, Charlemagne extended his empire south into Italy, west to the Pyrenees, north to Denmark and east to the Oder. His secular authority was bolstered by his coronation as the first **Holy Roman Emperor** in 800, a title bestowed on him by the Pope in order to legitimize his claim as the successor to the emperors of Imperial Rome.

The strength and stability of Charlemagne's court at Aachen spread to the Low Countries, bringing a flurry of building of superb Romanesque churches like Maastricht's St Servaas, and a trading boom, utilizing the region's principal rivers. However, unlike his Roman predecessors, Charlemagne was subject to the divisive inheritance laws of the Salian tribe of Franks, and after his death in 814, his kingdom was divided between his grandsons into three roughly parallel strips of territory, the precursors of France, the Low Countries and Germany.

THE GROWTH OF THE TOWNS

The tripartite division of Charlemagne's empire placed the Low Countries between the emergent French- and German-speaking nations, a dangerous location which was subsequently to decide much of its history. Amidst the cobweb of local alliances that made up early feudal western Europe in the ninth and tenth cen-

turies, however, this was not apparent. During this period, French kings and German emperors exercised a general authority over the region, but power was effectively in the hands of local lords who, remote from central control, brought a degree of local stability. From the twelfth century, feudalism slipped into a gradual decline, the intricate pattern of localized allegiances undermined by the increasing strength of certain lords, whose power and wealth often exceeded that of their nominal sovereign. Preoccupied by territorial squabbles, this streamlined nobility was usually willing to assist the growth of towns by granting charters that permitted a certain amount of autonomy in exchange for tax revenues, and military and labour services. The first major cities were the cloth towns of Flanders – Bruges, Ieper (Ypres) and Ghent. Meanwhile, their smaller northern neighbours concentrated on trade, exploiting their strategic position at the junction of several of the major waterways and trade routes of the day, Amsterdam being a case in point.

BURGUNDIAN RULE

By the late fourteenth century the political situation in the Low Countries was fairly clear: five lords controlled most of the region, paying only nominal homage to their French or German overlords. In 1419 **Philip the Good** of Burgundy succeeded to the countship of Flanders and by a series of adroit political moves gained control over Holland, Zeeland, Brabant and Limburg to the north, and Antwerp, Namur and Luxembourg to the south. He consolidated his power by establishing a strong central administration in Bruges and restricting the privileges granted in the towns' charters. During his reign Bruges became an emporium for the Hanseatic League, a mainly German association of towns who acted as a trading group and protected their interests by an exclusive system of trading tariffs. Philip died in 1467 to be succeeded by his son, Charles the Bold, who was killed in battle ten years later, plunging his carefully crafted domain into turmoil. The French seized the opportunity to take back Arras and Burgundy and before the people of Flanders would agree to fight the French they kidnapped Charles's daughter, Mary, and forced her to sign a charter that restored the civic privileges removed by her grandfather Philip.

THE HABSBURGS

After her release, Mary married the **Habsburg** Maximilian of Austria, who assumed sole authority when Mary was killed in a riding accident in 1482. Maximilian continued to implement the centralizing policies of Philip the Good, but in 1494, when he became Holy Roman Emperor, he transferred control of the Low Countries to his son, Philip the Handsome. The latter died in 1506 and his territories were passed on to Maximilian's grandson **Charles V**, who in turn became King of Spain and Holy Roman Emperor in 1516 and 1519 respectively. Charles was suspicious of the turbulent burghers of Flanders and, following in Maximilian's footsteps, favoured Antwerp at their expense; it soon became the greatest port in the empire, part of a general movement of trade and prosperity away from Flanders to the cities to the north.

Through sheer might, Charles systematically bent the merchant cities of the Low Countries to his will, but regardless of this display of force, a spiritual trend was emerging that would soon question not only the rights of the Emperor but also rock the power of the Catholic Church itself.

STIRRINGS OF THE REFORMATION

An alliance of Church and State had dominated the medieval world: pope and bishops, kings and counts were supposedly the representatives of God on earth, and they combined to crush religious dissent wherever it appeared. Much of their authority depended on the ignorance of the population, who were entirely dependent on their priests for the interpretation of the scriptures, their view of the world carefully controlled.

There were many complex reasons for the **Reformation**, the stirring of religious revolt that stood sixteenth-century Europe on its head, but certainly the **development of typography** was key. For the first time, printers were able to produce relatively cheap bibles in quantity, and the religious texts were no longer the exclusive property of the Church. A welter of debate spread across much of western Europe, led initially by theologians who wished to cleanse the Catholic church of its corruptions, superstitions and extravagant ceremony; only later did many of these same thinkers decide to support a breakaway church. Humanists like **Erasmus of Rotterdam** (1465–1536) saw man as the crowning of creation rather than the sinful creature of the Fall; and, most importantly, in 1517 **Martin Luther** produced his 95 theses against indulgences, rejecting among other things Christ's presence in the sacrament of the Eucharist, and denying the Church's monopoly on the interpretation of the Bible. His works and Bible translations were printed in the Netherlands and his ideas gained a following in a group known as the Sacramentarians. They, and other reforming groups branded as **Lutheran** by the Church, were persecuted and escaped the towns to form fugitive communes where the doctrines of another reformer, **John Calvin** (1509–64), became popular. Luther stated that the Church's political power was subservient to that of the state; Calvin emphasized the importance of individual conscience and the need for redemption through the grace of Christ rather than the confessional. The seeds of Protestantism fell on fertile ground among the merchants of the cities of the Low Countries, whose wealth and independence could not easily be accommodated within a rigid caste society. Similarly, their employees, the guildsmen and their apprentices, had a long history of opposing royal authority, and many were soon convinced of the need to reform an autocratic, venal church. In 1555, Charles V abdicated, transferring his German lands to his brother Ferdinand, and his Italian, Spanish and Low Countries territories to his son, the fanatically Catholic **Philip II**. In the short term, the scene was set for a massive confrontation, while the dynastic ramifications of the division of the Habsburg Empire were to complicate European affairs for centuries.

THE REVOLT OF THE NETHERLANDS

On his father's abdication, Philip decided to teach his heretical subjects a lesson. He garrisoned the towns of the Low Countries with Spanish mercenaries, imported the Inquisition and passed a series of anti-Protestant edicts. The opposition to these measures was, however, so widespread that he was pushed into a tactical withdrawal, recalling his soldiers and transferring control to his sister **Margaret of Parma** in 1559. Based in Brussels, the equally resolute Margaret implemented the policies of her brother with gusto. In 1561 she reorganized the Church and created fourteen new bishoprics, a move that was construed as a wresting of power from civil authority, and an attempt to destroy the local aristocracy's powers of religious patronage. Protestantism and Protestant sympathies spread to the nobility, who now formed the "League of the Nobility" to counter Habsburg policy. The League petitioned Philip for moderation but were dismissed out of hand by one of Margaret's Walloon advisers, who called them "ces geux" ("those beggars"), an epithet that was to be enthusiastically adopted by the rebels. In 1565 a harvest failure caused a winter famine among the workers, and in many towns, particularly Antwerp, they ran riot in the churches, sacking them of their wealth and destroying their rich decoration in the **Iconoclastic Fury**.

The ferocity of this outbreak shocked the higher classes into renewed support for Spain, and Margaret regained the allegiance of most nobles – with the principal exception of the country's greatest landowner, Prince William of Orange-Nassau, known as **William the Silent** (though William the Taciturn is a better translation). Of Germanic descent, he was raised a Catholic but the excesses and rigidity of Philip had caused him to side with the Protestant movement. A firm believer in individual freedom and religious tolerance, William became a symbol of liberty; but after the Fury had revitalized the pro-Spanish party, he prudently slipped away to his estates in Germany.

Philip II saw himself as responsible to God for the salvation of his subjects and therefore obliged to protect them from heresy. In 1567, keen to take advantage of the opportunity provided by the increased support for Margaret, he appointed the **Duke of Alva**, with an army of 10,000 men, to enter the Low Countries and suppress his religious opponents absolutely. Alva's arrival prompted Margaret to withdraw in a huff, and the Low Countries came under military rule. Alva's first act was to set up what the Protestants soon called the **Council of Blood**, a kangaroo court which tried and condemned 12,000 of those who had taken part in the rioting of the year before. Initially the repression worked: in 1568, when William attempted an invasion from Germany, the towns, garrisoned by the Spanish, offered no support. William

waited and conceived other means of defeating Alva. In April 1572 a band of privateers entered Brielle on the Maas and captured it from the Spanish. This was one of several commando-style attacks by the so-called **Waterguezen** or sea-beggars, who were at first obliged to operate from England, although it was soon possible for them to secure bases in the Netherlands, whose citizens had grown to loathe Alva and his Spaniards.

After the success at Brielle, the revolt spread rapidly: by June the rebels controlled the province of Holland and William was able to take command of his troops in Delft. Alva and his son Frederick fought back, taking Gelder, Overijssel and the towns of Zutphen and Naarden, and in June 1573 Haarlem, massacring the Calvinist ministers and most of the defenders. But the Protestants retaliated: utilizing their superior naval power the dykes were cut and the Spanish forces, unpaid and threatened with destruction, were forced to withdraw. Frustrated, Philip replaced Alva with Luis de Resquesens, who initially had some success in the south, where the Catholic majority were more willing to compromise with Spanish rule than their northern neighbours.

William's triumphant relief of Leiden in 1574 increased the confidence of the rebel forces, and when de Resquesens died in 1576, his unpaid garrison in Antwerp mutinied and attacked the town, slaughtering some 8000 of its people in what was known as the **Spanish Fury**. Though Spain still held several towns, the massacre alienated the south and pushed its peoples into the arms of William, whose troops now controlled most of the Low Countries. Momentarily, it seemed possible for the whole region to unite behind William, and the various provinces signed the **Pacification of Ghent** in 1576, an agreement that guaranteed freedom of religious belief. However, differences between Protestant north and Catholic south proved irreconcilable, with many Walloons and Flemings suspicious both of William's ambitions and his Calvinist cronies. Consequently, when another army arrived from Spain, under the command of Alexander Farnese, Duke of Parma, the south was reoccupied without much difficulty, beginning a separation that would lead, after many changes, to the creation of three modern countries.

In 1579 seven provinces (Holland, Zeeland, Utrecht, Groningen, Friesland, Overijssel and Gelderland) signed the **Union of Utrecht**, an alliance against Spain that was to be the first unification of the Netherlands as an identifiable country – the so-called **United Provinces**. The agreement stipulated freedom of belief in the provinces, an important step since the struggle against Spain wasn't simply a religious one: many Catholics disliked the Spanish occupation and William did not wish to alienate this possible source of support. This liberalism did not, however, extend to freedom of worship, although a blind eye was turned to the celebration of Mass if it was done privately and inconspicuously – giving rise to the "hidden churches" found throughout the country.

THE UNITED PROVINCES (1579–1713)

In order to follow the developments of the sixteenth and seventeenth centuries in what is now The Netherlands, it's necessary to have an idea of the organization of the **United Provinces**. Holland, today comprising North and South Holland, was by far the dominant province economically and politically, and although the provinces maintained a decentralized independence, as far as the United Provinces as a whole were concerned, what Holland said, pretty much went. The assembly of these United Provinces was known as the **States General**, and met at The Hague; it had no domestic legislative authority, and could only carry out foreign policy by unanimous decision, a formula designed to make potential waverers feel more secure. The role of **Stadholder** was the most important in each province, roughly equivalent to that of governor, though the same person could occupy this position in any number of provinces – and mostly did, with the Orange-Nassaus characteristically picking up five or six provinces at any one time. The Council Pensionary was another major post. The man who held either title in Holland was a centre of political power. Pieter Geyl, in his seminal *Revolt of the Netherlands*, defined the end result as the establishment of a republic which was "oligarchic, erastian (and) decentralized".

In 1584, a Catholic assassinated William the Silent at his residence in Delft. It was a grievous blow to the provinces and, as William's son **Maurice** was only 17, power passed to **Johan van Oldenbarneveldt**, the country's leading statesman and Council Pensionary of Rotterdam and later, Holland. Things were going badly in the war against the Spanish: Nijmegen had fallen and Henry III of France refused help even though the States General had made him tentative offers of sovereignty. In desperation, Oldenbarneveldt turned to Elizabeth I of England, who suggested the Earl of Leicester as governor general. Leicester was accepted, but completely mishandled the military situation, alienating the Dutch into the bargain. Short of options, Oldenbarneveldt and Maurice stepped into the breach and, somewhat to their surprise, drove the Spanish back. International events then played into their hands: in 1588, the English defeated the Spanish Armada and, the following year, the powerful and ambitious king Henry III of France died. Most important of all, Philip II of Spain, the scourge of the Low Countries, died in 1598, a necessary preamble to the **Twelve Year Truce** (1609–1621) signed between the Habsburgs and the United Provinces, which grudgingly accepted the independence of the new republic.

THE EARLY SEVENTEENTH CENTURY

In the breathing space created by the truce, the rivalry between Maurice and Oldenbarneveldt intensified and an obscure argument within the Calvinist church on predestination proved the catalyst for Oldenbarneveldt's downfall. The quarrel, between two Leiden theologians, began in 1612: Armenius argued that God gave man the choice of accepting or rejecting faith; Gomarus, his opponent, that predestination was absolute – to the degree that God chooses who will be saved and who damned with man powerless in the decision. This row between the two groups (known respectively as Remonstrants and Counter-Remonstrants) soon became attached to the political divisions within the republic. When a synod was arranged at Dordrecht to resolve the doctrinal matter, the province of Holland, led by Oldenbarneveldt, refused to attend, insisting on Holland's right to decide its own religious orthodoxies. At heart, he and his fellow deputies supported the provincial independence favoured by Remonstrant sympathisers, whereas Maurice sided with the Counter-Remonstrants, who favoured a strong central authority. The Counter-Remonstrants won at

Dordrecht and Maurice, with his troops behind him, quickly overcame his opponents and had Oldenbarneveldt arrested. In May 1619 he was executed in The Hague "for having conspired to dismember the states of the Netherlands and greatly troubled God's church".

With the end of the Twelve Year Truce in 1621, fighting with Spain broke out once again, this time part of the more general **Thirty Years' War** (1618–48), a largely religious-based conflict between Catholic and Protestant countries that involved most of western Europe. In the Low Countries, the Spanish were initially successful, but they were weakened by war with France and by the fresh attacks of Maurice's successor, his brother **Frederick Henry**. From 1625, the Spaniards suffered a series of defeats on land and sea that forced them out of what is today the southern part of the Netherlands, and in 1648 they were compelled to accept the humiliating terms of the **Peace of Westphalia**. This was a general treaty that ended the Thirty Years' War and under its terms the independence of the United Provinces was formally recognized. What's more, the Dutch were able to insist that the Scheldt estuary be closed to shipping, an action designed to destroy the trade and prosperity of Antwerp, which – along with the rest of modern-day Belgium – remained part of the Habsburg empire. By this act, the commercial expansion and pre-eminence of Amsterdam was assured, and the Golden Age began.

THE GOLDEN AGE

The brilliance of **Amsterdam**'s explosion onto the European scene is as difficult to underestimate as it is to detail. The size of the city's merchant fleet carrying Baltic grain into Europe had long been considerable and even during the long war with Spain it had continued to expand. Indeed, not only were the Spaniards unable to undermine it, but they were, on occasion, even obliged to use Dutch ships to supply their own troops – part of a burgeoning cargo trade that was another key ingredient of Amsterdam's economic success.

It was, however, the emasculation of Antwerp by the Treaty of Westphalia that launched a period of extraordinarily dynamic growth, and Amsterdam quickly became the emporium for the products of north and south Europe and the new colonies in the East and West Indies. Dutch banking and investment brought further prosperity, and by the mid-seventeenth century Amsterdam's wealth was spectacular. The Calvinist bourgeoisie indulged themselves in fine and whimsically decorated canal houses, and commissioned images of themselves in group portraits. Civic pride knew no bounds: great monuments to self-aggrandizement, such as the new town hall, were hastily erected, and, if some went hungry, few starved, as the poor were cared for in municipal almshouses. The arts flourished and religious tolerance extended even to the traditional scapegoats, the **Jews**, and in particular the Sephardic Jews, who had been hounded from Spain by the Inquisition but were guaranteed freedom from religious persecution under the terms of the Union of Utrecht of 1579 (see above). By the end of the eighteenth century, Jews accounted for ten percent of the city's inhabitants. Guilds and craft associations thrived, and in the first half of the seventeenth century the city's population quadrupled. Furthermore, although Amsterdam was the centre of this boom, economic ripples spread across much of the United Provinces. Dutch farmers were, for instance, able to sell all they could produce in the expanding city and a string of Zuider Zee ports cashed in on the flourishing Baltic trade.

Throughout this so-called **Golden Age**, one organization that kept the country's coffers brimming was the **East India Company**. Formed in 1602, this Amsterdam-controlled enterprise sent ships to Asia, Indonesia, and as far as China to bring back spices, woods and other assorted valuables. The States General granted the company a trading monopoly in all lands east of the Cape of Good Hope and, for good measure, threw in unlimited military powers over the lands it controlled. As a consequence, the company became a colonial power in its own right, governing, at one time or another, Malaya, Ceylon and parts of modern-day Indonesia. In 1621, the **West India Company** was inaugurated to protect Dutch interests in the Americas and Africa. Expending most of its energies in waging war on Spanish and Portuguese colonies from a base in Surinam, it never achieved the success of the East India Company, and was dismantled in 1674, ten years after its small colony of New Amsterdam had been captured by the British – and renamed New York. Elsewhere, the Netherlands held on to its colonies for as long as possible – **Java** and **Sumatra** remained under Dutch control until 1949.

Although the economics of the Golden Age were dazzling, the political climate was dismal. The United Provinces were dogged by interminable wrangling between those who hankered for a central, unified government under the pre-eminent **House of Orange-Nassau** and those who championed provincial autonomy. Frederick Henry died in 1647 and his successor, William II, lasted just three years before his death from smallpox. A week after William's death, his wife bore the son who would become William III of England, but in the meantime the leaders of the province of Holland seized their opportunity. They forced measures through the States General abolishing the position of Stadholder, thereby reducing the powers of the Orangists and increasing those of the provinces, chiefly Holland itself. Holland's foremost figure in these years was **Johan de Witt**, Council Pensionary to the States General. He guided the country through wars with England and Sweden, concluding a triple alliance between the two countries and the United Provinces in 1678. This didn't last, however, and when France and England marched on the Provinces two years later, the republic was in deep trouble – previous victories had been at sea, and the army, weak and disorganized, could not withstand an attack. In panic, the country turned to **William III of Orange** for leadership and Johan de Witt was brutally murdered by a mob of Orangist sympathisers in The Hague. By 1678 William had defeated the French and made peace with the English – and was rewarded (along with his wife Mary) with the English crown ten years later.

THE UNITED PROVINCES IN THE EIGHTEENTH CENTURY

Though King William had defeated the French, Louis XIV retained designs on the United Provinces and the pot was kept boiling in a long series of dynastic wars that ranged across northern Europe. In 1700, Charles II of Spain, the last of the Spanish Habsburgs, died childless, bequeathing the Spanish throne and control of the Spanish Netherlands to Philip of Anjou, Louis' grandson. Louis promptly forced Philip to cede the latter to France, which was, with every justification, construed as a threat to the balance of power by France's neighbours. The **War of the Spanish Succession** ensued with the United Provinces, England and Austria forming the Triple Alliance to thwart the French king. The war itself was a haphazard, long-winded affair distinguished by the spectacular victories of the Duke of Marlborough at Blenheim, Ramillies and Malplaquet. It dragged on until the **Treaty of Utrecht** of 1713 in which France finally abandoned its claim to the Spanish Netherlands.

However, the fighting had drained the United Provinces' reserves and its slow economic and political decline began, accelerated by a reactive trend towards conservatism. This in turn reflected the development of an increasingly socially static society, with power and wealth concentrated within a small elite. Furthermore, with the threat of foreign conquest effectively removed, the Dutch ruling class divided into two main camps – the Orangists and the pro-French "Patriots" – whose interminable squabbling soon brought political life to a virtual standstill. The situation deteriorated even further in the latter half of the century and the last few years of the United Provinces present a sorry state of affairs.

In 1795 the French, aided by the Patriots, invaded, setting up the **Batavian Republic** and dissolving the United Provinces and much of the control of the rich Dutch merchants. Effectively part of the Napoleonic empire, the Netherlands were obliged to wage unenthusiastic war with England, and in 1806 Napoleon appointed his brother Louis as their king in an attempt to create a commercial gulf between the country and England. Louis, however, wasn't willing to allow the Netherlands to become a simple satellite of France; he ignored Napoleon's directives and after just four years of rule was forced to abdicate. The country was then formally incorporated into the French Empire, and for three gloomy years suffered occupation and heavy taxation to finance French military adventures.

Following Napoleon's disastrous retreat from Moscow, the Orangist faction once more surfaced to exploit weakening French control. In 1813, Frederick William, son of the exiled William V, returned to the country and eight months later, under the terms of the **Congress** of Vienna, was crowned King William I of the United Kingdom of the Netherlands, incorporating both the old United Provinces and the Spanish (Austrian) Netherlands. A strong-willed man, he spent much of the latter part of his life trying to control his disparate kingdom, but he failed primarily because of the Protestant north's attempt to dominate the Catholic south. The southern provinces revolted against his rule and in 1830 the Kingdom of Belgium was proclaimed.

1830 TO WORLD WAR II

A final invasion of Belgium in 1839 gave William most of Limburg, and all but ended centuries of changes to borders and territory. The Netherlands benefited from this new stability, the trade surplus picked up and canal building linked Rotterdam and Amsterdam to the North Sea. The outstanding political figure of the times, **Jan Rudolph Thorbecke**, formed three ruling cabinets (1849–53, 1862–66 and 1872, in the year of his death) and steered the Netherlands through a profound change. The political parties of the late eighteenth century had wished to resurrect the power and prestige of the seventeenth-century Netherlands; Thorbecke and his allies resigned themselves to the country's reduced status of a small power and eulogized its advantages. For the first time, from about 1850, liberty was seen as a luxury made possible by the country's very lack of power, and the malaise which had long disturbed public life gave way to a positive appreciation of the narrowness of its national existence. One of the results of Thorbecke's liberalism was a gradual extension of the franchise, culminating in the Act of Universal Suffrage in 1917.

At the outbreak of **World War I** the Netherlands remained neutral, but suffered privations from the Allied blockade of ports through which Germany might be supplied. Similar attempts to remain neutral in **World War II** however, failed: the Germans invaded on May 10, 1940, destroying Rotterdam four days later. The Dutch were quickly overwhelmed, Queen Wilhelmina fled to London, and opposition to Nazi occupation was continued by the Resistance. Instrumental in destroying German supplies and munitions, they also helped many downed airmen escape back to England. A heavy price was paid for their contribution to the war effort: 23,000 resistance fighters were killed in the war years. In Amsterdam, the old Jewish community, swollen by those who had fled Germany to escape the persecution of the 1930s, was obliterated, leaving the deserted Jodenhoek and the diary of **Anne Frank** as testament to the horrors.

Liberation began in autumn 1944 with **Operation Market Garden**. This was a British plan to finish the war quickly by creating a corridor stretching from Eindhoven to Arnhem, gaining control of the three main rivers en route, isolating the occupying forces to the west in the Netherlands and pushing straight into Germany. It was a gamble, but if successful would hasten the end of hostilities. On September 17 the 1st Airborne Division parachuted into the countryside around Oosterbeek, a small village near the most northerly target of the operation, the bridge at **Arnhem**. German opposition was much stronger than expected, and after heavy fighting the Allied forces could only take the northern end of the bridge. The advancing British army was unable to break through fast enough, and after four days the decimated battalion defending the bridge was forced to withdraw.

With the failure of Operation Market Garden, the Allies were obliged to resort to more orthodox military tactics to clear the south and east Netherlands of the Germans, a slow process that took all the winter and spring of 1944–45. As the assault was concentrated on Germany itself, the coastal provinces of the country were left alone, but they suffered terribly from lack of food and fuel. Finally, on April 5, 1945, the German army surrendered to the Canadians at Wageningen.

1945 TO THE PRESENT DAY

The post-war years were spent patching up the damage of occupation. Rotterdam was rapidly rebuilt, and the dykes blown in the war – both by the Allies to slow the German advance and by the German army itself – were repaired. Two events were, however, to mar the late 1940s and early 1950s: the former Dutch colonies of Java and Sumatra, taken by the Japanese at the outbreak of the war, were now ruled by a nationalist Republican government that refused to recognize Dutch sovereignty. Following the failure of talks between The Hague and the islanders in 1947, the Dutch sent the troops in, a colonial enterprise that soon became a bloody débâcle. International opposition was intense and, after much condemnation and pressure, the Dutch reluctantly surrendered their most important Asian colonies, which were incorporated as **Indonesia** in 1950. Back at home, tragedy struck on February 1, 1953 when an unusually high tide was pushed over Zeeland's sea defences by a westerly wind, flooding 40,000 acres of land and drowning over 1800 people. The response was to secure the area's future with the **Delta Project**, closing off the western part of the Scheldt and Maas estuaries with massive sea dykes. A brilliant and graceful piece of engineering, the main storm surge barrier on the Oosterschelde was finally completed in 1986.

Elsewhere rebuilding continued; in Amsterdam all the land projected in 1947 for use by the year 2000 was in fact used up by the "garden cities" of the dormitory suburbs by 1970. Similarly, the reclaimed polders of Flevoland were soon built upon to absorb more of the excess urban population – Lelystad, the main town, now has a population of around 80,000. But growth wasn't only physical: the social consciousness and radicalism of the 1960s reached the country early, and the flower-power, psychedelic revolution was quick to catch on. It was quick to fade, too, replaced by the cynicism of the 1970s, but one manifestation of the radical brouhaha that did produce tangible change was the **squatting movement**. The squatters and associated activists objected to the wholesale destruction of low-cost (often old) urban housing as envisaged by most municipal planning departments, arguing that the country's city centres should not become the preserve of big business, holed up in mighty glass and concrete towers. Their campaign precipitated major riots in Amsterdam and other cities throughout the late 1960s and early 1970s, and although individual actions rarely defeated the developers, the squatters won the argument: by the mid-1980s urban planning had, by and large, become a much more thoughtful, consultative affair with due (or at least some) attention given to both the urban environment in general and the need to keep people living in the city centres in particular.

Today, the country's finely balanced system of proportional representation forces almost continuous political compromise and debate, but brings little rapid change, politics and politicking seeming a bland business conducted between the three main parties, the **Protestant-Catholic CDA coalition**, the **Liberal VVD** and the **Socialist PvdA**. A governmental system that has so effectively incorporated the disparate elements of a modern and diverse state – Catholic and Protestant, management and union, city and country, socialist and conservative – has earned the Netherlands a well-deserved reputation for comfortable toleration, and outbreaks of opposition, when they do appear, on such items as eco-issues, housing and racism, provoke a mad rush to the bargaining table.

AN INTRODUCTION TO DUTCH ART

The following piece is the very briefest of introductions to the subject, designed to serve only as a quick reference on your way round the major galleries. For the reasons already stated in the introduction to the "History" section, it inevitably includes reference to the early art of the whole region – the Low Countries – rather than just the Netherlands. For more in-depth and academic studies, see the recommendations in "Books" on p.375. For a list of where to find some of the artists mentioned here, turn to the box at the end of this section.

BEGINNINGS

Until the sixteenth century the area now known as the "Low Countries" was in effect one country, the most artistically productive part of which was Flanders in modern Belgium, and it was there that the solid realist base of later Dutch painting developed. Today the works of these early **Flemish painters** are pretty sparse in Holland, and even in Belgium few collections are as complete as you might expect; indeed, many ended up as the property of the ruling Habsburgs and were removed to Spain. Most Dutch galleries do, however, have a few examples.

Jan van Eyck (1385–1441) is generally regarded as the originator of Low Countries painting, and has even been credited with the invention of oil painting itself – though it seems more likely that he simply perfected a new technique by thinning his paint with the recently discovered turpentine, thus making it more flexible. His most famous work still in the Low Countries is the altarpiece in Ghent Cathedral (debatably painted with the help of his lesser-known brother, Hubert), which was revolutionary in its realism, for the first time using elements of native landscape in depicting biblical themes. His work was also rich in a complex symbolism, whereby everyday objects take on a disguised, usually religious meaning, the nature of which has generated analysis and discussion ever since. Van Eyck's style and technique were to influence several generations of Low Countries artists.

Firmly in the Van Eyck tradition were the **Master of Flemalle** (1387–1444) and **Rogier van der Weyden** (1400–64). The Flemalle master is a shadowy figure: some believe he was the teacher of Van der Weyden, others that the two artists were in fact the same person. There are differences between the two, however: the Flemalle master's paintings are stylistically close to Van Eyck's, whereas Van der Weyden shows a more emotional and religious intensity. Van der Weyden influenced such painters as **Dieric Bouts** (1415–75), who was born in Haarlem but worked in Leuven, and is recognizable by his stiff, rather elongated figures. **Hugo van der Goes** (d. 1482) was the next Ghent master after Van Eyck, most famous for the *Portinari Altarpiece* in Florence's Uffizi gallery. After a short painting career, he died insane and his late works have strong hints of his impending madness in their subversive use of space and implicit acceptance of the viewer's presence. Few doubt that **Hans Memling** (1440–94) was a pupil of Van der Weyden: active in Bruges throughout his life, he is best remembered for the pastoral charm of his landscapes and the quality of his portraiture, much of which survives on the rescued side panels of triptychs. **Gerard David** (1460–1523) was a native of Oudewater, but moved to Bruges in 1484, becoming the last of the great painters to work in that city, before it was overtaken in prosperity by Antwerp – which itself became the focus of a more Italianate school of art in the sixteenth century.

More renowned is **Hieronymus Bosch** (1450–1516), a native of 's Hertogenbosch, who lived for most of his life in Holland, though his style is closely aligned to that of his Flemish contemporaries. Frequently reprinted, his religious allegories are filled with macabre visions of tortured people and grotesque beasts, and appear at first faintly unhinged, though it's now clear that these are visual representations of what were then familiar sayings, idioms and parables. While their interpretation is far from resolved, Bosch's paintings draw strongly on subconscious fears and archetypes, giving them a lasting, haunting fascination.

THE SIXTEENTH CENTURY

At the beginning of the sixteenth century, the first signs that Flanders didn't have the monopoly on artistic talent began to show – in the northern towns. An early start was made in Haarlem, where **Geertgen tot Sint Jans** ("Little Gerard of the Brotherhood of St John"; 1465–1495) had initiated – in a strangely naïve style – an artistic tradition that would produce a string of fine artists. **Jan Mostaert** (1475–1555) took over after Geertgen's death, and continued to develop the divergent style. However, it was **Lucas van Leyden** (1489–1533) who was the first painter to effect significant changes in northern painting. Born in Leiden, his bright colours and narrative technique were refreshingly new, introducing a novel dynamism into what had by then become a rigidly formal treatment of devotional subjects. There was rivalry, of course. Eager to publicize Haarlem as the artistic capital of the northern Netherlands, Carel van Mander (see p.352) claimed Haarlem native **Jan van Scorel** (1495–1562) as the better painter, complaining, too, of Lucas's dandyish ways. Certainly Scorel's influence should not be underestimated. When the Bishop of Utrecht became Pope Hadrian VI, he took Scorel with him to Rome as court painter, giving him the opportunity to introduce Italian styles into what had been a completely independent tradition. Hadrian died soon after, and Van Scorel returned north, combining the ideas he had picked up in Italy with his native realism and passing them on to **Maerten van**

Heemskerck (1498–1574), who went off to Italy himself in 1532, staying there five years before returning to Haarlem.

Despite the emerging artists of the north however, artistic pre-eminence remained with Flanders, passing from Bruges to Antwerp, whose artists combined the influence of the Italian painters with the domestic Flemish tradition. **Quentin Matsys** (1464–1530) introduced florid classical architectural detail and intricate landscape backgrounds to his works, influenced perhaps by the work of Leonardo da Vinci. As well as religious works, he painted portraits and genre scenes, all of which have recognizably Italian facets, and paved the way for the Dutch genre painters of later years. His follower, **Joos van Cleve** (1485–1541) painted in a similarly refined and realistic manner. **Jan Gossaert** (c.1470–1533) made the pilgrimage to Italy, and his dynamic works are packed with detail, especially finely drawn classical architectural backdrops. He was the first Low Countries artist to introduce the subjects of classical mythology into his works, part of a steady trend through the period towards secular subject matter, which can also be seen in the work of **Joachim Patenier** (1485–1524), who painted small landscapes of fantastic scenery.

The latter part of the sixteenth century was dominated by the work of **Pieter Bruegel the Elder** (1525–69), whose gruesome allegories and innovative interpretations of religious subjects are firmly placed in Low Countries settings. Most famous are his paintings of peasant lowlife, though he himself was well connected in court circles in Antwerp and, later, Brussels. **Pieter Aertsen** (1508–75) also worked in the peasant genre, adding aspects of the still life: his paintings often show a detailed kitchen scene in the foreground, with a religious episode going on behind. Towards the latter half of the century the stylized Italianate portrait was much in vogue, its chief exponents being **Adriaen Key**, **Anthonis Mor** and **Frans Pourbus**.

RUBENS AND HIS FOLLOWERS

Pieter Paul Rubens (1577–1640) was the most influential Low Countries artist of the early seventeenth century and the most important exponent of Baroque painting in northern

Europe. Born in Siegen, Westphalia, his parents returned to their native Antwerp when Rubens was a child. He entered the Antwerp Guild in 1598, became court painter to the Duke of Mantua in 1600, and until 1608 travelled extensively in Italy, absorbing the art of the High Renaissance and classical architecture. By the time of his return to Antwerp in 1608 he had acquired an enormous artistic vocabulary: the paintings of Caravaggio in particular were to influence his work strongly. His first major success was *The Raising of the Cross*, painted in 1610 and kept today in Antwerp cathedral. A large, dynamic work, it caused a sensation at the time, establishing Rubens' reputation and leading to a string of commissions that enabled him to set up his own studio.

The division of labour in Rubens' studio, and the talent of the artists working there – who included Antony van Dyck and Jacob Jordaens – ensured quality and quantity. Indeed, the degree to which Rubens personally worked on a canvas varied considerably; and would determine its price. From the early 1620s onwards he turned his hand to a plethora of themes and subjects – religious works, portraits, tapestry designs, landscapes, mythological scenes, ceiling paintings (including that of the Banqueting Hall in Whitehall, London, a commission for Charles I, by whom he was knighted) – each of which was handled with supreme vitality and virtuosity. From his Flemish antecedents he inherited an acute sense of light, and used it not to dramatize his subjects (a technique favoured by Caravaggio and other Italian artists), but in organic association with colour and form. The drama in his works comes from the tremendous animation of his characters. His large-scale allegorical works, especially, are packed with heaving, writhing figures that appear to tumble out from the canvas.

The energy of Rubens' paintings was reflected in his private life. In addition to his career as an artist, he also undertook diplomatic missions to Spain and England on behalf of the governors of Holland, and used the opportunities to study the works of other artists and – as in the case of Velázquez – to meet them personally. In the 1630s, gout began to hamper his activities, and from this time his painting became more domestic and meditative. Hélène Fourment, his second wife, was the subject of many portraits and served as a model for characters in his alle-

gorical paintings, her figure epitomizing the buxom, well-rounded women found throughout his work.

Rubens' influence on the artists of the period was enormous. The huge output of his studio meant that his works were universally seen, and widely disseminated by the engravers he employed to copy his work. Chief among his followers was the portraitist **Antony van Dyck** (1599–1641), who worked in Rubens' studio from 1618, often taking on the depiction of religious figures in his master's works that required particular sensitivity and pathos. Like Rubens, he was born in Antwerp and travelled widely in Italy, though his initial work was influenced less by the Italian artists than by Rubens himself. Eventually van Dyck developed his own distinct style and technique, establishing himself as court painter to Charles I in England, and creating portraits of a nervous elegance that would influence the genre there for the next 150 years. Most of van Dyck's great portraiture remains in England and his best religious paintings are to be found in Belgium, but some of his canvases are exhibited in Dutch galleries, as is a small part of the oeuvre of **Jacob Jordaens** (1593–1678), another member of Rubens' studio, whose robustly naturalistic works have an earthy and sensuous realism that's quite distinct in style and technique.

Amongst several other artists working in Antwerp during the early seventeenth century – and greatly influenced by Rubens – were **Gerhard Seghers** (1591–1651), who specialized in painting flowers, usually around portraits or devotional figures painted by other artists, including Rubens himself. There was also **Theodor Rombouts** (1579–1637), who was strongly influenced by Caravaggio following a trip to Italy, but changed his style to fall in line with that of Rubens when he returned to Antwerp, and **Frans Snyders** (1579–1657), a still life genre specialist who took up where Aertsen left off, amplifying his subject – food and drink – onto even larger, more sumptuous canvases. Synders was also part of the Rubens art machine, painting animals and still life sections for the master's works.

THE GOLDEN AGE

To some extent at least, Dutch art begins with **Carel van Mander** (1548–1606), Haarlem painter, art impresario and one of the few chroniclers of the art of the Low Countries. His *Schilderboek* of 1604 put Flemish and Dutch traditions into context for the first time, and in addition specified the rules of fine painting. Examples of his own work are rare – though Haarlem's Frans Hals Museum weighs in with several (see p.144) – but his followers were many. Among them was **Cornelius Cornelisz van Haarlem** (1562–1638), who produced elegant renditions of biblical and mythical themes; and **Hendrik Goltzius** (1558–1616), who was a skilled engraver and an integral member of Van Mander's Haarlem academy. These painters' enthusiasm for Italian art, combined with the influence of a late revival of Gothicism, resulted in works that combined Mannerist and Classical elements. An interest in realism was also felt, and, for them, the subject became less important than the way in which it was depicted: biblical stories became merely a vehicle whereby artists could apply their skills in painting the human body, landscapes, or copious displays of food. All of this served to break religion's stranglehold on art, and make legitimate a whole range of everyday subjects for the painter.

In Holland (and this was where the north and the south finally diverged) this break with tradition was compounded by the **Reformation**: the austere Calvinism that had replaced the Catholic faith in the United (ie northern) Provinces had no use for images or symbols of devotion in its churches. Instead, painters catered to the burgeoning middle class, and visits to Italy were considered a useful extra rather than an intrisic element of the job; the real giants of the seventeenth century – Hals, Rembrandt, Vermeer – stayed in the Netherlands all their lives. Another innovation was that painting split into more distinct categories – genre, portrait, landscape – and artists tended (with notable exceptions) to confine themselves to one field throughout their careers. So began the greatest age of Dutch art.

HISTORICAL AND RELIGIOUS PAINTING

Italy continued to hold some sway in the Netherlands, not through the Renaissance painters but rather via the fashionable new realism of Caravaggio. Many artists – Rembrandt for one – continued to portray classical subjects, but in a way that was totally at odds with the Mannerists' stylish flights of imagination. The Utrecht artist **Abraham Bloemaert** (1564–1651), though a solid Mannerist throughout his career, encouraged these new ideas, and his students – **Gerard van Honthorst** (1590–1656), **Hendrik Terbrugghen** (1588–1629) and **Dirck van Baburen** (1590–1624) – formed the nucleus of the influential **Utrecht School**, which followed Caravaggio almost to the point of slavishness. Honthorst was perhaps the leading figure, learning his craft from Bloemaert and travelling to Rome, where he was nicknamed "Gerardo delle Notti" for his ingenious handling of light and shade. In his later paintings, however, this was to become more routine technique than inspired invention, and though a supremely competent artist, Honthorst remains somewhat discredited among critics today. Terbrugghen's reputation seems to have aged rather better: he soon forgot Caravaggio and developed a more individual style, his later, lighter work having a great influence on the young Vermeer. After a jaunt to Rome, Baburen shared a studio with Terbrugghen and produced some fairly original work – work which also had some influence on Vermeer – but today he is the least studied member of the group and few of his paintings survive.

But it's **Rembrandt** who was considered the most original historical artist of the seventeenth century, painting religious scenes throughout his life. In the 1630s, the poet and statesman Constantijn Huygens procured for him his greatest commission – a series of five paintings of the Passion, beautifully composed and uncompromisingly realistic. Later, however, Rembrandt received fewer and fewer commissions, since his treatment of biblical and historical subjects was far less dramatic than that of his contemporaries and he ignored their smooth brushwork, preferring a rougher, darker, more disjointed style. It's significant that while the more conventional Jordaens, Honthorst and Van Everdingen were busy decorating the Huis ten Bosch near The Hague for patron Stadholder Frederick Henry, Rembrandt was having his monumental *Conspiracy of Claudius Civilis* (painted for the new Amsterdam Town Hall) rejected – probably because it was thought too pagan an interpretation of what was an important symbolic event in Dutch history. **Aert van Gelder** (1645–1727), Rembrandt's last pupil and probably the only one to concentrate on historical painting, followed the style of his master closely, producing shimmering biblical scenes well into the eighteenth century.

GENRE PAINTING

Genre refers to scenes from everyday life, a subject that, with the decline of the church as patron, had become popular in Holland by the mid-seventeenth century. Many painters devoted themselves solely to such work. Some genre paintings were simply non-idealized portrayals of common scenes, while others, by means of symbols or carefully disguised details, made moral entreaties to the viewer.

Among early seventeenth-century painters, **Hendrik Terbrugghen** and **Gerard Honthorst** spent much of their time on religious subjects, but also adapted the realism and strong chiaroscuro learned from Caravaggio to a number of tableaux of everyday life. **Frans Hals**, too, is better known as a portraitist, but his early genre paintings no doubt influenced his pupil, **Adriaen Brouwer** (1605–38), whose riotous tavern scenes were well received in their day and collected by, among others, Rubens and Rembrandt. Brouwer spent only a couple of years in Haarlem under Hals before returning to his native Flanders, where he influenced the younger **David Teniers**. **Adriaen van Ostade** (1610–85), on the other hand, stayed in Haarlem most of his life, skilfully painting groups of peasants and tavern brawls – though his later acceptance by the establishment led him to water down the realism he had learnt from Brouwer. He was teacher to his brother **Isaak** (1621–49), who produced a large number of open-air peasant scenes, subtle combinations of genre and landscape work.

The English critic E.V. Lucas dubbed Teniers, Brouwer and Ostade "coarse and boorish" compared with **Jan Steen** (1625–79), who, along with Vermeer, is probably the most admired Dutch genre painter. You can see what he had in mind: Steen's paintings offer the same Rabelaisian peasantry in full fling, but they go their debauched ways in broad daylight, and nowhere do you see the filthy rogues in shadowy hovels favoured by Brouwer and Ostade. Steen offers more humour, too, as well as more moralizing, identifying with the hedonistic mob and reproaching them at the same time. Indeed, many of his pictures were illustrations of well-known proverbs – popular epithets on the evils of drink or the transience of human existence that were supposed to teach as well as entertain.

Gerrit Dou (1613–75) was Rembrandt's Leiden contemporary and one of his first pupils. It's difficult to detect any trace of the master's influence in his work, however, as Dou initiated a style of his own: tiny, minutely realized and beautifully finished views of a kind of ordinary life that was decidedly more genteel than Brouwer's – or even Steen's for that matter. He was admired, above all, for his painstaking attention to detail: and he would, it's said, sit out the settling dust in his studio before starting work. Among his students, **Frans van Mieris** (1635–81) continued the highly finished portrayals of the Dutch bourgeoisie, as did **Gabriel Metsu** (1629–67) – perhaps Dou's greatest pupil – whose pictures often convey an overtly moral message. Another pupil of Rembrandt's, though a much later one, was **Nicholaes Maes** (1629–93), whose early works were almost entirely genre paintings, sensitively executed and again with a didactic message. His later paintings show the influence of a more refined style of portrait, which he had picked up in France.

As a native of Zwolle, **Gerard ter Borch** (1619–81) found himself far from all these Leiden/Rembrandt connections; despite trips abroad to most of the artistic capitals of Europe, he remained very much a provincial painter all his life. He depicted Holland's merchant class at play and became renowned for his curious doll-like figures and his enormous ability to capture the textures of different cloths. His domestic scenes were not unlike those of **Pieter de Hooch** (1629–after 1684), whose simple depictions of everyday life are deliberately unsentimental, and, for the first time, have little or no moral commentary. De Hooch's favourite trick was to paint darkened rooms with an open door leading through to a sunlit courtyard, a practice that, along with his trademark rusty red colour, makes his work easy to identify and, at its best, exquisite. That said, his later pictures reflect the encroaching decline of the Dutch Republic: the rooms are more richly decorated, the arrangements more contrived and the subjects far less homely.

It was, however, **Jan Vermeer** (1632–75) who brought the most sophisticated methods to painting interiors, depicting the play of natural light on indoor surfaces with superlative skill – and the tranquil intimacy for which he is now internationally famous. Another recorder of the better-heeled Dutch households and, like De Hooch, without a tendency to moralize, he is regarded (with Hals and Rembrandt) as one of the big three Dutch painters – though he was, it seems, a slow worker. As a result, only about forty paintings can be attributed to him with any certainty. Living all his life in Delft, Vermeer is perhaps the epitome of the seventeenth-century Dutch painter – rejecting the pomp and ostentation of the High Renaissance to quietly record his contemporaries at home, painting for a public that demanded no more than that.

PORTRAITS

Naturally, the ruling bourgeoisie of Holland's flourishing mercantile society wanted to record and celebrate their success, and it's little wonder that portraiture was the best way for a young painter to make a living. **Michiel Jansz Miereveld** (1567–1641), court painter to Frederick Henry in The Hague, was the first real portraitist of the Dutch Republic, but it wasn't long before his stiff and rather conservative figures were superseded by the more spontaneous renderings of **Frans Hals** (1585–1666). Hals is perhaps best known for his "corporation pictures" – portraits of the members of the Dutch civil guard regiments that had been formed in most of the larger towns while the threat of invasion by the Spanish was still imminent. These large group pieces demanded superlative technique, since the painter had to create a collection of individual portraits while retaining a sense of the group, and accord prominence based on the importance of the sitter and the size of the payment each had made. Hals was particularly good at this, using innovative lighting effects, arranging his sitters subtly, and putting all the elements together in a fluid and dynamic composition. He also painted many individual portraits, making the ability to capture fleeting and telling expressions his trademark; his pictures of children are particularly sensitive. Later in life, his work became darker and more akin to Rembrandt's.

Jan Cornelisz Verspronck (1597–1662) and **Bartholomeus van der Helst** (1613–70) were the other great Haarlem portraitists after Frans Hals – Verspronck recognizable by the smooth, shiny glow he always gave to his sit-

ters' faces, Van der Helst by a competent but unadventurous style. Of the two, Van der Helst was the more popular, influencing a number of later painters and leaving Haarlem while still young to begin a solidly successful career as portrait painter to Amsterdam's burghers.

The reputation of **Rembrandt van Rijn** (1606–69) is still relatively recent – nineteenth-century connoisseurs preferred Gerard Dou – but he is now justly regarded as one of the greatest and most versatile painters of all time. Born in Leiden, the son of a miller, he was apprenticed at an early age to Jacob van Swanenburgh, a then quite important, though uninventive, local artist. He shared a studio with Jan Lievens, a promising painter and something of a rival for a while (now all but forgotten), before going to Amsterdam to study under the fashionable Pieter Lastman. Soon he was painting commissions for the city elite and became an accepted member of their circle. The poet and statesman Constantijn Huygens acted as his agent, pulling strings to obtain all of Rembrandt's more lucrative jobs, and in 1634 Rembrandt married Saskia van Ulenborch, daughter of the burgomaster of Leeuwarden and quite a catch for the still relatively humble artist. His self-portraits at the time show the confident face of security – on top of things and quite sure of where he's going.

Rembrandt would not always be the darling of the Amsterdam smart set, but his fall from grace was still some way off when he painted *The Night Watch*, a group portrait often – but inaccurately – associated with the artist's decline in popularity. Indeed, although Rembrandt's fluent arrangement of his subjects was totally original, there's no evidence that the military company who commissioned the painting was anything but pleased with the result. More likely culprits are the artist's later pieces, whose obscure lighting and psychological insight took the conservative Amsterdam burghers by surprise. His patrons were certainly not sufficiently enthusiastic about his work to support his taste for art collecting and his expensive house on Jodenbreestraat, and in 1656 possibly the most brilliant artist the city would ever know was declared bankrupt. He died thirteen years later a broken and embittered old man – as his last self-portraits show. Throughout his career Rembrandt maintained a large studio, and his influence pervaded the next generation of Dutch painters. Some – Dou and Maes – more famous for their genre work, have already been mentioned. Others turned to portraiture.

Govert Flinck (1615–60) was perhaps Rembrandt's most faithful follower, and he was, ironically, given the job of decorating Amsterdam's new town hall after his teacher had been passed over. However, he died before he could execute his designs, and Rembrandt was one of several artists commissioned to paint them – though his contribution was removed shortly afterwards. The work of **Ferdinand Bol** (1616–80) was so heavily influenced by Rembrandt that for a long time art historians couldn't tell the two apart. Most of the pitifully slim extant work of **Carel Fabritius** (1622–54) was portraiture, but he too died young, before he could properly realize his promise as perhaps the most gifted of all Rembrandt's students. Generally regarded as the teacher of Vermeer, he forms a link between the two masters, combining Rembrandt's technique with his own practice of painting figures against a dark background, prefiguring the lighting and colouring of the Delft painter.

LANDSCAPES

Aside from Bruegel, whose depictions of his native surroundings make him the first true Low Countries landscape painter, **Gillis van Coninxloo** (1544–1607) stands out as the earliest Dutch landscapist. He imbued the native scenery with elements of fantasy, painting the richly wooded views he had seen on his travels around Europe as backdrops to biblical scenes. In the early seventeenth century, **Hercules Seghers** (1590–1638), apprenticed to Coninxloo, carried on his mentor's style of depicting forested and mountainous landscapes, some real, others not: his work is scarce but is believed to have had considerable influence on the landscape work of Rembrandt. **Esaias van der Velde**'s (1591–1632) quaint and unpretentious scenes show the first real affinity with the Dutch countryside, but while his influence was likewise great, he was soon overtaken in stature by his pupil **Jan van Goyen** (1596–1656), a remarkable painter who belongs to the so-called "tonal phase" of Dutch landscape painting. Van Goyen's early pictures were highly coloured and close to those of his teacher, but it didn't take him long to develop a

markedly personal touch, using tones of green, brown and grey to lend everything a characteristic translucent haze. His paintings are, above all, of nature, and if he included figures it was just for the sake of scale. Long neglected, his fluid and rapid brushwork was only appreciated with the arrival of the Impressionists.

Another "tonal" painter and a native of Haarlem, **Salomon van Ruisdael** (1600–70) was also directly affected by Van der Velde, and his simple and atmospheric, though not terribly adventurous, landscapes were for a long time consistently confused with those of Van Goyen. More esteemed is his nephew, **Jacob van Ruisdael** (1628–82), generally considered the greatest of all Dutch landscapists, whose fastidiously observed views of quiet flatlands dominated by stormy skies were to influence European painters' impressions of nature right up to the nineteenth century. Constable, certainly, acknowledged a debt to him. Ruisdael's foremost pupil was **Meindert Hobbema** (1638–1709), who followed the master faithfully, sometimes even painting the same views (his *Avenue at Middelharnis* may be familiar).

Nicholas Berchem (1620–83) and **Jan Both** (1618–52) were the "Italianizers" of Dutch landscapes. They studied in Rome and were influenced by the Frenchman Claude Lorraine, taking back to Holland rich, golden views of the world, full of steep gorges and hills, picturesque ruins and wandering shepherds. **Allart van Everdingen** (1621–75) had a similar approach, but his subject matter stemmed from travels in Norway, which, after his return to Holland, he reproduced in all its mountainous glory. **Aelbert Cuyp** (1620–91), on the other hand, stayed in Dordrecht all his life, painting what was probably the favourite city skyline of Dutch landscapists. He inherited the warm tones of the Italianizers, and his pictures are always suffused with a deep, golden glow.

Of a number of specialist seventeenth-century painters who can be included here, **Paulus Potter** (1625–54) is rated as the best painter of **domestic animals**. He produced a fair amount of work in a short life, the most reputed being his lovingly executed pictures of cows and horses. The accurate rendering of **architectural** features also became a specialized field, in which **Pieter Saenredam** (1597–1665), with his finely realized paintings of Dutch church interiors, is the most widely known exponent.

Emanuel de Witte (1616–92) continued in the same vein, though his churches lack the spartan crispness of Saenredam's. **Gerrit Berckheyde** (1638–98) worked in Haarlem soon after, but he limited his views to the outside of buildings, producing variations on the same scenes around town.

In the seventeenth century another thriving category of painting was **still life**, in which objects were gathered together to remind the viewer of the transience of human life and the meaninglessness of worldly pursuits. Thus, a skull would often be joined by a book, a pipe or a goblet, and some half-eaten food. Again, two Haarlem painters dominated this field: **Pieter Claesz** (1598–1660) and **Willem Heda** (1594–1680), who confined themselves almost entirely to depicting these carefully arranged groups of objects.

THE EIGHTEENTH AND NINETEENTH CENTURIES

Accompanying Holland's economic decline was a gradual deterioration in the quality and originality of Dutch painting. The delicacy of some of the classical seventeenth-century painters was replaced by finicky still lifes and minute studies of flowers, or finely finished portraiture and religious scenes, as in the work of **Adrian van der Werff** (1659–1722). Of the era's big names, **Gerard de Lairesse** (1640–1711) spent most of his time decorating a rash of brand new civic halls and mansions, but, like the buildings he worked on, his style and influences were French. **Jacob de Wit** (1695–1754) continued where Lairesse left off, and also benefitted from a relaxation in the laws against the Catholics and decorated several of their newly legal churches. The period's only painter of any true renown was **Cornelis Troost** (1697–1750) who, although he didn't produce anything really original, painted competent portraits and some neat, faintly satirical pieces that have since earned him the title of "The Dutch Hogarth". Cosy interiors also continued to prove popular and the Haarlem painter **Wybrand Hendriks** (1744–1831) satisfied demand with numerous proficient examples.

Johann Barthold Jongkind (1819–91) was the first important artist to emerge in the nineteenth century, painting landscapes and seascapes that were to influence Monet and the early Impressionists. He spent most of his life in France and his work was exhibited in Paris with the Barbizon painters, though he owed less to them than to the landscapes of Van Goyen and the seventeenth-century "tonal" artists. Jongkind's work was a logical precursor to the art of the **Hague School**, a group of painters based in and around that city between 1870 and 1900 who tried to re-establish a characteristically Dutch national school of painting. They produced atmospheric studies of the dunes and polders around The Hague, nature pictures that are characterized by grey, rain-filled skies, windswept seas, and silvery, flat beaches – works that, for some, verge on the sentimental. **Hendrik Johannes Weissenbruch** (1824–1903) was a founding member, a specialist in low, flat beach scenes dotted with stranded boats. The banker-turned-artist **Hendrik Willem Mesdag** (1831–1915) did the same but with more skill than imagination, while **Jacob Maris** (1837–99), one of three artist brothers, was perhaps the most typical of the Hague School, with his rural and sea scenes heavily covered by grey, chasing skies. His brother **Matthijs** (1839–1917) was less predictable, ultimately tiring of his colleagues' interest in straight observation and going to London to design windows, while **Willem** (1844–1910), the youngest, is best known for his small, unpretentious studies of nature.

Anton Mauve (1838–88) is better known, an exponent of soft, pastel landscapes and an early teacher of Van Gogh. Profoundly influenced by the French Barbizon painters – Corot, Millet et al – he went to Hilversum in 1885 to set up his own group, which became known as the "Dutch Barbizon". **Jozef Israëls** (1826–1911) has often been likened to Millet, though it's generally agreed that he had more in common with the Impressionists, and his best pictures are his melancholy portraits and interiors. Lastly, **Johan Bosboom**'s (1817–91) church interiors may be said to sum up the nostalgia of the Hague School: shadowy and populated by figures in seventeenth-century dress, they seem to yearn for Holland's Golden Age.

Vincent van Gogh (1853–90), on the other hand, was one of the least "Dutch" of Dutch artists, and he lived out most of his relatively short painting career in France. After countless studies of peasant life in his native North Brabant – studies which culminated in the sombre *Potato Eaters* – he went to live in Paris with his art-dealer brother Theo. There, under the influence of the Impressionists, he lightened his palette, following the pointillist work of Seurat and "trying to render intense colour and not a grey harmony". Two years later he went south to Arles, the "land of blue tones and gay colours", and, struck by the harsh Mediterranean light, his characteristic style began to develop. A disastrous attempt to live with Gauguin, and the much-publicized episode when he cut off part of his ear and presented it to a local prostitute, led eventually to his committal in an asylum at St-Rémy, where he produced some of his most famous, and most expressionistic, canvases – strongly coloured and with the paint thickly, almost frantically, applied.

Like Van Gogh, **Jan Toorop** (1858–1928) went through multiple artistic changes, though he did not need to travel the world to do so; he radically adapted his technique from a fairly conventional pointillism through a tired Expressionism to Symbolism with an Art-Nouveau feel. Roughly contemporary, **George Hendrik Breitner** (1857–1923) was a better painter, and one who refined his style rather than changed it. His snapshot-like impressions of his beloved Amsterdam figure among his best work and offered a promising start to the new century.

THE TWENTIETH CENTURY

Most of the trends in the visual arts of the early twentieth century have, at one time or another, found their way to the Netherlands: of many minor names, **Jan Sluyters** (1881–1957) was the Dutch pioneer of Cubism. But only one movement was specifically Dutch – **De Stijl** (literally "the Style"). **Piet Mondrian** (1872–1944) was De Stijl's leading figure, developing the realism he had learned from the Hague School painters – via Cubism, which he criticized for being too cowardly to depart totally from representation – into a complete abstraction of form which he called **neo-plasticism**. He was something of a mystic, and this was to some extent responsible for the direction that De Stijl – and his paintings – took: canvases painted with grids of lines and blocks made up of the three primary colours and white, black and grey. Mondrian believed this freed the work of art from the vagaries of personal perception, making it possible to obtain what he called "a true vision of reality".

De Stijl took other forms too: there was a magazine of the same name, and the movement introduced new concepts into every aspect of design, from painting to interior design and architecture. But in all these media, lines were kept simple, colours bold and clear. **Theo van Doesburg** (1883–1931) was a De Stijl co-founder and major theorist: his work is similar to Mondrian's except for the noticeable absence of thick, black borders and the diagonals that he introduced into his work, calling his paintings "contra-compositions" – which, he said, were both more dynamic and more in touch with twentieth-century life. **Bart van der Leck** (1876–1958) was the third member of the circle, identifiable by white canvases covered by seemingly randomly placed interlocking coloured triangles. Mondrian split with De Stijl in 1925, going on to attain new artistic extremes of clarity and soberness before moving to New York in the 1940s and producing atypically exuberant works such as *Victory Boogie Woogie* – so named because of the artist's love of jazz, and now exhibited at The Hague's Gemeentemuseum.

During and after De Stijl, a number of other movements flourished, though their impact was not so great and their influence largely confined to the Netherlands. The Expressionist **Bergen School** was probably the most localized, its best-known exponent being **Charley Toorop** (1891–1955), daughter of Jan, who developed a distinctively glaring but strangely sensitive realism. **De Ploeg** ("The Plough"), centred in Groningen, was headed by **Jan Wiegers** (1893–1959) and influenced by Kirchner and the German Expressionists; the group's artists set out to capture the uninviting landscapes around their native town, and produced violently coloured canvases that hark back to Van Gogh. Another group, known as the **Magic Realists**, surfaced in the 1930s, painting quasi-surrealistic scenes that, according to their leading light, **Carel Willink** (1900–83), revealed "a world stranger and more dreadful in its haughty impenetrability than the most terrifying nightmare".

Postwar Dutch art began with **CoBrA**: a loose grouping of like-minded painters from Denmark, Belgium and Holland, whose name derives from the initial letters of their respective capital cities. Their first exhibition at Amsterdam's Stedelijk Museum in 1949 provoked a huge uproar, at the centre of which was **Karel Appel** (b. 1921), whose brutal Abstract Expressionist pieces, plastered with paint inches thick, were, he maintained, necessary for the era – indeed, inevitable reflections of it. "I paint like a barbarian in a barbarous age," he claimed. In the graphic arts the most famous twentieth-century figure is **Maurits Cornelis Escher** (1898–1972).

As for today, there's as vibrant an art scene as there ever was, best exemplified in Amsterdam by the rotating exhibitions of the Stedelijk and by the dozens of galleries and exhibition spaces throughout the city. Among contemporary Dutch artists, look out for the abstract work of **Edgar Fernhout** and **Ad Dekkers**, the reliefs of **Jan Schoonhoven**, the multimedia productions of **Jan Dibbets**, the glowering realism of **Marlene Dumas**, the imprecisely coloured geometric designs of **Rob van Koningsbruggen**, the smeary expressionism of **Toon Verhoef**, and the exuberant figures of **Rene Daniels** – to name only the most important figures.

DUTCH GALLERIES: A HIT LIST

In **Amsterdam**, the Rijksmuseum (see p.101) gives a complete overview of Dutch art up to the end of the nineteenth century, in particular the work of Rembrandt, Hals, and the major artists of the Golden Age; the Van Gogh Museum (see p.105) is best for the Impressionists and, of course, van Gogh; and, for twentieth-century and contemporary Dutch art, there's the Stedelijk (see p.106). Within easy reach of the city, the Frans Hals Museum (see p.144) in **Haarlem** holds some of the best work of Hals and the Haarlem School, whilst **Leiden**'s Stedelijk Museum de Lakenhal (see p.178) weighs in with a healthy sample of lesser-known sixteenth- and seventeenth-century Dutch painters, featuring the likes of Jan Lievens, Gerrit Dou and Lucas van Leyden. In **Utrecht**, the Centraal (see p.217) has paintings by van Scorel and the Utrecht School, and the Catharijne Convent Museum (see p.216) boasts an excellent collection of works by Flemish artists and by Hals and Rembrandt.

Further afield, **The Hague**'s Gemeentemuseum (see p.191) owns the country's largest set of Mondrians, and the outstanding Mauritshuis (see p.183) exhibits the work of all the major painters of the Golden Age, especially Rembrandt and Vermeer. In **Rotterdam**, the Boijmans-Van Beuningen (see p.202) has a weighty stock of Flemish primitives and surrealists, as well as works by Rembrandt and other seventeenth-century artists, and in nearby **Dordrecht**, the Dordrechts Museum (see p.211) offers an assortment of seventeenth-century paintings that includes work by Aelbert Cuyp, and later canvases by the Hague School and Breitner. In the east of the country, the Rijksmuseum Kröller-Müller (see p.293), just outside **Arnhem**, is probably the country's finest modern art collection, and has a superb collection of van Goghs; a little further east, **Enschede**'s Rijksmuseum Twente (see p.277) has quality works from the Golden Age to the twentieth century.

HOLLAND
IN FICTION

A reasonable range of Dutch literature has
been translated into English in recent years,
notably the work of Cees Nooteboom,
Marga Minco, Harry Mulisch and Simon
Carmiggelt. There's also, of course, English-
language fiction set in Amsterdam or the
Netherlands, of which the detective writer
Nicolas Freeling is perhaps the best-known
exponent. The following extracts illustrate
the width and depth of contemporary Dutch
writing and for variety we've also included
a short piece by Maria Stahlie, first published in the now-defunct Dutch English-
language publication, *The Magazine*.

SIMON CARMIGGELT

Humour is a frequent theme of Dutch literature, and Simon Carmiggelt was one of the
country's best-loved humorous writers – and
a true if singular poet of his favourite city,
Amsterdam. He moved to the city during the
war, working as a production manager and
journalist on the then illegal newspaper, *Het
Parool*. In 1946, he started writing a daily
column in the paper, entitled *Kronkel*, meaning "twist" or "kink". It was an almost
immediate success, and he continued to
write his *Kronkels* for several decades, in
the end turning out almost 10,000. They're a
unique genre – short, usually humorous
anecdotes of everyday life, with a strong
undercurrent of melancholy and a serious-
ness at their heart. They concern ordinary
people, poignantly observed with razor-
sharp – but never cruel – wit and intelligence. Some of the strongest have been bundled together in anthologies, two of which –
A Dutchman's Slight Adventures (1966) and
I'm Just Kidding (1972) – were translated into
English. Simon Carmiggelt died in 1989.

CORNER

In a café in the Albert Cuypstraat, where the
open-air market pulses with sounds and colour,
I ran into my friend Ben.

"Did you know Joop Groenteman?" he asked.
"You mean the one who sold fruit?" I replied.
"Yes. You heard about his death?"

I nodded. A fishmonger had told me. "It's a
shame," said Ben. "A real loss for the market.
He had a nice stall – always polished his fruit.
And he had that typical Amsterdam sense of
humour that seems to be disappearing. He'd say
"Hi" to big people and "Lo" to little ones. If
somebody wanted to buy two apples, he'd ask
where the party was. No one was allowed to
pick and choose his fruit. Joop handed it out
from behind the plank. Somebody asked him
once if he had a plastic bag, and he said, 'I got
false teeth. Ain't that bad enough?' He never
lost his touch, not even in the hospital."

"Did you go see him there?" I enquired.

"Yes, several times," Ben said. "Once his bed
was empty. On the pillow lay a note: 'Back in
two hours. Put whatever you brought on the
bed.' He had to go on a diet because he was too
fat. They weighed him every day. One morning
he tied a portable radio around his waist with a
rope, put his bathrobe over it, and got on the
scale. To the nurse's alarm he'd suddenly gained
eight pounds. That was his idea of fun in the
hospital. During one visit I asked him when he'd
get out. He said, 'Oh, someday soon, either
through the front door or the back.'"

Ben smiled sadly.

"He died rather unexpectedly," he resumed.
"There was an enormous crowd at his funeral. I
was touched by the sight of all his friends from
the market standing round the grave with their
hats on and each one of them shovelling three
spadesful of earth on to his coffin. Oh well, he
at least attained the goal of his life."

"What goal?" I asked.

"The same one every open-air merchant
has," Ben answered, "a place on a corner. If
you're on a corner, you sell more. But it's awful-
ly hard to get a corner place."

"Joop managed it, though?"

"Yes – but not in the Albert Cuyp," said Ben.
"That corner place was a sort of obsession to
him. He knew his chance was practically nil. So
then he decided that if he couldn't get one while
he was alive, he'd make sure of it when he died.
Every time the collector for the burial insurance
came along, he'd say 'Remember, I want a corner grave.' But when he did die, there wasn't a
single corner to be had. Well, that's not quite
right. It just happened that there was one corner
with a stone to the memory of someone who
had died in the furnaces of a concentration
camp. Nobody was really buried there. And the

cemetery people gave permission to have the stone placed somewhere else and to let Joop have that plot. So he finally got what he wanted. A place on the corner."

HERRING-MAN

It was morning, and I paused to buy a herring at one of those curious legged vending carts that stand along Amsterdam's canals.

"Onions?" asked the white-jacketed herring-man. He was big and broad-shouldered, and his hair was turning grey — a football believer, by the looks of him, who never misses Sunday in the stadium.

"No onions," I answered.

Two other men were standing there eating. They wore overalls and were obviously fellow-workers.

"There's them that take onions, and them that don't," one of the men said tolerantly. The herring-man nodded.

"Take me, now, I never eat pickles with 'em," said the other in the coquettish tone of a girl revealing some little charm that she just happens to possess.

"Give me another, please," I said.

The herring-man cut the fish in three pieces and reached with his glistening hand into the dish of onions.

"No, no onions," I said.

He smiled his apology. "Excuse me. My mind was wandering," he said.

The men in overalls also ordered another round and then began to wrangle about some futility or other on which they disagreed. They were still at it after I had paid and proceeded to a café just across from the herring-cart, where I sat down at a table by the window. For Dutchmen they talked rather strenuously with their hands. A farmer once told me that when the first cock begins to crow early in the morning, all the other roosters in the neighbourhood immediately raise their voices, hoping to drown him out. Most males are cut from the same cloth.

"What'll it be?" asked the elderly waitress in the café.

"Coffee." As she was getting it a fat, slovenly creature came in. Months ago she had had her hair dyed straw yellow, but later had become so nostalgic for her own natural brown that her skull was now dappled with two colours.

"Have you heard?" she asked.

"What?"

"The herring-man's son ran into a streetcar on his motorbike yesterday," she said, "and now he's good and dead. The docs at the hospital couldn't save him. They came to tell his pa about a half an hour ago."

The elderly waitress served my coffee.

"How awful," she said.

I looked across the street. The overalled quarrellers were gone, and the broad, strong herring-man stood cleaning his fish with automatic expertness.

"The kid was just seventeen," said the fat woman. "He was learning to be a pastry cook. Won third prize at the food show with his chocolate castle."

"Those *motorbikes* are rotten things," the waitress said.

"People are mysterious," a friend of mine once wrote, and as I thought of those words I suddenly remembered the onions the herring-man nearly gave me with my second fish, his smiling apology: "My mind was wandering."

GENIUS

The little café lay on a broad, busy thoroughfare in one of the new sections of Amsterdam. The barkeeper-host had only one guest: an ancient man who sat amiably behind his empty genever glass. I placed my order and added, "Give grandfather something, too."

"You've got one coming," called the barkeeper. The old man smiled and tipped me a left-handed military salute, his fingers at his fragile temple. Then he got up, walked over to me, and asked, "Would you be interested in a chance on a first-class smoked sausage, guaranteed weight two pounds?"

"I certainly would be," I replied.

"It just costs a quarter, and the drawing will take place next Saturday," he said.

I fished out twenty-five cents and put it on the bar, and in return he gave me a piece of cardboard on which the number 79 was written in ink.

"A number with a tail," he said. "Lucky for you."

He picked up the quarter, put on his homburg hat, and left the café with a friendly "Good afternoon, gentlemen." Through the window I saw him unlocking an old bicycle. Then, wheeling his means of transport, he disappeared from view.

"How old is he?" I asked.

"Eighty-six."

"And he still rides a bicycle?"

The barkeeper shook his head.

"No," he replied, "but he has to cross over, and it's a busy street. He's got a theory that traffic can see someone with a bicycle in his hand better than someone without a bicycle. So that's the why and the wherefore. When he gets across, he parks the bike and locks it up, and then the next day he's got it all ready to walk across again."

I thought it over.

"Not a bad idea," I said.

"Oh, he's all there, that one," said the barkeeper. "Take that lottery, now. He made it up himself. I guess he sells about a hundred chances here every week. That's twenty-five guilders. And he only has to fork over one sausage on Saturday evening. Figure it out for yourself."

I did so, cursorily. He really got his money's worth out of that sausage, no doubt of it.

"And he runs the drawing all by himself," the barkeeper went on. "Clever as all get out. Because if a customer says, 'I've bought a lot of chances from you, but I never win,' you can bet your boots he will win the very next Saturday. The old man takes care that he does. Gets the customer off his neck for a good long time. Pretty smart, huh?"

I nodded and said, "He must have been a businessman?"

"Well no. He was in the navy. They've paid him a pension for ages and ages. He's costing them a pretty penny."

All of a sudden I saw the old man on the other side of the street. He locked his bicycle against a wall and wandered away.

"He can get home from there without crossing any more streets," said the barkeeper.

I let him fill my glass again.

"I gave him a drink, but I didn't see him take it," I remarked.

The barkeeper nodded.

"He's sharp as tacks about that, too," he said. "Here's what he does. He's old and spry, and nearly everybody buys him something. But he never drinks more than two a day. So I write all the free ones down for him." He glanced at a notepad that lay beside the cash register. "Let's see. Counting the one from you, he's a hundred and sixty-seven to the good."

CEES NOOTEBOOM

Cees Nooteboom is one of Holland's best-known writers. He published his first novel in 1955, but it was only with his third novel, *Rituals*, published in 1980, that he became well-known. The central theme of all his work is the phenomenon of time: *Rituals* in particular is about the passing of time and the different ways of controlling the process. Inni Wintrop, the main character, is an outsider, a "dilettante" as he describes himself. The book is almost entirely set in Amsterdam, and although it describes the inner life of Inni himself, it also paints a vivid picture of the city. Each section details a decade of Inni's life; the one reprinted below describes an encounter from his forties.

RITUALS

There were days, thought Inni Wintrop, when it seemed as if a recurrent, fairly absurd phenomenon were trying to prove that the world is an absurdity that can best be approached with nonchalance, because life would otherwise become unbearable.

There were days, for instance, when you kept meeting cripples, days with too many blind people, days when you saw three times in succession a left shoe lying by the roadside. It seemed as if all these things were trying to mean something but could not. They left only a vague sense of unease, as if somewhere there existed a dark plan for the world that allowed itself to be hinted at only in this clumsy way.

The day on which he was destined to meet Philip Taads, of whose existence he had hitherto been unaware, was the day of the three doves. The dead one, the live one, and the dazed one, which could not possibly have been one and the same, because he had seen the dead one first. These three, he thought later, had made an attempt at annunciation that had succeeded insofar as it had made the encounter with Taads the Younger more mysterious.

It was now 1973, and Inni had turned forty in a decade he did not approve of. One ought not, he felt, to live in the second half of any century, and this particular century was altogether bad. There was something sad and at the same time ridiculous about all these fading years piling on top of one another until at last the millennium arrived. And they contained a contradiction, too: in order to reach the hundred, and in this case the thousand, that had to be completed, one had to add them up; but the feeling that went with the process seemed to have more to do with subtraction. It was as if no one, especially not Time, could wait for those ever dustier, ever higher figures finally to be declared void by a revolution of a row of glittering, perfectly shaped noughts, whereupon they would be relegated to the scrap heap of history. The only people apparently still sure of anything in these days of superstitious expectation were the Pope, the sixth of his name already, a white-robed Italian with an unusually tormented face that faintly resembled Eichmann's, and a number of terrorists of different persuasions, who tried in vain to anticipate the great witches' cauldron. The fact that he was now forty no longer in itself bothered Inni very much.

"Forty," he said, "is the age at which you have to do everything for the third time, or else you'll have to start training to be a cross-tempered old man," and he had decided to do the latter.

After Zita, he had had a long-lasting affair with an actress who had finally, in self-preservation, turned him out of the house like an old chair.

"What I miss most about her," he said to his friend the writer, "is her absence. These people are never at home. You get addicted to that."

He now lived alone and intended to keep it that way. The years passed, but even this was noticeable only in photographs. He bought and sold things, was not addicted to drugs, smoked less than one packet of Egyptian cigarettes a day, and drank neither more nor less than most of his friends.

This was the situation on the radiant June morning when, on the bridge between the Herenstraat and the Prinsenstraat, a dove flew straight at him as if to bore itself into his heart. Instead, it smashed against a car approaching from the Prinsengracht. The car drove on and the dove was left lying in the street, a gray and dusty, suddenly silly-looking little thing. A blonde-haired girl got off her bicycle and went up to the dove at the same time as Inni.

"Is it dead, do you think?" she asked.

He crouched down and turned the bird onto its back. The head did not turn with the rest of the body and continued to stare at the road surface.

"Finito," said Inni.

The girl put her bike away.

"I daren't pick it up," she said, "Will you?"

She used the familiar form of you. As long as they still do that, I am not yet old, thought Inni, picking up the dove. He did not like doves. They were not a bit like the image he used to have of the Holy Ghost, and the fact that all those promises of peace had never come to anything was probably their fault as well. Two white, softly cooing doves in the garden of a Tuscan villa, that was all right, but the gray hordes marching across the Dam Square with spurs on their boots (their heads making those idiotic mechanical pecking movements) could surely have nothing to do with a Spirit which had allegedly chosen that particular shape in which to descend upon Mary.

"What are you going to do with it?" asked the girl.

Inni looked around and saw on the bridge a wooden skip belonging to the Council. He went up to it. It was full of sand. Gently he laid the dove in it. The girl had followed him. An erotic moment. Man with dead dove, girl with bike and blue eyes. She was beautiful.

"Don't put it in there," she said. "The workmen will chuck it straight into the canal."

What does it matter whether it rots away in sand or in water, thought Inni, who often claimed he would prefer to be blown up after his death. But this was not the moment to hold a discourse on transience.

"Are you in a hurry?" he asked.

"No."

"Give me that bag then." From her handlebar hung a plastic bag, one from the Athenaeum Book Store.

"What's in there?"

"A book by Jan Wolkers."

"It can go in there then," said Inni. "There's no blood."

He put the dove in the bag.

"Jump on the back."

He took her bike without looking at her and rode off.

"Hey," she said. He heard her rapid footsteps and felt her jumping on the back of the bike. In the shop windows he caught brief glimpses of something that looked like happiness. Middle-aged gentleman on girl's bicycle, girl in jeans and white sneakers on the back.

He rode down the Prinsengracht to the Haarlemmerdijk and from a distance saw the barriers of the bridge going down. They got off, and as the bridge slowly rose, they saw the second dove. It was sitting inside one of the open metal supports under the bridge, totally unconcerned as it allowed itself to be lifted up like a child on the Ferris wheel.

For a moment Inni felt an impulse to take the dead dove out of the plastic bag and lift it up like a peace offering to its slowly ascending living colleague, but he did not think the girl would like it. And besides, what would be the meaning of such a gesture? He shuddered, as usual not knowing why. The dove came down again and vanished invulnerably under the asphalt. They cycled on, to the Westerpark. With her small, brown hands, the girl dug a grave in the damp, black earth, somewhere in a corner.

"Deep enough?"

"For a dove, yes."

He laid the bird, which was now wearing its head like a hood on its back, into the hole. Together they smoothed the loose earth on top of it.

"Shall we go and have a drink?" he asked.

"All right."

Something in this minimal death, either the death itself or the summary ritual surrounding it, had made them allies. Something now had to happen, and if this something had anything to do with death, it would not be obvious. He cycled along the Nassaukade. She was not heavy. This was what pleased him most about his strange life – that when he had gotten up that morning, he had not known that he would now be cycling here with a girl at his back, but that such a possibility was always there. It gave him, he thought, something invincible. He looked at the faces of the men in the oncoming cars, and he knew that his life, in its absurdity, was right. Emptiness, loneliness, anxiety – these were the drawbacks – but there were also compensations, and this was one of them. She was humming softly and then fell silent. She said suddenly, as if she had taken a decision, "This is where I live."

Translated by Adrienne Dixon
© Louisiana State University Press, 1983.

Rudi van Dantzig is one of Holland's most famous choreographers, and was, until 1991, artistic director of the Dutch National Ballet. *For a Lost Soldier*, **published in 1986, was his debut novel, an almost entirely autobiographical account of his experiences as a child during the war years. It's an extremely well-written book, convincingly portraying the confusion and loneliness of the 50,000-odd Dutch children who were evacuated to foster families during the cold winter at the end of World War II. The novel's leading character is Jeroen, an eleven-year-old boy from Amsterdam who is sent away to live with a family in Friesland. During the Liberation celebrations, he meets an American soldier, Walt, with whom he has a brief sexual encounter; Walt disappears a few days later. The extract below details Jeroen's desperate search for Walt shortly after his return to Amsterdam.**

FOR A LOST SOLDIER

I set out on a series of reconnoitring expeditions through Amsterdam, tours of exploration that will take me to every corner. On a small map I look up the most important streets to see how I can best fan out to criss-cross the town, then make plans on pieces of paper showing exactly how the streets on each of my expeditions join up and what they are called. To make doubly sure I also use abbreviations: H.W. for Hoofdweg, H.S. for Haarlemmerstraat. The pieces of paper are carefully stored away inside the dust-jacket of a book, but I am satisfied that even if somebody found the notes, they wouldn't be able to make head or tail of them. It is a well-hidden secret.

For my first expedition I get up in good time. I yawn a great deal and act as cheerfully as I can to disguise the paralysing uncertainty that is governing my every move.

"We're going straight to the field, Mum, we're going to build a hut," but she is very busy and scarcely listens.

"Take care and don't be back too late."

The street smells fresh as if the air has been scrubbed with soap. I feel dizzy with excitement and as soon as I have rounded the corner I start to run towards the bridge. Now it's beginning, and everything is sure to be all right, all my waiting and searching is about to come to an end; the solution lies hidden over there, somewhere in the clear light filling the streets.

The bright air I inhale makes me feel that I am about to burst. I want to sing, shout, cheer myself hoarse.

I have marked my piece of paper, among a tangle of crossing and twisting lines, with H.W., O.T., W.S.: Hoofdweg, Overtoom, Weteringschans.

The Hoofdweg is close by, just over the bridge. It is the broad street we have to cross when we go to the swimming baths. I know the gloomy houses and the narrow, flowerless gardens from the many times I've walked by in other summers, towel and swimming trunks rolled under my arm. But beyond that, and past Mercatorplein, Amsterdam is unknown territory to me, ominous virgin land.

The unfamiliar streets make me hesitate, my excitement seeps away and suddenly I feel unsure and tired. The town bewilders me: shops with queues outside, people on bicycles carrying bags, beflagged streets in the early morning sun, squares where wooden platforms have been put up for neighbourhood celebrations, whole districts with music pouring out of loudspeakers all day. An unsolvable jigsaw puzzle. Now and then I stop in sheer desperation, study my hopelessly inadequate piece of paper, and wonder if it would not be much better to give up the attempt altogether.

But whenever I see an army vehicle, or catch a glimpse of a uniform, I revive and walk a little faster, sometimes trotting after a moving car in the hope that it will come to a stop and he will jump out.

Time after time I lose my way and have to walk back quite far, and sometimes, if I can summon up enough courage, I ask for directions.

"Please, Mevrouw, could you tell me how to get to the Overtoom?"

"Dear me, child, you're going the wrong way. Over there, right at the end, turn left, that'll take you straight there."

The Overtoom, when I finally reach it, seems to be a street without beginning or end. I walk, stop, cross the road, search: not a trace of W.S. Does my plan bear any resemblance to the real thing?

I take off my shoes and look at the dark impression of my sweaty foot on the pavement. Do I have to go on, search any more? What time is it, how long have I been walking the streets?

Off we sail to Overtoom,
We drink milk and cream at home,
Milk and cream with apple pie,
Little children must not lie.

Over and over again, automatically, the jingle runs through my mind, driving me mad.

As I walk back home, slowly, keeping to the shady side of the street as much as I can, I think of the other expeditions hidden away in the dust-jacket of my book. The routes I picked out and wrote down with so much eagerness and trust seem pointless and unworkable now. I scold myself: I must not give up, only a coward would do that. Walt is waiting for me, he has no one, and he'll be so happy to see me again.

At home I sit down in a chair by the window, too tired to talk, and when I do give an answer to my mother my voice sounds thin and weak, as if it were finding it difficult to escape from my chest. She sits down next to me on the arm of the chair, lifts my chin up and asks where we have been playing such tiring games, she hasn't seen me down in the street all morning, though the other boys were there.

"Were you really out in the field?"

"Ask them if you don't believe me!" I run onto the balcony, tear my first route map up into pieces and watch the shreds fluttering down into the garden like snowflakes.

When my father gets back home he says, "So, my boy, you and I had best go into town straightway, you still haven't seen the illuminations."

With me on the back, he cycles as far as the Concertgebouw, where he leans the bike against a wall and walks with me past a large green space with badly worn grass. Here, too, there are soldiers, tents, trucks. Why don't I look this time, why do I go and walk on the other side of my father and cling — "Don't hang on so tight!" — to his arm?

"Now you'll see something," he says, "something you've never even dreamed of, just you wait and see."

Walt moving his quivering leg to and fro, his warm, yielding skin, the smell of the thick hair in his armpits...

I trudge along beside my father, my soles burning, too tired to look at anything.

We walk through the gateway of a large building, a sluice that echoes to the sound of voices, and through which the people have to squeeze before fanning out again on the other side. There are hundreds of them now, all moving in the same direction towards a buzzing hive of activity, a surging mass of bodies.

There is a sweet smell of food coming from a small tent in the middle of the street in front of which people are crowding so thickly that I can't see what is being sold.

I stop in my tracks, suddenly dying for food, dying just to stay where I am and to yield myself up to that wonderful sweet smell. But my father has already walked on and I have to wriggle through the crowds to catch up with him.

Beside a bridge he pushes me forward between the packed bodies so that I can see the canal, a long stretch of softly shimmering water bordered by overhanging trees. At one end brilliantly twinkling arches of light have been suspended that blaze in the darkness and are reflected in the still water. Speechless and enchanted I stare at the crystal-clear world full of dotted lines, a vision of luminous radiation that traces a winking and sparkling route leading from bridge to bridge, from arch to arch, from me to my lost soldier.

I grip my father's hand. "Come on," I say, "let's have a look. Come on!"

Festoons of light bulbs are hanging wherever we go, like stars stretched across the water, and the people walk past them in silent, admiring rows. The banks of the canal feel as cosy as candle-lit sitting-rooms.

"Well?" my father breaks the spell. "It's quite something, isn't it? In Friesland, you'd never have dreamed that anything like that existed, would you now?"

We take a short cut through dark narrow streets. I can hear dull cracks, sounds that come as a surprise in the dark, as if a sniper were firing at us.

My father starts to run.

"Hurry, or we'll be too late."

An explosion of light spurts up against the black horizon and whirls apart, pink and pale green fountains of confetti that shower down over a brilliant sign standing etched in the sky.

And another shower of stars rains down to the sound of muffled explosions and cheers from the crowd, the sky trembling with the shattering of triumphal arches.

I look at the luminous sign in the sky as if it is a mirage.

"Daddy, that letter, what's it for? Why is it there?" Why did I have to ask, why didn't I just add my own letters, fulfil my own wishful thinking?

"That W? You know what that's for. The W, the W's for Queen Wilhelmina..." I can hear a scornful note in his voice as if he is mocking me.

"Willy here, Willy there," he says, "but the whole crew took off to England and left us properly in the lurch."

I'm not listening, I don't want to hear what he has to say.

W isn't Wilhelmina: it stands for Walt! It's a sign specially for me...

Reprinted by permission of The Bodley Head.

MARGA MINCO

Marga Minco's *Empty House*, first published in 1966, is another wartime novel. During the German occupation her entire family, being Jewish, was deported and none survived the concentration camps. Minco herself managed to escape this fate and spent much of the war in hiding in Amsterdam. In 1944 she moved to Kloveniersburgwal 49, which served as a safe house for various Dutch artists during the ensuing winter; it's this house – or, rather, the house next door – that is the model for the various empty houses in the novel. In the following extract, the main character, Sepha, meets Yona, another Jewish survivor who is later to become a great friend, when travelling back from Friesland to the safe house.

AN EMPTY HOUSE

As soon as we were in the centre Yona put on her rucksack and tapped on the window of the cab. We'd been delayed a lot because the lorry which had picked us up at our spot beyond Zwolle had to go to all kinds of small villages and made one detour after another. We sat in the back on crates. Yona had grazed her knee heaving herself up over the tail-gate. I'd not seen it because I'd been making a place for us to sit.

"What have you done?" I asked.

"Damn it," she cried, "I'm not as agile as you. I told you. I spent all my time holed up in a kind of loft." She tied a hanky round her knee.

"One step from the door to the bed. Do you think I did keep-fit exercises or something?"

I thought of the fire-escape which I'd gone up and down practically every day. In the end I could do it one-handed.

"Have you somewhere to go to in Amsterdam?"

I expected her to say it was none of my business, but she seemed not to hear me. The lorry thundered along a road where they'd just cleared away barricades.

"Do you know," she said, "at first I didn't know where I was?" Suddenly her voice was much less sharp. "All I knew was that it was a low house with an attic window above the back door. 'You don't live here,' said the woman of the house. She always wore a blue striped apron. 'But I am here though,' I said. 'No,' she said, 'you must remember that you're not here, you're nowhere.' She didn't say it unpleasantly, she wished me no harm. But I couldn't get it out of my mind — you're nowhere. It's as if, by degrees, you start believing it yourself, as if you begin to doubt yourself. I sometimes sat staring at my hands for ages. There was no mirror and they'd whitewashed the attic window. It was only by looking at my hand that I recognized myself, proved to myself that I was there."

"Didn't anybody ever come to see you?"

"Yes. In the beginning. But I didn't feel like talking. They soon got the message. They let me come downstairs in the evenings occasionally, the windows were blacked out and the front and back doors bolted. It didn't impress me as being anything special. Later on, I even began to dislike it. I saw that they were scared stiff when I was sitting in the room. They listened to every noise from outside. I told them that I'd rather stay upstairs, that I didn't want to run any risks. You can even get used to a loft. At least it was mine, my loft."

While talking, she had turned round; she sat with her back half turned towards me. I had to bend forward to catch her last words. Her scarf had slipped off. Her hair kept brushing my face. Once we were near Amsterdam, she started talking about her father who went with her to the Concertgebouw every week, accompanied her on long walks and ate cakes with her in small tea-rooms. She talked about him as if he were a friend. And again I had to hear details of the house. She walked me through rooms and corridors, showed me the courtyard, the cellar

with wine-racks, the attic with the old-fashioned pulley. I knew it as if I had lived there myself. Where would she sleep tonight?

"If you want to, you can come home with me," I said. "I shan't have any time. I've so much to do. There's a case of mine somewhere as well. I can't remember what I put in it."

We drove across Berlage Bridge. It was still light. She'd fallen silent during the last few kilometres and sat with her chin in her hands. "The south district," I heard her say. "Nothing has changed here, of course."

I wrote my address on a little piece of paper and gave it to her. She put it in the pocket of her khaki shirt without looking at it.

"You must come," I shouted after her when she had got out at Ceintuurbaan. She walked away without a backward glance, hands on the straps of her rucksack, hunched forward as if there were stones in it. I lost sight of her because I was looking at a tram coming from Ferdinand Bolstraat. The trams were running again. There were tiny flags on the front. Flags were hanging everywhere. And portraits of the Queen. And orange hangings. Everyone seemed to be in the streets. It was the last evening of the Liberation celebrations. The driver dropped me off at Rokin. I'd not far to go. If I walked quickly, I could be there in five minutes. The door was usually open, the lock was broken — less than half a minute for the three flights of stairs. I could leave my case downstairs.

People were walking in rows right across the full width of the street. The majority had orange buttonholes or red, white and blue ribbons. There were a lot of children with paper hats, flags and tooters. Two mouth-organ players and a saxophonist in a traditional Volendammer costume drifted with the mass, though far apart. I tried to get through as quickly as possible. I bumped into a child who dropped his flag, which was about to be trodden underfoot. I made room with my case, grabbed the flag from the ground and thrust it into his hand. Jazz music resounded from a bar in Damstraat. The door was open. Men and women were sitting at the bar with their arms around each other. Their bodies shook. All that was left in the baker's window were breadcrumbs. Here it was even busier. Groups of Canadians stood at the corners, besieged by whores, black-market traders and dog-end collectors.

I'd not seen much of the Liberation in the Frisian village. The woman I'd stayed with baked her own bread; she had done so throughout the war and she just went on doing it. When I was alone in the kitchen with her she asked with avid interest about my experiences in the hunger winter. She wanted to know everything about the church with corpses, the men with rattles, the people suffering from beriberi on the steps of the Palace, the emaciated children who went to the soup-kitchen with their pans. I spared her no details. About the recycled fat which gave us diarrhoea, the rotten fen potatoes, the wet, clay-like bread, about the ulcers and legs full of sores. I saw it as a way of giving something back.

At last I was at the bridge. I looked at the house with the large expanses of window and the grimy door. At the house next door, the raised pavement and the neck gable. The windows were bricked up. The debris was piled high behind. All that was left were bare walls. I put down my case to change hands. It was as if, only then, that I felt how hungry I was, how stiff my knees were from sitting for hours on the crate. There was something strange about the houses, as if I'd been away for years. But it could have been that I'd never stopped on the bridge before, never looked at them from that angle. The barge was still there. An oil-lamp was burning behind the portholes.

Our front door was closed. The lock had been mended in the meantime. I ought to have had a key somewhere. I didn't want to ring. I'd never realized that the staircase was so dark when the front door was shut. Without thinking, I groped for the banister and banged my hand against the rough wall. "It's nice, soft wood," Mark had said as he sawed the banister into logs. "You can cut it nicely into pieces with a sharp knife." The steps on the upper flight grated as if there were sand on them. I pushed the door open with my case.

There was a black lady's handbag on the bed. A leather bag with a brass clasp. Who had a bag like that? The leather was supple and smooth, except for some creases on the underside. I walked to the table which was full of bottles and glasses. I saw a long dog-end lying in one of the ashtrays. The cigarette must have been carefully put out. Afterwards the burnt tobacco had been nipped off. I found the empty packet on the floor, Sweet Caporal. The divan was strewn with newspapers. Eisenhower standing in a car. Montgomery standing in a car. A new Bailey bridge built in record time.

I had to look among the piled-up crockery in the kitchen for a cup. I rinsed it a long time before I drank from it. I felt the water sink into my stomach; it gurgled as if it was falling into a smooth, cold hollow. The tower clock sounded the half-hour. The house became even quieter. There appeared to be nobody home on the other floors either. Half nine? It got dark quickly now. It was already dark under the few trees left along the canal. I opened one of the windows and leant outside. A man and a woman tottered along the pavement on the other side. They held each other firmly under the arm. They would suddenly lurch forward a few metres, slowly right themselves and start up again. The nine o'clock man always walked there too. I'd not heard him since the Liberation.

Reprinted by permission of Peter Owen Publishers, London.

NICOLAS FREELING

Creator of the Dutch detective Van der Valk, Nicolas Freeling was born in England but has lived most of his life in Europe, where the bulk of his novels are set. He actually left Amsterdam well over twenty years ago and nowadays rarely returns to the city. But in the Van der Valk novels he evokes Amsterdam (and Amsterdammers) as well as any writer ever has, subtly and unsentimentally using the city and its people as a vivid backdrop to his fast-moving action. The following extract is from *A Long Silence*, first published in 1972.

A LONG SILENCE

Arlette came out into the open air and saw that spring had come to Amsterdam. The pale, acid sun of late afternoon lay on the inner harbour beyond the Prins Hendrik Kade: the wind off the water was sharp. It gave her a shock. A succession of quick rhythmic taps, as at the start of a violin concerto of Beethoven. That she noticed this means, I think, that from that moment she was sane again. But it is possible that I am mistaken. Even if insane one can have, surely, the same perceptions as other people, and this "click" is a familiar thing. Exactly the same happens when one takes a night train down from Paris to the Coast, and one wakes somewhere between Saint Raphael and Cannes and looks out, and there is the Mediterranean. Or was.

The pungent salt smell, the northern, maritime keynotes of seagull and herring, the pointed brick buildings, tall and narrow like herons, with their mosaic of parti-coloured shutters, eaves, sills, that gives the landscapes their stiff, heraldic look (one is back beyond Brueghel, beyond Van Eyck, to the primitives whose artists we do not know, so that they have names like the Master of the Saint Ursula Legend). The lavish use of paint in flat bright primary colours which typifies these Baltic, Hanseatic quaysides is startling to the visitor from central Europe. Even the Dutch flags waving everywhere (there are no more determined flag-wavers) upset and worried Arlette: she had not realised how in a short time her eye had accustomed itself to the subtle and faded colourings of France, so that it was as though she had never left home. The sharp flat brightness of Holland! The painters' light which hurts the unaccustomed eye... Arlette never wore sunglasses in France, except on the sea, or on the snow, yet here, she remembered suddenly, she had practically gone to bed in them. It was all so familiar. She had lived here, she had to keep reminding herself, for twenty years.

She had no notion of where she wanted to go, but she knew that now she was here, a small pause would bring the spinning, whirling patterns of the kaleidoscope to rest. She crossed the road and down the steps to the little wooden terrace – a drink, and get her breath back! Everything was new – the pale heavy squatness of the Dutch café's cup-and-saucer, left on her table by the last occupant; the delightful rhythmic skyline across the harbour of the Saint Nicolaas church and the corner of the Zeedijk! Tourists were flocking into waterbuses, and now she was a tourist too. An old waiter was wiping the table while holding a tray full of empty bottles, which wavered in front of her eye.

"Mevrouw?"

"Give me a chocomilk, if at least you've got one that's good and cold."

Another click! She was talking Dutch, and as fluently as ever she had! He was back before she had got over it.

"Nou, mevrouwtje – cold as Finnegan's feet." His voice had the real Amsterdam caw to it. "You aren't Dutch though, are you now?"

"Only a tourist," smiling.

"Well now, by-your-leave: proper-sounding Dutch you talk there," chattily, bumping the glass down and pouring in the clawky chocomilk.

"Thank you very much."

"Tot Uw dienst. Ja ja ja, kom er aan" to a fussy man, waving and banging his saucer with a coin.

Neem mij niet kwa-a-lijk; een be-hoor-lijk Nederlands spreekt U daar. Like a flock of rooks. Yah, yah ya-ah, kom er a-an. And she was blinded by tears again, hearing her husband's exact intonation – when with her he spoke a Dutch whose accent sometimes unconsciously – ludicrously – copied hers, but when with the real thing, the rasecht like himself his accent would begin to caw too as though in self-parody.

Next door to her were sitting two American girls, earnest, quiet, dusty-haired, looking quite clean though their jeans were as darkly greasy as the mud the dredger over there was turning up off the harbour bottom. Scraps of conversation floated across.

"She's a lovely person, ever so quiet but really mature, you know what I mean, yes, from Toledo." Arlette knew that Van der Valk would have guffawed and her eyes cleared.

I see her there, at the start of her absurd and terrifying mission. She has the characteristic feminine memory for detail, the naively earnest certainty that she has to get everything right. Had I asked what those two girls were drinking she would have known for sure, and been delighted at my asking.

I have not seen Amsterdam for four or five years, and it might be as long again before I shall. This is just as well. I do not want my imagination to get in the way of Arlette's senses. Piet, whose imagination worked like mine, saw things in an entirely different way to her. We were sitting once together on that same terrace.

"Look at that dam building," pointing at the Central Station, a construction I am fond of, built with loving attention to every useless detail by an architect of the last century whose name I have forgotten (a Dutch equivalent of Sir Giles Gilbert Scott). "Isn't it lovely?" Lovely is not the word I would have chosen but it is oddly right.

"The Railway Age," he went on. "Make a wonderful museum – old wooden carriages, tuff-tuff locos with long funnels, Madame Tussaud figures of station-masters with beards, policemen wearing helmets, huge great soup-strainer moustaches, women with bustle and reticules…" Yes, indeed, and children in sailor suits. Arlette's mind does not behave like this.

I am changed, thought Arlette, and unchanged. I am the same housewife, familiar with these streets, these people. I am not pricked or tickled by anything here, like a tourist. I see all this with the coolness and objectivity of experience. I am not going to rush into anything stupid or imprudent. This is a town I know, and I am going to find myself perfectly able to cope with the problem. I am not alone or helpless; I have here many friends, and there are many more who were Piet's friends and who will help me for his sake. But I am no longer the thoughtless and innocent little wife of a little man in a little job, standing on the corner with shopping bag wondering whether to have a cabbage or a cauli. I am a liberated woman, and that is going to make a difference.

A tout was circling around the cluster of tables, sizing up likely suckers. A year or so ago he would have been handing out cards for a restaurant or hotel, looking for a quickie trip around the sights, with waterbus, Anne Frank and the Rembrandthuis all thrown in for only ten guilders. Now – he had closed in on the two American girls and she could hear his pidgin-German patois that is the international language of the European tout – selling live sex-shows. The two girls glanced up for a second with polite indifference, and went back to their earnest, careful, intense conversation, paying no further attention to him at all. He broke off the patter, circled backwards like a boxer and gave Arlette a careful glance: Frenchwomen, generally fascinated by the immoralities and debaucheries of these English and these Scandinavians – a likely buyer, as long as they have first done their duty with a really good orgy at Marks and Spencer's. Arlette met his eye with such a chill and knowing look that he shuffled back into the ropes and made off sideways: cow has been to the sex-show and has no money left. Amsterdam too has changed and not changed, she thought.

"Raffishness" was always the first cliché tourists used, the Amsterdammers were always

intensely, idiotically proud of their red-light district and since time immemorial a stroll to look at "the ladies behind the windows" was proposed to every eager tourist the very first night.

They have taken now with such relish to the new role of exhibitionist shop-window that it is hard not to laugh – the visitor's first reaction generally is roars of laughter. The Dutch have a belief that sex has made them less provincial somehow – for few attitudes are more provincial than the anxious striving to be modern-and-progressive. Paris doesn't exist any more, and London is slipping, they will tell one with a boastful pathos, and Holland-is-where-it's-at. A bit immature, really, as the two nineteen-year-olds from Dubuque were probably at that moment saying. Arlette was a humble woman. She saw herself as snobbish, narrow, rigid, French provincial bourgeois. Piet, born and bred in Amsterdam, used to describe himself as a peasant. This humility gave them both an unusual breadth, stability, balance. I remember his telling me once how to his mind his career if not his life had been an abject failure.

"But there," drinking brandy reflectively, being indeed a real soak and loving it, "what else could I have done?"

Arlette, walking through the lazy, dirty sun-shine of late afternoon in Amsterdam, was thinking too, "What else could I have done?" She had come to lay a ghost. Not that she – hardheaded woman – believed in ghosts, but she had lived long enough to know they were there. Piet was a believer in ghosts. "I have known malign influences outside the bathroom door," he used to say. He was delighted when I gave him to read the finely-made old thriller of Mr A.E.W. Mason which is called The Prisoner in the Opal: he saw the point at once, and when he brought it back he said that he too, with the most sordid, materialistic, bourgeois of enquiries, always made the effort "to pierce the opal crust". Poor old Piet.

Once we were having dinner together in a Japanese restaurant. We had had three pern-ods, big ones, the ones Piet with his horrible Dutch ideas of wit which he took for esprit described as "Des Grand Pers". We were watching the cook slicing raw fish into fine transparent slices.

"There is poetry," said Piet suddenly, "in those fingers." I turned around suspiciously, because this is a paraphrase from a good writer, whom Piet had certainly not read. I used the phrase as an epigraph to a book I once wrote about cooks – which Piet had not read either. "Poetry in the fat fingers of cooks" – I looked at Piet suspiciously.

"So," with tactful calm, "is that a quotation?"

"No," innocent, "Just a phrase. Thought it would please you, haw." That crude guffaw; completely Piet. The stinker; to this day I don't know whether he was kidding me. A skilful user of flattery, but damn it, a friend.

The Damrak, the Dam, the Rokin. Squalid remnants of food, flung upon the pavements. The young were unable or unwilling to spend much on food, she thought, and what they got for their money probably deserved to be flung: one could not blame them too much, just because one felt revolted. But one did blame them: beastly children.

The Utrechtsestraat. The Frederiksplein. And once out of the tourist stamping-ground, Arlette knew suddenly where she was going. She was heading unerringly and as though she had never been away straight towards the flat where she had lived for twenty years. It was a longish way to walk, all the way from the Central Station and carrying a suitcase too. Why had she done it? She would have said, "What else could I have done?" crossly, for when she got there she was very tired and slightly footsore, dishevelled, her hair full of dust, smelling of sweat and ready to cry.

"Arlette! My dear girl! What are you doing? – but come in! I'm so happy to see you – and at the same time, my poor child, I'm so sad! Not that we know anything – what one reads in the paper nowadays – Pah! And again Pah! come in, my dear girl, come in – you don't mean to say you walked… from the station? You didn't! You couldn't! Sit down child, do. The lavy? But of course you know where it is, that's not something you'll have forgotten. I'll make some coffee. My dear girl, marvellous to see you, and the dear boys? – no no, I must be patient, go and have a pee child, and a wash, do you good." The old biddy who had always had a ground floor flat, and still did… She taught the piano. It had been the most familiar background noise to Arlette's life throughout the boys' childhood; her voice carried tremendously.

"One, Two, not so hasty. Pedal there, you're not giving those notes their value, that's a

sharp, can't you hear it?" And coming back from shopping an hour later another one was being put through its hoops. "Watch your tempo, not so much espressivo, you're sentimentalising, this is the Ruysdaelkade, not the Wiener Wald or something."

"Lumpenpack," she would mutter, coming out on the landing for a breather and finding Arlette emptying the dustbin.

Old Mother Counterpoint, Piet always called her, and sometimes in deference to Jane Austen "Bates" ("Mother hears perfectly well; you only have to shout a little and say it two or at the most three times"). A wonderful person really. A mine of information on the quarter, possessor of efficient intelligence networks in every shop, an endless gabble on the telephone, forever fixing things for someone else. She could find anything for you; a furnished room, a second-hand pram scarcely used, a boy's bike, a shop where they were having a sale of materials ever so cheap – even if she didn't have her finger on it she knew a man who would let you have it wholesale. Warm-hearted old girl. Gushing, but wonderfully kind, and gentle, and sometimes even tactful.

"You take yours black, dear, oh yes, I hadn't forgotten – you think I'd forget a thing like that? Not gaga yet, thank God. Good heavens, it must be seven years. But you haven't aged dear, a few lines yes – badges of honour my pet, that's what I call them. Tell me – can you bear to talk about it? Where are you staying? By the look of you you could do with a square meal."

"I don't know, I was wondering…"

"But my poor pet of course, how can you ask, you know I'd be more than pleased and I've plenty of room, it's just can you bear all the little fussinesses of a frightened old maid – oh nonsense child, now don't be tiresome. Now I'll tell you what, no don't interrupt, I'm going to the butcher, yes still the same awful fellow, all those terrible people, how they'll be thrilled, just wait till he hears, I'll frighten him, he gave me an escalope last week and tough… my poor girl, since you left he thinks everything is permitted him. I'll get a couple of nice veal cutlets and we'll have dinner, just you wait and I'll get something to drink too, I love the excuse and what's more I'll make pancakes. I never bother by myself, you take your shoes off and put your feet up and read the paper, nonsense you'll do no such thing, I want to and anyway I'll enjoy it:

would you perhaps love a bath, my pet?" The voice floated off into the hallway.

"Where's my goloshes, oh dear, oh here they are now how did they get that way, oh wait till I tell the wretch the cutlets are for you, he'll jump out of his skin…" The front door slammed. Arlette was home.

It was a nice evening. Bates brought Beaujolais – Beaujolais! "I remember you used to buy it, child, I hope you still like it. Cutlets."

"He practically went on his knees when he heard, with the tears in his eyes he swore on his mother's grave you'd be able to cut them with a fork and I just looked and said 'She'd better', that's all."

"Bananas – I've got some rum somewhere, hasn't been touched in five years I'd say, pah, all dusty, do you think it'll still be all right dear, not gone poisonous or anything, one never knows now, they put chemicals in to make things smell better, awful man in the supermarket and I swear he squirts the oranges with an aerosol thing to make them smell like oranges, forlorn hope is all I can say."

The rum was tasted, and pronounced fit for pancakes.

"And how's Amsterdam?" asked Arlette, laughing.

It wasn't what it was; it wasn't what it had been. Arlette had been prepared to be bored with old-maidish gush about how we don't sleep safe in our beds of nights, not like when we had a policeman in the house, which did give someone a sense of security somehow. She ought to have known better really, because old mother Counterpoint had the tough dryness, the voluble energy, the inconsequent loquacity she expected – and indeed remembered, but the warm-hearted kindness was illuminated by a shrewd observation she had never given the old biddy credit for.

"Well, my dear, it would ill become me to complain. I'll have this flat for as long as I live and they can't put my rent up, I have to spread my butter thinner but I'm getting old and I need less of it. I have the sunshine still and the plants and my birds and they'll all last my time. I think it comes much harder on a girl your age, who can remember what things used to be, and who still has to move with the changes and accept them, whereas people expect me to be eccentric and silly. And I'm sorrier still for the young ones. They don't have any patterns to move by:

it must give a terrible sense of insecurity and I think that's what makes them so unhappy. Everyone kowtows to them and it must be horrid really. Look at the word young, I mean it used to mean what it said and no more, young cheese or a young woman and that was that – and now they talk about a young chair or a young frock and it's supposed to mean good, and when you keep ascribing virtue to people, and implying all the time that they should be admired and imitated, well dear, it makes their life very difficult and wearisome; I used to know a holy nun and she said sometimes that everybody being convinced one was good made a heavy cross to carry. When the young do wicked things I can't help feeling that it's because they're dreadfully unhappy. Of course there's progress, lots and lots of progress, and it makes me very happy. I don't have many pupils now, but I'm always struck when they come, so tall and healthy and active, so unlike the pale little tots when I was a young woman, and I remember very hard times, my dear, all the men drunk always because their lives were so hard, but they don't seem to me any happier or more contented and they complain more because they expect much more. I can't really see what they mean talking about progress because that seems to me that people are good and get better and the fact is, my pet, as you and I know, people are born bad and tend to get worse and putting good before evil is always a dreadful struggle dear, whatever they say. One is so vain and so selfish."

And Arlette, who had had a good rest, a delicious bath, and a good supper, found herself pouring out her whole tale and most of her heart.

"Well," said Bates at the end with great commonsense, "that has done you a great deal of good my dear, and that's a fact, just like taking off one's stays, girls don't wear stays any more and they don't know what they miss."

Arlette felt inclined to argue that it was a good thing to be no longer obliged to wear stays.

"Of course dear, don't think I don't agree with you, healthy girls with good stomach muscles playing tennis, and no more of that fainting and vapouring. But I maintain that it was a good thing for a girl to know constraint. Sex education and women's lib, all dreadful cant. Girls who married without knowing the meaning of the word sex were sometimes very happy and sometimes very unhappy, and I don't believe they are any happier now. I married a sailor, dear, and learned how to go without."

"It doesn't make me any happier now," said Arlette dryly.

"No dear, and that's just what I felt in 1940 when my ship got torpedoed. So now let's be very sensible. You've come here very confused and embittered, and you don't want anything to do with the police, and you're probably quite right because really poor dears they've simply no notion, but at the present you've no notion either. You'd never of thought about asking my advice because I'm a silly old bag but I'll give it you, and it is that you probably can find out who killed your husband, because it's surprising what you can do when you try, but it's as well to have friends you can count on, and you can count on me for a start, and with that my dear we'll go to bed, your eyes are dropping out."

"Did you join the resistance, in 1940 I mean?" asked Arlette.

"Yes I did, and what's more once I threw a bomb at a bad man in the Euterpestraat, and that was a dreadful place, the Gestapo headquarters here in Amsterdam and it was very hard because I was horribly frightened of the bomb, and even more frightened of the bad man who had soldiers with him and most of all because I knew they would take hostages and execute them, but it had to be done, you see."

"I do see," said Arlette seriously, "it wasn't the moment to take off one's stays and feel comfortable."

"Right, my pet, right," said old mother Counterpoint.

© Nicolas Freeling 1972.
Reprinted with the kind permission
of Curtis Brown Ltd.

MARIA STAHLIE

The Dutch author Maria Stahlie (b. 1955) began her career as a literary translator. She wrote her first novel, *Unisono*, in 1988. Since then, she has published, among other works, *In the Spirit of the Monadinis* and *The Sin of Death*. 1994 saw the appearance of her sixth novel, *The Beast with Two Backs*, a title taken from Rabelais's description of a couple making love. Inspired by Nabokov's *Lolita*, the novel deals with a 38-year-old journalist who falls in love with an 18-year-old; conscience and the integrity of human action are major themes. Maria Stahlie lives in Amsterdam.

A DUTCH CROSS

A Dutch critic wrote that my last book but one, The Plague of Butterflies, breathes an un-Dutch atmosphere. I took this as a compliment. But did I try to write an un-Dutch book? I think I did, for who would like to have a typically Dutch book flow from their pen? A typically Dutch book is full of realism, it is written in an economic style; the author sets out not so much to surprise as to convince. A typically Dutch book is small-minded and boring. Little wonder, then, that many a Dutch writer wants to shake off their Dutchness and express themselves in a grand and compelling way.

Unfortunately, there is a world of difference between literary flamboyance and a natural, real-life flamboyance. Even if I sometimes overindulge myself in florid extravagance, even if I allow imagination to triumph, and reconcile the irreconcilable, in everyday life I am, I'm afraid, Dutch to the core. This was thrown into sharp relief during the periods I spent living in foreign countries.

Together with my husband, my love, I twice had the good fortune to be in un-Dutch surroundings. For about eighteen months we lived and worked in America, in Minneapolis, and not long after that we sought contentment on a Greek island in the Aegean Sea. We visited the New World and we visited the Old World, but we never really managed to leave the Middle of the Road. Face-to-face with the pleasure in which Americans, in their own inimitable fashion, indulge, and face-to-face with the overwhelming heartiness, and equally overwhelming melancholy, of the Greeks, we had to conclude with some dismay, that, in our greyness, we were very fond of our privacy, and our certainty. It was these oppressive moments of insight which led us to the understanding that, despite all our travels, we were probably weighed down most by what can only be decribed as a typically Dutch sense of proportion.

It did not come as a surprise that our sense of proportion did not match the excess held up to be the norm in America. True, we could laugh about it all at the beginning, those enormous helpings, those extravagant colours, that shameless kitsch, the unassailable cheerfulness with which everybody passes the time of day to everybody, the enthusiasm with which the TV audience shows their approval or approbation. But the laugh began to stick in our throats.

On one occasion, during a speech I was giving at the university in front of students, colleagues and new friends, I made a small digression eulogising the imagination. "Yee-haa!" shouted at least ten voices in approval. Halfway through the speech I threw in a joke about airbags, which were a new phenomenon for American cars at the time. Two-thirds of the audience noisily approved. A warm sense of solidarity, almost of love, spread over my whole body. I finished my address with the statement that Minneapolis was capable of holding its own with any other city; all those present rose in unison to indicate, with whoops and applause, that they were in complete accord. The sense of warmth rose into my cheeks; blushing dèeply, I was ashamed. Looking through my emotion, on closer analysis I realized that the approval of my audience seemed over-done to me.

Two years later, our frugal Dutch character was brought home to us again. During a stay of ten months on the island of Paros, one of the Cyclades, we got acquainted with a peasant named Dimitri. Dimitri was eighty-four years old; he lived in accordance with age-old tradition, season by season. We first met him in the autumn, but it was winter when we saw him for a second time, Christmas Day to be exact. It was raining and the wind was nasty. I looked from the window, and in the distance I could see the silhouette of a donkey, loaded down and carrying a little man, coming closer. Only when they halted in front of our door did I recognize Dimitri. He had come more than four miles through the hills to bring us, the foreigners, some gifts – cheese and wine and bread and red-painted eggs. He knew that, for Westerners, Christmas was a more important celebration than Easter. Just before he left to plod through the wind and rain back to his farm in the middle of the island, Dimitri sang us a long and sad song, so that we could share in his wintry mood. He left us alone in confusion; our cosy sense of proportion finally dictated to us that Dimitri's unselfishness, his warm heartedness and understanding had been too much of a good thing.

This Dutch rationality, this thoroughly Dutch sense of proportion… we experienced it in Greece even more than we had done in America, a heavy cross to bear. We would have given anything to be able to react in kind, stylized and with a sense of drama, to the people and the situations that surrounded us. For it had become crystal-clear to us that what we regarded as over-done, or too much of a good thing, in truth did a lot more justice to the world than our highly personal, critical sense which whittled everything down to nothing.

In the weeks that followed Dimitri's visit, we somehow succeeded in lightening our load. Being Dutch, we had an excuse for our heavy cross: apart from the Second World War, our country has not gone through one single drama in the last three-and-a-half centuries. Geographically speaking, no spot is better sheltered on the entire globe, and, compared to other countries, Sloughs of Despond and Heights of Majesty are rather thin on the ground in Holland. It was to be our fate that our sense of drama got bogged down in an excess of certainty and security. But not only did we have an excuse for our behaviour, we even had a secret passage to scamper down: whenever we wanted to, we could write un-Dutch books, and, by doing so, leave the cheese-paring of the Low Countries far behind.

Meanwhile, I am well and truly back in Amsterdam. But every day, fleeing from my typically Dutch sense of proportion, I try to go too far and write as many un-Dutch sentences as possible. I dread that my secret passage of escape might just be leading me back to where I started from.

BOOKS

Most of the books listed below are in print and in paperback – those that are out of print (o/p) should be easy to track down in secondhand bookshops. Publishers are detailed with the British publisher first, separated by a semi-colon from the US publisher, where both exist. Where books are published in only one of these countries, "UK" or "US" follows the publisher's name; where the book is published by the same company in both countries, the name of the company appears just once.

HISTORY AND SOCIETY

Geoffrey Cotterell, *Amsterdam, The Life of a City* (US, o/p). Popularized, offbeat history giving a highly readable account of the city up to the late 1960s.

Mike Dash, *Tulipomania* (Gollancz; Crown). An examination of the introduction of the tulip into the Low Countries at the height of the Golden Age, and the extraordinarily inflated and speculative market in the many varieties of bulbs and flowers that resulted from this. There's a lot of padding and scene-setting, but it's an engaging enough read, and has nice detail on seventeenth-century Amsterdam, Leiden and Haarlem.

Pieter Geyl, *The Revolt of The Netherlands 1555–1609*; *The Netherlands in the Seventeenth Century 1609–1648*. (Cassell; US, o/p) Geyl's history of the Dutch-speaking peoples is the definitive account of Holland during its formative years, chronicling the uprising against the Spanish and the formation of the United Provinces. Quite the best thing you can read on the period.

Mark Girouard, *Cities and People: A Social and Architectural History* (Yale). Has an informed and well illustrated chapter on Amsterdam's social history.

Christopher Hibbert, *Cities and Civilisation* (Stewart, Tabori & Chang, US). Includes a chapter on Amsterdam in the age of Rembrandt. Some interesting facts about seventeenth-century daily life.

J.H. Huizinga, *Dutch Civilisation in the 17th Century* (o/p). Analysis of life and culture in the Dutch Republic by one of the country's most widely respected historians.

Carol Ann Lee, *Roses from the Earth: the Biography of Anne Frank* (Viking). Amongst a spate of recent publications trawling through and over the life of the young Jewish diarist, this is perhaps the best, written in a straightforward and insightful manner without sentimentality.

Geert Mak, *Amsterdam: A Brief Life of the City* (Harvill, UK). Recently published, this is a readable and evocative social history of Amsterdam written by a leading Dutch journalist. It's light and accessible enough to read from cover to cover, but its index of places makes it useful to dip into as a supplement to this guide too.

Geoffrey Parker, *The Dutch Revolt* (Penguin); *The Army of Flanders and the Spanish Road 1567–1659* (CUP); *Philip II* (Court); and *The Thirty Years' War* (Routledge; Kegan & Paul). Parker's various accounts of the struggle between the Netherlands and Spain make for compelling reading, particularly *The Army of Flanders*; the title may sound academic, but this book gives a fascinating insight into the Habsburg army which occupied the Low Countries for well over a hundred years – how it functioned, was fed and moved from Spain to the Low Countries along the so-called Spanish Road.

J.L. Price, *Culture and Society in the Dutch Republic in the 17th Century* (Yale). An accurate, intelligent account of the Golden Age.

Simon Schama, *The Embarrassment of Riches: An Interpretation of Dutch Culture in the Golden Age*. (Fontana; Vintage). Enthralling and highly readable account of the Golden Age, drawing on a vast range of archive sources.

Jan Stoutenbeek et al, *A Guide to Jewish Amsterdam* (o/p). Fascinating, if perhaps overdetailed, guide to just about every Jewish monument in the city. You can purchase a copy in better Amsterdam bookshops.

Sir William Temple, *Observations upon the United Provinces of The Netherlands* (o/p). Written by a seventeenth-century English diplomat, and a good, evocative account of the country at the time.

ART AND ARCHITECTURE

Svetlana Alpers, *Rembrandt's Enterprise* (University of Chicago Press). Intriguing study of Rembrandt, positing the theory – in line with the recent findings of the Leiden-based Rembrandt Research Project – that many previously accepted works are not by Rembrandt at all but merely the products of his studio.

Pierre Cabanne, *Van Gogh* (o/p). Standard mix of art criticism and biography, drawing heavily on the artist's own letters.

Kenneth Clark, *Civilisation* (Penguin, UK). Includes a warm and scholarly rundown on the Golden Age, with illuminating insights on the way in which the art reflected the period.

Eugene Fromentin, *The Masters of Past Time: Dutch and Flemish Painting from Van Eyck to Rembrandt* (Phaidon, UK). Entertaining essays on the major Dutch and Flemish painters.

R.H. Fuchs, *Dutch Painting* (Thames & Hudson). As complete an introduction to the subject – from Flemish origins to the present day – as you could wish for in just a couple of hundred pages.

Walter S. Gibson, *Bosch* and *Bruegel* (both Thames & Hudson). Two wonderfully illustrated titles on the most famous allegorical painters, the first containing everything you wanted to know about Hieronymus Bosch, his paintings and his late fifteenth-century milieu, and the latter taking a detailed look at Pieter Bruegel's art, with nine well-argued chapters investigating the various components.

H. L. C. Jaffe, *De Stijl: Visions of Utopia* (Harvard; Belknap). A good, informed introduction to the twentieth-century movement and its philosophical and social influences.

Guus Kemme (ed.), *Amsterdam Architecture: A Guide* (o/p). Illustrated guide to the architecture of Amsterdam, with potted accounts of the major buildings.

Melissa McQuillan, *Van Gogh* (Thames & Hudson). Extensive, in-depth look at Vincent's paintings, as well as his life and times.

Paul Overy, *De Stijl* (Thames & Hudson). Inventive reassessment of all aspects of the De Stijl movement. Clearly written and comprehensive.

Jacob Rosenberg et al, *Dutch Painting 1600–1800* (Yale). Full and erudite anthology of essays on the art and buildings of the Golden Age and after. For dedicated Dutch-art fans only.

Simon Schama, *Rembrandt's Eyes* (Penguin; Knopf). Published in 1999, this erudite work is an enchanting read, full of original insights into the life and times of one of the world's greatest artists.

Alastair Smart, *The Renaissance and Mannerism outside Italy* (o/p). A very readable survey that includes lengthy chapters on van Eyck and his contemporaries, their successors, Bosch and Bruegel, and the later, more Mannerist-inclined painters of the Low Countries. A fine introduction to a crucial period.

Irving Stone, *Lust for Life* (Mandarin; New American Library). Everything you ever wanted to know about Van Gogh in a pop genius-is-pain biography.

Mariet Westerman, *The Art of the Dutch Republic 1585–1718* (Everyman). This excellently written, well illustrated and enthralling book tackles its subject thematically, from the marketing of works to an exploration of Dutch ideologies.

Christopher White, *Rembrandt* (Thames & Hudson). The most widely available – and wide-ranging – study of the painter and his work, with wonderfully incisive commentary from the author.

LITERATURE

Simon Carmiggelt, *Kronkels* (o/p). Second collection of Carmiggelt's "slight adventures", three of which are reprinted on pp.360–362.

Tracey Chevalier, *Girl with a Pearl Earring* (Harper Collins; Dutton). One of a recent crop of novels set during the Golden Age, Chevalier's book is a fanciful piece of fiction, building a story around the subject of one of Vermeer's most enigmatic paintings. It's an absorbing read, slowly unfolding to its climax, and painting a convincing picture of seventeenth-century Delft and the society and values of the time.

Rudi van Dantzig, *For a Lost Soldier* (Gay Mens Press, UK). Honest and convincing tale, largely autobiographical, that tells of a young boy's sexual awakening against a background of war and liberation. See the extract on pp.364–366.

Anne Frank, *The Diary of a Young Girl* (Penguin; Bantam). Lucid and moving, the most revealing thing you can read on the plight of Amsterdam's Jews during the war years.

Nicolas Freeling, *Love in Amsterdam* (Carroll & Graf, US); *Dwarf Kingdom* (Chivers; G K Hall). *A City Solitary; Strike Out Where Not Applicable; A Long Silence* (all o/p). Freeling writes detective novels, and his most famous creation is the rebel cop, Van der Valk, around whom a successful British TV series was made. Light, carefully crafted tales, with just the right amount of twists to make them classic cops 'n' robbers reading – and good Dutch locations. There's an extract from *A Long Silence* on pp.368–372.

Etty Hillesum, *Etty: An Interrupted Life* (Persephone; Henry Holt). Diary of an Amsterdam Jewish young woman uprooted from her life in the city and taken to Auschwitz, where she died. As with Anne Frank's more famous journal, penetratingly written – though on the whole much less readable.

Richard Huijing (ed & trans.), *The Dedalus Book of Dutch Fantasy* (Hippocrene). A fun and artfully selected collection of stories that contains contributions from some of the greats of Dutch literature, including a number whose work does not as yet appear in translation anywhere else.

Margo Minco, *The Fall; An Empty House; The Glass Bridge* (all o/p). Prolific author and wartime survivor, Minco is one of Holland's leading contemporary authors. Her work (especially *The Fall*) focuses on the city's Jewish community, particularly in the war years. See the extract from *An Empty House* on pp.366–368.

Deborah Moggach, *Tulip Fever* (Vintage; Delacorte). At first Deborah Moggach's novel seems no more than an attempt to build a story out of her favourite domestic Dutch interiors, genre scenes and still life paintings. But ultimately the story is a basic one – of lust, greed,

mistaken identity, and tragedy. The Golden Age backdrop is well realized, but almost incidental.

Harry Mulisch, *The Assault* (Penguin; Random House). Set part in Haarlem, part in Amsterdam, this novel traces the story of a young boy who loses his family in a reprisal-raid by the Nazis. A powerful tale, made into an excellent and effective film.

Multatuli, *Max Havelaar: or the Coffee Auctions of the Dutch Trading Company* (Penguin, UK). Classic nineteenth-century Dutch satire of colonial life in the East Indies. Eloquent and, at times, amusing.

Cees Nooteboom, *Rituals* (Harvill; Harvest); *In the Dutch Mountains* (Penguin; Harvest); *The Following Story* (Harvill; Harvest). The first is an existential novel from the 1980s, mapping the empty life of a rich Amsterdammer who dabbles in antiques – bleak but absorbing; see the extract on pp.362–364. The later *In the Dutch Mountains* is similarly aloof in style, and not directly about Holland, but is nonetheless compelling, casting up offbeat philosophical musings. The last work is a typically adroit and economical exploration of the author's favourite themes of memory and the nature of reality. Its starting point is the startling image of a narrator who goes to sleep in one city and wakes up in a completely different place.

Jona Oberski, *Childhood* (o/p). First published in 1978, this is a Jewish child's eye-witness account of the war years, the camps and executions. Written with feeling and precision.

Janwillem van de Wetering, *Hard Rain* (St Martins; Soho). An offbeat detective tale set in Amsterdam and provincial Holland. Like Van de Wetering's other stories, it's a humane, quirky and humorous story, worth reading for the characters and locations as much as for the inventive narrative.

David Veronese, *Jana* (Serpent's Tail, US). A hip thriller set in the underworld of Amsterdam and London.

Jan Wolkers, *Turkish Delight* (M. Boyars, UK). Wolkers is one of The Netherlands' best-known artists and writers, and this is one of his early novels, a close examination of the relationship between a bitter, working-class sculptor and his young, middle-class wife. A compelling work, at times misogynistic and even offensive, by a writer who above all seeks reaction.

LANGUAGE

In the Netherlands, the principal language is Dutch. Most Dutch-speakers, however, particularly in the main towns of Holland and in the tourist industry, speak English to varying degrees of excellence. The Dutch have a seemingly natural talent for languages, and your attempts at speaking theirs may indeed be met with some amusement.

Dutch is a Germanic language – the word "Dutch" itself is a corruption of Deutsche, a label inaccurately given by English sailors in the seventeenth century. Though the Dutch are at pains to stress the differences between the two languages, if you know any German you'll spot many similarities. As noted above, English is very widely spoken, but in smaller towns and in the countryside, where things aren't quite as cosmopolitan, the following words and phrases of Dutch should be the most you'll need to get by; they can be supplemented with the detailed "Food Glossary" on pp.40–41.

Of the **phrase books and dictionaries** available, you'll find the *Rough Guide Dictionary and Phrasebook* an accessible and comprehensive companion. To continue your studies, take a look at *Colloquial Dutch* (Routledge).

PRONUNCIATION

Dutch is pronounced much the same as English. However, there are a few Dutch sounds that don't exist in English, which can be difficult to pronounce without practice.

Consonants

v is like the English f in **f**ar

w like the v in **v**at

j like the initial sound of **y**ellow

ch and *g* are considerably harder than in English, enunciated much further back in the throat; in Amsterdam at least, where the pronunciation is particularly coarse, there's no real English equivalent. They become softer the further south you go, where they're more like the Scottish lo**ch.**

ng is as in bri**ng**

nj as in o**ni**on

Otherwise double consonants keep their separate sounds – *kn*, for example, is never like the English "knight".

Vowels and Dipthongs

Doubling the letter lengthens the vowel sound:

a is like the English **a**pple

aa like c**a**rt

e like l**e**t

ee like l**a**te

o as in p**o**p

oo in p**o**pe

u is like the French t**u** if preceded but not followed by a consonant (eg *nu*); it's like w**oo**d if followed by a consonant (eg *bus*).

uu the French t**u**

au and *ou* like h**o**w

ei and *ij* as in f**i**ne, though this varies strongly from region to region; sometimes it can sound more like l**a**ne.

oe as in s**oo**n

eu is like the dipthong in the French l**eu**r

ui is the hardest Dutch dipthong of all, pronounced like h**ow** but much further forward in the mouth, with lips pursed (as if to say "oo").

DUTCH WORDS AND PHRASES

BASICS AND GREETINGS

Yes	*ja*	Goodbye	*tot ziens*
No	*nee*	See you later	*tot straks*
Please	*alstublieft*	Do you speak English?	*spreekt u Engels?*
(No) Thank you	(*nee*) *dank u* or *bedankt*	I don't understand	*Ik begrijp het niet*
Hello	*hallo* or *dag*	Women/men	*vrouwen/mannen*
Good morning	*goedemorgen*	Children	*kinderen*
Good afternoon	*goedemiddag*	Men's/women's toilets	*heren/dames*
Good evening	*goedenavond*		

OTHER ESSENTIALS

I want . . .	*Ik wil . . .*	Left/right	*links/rechts*
I don't want . . .	*Ik wil niet . . .* (+verb)	Straight ahead	*rechtuit gaan*
	Ik wil geen . . . (+noun)	Platform	*spoor* or *perron*
How much is . . . ?	*Wat kost . . . ?*	Ticket office	*loket*
Post office	*postkantoor*	Here/there	*hier/daar*
Stamp(s)	*postzegel(s)*	Good/bad	*goed/slecht*
Money exchange	*wisselkantoor*	Big/small	*groot/klein*
Cash desk	*kassa*	Open/closed	*open/gesloten*
How do I get to . . . ?	*Hoe kom ik in . . . ?*	Push/pull	*duwen/trekken*
Where is . . . ?	*Waar is . . . ?*	New/old	*nieuw/oud*
How far is it to . . . ?	*Hoe ver is het naar . . . ?*	Cheap/expensive	*goedkoop/duur*
When?	*Wanneer?*	Hot/cold	*heet* or *warm/koud*
Far/near	*ver/dichtbij*	With/without	*met/zonder*

DAYS AND TIMES

Sunday	*Zondag*	Year	*jaar*	3.20	*tien voor half vier*
Monday	*Maandag*	Month	*maand*	3.25	*vijf voor half vier*
Tuesday	*Dinsdag*	Week	*week*	3.30	*half vier*
Wednesday	*Woensdag*	Day	*dag*	3.35	*vijf over half vier*
Thursday	*Donderdag*	Hour	*uur*	3.40	*tien over half vier*
Friday	*Vrijdag*	Minute	*minuut*	3.45	*kwart voor vier*
Saturday	*Zaterdag*	What time is it?	*Hoe laat is het?*	3.50	*tien voor vier*
Yesterday	*gisteren*	It's . . .	*Het is . . .*	3.55	*vijf voor vier*
Today	*vandaag*	3.00	*drie uur*	8am	*acht uur 's-ochtends*
Tomorrow	*morgen*	3.05	*vijf over drie*	1pm	*een uur 's-middags*
Tomorrow	*morgenochtend*	3.10	*tien over drie*	8pm	*acht uur 's-avonds*
morning		3.15	*kwart over drie*	1am	*een uur 's-nachts*

NUMBERS

When saying a number, the Dutch generally transpose the last two digits:
for example, *drie guilden vijf en twintig* is ƒ3,25.

0	*nul*	9	*negen*	18	*achttien*	70	*zeventig*
1	*een*	10	*tien*	19	*negentien*	80	*tachtig*
2	*twee*	11	*elf*	20	*twintig*	90	*negentig*
3	*drie*	12	*twaalf*	21	*een en twintig*	100	*honderd*
4	*vier*	13	*dertien*	22	*twee en twintig*	101	*honderd een*
5	*vijf*	14	*veertien*	30	*dertig*	200	*twee honderd*
6	*zes*	15	*vijftien*	40	*veertig*	201	*twee honderd een*
7	*zeven*	16	*zestien*	50	*vijftig*	500	*vijf honderd*
8	*acht*	17	*zeventien*	60	*zestig*	1000	*duizend*

GLOSSARY

For the sake of convenience, we've divided the glossary into Dutch and architectural terms.

DUTCH TERMS

ABDIJ Abbey or group of monastic buildings.

AMSTERDAMMERTJE Phallic-shaped objects placed alongside Amsterdam streets to keep drivers off pavements and out of the canals.

A.U.B. *Alstublieft* – "please" (also shown as **S.V.P.**, from French).

BEGIJNHOF Similar to a hofje but occupied by Catholic women (Begijns) who led semi-religious lives without taking full vows.

BEIAARD Carillon chimes.

BELFORT Belfry.

BG *Begane grond* – "ground floor" ("basement" is **K** for *kelder*).

BRUG Bridge.

BTW *Belasting Toegevoegde Waarde* – VAT (sales tax).

FIETSPAD Bicycle path.

GASTHUIS Hospice for the sick or infirm.

GEEN TOEGANG No entry.

GEMEENTE Municipal, as in *Gemeentehuis* – town hall.

GERECHTSHOF Law Courts.

GESLOTEN Closed.

GEVEL Gable. The only decoration practical on the narrow-fronted canal house was on its gables. Initially fairly simple, they developed into an ostentatious riot of individualism in the late seventeenth century before turning to a more restrained classicism in the eighteenth and nineteenth centuries. The earliest gables were simple wooden frames, later renditions were of brick and stone – primarily spout-shaped, bell-shaped or crowstepped.

GEZELLIG A hard term to translate – something like "cosy", "comfortable" and "inviting" in one – which is often said to lie at the heart of the Dutch psyche. A long, relaxed meal in a favourite restaurant with friends is *gezellig*; grabbing a quick snack is not. The best brown cafés ooze *gezelligheid*; Amsterdam's Kalverstraat on a Saturday afternoon definitely doesn't.

GILD Guild.

GRACHT Canal.

GROTE KERK Literally "Big Church" – the main church of a town or village.

HALLE Hall.

HIJSBALK Pulley beam, often decorated, fixed to the top of a gable to lift goods, furniture etc. Essential in canal houses whose staircases were narrow and steep, hijsbalken are still very much in use today.

HOF Courtyard.

HOFJE Almshouse, usually for elderly women who could look after themselves but needed small charities such as food and fuel; usually a number of buildings centred around a small, enclosed courtyard.

HUIS House.

JEUGDHERBERG Youth hostel.

KERK Church; eg Grote Kerk – the principal church of the town; Onze Lieve Vrouwe Kerk – church dedicated to the Virgin Mary.

KONINKLIJK Royal.

LAKENHAL Cloth hall. The building in medieval weaving towns where cloth would be weighed, graded and sold.

LET OP! Attention!

LUCHTHAVEN Airport.

MARKT Central town square and the heart of most Dutch communities, normally still the site of weekly markets.

MOKUM A Yiddish word meaning "city", originally used by the Jewish community to indicate Amsterdam; now in general usage as a nickname for the city.

NEDERLAND/NEDERLANDS The Netherlands/Dutch.

OMMEGANG Procession.

OOST East.

PLEIN A square or open space.

POLDER An area of land reclaimed from the sea.

POSTBUS Post office box.

RAADHUIS Town hall.

RANDSTAD Literally "rim-town", this refers to the urban conurbation that makes up much of North and South Holland, stretching from Amsterdam in the north down to Rotterdam and Dordrecht in the south.

RIJK State.

SCHEPENZAAL Alderman's Hall.

SCHOUWBURG Theatre.

SCHONE KUNSTEN Fine arts.

SIERKUNST Decorative arts.

SPIONNETJE Small mirror on canal house enabling occupant to see who is at the door without descending stairs.

SPOOR Platform (on a train station).

STADHUIS The most common word for a town hall.

STEDELIJK Civic, municipal.

STEEG Alley.

STEEN Fortress.

STICHTING Institute or foundation.

STRAAT Street.

T/M *Tot en met* – "up to and including".

TOEGANG Entrance.

UITGANG Exit.

V.A. *Vanaf* – "from".

V.S. *Verenigde Staten* – "United States".

VOLKSKUNDE Folklore.

VVV Dutch tourist information office

WAAG Old public weighing-house, a common feature of most towns.

WEG Way.

WIJK District (of a city).

Z.O.Z. Please turn over (page, leaflet etc).

ZUID South

ARCHITECTURAL TERMS

AMBULATORY Covered passage around the outer edge of the choir of a church.

APSE Semicircular protrusion at (usually) the east end of a church.

ART DECO Geometrical style of art and architecture popular in the 1930s.

ART NOUVEAU Style of art, architecture and design based on highly stylized vegetal forms. Popular in the early part of the twentieth century.

BAROQUE High Renaissance period of art and architecture, distinguished by extreme ornateness, exuberance and complex spatial arrangement of interiors.

CABINET-PIECE Small, finely detailed painting of a domestic scene.

CARILLON A set of tuned church bells, either operated by an automatic mechanism or played by a keyboard.

CARYATID A sculptured female figure used as a column.

CAROLINGIAN Dynasty founded by Charlemagne; late eighth to early tenth century. Also refers to art, etc, of the time.

CLASSICAL Architectural style incorporating Greek and Roman elements – pillars, domes, colonnades etc – at its height in the seventeenth century and revived, as **Neoclassical** (see below), in the nineteenth century.

CLERESTORY Upper storey of a church, incorporating the windows.

FLAMBOYANT Florid form of Gothic (see below).

FRESCO Wall painting – durable through application to wet plaster.

GABLE The triangular upper portion of a wall – decorative or supporting a roof. See **Gevel**, above.

GOTHIC Architectural style of the thirteenth to sixteenth centuries, characterized by pointed arches, rib vaulting, flying buttresses and a general emphasis on verticality.

MEROVINGIAN Dynasty ruling France and parts of Germany from sixth to mid-eighth centuries. Refers also to art, etc, of the period.

MISERICORD Ledge on choir stall on which occupant can be supported while standing; often carved with secular subjects (bottoms were not thought worthy of religious ones).

NAVE Main body of a church.

NEOCLASSICAL Architectural style derived from Greek and Roman elements – pillars, domes, colonnades, etc – popular in the Low Countries during French rule in the early nineteenth century.

ROCOCO Highly florid, light and graceful eighteenth-century style of architecture, painting and interior design, forming the last phase of Baroque.

RENAISSANCE Movement in art and architecture developed in fifteenth-century Italy.

RETABLE Altarpiece.

ROMANESQUE Early medieval architecture distinguished by squat forms, rounded arches and naive sculpture.

STUCCO Marble-based plaster used to embellish ceilings, etc.

TRANSEPT Arms of a cross-shaped church, placed at ninety degrees to nave and chancel.

TRIPTYCH Carved or painted work on three panels. Often used as an altarpiece.

TYMPANUM Sculpted panel above a church door.

VAUBAN Seventeenth-century military architect – his fortresses still stand all over Europe and the Low Countries.

VAULT An arched ceiling or roof.

INDEX

Stay in touch with us!

ROUGH*NEWS* **is Rough Guides' free newsletter. In four issues a year we give you news, travel issues, music reviews, readers' letters and the latest dispatches from authors on the road.**

I would like to receive ROUGH*NEWS*: please put me on your free mailing list.

NAME . . . .

ADDRESS . . . .

Please clip or photocopy and send to: Rough Guides, 62–70 Shorts Gardens, London WC2H 9AB,
England or Rough Guides, 375 Hudson Street, New York, NY 10014, USA.

ROUGH GUIDES: Mini Guides, Travel Specials and Phrasebooks

MINI GUIDES
Antigua
Bangkok
Barbados
Big Island of
  Hawaii
Boston
Brussels
Budapest

Dublin
Edinburgh
Florence
Honolulu
Jerusalem
Lisbon
London
  Restaurants
Madrid
Maui
Melbourne
New Orleans
Rome
Seattle
St Lucia

Sydney
Tokyo
Toronto

TRAVEL SPECIALS
First-Time Asia
First-Time
  Europe
Women Travel

PHRASEBOOKS
Czech
Dutch

Egyptian Arabic
European
French
German
Greek
Hindi & Urdu
Hungarian
Indonesian
Italian
Japanese

Mandarin
  Chinese
Mexican
  Spanish
Polish
Portuguese
Russian
Spanish
Swahili
Thai
Turkish
Vietnamese

ROUGH GUIDES:
Reference and Music CDs

REFERENCE
Classical Music
Classical:
  100 Essential CDs
Drum'n'bass
House Music
Jazz
Music USA

Opera
Opera:
  100 Essential CDs
Reggae
Reggae:
  100 Essential CDs
Rock
Rock:
  100 Essential CDs
Techno
World Music
World Music:
  100 Essential CDs
English Football
European Football

Internet
Millennium

ROUGH GUIDE
MUSIC CDs
Music of the
  Andes
Australian
  Aboriginal
Brazilian Music
Cajun & Zydeco

Classic Jazz
Music of
  Colombia
Cuban Music
Eastern Europe

Music of Egypt
English Roots
  Music
Flamenco
India & Pakistan
Irish Music
Music of Japan
Kenya & Tanzania
Native American
North African
Music of Portugal

Reggae
Salsa
Scottish Music
South African
  Music
Music of Spain
Tango
Tex-Mex
West African
  Music
World Music
World Music Vol 2
Music of
  Zimbabwe